Readings in
Cooperative Learning
for
Undergraduate Mathematics

ISBN 0-88385-153-9

Library of Congress Catalog Number 97-71908

Printed in the United States of America

Current Printing

10 9 8 7 6 5 4 3 2 1

Readings in Cooperative Learning for Undergraduate Mathematics

Edited by

Ed Dubinsky
David Mathews
Barbara E. Reynolds

Published by

THE MATHEMATICAL ASSOCIATION OF AMERICA

011399-3970X8

MAA Notes Series

The MAA Notes Series, started in 1982, addresses a broad range of topics and themes of interest to all who are involved with undergraduate mathematics. The volumes in this series are readable, informative, and useful, and help the mathematical community keep up with developments of importance to mathematics.

MAA Notes

These volumes can be ordered from:
MAA Service Center
P.O. Box 91112
Washington, DC 20090-1112
800-331-1MAA   FAX: 301-206-9789

Introduction

In 1995, the Mathematical Association of America (MAA) formed Project CLUME (Cooperative Learning in Undergraduate Mathematics Education) for the purpose of helping collegiate mathematics faculty learn about the pedagogical strategies known as cooperative learning and how they might be implemented.

With substantial funding from the National Science Foundation,[1] Project CLUME conducts residential summer workshops, courses on the Web, minicourses at conferences and various presentations. It also maintains an email network of people who have participated in the workshops.

The workshops and courses are intensive programs in which participants study the theoretical background of cooperative learning, learn about and experience various short-term and long-term cooperative learning strategies, and look at the literature on this pedagogical approach.

The literature on this topic is vast and only experts can hope to be familiar with all of it. Naturally, a course can only deal with a small portion and it is necessary to make a selection. This anthology represents such a selection. Although we have used cooperative learning in our classes, worked with others to learn how to use it, and even done some research, we are not specialists in this field. Before deciding on which papers to include, we did make a survey of the literature, but we make no claims of completeness. We have relied on our experience and our taste to choose a set of papers that is large enough to represent a reasonable portion of what has been written about cooperative learning yet small enough that it can be read, assimilated and discussed in a short, but intensive course. We have also relied on feedback from our participants who have worked with these readings. This has led to revisions in our selections, and we intend to continue to revise this work as we continue to conduct our faculty development courses.

We have organized the 17 papers in the present selection into three categories that, we feel, represent the major points of view one should take in thinking about cooperative learning.

The papers in the first category, Constructivism and the Teacher's Role, are concerned with the theoretical basis for cooperative learning, how it relates to the traditional role of the teacher and how that role may change. Our own views about the importance of constructivism in theories of learning have certainly influenced our selections here.

In the second category, Research and Effectiveness, there are papers which tell us what has been found regarding the effectiveness of cooperative learning and how that compares with traditional pedagogical approaches. The conclusion seems clear. Cooperative learning sometimes leads to significantly improved learning, sometimes makes no difference that can be discerned, and is almost never worse than traditional teaching methods. Moreover, the difference between these outcomes seems to depend on certain implementation issues.

That leads to the final category, Implementation Issues. Here we consider examples of very specific issues: management structures and teaching cooperative skills; the very general issue of status; and finally, two examples of how cooperative learning can be integrated into an overall pedagogical approach.

We conclude this selection of papers with an extensive bibliography which points the interested reader toward a wider selection from the literature on small group resources in science, mathematics, engineering, and technology.

---

[1] NSF Award Number DUE-9455164 and DUE-9653383.

This book is the text for our courses in cooperative learning. We also hope that it is useful to the general reader who may want to use it in support of teaching with cooperative learning, or who just may be interested in a small snapshot of what the literature has to say about this innovative and challenging pedagogical strategy.

Ed Dubinsky
David Mathews
Barbara E. Reynolds
Directors, Project CLUME
Spring, 1997

Contents

PART I
Constructivism and the Teacher's Role

To a large extent, the initial source of interest in cooperative learning is a reflection, engaged in by the teaching profession, on the education enterprise. Hence, we begin our collection with four papers that look at how we teach, how we might teach, and what theoretical bases there might be for our teaching practice.

There is a traditional, or standard method of teaching. Although it has many variations, certain common themes can be discerned. There is also a widespread dissatisfaction with the learning that takes place in our mathematics courses. This is certainly the first reason why people are thinking about alternative pedagogical approaches such as cooperative learning.

Finkel and Monk open our story with a presentation, in the form of mythical anecdotes, of several different ways a class can operate including cooperative learning. They focus very strongly on the roles of the teacher, the roles of the students, and the relations among them. Guskin contemplates a more global restructuring of faculty roles within the context of our system of higher education. MacGregor continues the discussion of cooperative learning in relation to a more general reform of education and begins to focus our attention on theories of learning that can inform our teaching practice. It is here that we first read about constructivism which seems to be more of a category of theoretical perspectives rather than a specific theory. Finally, Asiala, Brown, DeVries, Dubinsky, Mathews, and Thomas describe the specific research and curriculum development work performed by one team which is attempting to sustain a long term effort by building a community of investigator-teachers. This group is trying to develop a very specific constructivist theory and apply it to a teaching practice in which cooperative learning is a key feature. Their overall approach implements fundamental changes in the teacher's role as well as in many other aspects of the post-secondary education enterprise.

Comments on the article by Finkel and Monk

The search for alternative pedagogical strategies is the direct result of dissatisfaction with the learning outcomes for students in traditionally-structured classrooms. Finkel and Monk introduce this problem in two vignettes which describe traditional learning environments which, in spite of careful structuring on the part of the instructor, fail to engage students with the course material in anything but a superficial manner. In a third vignette, the authors describe a classroom in which learning appears to be taking place in large measure, while little teaching (in the traditional sense) seems to be occurring.

The authors trace the difficulties of the two traditional approaches they describe to the prevailing social structure of the classroom. This existing structure stems from an often unconscious acceptance of the two-person model of education. The accepted roles of faculty and students, the authors argue, tend to prevent any increase in engagement of students with the course material. Indeed, these roles are so ingrained in existing classroom culture that attempts to change the roles of either students or faculty necessarily meet with resistance and often with failure.

The authors argue that the answer to reforming pedagogy lies in reorganizing the social climate of the classroom. They present an important distinction between the teacher's role and teaching functions. The authors contend that by focusing on teaching functions, and by accomplishing the teaching functions in a variety of innovative ways, faculty can become liberated from stifling roles and can create more positive learner-centered classrooms for their students.

Discussion Questions

1. Describe the two-person model of education. Does this describe your ideal of education? Do you think it describes your colleagues' ideal of education?
2. Summarize the cognitive and social aspects of the two-person model which tend to keep teachers as the central focal point of the classroom. Have you experienced any of these?
3. Near the end of their article, the authors give suggestions about how to get started in dissolving the Atlas Complex. Do these suggested steps seem vulnerable to the forces in question 2? Why or why not?
4. Finkel and Monk assert that some teaching functions can be performed just as well by students as by the teacher. Do you agree or disagree? If you agree, name some of these. If you disagree, explain why.

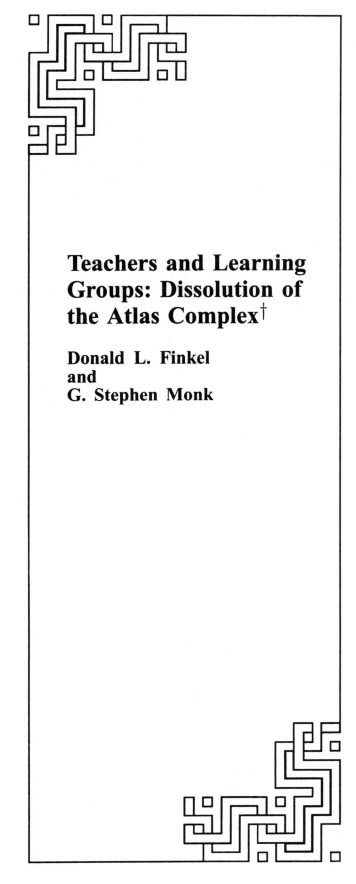

Teachers and Learning Groups: Dissolution of the Atlas Complex[†]

Donald L. Finkel
and
G. Stephen Monk

The Atlas Complex

Professor A is just concluding the culminating lecture on one of his favorite topics in his field. In earlier lectures, he painstakingly laid the groundwork, explaining each element and placing each detail of the theory in its proper relationship to the others. Today, he carefully ties the various components together to exhibit one of the most beautiful and powerful theories that he knows of. Each time that he lectures on this theory, he more clearly understands its depth and subtlety, and his lectures improve accordingly. Students find the theory difficult, and so he has learned to inject humor, personal views, and dramatic emphasis to get it across. Today, Professor A's pacing and timing work perfectly. He ends just in time to allow for his usual five minutes of questions. He asks, "Are there any questions?" A few students look up from their notebooks, but nothing else happens. He fills the silence by raising some questions that naturally arise from the theory. Then, he answers the questions. The students dutifully record the answers. One student asks a polite question about a specific fact in the lecture, and Professor A uses the occasion to expound still more on the theory. Another student asks the inevitable question about how much of the material will be on the exam. When the bell rings, Professor A is stirred by mixed emotions. He is pleased with how well he pulled the lecture together—it is easily the best version that he has given—but he is bothered by how little the students seem to have been moved by it. He has enough experience to know what the absence of real questions means. The students probably admire both his performance and the theory. But they do not feel the power of the theory, and they do not grasp how economically it answers so many deep questions. What must he do to get the excitement of his subject across to students?

Professor B is conducting a seminar in her own field of research. The topic for discussion is one of the seminal works in the field. Some students ask her to clarify certain passages, and she is able to do so clearly and completely. Then she asks a question that she believes to be central to the issues that underlie the work, and one of the brighter students responds in a very thorough and lengthy manner. But, inevitably, the student does not understand the full depth of the issue, and Professor B has a strong impulse to correct and clarify the student's answer. However, as an experienced seminar leader, she stifles this impulse and asks the students if they have any response to the first student's answer. Another student says that he disagrees with the first student and proceeds to give his own long and complete answer. Now, Professor B has two shallow and slightly incorrect answers to clear up. After doing so, she asks another question. She fixes her eye on one of the quieter students, and the student responds very tentatively, so that Professor B must encourage him and help to fill in the details missing from his answer. These separate, truncated dialogues between Professor B and each of her students continue until, out of something approaching desperation, she presses one student on what he means by one of his too neat, almost glib answers. As the student retreats into silence, a feeling of defeat overcomes Professor B. The work that they are discussing always stimulates her thinking with the freshness of its perspectives and insights. At each reading, it raises new questions in her mind. How can it fail to motivate a discussion as involving as those she has with fellow students in graduate school? The cause of the dry, ritualistic seminar before her must be herself, she reasons. She has not asked the right questions.

Both these teachers are the central figures in their classrooms. Like most of their colleagues, they assume full responsibility for all that goes on. They supply motivation, insight, clear explanations, even intellectual curiosity. In exchange, their students supply almost nothing but a faint imitation of the academic performance that they witness. Both teachers so thoroughly dominate the proceedings that they are cut off from what the students know or are confused about. For their part, the students form a group of isolated individuals who have no more in common than their one-to-one relationship with the same individual. While Professors A and B exercise their authority through control of the subject matter and the social encounter in the classroom, they lack the power to make things happen for their students. They are both caught in the middle of their classes by a host of mysterious forces– hidden assumptions, hidden expectations, and the results of their own isolating experience. We call this state the Atlas complex.

In this chapter, we first examine the phenomenon of the Atlas complex. In the next section, we describe a third teacher, Professor C, who is very present in his class but who is not caught in the middle. This example allows us to broaden our perspective on the social organization of the typical college course and on the particular hold that it has on the teacher. Finally, we show the many ways in which this social system can be modified to free teachers from the middle without violating their sense of themselves as teachers. Such modifications should broaden and enrich their view of what they can accomplish as teachers. The result should be a more fulfilling teaching experience and a greater sense of what is possible—in short, a dissolution of the Atlas complex.

The Two-Person Model

Most teachers and students conceive of the heart of education as a two-person relationship. The ideal relationship is that of tutor and tutee alone in a room. Classes are seen only as an economic or pragmatic necessity in which one person—the teacher—either simultaneously engaged in ten or three hundred two-person relationships with separate individuals or addresses a single undifferentiated entity—the audience. Teachers who view their classes as an elaboration of the two-person model are cut off from the potential energy and inspiration that lie in student-to-student interaction or in the mutual support that a group of individuals working toward a common goal can provide. Consequently, it becomes the responsibility of teachers to provide motivation, enlightenment, and a sense of purpose. Like Atlas, such teachers support the entire enterprise.

The sense of fixedness that stems from the two-person model of teaching has both a cognitive and a social component. The cognitive component stems from the teacher's expertise in subject matter, while the social component results from the teacher's occupying the role of group leader in the classroom. Teachers invest a large quantity of their time, energy, and hard work in becoming experts in their disciplines. They have a comprehensive understanding of their subjects and detailed knowledge of their subjects' intricacies and skills. How can they withhold these things? And if students do not get the point the first time, what can teachers do but give again or give more? By the very terms of the encounter, students lack something that the teacher has in abundance; thus, every activity in which the teacher does not give this "something" must play a secondary role. Teachers assume that their principal task is one of improving the ways in which they express their expertise: Clear and precise explanation can always be articulated and sharpened; penetrating questions can always be made more penetrating.

The social component of the sense of fixedness derives from the teacher's role of group leader. The literature on the social psychology of small groups (Slater, 1966) demonstrates that most groups in their early stages can be described precisely by the two-person model; that is, each member acts as if he or she were in an exclusive dyadic relationship with the leader. It is a long and arduous process for group members to break their dependence on the leader and to form mutual bonds with one another. But teachers are more than just leaders. Their expertise in the subject matter exacerbates the problem that all leaders face if they want to distribute responsibility to the individual members of the group. The teacher is the very embodiment of the group's goal—the subject matter. There is no doubt that teachers have all the answers. Why should students look to anyone else?

These forces hold teachers in place with their Atlas-like burden of responsibility. They prevent teachers from sharing some of their responsibilities with the group's members. But some teachers do try to make such a change. They allow individual students to take turns at leading the class, they form study groups of various kinds, they try to restrict their role in discussion to that of facilitator or resource person. And, when they encounter the intensity of the forces, they find themselves pushed back into the center by a cognitive force, by a social force, or by both.

The most striking consequence of allowing students to interact directly and collectively with subject matter without the teacher's mediation is that the teacher comes face to face with students' own partially formed and inadequate conceptions of the subject. As experts with carefully articulated and elaborate views of their subjects, and as representatives of their disciplines, teachers are bound to feel a strong personal discomfort in the presence of the kinds of imprecise, loosely connected, unintegrated comprehension that students have of their subjects. Thus, the very act of opening up and listening to students forces the teacher-expert back into the middle, because imprecise explanations cannot go unrefined, because all the connections have to be made, and because final conclusions have to be drawn. In short, the teacher returns to the center in order to mediate between the students and the material.

For their part, students are likely to resist the teacher's attempt to step out of the middle because they perceive this switch in roles as an attempt to abandon responsible leadership. Students who feel abandoned resent their teacher, and consequently they do not develop the enthusiasm necessary for learning. This in turn leads the teacher who tries to innovate and share responsibility for learning to become cynical about students. The primary reason for this sequence of reactions is that when teachers switch from the role of expert to the role of helper, their expertise gets lost. If students have no way to draw on the teacher's knowledge of the subject, it is natural that they learn less. The attempt to break the two-person model and to cause students to draw on the resources of the group can easily lead to a lowering of the intellectual goals of the class, in the eyes of both teacher and students. And since this is usually judged to be unsatisfactory, the teacher returns to the role of expert, and the students settle back into their seats to take in the teacher's illuminating words.

We have described the way in which the cognitive and social aspects of the two-person model keep teachers in the middle of their classes, carrying all the burden and responsibility of the course on their own shoulders. We have also described how the forces that typically operate on teachers, both from within and without, tend to move them back to the center when they try to leave it. People approach teaching with a set of conventional beliefs about the teacher's role that are strongly reinforced by being in the middle. Years of experience then fuse these beliefs into a whole, so that they cannot be differentiated, questioned, or tested. Instead, they form a complex—a monolithic and undifferentiated state of mind that gives teachers so much responsibility for everything that goes on in the class that they cannot move—a state of mind that we call the Atlas complex.

But a teacher who takes responsibility for all that goes on in the class gives students no room to experiment with ideas, to deepen their understanding of concepts, or to integrate concepts into a coherent system. Most teachers agree that these processes, together with many others are necessary if students are to understand a subject matter. Any teacher will say that the best way of learning a subject is to teach it—to try to explain it to others. Scientists agree that intellectual exchange, discourse, and debate are important elements in their own professional development. Almost anyone who has learned something well has experienced the particular potency that a collaborative group can have through its ability to promote and make manifest such intellectual processes as assimilating experience or data to conceptual frameworks, wrestling with inadequacies in current conceptions, drawing new distinctions, and integrating separate ideas. The evidence that collective work is a key ingredient to intellectual growth surrounds us. Yet, to judge the typical college course, most teachers do not believe that it is either appropriate or possible to foster these important processes in the classroom.

Professor C

Before we examine how the Atlas complex can be dissolved, we will describe a class that does not have a teacher in the middle and that still benefits from the teacher's expertise. This should show that change is possible—that the forces holding the teacher in the middle are not irresistible. It should also illustrate the point of view that we wish to advance in the next section.

Professor C walks into his class of forty students and hands out a dittoed "worksheet" to every student. The students continue to chatter as they glance at the worksheet, start to form groups of five (as the worksheet instructs them to do), and seat themselves around the tables in the room. Gradually, the noise level falls as students read through the worksheet. Then, it rises again as they begin to engage in discussion with one another over the questions on the sheet. After a few minutes, Professor C joins one group, where he quietly watches and listens, but does not talk. A few minutes later, he moves to another group. After listening to the discussion there, he suggests to group members that they are not getting anywhere because they misunderstand the example given in the first question. He tells them to draw out in pictures what the example describes, and as they do so, he makes clarifying comments. He listens as discussion resumes, then moves to yet another group. Meanwhile, many students are not only talking but also making notes as they do. Some groups are engaged in heated discussion; others are quieter, as individuals pause to think or to listen to a member who reads a passage aloud from reading that accompanies the worksheet. In one way or another, however, all the groups are working with the sequence of questions and instructions contained in the worksheet.

Professor C may seem to be a teacher with no real function; indeed, he may even seem irresponsible. But keeping a class of forty students actively involved with course material with a minimum of direct support from the teacher requires an artfully written set of instructions and questions. Professor C puts all his expert knowledge, his most provocative questions, and his insights about how students comprehend the material into the worksheets. Breaking his own finished knowledge of his discipline down into its component processes, then provoking students to discover these processes takes at least as much intellectual work as a finely crafted series of lectures would require. But, having done this work and set the students to interacting with one another and with the worksheet, he becomes free to perform a number of helping teaching functions as well as to expound, probe, or press on the basis of his expertise. He can also take time just to listen to students. He is free to choose. (For a more complete description of the worksheet approach and its uses, see Finkel and Monk, 1978, 1979.)

Professor C revises his worksheets after watching his class interact with them (this is where listening becomes important), just as Professor A revises his lectures every time that he gives them. The difference is that Professor C bases his revision on direct observation, while Professor A must rely on his own perception of how he has done, supplemented by a few polite questions and test results. Like Professor B, Professor C always feels that livelier and deeper conversation would result if he only could ask better questions. The difference is that Professor C has had the opportunity to be an outside observer of students' conversation without the concerns of a discussion leader; thus, Professor C can gain a clearer view of what actually happens than even most seminar leaders can.

We offer the example of Professor C not as a model for Professor A, Professor B, or any other teacher to imitate. Answers to teaching problems are never easy. The example of Professor C shows that a teacher can be in his class without being caught in the middle. We will use this example to illustrate a principle that lies behind a variety

of possible course restructurings and that helps to relieve the teacher of the Atlas complex.

From Roles to Functions

Professor C serves as an expert in his class primarily through his worksheet. Since students focus on it and not on him, he is free to give clear explanations, to press for clearer answers, and to encourage hesitant students. The power of this approach stems from a fundamental differentiation of the teaching functions that make up the role of teacher. When these functions are differentiated and then distributed throughout a course, many of the constricting features that come from the role of teacher disappear and with them, the peculiar symptoms of the Atlas complex.

Brown (1965, p. 153) observes that "roles are norms that apply to categories of persons." In this case, the category is *teacher*, and anyone who fills that role is expected to follow a certain set of norms in his behavior. Moreover, roles do not exist in isolation; they are defined in interlocking sets, within the context of a given institution. In defining the role of college teacher, we necessarily define norms for college student as well. Social life flows smoothly because of these sets of roles. People enter the social arena knowing in advance what to expect; they have to be confident that the range of unpredictable behavior is strongly limited. Teachers who want to teach in a strikingly different way, for pedagogical reasons, usually find themselves crossing the limits of their role, violating some of the rules that define it. Students will be the first to force them back into doing what teachers are supposed to do; that is, into the conventional role of teacher. Thus, the very predictability that we need from roles can become so rigid by force of habit that the roles of teacher and student become overly restrictive and actually exclude the usual needs of cognitive life in the classroom.

Suppose now that teachers focus not on how they are supposed to behave but on the job that they are supposed to accomplish. Most teachers understand this job to involve such things as getting the students to understand a given theory, having students examine certain phenomena from a new perspective, or teaching students how to perform new skills. Each goal leads to certain mental processes that must be carried out. These processes include organizing and synthesizing a variety of specific facts, ideas, and events into a general scheme; engaging the particulars of a context or experience while maintaining a perspective on its general qualities and compressing and crystallizing connections made within the discipline or between a discipline and the area that it describes. Each process requires a different form of work from students and a different form of assistance from the teacher. A teacher operates in quite different ways depending on whether students are to organize and synthesize, to engage, or to compress and crystallize. Even within each mental process, the teacher has to make choices to act. We call particular ways of operating in a classroom *teaching functions.*

For instance, to get students to organize and synthesize specific facts and events into a general scheme, the teacher can perform such teaching functions as asking students to give their current interpretations of the specific facts and events, laying out projects that allow students to devise their own schemes, responding to students' work, and presenting the teacher's own organizing scheme.

In designing his worksheet, Professor C performed such teaching functions as interpreting student misconceptions, setting goals and tasks, and analyzing his subject matter. In his classroom, professor C performs such teaching functions as listening to students, redirecting them, clearing up misunderstandings, and supporting students. Notice that analysis of classroom roles ties behavior to persons (teacher, students), while analysis of teaching functions ties behavior to tasks that must be accomplished. Some teaching functions can be performed just as well by students as by the teacher. Other teaching functions can be performed by groups. As we show in the next sections, a conscious decision about which teaching functions are to be performed by whom and where can be made as part of the design of the organization of the course.

The perspective of teaching functions makes the strong negative effects of thinking in terms of teaching roles quite clear. First, any role is inevitably confining. Many teachers acknowledge that a particular teaching function should be performed but that it is not. They say, "Such things are not done" or "Students won't stand for it." This is only a way of saying that their particular role does not permit it. And, because the role does not permit it, most teachers are not inclined consciously to articulate what teaching functions they deem most important for their students' learning.

Second, the language of roles itself creates dilemmas about the ways in which people are to behave. Teachers ask, Is my role of teacher one of expert or helper? as if they must choose between these two roles. The conflict disappears if the teacher performs functions that require expertise at one time and place and functions that require helping at others. To say that students must be *independent* (bold, skeptical, imaginative) and *dependent* (relying on the accumulated knowledge of past generations) sounds like a contradiction, because it is couched in the language of roles. The adjectives prescribe contradictory norms for a category of persons. But, if we say instead that some of the activities in which a student must engage require independence and that others require dependence, then the contradiction disappears. There is a time and a place for both independence and dependence when each characterizes a mode of engaging in a specific activity. But, as role descriptors they contradict each other.

Third, roles tend to generate their own work to be done, so that the teacher's activities are determined not by tasks but by roles and expectations. Thus, Professor A becomes a performer caught up in such functions as polishing, timing, and motivating, while Professor B becomes a stage manager of discussions who looks for the perfect sequence of questions so that the actors can play their parts.

Fourth, every role includes several distinct functions. When these functions are performed simply as part of the role, they tend to blur and merge; they are performed simultaneously, but none is performed particularly well. In trying to get feedback after he has spent forty-five minutes driving his points home, Professor A is fooling himself. Likewise, in trying to manage a discussion among students while maintaining high standards of rigor, Professor B performs neither function. A lecturer who gives illuminating examples to stimulate students' thought processes and then immediately gives her own perspective to explain these examples can think of herself as engaging students in a particular context and inviting them to form their own view of it, which she will then enrich. But, for students to perform such an activity in fact requires behavior from the lecturer that the students would tolerate. Thus, Professor B's students do not really go through the process, and she really performs just one function, exposition.

Distributing Teaching Functions in a Course

While most teachers acknowledge that their role is confining and wish to perform a wider array of teaching functions, they find that good intentions, even when backed by strong resolve, do not go far to promote change. To effect genuine change, a teacher must first differentiate teaching functions, then distribute them in the course so that the responsibility for learning is shared with students. Only then can the Atlas complex be dissolved. To do this, the various parts of the course must be clearly distinguished so that the functions appropriate to them can be distributed.

When we think of making structural changes in a formal organization, such as a corporation, the candidates for transformation are immediately apparent. For instance, we can alter channels of communication, or change the authority relations between officers, or merge or divide departments. Like a corporation, a course is a social system. However, when it is viewed simply as a teacher and some students, it seems to lack the structural components that a corporation has, and thus it seems to lack candidates for transformation.

To distribute teaching functions, the teacher needs to distinguish three components in his course: specific activities that serve general teaching functions, people responsible for performing these activities, and the "places" in the course where these activities are performed. For instance, a teacher who wants to perform the teaching function of giving his own perspective on the subject can choose among such activities as these: giving a lecture, having students study a few key examples that exemplify the significance of his own perspective, and asking a highly convergent sequence of questions that point to that perspective. Further, there are many choices as to who performs each particular activity. The typical choice is between the teacher and individual students. However, there are additional candidates for this responsibility: Small groups of students working together can take over some teaching functions. In some instances, the entire classroom group can do so. Finally, there is an enormous array of "places" in any course where various teaching functions can be located. The obvious places include class sessions, tests, homework assignments, office hours, lecturers, and quiz sections. These can be refined to include such places as Friday's class, critiqued but ungraded homework, files of past tests, required office conferences, and make-up tests.

Once teachers have differentiated the teaching functions to be performed and consciously distinguished the components of their courses that can be operated on, then they can make local decisions about the specific activities used to realize these functions, about, who performs each function, and about where in the course the activity should be carried out. With this strategy for change, teachers can preserve existing activities that already serve important teaching functions and test new activities that may be able to take the place of activities that have not worked out well.

Faced with the complexities of the course as a social system, teachers may well wonder how to get started in such a program for change—particularly since, by our analysis, teachers themselves play such a dominant role in the system. Student learning groups, in which small numbers of students work together in a class without constant assistance from the teacher, can restrict the problem of systematic change to a problem of manageable size. Professor C divided his class into small groups that worked together for two hours, guided by the instructions and questions on the worksheet, so that he became free in the class to perform many helping functions. Working in groups, the students perform such functions as asking and answering questions, giving support and reinforcement, and providing fresh perspectives on the subject. Each small group of students serves other important functions as well, such as providing carrying energy and bringing out low participa-

tors. But, the concept of learning group is extremely elastic. Learning groups can be permanent or temporary. They can work for five minutes, or two hours, or even longer at one time. They can be highly structured by the teacher or not. They can be required to devise group products, which are assigned group grades. Or, they can serve primarily as support groups for individuals.

Teachers who decide to use learning groups as part of a class, no matter on how small a scale, have taken a giant step out of the middle of their class, because in carrying out their decision, they distribute teaching functions, which forces them to deal with all the key issues involved in such a move. What concrete activities will be carried out in the groups? Who will have the responsibility for these activities? At what time and place in the course will learning groups be used?

Teachers who feel that a commitment to learning groups is too radical a step can take smaller steps in the same direction to divest themselves of some of their Atlas-like burden. For instance, Professor A could begin by distributing his beautifully polished lectures in advance and instruct students to read them as preparation for class. This puts him in a position to use the class time as an opportunity to serve a new teaching function. Since he is concerned with eliciting intelligent and informed questions from his students and with having a chance to respond to them, he can use the class period for just this purpose. He can have students bring prepared questions to class, where they can form the basis for a discussion, or he can simply respond to them publicly. He can take yet another step and use small temporary groups of students to drive the intellectual processes necessary for the assimilation and organization of ideas derived from his lecture. To do this, he can distribute a short list of conceptual questions along with his lecture, which each group of students can be responsible for answering. Student work of this nature would enable him to perform yet another teaching function: critiquing without grading the students' response to his lectures. This teaching function would not only be beneficial to the students; it would help Professor A to revise his lectures, because it would give him a sharper view of his students' conception of the subject matter.

In much the same way, Professor B could write her telling and penetrating questions out for students to work on as they do their reading. To reduce her dominant role in the seminar, she can choose a small number of teaching functions to perform during class, to the exclusion of all others. If she still feels that her expertise is not being drawn upon sufficiently she can designate a segment of the seminar (the last fifteen minutes of each class or the last class of each week) in which she answers student questions or comments on student answers. However, she must do this in such a way that students see clearly that the expected behavior for this segment of the seminar is different from the behavior expected in the rest of the seminar.

In the preceding paragraphs, we have made a number of recommendations about how a course can be changed by distribution of teaching functions. However, it is important to remember that, as a social system, a course is not just a variety of distinct structural components; these components are strongly linked. If a change in one part of the system is to have lasting effect, the teacher must consider how this change interacts with other parts of the system. Change that is not integrated into the system will either be isolated and nullified, or it will distort the entire system. For instance, if learning groups are introduced, then their relation to the evaluation structure of the course must be made very clear. Exams signal to students more clearly than anything else what the teacher really cares about, and students direct their behavior accordingly. Thus, if group work is to be taken seriously, the results of group work must be tested by exams. That is, there should be a clear payoff to students for putting their energies into the new activity. Similarly, if the teacher deems collaborative work among students to be important and the teacher works hard to foster it in class, it makes no sense to grade exams on a curve, since students see such grading as a clear message that they are competing with one another.

However far one goes in distributing teaching functions, it is extremely important to set up clear boundaries around the various "places" in the course to which distinct teaching functions have been assigned. Places can be marked off by such means as a designated day of the week or time in the day, a different classroom format, a different medium, a different physical location, or a different mode of evaluation. As long as teachers are absolutely explicit about the nature of the different tasks to be performed in the places marked off by such boundaries, they can ensure the predictability of behavior that people require when they drop stereotypical roles. A lecture carefully organized to give a highly polished overview of the subject indicates one set of behaviors for teacher and students, while a class period in which students work in groups on their first tentative explorations of the subject calls for another. A separate class period in which a panel of students presses the teacher with what they see to be the most important questions on the subject leads to yet another kind of behavior. As long as such class periods are clearly marked off, the diversity of expected behavior can create no confusion. There is a time and a place for students to be receptive and passive, curious and imaginative, challenging and doubting. Similarly, the teacher can assume an authoritative voice for a lecture, become a listener and helper in a worksheet class, and answer questions thoughtfully and carefully before a

panel of students. As one boundary after another is crossed in a course, teachers and students can alter their behavior quite radically. All flows smoothly—just as long as the boundaries are absolutely clear.

Dissolution of the Atlas Complex

The perception that each course is in fact a miniature social system is perhaps the key to teachers' dissolution of the Atlas complex. The Atlas complex is a state of mind that keeps teachers fixed in the center of their classroom, supporting the entire burden or responsibility for the course on their own shoulders. This state of mind is hardened by the expectations that surround teachers and by the impact of the experience that results from them. A direct assault on the complex is doomed to fail.

The solution that we propose here is indirect. By focusing teachers' attention on their course as a social system, not on themselves as filling a role, we suggest that teachers can take specific, concrete actions that enable them to share responsibilities in the classroom. To do this, teachers must distinguish the various components of a course—the structural parts that comprise the social system—and distribute teaching functions into them.

There is a continuum along which the teacher can make such changes, ranging from small moves that share responsibility with students as individuals, to use of learning groups, which allows small subgroups of students temporarily to assume a number of different teaching functions, to delegation of major responsibilities to the entire group. We have found that the middle course of action—learning groups—is the most effective way to begin, for it opens up a great number of local possibilities for change while allowing the teacher to keep the fundamental structure of curriculum and teaching intact.

Most teachers start with a small change, which enables them to experience their teaching in a different way and enriches their view of their course as a social system containing diverse teaching functions. This step leads to alterations in their own and their students' expectations of themselves, which deepen and expand their sense of further possible steps for change in the course. Each further step alters both their experience of teaching and their sense of what is possible. Only in this way is it possible to dissolve the Atlas complex

References

Brown, R. *Social Psychology.* New York: Free Press, 1965.

Finkel, D. L., and Monk, G. S. *Contexts for Learning: A Teacher's Guide to the Design of Intellectual Experience.* Olympia, Wash.: Evergreen State College, 1978.

Finkel, D. L., and Monk, G. S. "The Design of Intellectual Experience," *Journal of Experiential Education,* 1979, 38, 31–38.

Slater, P. *Microcosm: Structural, Psychological, and Religious Evolution in Groups.* New York: Wiley, 1966.

Comments on the article by Guskin

The previous article by Finkel and Monk may be characterized as an analysis of the difficulties which individual faculty members face in engaging students in the learning process by reflecting on unexamined assumptions about the relationship between teaching and learning. The next article, written by the chancellor of a university system, may be seen as an extension of this analysis. Guskin shifts our attention from the role of *individual faculty* in promoting learning to the role of *the faculty* as a whole with regard to learning.

Central to both articles is a vision of moving from a teaching paradigm of education to a learning paradigm. Like Finkel and Monk, Guskin details the new expectations of the instructor in this transformation, and the changing role of students away from passive learning toward active learning. An important observation is that cooperative learning strategies are seen as central to this transformation both by the previous authors as teachers and researchers, and by Guskin as a university administrator.

Guskin presents three "learning strategies": accumulation of information and knowledge, skill development, and conceptual development as general categories for the multifaceted educational outcomes which we intend for our students. His analysis of the role of cooperative learning in each of these categories can be seen as an elaboration of the discussion of teaching functions proposed by Finkel and Monk.

Guskin concludes his paper by reasserting that irrespective of the difficulty of affecting the changes he has outlined, such a transformation of the faculty role is necessitated by economics, technology, and societal pressure for increased accountability of higher education. Such changes, he argues, are necessary for the survival of higher education and can ultimately enhance student learning as well.

Discussion Questions

1. Do you agree with the author that restructuring the role of faculty will be a monumental undertaking? Why or why not?
2. What do you think that faculty would see as losses from such a restructuring of their roles? What would they see as gains?
3. What connections does the author describe between instruction and learning?
4. Discuss the role of cooperative learning in each of the three "learning strategies" detailed in this paper.
5. Do you agree with Guskin's premise that change to a technology-rich, student-active, cooperative-learning environment is essential? Why or why not?
6. How does Guskin's view of the role of cooperative learning in reformed pedagogy compare with that of Finkel and Monk?

Reducing Student Costs & Enhancing Student Learning

Part II
Restructuring the Role of Faculty†

Alan E. Guskin

In Part I of this article (in the July/August issue), I sketched out some of the major changes that higher education may undergo in the next five to 10 years as it tries to deal with increasingly unacceptable levels of student costs, rising institutional expenses, an emphasis on student learning outcomes, and the power of new electronic technologies to enhance student learning. To deal with these forces, I described significant changes in how administrative work is organized and argued that administrative cost reduction must precede major alterations in the academic area.

I also made clear that administrative reductions will not produce enough savings to significantly reduce student costs and that any significant reduction in university expenses will have to involve major cost savings in the academic area. In this second article, I extend the argument that significant increases in faculty productivity will only be possible by fundamentally restructuring the work of faculty members.

Restructuring the role of faculty members will, at first, prove to be a monumental undertaking. All of the incentives seem against doing so—except, in the end, survival. For over three decades faculty have been trained and rewarded to "do their own work"—namely, research, writing, consulting, and so on—often with a lightening of their teaching "load." During this same period, university governance structures have shifted powerfully to emphasize the primacy of the faculty and of individual faculty members themselves; it is the faculty who determine the nature of the curriculum, the priorities for faculty work, and even the faculty workload. Hence, the idea of increasing faculty productivity runs counter to the personal and professional interests of faculty and the way they (and almost everyone else in university life) have come to define a meaningful faculty role in educating students. The result is a university president's or dean's worst nightmare: the need is to convince faculty to change how and what they teach, but faculty themselves are in charge of the very decision-making processes that determine what they do.

Gordon Winston, writing last year in *Change* (January/February 1993) about the economics of colleges and universities, summed up the depth of this challenge:

> We've got a whole generation of faculty (and young administrators) who have never seen anything but the lush 1980s and a larger number who have persuaded themselves that the expansions of the '80s were normal...

† *Change,* 26 (5), pp. 16–25, 1994. Reprinted with permission of the Helen Dwight Reid Educational Foundation. Published by Heldref Publications, 1319 Eighteenth Street, NW, Washington, DC 20036-1802. Copyright © 1994.

The fundamental challenge to college administrators over the next few years, arguably, will be to induce a highly resistant community to understand that there's an economic reality within which they'll have to live, one that may include "downsizing" and "restructuring" and the biting of all sorts of personally painful bullets.

Higher education's predicament is not very different from that being faced in the corporate and health care worlds: survival depends on radical change, yet the people needing to change the most are in control of the decision-making processes that must deal with the change. On campus, as elsewhere, institutional leadership and strong doses of courage are required.

Our thinking about how to increase faculty productivity is undermined by unexamined assumptions about how faculty members influence student learning. In effect, the status quo is based on two overarching assumptions:

- that faculty members teaching groups of students in a classroom setting are essential for effective student learning; and, based on this assumption,
- that increasing the productivity of faculty members requires increasing the number of students taught in a particular class.

Some productivity gains can no doubt be produced by faculty just teaching more of what they now do. But I don't believe the volume of activity is the appropriate goal: the issue is not how many courses faculty teach, but how much students learn. A few more faculty members teaching more courses will not significantly reduce institutional expenses or increase student learning.

The reality is that faculty do work hard, and much of that work does not involve doing research. A good deal of their time is spent teaching, as well as in other non-research, non- teaching activities. Indeed, the significant changes and reduction in administrative expenses discussed in Part I, which are an essential first step in reducing university costs, will likely increase the amount of non-teaching work faculty members perform.

Tinkering with the balance between teaching and research won't radically alter institutional expenses; neither will reducing wasteful activity and meetings. Surely there can be modest gains as faculty teach a bit more and fewer people are hired as part-timers. But these savings will be small and will not, even in the short term, make a real difference in the underlying expense structure of a college or university.

By the same token, cutting departments or even entire schools won't solve the financial problem. We could make such cuts (and all the small changes above) and probably survive, but the reality would be an ever-increasing downhill struggle entailing big, new costs to the quality of faculty life and to opportunities for student learning.

What follows is one attempt to *begin* the discussion needed to answer the challenge of restructuring the role of faculty over the next five to 10 years. In this effort, there is no *one* model for success, except that faculty and administrators must work together to create alternatives to the present arrangements. In doing so, they must stimulate the human and financial benefits and costs of these alternatives. There is, however, *one* model for failure; that is, to deny the reality that we need to restructure the roles of administrators and faculty in order to reduce institutional expenses and student costs.

I venture into this arena not out of a deep understanding of all that could be done, but in an attempt to break through the generic assertion that "what we need to do is restructure what faculty do" but without giving any examples of what is meant by doing so. Further, there are now a number of articles appearing that appropriately stress the need to introduce the new information technologies, but don't develop examples of how this might be done—and especially how it relates to what we know about student learning. The following discussion attempts to begin meeting the challenge of rethinking the role of faculty and the use of new technologies in order both to enhance student learning and reduce student costs.

Restructuring the Role of Faculty

The alternative to the present role of faculty states the problem and challenge: *to create learning environments focused directly on activities that enhance student learning, we must restructure the role of the faculty to maximize essential faculty-student interaction, integrate new technologies fully into the student learning process, and enhance student learning through peer interaction.*

The radical restructuring of the faculty role called for here requires that we understand anew how faculty contribute best to student learning—an understanding that is readily available in our research literatures but that is uncommonly put into practice by faculty.

Let me begin with a set of summary conclusions:

- There are key elements of the student learning process that only can be accomplished effectively through the human interaction of students and faculty members.
- There are key elements of student learning process that can be accomplished effectively using electronic technologies, especially new information technologies.
- There are key elements of student learning process that can be accomplished effectively through peer interac-

tion without the presence of a faculty member and by students learning by themselves inside and outside the institution.

These propositions are the cornerstones of the proposals that follow, which aim to reduce the number of faculty while increasing student learning. My proposals in brief are that students will spend more time learning by themselves and with their peers and much more time engaged with powerful, interactive technologies, and will spend less actual time—but more creative, intensive, and focused time—with faculty members. Faculty, in turn, will work with greater numbers of students but "teach" much less.

Student Learning.

Student learning at the undergraduate level is very complex, both in our aims and in what is achieved, whether directly or indirectly. We want students to learn about a lot of things. We want them to accumulate information and knowledge in a host of fields, with depth in at least one. We expect students to develop skills not only in writing and communication but in the use of quantitative and scientific methods and in the learning of a foreign language. Even more importantly, we have strong expectations regarding students' conceptual learning—the development of conceptual, intellectual tools that enable them to compare and contrast the material they are acquiring and to make judgments about its relevance to other issues of concern.

These three types of learning—accumulation of information and knowledge, skill development, and conceptual development—occur more or less effectively in most institutional learning environments. Nevertheless, ample evidence exists that there are certain settings that foster such learning. Psychologist Donald Norman discusses the optimal environment for the individual student. Arthur Chickering and Zelda Gamson—both higher education researchers—refer to how faculty can increase student learning through better practices. Together these two approaches help us better understand what we might look at in order to enhance student learning.

Based on what we know today, Norman (1993) states that the optimal environment for learning exists when we

- provide a high intensity of interaction and feedback;
- have specific goals and established procedures;
- motivate;
- provide a continual feeling of challenge, one that is neither so difficult as to create a sense of hopelessness and frustration, nor so easy as to produce boredom;

- provide a sense of direct engagement, producing a feeling of directly experiencing the environment, directly working on the task;
- provide appropriate tools that fit the user and task so well that they aid and do not distract; and
- avoid distraction and disruptions that intervene and destroy the subjective experience.

Chickering and Gamson, in their influential article, "Seven Principles for Good Practices in Undergraduate Education," summarize many years of research on good practice in college teaching. They conclude that good practice

- encourages student/faculty contact;
- encourages cooperation among students;
- encourages active learning;
- gives prompt feedback;
- emphasizes time on task;
- communicates high expectations; and
- respects diverse talents and ways of learning.

These optimal settings present a clear message to most every college and university: that the primary learning environment for undergraduate students, the fairly passive lecture-discussion format where faculty talk and most students listen, is contrary to almost every principle of optimal settings for student learning. While the lecture and lecture-discussion formats are, overwhelmingly, the common practice at most universities where large classes, multiple-choice exams, and teaching assistants are the norm, this situation is also true for too much of the education that occurs in most smaller colleges. Intimate faculty/student contact that encourages feedback, that motivates students, and that allows students to perform is the exception, not the norm. Direct faculty-student engagement outside of class and other formal settings is not common, and students are only occasionally provided vehicles for real peer, collaborative learning with and without faculty.

Learning Strategies

In focusing on human and technological learning strategies that could help us think through alternative ways for faculty to practice their profession, both in classroom and non-classroom settings, this effort attempts to turn the typical discussion of the role of faculty upside-down. The focus is not on how faculty teach but on how students learn, and doing whatever it takes to enhance such learning.

I believe rethinking what faculty do can be accomplished because so much effort currently is expended using methods that are not very effective in producing high levels of student learning—namely talking at students in fairly large groups and imparting information to them. And, it is precisely this function that will be most easily and effectively performed by the new computer technologies.

I also believe that faculty spend precious little time involved in the activities that are unique to faculty and that have major impact on student learning—namely direct, individual faculty/student interaction, intense small group discussions, mentoring and advising—and in encouraging students to be involved in activities that are important for student learning but do not involve faculty—peer-group, team-oriented settings, peer tutoring and coaching, and experiential learning outside the institution (see Alexander Astin's [1992] research). Further, I believe faculty members can effectively and efficiently use new technologies in a way that will enhance and/or often substitute for a good deal of their present teaching method, thereby freeing them to spend time with more students and to have a greater impact on the learning of all these students.

All the above forms the context for the analyses that follow. The three following learning strategies borrow from Donald Norman's discussion of student learning in his 1993 book, *Things That Make Us Smart.*

1) Accumulation of Information and Knowledge

This learning strategy is rather straightforward and represents a good deal of what occurs in higher education today. The common format is the faculty lecture or lecture/discussion. In addition to using books, an old "tool" for maximizing this presentation of information, faculty sometimes use visual aids, like films, videos, and the like.

It is hard to imagine an area more ripe for the new information technologies, some of which already exist and many of which are forthcoming on a monthly basis. Over the next five to 10 years, sophisticated interactive software for college-level subject matter will be easily accessible. While the initial cost of developing such interactive technologies is high, the size of the higher education market will attract enterprising software developers and will lead to reasonable costs. In fact, as the market for software grows, the growth in software choices will probably be exponential.

Beyond interactive technology is the ready access to an "information superhighway"—the Internet—where students can gather information from all over the nation and world, access numerous library catalogs and databases, and communicate freely on their own with peers and experts. The growth of new "superhighways" will definitely happen within the next few years, as will the availability of vast amounts of information in a variety of formats.

The power of these new technologies is enormous, especially so for student learning and access. Students will be able to gain access to these storehouses of information, knowledge, and human-electronic interaction anytime and at any place, which will enable those with different learning styles to adapt the information and ideas received to their special needs.

A major faculty role, and especially the role of the librarian as information technology expert, will be to guide students to these sources by helping them learn how to ask the right questions. I believe the combination of good human and technological guides and well- developed electronically interactive formats will be essential in enabling students to explore the vast potential of the new electronic resources. Rather than the faculty member providing this information through lecture or lecture-discussion formats, a librarian/information technology expert and/or appropriate written and technology-based guides will be able to do so.

Courses as we now know them may be radically altered so that a student would learn a particular subject area in a series of "learning blocks," with one block focused on electronic sources, another on intensive interaction with a faculty member, a third on intensive lecture- discussion formats over brief periods of time, a fourth in real-life experiences or simulations, and even another block as a peer-study group. Evaluation of student learning in a particular area, then, would include separate assessments of the learning achieved in each of these blocks integrated into a total assessment of the learning demonstrated.

2) Skill Development

High-level skill development represents a good deal of the work of colleges and universities: from the more basic levels of math, quantitative methods, writing, communicating, and foreign languages, to the higher-level skills of research and scholarly methods, to the arts and communication technologies, skill development is very much a focus of our efforts.

Coaching.   A critical aspect of skill development, coaching is when an experienced individual uses a combination of tips, advice, and example to help a student avoid unnecessary pitfalls. What seemed insurmountable in the beginning (e.g., acquiring the speed of a native speaker in a foreign language) becomes readily understandable and easily performed as the skill is developed. The coach's role involves providing continuous feedback, encouragement, and in many cases, demonstration.

Obviously, coaching performed by a highly experienced expert may be desirable, but it is not always necessary. Communication-oriented foreign language training sessions can be led by relatively inexperienced native speakers and upper-division students fluent in a language, who have been taught a specific method of teaching languages. Having highly paid faculty teach grammar or even spoken language is less effective and more costly than a skill-oriented, spoken language program. The Peace Corps, for example, has been teaching languages this way for over 30 years.

The efficiency of this model can be very striking. At Antioch College, the number of languages taught using this approach tripled without increasing the number of faculty and by very modestly increasing the costs for assistants. The key to the program's success is its conception of language learning: the focus is on students' ability to use the language and native speakers' following a well-thought-out linguistic method that emphasizes communication.

In fact, a good argument can be made for coaching/tutoring in many skill areas where upper-level students are paired with lower-level ones in a fairly intimate learning environment. It may be that peer coaching in lower-level areas is more effective than faculty coaching because the older peer really understands how to overcome learning hurdles that are but faint memories to faculty members. Evidence shows that in such peer coaching situations both the upper- and lower-level students increase their learning. The combination of more effective learning and reduced expenses may well be a powerful motivation for increasing this learning method.

While interactive technology cannot substitute for human coaching, there are many skill areas—including language learning—where interactive technologies and computer analysis can be a major aid in reducing the time needed for human coaching by highly trained experts.

Simulation.   The advances just beginning to occur in software that simulates science laboratories could be a boon to colleges and universities. Using this software can reduce, significantly, the expense of costly laboratory materials and of maintaining extremely expensive specialized labs. While these simulated laboratories are only now in the early stages of development, it is highly likely that as universities seek to cut costs, the market for such software will grow significantly, thereby increasing the quantity and quality of the simulations.

The extent to which such simulation technology is developing was highlighted in a *New York Times* article (Oct. 31, 1993) that described how new virtual reality technology is being developed to train surgeons:

> Virtual reality, the use of electronic sensors and computer-generated images to give people the illusion of participating in fabricated events, is moving beyond the game room and into practical applications in medical schools and other real-life settings.

> Just as flight simulators have long been used to train pilots before they climb into actual airplanes, authorities in a variety of fields say virtual reality "environments" have a bright future as a training tool for students and as a way to give doctors and engineers a "dry run" through risky or costly procedures.

It is likely that because of the ease of use and the reduced need for lab staff, students using computer-simulated laboratories will be able to carry out more experiments and learn more about "doing science" than otherwise possible. And because these simulation experiences will be able to be carried out at any time and place—and will be easily repeated—students with different learning styles will be able to learn at their own pace and achieve the same level of understanding as those more attuned to the formal laboratory settings. It is possible that the flexibility and availability of computer-simulated laboratories actually will increase the quality of student work. Also, since small groups of students will be able to work together more easily at their own convenience, there is more potential for increasing learning.

The key to successfully using such simulated lab experiences in honing the skills of undergraduate science students will be understanding the balance needed between hands-on work in a lab and the use of computer simulation. How much real touching and feeling of the equipment and chemicals is necessary for a student to "do" science? Surely, some touching and feeling is necessary, but just how much is really needed if we focus on the learning needs of students and not the traditions and past practice of faculty members? It also must be emphasized that students entering college in the next five to 10 years will be attuned to working in computer-generated environments—whether from playing games, traveling the information superhighway, or working with interactive television systems.

An interesting by-product of changing the nature of science labs is the implication for academic calendars. Since the large blocks of time needed to schedule science labs are usually major impediments to serious calendar revisions, shortening the time spent in labs and increasing the time spent on computer simulations has profoundly positive implications for calendar changes as well as student learning.

3) Conceptual Development

Most educators would consider conceptual learning the cornerstone of a good undergraduate education. Conceptual learning is hard work; it not only requires a good deal of reflection, but it literally forces students to restructure how they think about a particular area of life and, as a result, to readjust the ideas they have about it.

As students advance through their undergraduate education, they are expected to form new conceptual abilities. Unfortunately, when the faculty use instructional strategies that are not consistent with a reflective mode of learning and that do not motivate students, such restructuring of conceptual frameworks is difficult to achieve. Norman (1993) writes:

> ...the trick in teaching is to entice and motivate the student into excitement and interest in the topic, and then give them the proper tools to reflect; to explore, compare, and integrate; to form the proper conceptual structures...
>
> ...the problem is to make students want to do the hard work that is necessary for reflection.

Motivation turns out to be the key. If a highly entertaining environment creates such motivation, fine, although most entertainment is not reflective in orientation. It turns out, Norman's studies show, that students who were highly motivated learned the material far better than those who were uninterested, irrespective of how the material was presented.

Faculty members who helped train the early groups of Peace Corps volunteers found, to their delight, that the volunteers were so motivated to learn that the faculty were unprepared to deal with them because of the faculty members' experiences in typical classroom settings. Many volunteers were average college graduates who were intensely focused on going overseas to serve, and thus hungry to learn anything they could about the country in which they were going to live and work for two years. Challenging questions were common, and students' attempts to project themselves into the reality of their new country led them to rethink their views about the Third World and their own country. As someone who went through the training, I know that this intense and challenging new learning was not easy, especially given the time pressure, but it was exciting for everyone because the volunteers were so highly motivated to learn.

The typical faculty/student lecture-discussion only rarely reaches these levels of motivation, even in the hands of the best faculty. Yet, we know that our students spend hours intensely involved in activities they care about. Norman (1993) writes about game makers:

> They obviously know how to capture interest sufficiently well that real learning takes place, albeit learning of irrelevant subjects.
>
> The solution is to merge what each group of people can do best. Educators know what needs

to be learned; they are simply pretty bad at figuring out how to get the intense, devoted concentration required for the learning to take place. The field of entertainment knows how to create interest and excitement. It can manipulate the information and images. But it doesn't know what to teach.

> Perhaps we could merge these skills. The trick is to marry the entertainment world's skills of perception and of capturing the user's engagement with the educator's skills of reflective, indepth analysis.

It is difficult to imagine the present generation of students sitting day after day and week after week, focusing on and listening primarily to lectures—even exciting ones involving discussion. It is more likely that they will be better focused and more motivated in well-designed settings using interactive technologies. The challenge for faculty members will be to integrate the new world of simulation and interactive technologies with their own unique role as mentors, coaches, facilitators, and teachers of student learning.

Simulation.   We've discussed the use of interactive technology and computer simulation in regard to other learning modes. Such technologies also can play an important role in reflective thought if they are designed well, allowing a student to delve deeper and deeper into areas of interest while encouraging reflection. Much of this level of highly sophisticated interactive technology is only a few years away. But when it does arrive it will find ready takers among the student body, if not as easily among the faculty.

Mentoring and Human Simulation.   Simulations involving interactive technologies are exciting ventures and will expand the learning environment for students while containing costs; so, too, will the use of human simulations.

There are many instances where creative faculty have redesigned their undergraduate courses as learning laboratories, using one or another simulated environment to motivate and challenge students to reflect on their beliefs and actions; for example, simulating school and city decision-making settings and developing research projects. A similar classroom strategy involves teaching through case studies, which, in creative hands, can simulate problem-solving activities. These strategies combine the excitement of experiential learning with the intensity and focus necessary for reflection, thereby creating powerful learning environments for conceptual development. Unfortunately, such courses are the exception and occur in the context of three or four other classes offered in the typical lecture-discussion format.

Mentoring and Small Group Intensive Discussions.
While there are many times when one-on-one faculty/student interaction facilitates reflection, small group discussions also can be very effective environments for such learning because students not only receive support from their peers for their new conceptions but can share their different perspectives and even feel comfortable remaining silent and thinking. At the same time, the pressure of peers can provide an intensity and excitement to discussions—if the faculty member knows how to lead small group discussions.

A faculty member serving as a mentor/group leader not only can provide students with the feedback and focus that challenge conceptual thinking, but can enable students to build a sense of confidence in their own ideas. This type of faculty-student interaction is obviously a labor-intensive activity, but it is very important for enhancing student learning. However, when these intense group discussions, which can take place over a limited period of time, are integrated with information and experiences acquired in settings without faculty presence, the goal of reducing expenses and enhancing student learning can occur. It is possible that by doing this faculty members can spend less time with more students than would be the case in most college courses while, I believe, having more impact on student learning.

Testing Ideas in Real-Life Experience and Reflection.
The growth of student interest in community service activities provides settings in which ideas can be tested through direct experience. Such off-campus activities, which enable students to apply ideas or experience new environments, are important but do not necessarily emphasize reflection and conceptual development. What converts these experiences into a setting for conceptual development is reflecting on the experience itself through the written work and/or presentations to, and reflection with, others.

Faculty and/or peer advisors can play a critical role in many ways in enhancing a student's reflection: raising questions, providing alternative conceptions from the student's, encouraging the student to tie together the student's intellectual studies and life experiences, and providing feedback throughout the student's experience. This is a labor-intensive activity, but, like small group discussions, it can be cost effective and can enhance student learning provided the institution views the student's experiential and reflective learning as legitimate parts of university learning. Linking experiential learning in real-life settings with student reflection through written reports and presentations, while faculty act as mentors/advisors, is learning in its broadest sense. Since the experiences occur beyond the campus, their actual institutional costs are small: substantial costs do occur, however, in the faculty-student interactions focused on encouraging students to reflect on their experiences.

One-on-One Advising and Faculty-Student Interaction.
Often faculty view advising as a limited exercise enabling students to understand which courses to register for to

SUMMARY TABLE			
Restructured Faculty Role and Use of New Technologies			
Types of Student Learning	Faculty Role	Peer-Group Role/ Individual Learning	Technology
Accumulation of Knowledge and Information	Faculty presenter; faculty or librarian as guide to resources; faculty assessment of learning	Independent learning; use of guides to access new technology and/or to help with independent learning	Interactive technologies; access to databases; communication technology network with others throughout country
Skill Development	Faculty coaching outside of class; faculty as group discussion leader; faculty as trainer of student coaches	Older and more experienced peers as coaches; action settings using skills	Interactive technologies; computer simulation
Conceptual Development	Faculty as mentor and model; small group discussion leadership; faculty as convener of cooperative learning groups; one-on-one advising; faculty-student interaction	Peer-group interaction—cooperative learning groups; testing ideas in real-life experience; independent learning	Simulation/virtual reality; human simulation; communication technology networks

meet institutional graduation requirements. However, the best faculty advisers use this role to mentor and coach as much as advise: they encourage students to see how new learning can relate to earlier learning; discuss with them students' concerns about their future, about relationships to other students; and provide adult experience and wisdom to a searching young (or older) student. All these provide the intimacy of faculty/student interaction that is long remembered by students.

Learning Independently and With Peers. It is probably obvious that many students learn in a reflective mode on their own or as a result of one of the instructional learning strategies discussed above. While there are considerable learning style differences in this regard—some people can reflect more effectively alone while others do so in small groups of peers—providing for such independent learning and legitimizing it as part of a student's education is important for conceptual development to take place. This type of learning obviously requires a relatively small expenditure of faculty and institutional resources.

Implications

The restructuring of the role of faculty and the integration of the new electronic technologies with these new roles will have significant impact on many aspects of academic life. I expect that the very nature of how we structure all aspects of educating students will change.

Probably the most significant implication will be in the university's expectations for the *role of the student in the learning process.* Too often, students today are treated as if they are expected to be passive recipients of information and knowledge, even though we know that the most effective learning occurs when students are active learners. Restructuring the role of faculty as outlined above—or in almost any other scenario—and integrating new computer technologies into the learning process will mean that students must not only be active but more independent learners. There also will be an increased emphasis on intrinsic motivation rather than external rewards, which, as discussed earlier, leads to more effective conceptual learning.

From passive to active learner, from an emphasis on learning primarily in larger groups to a focus on smaller, more intimate groups and independent learning, from being concerned with extrinsic rewards to a concern for internal motivation—these changes in the role of student as learner will not fall easily on students trained throughout their education to be passive learners in larger groups focused on grades. But besides learning more, the concrete benefits to the individual student will be considerable—namely greater

access to high-quality education at substantially reduced costs.

Faculty members will benefit from this new student role by having more exciting student learners and a university that can afford adequate faculty salaries and learning resources. The benefit to the society may well be better-educated students, who will be badly needed in the technologically intense and sophisticated 21st century.

A second implication of the new faculty role is that wholesale alterations will have to be made in the *academic calendar* as we now know it. The calendar will need to be more flexible not only to allow different subject matter to be taught and learned using different time patterns, but to encourage and enhance different learning styles. As mentioned earlier, in many areas students will learn a great deal of the subject matter using as a series of learning blocks, with different blocks focused on electronic sources; peer-study groups; intensive, faculty-led mini-lecture-discussion sessions; intensive, short-term, faculty-led seminar discussion sessions; or off-campus learning by doing.

For the most part, the present academic calendar is built to enable faculty to teach groups of students in classroom settings meeting two or three times per week. If the calendar becomes refocused to deal with the needs and tools of student learning, it will be very different than it is now.

Third, the undergraduate *curriculum* as presently organized will have to change from its present focus on faculty disciplinary interests to a focus on student learning. This will require a significant philosophical shift for almost all colleges and universities, even most small liberal arts colleges.

The restructuring of the faculty role over the next five to 10 years also will require significant changes in *assessment procedures.* If our primary focus is on student learning and if such learning occurs in a number of different settings—intense faculty/student interaction, teams of peers, the use of interactive technologies, reflection on experience—student assessment must focus on the individual faculty member evaluating a group of students by grades would be inappropriate. I expect a number of different methods might be tried with a focus on student proficiency that could be demonstrated in a number of different ways depending on the student's learning style. It is also possible that there will be more focus on student learning contracts developed in close interaction with faculty.

Maybe all this is just wishful thinking, but the assessment of student learning may become a primary area of faculty-student interaction—an interaction that could possibly have considerable positive impact on students.

Changes Needed

Colleges and universities are locked in an unexamined educational delivery system that is increasing in costs while, at best, maintaining a steady state in student learning. Even some of the better reforms being considered, which require years and a great deal of human energy to implement, will not produce significant increases in student learning nor stem the tide of increasing institutional expenses and student costs, if they accept as basic the present underlying educational process and relationship between faculty and students.

Restructuring the role of faculty is a monumental undertaking, more difficult and more significant than the administrative restructuring that must precede it. If successful, faculty members will change their present teaching practices and become primarily concerned with enhancing and facilitating student learning. To accomplish this, many faculty will need to acquire additional skills.

This is a difficult challenge, but one we must face. The unacceptability of student costs will drive us to change, the new technologies will challenge us to alter our practices, and the society will force us to be accountable. And if we do not reduce costs creatively, it will be done for us by federal and state governments or the marketplace. We must begin by asking ourselves, if in the next five to 10 years we have to cut faculty positions 25 to 30 percent without significantly increasing class size or faculty workload, how will we do it?

It is just possible that if we reduce administrative and student services expenses by 25 to 33 percent and the size of the faculty by 25 to 33 percent, we might be able to hold down student costs. And, if we carry out these changes creatively, we might accomplish this while also enhancing student learning.

Resources

Astin, Alexander, *What Matters in College? Four Critical Years Revisited,* San Francisco: Jossey-Bass, 1992.

Chickering, Arthur W. and Zelda Gamson. "Seven Principles for Good Practices in Undergraduate Education," in *New Directions in Teaching and Learning,* No 47, San Francisco: Jossey-Bass, 1991.

Norman, Donald. *Things That Make Us Smart: Defending Human Attributes in the Age of the Machine,* Reading, Mass: Addison-Wesley, 1993.

Winston, Gordon. "New Dangers in Old Traditions: The Reporting of Economic Performance in Colleges and Universities," *Change,* Vol. 25, No. 1, Jan//Feb. 1993.

Comments on the article by MacGregor

Although most of the discussion in the next paper is about collaborative learning, MacGregor is really writing about a larger theme—the overall reform of education. Her viewpoint is more general than that of Finkel and Monk but, like them, she focuses on specific changes that can be made by one teacher or group of teachers in one class or group of classes. She appears to feel that global change will begin to occur in response to changes at more local levels.

MacGregor begins her essay by using three descriptions of learning situations to situate herself within the broad spectrum of educational reform. Then she briefly refers to the theories of Dewey, Piaget and Vygotsky, the origins of cooperative learning, the recent work that has been done with learning communities, reform programs attached to specific disciplines, problem-centered approaches, collaboration in undergraduate education, and the epistemology of social constructionism. The purpose of these cameo statements seems to be to establish a theoretical and (recent) historical background for her views about reform.

Turning to collaborative learning, the author describes various ways in which one might go about implementing this strategy. She also points out several implementation issues.

The second half of the paper is devoted to changes in the overall educational enterprise that a strong use of cooperative learning is likely to entail. She considers separately the changes that will involve students and those that will be required of the teacher.

The paper ends with some generalities about the future of collaborative learning and its ultimate effects on education.

Discussion Questions

1. Give a succinct description of MacGregor's overall view of what education ought to be like.
2. Comment on MacGregor's theoretical and historical background for educational reform.
3. MacGregor is interested in describing a wide variety of approaches to cooperative learning. Can you see any specific themes that run through of the variations she discusses?
4. What changes in the student's role are advocated by MacGregor and what are your views about them?
5. What changes in the teacher's role are advocated by MacGregor and what are your views about them?
6. How do your feelings about the future of collaborative learning compare with those of MacGregor?

Collaborative Learning: Shared Inquiry as a Process of Reform†

Jean MacGregor

Having read a chapter on the origins of life in their introductory biology textbook, students arrive at class and pick up worksheets. They gather around the teacher, who, using the phospholipids in egg yolk to mix oil and water, is demonstrating hydrophobic and hydrophilic characteristics of phospholipids molecules. Then dividing in groups of three or four, the students start on the worksheet problems. They diagram possible arrangements of phospholipids in the "primordial soup" that might have led to the first cell membranes, and then they speculate on the sources of these molecules. The teacher circulates, observing the groups and posing questions occasionally if a group appears completed stalled. The class period ends with groups sharing answers to the questions and posing additional ones of their own: fodder for the following day's discussion.

In a learning community program entitled "Revolution and Reaction," the final text for a book seminar is Hannah Arendt's *On Revolution*. Freshman students are not only able to identify important concepts such as Arendt's contrast between pity and compassion, but they are also now able to restate the essence of these concepts in simple terms, communicate them to others, and lead their peers to an understanding of them. The faculty member is struck by the students' facility at comparing Arendt's ideas to ideas raised earlier in the quarter through other assigned texts, lecture material, research paper sources, and independent reading. Flipping back and forth through the text, the students are searching for passages that help them to draw comparisons to Plato, Machiavelli, and Marx.

In a writing class organized thematically around American social history, students are working in groups to plan, draft, and polish papers. They begin by reading a brochure and viewing a video on Irish immigration to the Five Points section of New York City in the 1850s. First in small groups and then in large ones, the students discuss the content and deepen their understanding of it by creating questions for each other and answering them. Working alternately in small groups and as a whole class with the teacher, the students move through a process of brainstorming possible paper topics, which range from stereotypes and prejudice then and now to how American values were played out in the immigrant experience in New York. The students and teacher, again working in small and in large groups, move next to narrowing the list to several workable topics, discussing various rhetorical structures to achieve different goals in writing on the topics. Later, the students move to a writing lab, where they work individually at word processors, but they also circulate to read each other's material and try out ideas. After several small group work sessions on each draft, papers begin to emerge.

In each of these three situations, students and teachers are engaged in collaborative learning. Students are working with each other, and frequently alongside their teachers, to grasp subject matter or to deepen their understanding of it. In the process, they are developing their social skills, and their intellectual skills as well. Students might be interpreting, questioning, creating, synthesizing, inventing, doubting, comparing, making connections, puzzling, or doing myriad other sorts of active, visible intellectual tasks. But this active learning takes place publicly, in partnership with others. Students and their teachers are involved in a common enterprise: the *mutual* seeking of understanding. Because many minds are simultaneously grappling with the material, while working toward a common goal, collaborative learning has the potential to unleash a unique intellectual and social synergy.

There have always been social dimensions to the learning process, but only in recent decades have specially designed collaborative learning experiences been regarded as an innovative alternative to the lecture-centered and teacher-as-single-authority approaches typical of most college classrooms. Today, work on collaboration comes from a broad array of disciplines and educational philosophies, and interest in collaborative approaches is growing both inside and beyond the academy. Nevertheless, while productive, engaged communities of learners are a worthwhile ideal, the work of collaboration can be demanding for teacher and student alike.

This chapter explores some of the historical underpinnings of collaborative learning and highlights the issues involved in designing collaborative approaches. It also raises important questions for those beginning to design collaborative intellectual experiences and examines how teaching and learning in collaborative modes entails, for faculty and students, a reframing of assumptions about teachers, learners, and knowledge.

Roots of Collaboration in Education

As the 1990s begin, interest in collaborative learning has probably never been greater. This expanding work, however, is not based on a single theoretical foundation or even a very clear history of practice. The work on collaboration in education is more like an arbor of vines growing in parallel, crossing and intertwining.

Dewey, Piaget, and Vygotsky.   Most of the collaborative learning vines are deeply rooted in experiential learning and student-centered instruction, the major proponents of which

in this century have been philosopher John Dewey and cognitive psychologists Jean Piaget and L. S. Vygotsky. They all struggled to understand how teachers can help learners deal with the tension between what students already know (their prior experience) and what is newly presented to them. They were strong advocates of learning as experiencing. They stressed how critical it is for the teacher not simply to transmit content but also to create a context where learners can discover on their own and successfully reconstruct their understanding of the world around them. While Piaget focused on cognitive development as an individual process, Dewey and Vygotsky were convinced that learning is fundamentally social in nature.

Cooperative Learning.   Many collaborative learning vines have additional roots in social psychology, particularly in the nature and power of small group theory. First articulated in the 1940s by pioneers such a Kurt Lewin and Martin Deutsch, small group theory has been applied to social interaction skills and learning in the context of team activity in workplaces and community arenas throughout the nation. Coupled with educational psychology, small group theory is in addition a principal foundation for the cooperative learning movement led by David Johnson and Roger Johnson at the University of Minnesota, and by Robert Slavin at Johns Hopkins University. This effort to develop cooperative (as opposed to competitive or individualized) goal structures for learning has developed rapidly in elementary and secondary schools. It is in this area that the most extensive evaluative research has occurred (Johnson and others, 1981; Slavin, 1983), generally corroborating the claim that students learn more in cooperative settings than they do in competitive or individualized ones.

Learning-Community Curricular Reform Efforts. Learning communities constitute another major vine in the collaborative learning arbor. This work grew out of important attempts to restructure college curricula for greater intellectual coherence and student engagement. At the University of Wisconsin in the late 1920s, philosopher Alexander Meiklejohn abandoned traditional courses in favor of an integrated, two-year, full-time program called the "Experimental College," in which students examined the classics and engaged in intensive dialogue about what it means to live in a democracy. This ground-breaking but short-lived experiment spawned several other curricular restructuring efforts, most notably Joseph Tussman's experiment at the University of California-Berkeley, St. John's and other "Great Books" colleges, and The Evergreen State College. The framers of these programs argued that the course structure itself is actually a barrier to effective learning because it abbreviates, fragments, and atomizes intellectual experience for student and professor alike. Their solution required a complete reconstruction of students' and teachers' curricular lives around full-time, integrated, interdisciplinary programs—mega-courses—usually involving both team teaching and collaborative discussion of primary texts. The threads of mutual responsibility and participation ran deep in these efforts, as they do today in expanding numbers of course-linking and curricular restructuring endeavors known as learning-community programs (Gabelnick, MacGregor, Matthews, and Smith, 1990).

Discipline-Based Efforts.   Other champions of classroom collaboration have emerged in recent years from successful group work in disciplinary contexts. Kenneth Bruffee and his colleagues at the City University of New York pioneered strategies for enabling students to work on their writing—and on their thinking—out loud, with each other. This has led to a rich peer-writing approach that has transformed the writing classroom into an active workshop where, as in the real world, writers work on their writing with other writers. More recently, Uri Treisman and others at the University of California-Berkeley have revolutionized the teaching of college mathematics by developing communities of students and faculty who work together intensively.

Problem-Centered Approaches.   Work in critical thinking and problem-centered learning constitutes another cluster of collaborative learning vines. Harvard University's Case Method, the work in Guided Design, McMaster University's problem-centered curricula, and a large array of home-grown simulations and "worksheet workshops"; all of these approaches involve carefully designed small group experiences. They ask teams of students to embark on tasks that challenge them to apply the ideas or practice the work of the discipline, with their teachers serving as coaches or providers of expert feedback.

Collaboration in Undergraduate Education.   During the 1980s, several informal networks with interests in collaborative learning have emerged in higher education. With support and recognition from organizations such as the Fund for the Improvement of Postsecondary Education (FIPSE), the American Association of Colleges, and the American Association for Higher Education, Collaboration in Undergraduate Education (CUE) is a network of individuals with interests not only in collaborative learning in the classroom but also in the broader issues of student-teacher collaboration in both research and curricular development or revision, teacher-to-teacher collaborative efforts, and collaborative approaches to academic administration (Romer, 1985). The CUE network mounts presentations and workshops at national higher education conferences, acts as a clearinghouse for information about collaborative work, publishes a newsletter, and works on publications. Additionally, the FIPSE-funded Collaborative Learning Resource Center at Lesley College in Cambridge, Massachusetts, is another clearinghouse, bringing together scholars, practitioners, and educational researchers interested in collaboration.

Collaborative Learning and Epistemological Theory

Those who structure their classrooms around collaboration can find philosophical confirmation of their approaches in recent scholarship in social constructionism and in feminist theory and pedagogy. Social constructionism, an expanding web of epistemological perspectives in several disciplines, springs from the assumption that knowledge is socially, rather than individually, constructed by communities of individuals. Knowledge is shaped, over time, by successive conversations, and by ever-changing social and political environments. The knowledge business should not be just the territory of competing scholars or experts, the social constructionists argue; the shaping and testing of ideas is something in which anyone can participate.

Theorists in the moral and intellectual development of women and in feminist pedagogy generally agree with the social constructionist view of knowledge creation and change. They believe that students cannot be regarded as a uniform body of isolated individuals poised to receive knowledge through uniform modes of information delivery. Rather, learners are diverse individuals whose understanding of reality is shaped by their gender, race, class, age, and cultural experience. Therefore, teaching is woefully inadequate if it is construed as an enterprise of "transmission" or "coverage." And learning is woefully limited if it is thought of as simply an exercise in "receiving" and "reflecting." To enable learners to move beyond superficial or merely procedural understanding of a subject, the teacher must invite them into a process of working out their own understandings and syntheses of the material, and developing their individual points of view toward it (Belenky, Clinchy, Goldberger, and Tarule, 1986).

Designing for Collaborative Learning

The glimpses of collaborative learning that opened this chapter suggest a broad range of formats and contexts in which these approaches flourish. During a lecture, students might be asked to turn to a neighbor to formulate responses, raise questions, or solve problems. Students might work in teams to conduct and write up a laboratory report, field study, or longer research project. Groups of students might meet regularly to prepare homework or critique each other's writing, hold seminar discussions, or prepare for a presentation. What is essential is positive interdependence between students, a product to which everyone contributes, and a sense of commitment and responsibility to the group's preparation, process, and product.

For the faculty member, designing collaborative learning experiences requires careful thought about what active learning might entail in one's course or discipline. Meaningful, lasting learning requires students to use what is known to them, and what is becoming known. This involves linking the gathering aspects of learning to doing, constructing, and creating. Gathering means the "taking in" part of learning: taking in new information or ideas, by reading, watching, or listening. Doing is the "using" part: using what is gathered either to construct one's own understanding of the material or to create something new, for example, a poem, a sculpture, or a response. Too often, college classrooms have made learning largely a gathering process, and have relegated the doing/constructing/creating portions to occasional performances on quizzes or tests.

Sketching in the Possibilities.   The first task for the teacher who is planning collaborative work for students is to examine the scope of a whole course and sketch the collaborative possibilities. Where and in how much of the course is collaboration appropriate? How can the gathering and the doing elements of the course be interwoven so that each element reinforces the other?

Developing the Collaborative Task.   Framing the actual tasks or problems for collaborative work requires thinking through the particular kind of intellectual experiences or thinking tasks that students might undertake together. Most teachers realize that unstructured, freewheeling explorations do not sufficiently focus student energy, or challenge students to use what they know. Students are most stimulated when confronted with absorbing or puzzling tasks or questions and a clear sense of the product that is expected of them: for example, a synthesis, a conceptual framework, a comparison, an argument, an array of personal responses, or a dramatization.

With experience, faculty members find that they get better and better at preparing students for collaborative work, that is, at providing them with a common framework or background from which to begin, questions or problems that stimulate and stretch them, and a clear sense of expected outcomes of the group work. It takes some practice, and repeated observation of students grappling with ideas, to find those points of access, or "zones of proximal development" as Vygotsky called them, where students are challenged to move from what they know into the realm of what they do not quite yet know.

Thinking Through How Evaluation Will Work.   A third design arena concerns feedback and accountability, critical elements in any collaborative enterprise. Several important issues should be addressed by faculty and students alike before the group work gets under way. If multiple small groups are working on problems or exploring issues simultaneously in a classroom, what will be the process for sharing or giving feedback on the results of work? When and how might the faculty member provide clarification, evaluation, or extension of the work that has been accomplished? Will the students have an opportunity to evaluate the nature of their own work, as well as their effort as an interdependent group? In what manner will they give the teacher feedback on the quality of the experience? How will the teacher carry out individual student evaluation when students are spending significant time working in teams?

Practice: The Best Teacher.   There are several resources on managing collaborative learning, but the richest guides for collaborative teachers are their own experiments with teaching, the advice and experience of colleagues, and, most importantly, formal and informal feedback from the students themselves. Indeed, the collaborative classroom, brimming with data about the content and quality of student learning, is an ongoing lab for classroom research. The public learning taking place provides immediate feedback for the discerning teacher to use in improving collaborative designs. For faculty who offer the same courses year after year, the use of group work is a sure hedge against staleness. Each refinement of a collaborative learning design, and each new class's experience with it, recreates the material in fresh and provocative ways.

Reframing the Student Role

A class with high expectations about participation and collaboration requires substantial role shifts for students. It is not unusual to encounter student resistance to group work. Embedded in student expectations about classroom culture, and in the inertia of their own ingrained habits, such resistance is real and should be taken seriously.

As they move into collaborative learning settings, students find themselves grappling with shifts such as the following: (1) from listener, observer, and note taker to active problem solver, contributor, and discussant; (2) from low to moderate expectations of preparation for class to high expectations, frequently having to do with reading and preparing questions or other assigned work in advance; (3) from a private presence in the classroom to a public one; (4) from attendance dictated by personal choice to that having to do with community expectation; (5) from competition with peers to collaborative work with them; (6) from responsibilities and self-definition associated with learning independently to those associated with learning interdependently; and (7) from seeing teachers and texts as the sole sources of authority and knowledge to seeing peers, oneself, and the thinking of the community as additional and important sources of authority and knowledge.

These shifts are especially problematic for younger college learners. To them, the adjective "cooperative" has unfortunate residual connotations from high school. With reference to authorities, being cooperative has to do with obedience; with reference to peers, it usually means cheating. The idea of cooperation as helping and sharing for positive goals is often a completely foreign notion. Many students also have difficulty accepting that collaborative learning with peers is real learning and has value, so conditioned are they to expecting teachers to be the sole source of knowledge in the classroom.

Moreover, there are the risks inherent in the public nature of collaborative work. Such work almost always entails talk, and a great deal of it. Learning collaboratively, students are working out loud, and the learning is "live"—on the air, as it were, bloopers and all.

The faculty member, then, needs to set the context for collaborative work so that students can understand and reflect on its rationale, value, and immediate goals. Many teachers feel it is essential to engage students in discussion about the risks and responsibilities of working in groups, the challenges and opportunities inherent in learning from diverse perspectives, and the interplay between individualism and community. With the students, many faculty members develop a set of group norms or ground rules for coming to class prepared, working together responsibly, and resolving differences. They also work to create a safe environment for risk taking, where students' offerings, even the most tentative ones, are listened to attentively, and where disagreements are aired with respect. Many teachers make a practice of giving public value to the group process as well as to the thinking tasks, by asking each collaborative student team to evaluate not only the quality of its intellectual work but also the quality of its team work. With time, patience, and understanding, students usually break through their cautiousness, fear, and skepticism about collaboration and discover the stimulation and power of working in concert with others.

Reframing the Teacher Role

Whether novice or veteran in the collaborative learning process, faculty members engaged in this work have their own reframing to do, with regard to coverage, classroom roles, evaluation, and a variety of other issues. Particularly challenging is the process of reconciling one's sense of responsibility about course coverage with one's commitment to enabling students to learn on their own. Too often, faculty members think of course coverage in zero-sum terms, neglecting to ask whether students are really comprehending and integrating all that is being covered. Teachers who build their courses around group work do not belittle or abandon coverage or skills; indeed, they and their students are seriously and directly confronting matters of understanding and comprehension all the time. But the burden of "covering" (and of explicating and relating) has shifted from the teacher alone to the teacher and students together.

If this shift of responsibility helps to "dissolve the Atlas complex" (Finkel and Monk, 1983), wherein the teacher feels endlessly responsible for the class's entire intellectual agenda, it also poses interesting questions. Authority and expertise, power and control—highly intertwined matters for any teacher—all come up for examination and redefinition in the collaborative classroom. As students together begin assuming more responsibility for their learning, and as classroom time is directed more to conversational inquiry, teachers begin to sense subtle but powerful shifts in their role. As students begin to take up their part in the learning enterprise, teachers begin to see that they are not so much relinquishing control as they are sharing it in new ways. They discover that the lines of authority are not so much blurred as they are reshaped.

For example, collaborating teachers want to share their expertise without eclipsing students' beginning attempts to develop their own. They may not be playing the center-stage expert role continuously, but they must then choose what alternate roles to play, and when it would be most productive to play which role. They might be active co-learners, who work with students as the more expert peers in a process of mutual inquiry. They might use their expertise as workshop architects or simulation designers, who present students with questions or problems; they then remove themselves from the process, allowing the students to explore on their own while they watch from the sidelines and give expert feedback only at the end. Or they might choose a role in between, where they are the stimulators of student group work, who move from group to group observing and entering occasionally into the picture as friendly kibitzers.

Teachers also must consider the issue of authority relative to grading and evaluation within the collaborative context. By observing student work in interactive settings, faculty discover how well they have come to know their students, and how much data they have acquired for evaluating them. Because this information is at once so much more rich and diverse than what would normally emerge from occasional discussions, papers, or exams, it makes the grading process both more interesting and more complex. What remains problematic, however, is that faculty members are still the expert witnesses of student learning, and the holders of power relative to the grading process. And, more than any other factor, instructors' evaluative processes act to divide students, and to press the classroom atmosphere back into a competitive mode. Teachers need to clarify, for themselves as well as for students, their assumptions and expectations about evaluation as it relates to the collaborative work in the class, and about what evaluative weight will be given to team work and to individual work throughout the course. Teachers find it crucial to build an understanding of the evaluation process at the outset, and to remain vigilant about students' perceptions of evaluation throughout the course. Many teachers build evaluation responsibilities and skills in their students by involving them in self-evaluation as well as in peer and faculty evaluation.

Collaborative Learning and the Future

Faculty involved with collaborative learning remain deeply committed to it, in spite of its challenges. Many of these teachers are inspired by larger social imperatives, such as the needs for greater multicultural understanding and a more participatory democracy. But many more teachers are simply excited about what collaborative learning helps them discover in their students and in themselves. They relish the ways students emerge as confident, competent learners, who in turn stimulate them to reexamine their own work and thinking. They value each class they teach as a unique community, enriched by the subject matter but enriching it as well. Preliminary efforts to evaluate collaborative learning are encouraging: these kinds of approaches have been found to have a positive impact on student retention, achievement, and intellectual development, as well as on attitudinal and affective change, particularly in the areas of self-esteem and sensitivity to racial, ethnic, and gender difference (Cooper and Mueck, in press; MacGregor, 1987).

What then, does the future hold for collaborative learning? Are the collaborative learning vines healthy? While recent evidence indicates a remarkable growth surge, the ground for collaborative learning is not entirely fertile. The prevailing structures on most colleges simply do not foster effective group work. Fifty-minute hours, large class sizes, and fixed seating arrangements are only a few of the struc-

tures that still assume a "transmission" model of college teaching and learning. Reward systems for college teachers do not yet give high priority to pedagogical excellence; even where they do, there is little recognition of teaching innovation or experimentation, and few opportunities for teachers to collaborate on different approaches. Stereotypes of what collaborative learning is or entails may deter many potentially interested teachers from ever trying it out. Others who do try collaborative approaches without adequate support or preparation may feel less than successful and turn away with a sense of discomfort or failure. But what can hold back collaborative learning the most is our cultural biases toward competition and individualism, also strong vines in the American arbor that have a particularly tenacious presence in our academic institutions. The task of the collaborative learning effort, then, is not only to share and document effective models of collaborative teaching and learning but also to articulate its role and value in American education and society.

While there are barriers to the spread of collaborative learning, other trends, both inside and outside the academy, propel the work forward. Collaborative learning networks, and learning community and other curricular efforts, are expanding. Many of these endeavors find reinforcement in major studies and reports on effective teaching and learning (Chickering and Gamson, 1987; National Institute of Education, 1984), and on student success in college (Tinto, 1987). While experience and sophistication develop on the practice side, there is growing commitment to collaboration from the general education sector. Social interaction skills, appreciation of racial, gender, and ethnic differences, and civic awareness and responsibility are emerging as essential outcomes of academic experience, not simply of student life activities.

These developments are modest, however, compared to the rapidly growing emphasis on social interdependence and collaboration both in the workplace and in public arenas. Horizontal and participatory forms of management have taken their places alongside more traditional vertical and authoritarian approaches in political contexts, and public involvement and partnership-building efforts are burgeoning worldwide. The arena of conflict resolution, once equated almost entirely with adversarial processes, has begun to include new, more collaborative forms of negotiated and mediated settlement processes. In what is becoming a daunting landscape of social and environmental predicaments, these new forms of management and problem solving represent small, promising sparks of constructive change. Workplaces, the nation, and the world will increasingly call for more responsible and responsive community builders and problem solvers, and all our educational systems will have to search for ways to meet this demand. All these trends may combine to create a much more favorable climate for the growth of collaborative learning approaches into the twenty-first century.

Shared Inquiry as a Process of Reform

As it becomes more widely practiced, collaborative learning has profound implications. It could change the nature of conventional undergraduate classrooms, and it could help to develop a much more civically active populace. Yet, the collaborative learning agenda is really about individual learners, and how it enables them to learn about learning and themselves. While there are larger educational and societal implications, collaborative learning can only begin and grow as a small-scale reform, the kind that springs within individuals, a few at a time. Collaboration in classroom settings can reveal that learning itself is always an occasion for reform. The process of shared inquiry invites students and teachers to develop the habit of seeing their knowledge as continuously evolving, indeed reforming, through dialogues with the self, others, and the world.

References

Belenky, M. F., Clinchy, B. M., Goldberger, N. R., and Tarule, J. M. *Women's Ways of Knowing.* New York: Basic Books, 1986.

Chickering, A. W., and Gamson, Z. "Seven Principles for Good Practice in Undergraduate Education." *American Association for Higher Education Bulletin,* 1987, 39, 3–7.

Cooper, J., and Mueck, R. "Student Involvement in Learning: Cooperative Learning and College Instruction." *Journal of Excellence in College Teaching,* in press.

Finkel, D. L., and Monk, G. S. "Teachers and Learning Groups: Dissolving the Atlas Complex." In C. Bouton and R. Y. Garth (eds.), *Learning in Groups.* New Directions for Teaching and Learning, no. 14. San Francisco: Jossey-Bass, 1983.

Gabelnick, F., MacGregor, J., Matthews, R. S., and Smith, B. L. *Learning Communities: Creating Connections Among Students, Faculty, and Disciplines.* New Directions for Teaching and Learning, no. 41. San Francisco: Jossey-Bass, 1990.

Johnson, D. W., and others. "Effect of Cooperative, Competitive and Individualistic Goal Structures on Achievement: A Meta-Analysis." *Psychological Bulletin,* 1981, 89, 47–62.

MacGregor, J. *Intellectual Development of Students in Learning Communities.* Washington Center Occasional Paper, no. 1 Olympia, Wash.: The Evergreen State College, 1987.

National Institute for Education. *Involvement in Learning: Realizing the Potential for Higher Education.* Final Report of the Study Group of the Conditions of Excellence in Higher Education. Washington, D.C.: National Institute for Education, 1984.

Romer, K. T. (ed.). CUE: *Models of Collaboration in Undergraduate Education.* Providence, R.I.: Brown University Press, 1985.

Slavin, R. E. "When Does Cooperative Learning Increase Student Achievement?" *Psychological Bulletin,* 1983, 94, 429–445.

Tinto, V. *Leaving College: Rethinking the Causes and Cures of Student Attrition.* Chicago: University of Chicago Press, 1987.

Comments on the article by
Asiala, Brown, DeVries, Dubinsky, Mathews and Thomas

As the title suggests, the following paper, by Asiala, Brown, DeVries, Dubinsky, Mathews, and Thomas describes a framework for research into how college students learn mathematics. Within this context, a process for developing curricula based on this research is presented. On your first reading of this article, you may want to focus on issues surrounding the design of curricula, and on a second (or later) reading consider how the design process is situated in the context of the framework for this research.

Theoretical perspectives of how individuals learn mathematics are influenced by an understanding of what it means to know mathematics. A statement of the theoretical perspective of this research group is given, and the implications of its components are discussed in the context of creating a learning environment in which students are encouraged to make the mental constructions which lead to learning mathematical concepts.

The ACE-cycle is described and discussed as an instructional strategy: *Activities* before the concept is presented formally, *Class discussion* about the concepts which the students are exploring, and follow-up *Exercises* for extended practice after the concepts have been formally presented. Several examples are given in which the ACE-cycle can lead students from an *action-understanding* of a concept (such as "function") through a *process-understanding* to an *object-understanding*. Problems presented in *activities* put the students into an intentionally disequilibrating environment which contains as much information as possible about the material to be studied. Cooperative learning groups provide a social context in which students are encouraged to reflect on the procedures they perform in working on problems. In these groups, students are supported in the process of making the necessary new mental constructions.

Discussion Questions

1. What has been your own experience of learning, particularly of learning mathematics? Would you say that this process has been "linear"—or has it been a process of gradually being able to draw on certain ideas more consistently, with greater ease, each time you've encountered a new problem to solve? Recall and reflect on some specific examples.
2. What characteristics of ISETL make it "an ideal environment for mathematical experimentation, reflection, and discussion"? What other programs or technologies are available which have similar characteristics?
3. The authors present several examples of a particular pedagogical strategy for presenting new concepts to students. Choose one of these examples and discuss how you could implement this in a course you are now teaching (or one you expect to teach soon).

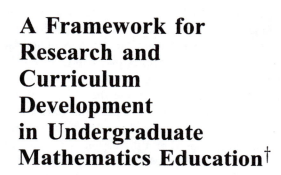

A Framework for Research and Curriculum Development in Undergraduate Mathematics Education[†]

**Mark Asiala, Anne Brown,
David J. DeVries,
Ed Dubinsky, David Mathews,
Karen Thomas**

Abstract. Over the past several years, a community of researchers has been using and refining a particular framework for research and curriculum development in undergraduate mathematics education. The purpose of this paper is to share the results of this work with the mathematics education community at large by describing the current version of the framework and giving some examples of its application.

Our framework utilizes qualitative methods for research and is based on a very specific theoretical perspective that is being developed through attempts to understand the ideas of Piaget concerning reflective abstraction and reconstruct them in the context of college level mathematics. Our approach has three components. It begins with an initial theoretical analysis of what it means to understand a concept and how that understanding can be constructed by the learner. This leads to the design of an instructional treatment that focuses directly on trying to get students to make the constructions called for by the analysis. Implementation of instruction leads to the gathering of data, which is then analyzed in the context of the theoretical perspective. The researchers cycle through the three components and refine both the theory and the instructional treatments as needed.

In this report the authors present detailed descriptions of each of these components. In our discussion of theoretical analyses, we describe certain mental constructions for learning mathematics, including actions, processes, objects, and schemas, and the relationships among these constructions. Under instructional treatment, we describe the components of the ACE teaching cycle (activities, class discussion, and exercises), cooperative learning and the use of a mathematical programming language. Finally, we describe the methodology used in data collection and analysis. The paper concludes with a discussion of issues raised in the use of this framework, followed by an extensive bibliography.

1. Introduction

The purpose of this paper is to set down a very specific methodology for research in the learning of mathematics, and curriculum development based on that research. We are concerned with theoretical analyses which model mathematical understanding, instruction based on the results of these analyses, and empirical data, both quantitative and qualitative, that can be used to refine the theoretical perspective and assess the effects of the instruction.

This report caps several years of research and development during which a framework for conducting this work has been developed and applied to various topics in collegiate mathematics. Now that the main outlines of our approach have stabilized, and the group of researchers using this framework has begun to grow, we wish to share our work with others in the mathematics education community,

[†] Reprinted with permission from CBMS Issues in Mathematics Education, Volume 6, 1996, pp. 1–32. Copyright © 1996 American Mathematical Society.

including potential collaborators.[1] We offer here the details of our approach, both as a report on what has taken place and as a possible guide to future efforts.

After a few general remarks in the introduction about paradigms, and about previous discussions of the specific framework we have been developing, we proceed to an overview of our approach as it now stands, and the goals we associate with it. Then, in the main portion of the paper, we describe in detail our framework and its components along with several examples. Next, we consider some larger issues that arise in connection with our framework. Finally, we summarize what has been said in this paper and point to what can be expected in future reports.

1.1 What is a paradigm and why is one needed?.

The seminal work of Thomas Kuhn [19] teaches us that scientific research proceeds according to what he calls *paradigms.*[2] *A paradigm is a collection of understandings (explicit or implicit) on the part of an individual or group of individuals about the kinds of things one does when conducting research in a particular field, the types of questions that are to be asked, the sorts of answers that are to be expected, and the methods that are to be employed in searching for these answers.*

We also learn from Kuhn that "paradigm shifts" do not come quickly or easily, but they do tend to be sharp. They are caused by what Kuhn calls a "crisis state" which can be the result of one of two different situations. One is that an event or discovery is so far reaching that it is impossible to assimilate it into the current paradigm, hence the need for a new paradigm. The second situation is a developing dissatisfaction with the current paradigm that reaches a level where answers to certain questions (often basic to the field) can not be easily or satisfactorily obtained. This brings about a sort of declared rejection of the current paradigm by individuals who begin to search for a new paradigm. Whatever the cause, the crisis state continues until an alternative can be agreed upon by the community and then the change *must* be a simultaneous rejection of the old paradigm and an acceptance of the new paradigm by the research community as a whole. Thus, dissatisfaction with a particular paradigm builds up gradually over a long period of time until there occurs a moment, or

"scientific revolution" in which the understandings change rather drastically and fairly quickly.

It seems that the second situation which causes Kuhn's scientific revolution has occurred for research in mathematics education. For a long time, research in this field consisted almost exclusively of statistical comparisons of control and experimental populations according to designs proposed by Sir R. A. Fisher some 60 years ago for the purpose of making decisions about agricultural activities [12]. In the last decade or so, there has been a growing concern with the impossibility of really meeting the conditions required to make application of statistical tests to mathematics education valid, a dissatisfaction with the small differences and unrealistic contexts to which these designs seem to lead, and a developing understanding that the fundamental mechanisms of learning mathematics are not as simplifiable and controllable as agricultural factors. Traditional statistical measures may apply, for example to paired-associate learning, but if one wishes to build on the work of Jean Piaget, and/or use the ideas of theoretical cognitive structures, then new methods of research, mainly qualitative, must be developed to relate those structures to observable behavior. (For a discussion of the implications of cognitive science on research methodology in education see Davis [4].) Workers in the field have stopped insisting on a statistical paradigm and have begun to think about alternatives.

This represents only the conditions for a scientific revolution and is not yet a paradigm shift because no single alternative point of view has been adopted to replace the accepted paradigm. The ideas of Jean Piaget have influenced many researchers to turn from quantitative to qualitative methods, but there are many forms of qualitative research that are being used at present. In considering the variety of approaches being used, there are two aspects which must be addressed. The first is the theoretical perspective taken by the researchers using a particular approach, and the second is the set of actual methods by which data is collected and analyzed.

Patton [20] lists some of the theoretical perspectives used by qualitative researchers. These include the ethnographic perspective, in which the central goal is to describe the culture of a group of people, and related perspectives including phenomenology and heuristics, in which the goals are to describe the essential features of a particular experience for a particular person or group of people. The tradition of ecological psychology seeks to understand the effect of the setting on the ways in which people behave, and the perspective of systems theory seeks to describe how a particular system (for instance, a teacher and a group of students in a given classroom) functions. In addition, there are orientational approaches (feminist, Marxist, Freudian,

---

[1] We have organized an informal community of researchers who use this framework, known as *Research in Undergraduate Mathematics Education Community* or *RUMEC*, with the intention of producing a series of research reports by various subsets of the membership. The present paper is the first in the *RUMEC* series.

[2] For a critical look at Kuhn's and others' philosophical views on the structure of scientific revolutions and theories see Suppe [30] or Gutting [16].

etc.) within each of these perspectives. Methods of data collection for qualitative studies vary widely, and in many of the theoretical perspectives it is considered important to use a wide variety of data collection methods, studying the phenomena of interest from all available angles in order to be able to triangulate data from many sources in reaching a conclusion. Romberg [24] discusses the use of interviews, which may range from informal discussions between researchers and participants to very structured conversations in which a predetermined list of questions is asked of each participant. He also discusses observational methods ranging from videotaping to the use of trained observers to participant observations. Patton [20] discusses other sources of data, including documents and files which may be available to the researcher, photographs and diagrams of the setting in which the research takes place, and the researchers' field notes.[3]

Thus we see that there is a wide variety of frameworks in which it is possible to work. In this paper we describe our choice which has been made consciously with concern for the theoretical and empirical aspects as well as applicability to real classrooms in the form of instructional treatments.

According to Kuhn, researchers shift to a new framework because it satisfies the needs of the times more than the existing paradigm. There are two reasons why we feel that researchers should make conscious choices about the framework under which they work.

One reason is necessity. The variety of qualitative research methodologies indicated above does not appear to be leading to any kind of convergence to a single approach (or even a small number of approaches) that has general acceptance. We are finding more and more that research done according to one framework is evaluated according to another and this is leading to some measure of confusion. Therefore, we feel that researchers should make explicit the framework they are using and the basis on which their work is to be judged. Consumers of the results of research need to have a clear idea of what they can and cannot expect to get out of a piece of research.

Second, we feel that a conscious attention to the specifics of one's framework is more in keeping with the scientific method as expressed by David Griese who interpreted science as "a department of practical work which depends on the knowledge and conscious application of principle" [15]. Griese decided 20 years ago that it was time to move computer programming to an endeavor in which it was possible to teach the principles so that they can be con-

sciously applied. We believe that it is important today that those who study the learning of post-secondary mathematics attempt to make available to others the methodologies under which they work.

1.2 Previous discussions of this framework.

Components of our framework have been discussed in several papers over the last several years: [2,5,7,8]. The overall framework with its three components have been discussed at length, especially the theoretical component, but only very fragmented discussions of the other two components, instructional treatments and gathering/analyzing data have been given. Moreover, the framework and its components are continuing to evolve as we reflect on our practice. Finally, the authors of this article are part of a larger community which is in the process of producing a number of studies of topics in calculus and abstract algebra using this framework. Therefore, it seems reasonable at this time to present a complete, self-contained and up-to-date discussion of the entire framework.

2. A framework for research and curriculum development

2.1 Overview of the framework.

The framework used in this research consists of three components. Figure 1 illustrates each of these components and the relationships among them. A study of the cognitive growth of an individual trying to learn a particular mathematical concept takes place by successive refinements as the investigator repeatedly cycles through the component activities of Figure 1.

Research begins with a theoretical analysis modeling the epistemology of the concept in question: what it means to understand the concept and how that understanding can be constructed by a learner. This initial analysis, marking the researchers' entry into the cycle of components of the framework, is based primarily on the researchers' under-

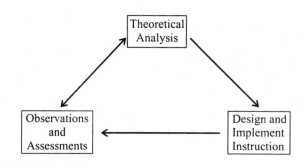

FIGURE 1
The Framework.

---

[3] For information on qualitative methods used in the social sciences see Jacob [17] or Patton [20]. For information on qualitative methods used in mathematics education research, see Romberg [24] or Schoenfeld [26].

standing of the concept in question and on their experiences as learners and teachers of the concept. The analysis informs the design of instruction. Implementing the instruction provides an opportunity for gathering data and for reconsidering the initial theoretical analysis with respect to this data. The result may well be a revision of the theoretical analysis which then lays the foundation for the next iteration of the study. This next iteration begins with the revised theoretical analysis and ends with a further revision or deeper understanding of the epistemology of the concept in question which may become the foundation for yet another repetition of the cycle. These repetitions are continued for as long as appears to be necessary to achieve stability in the researchers' understanding of the epistemology of the concept.

2.2 Goals and issues associated with the framework.

Research using this framework is inevitably a synthesis of "pure" and "applied" research. Each time the researchers cycle through the components of the framework, every component is reconsidered and, possibly, revised. In this sense the research builds on and is dependent upon previous implementations of the framework. We observe students trying to understand mathematics and offer explanations of successes and failures in terms of mental constructs and the ways in which they transform. Our specific goals are: to increase our understanding of how learning mathematics can take place, to develop a theory-based pedagogy for use in undergraduate mathematics instruction, and to develop a base of information and assessment techniques which shed light on the epistemology and pedagogy associated with particular concepts. The goals are thus associated with the three components of the framework.

There are many issues raised as a result of the use of this framework. In the component of theoretical analysis there are the following issues: 1. How does one go about developing the theoretical perspective? 2. How do we see the relationship between this theory and what actually happens; that is, to what extent can a theoretical analysis provide an accurate or even approximate picture of what is going on in the minds of the learners? In the component dealing with pedagogy there is the issue of explaining the relationship between the instructional treatments and our theoretical analysis. With respect to data analysis there are the following issues: 1. To what extent do our theoretical ideas work? 2. How much mathematics is being learned by the students? 3. What would it take to falsify specific conjectures or our theory in general? 4. Since data can come from this study but also from assessment of student learning which may not be part of this study, what is the appropriate use of these in drawing conclusions?

We will return to these issues later in this paper in Section 4, but in order to do so, it is important to develop more fully the description of the three components of the framework and their interconnections (as illustrated by the arrows in Figure 1).

3. The components of the framework

3.1 Theoretical analysis.

The purpose of the theoretical analysis of a concept is to propose a model of cognition: that is, a description of specific mental constructions that a learner might make in order to develop her or his understanding of the concept. We will refer to the result of this analysis as a genetic decomposition of the concept. That is, a genetic decomposition of a concept is a structured set of mental constructs which might describe how the concept can develop in the mind of an individual.

The analysis is initially made by applying a general theory of learning and is greatly influenced by the researchers' own understanding of the concept and previous experience in learning and teaching it. In subsequent iterations through the framework, the analysis of data increasingly contributes to the evolving genetic decomposition.

In working with this framework we make use of a very specific theoretical perspective on learning which has developed through our attempt to understand the ideas of Piaget concerning reflective abstraction and to reconstruct these ideas in the context of college-level mathematics. The initial development of this theory and its relationship to Piaget is described in some detail in [6]. The perspective is continuing to develop and we describe it here in its present form. We should note that, although our theoretical perspective is closely related to the theories of Piaget, this is not so much the case for the other components of our framework. Indeed, considerations of pedagogical strategies are almost absent from the totality of Piaget's work and our methodology for gathering and analyzing data is influenced in only some, but not all, of its aspects by the methodology which Piaget used.

3.1.1 Mathematical knowledge and its construction. Our theoretical perspective begins with a statement of our overall perspective on what it means to learn and know something in mathematics. The following paragraph is not a definition, but rather an attempt to collect the essential ingredients of our perspective in one place.

> An individual's mathematical knowledge is her or his tendency to respond to perceived mathematical problem situations by reflecting on problems and their solutions in a social context and by

constructing or reconstructing mathematical actions, processes and objects and organizing these in schemas to use in dealing with the situations.

There are, in this statement, references to a number of aspects of learning and knowing. For one thing, the statement acknowledges that what a person knows and is capable of doing is not necessarily available to her or him at a given moment and in a given situation. All of us who have taught (or studied) are familiar with the phenomenon of a student missing a question completely on an exam and then really knowing the answer right after, without looking it up. A related phenomenon is to be unable to deal with a mathematical situation but, after the slightest suggestion from a colleague or teacher, it all comes running back to your consciousness. Thus, in the problem of knowing, there are two issues: learning a concept and accessing it when needed.

Reflection, in the sense of paying conscious attention to operations that are performed, is an important part of both learning and knowing. Mathematics in particular is full of techniques and algorithms to use in dealing with situations. Many people can learn these quite well and use them to do things in mathematics. But understanding mathematics goes beyond the ability to perform calculations, no matter how sophisticated. It is necessary to be aware of how procedures work, to get a feel for the result without actually performing all of the calculations, to be able to work with variations of a single algorithm, to see relationships and to be able to organize experiences (both mathematical and non-mathematical).

From this perspective we take the position that reflection is significantly enhanced in a social context. There is evidence in the literature (see [32], for example) for the value to students of social interaction and there is also the cultural reality that virtually all research mathematicians feel very strongly the need for interactions with colleagues before, during, and after creative work in mathematics.

The statement describing our theoretical perspective asserts that "possessing" knowledge consists in a tendency to make mental constructions that are used in dealing with a problem situation. Often the construction amounts to reconstructing (or remembering) something previously built so as to repeat a previous method. But progress in the development of mathematical knowledge comes from making a reconstruction in a situation similar to, but different in important ways from, a problem previously dealt with. Then the reconstruction is not exactly the same as what existed previously, and may in fact contain one or more advances to a more sophisticated level. This whole notion is related to the well known Piagetian dichotomy of assimilation and accommodation [21]. The theoretical perspective which we are describing is itself the result of reconstruction of our

understanding of Piaget's theory leading to extension in its applicability to post-secondary mathematics.

Finally, the question arises of what is it that is constructed by the learner, or, in other words, what is the nature of the constructions and the ways in which they are made? As we turn to this issue, it should become apparent that our theoretical perspective, which may appear applicable to any subject whatsoever, becomes specific to mathematics.

3.1.2 Mental constructions for learning mathematics. As illustrated in Figure 2, we consider that understanding a mathematical concept begins with manipulating previously constructed mental or physical objects to form actions; actions are then interiorized to form processes which are then encapsulated to form objects. Objects can be de-encapsulated back to the processes from which they were formed. Finally, actions, processes and objects can be organized in schemas. A more detailed description of each of these mental constructions is given below.

In reading our discussion of these specific constructions, we would like the reader to keep in mind that each of the four is based on a specific construction of Piaget, although not always with exactly the same name. What we are calling actions are close to Piaget's *action schemes,* our processes are related to his *operations,* and *object* is one of the terms Piaget uses for that to which actions and processes can be applied. The term *schema* is more difficult, partly because Piaget uses several different terms in different places, but with very similar meanings, partly because of the difficulty of translating between two languages which both have many terms related to schema with subtle and not always corresponding distinction, and partly because our understanding of this specific construction is not as far as advanced as it is for the others. Our use of the term in this paper is close to what Piaget calls *schemata* in [22] where his meaning appears to be in some ways similar to the *concept image* of Tall and Vinner [31], and where he

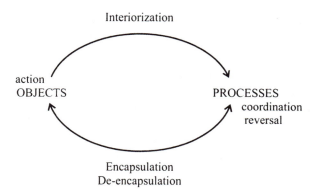

FIGURE 2

Constructions for mathematical knowledge.

talks about thematizing schemas which, essentially refers to making them objects. For a more detailed discussion of the relation between the theories of Piaget and (an early version of) our theoretical framework, the reader is referred to [6].

Action. An action is a transformation of objects which is perceived by the individual as being at least somewhat external. That is, an individual whose understanding of a transformation is limited to an action conception can carry out the transformation only by reacting to external cues that give precise details on what steps to take.

For example, a student who is unable to interpret a situation as a function unless he or she has a (single) formula for computing values is restricted to an action concept of function. In such a case, the student is unable to do very much with this function except to evaluate it at specific points and to manipulate the formula. Functions with split domains, inverses of functions, composition of functions, sets of functions, the notion that the derivative of a function is a function, and the idea that a solution of a differential equation is a function are all sources of great difficulty for students. According to our theoretical perspective, a major reason for the difficulty is that the learner is not able to go beyond an action conception of function and all of these notions require process and/or object conceptions. (See [1] for an elaboration of these issues.)

Another example of an action conception comes from the notion of a (left or right) coset of a group in abstract algebra. Consider, for example, the modular group $[Z_{20}, +_{20}]$— that is, the integers $\{0, 1, 2, \ldots, 19\}$ with the operation of addition mod 20—and the subgroup $H = \{0, 4, 8, 12, 16\}$ of multiples of 4. As is seen in [10] it is not very difficult for learners to work with a coset such as $2 + H = \{2, 6, 10, 14, 18\}$ because it is formed either by an explicit listing of the elements obtained by adding 2 to each element of H or applying some rule (e.g., "begin with 2 and add 4") or an explicit condition such as, "the remainder on division by 4 is 2". Understanding a coset as a set of calculations that are actually performed to obtain a definite set is an action conception. Something more is required to work with cosets in a group such as S_n, the group of all permutations on n objects where simple formulas are not available. Even in the more elementary situation of Z_n, students who have no more than an action conception will have difficulty in reasoning about cosets (such as counting them, comparing them, etc.) In the context of our theoretical perspective, these difficulties are related to a student's inability to interiorize these actions to processes, or encapsulate the processes to objects.

Although an action conception is very limited, the following paragraphs describe the way in which actions form the crucial beginning of understanding a concept. There-

fore, our learning-theory-based pedagogical approach begins with activities designed to help students construct actions.

Process. When an action is repeated, and the individual reflects upon it, it may be interiorized into a process. That is, an internal construction is made that performs the same action, but now, not necessarily directed by external stimuli. An individual who has a process conception of a transformation can reflect on, describe, or even reverse the steps of the transformation without actually performing those steps. In contrast to an action, a process is perceived by the individual as being internal, and under one's control, rather than as something one does in response to external cues.

In the case of functions, a process conception allows the subject to think of a function as receiving one or more inputs, or values of independent variables, performing one or more operations on the inputs and returning the results as outputs, or values of dependent variables. For instance, to understand a function such as $\sin x$, one needs a process conception of function since no explicit instructions for obtaining an output from an input are given; in order to implement the function, one must imagine the process of associating a real number with its sine.

With a process conception of function, an individual can link two or more processes to construct a composition, or reverse the process to obtain inverse functions [1].

In abstract algebra, a process understanding of cosets includes thinking about the formation of a set by operating a fixed element with every element in a particular subgroup. Again, it is not necessary to perform the operations, but only to think about them being performed. Thus, with a process conception, cosets can be formed in situations where formulas are not available. (See, for example, [10].)

Object. When an individual reflects on operations applied to a particular process, becomes aware of the process as a totality, realizes that transformations (whether they be actions or processes) can act on it, and is able to actually construct such transformations, then he or she is thinking of this process as an object. In this case, we say that the process has been *encapsulated* to an object.

In the course of performing an action or process on an object, it is often necessary to de-encapsulate the object back to the process from which it came in order to use its properties in manipulating it.

It is easy to see how encapsulation of processes to objects and de-encapsulating the objects back to processes arises when one is thinking about manipulations of functions such as adding, multiplying, or just forming sets of functions. In an abstract algebra context, given an element x and a subgroup H of a group G, if an individual thinks generally of the (left) coset of x modulo H as a process of operating with x on each element of H, then this process can be encapsulated to an object xH. Then, cosets are named, operations can be performed on them [10], and various actions on cosets of H, such as counting their number, comparing their cardinality, and checking their intersections can make sense to the individual. Thinking about the problem of investigating such properties involves the interpretation of cosets as objects whereas the actual finding out requires that these objects be de-encapsulated in the individual's mind so as to make use of the properties of the processes from which these objects came (certain kinds of set formation in this case).

In general, encapsulating processes to become objects is considered to be extremely difficult [22, 28, 29] and not very many pedagogical strategies have been effective in helping students do this in situations such as functions or cosets. A part of the reason for this ineffectiveness is that there is very little (if anything) in our experience that corresponds to performing actions on what are interpreted as processes.

Schema. Once constructed, objects and processes can be interconnected in various ways: for example, two or more processes may be coordinated by linking them (through composition or in other ways); processes and objects are related by virtue of the fact that the former act on the latter. A collection of processes and objects can be organized in a structured manner to form a schema. Schemas themselves can be treated as objects and included in the organization of "higher level" schemas. When this happens, we say that the schema has been *thematized* to an object. The schema can then be included in higher level schemas of mathematical structures. For example, functions can be formed into sets, operations on these sets can be introduced, and properties of the operations can be checked. All of this can be organized to construct a schema for function space which can be applied to concepts such as dual spaces, spaces of linear mappings, and function algebras.

As we indicated above, our work with, and understanding of, the idea of a schema has not progressed as much as some of the other aspects of our general theory. We are convinced, however, that this notion is an important part of the total picture and we hope to understand it better as our work proceeds. For now, we can only make some tentative observations concerning, for example, the distinction between a genetic decomposition and a schema.

A related question, on which our work is also very preliminary, has to do with relations between the mental constructs together with the interconnections that an individual uses to understand a concept, and the way in which an individual uses (or fails to use) them in problem situations. This is what we were referring to in our use of the term "tendency" in our initial statement. Now, a genetic decomposition for a mathematical concept is a model used by researchers to describe the concept. Our tentative understanding suggests that an individual's schema for a concept includes her or his version of the concept that is described by the genetic decomposition, as well as other concepts that are perceived to be linked to the concept in the context of problem situations.

Put another way, we might suggest that the distinction between schema and other mental constructions is like the distinction in biology between an organ and a cell. They are both objects, but the organ (schema) provides the organization necessary for the functioning of the cells to the benefit of the organism. An individual's schema is the totality of knowledge which for her or him is connected (consciously or subconsciously) to a particular mathematical topic. An individual will have a function schema, a derivative schema, a group schema, etc. Schemas are important to the individual for mathematical empowerment, but in general, we are very far from knowing all of the specifics, nor have we studied much about how this organization determines mathematical performance. All we can do now is to link together mental constructions for a concept in a generic road-map of development and understanding (genetic decomposition) and see how this is actualized in a given individual (schema). Clearly, an individual's schema may include actions or knee-jerk responses such as, "whenever I see this symbol I do that."

3.2 Instructional treatments.

The second component of our framework has to do with designing and implementing instruction based on the theoretical analyses. The theoretical perspective on learning we have just described influences instruction in two ways. First, as we have indicated earlier, the theoretical analysis postulates certain specific mental constructions which the instruction should foster. Later in the paper (Section 3.2.2) we will consider that effect in relation to specific mathematical content. Before doing that however, we shall describe a second, more global way in which the general theory influences instruction.

3.2.1 Global influences of the theoretical perspective. Returning to our formulation of the nature of mathematical knowledge and its acquisition (Section 3.1.1) we consider four components: the tendency to use one or another mathematical construct, reflection, social context, and constructions or reconstructions.

When confronted with a mathematical problem situation, it has frequently been observed that an individual is not always able to bring to bear specific ideas in her or his mathematical repertoire. (See, for instance, [25] for a very sharp example of students clearly possessing certain knowledge, but not being able to use it.) An individual's mathematical knowledge consists in a tendency to use certain constructions, but not all relevant constructions are recalled in every situation. This is one of the reasons that we cannot expect students to learn mathematics in the logical order in which it can be laid out. In fact, according to our theoretical perspective, the growth of understanding is highly nonlinear with starts and stops; the student develops partial understandings, repeatedly returns to the same piece of knowledge, and periodically summarizes and ties related ideas together [27]. Our general instructional approach acknowledges this growth pattern by using what we call an *holistic spray,* which is a variation on the standard spiral method [10].

In this variation, students are thrust into an intentionally disequilibrating environment which contains as much as possible about the material being studied. The idea is that everything is sprayed at them in an holistic manner, as opposed to being sequentially organized. Each individual (or cooperative learning group) tries to make sense out of the situation—that is, they try to solve problems, answer questions or understand ideas. Different students may learn different pieces of the whole at different times. In this way the students enhance their understanding of one or another portion of the material bit by bit. The course keeps presenting versions of the whole set of material and the students are always trying to make more sense, always learning a little more.

The social context to which our theoretical perspective refers is implemented in our instruction through the use of cooperative learning groups. Students are organized at the beginning of the semester in small groups of three to five to do all of the course work (computer lab, class discussion, homework and some exams) cooperatively. For details see [23]. One consequence of having students work in cooperative groups is that they are more likely to reflect on the procedures that they perform [32].

A critical part of our approach is to implement the results of our theoretical analysis in regular classrooms and to gather data on what happened in those classrooms. Consequently, our curricular designs are tied to the current curricular structures of the semester or quarter system in which we operate. Today, many people are thinking seriously about alternative ways to organize the entire educational enterprise—from kindergarten through graduate school. As new structures emerge, the generality of our approach will be indicated by the extent to which it can be adapted to these new forms.

Our instructional strategies also try to get students to reflect on their work through the overall structure of a course. A particular pedagogical approach we use, which we refer to as the *ACE Teaching Cycle,* and which we now

describe, is not a necessary consequence of the theoretical perspective but is one possible overall design supporting our theoretical analyses. In this design, the course is broken up into sections, each of which runs for one week. During the week, the class meets on some days in the computer lab and on other days in a regular classroom in which there are no computers. Homework is completed outside of class. As indicated above, the students are in cooperative groups for all of this work.

Thus there are three components of the ACE cycle: activities, class discussion, and exercises.

Activities. Class meets in a computer lab where students work in teams on computer programming tasks designed to foster specific mental constructions suggested by the theoretical analysis. The lab assignments are generally too long to finish during the scheduled lab and students are expected to come to the lab when it is open, or work on their personal computers, or use other labs to complete the assignment. It is important to note that there are major differences between these computer activities and the kinds of activities used in "discovery learning." While some computer activities may involve an element of discovery, their primary goal is to provide students with an experience base rather than to lead them to correct answers. Through these activities students gain experience with the mathematical issues which are later developed in the classroom phase. We will discuss the computer work in more detail below.

Class Discussion. Class meets in a classroom where students again work in teams to perform paper and pencil tasks based on the computer activities in the lab. The instructor leads inter-group discussions designed to give students an opportunity to reflect on the work they did in the lab and calculations they have been making in class. On occasion, the instructor will provide definitions, explanations and overviews to tie together what the students have been thinking about.

Exercises. Relatively traditional exercises are assigned for students to work on in teams. These are expected to be completed outside of class and lab and they represent homework that is in addition to the lab assignments. The purpose of the exercises is for students to reinforce the ideas they have constructed, to use the mathematics they have learned and, on occasion, to begin thinking about situations that will be studied later.

One must consider the question of how our pedagogical strategies are supported by the textbook for the course. We have found that traditional textbooks are not very helpful. For example, template problems (usually a key feature of a textbook) circumvent the disequilibration and formation of rich mental constructions which we consider necessary for meaningful understanding. Also, as we have indicated, mathematics is not learned in the logical order in which it is presented in most textbooks. It has therefore been necessary to produce appropriate texts for various courses. This has been done, using essentially the same style, for courses in Discrete Mathematics, Precalculus, Calculus, and Abstract Algebra. Other works are in progress. The textbooks are designed to support the constructivist approach to teaching that is described in this paper.

Our textbooks are arranged according to the ACE Cycle. Each book is divided into sections, each of which begins with a set of computer activities, followed by a discussion of the mathematics involved in these activities, and ending with an exercise set. It is expected that a section will be covered in one week with the students doing the computer activities in the lab, and possibly during "open hours," working through the discussion material in class and doing the exercises as homework.

The textbooks have certain features that, although not always popular with students or teachers, we feel are necessary to relate to how learning actually takes place. There are almost no cases of "worked problems" followed by drills in the exercises and no answers to exercises in the back of the book. Wherever possible, the student is given an opportunity to figure out for her or himself how to solve a problem using the ideas that are being learned. In the computer activities, the students are often asked to solve problems requiring mathematics they have not yet studied. They are encouraged to discuss these issues with their group members or other colleagues, read ahead in the text (where explanations can be found, although usually not directly), or even consult other texts. In other words, the students are forced to *investigate* mathematical ideas in order to solve problems. The explanations that are given in the discussion section are interspersed with many questions whose answers are important for understanding the concepts. These questions are not always answered in the texts (at least not right away) but they are generally repeated in the exercise set.

Although we feel that our textbooks make a major contribution to student learning, the books we produce are not as good for later reference. To overcome this, we try to include an extremely detailed and complete index, but also expect that the student might find some other text which is not so helpful for learning, but may be a better reference book.

3.2.2 Mental constructions.

Our main strategy for getting students to make mental constructions proposed by our theoretical analysis is to assign tasks that will require them to write and/or revise computer code using a mathematical programming language. In the sequel, we will refer to this as an *MPL*. The idea is that when you do something on a computer, it affects your mind. This effect occurs in three ways. First, we attempt to orchestrate the effect of these tasks so that we foster the specific mental constructions proposed by our theoretical analyses. Second, the computer tasks which we assign can provide a concrete experience base paving the way for later abstraction. Finally, there is an indirect effect from working with computers which has been reported and is less clearly understood.

Fostering mental constructions directly. This general discussion of our strategy is organized around actions, processes, objects, and schemas. The initial activities included in this section show how students familiarize themselves with the syntax of the programming language. At the same time, since the activities involve direct calculations of specific values, students gain experience constructing actions corresponding to selected mathematical concepts. This experience is built upon in subsequent activities where students are asked to reconstruct familiar actions as general processes. Later activities presented exemplify those that are intended to help students encapsulate processes to objects; these activities typically involve writing programs in which the processes to be encapsulated are inputs and/or outputs to the program. Finally, we describe a more complicated activity in which students need to organize a variety of previously constructed objects into a schema that can then be applied to particular problem situations.

Although our choice for a language in which to work is *ISETL*, there are other possibilities such as *Mathematica* and *Maple*. Because the syntax of *ISETL* is so close to that of standard mathematical notation, the programming aspects of the language are particularly easy to learn. This does not mean, however, that learning to write correct mathematics in *ISETL* is easy. On the contrary, students encounter a great many difficulties in using the language—difficulties that are most often directly associated with mathematical difficulties. For this reason, *ISETL* provides an ideal environment for mathematical experimentation, reflection, and discussion.

For those who know mathematics and have some experience with programming, little explanation is necessary in describing examples of the use of *ISETL*. Hence we will minimize our explanations of syntax in the sequel. (See [8] for a discussion of the use of this language and [3] for details on its syntax.)

Actions. We begin with activities in which students try to repeat on their terminal screens what is written in the text, or to predict what will be the result of running code that is given to them, or to modify code they have been given.

Following is a set of *ISETL* instructions as they would appear on the screen followed by the computer's response.

It is taken from the first pages of the textbook used in the C^4L calculus project [11].

The $>$ symbol is the *ISETL* prompt and lines which begin with this symbol or $>>$, which indicates incomplete input, are entered by the user. Lines without these prompts are what the computer prints on the screen.

```
>     7+18;
25;
>     13*(233.8);
3039.400000;
>     5 = 2.0 + 3;
true;
>     4 >= 2 + 3;
false;
>     17
>>    + 23.7 - 46
>>    *2
>>    ;
-51.300000;
>     x := -23/27;
>     x;
-0.851852;
>     27/36;
0.750000;
>     p := [3,-2]; q := [1,4.5];
>     r := [0.5,-2,-3];
>     p; q; r;
[3, -2];
[1, 4.500000];
[.500000, -2, -3];
>     p(1); p(2); q(2); r(3);
3;
-2;
4.500000;
-3;
>     p(1)*q(1) + p(2)*q(2);
-6.000000;
>     length := 0;
>     for i in [1..3] do
>>        length := length + r(i)**2;
>>        end;
>     length := sqrt(length);
>     length;
3.640055;
```

Students are asked to do these exercises for the purpose of becoming familiar with their *MPL*, but at the same time, there are several mathematical concepts which they have an opportunity to construct at the action level. For example, there are simple propositions, the formation of pairs and triples of numbers and the action of picking out an indexed term of a given sequence. Also the concept of dot product appears as an action. Finally, the algorithm for computing the length of a vector in three dimensions appears as an action because the calculation is explicit and is applied to a single vector.

Processes. In the previous paragraph we indicated how students might be led to construct actions by writing code that makes a computation once with specific numbers. Now we try to get them to build on these actions by performing activities intended to help them reconstruct their actions as processes. For example, students are led to interiorize actions to processes when they replace code written to perform a specific calculation by a computer function which will perform the action for any values. Thus, for the calculation of the length of a three-dimensional vector (which is our last example above), we might ask students to write the following computer function. (The last two lines assume that r has been defined previously as above, or as any three-dimensional vector.)

```
>     length := func(v);
>>    l := 0;
>>    for i in [1..3] do
>>        l := l + v(i)**2;
>>        end;
>>    return sqrt(l);
>>    end;
>     length(r);
3.64005;
```

There are a variety of ways that programming activities can be used to help students to understand functions as processes. Research suggests that students who write code to implement the point-wise sum, product, and composition of functions tend to make progress in developing a process conception of function [1]. Programming activities have also been used to help students get past the well-known difficulty many have in seeing that a piece-wise defined function is still a function, and that properties can be studied at the seam points as well as other places. A process conception of function emerges as students write programs in which the definition of a piece-wise function is implemented through the simple use of a conditional:

```
f := func(x);
    if x <= 1 then return 2-x**2;
    else return x/2 + 1.5;
    end;
end;
```

Following is how the code would look in *Maple*.

```
f:=proc(x);
if x<=1 then 2-x**2;
else x/2 + 1.5;
fi;
end;
```

A completely different approach considered by Kaput has students (in grades 3–13) *begin* with piecewise-defined functions and deal with them graphically using what is referred to as SimCalc simulations. (See [18] for details.)

We can also mention the example of boolean-valued functions of the positive integers. Our research suggests that one of the difficulties students have with proof by induction is at the very beginning. A student is faced with a problem: show that a certain statement involving an arbitrary integer is true for all (sufficiently large) values of the integer. This kind of problem is very new and difficult for most students. It really is a (mental) function which accepts a positive integer and plugs it into the statement to obtain a proposition which may be true or false—and the answer could be different for different values of n. Once again, expressing this problem as a function in an *MPL* is a big help for students in figuring out how to begin.

Suppose, for example, that the problem is to determine if a gambling casino with only $300 and $500 chips can represent (within the nearest $100) any amount of money beyond a certain minimum. We encourage students to begin their investigation by writing a computer program that accepts a positive integer and returns a boolean value. The following is one solution they generally come up with in our elementary discrete mathematics course.

```
P :=func(n);
  if is_integer(n) and n > 0
  and exists x,y in [0..n div 3] |
  3*x + 5*y = n
  then return true;
  else return false;
  end;
end;
```

Objects. Objects are obtained by encapsulation of processes, and an individual is likely to do this when he or she reflects on a situation in which it is necessary to apply an action to a dynamic process. This presents a difficulty because the action cannot be applied to the process until after the process has been encapsulated to an object. But, as we have said before, mental constructions do not seem to occur in simple logical sequences. In fact, the following three things can all be happening at the same time, initially in some amorphous combination:

1. the need to create an object (in order to apply an action to a process),
2. the encapsulation of the process to form the object, and
3. the application of an action to that object.

Gradually, as the learner reflects, he or she is able to differentiate, reorganize, and integrate the components of this experience so that a clear application of the action to the object is apparent.

Consider, for example, a student who has just learned what a permutation of $\{1, \ldots, n\}$ is, and is now faced with composing permutations. On the one hand, he or she could focus on permutations as processes, and simply perform the linking of the processes to get the composition. That would require only a process, but not an object conception of permutation. At a higher level, though, if the student is trying to think of composition as a binary operation, he or she would begin to see permutations as inputs to the binary operation process, and thus as objects.

Getting students to do all of this is another matter and there are very few effective pedagogical methods known. As we have indicated, one such method is to put students in situations where a problem must be solved or a task must be performed by writing programs in which the processes to be encapsulated are inputs to, and/or outputs of, the programs. Thus, in addition to having syntax similar to standard mathematical notation, we require that an *MPL* treat functions as first-class data types, that is, as entities which can be passed as input or output parameters to and from other student-defined procedures.

Continuing with our treatment of mathematical induction, we can report that students learn to treat propositions about natural numbers as objects. At the same time they develop an understanding of the "implication from n to $n + 1$", that is, $P(n) \rightarrow P(n + 1)$ understood as an object whose truth value as n varies is to be considered. Our approach is to have them write and apply the following program which accepts a function whose domain is the positive integers and whose range is the two element set $\{$true, false$\}$. This program returns the corresponding implication valued function. (The symbol $ refers to a comment and anything after this symbol on the line in which it appears is ignored by *ISETL*.)

```
$ P is a boolean-valued function.;
implfn := func (P);
  return func(n);
  return P(n) impl P(n+1);
  end;
end;
```

In calculus, two extremely important examples of construction of objects occur in connection with derivatives and integrals. Although it is very simple for mathematicians, our experience suggests that the idea that the derivative of a function is a function is not immediate for students. Writing a program such as the following, which accepts a function and returns an approximation to its derivative appears to help.

```
df := func (f);
 return func (x);
  return (f(x + 0.00001) - f(x))/0.00001;
 end;
end;
```

In this program, f is the variable and so it does not need to be defined before the program is run. Once it has been run, a function can be defined and given any name, for example g and then $df(g)$ will be a function that can be evaluated, assigned to be the value of a variable, graphed or treated in any other way that functions are treated.

It is important to note that the reason we are using *ISETL* here is because there are essential understandings we are trying to get students to construct as specified by our genetic decomposition, and we cannot do this with many other systems. For example, writing a program that constructs a function for performing a specific action in various contexts tends to get students to interiorize that action to a process. Perhaps even more critical is our method of getting students to make a function an object in their minds by using function programs as input to another program which students write. This latter program performs a process and returns a function as output. This can also be done using systems such as *Maple* or *Mathematica* as alternatives to *ISETL*. For example, if f is a simple proc in *Maple*, then the following *Maple* version of df could be used in a similar manner.

```
with (student);
df:=proc(f) local dq;
dq:=(f(x+.00001)-f(x))/.00001;
makeproc(dq,x);
end;
```

Integration is more difficult. The idea of defining a function by using the definite integral with one limit of integration fixed and the other allowed to vary is a major stumbling block for calculus students. In our treatment of integration, students have written a program called *Riem* which accepts a function and a pair of numbers, and computes an approximation to the integral of the function over the interval determined by the points. The students are then asked to write the following program.

```
Int := func (f,a,b);
 return func(x);
if a <= x and x <= b then return Riem(f,a,x);
 end;
end;
```

Using this program, students are able to construct and study approximations to the logarithm function and inverse trigonometric functions.

Schemas. Our use of programming activities to help students form schemas to organize collections of individual constructs and other schemas is, at the time of this writing, somewhat ad hoc. Some progress is being made, and has been reported in [2] for a limit schema. Roughly speaking, we ask students to write a set of computer programs that implements a mathematical concept and then to apply their code to specific situations.

For example, developing a schema for the Fundamental Theorem of Calculus requires very little code but it is extremely complicated. Having written the two computer functions df to approximate the derivative and Int to approximate the integral (see above), students are asked to write code that will first do one and then the other, in both orders. This problem gives the students considerable difficulty and they struggle with it for a long time. We feel that this is a useful struggle because it has to do with their ability to interpret functions as objects, to develop processes corresponding to differentiation and integration, and to put it all together in what is essentially a statement of the Fundamental Theorem.

The actual code to solve this problem is very short:

```
> df (Int (f (a,b));
```

```
> Int (df (f),a,b);
```

We ask students to apply their code to a specific function and to construct a table with four columns: values of the independent variable, corresponding values of f, and corresponding values of the above two lines of code. When the example is a function that does not vanish at a, then the second and third columns are identical, but the fourth is different. The students see the point right away—all three columns are supposed to be the same, but they feel they have made an error in connection with the last column. After some investigation, many students tend to discover on their own the idea of the "constant of integration."

We should note here that it is not our intention to suggest that the approach we are describing is the *only* way to help students understand the ideas surrounding the Fundamental Theorem of Calculus, such as velocity and accumulation and the relationship between them. There are other approaches, such as that being pursued by Jim Kaput [18] in which children control simulated motions on a computer screen. In this case, the functions are defined graphically rather than analytically. It would be interesting to see whether the theoretical framework we are using would apply in the same way to describe student understanding of functions.

Sometimes we don't ask students to write code but rather to investigate code which we provide. We do this in situations where the particular code involves more in the way of programming issues than mathematical issues. This is the case for the following example which simulates the operation of induction. This code makes use of the computer function, `implfn`, which they have written (see above) and is applied to a boolean-valued function P. The first few lines find a starting point and the rest of the code runs through the induction steps. If the proposition does hold from the selected starting point on, then the code will run forever.

```
start := 1;
while P(start) = false do
    start := start + 1;
end;

L := [];
n := start; L(n) := true;
while L(n) = true and implfn(P)(n) = true do
    L(n+1) := true;
    n := n+1;
    print "The proposition P is true
        for n = ", n;
end; print "P is not proven for n = ", n+1;
```

Making the abstract concrete. A second way in which working with an appropriate computer language can help students construct mathematical concepts is that the computer can provide an environment where students are able to make certain abstract notions concrete. Consider, for example, the statement that a function f maps its domain D onto a set S:

For each $y \in S$ there exists an x in D such that $f(x) = y$.

Students may consider such a precise definition to be a difficult abstraction. They can be helped by working with a *MPL* such as *ISETL* in which such a statement can be made, run, tested, and reasoned about. Following is *ISETL* code that expresses the same mathematical statement.

```
forall y in S | (exist x in D | f (x)=y);
```

If S, D, and f are defined, then this code can be run to return the value `true` or `false`.

Our way of using this feature in instruction is to begin with a somewhat vague discussion of the essential idea, perhaps in the context of students working on a problem that requires this idea. Then we ask students to write a program such as the above and use this program in solving problems. It appears that writing and working with a program that he or she has written helps the student make concrete the ideas embodied in the program.

Indirect effects of working with the computer. One example of an indirect effect on students is reported in [1]. Students were asked at the beginning of a discrete mathematics course to give examples of functions. A very high percentage of their responses were functions defined by simple expressions such as $x^2 + 1$ and many students displayed no more than an action conception of function, or even no useful conception at all. After several weeks

of work with a mathematical programming language involving procedures, sets, and finite sequences, but before any explicit study of functions in the course, students were asked again to provide examples. This time the examples given were much richer and more varied, with a number of students' responses indicating they were moving from action conception or no conception to a process conception of function.

3.3 Data.

The third component of the framework has to do with the collection and analysis of data.

There are several kinds of data which must be gathered in studies under this framework. There must be information about the students and the course(s) taken. In some cases, we gather data about students who have previously studied the mathematics we are concerned with under traditional instruction. In other cases, we will study students who have experienced the kind of instruction we describe in this paper. Where appropriate, we will summarize rough comparisons of performances of the two kinds of students. Sometimes, students' attitudes about mathematics and about the particular subject matter is of concern in the study. Most important, of course, is data that allows us to analyze the students' relationship to the particular material; it is this last category that we will consider now in some detail.

3.3.1 Forms of data. We see two reasons to gather a number of different kinds of data about the students' relationship to the material. First, the methods used do not provide precise information leading to inescapable conclusions. The best we can hope for is data that is illustrative and suggestive. Our confidence in any tentative conclusions that might be indicated is increased as we widen the sources of information about student knowledge and how it develops. The second reason is that we are interested in two different kinds of issues: what mental constructions students might be making and how much of what mathematics do they seem to be learning and using? That is, we are comparing the mental constructions the students appear to be making with those called for in the theoretical analyses, and at the same time we are searching for the limits of student knowledge. Often, the same information will shed light on both questions, but sometimes it is necessary to use different kinds of data to investigate these different issues.

In our studies we gather data using three kinds of instruments: written questions and answers in the form of examinations in the course or specially designed question sets; in-depth interviews of students about the mathematical questions of concern; and a combination of written instruments and interviews. For purposes of data analysis, all of our data is aggregated across the set of students who participated in the study.

The written instruments contain fairly standard questions about the mathematical content and they are analyzed in relatively traditional ways. We grade the responses on appropriate scales from incorrect to correct with partial credit in between, and then count the scores. Where appropriate we list the specific points (both correct and incorrect) in the responses of all the students and collate those points. This information tells us about what the students may or may not be learning and also about possible mental constructions.

The interviews of students form the most important and the most difficult part of our observation and assessment activity. The audio-taped transcripts of the interviews complement the record of written work which the student completes during the interview. An even more complete picture might be obtained by videotaping the interviews, but we have not yet added this component to our interviews. One reason why the interviews are far more valuable than written assessment instruments used alone is that for one student the written work may appear essentially correct while the transcript reveals little understanding, while for another student the reverse may be true. There is no set recipe for designing interview questions. The research team proposes, discusses, and pilots questions intended to test the hypotheses set forth by the current version of the genetic decomposition for the topic under study. An instrument is then put together which is administered to a number of students by a number of researchers. Communication among the interviewers before and between interviews is important to increase consistency.

A second combination of written instruments and interviews is used in the following way. The written instrument is administered to a total population and the responses are used in designing interview questions. For example, the student might be asked in the interview to explain what was written, or if he or she wished to revise the response. If the written instrument were administered to a group (as in a group examination such as described in [23]), we would ask whether the interviewee was fully in accord with and understood the group response. Individuals are selected for interview based on their responses. The idea is that it may not be necessary to interview all of the students who gave a certain written response. In selecting students to interview, we try to access the full range of understanding by including students who gave correct, partially correct, and incorrect answers on the written instruments. We also routinely select students who appear to be in the process of learning some particular idea rather than those who have clearly mastered it or those who had obviously missed the point. In this way, it is possible to interview only a small percentage of the total population, but still investigate every

written response that appeared. Usually it is feasible, for each specific response, to interview more than one student who made that response. A combination of the two kinds of instruments is discussed in [10].

3.3.2 Analyses of interview data. One of the most serious practical difficulties in doing qualitative research is the very large amount of data that is generated and that must be analyzed. We believe that our framework offers an alternative to the approach used by some researchers (see, for example, [27]) who attempt to make a full analysis of the total set of data. In the following paragraphs we begin by discussing the goals of our analyses of interviews and then describe the specific steps by which we attempt to achieve these goals.

Goals of the data analyses. Consider, in Figure 1 the bi-directional arrow connecting the theoretical analyses with the observations and assessments. What the data tells us can support, or lead to revisions of, the particular analyses that have been made of the concept being studied, and even the general theoretical perspective. This is the meaning of the arrowhead pointing up towards the theoretical analysis in the figure.

On the other hand, the arrowhead in the opposite direction, pointing down, indicates our method of using the analysis of the concept to focus our investigation of the data. In other words, the theoretical analysis tells us what questions to ask of the data. More specifically, our study of the data is narrowed by focusing on the question of whether the specific constructions proposed by the theoretical analysis (which are the main determinant of the design of instruction) are in fact being made by the students who succeed in learning the concept. Put another way, we ask if making, or failing to make, the proposed constructions is a reasonable explanation of why some students seemed to learn the concept and others did not.

Of course, actual student learning is seldom characterizable in binary, yes/no terms. Students range on a spectrum from those who seem to understand nothing (about the particular piece of mathematics) to those who indicate a mature understanding compatible with the understanding of mathematicians. The goal of our analysis of the data is to establish a parallel spectrum of mental constructions, going from those who appeared to construct very little, through those who constructed bits and pieces, to those who seemed to have made all of the constructions proposed by the theoretical analysis.

It is easy to see how such an approach requires iterating through the steps in Figure 1 as the parallel spectra of mathematical understanding and mental constructions are unlikely to be completely similar initially and the researcher must endeavor, in the repetitions, to try to bring them in line with each other.

Steps of the data analyses. Our interviews are audio-taped and transcribed. These transcriptions, together with any writing performed by the interviewee and any notes taken by the interviewer, make up the data which are to be analyzed. We do this in five steps.

1. Script the transcript. The transcript is put in a two-column format. The first column contains the original transcript and the second column contains an occasional brief statement indicating what is happening from that point until the next brief statement. It is convenient to number the paragraphs at this point.

2. Make the table of contents. A table of contents is constructed. The statements in the scripting should be a refinement of the items in the table of contents.

These first two steps are designed to make the transcript more convenient to work with and to give the researcher an opportunity to become familiar with its contents.

3. List the issues. By an issue we mean some very specific mathematical point, an idea, a procedure, or a fact, for which the interviewee may or may not construct an understanding. For example, in the context of group theory one issue might be whether the student understands that a group is more than just a set, that is, it is a set together with a binary operation.

The researcher begins to generate the list of issues by reading carefully through the transcript for each interviewee writing down each issue that seems to be discussed and noting the page numbers (or paragraph numbers) where it appears. These lists of issues for individuals are then transposed to form a single list of issues and, for each, a list of the specific transcripts (and location) in which it occurred. We believe that the best results are obtained at this step if these lists are generated independently by several researchers with subsequent negotiations to reconcile differences. Since the list of issues varies widely from one set of interviews to another, and since the issues are often not characterizable in terms of number or type of occurrence, we have not attempted to produce information such as inter-rater reliabilities. However, we have found that in most cases, the various researchers independently produce lists of issues which are very similar, and that differences in these lists are often a matter of a single issue being referred to by several different names. Negotiation amongst the researchers serves both to reconcile these differences and to clarify the issues and the terminology being used to describe them.

At this point a selection is made. If an issue occurs for only a very small number of interviewees, and at only a few isolated places, then it is unlikely that this data will shed much light on that issue. There are several reasons why this might occur. Perhaps no student came close to understanding the concept; perhaps all students were well beyond their struggles to understand that concept; or, it is possible that the interview questions were not successful in getting many students to confront these issues very often. In the latter case, it is natural to relegate the issue to future study.

The research team chooses for further study those issues which occur the most often for the most interviewees, and for which there is the largest range of successful, unsuccessful, and in-between performance to be explained.

4. Relate to the theoretical perspective. Each issue is considered in detail. The researchers try to explain the differences between the performances of individual students on the issue in terms of whether they constructed (or failed to construct) the actions, processes, objects, and schemas proposed by the theoretical analysis. If it is necessary to bring the theoretical analysis more in line with the data, the researchers may drop some constructions from the proposed genetic decomposition, or look for new ones to add to the theoretical analysis.

Focusing on the successes which have occurred, the researchers attempt to reconcile the way in which successful students appear to be making use, in their thinking, of the constructions predicted by the theoretical analysis. Again, adjustments in that analysis are made as necessary.

If the data appear to be too much at variance with the general theoretical perspective, consideration is given to revisions of the perspective. This can take the form of adding new kinds of constructions, or revising the explanations of constructions already a part of the theory.

If drastic changes are required very often, or if each new iteration of the framework continues to require major changes and the process is more like an oscillation than a convergence, then consideration must be given to rejecting the general theoretical perspective.

In each of these steps, each member of the research team makes an independent determination and all differences are reconciled through negotiation. Nothing appears in the final report that is not agreed to by all authors. This is the closest we come to objectivity in these considerations, and it is one reason why our papers tend to have long lists of authors.

5. Summarize performance. Finally, the mathematical performance of the students as indicated in the transcripts is summarized and incorporated in the consideration of performance resulting from the other kinds of data that were gathered.

4. Discussion of accuracy and assessment

We return now to the issues raised in Section 2.2.

We have already discussed the development of our theoretical perspective beginning with its origins in the ideas of Piaget and as a result of our work within the framework (Section 2.1). We also explained in some detail how the theoretical analysis influences our instructional treatment Section 3.2) and the relationship between the theoretical analysis and the analysis of data (Section 3.3.2). Regarding the use of data from other studies, our approach is to use all data that is available to the researchers at the time that they make their analyses.

There are two main issues that remain to be discussed: the relation between our theoretical perspective and accuracy about what is going on in the mind of the student, and the question of assessment, including a consideration of the circumstances under which our theory could be falsified.

4.1 Our theory and reality.

It is important to emphasize that, although our theoretical analysis of a mathematical concept results in models of the mental constructions that an individual might make in order to understand the concept, we are in no way suggesting that this analysis is an accurate description of the constructions that are actually made. We believe that it is impossible for one individual to really know what is going on in the mind of another individual. In this respect our theoretical framework is like its underlying radical constructivist perspective which Glasersfeld notes, "is intended, not as a metaphysical conjecture, but as a conceptual tool whose value can be gauged only by using it" [14]. All we can do is try to make sense out of the individual's reactions to various phenomena.

One approach would be to try to make inferences from these reactions about the actual thinking processes of the respondent. We reject this because there is no way that we could check our inferences. Rather, we take something of the view of Glasersfeld [13] and consider only whether our description of the mental constructions is compatible with the responses that we observe. That is, we ask only whether our theoretical analysis is a reasonable explanation of the comments and written work of the student. With respect to the instructional treatment, we confine ourselves to asking whether those strategies that are derived from our explanations appear to lead to the student learning the mathematical concept in question.

4.2 Assessment.

We make both an internal and external assessment of our results as the work proceeds.

Internally, we ask whether the theoretical analysis and resulting instruction "work" in the sense that students do (or do not) appear to be making the mental constructions proposed by the theory. That is, are the students' responses reasonably consistent with the assertion that those mental constructions are being made?

Externally, we ask if the students appear to be learning the mathematical concept(s) in question. We ask and answer this question in more or less traditional terms through the results of examinations and performance on the mathematical questions in our interviews.

Finally, at the extreme end of assessment is the question of falsification. Any scientific theory must contain within it the possibility that an analysis, or even the entire theory should be rejected. In our framework, revisions including major changes in, or even rejection of, a particular genetic decomposition can result from the process of repeating the theoretical analyses based on continually renewed sets of data. As we indicated above (Section 4), the need for continual and extensive revisions could lead to complete rejection of the general theory and, presumably, the entire framework with which we are working.

In a more positive vein, the continual revisions of our theoretical analyses and the applications to instruction in ongoing classes with, presumably, successful results over a period of time tends to ensure that the longer the work continues, the less likely that our framework and the general theoretical perspective it includes will turn out to have been totally useless. This is not to say, of course, that in the future, some more effective and more convenient framework and/or theory might not emerge and replace what we are using.

This paper has focused on the research methodology in a general approach to research and development in undergraduate mathematics education. It is closely related and complementary to two other papers about this same approach: [8] and [9]. The former concentrates on a somewhat historical description of the programming language *ISETL* and the latter focusses on the pedagogical aspect.

5. Conclusion

In conclusion, we would like to make one final point about the use of the framework described in this paper. Throughout our discussion we have given examples from previous studies in which developing forms of this framework were applied. These investigations had to do with the concept of function, mathematical induction, and predicate calculus. In subsequent publications, we expect to report on studies of students learning concepts in calculus and abstract algebra. Taken as a totality, these papers express a particular approach to investigating how mathematics can be learned and applying the results of those investigations to help real students in real classes. It is our intention to provide enough information in these reports to allow the reader to decide on the effectiveness of our method for understanding the learning process and for helping students learn college level mathematics.

References

1. Breidenbach, D., Dubinsky, E., Hawks, J., & Nichols, D. (1992). Development of the process conception of function. *Educational Studies in Mathematics, 23,* 247–285.

2. Cottrill, J., Dubinsky, E., Nichols, D., Schwingendorf, K., Thomas, K., & Vidakovic, D. (in press). Understanding the limit concept: Beginning with a coordinated process schema. *Journal of Mathematical Behavior.*

3. Dautermann, J. (1992). *Using ISETL 3.0: A Language for Learning Mathematics.* St Paul: West.

4. Davis, R. (1984). *Learning Mathematics: The Cognitive Science Approach to Mathematics Education.* Norwood, NJ: Ablex Publishing Corporation.

5. Dubinsky, E. (in press). On learning quantification. *Journal of Computers in Mathematics and Science Teaching.*

6. —— (1991). Reflective abstraction in advanced mathematical thinking. In D.Tall (Ed.), Advanced Mathematical Thinking (pp. 231–250). Dordrecht, The Netherlands: Kluwer.

7. —— (1994). A theory and practice of learning college mathematics. In A. Schoenfeld (Ed.), *Mathematical Thinking and Problem Solving* (pp. 221–243). Hillsdale, NJ: Erlbaum.

8. —— (1995). ISETL: A Programming Language for Learning Mathematics, *Communications in Pure and Applied Mathematics, 48,* 1–25.

9. —— (in preparation). Programming to Learn Advanced Mathematical Topics: One of Many Computational Environments.

10. Dubinsky, E., Dautermann, J., Leron, U., & Zazkis, R. (1994). On learning fundamental concepts of group theory. *Educational Studies in Mathematics, 27,* 267– 305.

11. Dubinsky, E., Schwingendorf, K. E., & Mathews, D. M. (1995). *Calculus, Concepts and Computers* (2nd ed.). New York: McGraw-Hill.

12. Fisher, Sir R. A. (1932). *Statistical Methods for Research Workers.* Edinburgh: Oliver & Boyd.

13. Glasersfeld, E. von (1987). Learning as a constructive activity. In C. Janvier (Ed.), *Problems of Representation in the Teaching and Learning of Mathematics* (pp. 41–69). Hillsdale, NJ: Erlbaum.

14. Glasersfeld, E. von (1995). *Radical Constructivism: A Way of Knowing and Learning.* New York: Falmer Press. p. 22.

15. Griese, D. (1981). *The Science of Programming.* New York: Springer-Verlag.

16. Gutting, G. (Ed.) (1980). *Paradigms and Revolutions: Appraisals and Applications of Thomas Kuhn's Philosophy of Science.* Notre Dame, IN: University of Notre Dame Press.

17. Jacob, E. (1988). Clarifying qualitative research: A focus on traditions. *Educational Researcher,* 17(1), 16–24.

18. Kaput, J. & Roschelle J. (unpublished). *Year 2 Annual Report to NSF: SimCalc Annual Report to NSF: Materials, Tests, and Results, 1995.* (Available from first author at Department of Mathematics, Umass Dartmouth, No. Dartmouth, MA 02747.)

19. Kuhn, T. (1970). *The Structure of Scientific Revolutions* (2nd ed.). Chicago: University of Chicago Press.

20. Patton, M. Q. (1990). *Qualitative Evaluation and Research Methods.* Newbury Park: Sage Publications.

21. Piaget, J. (1972). *The Principles of Genetic Epistemology* (W. Mays, Trans.). London: Routledge & Kegan Paul. (Original work published 1970)

22. Piaget, J. & Garcia, R. (1989). *Psychogenesis and the History of Science* (H. Feider, Trans.). New York: Columbia University Press. (Original work published 1983)

23. Hagelgans, N., Reynolds, B., Schwingendorf, K., Vidakovic, D., Dubinsky, E., Shahin, M., & Wimbish, G. (1995). *A Practical Guide to Cooperative Learning in Collegiate Mathematics* (MAA Notes Number 37). Washington, DC: The Mathematical Association of America.

24. Romberg, T. (1992). Perspectives on scholarship and research methods. In D. A. Grouws (Ed.), *Handbook of Research on Mathematics Teaching and Learning* (pp. 49–64). New York: Macmillan.

25. Schoenfeld, A. H. (1986). On having and using geometric knowledge. In H. Hiebert, (Ed.), *Conceptual and procedural knowledge: The case of mathematics* (pp. 225–264). Hillsdale, NJ: Erlbaum.

26. —— (1994). Some notes on the enterprise (Research in collegiate mathematics education, that is). *Research in Collegiate Mathematics Education I,* 1–19.

27. Schoenfeld, A. H., Smith, J. P., III, & Arcavi, A. (1993). Learning — the microgenetic analysis of one student's understanding of a complex subject matter domain. In R. Glaser (Ed.), *Advances in Instructional Psychology,* 4 Hillsdale, NJ: Erlbaum.

28. Sfard, A. (1987). Two conceptions of mathematical notions, operational and structural. In A. Borbàs (Ed.), *Proceedings of the Eleventh Annual Conference of the International Group for the Psychology of Mathematics Education* (pp. 162-169). Montreal: University of Montreal.

29. —— (1991). On the dual nature of mathematical conceptions. *Educational Studies in Mathematics, 22,* 1–36.

30. Suppe, F. (Ed.) (1977). *The Structure of Scientific Theories* (2nd Ed.). Urbana, IL: University of Illinois Press.

31. Tall, D. & Vinner, S. (1981). Concept image and concept definition in mathematics with particular reference to limits and continuity. *Educational Studies in Mathematics, 12,* 151–169.

32. Vidakovic, D. (1993). *Differences between group and individual processes of construction of the concept of inverse function.* Unpublished doctoral dissertation, Purdue University, West Lafayette, IN.

PART II
Research and Effectiveness

Teaching, like parenting, will probably always remain a human activity that we engage in because we must and because we want to, an activity that we profoundly need to do as well as possible, and an activity whose ultimate effectiveness will never be completely understood. Our children turn out well or badly in later life. Our students succeed or fail in their careers. We don't really know why, or if what we did helped or hindered, or made much of a difference at all. All we can do in both endeavors is to reach deeply into the fullness of our resources to try to understand what we are doing, to do it as well as we possibly can, and to hope for the best.

We can never rely entirely on research because as intelligent, sensitive, creative human beings, what we have to offer our students is vastly more than what can be contributed through formal research. Teaching will always be largely an art with aspects of a craft and hopefully an increasing flavor of a science—in Gries conceptualization of science as the conscious application of general principles to concrete situations.

Having said all that, we cannot deny that research can make a substantial contribution to our reflections on how our students learn and what we might do to help. There are two kinds of research and although any good investigation will have substantial components of both theoretical and empirical considerations, we can make characterizations in terms of the relative weight of each. In theoretically-oriented research the goal can be to understand the process by which learning can take place and see if instruction can be designed to reflect that understanding. The framework paper of Asiala et al. discussed in the previous section is of this nature. In more empirical investigations the researchers try to determine the effect on learning of manipulating different variables including, of course, aspects of the pedagogical methodology. Several of the papers in this section are empirically oriented.

Davidson presents an overview of research that tries both to show how varied can be pedagogy which is referred to as cooperative learning and to compare the effectiveness of these strategies with traditional teaching. The three papers by Slavin, Graves, and Good and Marshall look at specific issues related to cooperative learning. Slavin is concerned with the issue of group vs. individual rewards whereas Graves considers the question of whether there should be rewards at all. Good and Marshall discuss a different but still specific issue—whether groups should be homogenous or heterogeneous with respect to ability. The paper of Lou et al. presents a meta-analysis of cooperative learning research in which authors summarize results of studies of the effectiveness of placing students in small groups, of the critical factors in these findings and of the effects of different types of groups.

In the next paper, Cohen takes an entirely different view and suggests that rather than try to decide between cooperative learning and some other approach, or even to pick between one or another kind of cooperative learning, it would be better to study the conditions under which one or another strategy can be productive.

The last two papers in this section return to more of a theoretical emphasis. Heller, Keith and Anderson study cooperative learning in physics classes. They try to learn about the nature of students' problem solving abilities and how that might be affected by group work. Finally, Vidakovic, working in the constructivist framework of Asiala et al., asks how working in a group affects the way in which an individual constructs her or his understanding of a mathematical concept.

Comments on the article by Davidson

The following review by Davidson of the research concerning cooperative learning in mathematics clearly shows that there exists a great diversity of activities grouped together under the umbrella term "cooperative learning." Students could work in groups whose sizes range from two to six members, and may work together for greatly varying lengths of time on very different types of tasks. From these multiple implementations of cooperative learning, Davidson begins by teasing out some of the common basic notions concerning what students might be expected to do in cooperative learning groups, and also what faculty using these groups might do. In this context, Davidson gives a rather more detailed list of "teaching functions" than Finkel and Monk gave in their paper in this collection.

Since a multitude of educational arrangements are included in the general category of cooperative learning, attempts to answer the question of "Does cooperative learning in mathematics work better than the lecture method?" requires us to first distinguish among the different manifestations of cooperative learning. Also, as there is not just a single outcome of a mathematics course, but rather many outcome variables including problem solving ability, skill acquisition, retention, and attitude toward mathematics to name a few, we must refine our questions of effectiveness to a particular set of educational outcomes. Through his review of the literature, Davidson provides us with partial answers to numerous questions of effectiveness from research conducted up to the mid 1980's. In this survey, he brings together research results from elementary school mathematics through collegiate mathematics.

As we see in Davidson's summary, the interrelationships of input variables of pedagogical practice and output variables of educational outcome are extremely complex. As in the paper by Cohen in this section, one sees that conclusive proof that cooperative learning strategies of one particular type are universally better than lecture-based instruction is not likely to be provided by one single study. The complexity of the problems of teaching and learning mathematics indicates that rather than being provided with conclusive proof, we will almost certainly have to settle for a preponderance of evidence.

Discussion Questions

1. What categories of articles surveyed by Davidson do you find the most compelling? The least compelling? Why?
2. Describe the characteristics of a research study that would provide you with compelling or conclusive evidence that cooperative learning is more effective than lecture-based instruction in a collegiate mathematics course.
3. Would the above study also convince your colleagues? Why or why not?
4. What educational outcomes are the most important to you, and how do different cooperative learning strategies affect these? Are these goals the same or different across the spectrum of undergraduate mathematics courses?

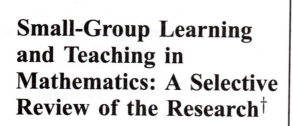

Small-Group Learning and Teaching in Mathematics: A Selective Review of the Research[†]

Neil Davidson

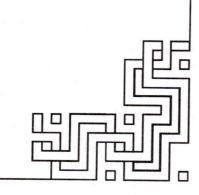

Since the late 1960s, a variety of types of cooperative learning procedures have been used in teaching many different mathematics courses, ranging from elementary school through graduate school. The procedures include small-group interaction in which students work together in groups of three to six members, partner learning taking place in dyads, and a peer-tutoring variation of partner learning in which one student is assigned to tutor another. Peer tutoring includes both same-age tutoring and cross-age tutoring, in which an older student tutors a younger one.

At present, there is a substantial body of research on small-group learning and teaching of mathematics. This chapter presents a selected sample, as opposed to a comprehensive review, of that research. Studies of peer tutoring are not included in this review, as that body of research can be found in other places (e.g., Devin-Sheehan, Feldman, & Allen, 1976).

The various small-group learning procedures have in common the following basic notions. First, the class is divided into small groups, of two to six members apiece. Each group has its own working space, which may or may not include a section of the blackboard. Each group is involved in discussing mathematical concepts and principles, in practicing mathematical techniques, and in solving problems. The teacher moves from group to group, checks the student's work, and provides assistance in varying degrees. The groups sometimes gather outside class to work on projects.

In each type of small-group teaching, there are certain basic leadership and management functions that must be performed—many of them by the teacher. How these functions are performed varies considerably, depending on the model of small-group instruction that is used. The basic set of functions is as follows:

Initiate group work
Present guidelines for small-group operation
Form groups
Prepare and introduce new material in some form
 Orally to entire class
 Orally to separate groups
 Via written materials
  Worksheets, activity packages, text materials, special texts designed for groups
Interact with small groups in various possible ways:
 Observe groups, check solutions, give hints, clarify notations, ask and answer questions, point out errors, provide encouragement, help groups

[†] Reprinted with permission from R. E. Slavin, S. Kagan, R. Hertz-Lazarowitz, C. Webb, and R. Schmuck, *Learning to Cooperate, Cooperate to Learn.* New York: Plenum, 1985, pp. 211–230.

to function, furnish overall classroom management

Tie ideas together

Make assignments of homework or in-class work

Evaluate students performance

As stated earlier, each of these functions can be performed in various ways and to varying degrees, depending on the model of small-group instruction in effect.

Several texts have been designed for small-group learning in mathematics. There are texts in elementary algebra (Stein & Crabill, 1972), plane geometry (Chakerian, Crabill, & Stein, 1972), abstract algebra (Davidson & Gulick, 1976), and mathematics for elementary-education or liberal-arts majors (University of Maryland Mathematics Project, 1978; Weissglass, 1979).

Main Effects of Small-Group Methods

Small-Group Discovery Method

Davidson (1971a, b, 1979) developed and tested a small-group discovery method in a year-long course in elementary calculus. The method was based on the educational philosophy of Dewey (1916/1966, 1938/1963) with supporting practices from social psychology (Deutsch, 1960; White & Lippitt, 1960).

The instructor introduced new material with brief lectures at the beginning of class, during which he posed problems and questions for investigation. For most of the class time, the students worked together cooperatively at the blackboard in four-member groups. The students discussed mathematical concepts, proved theorems, made conjectures, constructed examples and counterexamples, and developed techniques for problem solving. The instructor provided guidance and support for the small groups, employing all the practices described earlier for interaction with small groups.

The instructor stated the following guidelines for group behavior: (1) Work together in groups of four; (2) cooperate with other group members; (3) achieve a group solution for each problem; (4) make sure that everyone understands that solution before the group goes on; (5) listen carefully to others, trying whenever possible to build on their ideas; (6) share the leadership of the group; (7) make sure that everyone participates and no one dominates; and (8) take turns writing problem solutions on the board.

In the initial study, the students chose their own groups and switched the membership after each unit. The students were evaluated by means of take-home exams and an in-class final. There was no significant difference in performance on the final between the students in the experimental

class and those in the control classes taught by the lecture method. A questionnaire showed highly positive attitudes in the experimental class.

Two other investigations examined the effects of the small-group discovery method in elementary calculus. Loomer (1976) modified the method by including some of the Polya (1965) heuristic strategies for problem solving. He compared achievement in this modified method with that in a lecture control class. On five of six measures, there was no significant difference. However, in a delayed retest of problem solving, the control class scored marginally significantly higher ($p < .10$) than the small-group class. Unfortunately, one cannot separate the effects of the small groups from those of the heuristics.

Brechting and Hirsch (1977) employed modifications of the small-group discovery method and of Davidson's calculus course notes. The students in their small-group treatment scored significantly higher than those taught by traditional methods on a test of manipulative skills. There was no significant difference on a concept measure.

Laboratory and Data Collection

A second category of cooperative learning involves the use of data collection, manipulative materials, and laboratory equipment in small groups. Weissglass (1977, 1979) used a small-group laboratory method in a course in mathematics for elementary teaching. His approach was based on the theory of reevaluation counseling (Jackins, 1978). The course involved a sophisticated treatment of the mathematical concepts taught in elementary or junior high school and used a variety of study guides and laboratory activities. The groups investigated mathematical concepts with equipment including attribute blocks, Cuisenaire rods, geoboards, tangrams, geoblocks, and dice. In a comparison of the laboratory class with a lecture class, there was no significant difference on an achievement test. There was evidence indicating that the laboratory approach was more successful in "motivating those students with more mathematical knowledge and skills" (Weissglass, 1977, p. 382).

Computer-Assisted Instruction

Group work can be used in conjunction with computers. Golton (1975) studied the use of computer-assisted instruction (CAI) in probability and statistics at the sixth-grade level. In the experimental group, the students worked in pairs selected by free choice; in the control group, the students used the equipment alone. No significant differences were found between treatment and control on an achievement and retention test. Golton concluded that the cost of CAI can be halved by pairing students.

Remedial Mathematics

Small groups can be used in remedial courses. Chang (1977a, b) worked with remedial students in arithmetic and algebra in community colleges. In the experimental section, the students discussed mathematics in small groups with three or four members. The control section used the lecture-demonstration approach. The treatment group scored significantly higher than the control group on tests of arithmetic and algebra and on a combined test. Of the experimental students, 75% received a mark of C or better in the next math course, compared to only 47% of the control students.

Gilmer (1978) experimented with a developmental algebra course in a technical college. The experimental class used small-group discussions; the control class used an individual self-pacing approach. There were no significant differences in achievement or intellectual involvement. Pacing was faster in the control group. The experimental group had significantly higher course interest and attitude, as well as a trend toward a lower withdrawal rate, than the control group ($p < .07$).

Review

Pence (1974) compared the effects of small-group versus individual review on subsequent individual performance. Sixth-grade students were assigned to different treatments for the review of topics that they had failed on diagnostic tests. Three types of small-group review were contrasted with individual review. There were nonsignificant trends in achievement scores in favor of small-group review over individual review. Additionally, small-groups review required more time.

Goal Structures

Johnson and Johnson (1974, 1975) have differentiated among cooperative, competitive, and individualistic goal structures and have developed "learning-together" methods for the cooperative goal structure. They have conducted a number of studies in diverse subject areas comparing the effects of the three goal structures.

In one such study in mathematics, Johnson, Johnson, and Scott (1978) compared cooperative and individualistic methods involving high-achieving fifth- and sixth-grade students in an advanced math class, studying one hour per day for 50 days. In the cooperative condition, the students were told to work together as a group of four and to complete one assignment pamphlet and record slip for their entire group, with all students contributing ideas and seeking assistance from each other, not from the teacher. The teacher "praised and rewarded" the group as a whole. In the individualized condition, the students were told to work on their own and to complete individual assignment pamphlets and record slips, to avoid interaction with other students, and to seek help and clarification from the teacher. The teacher praised and rewarded each student individually.

The students in the cooperative groups in comparison with the students working individually, had more positive attitudes toward heterogeneity among their peers, believed that they were doing a better job of learning in school, and performed their daily tasks faster and more accurately. When the students in the cooperative treatment were tested in their groups and could help one another with their tests, they scored significantly higher than did the individualized students tested individually, on two of three final unit tests and on a retention test two months later. However, when all the students were tested individually, the students in the individualized treatment scored significantly higher than the students in the cooperative treatment in about 50% of the comparisons.

Robertson (1982) evaluated the Johnsons' methods in second- and third-grade mathematics courses and found no significant differences in mathematics achievement between the experimental and the control groups.

Group Rewards for Individual Learning

Slavin (1980a, 1983a, b) has presented and reviewed an extensive body of research dealing with three methods of cooperative learning in which there is both group study and a group reward for individual learning. These are Teams-Games-Tournaments (TGT), Student Teams-Achievement Divisions (STAD), and Team-Assisted Individualization (TAI). STAD and TGT are described as follows:

> These methods typically involve students working in small groups to master worksheets or other information initially presented by the teacher. Following the group study time, the students are individually assessed, and the group members' scores are summed to form group scores. These are recognized in class newsletters, or qualify the groups for certificates, grades, or other rewards... In STAD, the teacher presents a lesson, and then students study worksheets in four-member teams that are heterogeneous on student ability, sex, and ethnicity. Following this, students take individual quizzes, and team scores are computed based on the degree to which each student improved over his or her own past record. The team scores are recognized in class newsletters. TGT is the same as STAD, except that instead of taking quizzes, students compete against members of other teams who are similar in past performance to add points to their team scores. (Slavin, 1983b, p. 432)

In TAI, the students work in heterogeneous teams and form pairs or triads within their teams. They work on individualized curriculum materials at their own levels and rates. The students exchange answer sheets with their partners within the teams; the partners check each other's answers after solving four problems on a skill sheet. The team members help one another with problems. The students must solve a block of four problems correctly before they can go on to the next skill sheet, and eventually, they take various tests. The teams receive certificates based on the number of units completed and on the members' performance on the final tests. TAI is an individualized program that can be managed by a single teacher without an aide, as the students themselves manage the routine checking and procedures of the program. The TAI program and research on it are described in more detail in the preceding chapter.

The four studies of TGT in mathematics have been conducted with seventh-grade students by Edwards and DeVries (1972, 1974); Edwards, DeVries, and Snyder (1972); and Hulten and DeVries (1976). In three of the four studies, there was a significant difference in achievement gains favoring the TGT group over the control group taught by traditional large-group instruction. In the three studies involving integrated schools, effects on race relations were measured by asking the students to name their friends of the opposite race. In two of these three studies, the TGT students gained significantly more on the race relations criteria than did the control students. A measure of mutual concern examined the students' liking of their classmates and feelings of being liked by them. In both studies measuring this variable, there was a significant difference in mutual concern in favor of the TGT treatment over the control treatment.

The three studies of STAD in mathematics were carried out by Madden and Slavin (1983), Slavin and Karweit (1982), and Huber, Bogatzki, and Winter (1982). The grade levels were 3-6, 9, and 7, respectively. In all three studies, the student gains in achievement were significantly higher in STAD than in the traditionally taught control group.

One combined program employed three cooperative learning methods with the same fourth- and fifth-grade students in three different subject areas (Slavin & Karweit, 1981). TGT was used in mathematics. There was no significant difference in mathematics achievement scores between the TGT students and the controls. However, the TGT mutual concern scores were significantly higher than those of the controls.

Six studies of TAI in mathematics were conducted. These are reviewed in the preceding chapter. In five of these studies, the gains in achievement scores in the TAI approach were significantly higher than in the large-group control approach on the mathematics portion of the Com-

prehensive Test of Basic Skills (CBTS). However, the TAI students' scores were not significantly higher than the scores of students working individually with the TAI materials (Slavin, Leavey, & Madden, 1984). Several studies showed positive effects of TAI on affective variables, as described in the preceding chapter.

One of the TAI studies (Slavin, Madden, & Leavey, 1984a) compared the effects of TAI, an individualized program using TAI materials, and a traditional control method on the social acceptance, the behavior, and the achievement of mainstreamed, mildly academically handicapped children. The use of TAI and of the individual program with TAI materials significantly improved the social acceptance of the mainstreamed students; this improvement was indicated by the increased numbers of choices that they received as "best friends" and by the decreased numbers of received "rejections." The TAI mainstreamed students were rated as having significantly fewer behavioral problems than the mainstreamed students in the control class. This finding did not hold for the individualized students using TAI materials. No significant differences in the achievement of the mainstreamed students were found among the treatments; however, achievement data from a later study (Slavin, Madden, & Leavey, 1984b) with a larger sample of mainstreamed students showed gains in achievement that were significantly higher in TAI than in the control treatment.

In summary, throughout the set of studies comparing TGT, STAD, or TAI with traditional total-class instruction, significant differences in gains in student achievement in favor of the small-group treatment occurred in 11 out of 14 studies. For the most part, these were obtained on measures of basic skill learning and on simple application problems.

Reviews of team learning usually include an additional method: Aronson's Jigsaw (1978) and its variation, Jigsaw II (Slavin, 1980b). In these approaches, the material to be learned in each group is divided into several parts, each of which is assigned to one group member. The group members learn their own parts of the material by studying them with others who are also to become "experts" on the same topic. The experts then return to their own groups and teach the material to the other group members. As the Jigsaw methods have not been used in mathematics instruction, their results are not described here.

Research on Internal Dynamics in Cooperative Learning

Group Formation Procedures

The research on internal dynamics in cooperative learning includes several studies investigating different procedures in forming small groups. Stam (1973) compared sociometric choice grouping with random grouping in fifth-grade classes. The outcome measures were tasks requiring convergent thinking and divergent thinking. On the divergent-thinking tasks, the sociometric groups performed significantly better than the random groups. There were no significant differences on the convergent-thinking tasks.

Grant (1975) compared three grouping procedures in a course for prospective elementary teachers taught by the small-group discovery method. The first procedure used sociometric choice in conjunction with group dynamics exercises for two weeks. The second was based on interpersonality compatibility as measured by the Fundamental Interpersonal Relations Orientation-Behavior (FIRO-B) (Schutz, 1966). The third involved students choosing their groups in class. The groups using sociometric choice with group dynamic exercises scored significantly higher than the groups formed by in-class choice on a composite measure of achievement, mathematical attitude, and small-group attitude. There was no significant difference between the groups formed with the FIRO-B and those formed by means of the other procedures.

Webb (1977) compared the effects of problem practice on complex tasks performed in mixed-ability groups, in uniform-ability groups, or by individuals. Eleventh-grade students worked in four-person groups. Overall, the results on individual tests showed the following order from best to worst conditions: mixed-ability grouping, individual learning, and uniform-ability grouping. Webb found an aptitude-treatment interaction. The above order held for low-ability students but was reversed for medium-ability students. High-ability students performed less well in uniform-ability groups than in the other conditions.

Group-Process and Aptitude-Treatment Interactions

Webb (1980a, b, c, 1982a) has conducted a number of correlational studies relating group process to student achievement in mathematics. Much of this work is summarized elsewhere in this volume. Webb's presentation (1982b) summarized the results of four of these studies. One of them involved eleventh-grade students learning material on probability, algebra, and geometry. The other three studies involved seventh-, eighth-, or ninth-grade students learning general mathematics. In three of the four studies, all group work was tape-recorded, and interaction was coded from the tape transcripts. This procedure yielded much more useful information than a process of coding the interaction directly from observations of the students in class.

Webb (1982b) distinguished among all instances of help, explanation, and terminal responses. Explanations generally consisted of step-by-step descriptions or detailed accounts of problem solutions or error corrections. Terminal responses were forms of "help" that did not include these detailed descriptions, for example, giving an answer without an explanation or simply pointing out an error.

Webb's studies consistently showed that giving explanations was positively related to achievement, that is, that explaining to others helped one's own learning. However, giving terminal responses was negatively related to achievement, as was receiving no response to a request for help. The results for receiving explanations were not completely consistent but did suggest that receiving explanations tended to benefit achievement.

Janicki (1979) compared the effects of individual and small-group instruction. The students were fourth- and fifth-graders learning a two-week unit on fractions. In one treatment, the students worked on seatwork individually and were given a homework assignment at the end of class. In the other treatment, the students did seatwork in mixed-ability groups of four students; those who completed the seatwork could choose to do their homework or to play math games in their small group. No main effects of the treatments were found, but there was an aptitude-treatment interaction. The students who had a positive attitude and an internal locus of control performed better on the achievement and retention tests in the small-group approach. The students who had a less positive attitude and an external locus of control performed better in the individual approach.

Peterson and Janicki (1979) investigated aptitude-treatment interactions with students learning in large-group and mixed-ability small-group approaches. Fourth-, fifth-, and sixth-grade classes studied fractions for two weeks; each class used only one of the two instructional approaches.

Again, no main effects of treatment on achievement were found, but aptitude-treatment interactions did occur. Students of high ability retained more in the small-group approach than in the large-group approach. Students of low ability retained more in the large-group approach. Students who initially preferred one of the approaches (small-group or large-group) did better on the retention test in the other, nonpreferred approach. High-ability students had a more positive attitude toward mathematics in the small-group approach, and low-ability students had a more positive attitude in the large-group approach. Both high-ability and low-ability students had a more positive attitude toward the instructional approach in the small-group treatment, but medium-ability students had a more positive attitude toward instruction in the large-group treatment. Overall, the attitudes toward instruction were more positive in the large-group approach.

The aptitude-treatment interactions were explained through observations of group process as follows: The high-ability students probably liked math better and retained more in the small-group approach "because they were actively involved in explaining the math problems and helping others." The low-ability students probably liked math better and retained more in the large group "because the teacher provided direction and help" (Peterson & Janicki, 1979, p. 686).

Peterson, Janicki, and Swing (1981) investigated aptitude-treatment interactions with students learning in large-group and mixed-ability small-group approaches. Fifth- and sixth-grade classes studied a two-week unit on geometry, using one of the two instructional approaches in each class. There were no significant differences on achievement and retention tests between the two treatments. However, both high-ability and low-ability students performed better in the small-group approach than in the large-group approach. Medium-ability students tended to do slightly better, but not significantly so, in the large-group approach. These results were explained on the basis of classroom observations. The high-ability students spent more time giving explanations than the low-ability students; both spent more time explaining than the medium-ability students. The more time spent explaining to others, the better the student's performance; that is, the students learned by teaching. This finding was consistent with the prior results of Peterson and Janicki (1979) and Webb (1980a, b, c, 1982a).

Students had a more positive attitude toward instruction overall in the large-group approach. Students with better-than-average ability had a more positive attitude toward the instructional method in the large-group approach than in the small-group approach. This interaction, which was inconsistent with the prior result of Peterson and Janicki (1979), was explained by a group-process observation that the high-ability students "worked much harder" in the small-group approach by giving explanations to other group members.

In all the studies reviewed in this section, there was a consistent positive relationship between giving help and achievement. However, in two of the studies (Peterson & Janicki, 1979; Peterson et al., 1981), there was no significant relationship between receiving help and achievement. Webb (1982b) commented that the help received may have included both explanations and terminal responses, the effects of which canceled each other out.

In two studies (Peterson & Janicki, 1979; Peterson et al., 1981), overall student attitudes toward instruction were more positive in the large-group than in the small-group approach. However, the interactions involving student attitudes were not consistent across the studies.

Group Testing, Brainstorming, and Cognitive Development

Klingbeil (1974) examined the effects of group testing in a mathematics course for prospective elementary teachers. All sections learned by the small-group discovery method. Klingbeil stated the following guidelines for small-group examinations:

1. *All* group members must contribute in some way to the mathematical solution of each problem on the exam.
2. All problems should be worked out on the blackboard.
3. Each group must do its own work and cannot use information obtained from other groups.
4. The task of writing down the group solution must be rotated within the group for each exam.
5. All copies of the exam sheet including a copy with the group solutions (which is the only one that will be graded) must be handed in at the end of the hour. (p. 29)

There were three examination treatments: In one section, the students took all exams individually. In a second section, the students took all exams together in their small groups. In the third, the students alternated between individual and group exams for the six exams. There were no significant differences among the treatments on an individual final exam and on attitude measures. Strong but nonsignificant tendencies were found for the alternating individual–group exam procedure to result in lower test anxiety than the other treatments. On each test, the group exam scores were dramatically higher than the individual exam scores, presumably because the students could work together. Klingbeil recommended the limited use of group tests as part of an evaluation system.

Brainstorming

Gallicchio (1976) investigated the effects of brainstorming in mathematics classes for elementary education majors taught by the small-group discovery method. In the experimental group, there were 11 problem-solving sessions in which small groups used brainstorming. In the control section, small groups solved the same problems without brainstorming. The following guidelines were stated for group brainstorming:

1. List all ideas, such as facts given or possible strategies, on the chalkboard using the following brainstorming rules:

a. Quantity is wanted. The more ideas you have, the higher chance you have of solving the problem.

b. Wild ideas are acceptable.

c. Combination and improvement of ideas are sought.

d. No criticism is permitted of your own or other group member's ideas.

2. No idea may be evaluated until the brainstorming list is completed.

3. Each person in the group participates and no one dominates.

4. Each group should do its own work and should not use information obtained from other groups.

5. The group will be asked to hand in the brainstorming list as well as the solution(s) to the problem at the end of the session. (pp. 43–44)

Brainstorming did not significantly enhance mathematical creativity, achievement, or attitude or reduce test anxiety. However, the data obtained by observations and questionnaires indicated that brainstorming encouraged small-group interaction and helped the students to become more confident in their problem-solving ability.

Cognitive Development

Shearn (1982) examined the effects of small-group learning on students' cognitive development, as measured by the Perry (1970) sequence of stages. In Perry's scheme, students in Positions 1 and 2 (dualism) believe that all questions have right or wrong answers, that authority figures possess knowledge and answers, and that the opinions of peers in learning are not to be taken seriously. In Positions 3 and 4 (multiplicity), students become more accepting of a diversity of viewpoints, move toward less dependence on authorities, and have more respect for the views of their peers. In Position 5 (contextual relativism), students reason within different contexts, view the instructor more as a colleague than as an authority, and have respect for the opinions of their peers when supported by logic or by evidence. The later positions in Perry's scheme deal with ethical issues related to commitments. Although most research to date on Perry's scheme has dealt with college students (Widick, Knefelkamp, & Parker, 1975), it is clear that the stages are also pertinent to younger students.

Shearn's study (1982) involved the use of two forms of the small-group discovery method in a one-semester course in mathematics for prospective elementary teachers; most of the students were college sophomores. Although the study had several aspects, the finding pertinent to this review is

that the students in small-group learning progressed significantly in cognitive development, as measured by ratings of Perry's stages before and after the course. Such a developmental movement would not typically occur without an instructional intervention. Some future studies assessing cognitive development in small groups need to include a traditional control treatment for comparison.

Summary and Recommendations for Research

Summary of Findings

Considerable progress in the development of small-group teaching procedures in mathematics has occurred since the late 1960s. Small-group interaction has been used in conjunction with discovery learning, laboratory and data collection methods, computer-assisted instruction, peer tutoring, remedial work, review, group testing, and brainstorming. Instructional materials have been developed for several courses, as have programs to train teachers to use small-group instructional procedures. A summary of findings based on the research in small-group teaching of mathematics follows:

1. Considering all the studies comparing student achievement in small-group instruction and traditional methods in mathematics, the majority showed no significant difference. When significant differences were found, they almost always favored the small-group procedure. Only two studies (Loomer, 1976; Johnson et al., 1978) provided limited partial support for the superiority of the control procedure. No evidence showed that either small-group instruction or the control procedure was superior in fostering the learning of higher order concepts and principles or the solution of nonroutine problems.

If the term *achievement* refers to computational skills, simple concepts, and simple application problems, the studies at the elementary and secondary levels in mathematics support Slavin's (1983b) conclusions: (a) "Cooperative learning methods that use group rewards and individual accountability consistently increase student achievement more than control methods in . . . elementary and secondary classrooms" and (b) "Cooperative learning methods that use group study but not group rewards for individual learning do not increase student achievement more than control methods" (p. 443).

Although Conclusions (a) and (b) hold for the main effects of treatment, the situation is more complex when aptitude-treatment interactions are taken into account. In studies that did *not* involve group rewards for individual learning, Peterson and Janicki (1979) and Peterson et al. (1981) found that students of high ability in mathematics achieved significantly more in small-group than in large-group approaches.

Slavin did not extend his conclusions to the college level, as he did not review that literature. Indeed, Conclusion (a) has not been tested at the college level in mathematics; the studies have not examined the effects of group rewards on individual learning. Conclusion (b) cannot be completely extrapolated to the college level in mathematics, as shown by the studies of Chang (1977) and Brechting and Hirsch (1977), which obtained significant differences in achievement without using group rewards.

2.   The issue of student attitudes toward the subject matter and the method of instruction is rather clouded. In some studies (e.g., Gilmer, 1978), students preferred a small-group treatment, and in others (e.g., Peterson & Janicki, 1979), they preferred a large-group treatment. The interactions between student ability level and attitudes toward instruction were not consistent across the studies. In one study (Peterson & Janicki, 1979), the students learned less in the method that was their initial preference.

3.   There is evidence that the use of TGT in mathematics has positive effects on measures of mutual concern and on race relations in integrated schools. The evidence of these effects of TGT and also STAD has been gathered more extensively in subject areas other than mathematics.

4.   In terms of group formation procedures, two studies (Stam, 1973; Grant, 1975) showed some positive effects on learning when groups were formed by sociometric choice procedures. In one study (Webb, 1977), the use of mixed-ability groups led to higher achievement than the use of uniform-ability groups; however, the effects of the group formation procedure interacted with the ability level of the students. Forming groups heterogeneously by ability, sex, and ethnicity led to increased mutual concern and race relations in several studies reviewed by Slavin (1980a, 1983a).

5.   In several studies summarized by Webb (1982b), students' giving explanations in small groups was positively related to their achievement, whereas giving terminal responses was not so related. Receiving terminal responses or no responses to request for help was negatively related to student achievement.

6.   In two studies (Klingbeil, 1974; Johnson et al., 1978), the scores on small-group exams were significantly higher than the scores on the same exams taken individually. There is considerable controversy about the desirability of allowing group exam scores for evaluation.

7.   None of the following practices led to significant differences in individual student achievement: laboratory work, group review, group testing, and group brainstorming. However, for each practice, only one or two studies were available for consideration.

Recommendations for Research

Not surprisingly, this review of research has led to a number of further issues for investigation. Each of the following appears to offer a promising line of inquiry:

1.   Attempting to extend the range of TGT, STAD, and TAI methods upward to geometry, algebra II and trigonometry, calculus, and perhaps other college-level courses. This extension may require modifications of the methods to handle material that is more complex and less skill-oriented.

2.   Directly contrasting TAI with individualized programs that do not use group interaction or student management of learning.

3.   Implementing the Jigsaw or Jigsaw II model in mathematical problem-solving.

4.   Assessing the outcomes of methods such as TGT, STAD, and TAI in skills-oriented courses, which might prepare students better for various state-required functional math tests.

5.   Examining the results of various small-group procedures used in conjunction with microcomputers.

6.   a. Searching further for aptitude-treatment interactions related to small-group learning.

b. Seeking limited generalizations that give specific outcomes of particular combinations of characteristics related to the student, the type of task and content, the method of instruction, and the environment. Such studies seem especially pertinent to seeking conditions under which discovery or laboratory procedures enhance student learning; they do not do so across the board.

7.   Studying the group-process variables, for example, students' giving explanations, which may be predictors of student learning or may help explain aptitude-treatment interactions.

8.   Looking more closely at the effects of different procedures for small-group formation, including, for example, an instrument such as the Myers-Briggs Type Indicator (Briggs & Briggs Myers, 1977), which has not been previously used for this purpose in mathematics.

9.   Examining the cognitive, affective, and behavioral outcomes of training students to cooperate more effectively in groups, in contrast to promoting intragroup cooperation by means of intergroup competition.

10.   Implementing curriculum development models that allow for the identification of stylistic differences in learning mathematics and the incorporation of student-generated learning sequences.

11.   Designing small-group instruction to enhance student ability to solve nonroutine problems and to learn higher order concepts and principles, and testing the extent to which these goals are achieved.

12. Assessing the effects of various forms of small-group teaching on cognitive development, using progression through the Perry (1970) cognitive development stages as an outcome variable.

In conclusion, professionals involved in the research and development of small-group teaching in mathematics have included mathematics educators, mathematicians, classroom teachers, social psychologists, and educational psychologists. Although many of the workers in the field have been unaware of the efforts of others, a number of instances of collaborative efforts are found, often involving professionals within the same general category. One may hope that this review will lead to a greater degree of mutual awareness and cooperation in directing future efforts in the field. Indeed, many of the proposed questions cannot be addressed without such cooperation.

References

Aronson, E. *The Jigsaw classroom.* Beverly Hills, Calif.: Sage, 1978.

Brechting, Sister M. C., & Hirsch, C. R. The effects of small-group discovery learning on student achievement and attitudes in calculus. *AMATYC Journal,* 1977, 2, 77–82.

Briggs, K. & Briggs Myers, I. *Myers-Briggs Type Indicator.* Palo Alto, Calif.: Consulting Psychologists Press, 1977.

Chakerian, G. D., Crabill, C. D., & Stein, S. K. *Geometry: A guided inquiry.* Boston: Houghton Mifflin, 1972.

Chang, P-T. *On relationships among academic performance, sex difference, attitude and persistence of small groups in developmental college level mathematics courses.* Doctoral dissertation, Georgia State University, School of Education, Atlanta, Georgia, 1977. (a)

—— Small group instruction: A study in remedial mathematics. *AMATYC Journal,* 1977, 2, 72–76. (b)

Davidson, N. The small-group discovery method as applied in calculus instruction. *American Mathematical Monthly,* August-September 1971, 789–91. (a)

—— *The small-group discovery method of mathematics instruction as applied in calculus.* Doctoral dissertation, University of Wisconsin, 1970. Technical Report No. 168. Wisconsin Research and Development Center for Cognitive Learning, Madison, 1971. (b)

—— The small-group discovery method: 1967–77. In *Problem Solving Studies in Mathematics.* J. Harvey & T. Romberg (Eds.), Wisconsin Research and Development Center for Individualized Schooling, University of Wisconsin, Madison, 1979.

Davidson, N., & Gulick, F. *Abstract algebra: An active learning approach.* Boston: Houghton Mifflin, 1976.

Davidson, N., McKeen, R. & Eisenberg, T. Curriculum construction with student input. *Mathematics Teacher,* 1973, 66(3), 271–275.

Deutsch, M. The effects of cooperation and competition upon group process. In D. Cartwright & A. Zander (Eds.), *Group Dynamics: Research and theory* (2nd ed.). New York: Harper & Row, 1960.

Devin-Sheehan, L., Feldman, R., & Allen, V. L. Research on children tutoring children: A critical review. *Review of Educational Research,* 1976, 46, 335–385.

Dewey, John. *Democracy and education.* New York: Free Press, 1966. (Originally published, 1916.)

—— *Experience and education.* New York: Collier, 1963. (Originally published, 1938.)

Edwards, K. J., & DeVries, D. L. *Learning games and student teams: Their effects on student attitudes and achievement.* Center for Social Organization of Schools, The Johns Hopkins University, 1972, Report No. 147.

—— *The effects of Teams-Games-Tournaments and two structural variations on classroom process, student attitudes, and student achievement.* Center for Social Organization of Schools, The Johns Hopkins University, 1974, Report No. 172.

Edwards, K. J., DeVries, D. L., & Snyder, J. P. Games and teams: A Winning combination. *Simulation and Games* 1972, 3, 247–269.

Gallicchio, A. *The effects of brainstorming in small group mathematics classes.* Doctoral dissertation, University of Maryland, College Park, 1976.

Gilmer, G. F. *Effects of small discussion groups on self-paced instruction in a developmental algebra course.* Doctoral dissertation, Marquette University, Milwaukee, Wis., 1978.

Golton, R. F. *The effect of student interaction on computer-assisted instruction in mathematics at the sixth grade level.* Doctoral dissertation, University of California, Berkeley, Calif., 1975.

Grant, S. *The effects of three kinds of group formation using FIRO-B compatibility, sociometric choice with group dynamics exercises, and in-class choice on mathematics classes taught by the small-group discovery method.* Doctoral dissertation, University of Maryland, College Park, 1975.

Huber, G., Bogatzki, W., & Winter, M. *Cooperation: Condition and goal of teaching and learning in classrooms.* Unpublished manuscript, University of Tübingen, West Germany, 1982.

Hulten, B. H., & DeVries, D. L. *Team competition and group practice: Effects on student achievement and attitudes.* Center for Social Organization of Schools, Johns Hopkins University, 1976, Report No. 212.

Jackins, H. *The human side of human beings* (2nd ed.). Seattle: Rational Island Publishers, 1978.

Janicki, T. C. *Aptitude-treatment interaction effects of variations in direct instruction.* Unpublished doctoral dissertation, University of Wisconsin, Madison, 1979.

Johnson, D. W., & Johnson, R. T. Instructional goal structure: Cooperative, competitive, or individualistic. *Review of Educational Research,* 1974, 44, 213–240.

—— *Learning together and alone.* Englewood Cliffs, N.J.: Prentice-Hall, 1975.

Johnson, D. W., Johnson, R. T., & Scott, L. The effects of cooperative and individualized instruction on student attitudes and achievement. *Journal of Social Psychology,* 1978, 104, 207–216.

Klingbeil, D. *An examination of the effects of group testing in mathematics courses taught by the small-group discovery method.* Doctoral dissertation, University of Maryland, College Park, 1974.

Loomer, N. J. *A multidimensional exploratory investigation of small-group heuristic and expository learning in calculus.* Doctoral dissertation, University of Wisconsin, Madison, 1976.

Madden, N. A., & Slavin, R. E. Effects of cooperative learning on the social acceptance of mainstreamed academically handicapped students. *Journal of Special Education,* 1983, 17, 171–182.

Pence, B. M. J. *Small group review of mathematics: A function of the review organization, structure, and task format.* Doctoral dissertation, Stanford University, Stanford, Calif., 1974.

Perry, W. G. *Forms of intellectual and ethical development in the college years: A scheme.* New York: Holt, Rinehart and Winston, 1970.

Peterson, P. L., & Janicki, T. C. Individual characteristics and children's learning in large-group and small-group approaches. *Journal of Educational Psychology,* 1979, 71, 677–687.

Peterson, P. L., Janicki, T. C., & Swing, S. R. Ability × treatment interaction effects on children's learning in large-group and small-group approaches. *American Educational Research Journal,* 1981, 18, 453–473.

Polya, G. *Mathematical discovery,* Vol. 2. New York: Wiley, 1965.

Robertson, L. *Integrated goal structuring in the elementary school: Cognitive growth in mathematics.* Unpublished doctoral dissertation, Rutgers University, New Brunswick, N.J., 1982.

Schutz, W. C. *The interpersonal underworld.* Palo Alto, Calif.: Science and Behavior Books, 1966.

Shearn, E. L. *Adapting the developmental instruction model, based on Perry's theory, to a mathematics content course for preservice elementary teachers to enhance attitudes toward mathematics, cognitive development, and achievement.* Unpublished doctoral dissertation, University of Maryland, College Park, 1982.

Slavin, R. E. Cooperative learning. *Review of Educational Research,* 1980, 50, 315–342 (a).

—— *Using student team learning (rev. ed.),* Baltimore, Md.: Center for Social Organization of Schools, The Johns Hopkins University, 1980. (b)

—— *Cooperative learning.* New York: Longman, 1983. (a)

—— When does cooperative learning increase student achievement? *Psychological Bulletin,* 983, 94, 429–445. (b)

Slavin, R. E., & Karweit, N. L. Cognitive and affective outcomes of an intensive student team learning experience. *Journal of Experimental Education,* 1981, 50, 29–35.

—— *Student teams and mastery learning: An experiment in urban Math 9 classes.* Paper presented at the Annual Convention of the American Educational Research Association, New York, March 1982.

Slavin, R. E., Leavey, M., & Madden, N. A. *Combining student teams and individualized instruction in mathematics: An extended evaluation.* Paper presented at the Annual Convention of the American Educational Research Association, Montreal, April 1983.

—— Combining cooperative learning and individualized instruction: Effects on student mathematics achievement, attitudes, and behaviors. *Elementary School Journal,* 1984, 84, 409–422.

Slavin, R. E., Madden, N. A., & Leavey, M. Effects of cooperative learning and individualized instruction on mainstreamed students. *Exceptional Children,* 1984, 50, 434–443. (a)

—— Effects on Team Assisted Individualization on the mathematics achievement of academically handicapped and non-handicapped students. *Journal of Educational Psychology,* 76, 813–819, 1984 (b).

Stam, P. J. *The effect of sociometric grouping on task performance in the elementary classroom.* Doctoral dissertation, Stanford University, Stanford, Calif. 1973.

Stein, S., & Crabill, C. *Elementary algebra: A guided inquiry.* Boston: Houghton Mifflin, 1972.

University of Maryland Mathematics Project (UMMaP). *Unifying concepts and processes in elementary mathematics.* Boston: Allyn and Bacon, 1978.

Webb, N. M. *Learning in individual and small-group settings.* Technical Report No. 7. Stanford, Calif.: Aptitude Research Project, School of Education, Stanford University, 1977.

—— An analysis of group interaction and mathematical errors in heterogeneous ability groups. *British Journal of Educational Psychology,* 1980, 50, 1–11. (a)

—— Group process: The key to learning in groups. *New Directions for Methodology of Social and Behavioral Science: Issues in Aggregation,* 1980, 6, 77–87. (b)

—— A process-outcome analysis of learning in group and individual settings. *Educational Psychologist,* 1980, 15, 69–83. (c)

—— Group composition, group interaction and achievement in cooperative small groups. *Journal of Educational Psychology,* 1982, 74, 475–484. (a)

—— *Student interaction and learning in small groups: Research summary.* Paper presented at the Meeting of the International Association for the Study of Cooperation in Education, Provo, Utah, 1982. (b)

Weissglass, J. Mathematics for elementary teaching: A small-group laboratory approach. *American Mathematical Monthly,* May 1977, 377–382.

—— *Exploring elementary mathematics: A small-group approach for teaching.* San Francisco: W. H. Freeman, 1979.

White, R., & Lippitt, R. Leader behavior and member reaction in three "Social Climates". In D. Cartwright & A. Zander (Eds.), *Group dynamics: Research and theory.* New York: Harper & Row, 1960.

Widick, C., Knefelkamp, L., & Parker, C. The counselor as a developmental instructor. *Counselor Education and Supervision,* 1975, 14, 286–296.

Comments on the article by Slavin

Although many people engaged in education, including the editors of this volume, are convinced that cooperative learning is a pedagogical strategy that has tremendous potential for serious improvement in student learning, it is certainly not the case that the literature reports unbridled success with this method. Generally speaking, a given research study reports either large, small, or no improvement when cooperative learning is used. It is rare to see a research report of results that are worse with cooperative learning although there is a fair amount of anecdotal information from individual teachers telling us that they did not always succeed in making a class with cooperative learning work in the way in which they would like it to work. In some but not all such cases, the learning outcomes can be worse than when cooperative learning is not tried.

We would like to distinguish between the difficulties of making cooperative learning work (and how they might be overcome) and the question of what effect this strategy has when we are able to make it work. In the present paper the author is concerned with the latter. One possible response to varying results with cooperative learning is to ask if there are specific conditions under which it is more or less likely that this strategy will improve learning. Several authors have considered this question and this paper is one example.

In this paper, Slavin reviews a certain specific portion of the literature and comes to a definite conclusion: cooperative learning has a positive effect on student performance when the entire group is rewarded for the individual performances of its members and when these group rewards are complemented by individual accountability. When such rewards are not present, little difference is found.

Slavin restricts his review to papers reporting on studies of situations satisfying four criteria: cooperative learning was compared with a control group that could be considered initially equivalent; cooperative learning was used continually for at least two weeks; the study took place in elementary or secondary schools; and in the assessment, both cooperative learning and control groups were tested on similar material. There were 46 studies which met these criteria and were considered.

Finally, Slavin considers the causes for the effects he describes. He concludes that there is research support for the causal mechanism of the creation of peer norms and sanctions. Based on his review of the literature, he hypothesizes that if cooperative learning is used then interpersonal sanctions will be directed at increasing the academic performances of all group members only if group rewards are based on the sum of individual learning performances.

Discussion Questions

1. How well does the literature reported justify Slavin's conclusions?
2. To what extent do Slavin's results carry over to post secondary situations?
3. What implications do the results of this paper have for our system of testing and grading?
4. Slavin's conclusion is that positive results come from a combination of group incentives (the group as a whole is rewarded for the performances of its individual members) and individual accountability. What do you think is the relative value of these two factors?

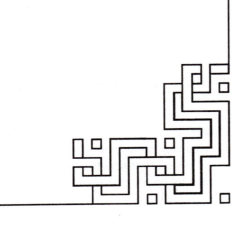

When Does Cooperative Learning Increase Student Achievement?[†]

Robert E. Slavin

Over the past 30 years there has been a considerable quantity of research concerning the effects of cooperative, competitive, and individualistic incentive structures on individual and group productivity. A *cooperative incentive structure* is one in which two or more individuals are rewarded based on their performance as a group; a *competitive incentive structure* indicates that two or more individuals are compared with one another, and those performing best are rewarded; and an *individualistic incentive structure* is one in which individuals are rewarded based on their own performance, regardless of others' performances. The research on these incentive structures has been reviewed on several occasions (e.g., Johnson & Johnson, 1974; Michaels, 1977; Miller & Hamblin, 1963; Slavin, 1977). All of these reviewers agreed that research relating different incentive structures to performance produces inconsistent findings. Some studies find that cooperative incentive structures produce the best performance, and others find that competitive or individualistic incentive structures are superior. However, the reviewers disagreed about the conditions under which cooperative incentive structures enhance performance. For example, Miller and Hamblin (1963) held that cooperative incentive structures were most effective for inherently interdependent tasks, whereas competitive or individualistic incentive structures were most effective for independent tasks. Johnson and Johnson (1974) disagreed, maintaining that cooperative incentive structures are best for all but the most mechanical of tasks, such as speeded drills. Michaels (1977) concluded that the methodologically adequate studies tended to favor competition over cooperation. Slavin (1977) proposed that in short experiments, cooperation was likely to be associated with greater productivity only if efficient task completion absolutely required coordination of efforts. However, he held that over the course of longer interventions, development of group sanctions favoring performance would ultimately make cooperation more effective whether or not coordination of efforts was critical to task completion.

The latest entry in this continuing discussion is a meta-analysis published recently by Johnson, Maruyama, Johnson, Nelson, and Skon (1981), which came to the same conclusion as the earlier Johnson and Johnson (1974) review: Cooperation is better for productivity than competition or individualization for all but rote-decoding tasks. The Johnson et al. review concluded as follows: "the overall effects stand as strong evidence for the superiority of cooperation in promoting achievement and productivity. . . .

† Originally appeared in *Psychological Bulletin,* 94, 429–445. Copyright © 1983 by the American Psychological Association. Reprinted with permission.

Educators may wish to considerably increase the use of cooperative learning procedures to promote higher student achievement" (Johnson et al., 1981, p. 58).

This conclusion has been sharply attacked by Cotton and Cook (1982) and by McGlynn (1982), who pointed out that the blanket conclusion that cooperation is most effective for achievement and productivity is contradicted in the meta-analysis itself, which found statistically significant interactions on productivity and achievement outcomes between cooperation/competition and 10 different factors, including type of task, resource sharing, task interdependence, and other factors (Cotton & Cook, 1982).

It is questionable whether an overall generalization concerning the effectiveness of cooperative, competitive, and individualistic reward structures is either feasible or useful. The Johnson et al. meta-analysis and all previous reviews have concluded that different tasks and outcome measures are associated with different results in this area. Under these circumstances, it is probably more useful to focus on research in small well-defined areas of some theoretical or practical importance rather than to attempt to generalize across widely divergent tasks, settings, outcome measures, and other features repeatedly found to have divergent effects on productivity and achievement outcomes.

This article reviews research on cooperative, competitive, and individualistic reward structures in a narrowly defined but practically important area: student achievement in elementary and secondary schools. Less than a third of the studies that constituted the Johnson et al. meta-analysis had individual achievement as a dependent measure. Almost all of the rest of the studies involve group productivity (e.g., the ability of a *group* to solve a problem, maze, or puzzle). Thus, the conclusions of the meta-analysis are strongly influenced by the results of these group productivity studies. This would not be a problem if group productivity resembled individual achievement as an outcome, but these outcomes are fundamentally different. Groups are inherently superior to individuals for solving problems, because if any group member solves the problem, he or she will tell the answer to the rest of the group. In fact, several studies (e.g., Faust, 1959; Marquart, 1955; Ryack, 1965) have compared the problem-solving scores of groups who really worked together to those of "nominal" groups composed of individuals who actually worked separately, but were credited with having solved a problem if any one of them solved it. In each case, the real groups' scores were higher than those of the individuals, but not than those of the "nominal" groups. This would indicate that it is sharing answers per se, not any emergent property of group interaction, that explains the increased productivity of groups in such group problem-solving experiments (see Hill, 1982, for more on this.)

School achievement bears little relationship to group problem solving. Learning is a completely individual outcome that may or may not be improved by cooperation, but it is clearly not obviously improved by cooperation in the same way as group problem solving is superior to individual problem solving. Two or more individuals who take a test together will get a better average score than individuals who take the test by themselves, but how much will each person *learn* from this experience? It may well be that working in a group under certain circumstances does increase the learning of the individuals in that group more than would working under other arrangements, but a measure of group productivity provides no evidence one way or the other on this. Only an individual learning measure that cannot be influenced by group member help can indicate which incentive or task structure is best. If a group produces an excellent lab report, but only a few students really contributed to it, it is unlikely that the group as a whole learned more than they might have learned had they each had to write their own (perhaps less excellent) lab reports.

Considering the range of performance outcomes that have been studied in research on cooperation, individual academic achievement is rather atypical. It is one of very few outcome measures that have meaning or importance only at the level of the individual. Further, the characteristics of elementary and secondary classrooms and the nature of the material taught in these settings have little in common with the tasks and settings of the short-term laboratory studies that constitute most research on cooperative, competitive, and individualistic reward structures. This article reviews the research on the achievement effects of cooperative incentive structures in elementary and secondary schools, with an emphasis on discovering the features of various cooperative programs that make them effective.

Cooperative Learning

In the last 12 years there has been a substantial awakening of interest in applying principles of cooperation to the classroom as a primary means of teaching traditional school subjects. A wide variety of such techniques, called *cooperative learning* methods, have been evaluated in school settings (see Sharan, 1980; Slavin, 1980a; Slavin, 1983). What characterizes these methods is that students spend much of their class time working in small, heterogeneous learning groups, in which they are expected to help one another learn. In all other respects, cooperative learning methods vary considerably.

It is important to note that although this article focuses exclusively on the effects of cooperative learning methods on school achievement, many researchers and practitioners would hold achievement to be an important but secondary goal of these methods. Cooperative learning methods have been found to have strong and consistent positive effects on such outcomes as race relations, attitudes toward academically handicapped classmates, self-esteem, and predisposition to cooperate in other settings (Slavin, 1983). Many would argue that as long as cooperative learning methods do not have negative effects on student achievement, their positive effects on social and attitudinal outcomes would justify their use.

Cooperative Learning Methods

There are two primary components of cooperative learning methods: A *cooperative incentive structure* and a *cooperative task structure*. Cooperative incentive structure, discussed at the beginning of this article, is what most theorists mean when they refer to cooperation (see, for example, Deutsch, 1949). The critical feature of a cooperative incentive structure is that two or more individuals are interdependent for a reward they will share if they are successful as a group. For example, if three people traveling in a car help push the car out of the mud, all of them benefit from each other's efforts (by being able to continue their trip). Either all of them will be rewarded or none of them will be, depending on whether they succeed. Group competition, as in team sports, is also a cooperative incentive structure, because the group's success depends on the efforts of the group members, and all group members share the same consequences (winning or losing).

Cooperative task structures are situations in which two or more individuals are allowed, encouraged, or required to work together on some task, coordinating their efforts to complete the task. Cooperative incentive structures usually involve cooperative tasks, but the two are conceptually distinct. For example, contributors to an edited volume are under a cooperative incentive structure (they all benefit if the book does well) even if they never meet or talk with one another (i.e., they are not under a cooperative task structure).

Cooperative learning methods used in classrooms always involve cooperative tasks, but not all of them involve cooperative incentives. The forms of the tasks and incentives vary considerably across different methods. The task structures used in cooperative learning methods can be divided into two categories: *task specialization* and *group study*. In methods that use task specialization, each group member is responsible for a unique part of the group activity; in group study methods, all group members study together and do not have separate tasks.

The incentive structures used in cooperative learning methods can be summarized in three categories, depending on whether or not rewards are given to groups, and if so, whether they are given on the basis of individual learning or a single group product. In methods that use group rewards for individual learning, rewards such as recognition (e.g., newsletters, certificates), grades, praise, or tangible rewards are given to students in groups who achieve some standard, such as making one of the highest group scores in the class or exceeding a preset criterion. The group score is the average score received by group members on an assessment of individual learning, such as a quiz. In methods that use group rewards for group products, similar group rewards are provided, but they are given based on the quality of a single group worksheet or report to which all group members contributed, rather than on individual learning. Cooperative learning methods that use individual rewards have students work together and instruct them to help one another, but provide only individual grades to students based on their own performance.

Thus, all of the cooperative learning methods can be located in a 3×2 table produced by the two factors incentive structure and task structure. This is depicted in Table 1. The methods in the six resulting cells are described below.

Group Study with Group Reward for Individual Learning

Methods in this cell typically involve students working in small groups to master worksheets or other information initially presented by the teacher. Following the group study time, the students are individually assessed, and the group members' scores are summed to form group scores. These are recognized in class newsletters, or qualify the groups for certificates, grades, or other rewards. Cooperative learning methods categorized in this cell include three developed at Johns Hopkins University: Student Teams-Achievement Divisions (STAD; Slavin, 1978a); Teams-Games-Tournament (TGT; DeVries & Slavin, 1978); and Team Assisted Individualization (TAI; Slavin, Leavey, & Madden, in press; Slavin, Leavey, & Madden, Note 4). In STAD, the teacher presents a lesson, and then students study worksheets in four-member teams that are heterogeneous on student ability, sex, and ethnicity.

Following this, students take individual quizzes, and team scores are computed based on the degree to which each student improved over his or her own past record. The team scores are recognized in class newsletters. TGT is the same as STAD, except that instead of taking quizzes, students compete against members of other teams who are similar in past performance to add points to their team

Task structure	Incentive structure		
	Group reward for individual learning	Group reward for group product	Individual reward
Group study (No task specialization)	STAD, TGT, TAI, Humphreys, Johnson, & Johnson (1982) methods, Hamblin, Hathaway & Wodarski (1971) methods Lew & Bryant (Note 1) methods	Learning Together, Wheeler & Ryan (1973) methods	Peterson & Janicki (1979) methods, Webb & Kenderski (in press) methods, Starr & Schuerman (1974) methods Huber, Bogatzki, & Winter (Note 2) methods
Task specialization	Jigsaw II	Group investigation, Wheeler (Note 3) methods	Jigsaw

Note: STAD = Student Teams-Achievement Division; TGT = Teams-Games-Tournament; TAI = Team Assisted Individualization. Adapted from *Cooperative Learning* by R. E. Slavin, New York: Longman, 1983. Copyright 1983 by Longman. Reprinted by permission.

TABLE 1. Categorization of Cooperative Learning Methods by Incentive and Task Structures

scores. In TAI, students work in heterogeneous teams, but they work on individualized curriculum materials at their own levels and rates. Teams receive certificates based on the number of units completed and the accuracy of their members' final tests.

Humphreys, Johnson, and Johnson (1982) evaluated a method in which students studied in small groups but were tested individually. Students' grades depended on the average of the group members' test scores. Hamblin, Hathaway, and Wodarski (1971) implemented methods in which students studied together and received tangible rewards (e.g., candy, toys, books) based on either the average of individual test scores, the highest three scores in the group, or the lowest three scores in the group. Lew and Bryant (Note 1) gave groups special free time if all group members achieved mastery (80%) on tests given weekly.

Group Study with Group Reward for Group Product

In these methods, students are asked to work or study together, and the group produces a single worksheet or test, which is the basis for evaluation of the group. The largest number of such studies involved methods developed by David and Roger Johnson, called "Learning Together" methods (from the title of their book, *Learning Together and Alone,* 1975). In most of the Learning Together studies, students in small, heterogeneous groups worked together to complete a single worksheet and were praised and rewarded as a group. In one of the Learning Together studies (Humphreys, Johnson, & Johnson, 1982), students received grades based on their group's average score on individual tests, so this study is included under the group study, group reward for individual learning category (see above). However, the methods used by Johnson, Johnson, Johnson, and Anderson (1976), Johnson, Johnson, and Scott (1978), and Robertson (1982) did not provide specific group rewards for individual learning, but gave students grades on the basis of the quality of the group worksheet, test, or other product. Wheeler and Ryan (1973) had students work together to produce a single report; as in the Learning Together studies, there was no way to determine how much each group member contributed to the final product.

Group Study with Individual Reward

In the group study method most commonly seen in practice, students work or study in small groups, with no group rewards. Students are graded solely on the basis of their own work. Most studies of cooperative learning at the postsecondary level involve this type of arrangement, and a few such studies (Huber, Bogatzki, & Winter, Note 2; Peterson & Janicki, 1979; Peterson, Janicki, & Swing, 1981; Starr & Schuerman, 1974; Webb & Kenderski, in press) involved elementary and secondary students.

Task Specialization with Group Reward for Individual Learning

Only one study (Ziegler, 1981) appears in this cell. This study used Jigsaw II (Slavin, 1980c), an adaptation of Aronson's (1978) Jigsaw method (see below). In Jigsaw II, each student in a heterogeneous team is given a unique topic on which to become an "expert." The students from different teams with the same topics meet in "expert groups" to discuss their topics, and then return to their teams to teach their teammates what they have learned. Finally, all students are tested on a quiz that covers all topics, and the quiz scores are summed to form team scores.

In the Ziegler (1981) study, students received grades based in part on their team scores.

Task Specialization with Group Reward for Group Product

Several cooperative learning studies have evaluated methods that use task specialization, but give group rewards or evaluations based on a single group product or report rather than on individual learning. Sharan, Hertz-Lazarowitz, and Ackerman (1980), Sharan (in press), and Hertz-Lazarowitz, Sapir, and Sharan (Note 5) evaluated a method called Group Investigation (Sharan & Sharan, 1976), in which small groups choose subtopics from a unit being studied by the entire class, and then students within the group choose subtasks within the group topic. The groups then prepare reports on their topics and present them to the rest of the class. Students are evaluated in large part based on the quality of their group presentations or other group products. Wheeler (Note 3) evaluated a method in which students performed separate subtasks in preparing group reports. The groups presenting the best reports received prizes.

Task Specialization with Individual Reward

This cell contains only Aronson's (1978) original Jigsaw model. This method is essentially the same as Jigsaw II (described above), except that instead of receiving grades based in part on the average of group members' quiz scores as in Jigsaw II, students in the original Jigsaw method receive only individual grades based on their own test scores.

Criteria for Inclusion of Studies

This paper reviews all available published and unpublished studies of cooperative learning methods that met the following criteria:

1. A cooperative learning method was compared with a control group that could be considered initially equivalent (because of random assignment or matching plus analysis of covariance), or appropriate single-subject designs were used (Hersen & Barlow, 1976). This requirement excluded a very small number of studies (all unpublished) that failed to use control groups.

2. The study took place in regular elementary or secondary schools for at least 2 weeks (10 class periods). This excluded a large number of studies of cooperative learning interventions that were in place for five class periods or less. Such studies were considered laboratory studies in

field settings rather than true field experiments because of their brief durations, use of tasks that are not typical of most school learning tasks (e.g., solving Rasmussen triangles), and artificial procedures (e.g., alternating periods of group work and individual interviews). This requirement also excluded several studies at the postsecondary level and two studies in self-contained special education classes.

3. Achievement measures fairly assessed learning in the experimental and control groups, and the tests used as dependent measures were given to individuals after the group experience. This excluded analyses presented in a small number of studies in which a control group was never exposed to the content studied by the experimental group and assessed by the final test, or in which students in the cooperative group were able to take the final tests in their groups (and could help one another) whereas the students in the control group took the tests by themselves.

Most of the cooperative learning studies partially controlled teacher effects by having the same teachers teach experimental and control classes, or by randomly assigning a large number of teachers to each treatment from among a pool of volunteers.

Field Experimental Research on Cooperative Learning and Achievement

Forty-six studies met the duration, setting and methodological adequacy criteria outlined above. In two studies (Huber et al., Note 2; Sharan, in press), two different methods were compared with control groups, so these are each presented as two studies, one for each comparison of a cooperative learning method with a control method. The characteristics and results of these studies are summarized in Table 2.

The achievement results of the forty-six studies are presented in the last column of Table 2. A + sign indicates that a statistically significant ($p < .05$) positive achievement effect was found, meaning that the cooperative learning group scored significantly higher than the control group on a test of content to which both were exposed. For studies that used multiple measures of achievement, a + was recorded if at least half of the measures showed significant positive effects for the cooperative treatment and none of the rest showed significant effects favoring the control group. A (+) sign indicates a marginally significant positive effect ($p < .10$), a 0 signifies no differences, and a − sign indicates that a control group significantly exceeded an experimental group in achievement ($p < .05$). The entries in Table 2 are the main effects for the entire samples involved in the studies, unless otherwise noted.

Taken together, the effects of cooperative learning methods on student achievement are clearly positive. Of

Major reports	N	Grade level	Duration (weeks)	Level of random assignment	Location	Subject area	Achievement effects
Group study with group reward for learning							
Student Teams-Achievement Divisions (STAD)							
Slavin, 1978b	205	7	10	Class	Rural town East	Language arts	0
Slavin, Note 6	62	7	10	Class	Urban East	Language arts	+
Slavin, 1980b	424	4	12	Class	Rural East	Language arts	+
Slavin, 1979	424	7–8	12	Class	Urban East	Language arts	0
Slavin & Oickle, 1981	230	6–8	12	Class	Rural East	Language arts	
Black students							+
White students							0
Madden & Slavin, in press	175	3–6	6	Class	Urban East	Mathematics	+
Allen & VanSickle, Note 7	51	9	6	Class	Rural South	Geography	+
Slavin & Karweit, Note 8	569	9	30	Teacher	Urban East	Mathematics	+
Huber, Bogatzki, & Winter, Note 2	170	7	3	Class	Urban Germany	Mathematics	+
Sharan, in press	436	7	16	Teacher	Urban Israel	English as a second language	+
Teams-Games-Tournament (TGT)							
Edward, DeVries & Snyder, 1972	96	7	9	Class	Urban East	Mathematics	+
Edwards & DeVries, Note 9	117	7	4	Student	Urban East	Mathematics	0
Edwards & DeVries, Note 10	128	7	12	Student	Urban East	Mathematics	+
						Social studies	0
Hulten, & DeVries, Note 11	299	7	10	Class	Urban East	Mathematics	+
DeVries, Edwards, & Wells, Note 12	191	10–12	12	Class	Suburban South	Social studies	(+)
DeVries & Mescon, Note 13	60	3	6	Student	Suburban East	Language arts	+
DeVries, Mescon, & Shackman, Note 14	53	3	6	Student	Suburban East	Language arts	+
DeVries, Mescon, & Shackman, Note 15	53	3	5	Student	Suburban East	Reading	+
DeVries Lucasse, & Schackman, Note 16	1742	7–8	10	Teacher	Suburban Midwest	Language arts	+
Combined student team learning program (STAD + TGT + Jigsaw II)							
Slavin & Karweit, 1981	559	4–5	16	Nonrandom (matched)	Rural East		
Language arts (STAD)							+
Mathematics (TGT)							0
Social studies (Jigsaw II)							0
Reading (STAD, Jigsaw II)							+
Team Assisted Individualization (TAI)							
Slavin, Leavey, & Madden, in press							
Experiment 1	506	3–5	8	School	Suburban East	Mathematics	+
Experiment 2	320	4–6	10	Nonrandom (matched)	Suburban East	Mathematics	+
Slavin, Leavey, & Madden, Note 4	1317	3–5	24	Nonrandom (matched)	Suburban East	Mathematics	+
Other							
Humphreys, Johnson, & Johnson, 1982 (Learning Together with Group Reward for Learning)	44	9	6	Student	Suburban Midwest	Science	+
Hamblin, Hathaway, & Wodarski, 1971							
Experiment 1	34	4	3	Nonrandom: Latin square	Urban Midwest	Spelling, mathematics, reading	+
Experiment 2	60	5	3	Nonrandom: Latin square	Urban Midwest	Mathematics	+
Lew & Bryant, Note 1	27	4	9	Nonrandom: ABABAB design	Suburban East	Spelling	+

Major reports	N	Grade level	Duration (weeks)	Level of random assignment	Location	Subject area	Achievement effects
				Group study with reward for group product			
Learning Together							
Johnson, Johnson, Johnson & Anderson, 1976	30	5	4	Student	Urban Midwest	Language arts	0
Johnson, Johnson, & Scott, 1978	30	5–6	10	Student	Suburban Midwest	Mathematics	-
Robertson, 1982	166	2–3	6	Class	Suburban East	Mathematics	0
Other							
Wheeler & Ryan, 1973	88	5–6	4	Student	Suburban Midwest	Social Studies	0
Peterson & Janicki, 1979	100	4–6	2	Student	Rural Midwest	Mathematics	0
				Group study with individual reward			
Peterson, Janicki, & Swing, 1981	93	4–5	2	Student	Rural Midwest	Mathematics	0
Webb & Kinderski, in press	107	7–8	3	Nonrandom (matched)	Urban California	Mathematics	0
Starr & Schoerman, 1974	48	7	3	Class	Suburban Midwest	Life science	0
Huber, Bogatzki, & Winter, Note 2	204	7	3	Class	Urban Germany	Mathematics	0
				Task specialization with group reward for learning			
Jigsaw II							
Ziegler, 1981	146	6	8	Class	Urban Canada	Social studies	+
				Task specialization with group reward for group product			
Group investigation							
Sharan, Hertz-Lazarowitz, & Ackerman, 1980	217	2–6	3	Nonrandom (matched)	Urban Israel	Social studies	
						Grades 2, 4, 6	+
						Grades 3, 5	0
Hertz-Lazarowitz, Sapir, & Sharan, Note 5	67	8	5	Nonrandom (matched)	Urban Israel	Arabic language and culture	0
Sharan, in press	467	7	18	Teacher	Urban Israel	English as a second language	+
Other							
Wheeler, Note 3	88	5–6	2	Student	Rural town South	Social Studies	+
				Task specialization with individual reward			
Jigsaw							
Lucker, Rosenfield, Sikes, & Aronson, 1976	303	5–6	2	Nonrandom (matched)	Urban Southwest	Social studies	
Black and Hispanic students							+
Anglo-American students							0
Baird, Lazarowitz, Hertz-Lazarowitz, & Jenkins in press							
Experiment 1	113	10–12	6	Nonrandom (matched)	Rural town West	Biology	0
Experiment 2	83	10–12	3	Class	Rural town West	Geology	0
Experiment 3	69	10–12	2	Class	Rural town West	Genetics	-
Gonzales, Note 17	182	3–4	20	Nonrandom (matched)	Rural California (bilingual classes)	Social studies	0

Note: Geographical designations refer to areas of the United States. 0 indicates no differences; + indicates a statistically significant ($p < .05$) positive achievement effect; (+) indicates a marginally significant ($p < .10$) positive effect; − indicates that a control group significantly exceeded an experimental group in achievement. Adapted from *Cooperative Learning* by R. E. Slavin, New York: Longman, 1983. Copyright 1983 by Longman. Reprinted by Longman. Reprinted by permission.

TABLE 2. Characteristics and Achievement Outcomes of Cooperative Learning Field Experiments

the 46 studies, 29 (63%) showed cooperative learning methods to have significantly positive (or, in one case, marginally positive) effects on student achievement, 15 (33%) found no differences, and 2 (4%) found significantly higher achievement for a control group than for a cooperative treatment.

However, the overall picture masks important differences between studies. Table 3 illustrates these differences by breaking down the achievement results by type of incentive and type of task (group study vs. task specialization). As can be seen in the top half of Table 3, there is a dramatic difference in achievement outcomes among the group study methods depending on their use of rewards. Of 27 studies that used group study and group rewards for individual learning, 24 (89%) found positive effects on student achievement, whereas 3 (11%) found no differences. In contrast, none of the nine studies of group study methods that did not use group rewards for individual learning found positive effects on student achievement. One (Johnson, Johnson, & Scott, 1978) found that an individualistic control group learned more than the cooperative experimental group, and the rest found no differences.

The results for studies that used task specialization are less clear because of the much smaller number of studies (10) that used this task structure. However, there is an interesting pattern to the findings. The only study to use task specialization and group rewards for individual learning (Ziegler, 1981) found strong effects on student achievement, which were maintained in a 5-month follow-up. Three of the four task specialization studies in which students were rewarded on the basis of a group product found positive achievement results. In contrast, there is little evidence to indicate that the original Jigsaw method (which uses no group rewards) increases student achievement more than control methods. The one Jigsaw study to find positive achievement effects (Lucker, Rosenfield, Sikes, & Aronson, 1976) found them only for a small subsample of minority students in a very brief study (2 weeks). No positive effects were found for Anglo-Americans in that study, or for Anglo-American or minority students in the other Jigsaw studies. Thus, this evidence suggests that the effects of tasks specialization methods on achievement depend on the use of group rewards, regardless of whether the rewards are based on individual learning or group performance.

Component Analyses

The evidence summarized in Table 2 presents strong support for the observation that group rewards for individual learning are critical to the effectiveness of cooperative learning methods. Restricting attention to the group

| | Incentive structure | | | | | | | |
| | Group reward for individual learning | | Group reward for group product | | Individual reward | | Total | |
Task structure	n	%	n	%	n	%	n	%
Group study (No task specialization								
Positive	24	89	0	0	0	0	24	67
No effect	3	11	3	75	5	100	11	31
Negative	0	0	1	25	0	0	1	3
N of studies	27		4		5		36	
Task specialization								
Positive	1	100	3	75	1	20	5	50
No effect	0	0	1	25	3	60	4	40
Negative	0	0	0	0	1	20	1	10
N of studies	1		4		5		10	
Total								
Positive	25	89	3	38	1	10	29	63
No effect	3	11	4	50	8	80	15	33
Negative	0	0	1	13	1	10	2	4
N of studies	28		8		10		46	

Note. Adapted from *Cooperative Learning* by R. E. Slavin, New York: Longman, 1983. Copyright 1983 by Longman. Reprinted by permission.

TABLE 3
Achievement Outcomes of Cooperative Learning Studies by Categories of Incentive and Task Structures

study methods, the presence or absence of group rewards for individual learning clearly discriminates methods that increase student achievement from those that do no better than control methods. Component analyses and comparisons of similar methods further bear out the importance of this factor. Slavin (1980b) varied rewards (team vs. individual) and tasks (group vs. individual) in a study of STAD. The results of this study indicated that providing recognition based on the team scores (the mean of the members' improvement scores) increased student achievement regardless of whether or not the students were allowed to study together. The students who could study in groups but received no group rewards learned less than all other students, including those who studied individually and received only individual rewards. This study also found that when students in interacting groups were working toward a team reward, they helped each other substantially more than when they could work together but received no team rewards. Huber et al. (Note 2) also compared STAD with group study without group rewards and with individual study. They found that STAD students learned more than the group study and individual work students, but there were no differences between the group study and individual study conditions. Finally, a study of TGT (Hulten & DeVries, Note 11) found that providing recognition based on team scores (the mean of the members' game scores in the TGT tournaments) improved achievement whether or not students were permitted to study together. Group study itself had no effects on student achievement. Thus, these component analyses add three more evaluations of methods that use group study but not group rewards. In no case did students in the group study conditions learn more than those in control conditions, and in one case (Slavin, 1980b) they learned less. However, in all three studies, the addition of specific group rewards based on members' learning made the methods instructionally effective.

The importance of group rewards for individual learning is also shown in a comparison of the four Learning Together studies. Johnson et al. (1976, 1978) and Robertson (1982) evaluated a group study method in which students worked in small groups to complete a single group worksheet. The groups were "praised and rewarded" for working together, but there was no way for group members to see exactly how much each student learned or contributed to the group worksheet. Individual student learning was not a criterion for rewards. The Johnson et al. (1978) study found greater learning for a control group than for the cooperative learning group, and there were no differences between experimental and control groups in the Johnson et al. (1976) and Robertson (1982) studies.

In contrast, Humphreys et al. (1982) evaluated an experimental treatment that was identical to that used in the earlier Learning Together research in every respect but one; instead of being praised and rewarded as a group for completing a single worksheet, students studied together but took individual quizzes. They then received grades based on the average of their group's quizzes. Students in this treatment learned significantly more than students in an individualistic control group similar to the control groups used in the earlier Learning Together studies. Since the use of grades based on the average group members' learning is the only feature distinguishing the Humphreys et al. method from the other Learning Together methods, it can be inferred that it was the group reward for individual learning that made the difference.

The pattern of results for the studies that used a group study task, both across the different methods and within the component analyses, support an unexpected conclusion: The opportunity for students to study together makes little or no contribution to the effects of cooperative learning on achievement. Providing an opportunity for group study without providing further structure in the form of individual assessment and group reward has not been found (among the studies that meet the criteria for inclusion applied in this article) to increase student achievement more than having students work separately. In two cases (Johnson et al., 1978; Slavin, 1980b), allowing students to work together without giving them a group goal or making them dependent on one another's achievement in some other way resulted in lower achievement than was seen in conditions in which students worked alone. On the other hand, studies of group study methods in which students could earn group rewards based on group members' individual academic performance were relatively consistent in showing the superiority of these methods to individualistic, competitive, or traditional control methods. There is some suggestion that group rewards based on group members' learning increase student achievement even in the absence of group interaction (Hulten & DeVries, Note 11; Slavin, 1980b).

Setting and Design Differences Between Studies

It could be argued that setting and design differences between studies may explain some differences in achievement outcomes. Table 4 summarizes the outcomes of the cooperative learning studies broken down by important methodological characteristics.

As is apparent in Table 4, grade level has little bearing on study outcomes. Positive effects were only slightly more likely to be found at the elementary level (Grades 2–6) than at the secondary (Grades 6–12) level. Study duration (longer or shorter than 7 weeks) and study sample

| | Effects on achievement | | | | | | |
| | Positive | | No effect | | Negative | | |
Characteristic	n	%	n	%	n	%	No. of Studies
All studies	29	63	15	33	2	4	46
Elementary (Grades 2–6)	16	57	6	39	1	4	23
Secondary (Graces 6–12)	13	70	9	26	1	4	23
Shorter than 7 weeks	12	48	12	48	1	4	25
Longer than 7 weeks	17	81	3	14	1	5	21
Sample size ≤ 117	11	48	10	44	2	9	23
Sample > 117	18	78	5	22	0	0	23
Random assignment of students	6	50	5	42	1	8	12
Random assignment of classes/teachers/schools	15	68	6	27	1	5	22
Nonrandom assignment (matching)	5	56	4	44	0	0	9
Single-subject designs	3	100	0	0	0	0	3

Note. Adapted from *Cooperative Learning* by R. E. Slavin, New York: Longman, 1983. Copyright 1983 by Longman. Reprinted by permission.

TABLE 4

Summary of Effects of Cooperative Learning on Achievement Broken Down by Setting and Design Characteristics

size (less than or greater than the median, 117.5) each had some effect on study outcomes. Longer and larger studies were more likely than shorter or smaller ones to find positive effects. Also, studies that used random assignment of classes, teachers, or schools, or single-subject designs, were somewhat more likely than those using matching or random assignment of students to find positive achievement effects.

However, these methodological differences do not affect the substantive conclusions. For example, 10 of the 11 smaller-than-median group reward for individual learning studies found positive effects on student achievement, whereas none of the 7 smaller-than-median studies of group study that did not use rewards based on individual learning found positive effects. Nine of the 10 shorter-than-median studies of group study with group reward for individual learning found positive achievement effects, but none of the other 8 shorter-than-median studies found positive effects.

Discussion

Cooperative Incentives Versus Group Tasks

The most striking conclusion from the cooperative learning research reviewed here is that among methods that do not use task specialization, it is the cooperative incentive structure that substantially explains the effectiveness of the cooperative learning methods. There is no evidence as of yet that group study per se makes any difference in student achievement. Perhaps this should not be surprising. The theory on which cooperative learning is based is a theory of incentive structures, not of task structures. Almost all of the early laboratory studies on cooperation involved giving money, prizes, or grades to individuals operating under various sets of cooperative, competitive, or individualistic rules. Deutsch's (1949) theory of cooperation and competition clearly assumes that the performance outcomes of these incentive systems depend on the relationship between others' behaviors and one's own rewards. Later theoretical statements (e.g., Johnson & Johnson, 1974; Slavin, 1977) also clearly focused on the reward consequences of actions taken to help or hinder others in cooperative, competitive, and individualistic incentive systems. Task interdependence (Miller & Hamblin, 1963) and type of task (Johnson & Johnson, 1974; Slavin, 1977) have been considered as conditioning or enabling components of a cooperative reward structure. Theories of task structures that would support an expectation that individuals working together without cooperative goals would perform or learn better than individuals working separately have had little impact on research. Thus, it should not come as a surprise that the coopera-

tive learning research does not find that students working in small groups learn better, unless the group members are given clear incentives for doing well as a group.

Individual Accountability

It is apparent from the results of the cooperative learning research reviewed here that cooperative incentives themselves are not sufficient to increase student achievement. Group study methods that provide group rewards, based on the quality of a group product have not been found to improve student achievement. The second ingredient that is apparently needed to make cooperative learning methods instructionally effective is *individual accountability.* That is, the best learning efforts of every member of the group must be necessary for the group to succeed, and the performance of each group member must be clearly visible and quantifiable to the other group members. In group study with reward for group product, groups are evaluated on the basis of a single worksheet, test, or project. As a result, it is possible for a single group member to do all the work. Contributions of less able group members may be considered useless at best by the group; at worst, they may be considered interruptions. Methods that fall in this category (principally the Johnson and Johnson (1975) Learning Together methods) instruct groups to encourage the participation of all members and have group members sign the group worksheet to indicate that they participated in and understood the group task. However, this may be inadequate to motivate the group members to encourage and help all members to learn the material. Ultimately, the most efficient strategy may be to poll the group's membership on each worksheet item, and to accept the answer agreed on by the more able group members. If a student asks for an explanation of the answer, it is probably inefficient to provide it. Webb's (1982) process studies of cooperating groups indicate that giving and receiving elaborated explanations are the best predictors of individual learning in group study tasks; receiving no answers or brief answers ("terminal responses") is negatively associated with learning gain. If there is little incentive for group members to provide such explanations, there is little reason to expect that they will do so. There is evidence to suggest that students believe that the purpose of worksheets is to finish them, not to learn from them (Anderson, Note 18). To expect students to altruistically care how much their classmates are learning from a worksheet is to ask a great deal.

In contrast, in group study methods in which groups are rewarded based on the sum or average of individual learning performances, there is good reason for students to care about the learning of their groupmates, because their own rewards depend on their partners' learning. A study by Hamblin et al. (1971) clearly showed that the students who learned the most from a cooperative learning experience were the ones on whom the group's success depended. When groups were given tangible rewards based on the average of the highest three scores in the group, high achievers learned much more than average or low achievers. When the rewards were given based on the average of the lowest three scores, low achievers achieved the most.

Analogously, when group success depends on the learning of all group members, all group members will learn, as is evidenced by the consistent positive achievement results of group study with group reward for individual learning.

Individual accountability in cooperative learning methods can be created in two principal ways. Averaging individual learning performances, discussed above, is one. The other is to give each student in the group a unique task. Task specialization methods are inherently high in individual accountability, because the group's success depends on the adequacy of each group member's contribution. However, the results of the task specialization studies suggest that individual accountability by itself is insufficient to increase student achievement. Group rewards are also needed. Without group rewards, there is little reason for group members to care about their groupmates' learning. In a method such as Jigsaw, students are interdependent for information, but they have little incentive to make sure that their groupmates have learned the information they have provided to them.

Thus, there are two factors that must be present if cooperative learning methods are to be more instructionally effective than traditional methods: group rewards and individual accountability. All but 4 of the 32 field experiments that used this combination of factors found significantly higher achievement for the cooperative groups than for control groups. Only 1 of the 14 studies that failed to include both group rewards and individual accountability found positive achievement effects, compared with control conditions.

Why Do Group Rewards and Individual Accountability Increase Student Achievement?

Peer norms and sanctions. The causal mechanism linking use of group rewards and individual accountability to increased student achievement in cooperative learning that has the greatest empirical as well as theoretical support is that provision of rewards based on group performance creates group member norms supporting performance. That is, if group success depends on the learning performance of all group members, group members try to make the group successful by encouraging each other to excel. Even though rewards given to groups are likely to be less finely tuned to individual performance than rewards given to individuals (see Slavin, 1977), group members are hypothesized to create a very sensitive and effective reward system for each other when the efforts of all group members are required for group success. Under these conditions, group members pay a great deal of attention to one another's efforts and socially reinforce efforts that help the group achieve its goal (see Deutsch, 1949). They are likely to pay attention to one another's learning efforts and to reinforce one another for outstanding learning performance, and to apply social disapproval to group members who are goldbricking or clowning instead of learning.

The occurrence of peer norms supporting classmates' achievement has been documented in several of the STAD and TGT studies in which students who have experienced cooperative learning are much more likely than control students to agree with such statements as, "other children in my class want me to work hard" (Edwards & DeVries, Note 10; Hulten & DeVries, Note 11; Madden & Slavin, in press; Slavin, 1978b). Students' perceptions that their classmates want them to excel probably have a strong effect on their own motivations to do so, and contrast sharply with the situation in classrooms in which individual competition for grades leads students to express norms against academic excellence (see Coleman, 1961; Slavin, Note 19). Peer norms for or against academic efforts may be more important for many students than teacher or parent pressure to achieve, especially for adolescents and for lower-class students (see Spilerman, 1971). In such cases, changing peer norms to favor academic efforts may be especially important.

In theory, group rewards based on group performance, however defined, should create group member norms favoring performance. However, this theory only applies to group member behaviors that are actually critical for the group to be successful. Therefore, it is hypothesized that in cooperative learning, only if the group reward is based on the sum of individual learning performances will interpersonal sanctions be directed at increasing the academic performance of *all* group members. If, for example, groups are judged based on a single worksheet or test produced by the group, pro-performance norms may be produced, but they should (in theory) apply only to the performance of those group members deemed by the group to have the most to contribute to the group product.

Conclusions

The results of the field experimental research on cooperative learning methods support the following conclusions:

1. Cooperative learning methods that use group rewards and individual accountability consistently increase student achievement more than control methods in many academic subjects in elementary and secondary classrooms.

2. Cooperative learning methods that use group study but not group rewards for individual learning do not increase student achievement more than control methods; there is no evidence that studying in groups per se is more or less effective than studying individually. The effects of group study depend entirely on the incentive structure used.

3. Cooperative learning methods that use task specialization and group rewards (however defined) apparently increase student achievement more than control methods, but methods that use task specialization and individual rewards do not have this effect. However, because the number of task specialization studies is small, more research of this kind will be needed before firm conclusions can be drawn.

As in earlier reviews of the general relationships between cooperative, competitive, and individualistic incentive structures and performance, the evidence summarized in this article makes it clear that research on these incentive structures must be directed at understanding the conditions under which they are most and least effective. Even in considering a relatively narrow set of outcome, setting, and implementation characteristics (studies of cooperative learning effects on individual student learning in elementary and secondary schools in field experiments of at least 2 weeks' duration), there are still important systematic differences in outcomes depending on even finer distinctions, in particular the use of group rewards based on individual learning performance.

For practitioners, the research summarized in this article clearly suggests that student achievement can be enhanced by use of cooperative learning methods that use group study and group rewards for individual learning, and possibly by other cooperative learning methods that maintain high individual accountability for students. However, as noted earlier, cooperative learning methods have been found to have positive effects on a wide range of social and emotional outcomes, such as student self-esteem, race relations, and acceptance of mainstreamed academically handicapped students (see Slavin, 1983). These noncognitive outcomes do not appear to depend to the same extent on particular incentive or task structures, and for many practical applications, these outcomes might justify the use of cooperative learning methods as long as they do not reduce student achievement.

The challenge for future research on cooperative learning and student achievement will be to understand more about how cooperative incentives function as motivators, to understand how cooperative incentives interact with variously constructed tasks to enhance student achievement,

and to understand how these cooperative incentives and tasks affect actual student behavior within cooperating groups. Also, there is a continuing need for development and evaluation of new cooperative learning methods, both to solve practical problems of instruction and to expand the range of operationalizations of cooperative learning. This review wold have been impossible if there had not been a wide range of cooperative learning methods evaluated in classroom settings. It is to be hoped that new methods and modifications of existing methods will be evaluated in the next several years to further increase the range of instructional alternatives in this important area.

Reference Notes

1. Lew, M., & Bryant, R. *The use of cooperative groups to improve spelling achievement for all children in the regular classroom.* Paper presented at the Massachusetts Council for Exceptional Children, Boston, April 1981.
2. Huber, G., Bogatzki, W., & Winter, M. *Cooperation: Condition and goal of teaching and learning in classrooms.* Unpublished manuscript, University of Tubingen, West Germany, 1981.
3. Wheeler, R. *Predisposition toward cooperation and competition: Cooperative and competitive classroom effects.* Paper presented at the Annual Convention of the American Psychological Association, San Francisco, September 1977.
4. Slavin, R. E., Leavey, M., & Madden, N. A. *Combining student teams and individualized instruction in mathematics: An extended evaluation.* Paper presented at the Annual Convention of the American Educational Research Association, Montreal, April, 1983.
5. Hertz-Lazarowitz, R., Sapir, C., & Sharan, S. *Academic and social effects of two cooperative learning methods in desegregated classrooms.* Unpublished manuscript, Haifa University, Israel, 1981.
6. Slavin, R. E. *Student learning team techniques: Narrowing the achievement gap between the races* (Rep. No. 228). Center for Social Organization of Schools, Johns Hopkins University, 1977.
7. Allen, W., & VanSickle, R. *Instructional effects of learning teams for low achieving students.* Unpublished manuscript, University of Georgia, 1981.
8. Slavin, R. E., & Karweit, N. *Student teams and mastery learning: An experiment in urban math 9 classes* (Rep. No. 320). Center for Social Organization of Schools, Johns Hopkins University, 1982.
9. Edwards, K. J., & DeVries, D. L. *Learning games and student teams: Their effects on student attitudes and achievement* (Rep. No. 147). Center for Social Organization of Schools, Johns Hopkins University, 1972.
10. Edwards, K. J., & DeVries, D. L. *The effects of Teams-Games-Tournament and two structural variations on classroom process, student attitudes, and student achievement* (Rep. No. 172). Center for Social Organization of Schools, Johns Hopkins University, 1974.

11. Hulten, B. H., & DeVries, D. L. *Team competition and group practice: Effects on student achievement and attitudes* (Rep. No. 212). Center for Social Organization of Schools, Johns Hopkins University, 1976.

12. DeVries, D. L., Edwards, K. J., & Wells, E. H. *Teams-Games-Tournament in the social studies classroom: Effects on academic achievement, student attitudes, cognitive beliefs, and classroom climate* (Rep. No 173). Center for Social Organization of Schools, Johns Hopkins University, 1974.

13. DeVries, D. L., & Mescon, I. T. *Teams-Games-Tournament: An effective task and reward structure in the elementary grades* (Rep. No. 189). Center for Social Organization of Schools, Johns Hopkins University, 1975.

14. DeVries, D. L., Mescon, I. T., & Shackman, S. L. *Teams-Games-Tournament (TGT) effects on reading skills in the elementary grades* (Rep. No. 200). Center for Social Organization of Schools, Johns Hopkins University, 1975.

15. DeVries, D. L., Mescon, I. T., & Shackman, S. L. *Teams-Games-Tournament in the elementary classroom: A replication* (Rep. No. 190). Center for Social Organization of Schools, Johns Hopkins University, 1975.

16. DeVries, D., Lucasse, P., & Shackman, S. *Small group versus individualized instruction: A field test of their relative effectiveness.* Paper presented at the Annual Convention of the American Psychological Association, New York, September, 1979.

17. Gonzales, A. *Classroom cooperation and ethnic balance.* Paper presented at the Annual Convention of the American Psychological Association, New York, September 1979.

18. Anderson, L. M. *Student response to seatwork: Implications for the study of students' cognitive processing.* Paper presented at the Annual Convention of the American Educational Research Association, Los Angeles, April, 1981.

19. Slavin, R. E. *Cooperative learning: Changing the normative climate of the classroom.* Paper presented at the Annual Convention of the American Educational Research Association, Los Angeles, April, 1981.

References

Aronson, E., *The jigsaw classroom.* Beverly Hills, CA: Sage, 1978.

Baird, J. H., Lazarowitz, R., Hertz-Lazarowitz, R., & Jenkins, T. Cooperative learning comes to high school science classes. In R. Slavin et al. (Eds.), *Learning to cooperate, cooperating to learn.* New York: Plenum Press, in press.

Coleman, J. S. *The adolescent society.* New York: Free Press of Glencoe, 1961.

Cotton, J., & Cook, M. Meta-analyses and the effects of various systems: Some different conclusions from Johnson et al. *Psychological Bulletin,* 1982, 92, 176–183.

Deutsch, M. A theory of cooperation and competition. *Human Relations,* 1949, 2, 129–152.

DeVries, D. L., & Slavin, R. E. Teams-Games-Tournament (TGT): Review of ten classroom experiments. *Journal of Research and Development in Education,* 1978, 12, 28–38.

Edwards, K. J., DeVries, D. L., & Snyder, J. P. Games and teams: A winning combination. *Simulation and Games,* 1972, 3, 247–269.

Faust, W. Group vs. Individual problem-solving. *Journal of Abnormal and Social Psychology,* 1959, 59, 68–72.

Hamblin, R. L., Hathaway, C., & Wodarski, J. S. Group contingencies, peer tutoring, and accelerating academic achievement. In E. Ramp & W. Hopkins (Eds.), *A new direction for education: Behavior analysis.* Lawrence, Kansas: The University of Kansas, Department of Human Development, 1971.

Hersen, M., & Barlow, D. *Single case experimental designs.* New York: Pergamon Press, 1976.

Hill, G. Group versus individual performance: Are $N + 1$ heads better than one? *Psychological Bulletin,* 1982, 91, 517–539.

Humphreys, B., Johnson, R., & Johnson, D. W. Effects of cooperative, competitive, and individualistic learning on students' achievement in science class. *Journal of Research in Science Teaching.* 1982, 19, 351–356.

Johnson, D. W., & Johnson, R. T. Instructional goal structure: Cooperative, competitive, or individualistic. *Review of Educational Research,* 1974, 44, 213–240.

—— *Learning together and alone.* Englewood Cliffs, NJ: Prentice-Hall, 1975.

Johnson, D. W. Johnson, R. T., Johnson, J., & Anderson, D. The effects of cooperative vs. individualized instruction on student prosocial behavior, attitudes toward learning, and achievement. *Journal of Educational Psychology.* 1976, 68, 446–452.

Johnson, D. W., Johnson, R. T., & Scott, L. The effects of cooperative and individualized instruction on student attitudes and achievement. *Journal of Social Psychology,* 1978, 104, 207–216.

Johnson, D. W., Maruyama, G., Johnson, R., Nelson, D., & Skon, L. Effects of cooperative, competitive, and individualistic goal structures on achievement: A meta-analysis. *Psychological Bulletin.* 1981, 89, 47–62.

Lucker, G. W., Rosenfield, D., Sikes, J., & Aronson, E. Performance in the interdependent classroom: A field study. *American Educational Research Journal,* 1976, 13, 115–123.

Madden, N. A., & Slavin, R. E. Cooperative learning and social acceptance of mainstreamed academically handicapped students. *Journal of Special Education,* in press.

Marquart, D. I. Group problem solving. *Journal of Social Psychology,* 1955, 41, 103–113.

McGlynn, R. A comment on the meta-analysis of goal structures. *Psychological Bulletin,* 1982, 92, 184–185.

Michaels, J. W. Classroom reward structures and academic performance. *Review of Educational Research,* 1977, 47(1), 87–98.

Miller, L. K., & Hamblin, R. L. Interdependence, differential rewarding, and productivity. *American Sociological Review,* 1963, 28, 768–778.

Peterson, P. L., & Janicki, T. C. Individual characteristics and children's learning in large-group and small-group approaches. *Journal of Educational Psychology,* 1979, 71, 677–687.

Peterson, P. L., Janicki, T., & Swing, S. Ability × Treatment interaction effects on children's learning in large-group and small-group approaches. *American Educational Research Journal,* 1981, 18, 453–473.

Robertson, L. Integrated goal structuring in the elementary school: Cognitive growth in mathematics. Unpublished doctoral dissertation, Rutgers University, 1982.

Ryack, B. A comparison of individual and group learning of nonsense syllables. *Journal of Personality and Social Psychology,* 1965, 2, 296–299.

Sharan, S. Cooperative learning in small groups: Recent methods and effects on achievement, attitudes, and ethnic relations. *Review of Educational Research,* 1980, 50, 241–271.

—— Cooperative learning in the classroom: Research in desegregated schools. Hillsdale, N.J.: Erlbaum, in press.

Sharan, S., Hertz-Lazarowitz, R., & Ackerman, Z. Academic achievement of elementary school children in small-group vs. whole class instruction. *Journal of Experimental Education,* 1980, 48, 125–129.

Sharan, S., & Sharan, Y. *Small-group teaching.* Englewood Cliffs, N.J.: Educational Technology Publications, 1976.

Slavin, R. E. Classroom reward structure: An analytic and practical review. *Review of Educational Research,* 1977, 47(4), 633–650.

—— Student teams and achievement divisions. *Journal of Research and Development in Education,* 1978, 12, 39–49. (a)

—— Student teams and comparison among equals: Effects on academic performance and student attitudes. *Journal of Educational Psychology,* 1978, 70, 532–538. (b)

—— Effects of biracial learning teams on cross-racial friendships. *Journal of Educational Psychology.* 1979, 71, 381–387.

—— Cooperative learning. *Review of Educational Research,* 1980, 50, 315–342. (a)

—— Effects of student teams and peer tutoring on academic achievement and time on-task. *Journal of Experimental Education,* 1980, 48, 252–257. (b)

—— *Using student team learning: Revised edition.* Baltimore, Md.: Center for Social Organization of Schools, The Johns Hopkins University, 1980. (c)

—— *Cooperative learning.* New York: Longman, 1983.

Slavin, R. E., & Karweit, N. Cognitive and affective outcomes of an intensive student team learning experience. *Journal of Experimental Education,* 1981, 50, 29-35.

Slavin, R. E., Leavey, M., & Madden, N. A. Combining cooperative learning and individualized instruction: Effects on student mathematics achievement, attitudes, and behaviors. *Elementary School Journal,* in press.

Slavin, R. E., & Oickle, E. Effects of cooperative learning teams on student achievement and race relations: Treatment by race interaction. *Sociology of Education,* 1981, 54, 174–180.

Spilerman, S. Raising academic motivation in lower class adolescents: A convergence of two research traditions. *Sociology of Education,* 1971, 44, 103–118.

Starr, R., & Schuerman, C. An experiment in small-group learning. *The American Biology Teacher,* 1974 (March), 173–175.

Webb, N. Student interaction and learning in small groups. *Review of Educational Research,* 1982, 52, 421–445.

Webb, N., & Kenderski, C. Student interaction and learning in small group and whole class settings. In P. Peterson, L. Cherry Wilkinson, & M. Hallinan (Eds.). *The social context on instruction: Group organization and group processes.* San Francisco: Academic Press, in press.

Wheeler, R., & Ryan, F. L. Effects of cooperative and competitive classroom environments on the attitudes and achievement of elementary school students engaged in social studies inquiry activities. *Journal of Educational Psychology,* 1973, 65, 402–407.

Ziegler, S. The effectiveness of cooperative learning teams for increasing cross-ethnic friendship: Additional evidence. *Human Organization,* 1981, 40, 264–268.

Comments on the article by Graves

In the previous paper, Slavin argues that the literature provides research supporting the practice of group rewards in a cooperative learning situation. In this paper we see that not every worker in the field supports this position. There is another point of view, put forward for example by Kohn, according to which the use of group rewards can detract from our efforts to develop a richer and intrinsically motivating curriculum that expects more from students than good test scores. In the following paper, Graves describes an ongoing debate on this issue and reports on supporting research for each side.

The position of Graves is that rather than simply deciding whether to have group rewards (or rewards at all) or not, it is important to think about the conditions under which group rewards might be helpful. He describes some of these conditions.

Discussion Questions

1. How do you feel about the issue of focusing on group rewards as a means of getting cooperative learning to work?
2. Are there other, more intrinsic rewards that can complement, or replace the kinds of rewards advocated by Slavin?
3. What are some conditions under which group rewards might be helpful? Harmful?
4. Does the existence of group rewards in class necessitate the existence of individual rewards for other tasks? Why or why not?
5. If an instructor uses a mix of group and individual rewards, what is an appropriate balance? Why?

The Controversy over Group Rewards in Cooperative Classrooms[†]

Ted Graves

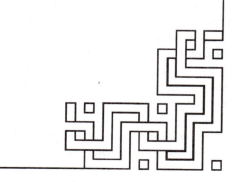

Academic controversy can be constructive and useful when the parties involved conduct a dialogue with the goal of understanding each other and arriving at a synthesis that takes all points of view into consideration. This requires listening carefully to each other's arguments and looking for their strengths rather than their weaknesses (as in a debate), the value of their insights, and the purposes they are trying to achieve. The recent exchange between Alfie Kohn and Robert Slavin concerning the use of group rewards in cooperative learning, published in the February issue of *Educational Leadership* (Kohn 1991a and 1991b, and Slavin 1991a and 1991b), represents only the first stage in this process.

A constructive controversy around this topic has been going on in the pages of *Cooperative Learning* magazine (Kohn 1990a, Slavin 1990, Schaps 1990) for several months, culminating last July in a roundtable session at the convention of the International Association for the Study of Cooperation in Education (IASCE) in Baltimore.[1] A summary of that session was published in the December 1990 issue of *Cooperative Learning* (Graves 1990). My purpose here is to carry that discussion another step forward, to discuss its applications for practitioners.

Polar Positions

Slavin and Kohn represent polar positions on the issue of group rewards. Slavin is concerned with increasing student achievement, and he believes the only demonstrably effective cooperative learning strategies are those that use group rewards based on the individual achievement of each group member (Slavin 1989, 1990, 1991a, 1991b). Kohn is concerned with fostering love of learning among students, and he believes that external rewards should never be used because they will undermine students intrinsic motivation to learn (Kohn 1990a, 1990b, 1991a, 1991b).

From his reading of the research (much of which he has conducted himself), Slavin sees little evidence that achievement gains through cooperative learning are possible without the use of group rewards, although he ac-

[†] Reprinted with permission from *Educational Leadership*, 48 (7). (ERIC Document Reproduction Service No. EJ424424.) pp. 77–79.

[1] In addition to Kohn and Slavin, four other leaders in the field participated: Elizabeth Cohen, Professor of Education and Sociology at Stanford University and author of *Designing Groupwork* (1986); Spencer Kagan, known for his "structural" approach to cooperative learning and author of *Cooperative Learning Resources for Teachers* (1985); Dee Dishon, well-known consultant and staff developer and co-author (with Pat Wilson O'Leary) of *A Guidebook for Cooperative Learning* (1984); and Daniel Solomon, Director of Research of the Child Development Project in San Ramon, California, who is often cited by Kohn as an exemplar of his point of view (Kohn 1990b).

knowledges a few important exceptions, most notably Sharan's use of Group Investigation (Slavin 1989 and 1991a). In the roundtable last July, the Child Development Project and the program of "complex instruction" at Stanford were cited as additional examples (Graves 1990). In both cases, educators have made deliberate efforts to foster intrinsic motivation among students to work hard and to help their teammates, by using appealing curriculum materials, by establishing student norms for achievement and for helping others achieve, and by teaching students the appropriate skills to achieve those norms. This process is difficult and costly, however, and the research evidence for its success is still weak.

To bolster his arguments against the use of group rewards, Kohn cites a body of research evidence showing that extrinsic rewards undermine intrinsic motivation (Kohn 1990a, 1991a, 1991b). Unfortunately, this evidence is mixed and subject to alternative interpretations. A careful meta-analysis and best-evidence synthesis of this literature is still needed. The best approximation I know of at this time is Lepper (1988).

Three Questions to Guide Practice

Obviously these issues need to be settled. In the meantime, however, the business of schooling must go on, and classroom teachers need the best guidance we can give based on available evidence and practical experience. Accordingly, we will consider these three questions that broaden this debate concerning the use of extrinsic rewards in the classroom:

1. Are there forms of group rewards that minimize possible negative effects on intrinsic motivation?
2. Under what conditions will reliance on intrinsic motivation be most likely to achieve our academic goals?
3. Under what conditions may extrinsic group rewards continue to be necessary and useful?

Minimizing negative effects.   Extrinsic rewards appear to have their most damaging effects on intrinsic motivation under two conditions:

1. When students would be willing to engage in the activities without the use of these rewards;
2. When the rewards may be seen by students as an attempt to manipulate and control their behavior.

Extrinsic rewards appear to have their least damaging effect on intrinsic motivation (and may actually enhance it) under the following conditions:

1. When the tasks are ones students would be unwilling to do on their own;
2. When the rewards are largely symbolic in form, serving more to communicate to students how well they are doing and their teachers pride in their accomplishments, than as "payment" for their performance;
3. When the rewards are social rather than tangible;
4. When they are unanticipated.

A number of practical recommendations for the classroom follow from these observations. As Slavin correctly points out, however, the vast majority of tasks we expect students to perform are not ones they would be motivated to do on their own. When students are unmotivated and the tasks are routine, some forms of group rewards may be helpful.

When extrinsic incentives seem necessary, try using symbolic rewards such as certificates of group achievement, stars, and smiley stickers, which communicate your pleasure in and appreciation of your students efforts, rather than tangible rewards, such as small gifts and treats, which are more likely to become the focus of their attention.

Avoid the appearance of manipulation. Behavior modification is a powerful psychological tool and there are classroom situations so chaotic that its use may be justified to create sufficient order for learning to occur. But try to involve students as much as possible in setting their own goals and reward them for achieving these. Encouraging students to pursue their own goals is a form of social reward likely to increase their intrinsic motivation to learn.

Most students find the pleasure of working together in cooperative groups a reward in itself. The "social rewards" of working cooperatively probably enhance intrinsic motivation, and are among the great advantages of using cooperative learning strategies. Many teachers find that after awhile students no longer seem to need the group certificates and other external incentives that induced them to work together effectively. Kohn is skeptical that students can be weaned away from extrinsic rewards once these have been used. But the practical experience of many teachers suggests it is really quite easy. In fact, it may be more difficult to wean *teachers* away from routinely using these rewards even when they are no longer necessary.

Finally, unanticipated rewards, whether simply in the form of teacher recognition, a class party, or free time at the end of the day for pure fun after the class has worked hard and effectively, are powerful tools for enhancing student motivation.

Using intrinsic rewards.   Group rewards do serve to motivate students to undertake routine academic tasks, such as basic skills acquisition. Increasingly, however, educators are urging discovery and problem solving approaches in science and math, whole language learning, and simulations and role plays in social studies. With these approaches, basic skills are acquired in context, while students undertake engaging activities. Clearly, we need to make our lessons as intrinsically interesting as possible and be alert for whether their inherent fascination is sufficient to motivate our students. A continuing need for extrinsic rewards may serve as a useful indicator that our curriculum requires further examination in this regard.

Slavin (1991b) is justly concerned that in group situations the more able students may do most of the work or simply share answers with their teammates. Group rewards based on the individual achievement of each group member is one way to ensure that able students take the trouble to help their teammates really learn and not just complete their group project or worksheet. Such rewards may also serve to "give permission" to students to ask for help when they need it, since otherwise they might let down their teammates.

Without group rewards, we would need to find some other means to accomplish these goals. Fostering internalized norms for high quality academic performance and helping others is a slow and difficult task, but this behavior should transfer to other situations where group rewards are not provided. The Child Development Project (Solomon 1990) and the Stanford Program for Complex Instruction (Cohen 1986) provide models for how to proceed.

Teaching students the skills to help each other effectively is also necessary—and something that Slavin's Student Team Learning approach (Slavin 1989) does not include. Good helping behavior is not automatic; it needs to be defined, modeled, and practiced. But it is a skill that will particularly benefit and challenge the more able students—and it is one they would not be likely to acquire in special programs for the gifted.

Conditions that call for extrinsic rewards. All our efforts to improve our curriculums may still leave us with a large portion of school activities students may be reluctant to engage in without some form of extrinsic reward. This is true for most adult jobs; why should we expect school to be different? The use of cooperative learning groups, with small, largely symbolic certificates of group achievement based on the individual achievement of each group member, will usually increase student scores on standardized tests; and these learning teams can make the effort more fun. When improved test scores are our goal, we now have a proven means to attain them.

But many of us aspire to much more for our students. Slavin's Student Team Learning strategies are ideal for non-contextual basic skills acquisition. They are not ideally

suited for whole language learning, mathematics problem solving, and the development of higher-order thinking skills in science and social studies. Other cooperative learning strategies are available for these purposes, however, such as Group Investigation (S. Sharan 1990, Y. Sharan 1990) and jigsaw modifications developed mainly by Australian and Canadian educators that involve groups in synthesizing and applying the information their members teach each other (Clarke et al. 1990, Kagan 1985, Reid et al. 1989). Research conducted by Shlomo Sharan and his colleagues (Sharan and Shachar 1988) with Group Investigation, in which they carefully measured higher-order thinking skills, verbal fluency, and other rich intellectual outcomes, amply demonstrates the effectiveness of this approach. There is almost no formal research on achievement outcomes from the variety of other cooperative/collaborative learning strategies available, but teachers almost universally report their students are thinking more deeply as a result of their use. These informal observations, though unreported in the research journals, should not be ignored–they probably carry more weight with teachers than formal research findings.

A Shared Vision

Many of the differences between Slavin and Kohn are a matter of where they stand along a pragmatic/idealistic continuum. Both share a vision of what education should be: not simply the acquisition of knowledge, but the development of intellectual curiosity, creativity, and problem-solving skills. By systematically using group rewards based on the individual achievement of each group member, Slavin has developed and refined cooperative learning strategies that work successfully for the vast majority of learning tasks he finds teachers giving their students. Kohn fears that this very success may detract from our efforts to develop a richer and intrinsically motivating curriculum and to expect more from our students than good test scores. The contrast between Kohn's and Slavin's approaches sharpens our awareness of the implications of our instructional practices and helps us to make our choices more consciously. By focusing on the variety of forms that group rewards can take and the conditions under which these may appropriately be used, however, we can move the debate forward to address the complexities of daily practice.

References

Clarke, J., R. Wideman, and S. Eadie. (1990). *Together We Learn.* Toronto: Prentice-Hall.

Cohen, E. (1986). *Designing Groupwork.* New York: Teachers College Press.

Dishon, D., and P.W. O'Leary. (1984). *A Guidebook for Cooperative Learning.* Holmes Beach, Fla.: Learning Publications, Inc.

Graves, T. (1990). "Are External Rewards Appropriate or Desirable in a Cooperative Classroom?" *Cooperative Learning* 11, 2: 15-17.

Kagan, S. (1985). *Cooperative Learning Resources for Teachers.* Riverside, Calif.: University of California.

Kohn, A. (1990a). "Effects of Rewards on Prosocial Behavior." *Cooperative Learning* 10, 3:23–24.

Kohn, A. (1990b). *The Brighter Side of Human Nature: Altruism and Empathy in Everyday Life.* New York: Basic Books.

Kohn, A. (1991a). "Group Grade Grubbing Versus Cooperative Learning." *Educational Leadership* 48, 5:83–87.

Kohn, A. (1991b). "Don't Spoil the Promise of Cooperative Learning." *Educational Leadership* 48, 5:93–94.

Lepper, M. (1988). "Motivational Consideration in the Study of Instruction." *Cognition and Instruction* 5, 4: 289–309.

Reid, J., P. Forrestal, and J. Cook. (1989). *Small Group Learning in the Classroom.* Scarborough, Western Australia: Chalkface Press.

Schaps, E. (1990). "Response to Kohn." *Cooperative Learning* 10, 4: 17–18.

Sharan, S. (1990). "The Group Investigation Approach to Cooperative Learning: Theoretical Foundations." In *Perspectives on Small Group Learning,* edited by M. Brubacher, R. Payne, and K. Rickett. Oakville, Ontario Rubicon Publishing Co.

Sharan, S., and H. Shachar. (1988). *Language and Learning in the Cooperative Classroom.* New York: Springer-Verlag.

Sharan, Y. (1990). "Group Investigation: Expanding Cooperative Learning." In *Perspectives on Small Group Learning,* edited by M. Brubacher, R. Payne, and K. Rickett. Oakville, Ontario Rubicon Publishing Co.

Slavin, R. (1989). *Cooperative Learning. Theory, Research, and Practice.* Englewood Cliffs, N.J.: Prentice-Hall.

Slavin, R. (1990). "Response to Kohn." *Cooperative Learning* 10, 4: 17.

Slavin, R. (1991a). "Synthesis of Research on Cooperative Learning." *Educational Leadership* 48, 5: 71–82.

Slavin, R. (1991b). "Group Rewards Make Groupwork Work." *Educational Leadership* 48, 5: 89–91.

Solomon, D. (1990). "Cooperative Learning and the Child Development Project." *Cooperative Learning* 10, 3: 18–19.

Comments on the article by Good and Marshall

Although the next paper is not directly about cooperative learning, it raises a question and comes to a conclusion, based on research, that is relevant for cooperative learning and warrants discussion. Unfortunately, there are two factors that reduce the relevance of this paper for cooperative learning in undergraduate mathematics education. First, all of the studies reported here are in pre-college settings. Second, according to Good and Marshall, there are serious difficulties with the studies that have been made and this prevents a simple summary of the literature. In spite of these factors, we have decided to include this paper because it draws some conclusions that could transfer to our context and because the authors discuss the difficulties in some detail. Although these difficulties weaken the extent to which we should rely on this literature, there is still much to be learned from it.

The question considered by Good and Marshall is whether students should be taught in heterogeneous classes or grouped according to their abilities—either in separate classrooms (tracking) or within a single classroom (ability grouping). This question is obviously related to one of the important considerations in forming cooperative learning groups. Should a group be heterogenous or homogenous? Clearly there will be different answers for different characteristics of a student. What Good and Marshall report about what is in the literature may well help us answer this question with respect to the characteristic of student ability.

Even though the authors consider tracking and ability grouping separately, the conclusions they draw regarding the two strategies are similar. Good and Marshall are quite negative with respect to tracking although they admit that there are are some special situations (particularly in high school) where different personal and curriculum content goals may justify tracking. The main concern expressed about ability grouping is that, according to the research, dividing a classroom into groups of students based on ability appears to make instruction more difficult.

Finally, Good and Marshall discuss some studies of classes in which students of high and low ability worked together, and how this was affected by various pedagogical strategies (such as group work, visual presentations, seatwork, class discussions, lectures). They present some interesting results from the literature, but they do not feel that the research is complete enough to draw any conclusions about the effects of these approaches other than that there seem to be important effects that warrant study.

A last point to be made is that this report is not very current and there is certainly a need for a survey of the literature that updates it.

Discussion Questions

1. What are some of the difficulties with the studies on which the paper reports and what affect do they have on any conclusions that might be drawn?
2. Could the difficulties with the studies be overcome in future research and, if so, how might this be done?
3. To what extent are any conclusions from these studies transferable to the collegiate context?
4. What relevance does this study have to cooperative learning?
5. What are the negative features of tracking?
6. What are the positive features of tracking?
7. What are the negative features of ability grouping?
8. What are the positive features of ability grouping?
9. Does teacher behavior determine student behavior or vice-versa?

Do Students Learn More in Heterogeneous or Homogeneous Groups?[†]

Thomas L. Good
Susan Marshall

Introduction

A key aspect of educational programs is the assignment of students to classrooms. Beliefs about how students should be assigned are varied and often contradictory, and important questions (Should high and low achievers be taught in the same class or in homogeneous groups within a class? Should second and third graders be taught together?) are answered in different ways by various educators and writers. Research studies and reviews of research have yielded complex responses to questions about whether students should be taught in homogeneous or heterogeneous settings.

Research on *tracking* (students are assigned to separate classes on the basis of ability) and on *ability grouping* (students are assigned to separate groups within the same classroom) illustrates that the ability of learners in a class or group has complex relationships to students' achievement and attitudes (Esposito, 1973; Persell, 1977; Rosenbaum, 1976). Indeed, Webb (1982) found that the effects of assignment to heterogeneous groups for instruction are mediated by the quality of instruction and the participants willingness to seek assistance from other students, as well as the gender, personalities, and abilities of students.

Our original purpose in writing this paper was to review existing research on ability grouping and tracking, and to summarize some of the consequences of heterogeneous and homogeneous grouping practices for high- and low-achieving students. We realized that others had found that the effects of grouping were complex, but we had hoped to be able to identify new trends by examining several variables at the same time. That is, rather than take a "one variable" approach (effects of homogeneous grouping versus heterogeneous grouping), we wanted to study the effects of other variables (e.g., age of students, subject matter, class-group size as well). We intended to emphasize studies that included observational data on instruction; however, we were unable to integrate research on ability grouping, largely because so few researchers actually observed instructional process.

Goals of Chapter

In the first section we discuss factors that prevent a simple summary of the literature, including the lack of observation, the need for more careful definitions of terms (e.g., heterogeneous, homogeneous), and the need to consider differences in societal views about the importance of

[†] Reprinted with permission from P. E. Peterson, L. C. Wilkinson, and M. T. Hallinan (eds.), *Student Diversity and the Organization, Process, and Use of Instructional Groups in the Classroom*, New York: Academic Press, 1984, pp. 15–38.

schooling during various eras when ability grouping data have been collected.

In the second section of the chapter, we discuss tracking studies that include classroom observational data. In the third part of the chapter, studies of ability grouping that include observational measures of classroom processes are examined. Although the complete literature on ability grouping is complex, tracking and ability group studies that include observational measures generally indicate that tracking and ability grouping have few desirable consequences for low-ability students. In this section we seriously question the value of tracking and ability grouping within classrooms.

In a fourth section of the chapter we discuss some new research on classroom composition, the potential contributions of these studies, and the need for future studies in this area. In particular, we advocate the integration of classroom composition studies with task-structure and task-demand research (Doyle, 1979).

A Review of the Literature—Some Difficulties

There are numerous reasons why it is difficult to compare and to integrate studies of ability grouping and teaching. First, the studies vary considerably in scope and purpose. Studies also differ in the number of students, the number of groups, and the size of the classes involved (and sometimes it is impossible to obtain this information). Such variation in samples makes it difficult to determine whether results are dependent upon class size and/or the combination of students in a classroom. Simply put, the effect of class homogeneity and/or heterogeneity may be mediated by class size, and in some studies these variable are confounded or unspecified, or both.

Goldberg, Passow, and Justman (1966) note that studies provide different instruction with regard to holding the curriculum and methods of teaching constant. In some studies teachers were requested to keep content and teaching method the same for all groups. However, in other studies enrichment materials and increased pace were provided for bright students; in yet other studies program modifications were made for slower but not for faster ones. Sometimes teachers were given specific instructions about how to vary their behavior, but some researchers provided no explicit directions. Obviously, such procedural variations among studies make it impossible to determine whether (and how) variation in student ability, class size, instruction, or materials affects outcome measures. Goldberg, Passow, and Justman also point out that researchers often ignore the teacher factor in designing experiments. Thus,

there often was no way to separate teacher qualities from organizational-student composition factors.

In our review of the literature, we are impressed by differences between societal views of education that existed in the 1920s and the 1930s, and those of the 1960s (and subsequently). These views must be considered when interpreting the results of studies. Early studies suggest that students most likely to be "victimized" by ability group assignments were high-ability students; more recent research indicates that students most likely to be "victimized" by group assignments are low-ability students (although studies at any time have produced mixed results). Some reasons for these discrepant findings are discussed here subsequently.

Perhaps the most important difference between school practices in the 1920s and recent practices is related to the fact that in the past there were many *other* socially acceptable options available to students who did not complete high school or college. There were apprentice programs for plumbers, electricians, bricklayers, and so on, which enabled students to leave school and find meaningful employment. Assignment to a low group probably did not have the negative consequences that it may have in the 1960s and later, when high school graduation was mandatory and a college degree almost required for satisfactory employment. For both students and teachers, the perceived consequences of assignment to low groups may have been less significant than they are presently.

There are other difficulties in comparing studies conducted in the 1920s and 1930s with research in the 1960s. In the 1920s and 1930s a somewhat smaller percentage of students was enrolled in public schools. In the 1920s schools were more likely to expel students for serious misbehavior. Furthermore, the retention of students who failed to achieve satisfactorily was a much more common practice in earlier times. The low achievers present in classrooms during the 1920s probably varied considerably from low achievers of today. Furthermore, the average number of pupils in a classroom has varied considerably from time to time in this century. Conclusions based on studies that are more than 10 years apart appear to be precarious.

In addition to the problems just described, the literature is further weakened by the fact that a rather narrow approach has been taken. We were struck by the fact that the homogeneous-heterogeneous question was typically approached as a one-variable problem. That is, much of the research is based on the belief that there is a single answer to the question, Is homogeneous or heterogeneous grouping better?, at least for particular types of students. This belief has probably led many investigators to study class heterogeneity without carefully considering the types of students involved, the community being served, the quality of instruction, and many other variables. As a result of focusing on one variable, poor definitions of heterogeneous and homogeneous classes abound, and most researchers have not observed classroom instruction. In our opinion, unspecific definitions of terms and lack of classroom observation are major impediments to summarizing this literature.

Defining Homogeneous and Heterogeneous Conditions

The descriptions of student samples in the literature (especially older studies) are often so vague that it is difficult to define what is meant by the terms *homogeneous* and *heterogeneous*. We suspect that in some studies classes that were labeled heterogeneous were in fact more homogeneous than classes labeled as homogeneous in other studies. For example, because the students in the school studied by Goldberg *et al.* (1966) were primarily middle-class, it is likely that some of the classrooms that were called heterogeneous in this sample would in fact be called homogeneous in studies of schools that served more heterogeneous populations.

Because descriptions of the characteristics of students in particular *classrooms* were seldom given, it was impossible to tell in many cases whether the students were labeled as heterogeneous because of criteria relative to the particular sample from which they were drawn, or more absolute standards. Defining homogeneity and heterogeneity is especially difficult in nonexperimental studies. Here attempts to achieve homogeneity are constrained by the variation in the student population from which instructional groups are formed. This means that grouping or non-grouping may achieve very different degrees of homogeneity-heterogeneity across schools differing in their student body composition.

There are many reasons why a class might be labeled heterogeneous. For example, a class (Type A) might have one-third high-aptitude students (IQ of 125 or better), one-third students with aptitudes ranging from 100 to 124, and one-third of students ranging from 85 to 99. Another heterogeneous class (Type B) could have one-half the students with IQs between 115 and 130, and the other half with IQs ranging between 85 and 100. Indeed, the *mean ability* of these two classes would be similar in many cases, although the teaching demands would be quite different in the two situations.

On the other hand, two classes could be heterogeneous (e.g., either Type A or Type B), but their overall ability levels could be very different. One class could have high ability and little variation or variation in both ability and range of student ability. Similarly, the composition (variation and mean ability) of homogeneous classes can vary widely as well.

Yet another type of heterogeneous class (Type C) might contain 25 of 30 students at grade level, one student two grades above grade level, and four students three grades below grade level. This heterogeneous class is different from Types A and B, and as such it would require dissimilar instruction. There are many types of heterogeneous and homogeneous classes and most studies can ask only one of the many variations of the general question, Do students learn more in heterogeneous or homogeneous classes?

Unfortunately, in addition to the tendency some investigators have to overgeneralize their data, many often report their samples so inadequately that it is impossible to determine which specific question they are addressing.

A Case Study.   Although in many studies the sample descriptions were woefully inadequate, some researchers did describe their samples adequately. Still, it is difficult to compare studies. As a case in point, we describe a study (Drews, 1962) designed to assess the effects of homogeneous and heterogeneous grouping on students at three ability levels in ninth-grade English classes. In the study, 101 superior, 251 average, and 80 slow students were assigned to homogeneous and heterogenous classes. Drews attempted to maintain a ratio in heterogeneous classes of 2-3 superior students, 25-30 average students, and 2-3 slow students. It is clear that this definition of heterogeneity was closest to the *Type C* definition described here previously. Obviously, this study only narrowly addresses the relative advantages and disadvantages of heterogeneous grouping.

There were 30–35 students in each class, except for the homogeneous slow classes (15–20). Superior students had an average IQ of 135, average students an average IQ of 100, and slow students an IQ of 86 (the term *slow* was used by Drews). At first glance it seems that we have a reasonable definition of the independent variable. But do we? The IQs within the superior group had to vary somewhat, and it may be that one heterogeneous class had two students with IQs of 125, but another heterogeneous class might have contained two superior students with IQs of 140. Indeed, average students often show considerable variation as well and it is likely that the mean ability and the range of ability will vary to some extent (and in some individual classes perhaps considerably) within heterogeneous classes. These subtle differences in the composition of classes might affect the effectiveness of homogeneous and heterogeneous groups, but unfortunately, many investigators report data for homogeneous or heterogeneous classes as a group and do not examine the distribution of ability within individual classes. The description provided in the Drews study is reasonable, but does not provide sufficient detail for comparing her research with others.

Drews found that teachers in both heterogeneous and homogeneous classes formed the same number of groups in their classrooms. Teachers based their instruction on three to five student-levels, independent of whether the class had a 5-grade range (homogeneous) or a 13-grade range (heterogeneous). Although this finding is interesting, the possibility that the labels (a 5-grade range vs. a 13-grade range) may be somewhat misleading must be considered. Recall that in each heterogeneous class a teacher only had to accommodate two or three superior students and two or three slower students. Hence, if we compare the results of this study to other studies (where it is even more difficult to specify the composition of particular classrooms), an 8-grade range in a different study might produce a more difficult teaching situation if there were *more* high and low students that teachers had to accommodate (for example, consider the Type A and Type B heterogeneous classrooms that we discussed previously). Still, it is significant that the presence of heterogeneous or homogeneous groups of students in this study had little effect on teachers' decisions about the number of groups they would form for instruction.

The verbal behavior of teachers in heterogeneous classes was similar to that of teachers in the superior homogeneous classes, although high-achieving students dominated discussion in heterogeneous classes. In contrast, homogeneous grouping increased participation and involvement in academic and social activities for most students, especially for slow learners.

Our interpretation of the study is that the demand characteristics of teaching in heterogeneous classrooms in which there are some capable students make it more likely that teachers will present more theory and conceptualization than they will when teaching homogeneous groups of average and slow students. However, this interpretation is dependent upon the particular distribution of students in this study. There were many average students in these classrooms and only a few superior and slow students. Two or three superior students in a class otherwise filled with below-average students might not have any desirable effects on classroom processes and achievement.

The Drews study also suggests that although low and average students benefitted from the higher level of thought usually present in heterogeneous classes, the lows also suffered the consequences of less direct participation in social and academic affairs in these classrooms. Unfortunately, observational data present are too meager to allow any firm conclusions. Furthermore, it is impossible to determine whether teachers responded to relative or absolute student differences. That is, were differences in achievement and teacher behavior due to the student composition of the classroom or to the teacher's perceptions of the relative heterogeneity of the class (his or her perception of how the class should be taught)?

Need for More Observation: A Case Study. Goldberg et al. (1966) classified 3000 fifth-graders in 45 elementary schools into five IQ levels varying from low-average to gifted (the five levels were: 130 and higher, 129–20, 119–110, 109–100, and 99 and below). The school district largely served a middle-SES population. Eighty-six fifth-grade classes were eventually organized on the basis of 15 ability grouping patterns. Each pattern was classified as representing one of three IQ ranges: narrow (an IQ spread of about 20 points), medium (an IQ spread of at least 30 points), and broad (an IQ spread of at least 40 points).

The investigators reported that there were significantly greater achievement gains in heterogeneous, broad-range classes than in medium- or narrow-range classes, across all five ability-levels. Achievement increments were seen in social studies, reading vocabulary, and three areas of mathematics. However, differences among the three types of classes were generally quite small.

Certain types of students affected general classroom achievement. Regardless of the class ability-range, the presence of gifted students (IQ 130 or above) affected the achievement of other students in science and to some extent in social studies. Conversely, low-average students tended to have a positive effect on the arithmetic computation scores of other classmates. Goldberg et al. argue that these findings may shed some light on the generally superior attainment of all ability levels in the broad-range classes.

At a minimum, these data suggest that high- and low-achieving students can learn when taught together in the same class (at least under certain conditions). Goldberg, Passow, and Justman argued that narrowing the range of student ability and teaching many low students in the same class led teachers to set lower standards.

Goldberg et al. also examined the effect of being in a particular classroom and found that for most pupils *specific classroom membership influenced achievement* as much as the ability pattern of the class. That is, within different types of homogeneous and heterogeneous classes, achievement variation within an ability pattern was as wide as were variations across ability patterns. *Teaching effects* were quite obvious; within a grouping condition, some teachers obtained more achievement from students than did other teachers.

Teachers' effects on different types of students were stronger than teachers' ability to get gains across different subject areas. Simply expressed, teachers who were getting good achievement gains in a particular subject obtained those gains from most of the students in their classrooms. However, teachers' ability to obtain achievement varied considerably from one subject area to another.

As we noted in the previous study (and as in most ability studies), heterogeneity has advantages and disadvantages. Goldberg *et al.* found that slow pupils self-concepts were lower in broad-range (i.e., heterogeneous) classes than in others. In explaining the drop in self esteem for slow pupils in the heterogeneous classes, Goldberg *et al.* suggest that despite their higher achievement than comparable students in homogeneous classes, the only thing slow pupils in these classes had to compare their behavior to was that of their brighter classmates.

What is known in this study is that teacher effects were as important as were grouping effects; however, we do not know how the behavior of teachers who generally got more gain from students was different from the behavior of teachers who achieved less with their classes. Also, we know that in general, across all ability levels of students, achievement was higher in heterogeneous than in homogeneous classes and this was particularly the case for low students. However, we do not know *how* these results were achieved because there are no process data to describe the instruction and curriculum that was presented. In conclusion, it seems clear that research will not be able to respond to the question, Do students learn best in homogeneous or heterogeneous classes? until student heterogeneity is defined more carefully and unless we observe classroom conditions more carefully than we have in the past.

Observational Studies of Tracking

Sophisticated studies of classroom process in tracked schools were very rare until recently in American schools. Recent observational studies of tracking suggest (a) that the assignment of students into lower tracks (where they receive all instruction only with other low-achieving students) generally leads to inferior teaching and opportunity to learn (b) that, at a minimum, assignment into a low track maintains or sustains student performance at a low level (and often may lead to deterioration).

Because of space limitations, only one observational study of tracking is discusses here. A study by Schwartz (1981) was chosen for illustrative purposes because it examines school process in tracked classrooms across a number of different process variables. We have not reproduced details of his methodology here, because those are available elsewhere (Schwartz, 1981). Briefly, the research was conducted primarily in one New York City elementary school and secondarily in three Philadelphia schools (one junior high and two elementary). The four schools studied differed in size and ethnic composition; however, all four schools served predominantly working-class populations.

Peer Effects

Schwartz found consistent differences in student behavior in high- and low-track classes throughout the sample. For example, during whole-class discussion, he found that students' behavior in low-track classrooms could be characterized as challenging teachers, obstructing academic activity, and misusing educational resources.

Schwartz (1981) found that during seatwork students in the high track took advantage of the situation in order to engage in minor misbehavior. However, he argues that their behavior was still basically task-oriented during seatwork and that although they competed during seatwork, high-track students still facilitated each other's academic efforts.

In contrast, when students in the low track were assigned independent seatwork and freed from the potential need to defend themselves against public academic humiliation and failure, they tended to discuss among themselves social and other events outside of school. Hence, tracking in this study was associated with a peer culture that promoted academic goals in high-track classes but impeded them in the low-ability classes.

Schwartz also reports evidence to illustrate the devastating impact of tracking on low-ability students and their rejection by peers. He found that 50% of lower-track students chose more high- than low-rank peers to "hang around with most." In marked contrast, less than 1% of high-track students chose to spend time with low-track over high-track classmates.

Although research is needed, it is our belief that peer influences in low-ability groups tend to be unavoidable and strong enough to overwhelm the potential instructional advantages of grouping (i.e., few teachers are capable of teaching low groups effectively, especially in secondary schools). Appropriate teacher expectations, instructional behavior, and group management may allow low groups to be taught effectively in some instances, but we suspect that the structural effects of teaching lows together in a large group are difficult to overcome. We now turn to a discussion of some research that has examined teacher behavior and attitudes in tracked classes.

Teacher Behavior and Attitudes

Schwartz found that teachers in low-track classrooms made fewer demands on students and applied less exacting standards both to students' performances as well as to their own teaching. He interpreted this finding to mean that teachers in low-track classrooms did not want to risk failure with pupils whom they viewed as difficult if not impossible to motivate. Others, too, have commented on the fact that teachers appear to be less serious when interacting with low-track than with high-track students (see, for example, Keddie, 1971; Leacock, 1969).

In addition, teacher comments on students' record cards indicated to Schwartz that teachers commitments to an evaluation of high- and low-track students varied notably. Over the course of the study he found a progressive disparity in the length and nature of teachers' year-end comments about high- and low-ability students. In general, teachers became more positive in their comments about high-track students and made more elaborate and lengthy comments about them. In contrast, students in low-track classrooms were progressively described in briefer and more pejorative terms. These students often received only one-word comments on their record cards.

Schwartz also found that the standards and sanctions utilized for high- and low-track students varied. Teachers complained more about low-ranked students' behavior but actually punished students in high classes more frequently. Indeed, teachers followed through on punishments and discipline three times more often in high than in low sections, even though students were warned about misbehavior more frequently in low than in high classes. However, students in high tracks were more likely to be praised and rewarded for academic achievement than students in low classes. These data again suggest that when teachers instruct high sections they are more serious and more careful about their own behavior as well as that of students.

Similarly, Hargreaves (1967) reports that teachers in one English comprehensive school had lower standards for the lower-stream students than for the higher-stream ones. Keddie (1971) also found that teachers' classroom behaviors indicated that they held lower standards, and, indeed, teachers' self-reports also supported the contention that low-track students received less demanding and less interesting curriculum assignments than students in other tracks. Keddie (1971) argues that the structural influence of grouping is so powerful that once inside the low-ability classrooms even those teachers who most actively oppose tracking on moral and or philosophical grounds become unwittingly ensnared in its framework.

Instructional Content

Surprisingly, Schwartz did not find much difference in the actual content of instruction that was offered to high-track and low-track students, although the abstractness of the content presented did vary between high and low classes. For example, in the junior high schools teachers often presented the *same material* with different emphases to high and low classes.

It is commonly argued that the content taught in a heterogeneous class must be so diverse for students of various abilities that there is a *need* to track students by ability so that content can be adjusted more easily. In this study, Schwartz found that students were asked to suffer the social consequences of being labeled (as members of the low-track classroom) but received neither a distinctive nor an appropriate curriculum.

In a study of tracking in British schools, Heathers (1967) found that teachers stressed basic skills and facts and used drill much more when interacting with "slow" learners, whereas they emphasized conceptual learning and independent projects with highs. Similar instructional differences were noted by Keddie (1971) in a study of a British comprehensive school. She found that the content assigned to high- and low-track students might be superficially similar, but that the emphasis was quite different for the students. For example, students in both tracks might study taxation, but the high-track class would study how different types of taxation work and the low-track classroom would learn how to fill out the forms.

Hargreaves (1967) found that in many schools poorer teachers were often assigned to teach low-ability classes and that both teachers and students knew this. Rosenbaum (1976) found that teachers reported that they prepared more for college-track than for non-college track classes and that they perceived that lower-business and general-track classes were so undemanding as to require little or *no* preparation at all. Thus, even when non-college track students had the same teachers as college-track students, they did not get as much attention, concern, or effort from their teachers. Observational data in Rosenbaum's study provide prima facie evidence that the academic needs of low-track students were simply not being met in low-track classes.

Evertson (1982) compared average- and low-ability classes taught by the same teachers in junior high schools and found that lower-ability classes tended to have more off-task, inappropriate, and disruptive student behavior. Also, teachers in low classes were less consistent in handling behavioral problems, less clear in instruction, and less effective in adjusting instruction to fit students interests and backgrounds than when they taught average ability classes. Metz (1978) also controlled for teacher effects by observing the same teachers instructing classes dissimilar in ability and reached conclusions similar to those reported by Evertson and Schwartz.

General Conclusions

Other studies that have examined instructional processes in schools that practice tracking have yielded somewhat similar conclusions. For example, in a review of tracking literature, Persell (1977) has noted that students in low-track classes tend to receive less appropriate student-teacher interaction, instruction and resource materials, and student-student interaction.

Rosenbaum (1976) studied the effects of tracking in a relatively *homogeneous* working-class neighborhood and found process dimensions associated with class placement similar to those reported by Schwartz. Lower-track placement was associated with *easier* and more *boring* work. In addition, grades were less variable and lower in these classes, despite the fact that content was less challenging.

Most of the observational data describing what takes place in track classes is recent. *Observational* studies of tracking show a consistent pattern of deprivation for low students in schools that practice tracking. Considering this evidence and the fact that there is *not* a single observational study to show positive consequences for low-track students, it seems unthinkable to support tracking educational policies generally. The evidence consistently suggests that low-track students may be placed into difficult situations that hinder their academic progress.

There appears to be little justification for tracking in elementary or middle schools. The issues in high schools are more complex and merit additional research. Because of present schooling practices, high-school students often become quite differentiated in terms of their abilities and interests. Some students are headed for college and want and need courses in language and advanced courses in mathematics and science; other students want specialized business or industrial courses. A key aspect is the difference between presenting the same content to all students versus presenting clearly diverse content to various students because they want to concentrate in different subject matter areas. Tracking (assuming that all students are actively taught) may make sense in secondary schools when personal and curriculum *content* goals are different.

Observational Research on Ability-Grouped Instruction

Having examined some of the observational literature on tracked classes, we now discuss observational studies of heterogeneous classes in which students receive portions of their instruction in ability groups within classrooms. Most of this research has been conducted in elementary schools, and most of it has focused on reading group instruction. In this section we discuss research on elementary classes in which students are grouped by ability for reading instruction.

In general, observational studies of reading instruction indicate that most teachers allocate equal time to different reading groups, although researchers have obtained other results on occasion. McDermott (1976) found that the differences in time allocation were in part due to student behavior. He found that students in the low group had less time to read because of interruptions from other students in the class. He also concluded that the behavior of students in the low group made it easy for other students in the class to interrupt them.

Recent observational research has consistently shown that teacher and student behavior, and thus the quality of instruction, varies in high and low reading-groups (Allington, 1983). However, it is not always clear whether differences in teacher behavior toward highs and lows are appropriate or not, and how such differences affect student achievement. From research conducted thus far, one cannot ascertain whether teacher behavior determines student behavior, or whether student needs and abilities dictate teacher perceptions and behavior.

Most researchers who have observed reading-group behavior have found differences between high and low groups that appear to be pejorative and unnecessary. In many cases these differences involve the same types of behaviors that others might interpret as appropriate.

A case in point is Alpert's (1974) study in which she observed the top and bottom reading-group sessions in 15 second-grade classrooms on three occasions to determine whether teachers adapted methods and materials to the two groups of students. She found that teachers used a great variety of readers and emphasized meaning (rather than decoding) when teaching high groups. Alpert interprets this as appropriate teacher behavior and argues that this behavior is consistent with students' needs. Because high pupils had mastered basic decoding skills, an emphasis on comprehension in these groups was appropriate. More work on decoding was needed in low groups because they did not possess these skills. These results illustrate the interpretation (causation) problem mentioned previously. Alpert interprets the differential behavior and materials given low-group students as appropriate; however, we wonder if any instructional approach can be useful if it does not stress the meaning and substance of the assignment. If teachers do not emphasize meaning, students may only mechanically respond to material with little interest in reading for meaning or enjoyment.

One of the most interesting studies of instruction in high and low first-grade reading groups in one classroom was conducted by Eder (1981). She found that students who were likely to have difficulty in learning to read generally were assigned to groups whose *social context* was not very conducive to learning. In part, this was because assignments to first-grade reading groups were based upon kindergarten teachers' recommendations, and a major criterion of placement was the *maturity* of the students as well as their perceived ability.

Most of the students in the study were relatively homogeneous in terms of their academic ability and socioeconomic background (students were from middle-class homes). More important, none of the students could read prior to entering first grade. Despite the relatively *homogeneous* nature of this student population, the first-grade teacher still grouped pupils for reading instruction.

In the early grades, it is probably necessary to group for instruction in reading. For example, it is important for teachers to elicit frequent overt responses from each individual pupil and in this sense grouping is probably necessary. However, this purpose (small instructional groups) can be achieved without ability grouping. Where grouping is necessary to allow teachers to deal with manageable numbers of students, such grouping need not yield high-, middle-, and low-ability groups. Despite the possibility of random or deliberately heterogeneously formed groups, teachers routinely assign students to groups on the basis of perceived ability—even when the objective differences between students are small (as Eder found).

Behavioral Differences

Eder found that the teacher discouraged interruptions of a student's oral reading turn within the high group but not in the low group. She believes that the teacher may have been concerned with maintaining the interest of the low group during other students' reading turns (in general, their reading turns tended to be longer and filled with more pauses); the teacher may also have thought that lows had less intrinsic interest in the material; therefore, the teacher was more willing to encourage most forms of participation or responses from low students but demanded more appropriate behavior and responses from highs.

Eder (1981) reports that because the most immature, inattentive students were assigned to low groups, the teacher was almost certain to have more managerial problems (e.g., distractions) with these groups than with others, especially early in the year. Indeed, because the teacher was often distracted from a student reader in the low group who was responding (because of the need to manage other students in the group), students often provided the correct word for the reader. Readers were not allowed time to ascertain words on their own, even though less than a third of the students interviewed reported that they liked to be helped, because they thought this interfered with their own learning. Eder's work indicates that low students had less time than highs to correct their mistakes before other students and/or the teacher intervened.

Eder also found that students in the low group spent 40% of their listening time not attending to the lesson (vs. 22% in the high group). Low students frequently read out of turn, adding to the general confusion. Eder reports twice as many teacher managerial-acts in the low group as in the high group (157 versus 61), and found that turn interruption increased over the course of the year.

Similar findings have been reported by other researchers. As noted here previously, McDermott (1976) found in one classroom that the low group was interrupted more frequently by other students in the class than was the high group. Allington (1980) found that teachers were more likely to interrupt low-group readers during reading than they were high-group readers, especially when lows made oral reading mistakes.

Allington (1983) found that good readers read about three times as many words as poor readers and that three-fourths of their reading was done silently. In contrast, poor readers usually read orally (and therefore more slowly). Although results vary somewhat from study to study, the general findings are that both the form and quality of instruction vary between high and low groups. Perhaps the most common finding reported across studies is that low students are interrupted by teachers and other pupils in the group proportionately more often following errors than are other students.

Effects of Group Placement

In many studies, initial differences between readers in high and low groups within classrooms are not particularly large, and the criteria for placement into particular groups often involve students social maturity as much as their cognitive ability or their perceived reading ability. Even after students are placed into reading groups, teachers may inadvertently evaluate skills other than reading performance per se (i.e., ability to talk about a story not because of general information gained from the story, but because of more generalized information; ability to anticipate teacher expectations). However, the effects of differential teacher behavior and instructional content may unnecessarily increase achievement differences between high and low groups.

It may be that limited instructional opportunities encourage students placed into low groups to become passive learners. To take but one variable, for example, frequent interruptions may encourage students to depend on others when they encounter difficulty rather than to think actively and attempt to solve problems themselves. Good (1981) has noted that during general discussions in some classrooms, lows have fewer opportunities to respond, but must answer more quickly when they are called on. If lows respond correctly, they are less likely than other students to be praised, and they are more likely to be criticized when they are incorrect. Furthermore, if they do not respond, lows are more likely to be given the answer by the teacher or someone else.

Although researchers are beginning to collect data that describe in detail what instruction is like for high and low reading-groups, several studies indicate that group placement is extremely important—that is, being placed into a higher reading group can have a significant, positive effect on achievement. Weinstein (1976) found that reading group membership contributed a significant increment of 25% to the prediction of achievement over and above initial readiness differences among children. Although the mediating effects of group membership were not identified in the Weinstein study, more recent studies (e.g., Eder, 1981) provide important clues about some of the ways in which group membership affects the academic performance of high and low students. It is becoming increasingly clear that differences in instruction of high and low reading-groups in many first-grade classrooms are likely to sustain the poor performance of slower students and to increase the disparity between the two groups.

Some Suggestions

We suspect that in many classes reading instruction delivered to low students should be altered; however, research has not documented successful ways for doing this. Still, there are many clues in the literature as to how teachers might proceed, and different individuals have offered suggestions for improving reading instruction. It is possible to offer suggestions but the effects of suggested changes upon students attitudes and performance have not been tested in research.

Eder recommends that low students receive more individualized attention and instruction in first-grade reading groups and Allington (1983) argues that teachers need to treat all readers more similarly. In particular, he states that poor readers develop more slowly partly because they are treated differently than are readers who have more skills when they enter first grade. In other words, differential instruction increases what may be relatively minor differences among students at the beginning of first grade.

In addition to these suggestions, we believe that most low-achieving first-grade students would be better off receiving some instruction in somewhat more heterogeneous groups than they presently do. Mixed groups would probably present fewer managerial difficulties, and students could move more quickly through the curriculum and focus more on the meaning of the material being examined. More diverse grouping might be particularly useful if, in addition to a general reading session in the morning, students

who have low readiness scores receive extra instruction and special sessions in the afternoon. Although the argument against ability group instruction in first-grade reading is not as strong as that against tracking (as argued in a previous section), research evidence is sufficient to question the value of ability grouping and to wonder if other formats for instruction might be more practical or effective.

Although it is possible to find a few studies that show that elementary students' achievement scores can be increased when students are assigned to higher ability groups (e.g., Dewar, 1963), research that includes systematic observation of instructional process as well as student achievement data has not shown a pattern of achievement gains associated with the assignment of students to ability groups, and, indeed, such research has raised questions about the adequacy of instruction that students placed into low groups receive. At the secondary level there are some data to suggest that high-ability students may obtain slight gains when they are in homogeneous classes and simultaneously receive an enriched curriculum. Again, however, examination of the instruction afforded low students taught in homogeneous groups (e.g., Metz, 1978) has raised serious questions about the efficacy of grouping.

Why Does Ability Grouping Not Work More Effectively?

According to Good and Stipek (1983), ability grouping within classrooms is the most common procedure used to accommodate individual differences in rates of learning. However, they note that there are difficulties posed by most such attempts to compensate for individual differences. Indeed, ability grouping apparently causes as many problems as it solves. The most common criticism of homogeneous ability grouping is that is stigmatizes children in lower groups, often causing them to develop negative self-concepts. Teachers tend to be less motivated to teach low-ability groups, and their expectations, behavior toward these children, and perceptions of students performances and instructional needs may be largely determined by these students placement in low groups. Evidence that group placement is highly stable over time suggests that ability grouping is less flexible than would be expected if children were all learning at an optimum rate.

Are More Varied Groups Less Teachable?

Much of the process-product research conducted in the late 1970s involved teachers who were instructing large groups of students because earlier naturalistic research had indicated that teachers who obtained the highest student achievement gains in mathematics used large-group formats. However, teachers who had the lowest achievement scores also used whole-class instructional techniques (Good, Grouws, & Ebmeier, 1983). Thus, despite many arguments that students need to be taught in instructional groups in order to achieve a better match between the content presented and the needs of individual learners, a number of studies conducted in the 1970's suggest that whole-class instruction is associated with more extreme effects on student achievement than individualized and group methods.

Indeed, in one program of research it was found in three different school districts that teachers who generally obtained the most extreme achievement effects (both positive and negative) taught students basically in large groups or in whole-class instruction (Good et al., 1983). Because subsequent research focused upon extreme teachers (those who were getting the best or worst results), most of the process studies that followed examined how teachers who were relatively effective and ineffective using whole-group instruction varied in their behavior. Thus, we have little information about variation in teacher behavior within group and individualized instructional formats, in elementary schools.

The data collected by Good *et al.* (1983) in the Missouri Mathematics Program of research make it clear that some teachers obtain more achievement from students than others and that teachers can be taught behaviors and principles that improve their effectiveness in using whole-class-large-group teaching techniques (Good, *et al.,* 1983). We cite this evidence in the present chapter because we want to explore the relationship between class heterogeneity and achievement. One of the oft-cited virtues of ability grouping is that it allows teachers to reduce variance in learners abilities so that the class is easier to instruct. It would seem, then, that teachers who use whole-class methods do so because the variance of learners' ability in their classes is less extreme than the variance in classes of teachers who use individualized or small-group techniques. However, in two different samples used to compare molar teaching orientations (whole class, individualized, small group), we found that the correlation between variation in student achievement and the selection of a whole-class-large-group teaching technique is very small but positive. That is, teachers in these samples had a slight tendency to use large-group teaching techniques when the variance in learners was greater.

Although teachers who group for instruction may be attempting to form groups of students with comparable instructional needs, the relationship between grouping practices and the variance in student ability suggests that many teachers do not group in order to accommodate more heterogeneous classes. Rather, the decision to group may be influenced by a number of other factors; information pre-

sented in teacher education programs, existing practices in a particular school, and the personal philosophy of a teacher.

Ebmeier recently reanalyzed data collected in the Missouri Mathematics Program (Ebmeier & Good, 1979; Good & Grouws, 1979) and correlated the variance in student ability that existed at the start of the year in each classroom with end-of-year residual achievement data. He found low but positive correlations between variance in student ability and mean residual achievement. That is, classrooms that showed the most achievement gain tended to begin the year with slightly *more* variation in student ability. One weakness of this analysis is that it utilized a linear model, and it is quite possible that there is an optimal level of variation. At some point variation may be so great as to impede student achievement. A second problem is that Ebmeier's reanalysis concerned only general variation and achievement of many classrooms. As we noted earlier in this chapter, there are different types of classrooms that might be labelled *heterogeneous.*

Obviously, we do not believe that increased heterogeneity of learners is always associated with increases in achievement for all students. Too much heterogeneity may create instructional problems, and there are probably limits on the amount of class heterogeneity that a teacher can reasonably handle (although an important variable will be the number of extreme performers in the class). In practice, the most prevalent problem is that ability-group membership lines are too tightly drawn. Lows in general need more opportunity to learn with highs.

Good and Stipek (1983) note that homogeneous groups are *not* necessarily easier to teach than diverse ones. Tyler (1962) found that homogeneous grouping on a *single* ability measure did not reduce variance in students other abilities. One danger of homogeneous ability grouping is that some teachers believe that students who have been grouped together will benefit from the same treatment. Good and Stipek contend that some teachers who instruct larger, more diverse classes may feel a stronger need to ascertain whether they have been understood by all students than if they taught homogeneous classes or groups of slow learners.

Furthermore, research on large-group instruction has shown that the ability to determine whether or not students have comprehended material is related to student achievement. Relatively ineffective teachers do not carefully monitor students' progress or their conceptual understanding of material (Good, 1982; Good *et al.,* 1983).

Summary

In this section we have examined studies of instruction in high- and low-ability groups within classrooms, especially reading groups. Research consistently shows that high students receive more active instruction, particularly instruction concerning the meaning of what is read. In contrast, teachers emphasize practice and skills when teaching low groups. Although the question of *appropriateness* is difficult to assess because data in these studies were correlational, we believe that research indicates that in many classrooms teachers err by holding expectations that are too low, by pacing instruction too slowly, and by ignoring or under-emphasizing the substantive aspects of tasks when instructing low groups. We believe that teachers' behavior towards low groups is influenced by their expectations for these pupils as well as the social difficulties that exist when many relatively immature students are taught at the same time (Eder, 1981).

Although studies reviewed in this section do not suggest that ability grouping within classrooms should be abandoned, they do show that dividing students into groups for instruction does not necessarily make instruction easier; in fact, slow students are often more difficult to instruct in groups. Teachers who group students by ability need to assess carefully their reasons for grouping and how adequately grouping enables them to meet instructional goals. Furthermore, teachers must periodically assess their behavior to be sure that students in the low group are receiving appropriate instruction.

Obviously, more research is needed, particularly experimental research that varies the composition of reading groups and assesses the effects of composition on student achievement and attitudes. We believe that teachers often overrespond to initial variance in learner s abilities and that some teachers rely upon grouping when teaching students with varied ability levels. We suspect that higher quality and more thoughtful teaching of mixed groups of learners can lead to better outcomes than can fragmented teaching of a number of different groups.

Composition Studies

Beckerman and Good (1981) studied the ratio of high- and low-achieving students in classrooms using a sample drawn from a large metropolitan school district that basically served a middle-class population in neighborhood schools. They defined classrooms with *more favorable* teaching situations as those in which more than a third of the students were high aptitude and less than a third were low aptitude. Less favorable classrooms were those in which less than a third of the students were high aptitude and more than a third were low aptitude.

Beckerman and Good found that both low-and high-aptitude students in favorable classrooms had higher achievement scores than the two groups in unfavorable classrooms. This effect was observed in both third- and fourth-grade classrooms, although the effect was not significant for high-aptitude, third-grade students. In this study, being in a classroom with many high-aptitude students was more beneficial than being in a low-aptitude classroom for low-aptitude students and some high-aptitude students.

Veldman and Sanford (1982) also found evidence that classroom composition might influence student achievement. They measured classroom composition in seventh and eighth grades in nine junior high schools by determining the mean achievement level for each class at the beginning of the year. Veldman and Sanford report that significant interaction effects were found, indicating that both high- and low-ability pupils do better in high-ability classes and that the effects of class ability are more pronounced with low-ability students. These results, although obtained with different methods, resulted in conclusions that were very similar to Beckerman and Good's. Veldman and Sanford also found that lower-ability students were more affected by group placement than highs. They argue that lower-ability students are more likely than highs to conform to the behavior of the majority of their classmates and that low-ability classes can be described as poor learning environments, which are frequently disrupted.

According to these researchers, changes in class composition or other context variables are unlikely to convert a very effective teacher into a totally ineffective one. Although composition is important, the *quality* of instruction is a crucial variable that also affects achievement. No doubt research will show quality of teaching, class ability-level, and variations in learners ability in the classroom are interrelated.

Results of these studies challenge the simple suggestion that variability in student achievement levels within a class requires that students be grouped on the basis of ability. We do not believe that teachers should never group, for we feel that for certain students and for some academic goals grouping is appropriate. However, we do challenge the assumption that high- and low-achieving students must be taught separately.

Earlier we suggested that one way to alter the structural constraints of low reading-groups was to teach high- and low-reading students together for at least a short time each day. Furthermore, there is clinical evidence that putting a student into a higher group and altering instructional behavior can be associated with improved achievement.

For example, Shavelson (1982) reports that changing the textbook used in the low group from one that was one grade below level to a book that was grade level (and a book that looked more sophisticated), altering the instructional focus from teacher reading to student reading, and emphasizing the content of assignments rather than format were effective in increasing students' effort and performance in reading as well as their interest. Weinstein (1982) found that moving a student from a low to a higher reading-group was associated with an increase in expectations and performance that was quite dramatic. Although the findings of Weinstein and Shavelson are anecdotal, they clearly demonstrate that when processes within a group are changed, or when a student is moved from a low group to a higher one, some of the negative influences of low-group membership are either eliminated or reduced (at least temporarily). (See also, Eder & Felmlee, Chapter 11, this volume.) There is growing evidence that the ability level and motivation of other students present in a class or group affects the achievement of individual students.

Classroom Composition and Task Structure

Future researchers should carefully examine the relationships of composition variables to recently identified factors such as task structure and grouping practices. In this section, we discuss the potential effects of student composition on task structure in order to illustrate more fully how student characteristics can influence educational outcomes.

Bossert (1979) has studied the distinctive types of work organization that exist in classrooms and how they influence outcomes of schooling (achievement, friendship patterns, etc.). Bossert analyzes the conditions under which classroom tasks are carried out, and argues that task structure influences students self-perceptions and achievement in important ways. He examines the influence of various structural dimensions (public vs. private evaluations; all students working on the same task vs. students working on different tasks and receiving evaluation related to the work; teacher-assignment of tasks vs. student selection; and many other variables). Some of the data suggest that specific task structures may encourage certain teacher and student perceptions and behaviors. This is important research, and it provides a method of exploring classroom work conditions that may influence classroom behavior. However, Bossert's data were collected in a laboratory school in which most of the students were reasonably bright and from fairly affluent homes. One wonders what influence the *relatively* homogeneous population of students had on his finding. The effects of an activity structure may vary according to the population of students in a class, and we suspect this variation is more problematic than Bossert's initial work suggests.

In a related study, Anderson and Scott (1978) found that diverse teaching strategies (group work, visual presentations, seatwork, class discussions, lectures) variously af-

fected the attention of students with different aptitudes and self-concepts. A comparison of the two studies suggests that student styles, teacher styles, curriculum, and activity structure are all important dimensions of classrooms and that an exclusive focus on one dimension does not provide a complete picture of classrooms.

Task Structure: Another Perspective

Doyle (1979) advocates the examination of classroom tasks and activity structures because he believes that the two differ within some, and possibly many, classrooms.[1] Doyle contends that what students do in classrooms (and their perceptions of what they are doing and why) may sometimes be discrepant with the actual task that the teacher has in mind. That is, students sometimes even practice the wrong operations. For example, a teacher may spend much class time having students *diagram* sentences; however, the teacher might choose not to test whether students can apply this skill (e.g., on the test, students are required to *write* original sentences). In this case, from Doyle's perspective, having students practice diagraming sentences would be an activity and not a task since it was not functionally related to the intended outcome. Doyle suggests the need to study broader relationships among classroom tasks and activities and points out that one can misinterpret classroom events if a process that occurs at one point in time is examined without a clear understanding of what *preceded* or what will *follow*.

As an explicit case in point, Doyle (1979) notes that teachers have been found to praise inappropriate student responses. Reasons for such teacher behaviors may be laudable (e.g., to encourage classroom participation); however, the discrepancy between stated teacher behavior (get thoughtful answers) and accepted behavior (wrong answers) may teach students that the real task is to respond quickly and not to think. Such discrepancies between activity and task demands may communicate low expectations for student learning. We agree with his contention; however, it is likely that certain teachers can teach their students to tolerate more risk than other teachers.

The studies by Bossert and Doyle are important steps toward integrating classroom environment (e.g., classroom structure) and molar curriculum variables (e.g., What is the real task for the student?). These perspectives will be better understood when they are applied in a variety of ed-

---

[1] From Doyle's perspective, a task consists of two elements: (a) a goal and (b) a set of operations necessary to achieve the goal. He argues that there are two consequences to accomplishing a task. First, the person develops information (e.g., facts and principles) and also the person will practice operations (e.g., memorizing and analyzing).

ucational settings. We believe that Bossert's and Doyle's perspectives need to consider teaching quality as well. Numerous studies using diverse research methods show that teacher effects are quite prevalent. Recall that Goldberg *et al.* (1966) found that the teacher to whom a student was assigned was more important than a particular ability grouping pattern to which he or she was assigned. Research also demonstrates that students' perceptions of ability and activity structures within classrooms are related (Rosenholtz & Wilson, 1980), but there are also data that indicate that an individual teacher can mediate this effect (Rosenholtz and Rosenholtz, 1981).

Student composition variables have been poorly defined and seldom studied in any systematic way. The number of potential composition questions is vast and wide-ranging in scope, and much research conducted in the past could have profited from more consideration of student composition factors. To illustrate more fully the range of possible research questions in this area, we suggest that the assignment of students to a class (e.g., the composition of students in the class) may have direct effects on grouping practices within the classroom.

At present, in many American schools, because of declining student enrollment, students have to be grouped across grade levels in order to have enough students to justify hiring a teacher. In such cases, we suspect that grouping too often begins with an organizational or institutional need rather than a question about how best to serve the educational needs of students.

As a case in point, one of the authors had a chance to observe the effects of such decision making on the school lives of second- and third-grade students in a small school serving a diverse student population. There were enough second- and third-grade students to justify the formation of three classes (one mixed, one second grade, and one third grade). In this particular case, a decision was made to *form* the mixed class on the basis of student *maturity* (capacity to work independently) as opposed to *ability*.

The principal wanted mature third-and second-grade students in one classroom so that one group could work independently while the teacher worked with the other group. Had the principal formed classes according to ability there would have been more pressure on the teacher to use whole-class and large-group teaching. Had the principal used more dynamic individual characteristics (sociability-works well in groups), or stressed a more social outcome (learn to work well with others who are diverse), the teacher might have made greater attempts to have second- and third-grade students interact.

In this case, the independent worker model and the demand characteristics communicated to the teacher by such a grouping virtually guaranteed that the teacher would in-struct the second- and third-grade students as separate, *intact* groups (no social or academic contact between groups) and that comparatively little social interaction could be allowed *within* groups because their group role was institutionalized as individual work.

This class contained 16 second- and third-grade students. The 4 third-grade girls appeared to be socially isolated, in part because of peer expectations (i.e., social interaction occurs with same-sex, same-age classmates and the teacher did little to alter this peer norm) and in part because the girls were from diverse backgrounds.

This example clearly illustrates the need to study a variety of variables if classroom life is to be understood more fully. It is likely that the principal's decision about how to assign students was influenced to some extent by perception of the teacher's style and ability. No doubt, the teacher's classroom strategies were influenced *by* both the composition of students as well as the assumptions and expectations about the principal's motivation in assigning students for instruction in this way. A different teacher and another four girls would, we believe, have led to different consequences.

Historically, educational research has made too much ado about too few variables. Teacher effects are real, as are student variables, structural settings, curriculum tasks, student composition factors, as well as school effects. And all of these variables are relevant to the question, Do students learn more in heterogeneous or homogeneous settings? And it is because of this complexity that composition variables have to be considered along with quality of teaching (e.g., Good, 1982), task structure of the classroom environment (e.g., Bossert, 1979), and task demands of assigned work (e.g., Doyle, 1979).

References.

Allington, R. Teacher interruption behaviors during primary grade oral reading. *Journal of Educational Psychology,* 1980, 73, 371–377.

Allington, R. The reading instruction provided readers of differing reading ability. *Elementary School Journal,* 1983, 83, 548–559.

Alpert, J. L. Teacher behavior across ability groups: A consideration of the mediation of Pygmalion effects. *Journal of Educational Psychology,* 1974, 66,(3), 348–353.

Anderson, L., & Scott, C. The relationship among teaching methods, student characteristics, and student involvement in learning. *Journal of Teacher Education,* 1978, 29, 52–57.

Beckerman, T., & Good, T. The classroom ratio of high- and low-aptitude students and its effect on achievement. *American Educational Research Journal,* 1981, 18, 317–327.

Bossert, S. *Task and social relationships in classrooms: A study of classroom organization and its consequences.* (American Sociological Association, Arnold and Caroline Rose Monograph Series). New York: Cambridge University Press, 1979.

Dewar, J. Grouping for arithmetic instruction in sixth grade. *Elementary School Journal,* 1963, 63, 266–269.

Doyle, W. Classroom task and students' abilities. In P. Peterson & H. Walberg (Eds.), *Research on teaching: Concepts, findings, and implications.* Berkeley, California: McCutchean, 1979.

Drews, E. *The effects of heterogeneous and homogeneous grouping upon children of three ability levels in ninth-grade English classes.* A report to the Lansing, Michigan Public Schools, 1962.

Ebmeier, H., & Good, T. The effects of instructing teachers about good teaching on the mathematics achievement of fourth grade students. *American Educational Research Journal,* 1979, 16, 1–16.

Eder, D. Ability grouping as a self-fulfilling prophecy: Micro-analysis of teacher-student interaction. *Sociology of Education,* 1981, 54, 151–161.

Esposito, D. Homogeneous and heterogeneous ability grouping: Principle findings and implications for evaluating and designing more effective educational environments. *Review of Educational Research,* 1973, 43, 163–179.

Evertson, C. Differences in instructional activities in average- and low-achieving junior high English and math classes. *Elementary School Journal,* 1982, 82, 329–350.

Goldberg, M., Passow, A., & Justman, J. *The effects of ability grouping.* New York: Teachers College Press, 1966.

Good, T. Teacher expectations and student perceptions: A decade of research. *Educational Leadership,* 1981, 38, 415–421.

—— Classroom research: What we know and what we need to know (Tech. Rep. 9018). Austin, Texas; Research and Development Center for Teacher Education, 1982.

Good, T., & Grouws, D. The Missouri mathematics effectiveness project: An experimental study in fourth grade classrooms. *Journal of Educational Psychology,* 1979, 71, 355–362.

Good, T., Grouws, D., & Ebmeier, H. *Active mathematics teaching: Empirical research in elementary and secondary classrooms.* New York: Longman, 1983.

Good, T., & Stipek, D. Individual differences in the Classroom: A psychological perspective. In M. Fernstermacher & J. Goodlad (Eds.), *1983 NSSE Yearbook,* 1983.

Hargreaves, D. *Social relations in a secondary school.* London: Routledge & Kegan Paul, 1967.

Heathers, G. *Organizing schools through the dual progress plan.* Danville, Illinois: Interstate, 1967.

Keddie, N. Classroom knowledge. In M. Young (Ed.), *Knowledge and control: New directions for the sociology of education.* London: Collier MacMillan, 1971.

Kulik, C., & Kulik, J. Effects of ability grouping on secondary school students: A meta analysis of evaluation findings. *Review of Educational Research,* 1982, 19, 415–428.

Leacock, E. *Teaching and learning in city schools.* New York: Basic Books, 1969.

McDermott, R. *Kids make sense: An ethnographic account of the interactional management of success and failure in one first-grade classroom.* Unpublished doctoral dissertation, Stanford University, 1976.

Metz, M. *Classrooms and corridors: The crisis of authority in desegregated secondary schools.* Berkeley, California: University of California Press, 1978.

Persell, C. *Education and inequality: The roots and results of stratification in America's schools.* New York: The Free Press, 1977.

Rosenbaum, J. *Making inequality: The hidden curriculum of high school tracking.* New York: Wiley, 1976.

Rosenholtz, S., & Rosenholtz, S. Classroom organization and the perception of ability. *Sociology of Education,* 1981, 54, 132–140.

Rosenholtz, S., & Wilson, B. The effect of classroom structure on shared perceptions of ability. *American Educational Research Journal.* 1980, 17, 75–82.

Schwartz, F. Supporting or subverting learning: Peer group patterns in four tracked schools. *Anthropology and Education Quarterly,* 1981, 12, 99–121.

Shavelson, R. *One psychologist's (not very representative) view of teachers' decisions about grouping students: Alia status.* A paper presented at the Annual Meeting of the American Educational Research Association, New York, 1982.

Tyler, F. Intra-individual variability. In N. Henry (Ed.), *The sixty-first yearbook of the National Society for the study of education,* (Part 1). Chicago: University of Chicago Press, 1962.

Veldman, D., & Sanford, J. The influence of class ability level on student achievement and classroom behavior (Tech. Rep.). Austin, Texas: Research and Development Center for Teacher Education, 1982.

Webb, N. *Predicting learning from student interaction: Defining the variables.* Paper presented at the Annual Meeting of the American Educational Research Association, New York City, 1982.

Weinstein, R. Reading group membership in first grade: Teacher behaviors and pupil experience over time. *Journal of Educational Psychology,* 1976, 68, 103–116.

—— *Expectations in the classrooms: The student perspective.* Paper presented at the Annual Meeting of the American Educational Research Association, New York City, 1982.

Comments on the article by
Lou, Abrami, Spence, Poulsen, Chambers, and d'Apollonia

In this meta-analysis of cooperative learning research, the authors provide us with an up-to-date synthesis of quantitative research concerning different aspects of within-class grouping of students for instruction. Specifically, the authors ask three broad questions about the use of cooperative learning strategies in the classroom:

1. How much, if any, does placing students in small groups facilitate their learning and other outcomes, such as attitudes and self-concept?
2. Which factors explain variability in study findings?
3. Which type of grouping is best and under what conditions?

As noted by the authors, research on the effectiveness of cooperative learning has been conducted for quite some time. In fact, the section of this paper entitled "Within-Class Grouping Then and Now" nicely contextualizes some of the other, older papers which are included in this volume. In an attempt to make sense of the variability of findings by individual studies, the authors conducted a careful and systematic analysis of the existing research literature.

Combining the results from 51 studies involving a total of 16,073 students, the authors conclude that "On average, students learning in small groups within classrooms achieved significantly more than students not learning in small groups." Perhaps more interesting however, are the large number of factors which were identified which moderated the effects of within-class grouping on student achievement. Teacher training, grouping strategies, group size, intensity of treatment, subject area, and many other issues were examined in this meta-analysis for their possible effects on achievement outcomes.

In addition to performance measures, outcomes other than achievement (in particular student attitudes and student self-concept) were analyzed and reported separately in this meta-analysis.

Discussion Questions

1. Do you find a meta-analysis such as this more or less convincing than a single careful study? Why?
2. What are the authors' conclusions relating the "treatment intensity" and positive effects of within-class grouping?
3. What conclusions do the authors draw about the effects of within-class grouping on attitudes and self concept? How do these outcomes compare in importance with achievement?
4. The authors report that "Within-class grouping positively affected student learning in all subject areas." The effects were not uniform across all subject areas, however. What conclusions were drawn about mathematics in particular? Why might this be the case?
5. The authors state that "No review of empirical research can resolve differences in educational policy which arise from differences in educational values and philosophy." How does this assertion relate to pedagogical choices you make in college-level mathematics courses?

Within-Class Grouping: A Meta-Analysis[†]

Yiping Lou, Philip C. Abrami, John C. Spence, Catherine Poulsen, Bette Chambers, Sylvia d'Apollonia

Contemporary classrooms are notable for the number and diversity of students who occupy them. Economic pressures in many regions have resulted in increased class sizes. Detracking or destreaming, the mainstreaming of students with special needs, and the reduction of special programs for gifted students make it likely that teachers face students who have a broad spectrum of needs, abilities, goals, and interests and who may differ along racial, ethnic, linguistic, and economic lines. The mosaic of students who populate classrooms means that teachers face difficult pedagogical decisions if students are to learn effectively and enjoyably. One decision concerns whether to group students for instruction within class and teach them accordingly.

The term *small-group instruction* has different meanings. In the loosest sense it means the physical placement of students into groups for the purposes of learning. Gamoran (1987) refers to this placement as the organizational structure of the classroom. In the strictest sense, however, small-group instruction means the use of specific instructional strategies when students are placed together to learn. Gamoran refers to this as the instructional processes occurring within classes and groups. In this article we will use the term *small-group instruction* in the loosest sense and interchangeably with *within-class grouping* and *intraclass grouping,* although we also attempt to explore the influence of instructional strategies on small groups.

The effects of within-class grouping have been the focus of educational research for some time. However, individual study findings appear quite varied and therefore call for a careful and systematic review. Previous meta-analyses (Kulik & Kulik, 1987, 1991; Slavin, 1987)[1] explored whether within-class grouping was superior to whole-class instruction in promoting student learning. While positive effects of grouping were reported in each review, the average effects were not consistent in size. Slavin (1987) reported an average effect size of +0.32; Kulik and Kulik (1987) reported an average effect size of +0.17, while Kulik and Kulik (1991) reported an average effect size of +0.25. Furthermore, the samples of studies included were small and varied from review to review (7 in Slavin, 1987; 15 in Kulik & Kulik, 1987; 11 in Kulik & Kulik, 1991). In addition, the reviews concentrated on the effects of within-class grouping versus no grouping; the effects of homogeneous grouping and heterogeneous grouping were not compared. Finally, no review determined whether the set of findings was uniform or probed the effects to determine when grouping was best and under what conditions.

[†] *Review of Educational Research,* Winter 1996, vol. 66, no. 4, pp. 423–458. Copyright © 1996 by the American Educational Research Association. Reprinted by permission of the publisher.

Therefore, the primary objective of this study is to integrate quantitatively the research findings on the effects of within-class grouping and to explain study-to-study variability in outcomes. Specifically, we ask three broad questions about grouping. First, how much, if any, does placing students in small groups facilitate their learning and other outcomes, such as attitudes and self-concept? Second, which factors explain variability in study findings? Third, which type of grouping is best and under what conditions? In sum, our meta-analysis is designed to be more comprehensive and thorough than previous reviews.

Arguments for Whole-Class Instruction

Whole-class instruction means the students are taught as a single, large group. In whole-class instruction, there is an emphasis on the uniformity of instruction rather than on the diversity of instruction. For example, it is common for the teacher utilizing whole-class instruction to provide a single, detailed explanation to the class followed by the assignment of individual seatwork. In whole-class instruction, the emphasis is on teacher explanations and encouragement, rather than on peer explanations and encouragement, to promote student learning. There are several reasons for utilizing whole-class instruction. First, the uniformity of instruction means that teachers may spend preparation time on developing a single set of instructional materials appropriate to the content to be learned rather than spend time developing many sets of materials. Second, whole-class instruction means that teachers may emphasize a single set of instructional objectives for all students, objectives which are sometimes encountered in a required or core curriculum. The adherence to specified objectives also implies a fixed pace of instruction for all students. Third, teachers may utilize their content and pedagogical expertise to explain new material orally to all students. Students may use seatwork to practice the skills taught by the instructor and to explore content further. Thus, learning may be facilitated by direct instruction from the teacher (since instructional time is maximized) and by guided, individual practice. Fourth, students may be motivated to learn by tangible or symbolic incentives provided by the teacher, which sometimes places students in competition with one another to excel. Fifth, whole-class instruction means that all students may be exposed to the same learning opportunities, emphasizing the open, democratic principles of the educational system and the realities of life in a world that operates according to the survival of the fittest.

Arguments for Small-Group Instruction

Small-group instruction means that a class of students is taught in several small groups. In small-group instruction, there is often an emphasis on diversity of instruction rather than on uniformity of instruction. The teacher may provide either a single, brief explanation to the class as a whole or give different instructions to each group. The teacher may either assign the same seatwork to each group or vary the assignment from group to group. In small-group instruction, peer helping is often encouraged to promote student learning. There are several reasons for utilizing small-group instruction. First, the emphasis on peer learning means that the teacher may have more time to provide either remedial assistance to students experiencing difficulties or enrichment activities to students who have already mastered prescribed content. Second, using within-class grouping means that teachers may have greater flexibility in adjusting the learning objectives and the pace of instruction to meet individual learning needs. Using homogeneous ability groups means that the teacher can increase the pace and level of instruction for high achievers and provide more individual attention, repetition, and review for low achievers. Third, students in small groups may engage in such activities as orally rehearsing material, explaining material to others, discovering solutions, and debating and discussing content and procedural issues. Thus, teachers may capitalize on the social aspects of cognitive growth (Piaget, 1954; Vygotsky, 1978) emphasizing the development of higher-order thinking skills. Fourth, students who learn together in small groups may be motivated by cooperative, as opposed to competitive, incentive structures. Fifth, small-group instruction means that students may have the opportunity to develop social and communication skills because of the need and opportunity to work with others to learn.

Within-Class Grouping Then and Now

While classroom teachers have been dividing students into learning groups for some time, the research evidence is more recent. Few studies existed at the time of Petty s (1953b) review, but the situation changed thereafter. In the late 1950s and 1960s, researchers most often examined the effects of homogeneous within-class grouping where teachers would divide a class into subgroups for specific activities and purposes, especially for elementary instruction in reading and sometimes for instruction in mathematics.

In a typical study, Dewar (1963) explored the effects of within-class grouping on the learning of arithmetic among classes of sixth-grade students. Each class was divided into three groups on the basis of test results, school records, and teacher judgment. Membership in the groups remained constant for the term, and teachers used specially prepared materials along with textbooks from Grades 4–8. The highest-scoring students used sixth-, seventh-, and eighth-grade materials; the middle-scoring groups used fifth-, sixth, and seventh-grade materials; and the lowest-scoring groups used fourth-, fifth-, and sixth-grade materials. Each teacher spent almost an hour per day on mathematics instruction. The teacher presented material to a group for approximately 15 minutes before moving on to another group. While the teacher was presenting material to one group, all other groups worked on their assignments.

By the late 1970s and 1980s, researchers were again examining the effects of within-class grouping, but with a particular emphasis on cooperative learning. In many of these studies, teachers would most often divide students into heterogeneous ability groups.

Cooperative learning is one form of small-group instruction which utilizes both positive interdependence and individual accountability to encourage students to learn (Abrami et al., 1995). Positive interdependence exists when individual accomplishments contribute positively to the accomplishments of others—for example, when the members of a group all receive the same recognition for the group's accomplishments. Individual accountability exists when students are responsible for their own learning and the learning of other group members—for example, when each member of a group has clear tasks or roles to accomplish.

In a typical study, Bejarano (1987) compared the effects of a cooperative learning technique known as Student Teams and Achievement Divisions (STAD) with those of whole-class instruction. The STAD technique had several components: (a) assignment of students to teams, where each team consisted of members who were heterogeneous in ability; (b) brief, whole-class instruction; (c) team study using worksheets common to all teams; (d) individual quizzes; (e) calculation of quiz results in the form of improvement points noting personal gains; and (f) team recognition based on the combination of individual improvement points. Of particular note, the STAD technique emphasized both an individual's responsibility for his or her own learning and the importance of contributing to the learning success of teammates.

Duration and Composition of Within-Class Groups

Teachers may use small groups for only a portion of class time, for only a fraction of a semester, or for selected activities. For example, Coldiron, Braddock, and McPartland (1987) found that almost all (about 90%) elementary school students in Pennsylvania were exposed to within-class ability grouping for reading, but only about one third of the students were exposed to grouping in mathematics. These dif-

ferences in pervasiveness and duration are worth exploring to find the optimal conditions for small-group instruction and to test for the presence of novelty effects.

Grouping for instruction can be accomplished in a variety of ways. Students may be self-assigned, randomly assigned, or instructor assigned to groups. Groups may be formed on the basis of (a) common interests, common skills, or friendships or (b) diverse interests, diverse skills, or unfamiliarity. Groups formed on the basis of common interests may be intrinsically motivated to work together to learn. Homogeneous ability groups may encourage learning as students attempt to maintain a pace commensurate with other group members. Friendship groups may be motivated to learn by the effects of group cohesiveness. In contrast, groups formed on the basis of diverse interests may enhance learning if multiple perspectives facilitate goal attainment or stimulate creative controversy. Heterogeneous ability groups may foster learning through the use of elaborated explanations whereby the more able students tutor the less able ones. Placing strangers together may better integrate all students into the classroom milieu, avoid outcasts, and teach students tolerance, acceptance, and strategies for working successfully with a diversity of partners.

Clearly, one issue underlying group composition is whether or not groups should be heterogeneously composed according to ability, interests, liking, gender, ethnicity, and so on. Unfortunately, a scant number of studies exist to integrate findings on group composition criteria other than relative ability or prior achievement. This may be satisfactory if relative ability is the most salient quality to consider when forming groups. Wilkinson (1986), however, concluded that teachers need to consider many factors when they assign students to instructional groups and that individual students' needs and characteristics, such as developmental level, are the most important.

In the absence of sufficient primary research, this integration is restricted to an examination of the extent to which small groups composed of students who are relatively similar in ability or prior achievement achieve in comparison to small groups composed of students who are relatively dissimilar in ability or prior achievement. In addition, the integration explores the extent to which type of ability grouping affects learning for students relatively high in ability, medium or average in ability, and low in ability.

A second issue in group composition concerns the nature of the task required of students learning in small groups. Noddings (1989) argued that the composition of classroom groups interacts with the nature of the learning task to affect student learning. For many academic tasks, Noddings noted that teachers frequently assign students to homogeneous ability groups, such as traditional reading groups.

In traditional reading and other group activities, student placement can be relatively stable and long-term, depending almost entirely on the results of initial achievement or ability testing (Hallinan, 1984). Across homogeneous groups, the nature of the task and pace of learning often require adjustment to suit the learners. If adjustments are not made it is possible that (a) some groups will be unable to accomplish the task because no member has the requisite skills for learning, and (b) some groups will too readily accomplish the task because all members have already acquired the skills which the task was designed to develop. Indeed, Kulik and Kulik (1991) concluded that homogeneous within-class grouping would be pointless without adapting the curriculum materials to the needs and abilities of students in each group.

Noddings (1989) also noted that when the task is a typical academic one and groups are heterogeneously formed, the group members often turn to the most able student for help. When this happens, there may be little interaction and limited engagement, thereby minimizing understanding even though students appear to get the answer right. Webb (1989) also found that merely giving or receiving answers was insufficient and could interfere with learning if and when such behavior circumvented cognitive engagement. Giving and receiving elaborated explanations, on the other hand, was positively related to achievement.

Methodological Considerations

Good and Marshall (1984) commented on the tendency for studies to manipulate factors along with small-group instruction. For example, curriculum and teaching method were not always held constant across conditions. In some studies, teachers were requested to keep content and teaching method the same. In other studies, special materials and pace were made available for students according to their group placement. In yet other studies, teachers using small groups were given special training, while control teachers using whole-class instruction were not.

One solution to the problem of confounded effects is to exclude studies where grouping method varies with other factors. Slavin (1987) dealt with the confounding problem in exactly this way. His review of studies of gifted and special education students excluded studies in which curriculum, class size, resources, and goals varied along with the between-class grouping plan. He found no large effects in the studies that remained. Critics (e.g., Allan, 1991) responded that this finding was used by educational administrators to make decisions about all special education and gifted programs, including those not studied. For the comparison of small-group instruction to no grouping, we did not exclude studies in which grouping practices, in-

struction, and curriculum varied. Instead, we attempted to identify, code, and analyze the effects of factors that varied along with the use of small-group instruction.

Policy Issues in Grouping Students for Instruction

There are strong and emotional arguments both for (e.g., Allan, 1991) and against (e.g., Oakes, 1985) between-class grouping. Many of the arguments about group composition between classes apply to within-class grouping. For example, there is a concern that it is unethical to stigmatize low-ability students by using a system of within-class tracking whereby students are segregated according to ability or prior achievement. In particular, there is the fear that low-ability students placed in homogeneous ability groups will be denied opportunities to learn and be unmotivated to learn because of peer, personal, and teacher expectations of poor performance.

On the other hand, there is a concern that it is unethical to retard the achievement of high-ability students by assigning them to heterogeneous within-class groups, in which students are integrated according to ability. In particular, there is the fear that high-ability students placed in heterogeneous groups will be denied opportunities to learn because much of the material has already been mastered by them, because the pace of learning in the group is below their capacity, and because their role in the group is not to learn but to instruct less able students.

No review of empirical research can resolve differences in educational policy which arise from differences in educational values and philosophy. For example, in an early narrative review of the literature on within-class grouping, Petty (1953b) argued that grouping students for instruction was then viewed as "a democratic instructional procedure designed to adapt the curriculum and learning environment to the abilities and needs of individual pupils and to provide appropriate means for fostering their continuous development" (p. 7). More recently, other (e.g., Rosenbaum, 1976) have argued that the use of ability grouping may serve to increase divisions along ethnic, racial, and class lines.

Still others (Good & Marshall, 1984; Kulik & Kulik, 1987) have noted that these values change over time. For example, during the 1950s "excellence" was a byword in education, and between-class grouping was seen as beneficial for high-ability students. In the 1960s and 1970s, concerns about equal opportunity increased, and between-class grouping was seen as beneficial for high-ability students. In the 1960s and 1970s, concerns about equal opportunity increased, and between-class grouping was seen as harmful for disadvantaged students. What a review can do is help inform policy by exploring the empirical basis of beliefs which underlie a particular philosophy and by suggesting directions for future research if the evidence is lacking. The present review was undertaken, in part, with this purpose in mind.

Method

This meta-analysis primarily examined the effects of within-class grouping on student achievement at the elementary, secondary, and postsecondary levels. However, outcomes other than achievement were included, when they were available, and analyzed separately. Two groups of studies were identified and analyzed independently. Analysis 1 included studies which compared within-class grouping with no grouping. Analysis 2 included studies which directly compared homogeneous within-class grouping with heterogeneous within-class grouping. The procedures employed to conduct the quantitative integrations are outlined below under the following headings: Literature Search, Inclusion/Exclusion Criteria, Study Features Coding, Number of Findings Extracted, Effect Size Calculations, and Data Analyses.

Literature Search

The studies used in this meta-analysis were located via a comprehensive search of the literature. Electronic searches were performed on the ERIC (1966–1994), PsycLIT (1974–1994), Sociofile (1974–1994), Dissertation Abstracts (1965–1994), and Social Sciences Citation Index (1989–1994) databases. Although the search strategy varied depending on the database, search terms included *group composition, grouping for instructional purposes, small group, team learning, team instruction, heterogeneous/homogeneous grouping, group structure, ability grouping, peer tutoring,* and *cooperative learning.* Through branching from primary studies and review articles, other citations were found and included. In total, the search uncovered over 3,000 published articles concerning within-class grouping.

Inclusion/Exclusion Criteria

To be included in this review a study had to meet the following criteria.

(1) The research must have occurred within the classroom at the elementary, secondary, or postsecondary school level. Consequently, within-class grouping studies of organizational behavior (e.g., in a business setting) or social psychology (e.g., group therapy) were excluded.

(2) The research had to involve within-class ability grouping, either homogeneous ability grouping or heterogeneous ability grouping. The same teacher had to instruct a classroom of groups that were working in close proximity to one another. Studies were not included if they involved between-class tracking or grouping in a laboratory setting outside the classroom.

(3) The minimum group size was 2 students, and the maximum group size was 10 students.

(4) Grouping had to be in place for more than 1 day. Thus, studies involving only one session (e.g., a 1-hour lesson) were not included.

(5) If training of any kind was offered to the students, then all group members must have received it.

(6) The research had to report measured outcomes from both experimental and control groups. Studies reporting only single-group pretest and posttest comparisons were initially coded, but the results were eventually excluded for two reasons. First, the methodological shortcomings inherent in this design make unambiguous interpretations of outcomes tenuous. Second, the gain score results from these studies were significantly different from the results of studies employing experimental and control groups. One-shot case studies were also excluded a priori on methodological grounds.

(7) Achievement, attitudes, and self-concept were included, but each was analyzed separately. Classroom behaviors and interrelationships among measures were initially included but not analyzed for this meta-analysis.

(8) Finally, research primarily involving either children with learning disabilities or enrichment programs for gifted students were excluded.

The searches identified more than 500 studies on cooperative learning (cf. Johnson & Johnson, 1989), most employing heterogeneous grouping. In order to balance the number of grouping studies using this instructional method with grouping studies using other instructional methods, we included only those studies identified by the search term *cooperative learning* and the term *homogeneous/heterogenous grouping* or *ability grouping or group composition.*

Most studies on peer tutoring were excluded because we considered the group dynamics of tutoring to be quite different from other grouping methods. Members of peer tutoring dyads often functioned as learner (tutee) and teacher (tutor), effectively creating learning groups of one. Also, tutors often received special training and extra rewards (e.g., free time during a regular class, extra credit, etc.). Therefore, studies of cross-age/cross-class tutoring, tutoring outside classrooms or for remuneration, and one-way tutoring (i.e., one tutor taught one student) were excluded.

Studies	Slavin (1987)[*]	Slavin (1990)[*]	Kulik & Kulik (1987)[*]	Kulik & Kulik (1991)[*]	The present meta-analysis		
					Analysis	Outcome	Reason for excluding
Abu (1993)					1b	A,B	
Allen & VanSickle (1984)					1b	A,C	
Amaria et al. (1968)					1a, 1b, 2	A	
Armstrong (1993)					2	A,C	
Ballman (1988)					1b	A	
Bejarano (1987)					1b	A	
Berge (1990)					1b	A	
Bierden (1970)			x				II
Blaney et al. (1977)					1b	B,C	
Bright et al. (1980)					2	A	
Campbell (1964/1965)		x	x	x	1a	A	
Carter & Jones (1993)					2	A	
Chang (1993)					1b	A,B,C	
Cignetti (1974)			x	x	1a	A	
DeVries & Edwards (1973)					1b	B	
Dewar (1963)	x		x	x	1a	A	
Eddleman (1971)			x	x			III
Evans (1942)					1a	A	
Fantuzzo et al. (1990)					1a	A	
Hallinan & Sorensen (1985)					1a	A	
Harrah (1955/1956)		x	x		2	A	
Hay (1980/1981)					1b	A	
Heller & Fantuzzo (1993)					1b	A,B,C	
Hudgins (1960)					1b	A	
Hulten & DeVries (1976)					1b	A,B,C	
Janicki & Peterson (1981)					1b	A,B	
Johnson et al. (1979)					1b	A,B	
Jones (1948)	x		x	x	1a	A	
Kamil & Rauscher (1990)					1a	A	
Kassem (1990)					1b	A,B	
Kenny (1975)					1b	A,B	
Knupfer (1993)					2	A	
Krieder (1992)					1b	A,B	
Lawrenz (1985)/Lawrenz & Munch (1984)					2	A,B	
Macdonald et al. (1966)					1a	A,B,C	
Marita (1965)					1a	A,B	
McHugh (1959)					1a	A	
Mehta (1993)					1b	A	
Merritt (1972)					1a	A,B,C	
Mevarech (1985)					1b	A	
Mevarech (1991)					1b	A	
Mevarech & Susak (1993)					1b	A	
Monroe (1922)			x				I
Moody & Gifford (1990)					2	A	
Mortlock (1969)			x		1a	A	

Studies	Slavin (1987)[*]	Slavin (1990)[*]	Kulik & Kulik (1987)[*]	Kulik & Kulik (1991)[*]	The present meta-analysis		
					Analysis	Outcome	Reason for excluding
Park (1993)					1a	A,B	
Peterson & Janicki (1979)					1b	A,B	
Peterson et al. (1981)					1b	A,B	
Petty (1953a, 1953b)					1a	A	
Putbrese (1971/1972)			x	x	1a	A	
Sandby-Thomas (1983)					1a	A	
Shields (1927)			x	x			I
Slavin (1978)					1b	A,B,C	
Slavin & Karweit (1984a)					1b	A	
Slavin & Karweit (1984b, 1985)	x		x	x			I
Smith (1960/1961)	x		x	x	1a	A	
Spence (1958)	x		x	x			I
Stern (1971/1972)	x				1a	A,B	
Terwel et al. (1994)					1b	A	
Tingle & Good (1990)					1b	A	
Wallen & Vowels (1960)	x		x	x	1a	A	
Watson (1988)					1b	A	
Webb (1982a)					2	A	
Webb (1982b)					2	A	
Webb (1984)					2	A	
Webb et al. (1990)					1b	A	
Wright & Cowen (1985)					1b	A,B,C	
Yager et al. (1985)					1b	A	
Yueh & Alessi (1988)					2	A	
Ziegler (1981)					1b	A,B	
Zisk (1993)					1b	C	

Note. For analysis: 1a = homogeneous ability grouping versus no grouping, 1b = heterogeneous ability grouping versus no grouping, 2 = homogeneous ability grouping versus heterogeneous ability grouping. For outcome: A = achievement, B = attitudes, C = self-concept. For reason for excluding: I = group size > 10, II = within-group design, III = study confounds group composition with other factors.

[*] Only one type of analysis (namely, homogeneous ability grouping versus no grouping) and only one type of outcome (namely, student achievement) were included in Slavin's (1987, 1990) and Kulik and Kulik's (1987, 1991) meta-analyses on within-class grouping.

TABLE 1
Within-class grouping studies included in the previous and present meta-analyses

However, paired learning and reciprocal tutoring, in which two students alternated between the roles of tutor and tutee, were included.

Studies on group-based mastery learning were included if they met the inclusion/exclusion criteria (e.g., students were placed together in small groups for the purposes of learning, group size smaller than 10, etc.). Thus, group-based mastery learning studies were excluded if students did remediation or enrichment work individually.

Using the above criteria, abstracts from electronic searches and references from primary studies and reviews were first examined by two researchers to identify potential studies to include. Differences between the independent judgments of the two researchers were resolved through discussion. If there was a doubt, the study was collected. Next, the collected studies were each read by two researchers for possible inclusion. Any study that was considered for exclusion by one researcher was cross-checked by the other researcher. Sixty-six studies met the inclusion criteria and were included in this review. Table 1 lists the studies included in this meta-analysis, those included in previous meta-analyses, and the reasons for study exclusions. Six studies that were included in Slavin (1987, 1990) or Kulik and Kulik (1987, 1991) were excluded for failing to meet one or more of the criteria specified here.

Study Features Coding

Literature reviews are often unnecessary when the findings on a phenomenon appear uniform across studies. Instead, it is the apparent inconsistency of findings that motivates the search for factors which explain differences among studies. The purpose of coding study features is to identify those methodological and substantive characteristics which may be responsible for significant variations in the findings. In this review, nomological coding was used first to objectively identify salient study features in the literature, thereby avoiding reviewer bias (Abrami, Cohen, & d'Apollonia, 1988; Abrami, d'Apollonia, & Cohen, 1990). Features with more than three substantive occurrences in a random sample of 25% of the primary literature and review articles were included for nomological coding. Forty-five study features were initially identified and were organized into three major categories: outcome features, methodological features, and substantive features. Outcome features were generally concerned with the nature of the dependent measures analyzed in the study. Methodological features were generally concerned with the quality of the research design and the fidelity of the treatment. Substantive features included grouping characteristics, instructor and instructional characteristics, student characteristics, setting, and scope. Unfortunately, many features had too few cases to be included in the analyses and were subsequently dropped. (See Table 2 for a description of the 26 study features that were coded and used in this review.)

Study features coding was performed independently by two coders. Their initial coding agreement was 88.24%. Disagreements between the two coders were resolved through discussion and further review of the disputed studies.

Number of Findings Extracted

Effect sizes were extracted and are reported separately for each major outcome category, primarily achievement but also student attitudes and self-concept. For each major outcome category, several effect sizes were often extracted from a single study as long as they were distinguishable at the level of study features (e.g., effect sizes reported separately for each of three grade levels). When not distinguishable by any study feature, effect sizes were averaged. Multiple effect sizes extracted from single studies can be problematic because methods of research integration normally assume that effect sizes are independent. This problem is, in our opinion, not especially pronounced when different subjects from a study provide separate measures of effect size. Such a condition arises in factorial designs, for example, when different effect sizes are extracted for male and female participants. In our analyses, each effect size was weighted by sample size, so that a study with two effect sizes based on 50 subjects each had the same overall weight as a study with a single effect size based on 100 subjects.

Dependence among effect sizes is pronounced when the same subjects from a study provide separate measures of effect size—a situation where within-group or repeated factors are present. For example, in this review we collected achievement data measured at mid-treatment, posttest, and delayed posttest. Ignoring the dependence and treating the within-group effects as independent would increase the Type I error rate of the homogeneity of effect size tests (i.e., tests of the variability in effect sizes) (Gleser & Olkin, 1994). Discarding the data would have the opposite effect, increasing the likelihood of committing a Type II error. In this meta-analysis, the problem was overcome by taking a single, random sample from the set of correlated effect sizes per feature for each affected study. This had the desirable effect of ensuring that all levels of a study feature were represented. For example, for the analysis of measure source, the selection of within-group findings was made randomly from among outcomes based on standardized tests, teacher-made tests, and researcher-made tests. This method was applied after all the study findings had been extracted and coded.

The study findings were extracted by two coders separately. The initial coding agreement on the number of findings to extract per study was 80.29%. Disagreements between the coders were resolved through subsequent discussion and further review of the disputed findings. Overall, there were 266 findings extracted prior to random sampling within studies. After random sampling, 165 independent findings were selected for analysis.

Effect Size Calculations

The basic index used for the effect size calculation was the mean of the experimental group minus the mean of the control group divided by the pooled standard deviation (PSD). The main reason for using the PSD is that often the assumption of homogeneity of variance in the population is reasonable, in which case the PSD is more stable and provides a better estimate of the population variance than the control group SD alone (Hedges & Olkin, 1985; Hunter & Schmidt, 1990; Rosenthal, 1991). Another reason for the choice of the PSD is that estimated effect sizes based on incomplete results (e.g., t values, F values, ANOVA tables, or p levels) are more readily comparable to calculated effect sizes. Finally, the PSD is a more appropriate measure when it is unclear which group is the control condition, such

Study feature	Description
	Outcome features
Measure source	Was the outcome measure standardized, researcher made, or teacher made?
Measure type	What type of outcome was measured?
Contrast type	Which of three questions about grouping was explored: homogeneous grouping versus no grouping, heterogeneous grouping versus no grouping, or homogeneous grouping versus heterogeneous grouping?
	Methodological features
Student equivalence	What attempts were made to achieve the equivalence of students in experimental and control conditions?
Teacher equivalence	What attempts were made to achieve the equivalence of teachers in experimental and control conditions?
School equivalence	What attempts were made to achieve the equivalence of schools in experimental and control conditions?
Overall design quality	Using a composite of student equivalence, teacher equivalence, and school equivalence, what is the overall design quality?
Teacher training equivalence	Did experimental teachers receive more or different training than control teachers?
Materials equivalence	Did experimental groups receive more or different material than control groups?
Rewards/grades equivalence	Did the experimental groups experience different rewards or grade structures than the control groups?
Overall instructional equivalence	Using a composite of teacher training equivalence, materials equivalence, and rewards/grades equivalence, what is the overall instructional equivalence?
Publication bias	Was the study published or unpublished?
	Substantive features
	Grouping characteristics
Grouping basis	What method(s) of assessment was used to group students?
Grouping specificity	Was grouping based on specific or general measures?
Group size	What was the average number of students in groups?
Group stability	Did group members stay together throughout the implementation?
	Instructor characteristics
Experimental teacher training	What was the amount of training (or experience in the strategy) given to the experimental teachers?
	Instructional characteristics
Type of small-group instruction	Was a cooperative learning strategy used in the experimental condition?
Control method of instruction	What instructional method was used in the control condition?
Goal structure of control condition	What was the goal structure (competitive, individualistic) used in the control condition?
	Student characteristics
Relative ability of students	What was the relative ability level of students in the class?
	Setting
Subject area	What was the subject area studied by the students?
Grade level	What was the students' grade level?
Class size	What was the average class size?
	Scope
Duration of treatment	What was the length of the experimental treatment?
Intensity of treatment	What was the intensity of the experimental treatment (e.g., hours per week)?

Note. The following study features were also coded but dropped from analyses due to 90% missing data or almost no variability: whose outcome was measured, outcome measure timing, type of experimental design, student expectations about grouping, teacher expectations about grouping, teaching experience, teacher gender, experimental method of instruction, medium of instruction, absolute ability level of the class, homogeneity of class ability, student race, student socioeconomic status, student gender, student attitudes toward subject, student attitudes toward experimental method, student self-concept, student locus of control, and country of implementation.

TABLE 2
Study features coded

as occurs when heterogeneous grouping and homogeneous grouping are compared.

In studies that report posttest data only, we used the posttest mean difference in the numerator and the posttest PSD in the denominator. In studies that provided gain scores or both pretest and posttest data, we used the gain score difference in the numerator to control for pretest differences, but the posttest PSD was used in the denominator rather than the gain score PSD since the gain score PSD is usually smaller than the posttest PSD (Glass, McGaw, & Smith, 1981). When the posttest SDs were not provided in the study, we tried to estimate the posttest PSD whenever possible. Such estimation requires r, which is, unfortunately, not usually reported in studies. In one case, we obtained $r = .88$ for the Stanford Achievement Test (1953 revision) from the Fifth Mental Measurements Yearbook (Gage, 1959). In other cases, we had to estimate a 'typical' reliability for the class of measures based upon our knowledge of the literature. Specifically, we estimated $r = .85$ for standardized tests and $r = .75$ for unstandardized tests.

In two studies that used the Metropolitan Achievement Test and reported only grade equivalence data, we transformed the grade equivalence using a regression equation computed from technical information about the test (Hildreth, 1948). We also used means and SDs of the test norms to estimate the control group data for one study and the PSD for another study.

In studies that compared homogeneous grouping and heterogeneous grouping, the control group was the heterogeneous group. There were two reasons for this choice. First, the whole-class situation, which is a typical control condition, is usually heterogeneous. Second, meta-analyses on between-class ability grouping (e.g., Kulik & Kulik, 1987; Slavin, 1987) used the heterogeneous class as the control group.

Effect sizes from data in such forms as t tests, F tests, p levels, frequencies, and r values were computed via conversion formulas provided by Glass et al. (1981) and Hedges, Shymansky, and Woodworth (1989). When results were not significant, studies occasionally reported only a significance level. When the direction of the effect was not available, we estimated the effect size to be zero. For example, when the direction was reported, we used a 'midpoint' approach (Sedlmeier & Gigerenzer, 1989) to estimate a representative t value (i.e., midpoint between 0 and the critical t value for the sample size to be significant). Statistical tests were performed on preliminary data sets to check whether estimated and unestimated effect sizes might be different. The nonsignificance of the test results confirmed that this effect size estimating procedure was reasonable.

Formulas for calculating effect sizes were entered into the Excel (Microsoft Corporation, 1993) computer program. Raw data for each finding were extracted by two coders separately and then checked for reliability. The initial coding agreement between the two coders was 65.51%. Disagreements between the two coders were subsequently resolved through discussion and further review of the disputed study finding.

Data Analyses

Data screening was performed using the SPSS (1994) frequency and descriptive procedures. Several study features with over 90% missing data or almost no variability (e.g., almost all teachers had over 2 years of experience) were dropped from further analysis. Categories within some variables (e.g., group size, subject area, grade) were combined based on frequency distributions and the preliminary results from the homogeneity analyses.

The homogeneity tests (Hedges & Olkin, 1985) were performed using DSTAT (B. T. Johnson, 1989), a meta-analysis computer program designed to integrate findings and analyze their variability. Effect sizes extracted from studies were corrected for bias and weighted by their sample sizes via formulas provided by Hedges and Olkin (1985). This approach not only provided a sample size weighted estimate of the overall effect of within-class grouping, but also allowed testing for heterogeneity in the aggregated effect sizes. When the homogeneity of the effect sizes was rejected (i.e., a significant chi-square value was obtained for Q_T, further exploration of the findings was done through the analysis of study features. A significant Q_B indicated that the study feature significantly moderated the magnitude of the effect sizes. When there were more than two levels of a study feature, Scheffé, post hoc comparisons were performed to test for significant differences between levels. A significant Q_W for a level of the study feature indicated that the subset of effects sizes was heterogeneous.

Two major sets of analyses were performed. Analysis 1 involved effect sizes from studies that compared the effects of grouping with those of no grouping. Analysis 2 involved studies that directly investigated the effect of group ability composition on student achievement; no other outcomes could be analyzed. Effect sizes from these studies were based on direct comparisons of homogeneous ability grouping (i.e., students with a narrow range of relative abilities grouped together) with heterogeneous ability grouping (i.e., students with a wide range of relative abilities grouped together). Only three findings were extracted from studies in which method of instruction was confounded with group composition; these confounded effects were dropped from

	Type of analysis	
Outcome	Grouping vs. no grouping	Homogeneous grouping vs. heterogeneous grouping
Achievement	103 (51)	20 (12)
Attitudes	30 (21)	
Self-concept	12 (10)	

Note. Values in parentheses are the numbers of studies from which the findings were extracted. Some studies provided outcomes in more than one category.

TABLE 3
Maximum number of findings and studies analyzed per analysis for each category of outcomes

Analysis 2. Study features analyses were conducted for factors where sufficient variability existed.

Results

The outcome categories and analysis types extracted from each study are listed in Table 1. The number of independent findings and number of studies analyzed for each analysis type and outcome category are presented in Table 3.

Analysis 1: Grouping Versus No Grouping

For Analysis 1, three major categories of outcomes (achievement, attitudes, and self-concept) were examined separately for the effect of within-class grouping. Full study feature analyses were performed on the achievement data only. Insufficient data were available for such analyses on the other outcomes.

Overall Effects of Within-Class Grouping on Student Achievement. The overall effect of within-class grouping on student achievement was based on 103 independent effect sizes extracted from 51 studies involving a total of 16,073 students. Student achievement measures included general ability tests, standardized subject matter achievement tests, and locally developed or teacher-made achievement tests. The mean sample size weighted effect size $(d+)$ for within-class grouping was $+0.17$, which was significantly different from zero (95% confidence interval is $+0.16$ to $+0.23$). The mean effect size for the study findings randomly excluded from the analysis to avoid dependence problems was computed $(d+ = +0.20, n = 55)$ and was not significantly different from the effects included.

On average, students learning in small groups within classrooms achieved significantly more than students not learning in small groups. In general, average students (i.e., those at the 50th percentile) in small-group classrooms performed at slightly above average (i.e., at about the 57th percentile) compared to students learning in classrooms without grouping. However, the homogeneity test showed that the effect sizes were heterogeneous, $Q_T(103) = 431.62$, $p < .05$. Examination of the individual findings revealed 74 effect sizes above zero, 5 equal to zero, and 24 effect sizes below zero. The range of effect sizes was from a low of -1.96 to a high of $+1.52$. Therefore, further exploration of the findings through the analysis of study features was warranted and is presented below.

What Factors Moderate the Effect of Within-Class Grouping on Student Achievement? Study features analyses were performed on the 103 findings comparing the effects of homogeneous or heterogeneous grouping versus no grouping on achievement. Results of the analyses are described below in three major categories: outcome features, methodological features, and substantive features.

Outcome features. Table 4 presents the results of the homogeneity tests on several outcome features: measure

Variables	Q_B	n	$d+$	95% CI	Q_w
Measure source	70.02*	98			
Standardized tests		61	$+0.07$	$+0.03$ to $+0.11$	134.92*
Teacher-made tests		16	$+0.42$	$+0.26$ to $+0.59$	60.56*
Researcher-made tests		21	$+0.34$	$+0.28$ to $+0.39$	145.78*
Measure type	59.24*	103			
Not geared to instruction		56	$+0.08$	$+0.04$ to $+0.12$	137.83*
Geared to instruction		47	$+0.34$	$+0.29$ to $+0.39$	234.55*
Contrast type	0.94	103			

$^* p < .05$

TABLE 4
Outcome features analyses: Grouping versus no grouping findings

Variables	Q_B	n	$d+$	95%CI	Q_W
Student equivalence	5.83	103			
Teacher equivalence	0.13	99			
School equivalence	18.04*	86			
Experimental control		73	+0.12	+0.08 to +0.17	168.75*
Statistical control		13	+0.27	+0.22 to +0.33	196.96*
Overall design quality	3.38	103			
Teacher training equivalence	74.74*	56			
More or different		11	+0.42	+0.36 to +0.49	92.04*
Not different		45	+0.08	+0.04 to +0.13	138.73*
Materials equivalence	19.11*	69			
More or different		23	+0.26	+0.21 to +0.31	224.30*
Not different		76	+0.14	+0.10 to +0.18	188.70*
Rewards/grade equivalence	11.59*	99			
More or different		27	+0.29	+0.22 to +0.37	68.83*
Not different		51	+0.11	+0.06 to +0.15	154.39*
Overall instructional equivalence	18.78*	39			
Different treatment		23	+0.25	+0.19 to +0.31	83.89*
Not different treatment		16	+0.02	+0.07 to +0.11	27.68*
Publication bias	0.78	103			

    * $p < .05$

TABLE 5
Methodological features analyses: Grouping versus no grouping findings

source, measure type, and contrast type. Measure source was a significant predictor, $Q_B(2) = 70.02$, $p < .05$. Post hoc analyses indicated that the mean weighted effect sizes for researcher-made tests ($d+ = +0.34$) and teacher-made tests ($d+ = +0.42$) were both significantly higher than for standardized tests ($d+ = +0.07$). Measure type was also significant. The effect sizes were larger when outcome measures were specifically geared to instructional content ($d+ = +0.34$) than when the outcome measures were not geared to what was taught ($d+ = +0.08$).

No significant effect was found for contrast type. The mean effect of homogeneous grouping compared to no grouping ($d+ = +0.16$) was similar to the mean effect of heterogeneous grouping versus no grouping ($d+ = +0.19$). Both mean weighted effect sizes were significantly positive, yet each set of findings was not uniform. A significant amount of within-group variability remained within each type of grouping; for homogeneous grouping, $Q_W = 246.51$, $p < .05$, and for heterogeneous grouping, $Q_W = 184.17$, $p < .05$.

Methodological features. Analyses of nine methodological features are presented in Table 5. Overall design quality (a composite of student equivalence, teacher equivalence, and school equivalence between experimental and

control conditions) was not significantly related to the variability in effect sizes, $Q_B(1) = 3.38$, $p > .05$. Studies using either experimental control or statistical control showed significant positive effects for within-class grouping. However, overall instructional equivalence (a composite of teacher training equivalence, material equivalence, and reward equivalence between experimental and control conditions) was significantly related to the magnitude of the effect sizes. Greater achievement gains for within-class grouping occurred in studies that provided different instruction to the experimental condition ($d+ = +0.25$) than in studies that provided the same treatment ($d+ = +0.02$). Each of the three composite factors was significantly related to effect size variability. The effect of within-class grouping was higher when teachers in the grouped condition received more or different training as compared to those in the ungrouped condition ($d+ = +0.42$) than when teacher training was the same across conditions ($d+ = +0.08$). The within-class grouping effect was higher when grouped classes employed more or different materials as compared to ungrouped classes ($d+ = +0.26$) than when the same materials were used across the two conditions ($d+ = +0.14$). Similarly, the within-class grouping effect was higher when grouped classes implemented more or dif-

Variables	Q_B	n	$d+$	95%CI	Q_W
Grouping basis	68.84*	81			
Standardized tests		48	+0.10	+0.03 to +0.17	97.04*
Teacher tests or judgment		12	−0.02	−0.09 to +0.05	65.11*
Mixed sources		21	+0.33	+0.28 to +0.38	127.63*
Grouping specificity	18.12*	84			
Ability specific to subject		58	+0.19	+0.15 to +0.24	297.79*
General ability		9	+0.19	−0.02 to +0.40	13.79
Both specific & general ability		8	+0.10	+0.02 to +0.18	15.57*
Specific/general ability + other		9	+0.39	+0.28 to +0.49	18.62*
Group size	31.99*	92			
Pairs		13	+0.15	+0.06 to +0.24	34.94*
Small (3–4)		38	+0.22	+0.22 to +0.16	132.30*
Medium (5–7)		17	−0.02	−0.02 to −0.09	75.28*
Large (8–10)		24	+0.11	+0.01 to +0.21	32.78*
Group stability	0.14	40			

* $p < .05$

TABLE 6
Substantive features analyses (grouping characteristics): Grouping versus no grouping

ferent reward strategies as compared to ungrouped classes ($d+ = +0.29$) than when the same reward strategies were utilized across the two conditions ($d+ = +0.11$). Finally, whether findings were from published journals or from unpublished dissertations or reports was not related to the overall effect of within-class grouping.

Substantive features. Several groups of substantive features were analyzed. These were grouping characteristics, instructor characteristics, instructional methods, student characteristics, setting factors, and scope of the treatment.

Table 6 presents the results of the study features analyses on *grouping characteristics*. First, grouping basis was significantly related to the variability in effect sizes. Post hoc comparisons indicated that the mean weighted effect size was significantly higher when grouping was based on mixed sources ($d+ = +0.33$) than on either standardized tests alone ($d+ = +0.10$) or teacher-made tests or teacher judgement alone ($d+ = -0.02$). Second, grouping specificity significantly explained variability in the effect sizes. The mean effect size was highest when grouping was based on assessment of specific or general ability plus other factors ($d+ = +0.39$). Third, group size was significantly related to the magnitude of the effect sizes; the average effect size for 3–4 member groups ($d+ = +0.22$) was significantly higher than that for 5–7 member groups ($d+ = -0.02$). Finally, group stability did not significantly explain the variability in the effect sizes.

Study features analyses on *instructor and instructional characteristics* are presented in Table 7. Teacher experience with, or amount of training received for, the experimental treatment was related to the magnitude of the effect sizes. The average effect size was +0.17 for no experience or training, +0.24 for information only, +0.31 for minimal training or experience, and +0.57 for extensive training or experience. All four effect sizes were significantly different from zero. The average effect size for moderate experience or training was +0.02, which was not significantly different from zero.

The experimental method of instruction explained a significant amount of variability in effect sizes, $Q_B(9) = 42.96$, $p < .05$, but there were too few cases to reliably examine most methods. Consequently, we divided the studies into two types of small-group instruction: cooperative learning and other. Type of instruction was significantly related to the size of the treatment effect. Small groups using cooperative learning with outcome interdependence ($d+ = +0.28$) achieved significantly higher than other small groups without outcome interdependence ($d+ = +0.15$).

The method of instruction used in the control condition was also significantly related to the size of the grouping effect. The effect of placing students in small groups was superior when the control method of instruction was either traditional, frontal teaching ($d+ = +0.24$) or individualized mastery learning ($d+ = +0.15$). However,

Variables	Q_B	n	$d+$	95%CI	Q_W
Experimental teacher training	55.72*	61			
None		2	+0.17	+0.06 to +0.28	0.25
Info. only		9	+0.24	+0.15 to +0.34	22.13*
Minimal		36	+0.31	+0.25 to +0.36	160.74*
Moderate		11	+0.02	−0.05 to +0.08	74.42*
Extensive		3	+0.57	+0.32 to +0.82	0.23
Type of small-group instruction	10.27*	103			
Cooperative learning		25	+0.28	+0.21 to +0.34	57.63*
Other		77	+0.15	+0.11 to +0.19	360.70*
Control method of instruction	56.46*	102			
Traditional		77	+0.24	+0.20 to +0.28	314.36*
Individualized mastery learning		15	+0.15	+0.07 to +0.24	20.88
Other		10	−0.12	−0.20 to −0.03	36.90*
Goal structure of control condition	0.51	67			

* $p < .05$

TABLE 7
Substantive features analyses (instructor and instructional characteristics): Grouping versus no grouping findings

Variables	Q_B	n	$d+$	95%CI	Q_W
Relative ability of students	6.20*	53			
Low		24	+0.37	+0.30 to +0.44	104.44*
Medium		11	+0.19	+0.06 to +0.32	26.35*
High		18	+0.28	+0.15 to +0.41	47.07*
Subject area	4.52*	103			
Math/science		65	+0.20	+0.16 to +0.24	316.02*
Reading/language arts/other		38	+0.13	−0.09 to +0.18	111.08
Grade level	27.55*	98			
Early elementary (1–3)		30	+0.08	+0.02 to +0.14	157.81*
Late elementary (4–6)		36	+0.29	+0.24 to +0.35	132.05*
Secondary (7–12)		25	+0.17	+0.12 to +0.23	85.98*
Postsecondary		7	+0.19	−0.03 to +0.42	8.55
Class size	46.70*	103			
Small (less than 25)		33	+0.22	+0.17 to +0.27	114.80*
Medium (26–35)		50	+0.06	+0.01 to +0.11	178.46*
Large (more than 35)		20	+0.35	+0.28 to +0.42	91.66*
Duration of treatment	0.34	103			
Intensity of treatment	14.49*	103			
Low ($\leq$ 1 period/week)		40	+0.08	+0.03 to +0.14	141.83*
High (> 1 period/week)		63	+0.22	+0.18 to +0.25	275.30*

* $p < .05$

TABLE 8
Substantive features analyses (student characteristics, setting, and scope): Grouping versus no grouping findings

when within-class grouping was compared to other methods of instruction such as experiential learning, within-class grouping was not superior ($d+ = -0.12$). Finally, the goal structure (competitive, individualistic) used in the control condition was not related to effect size variability.

Table 8 presents the results of the study features analyses of *student characteristics, setting, and scope of the treatment*. The relative ability of students was significantly related to the within-class grouping effect sizes. $Q_B(2) = 6.20$, $p < .05$. While low-ability students,

Variables	n	$d+$	95%CI	Q_T
Overall student attitudes	30	+0.18	+0.13 to +0.23	327.04*
Attitudes toward subject	16	+0.18	+0.13 to +0.24	280.76*
Attitudes toward instructional approach	5	−0.13	−0.33 to +0.06	18.39*
Other attitudes	9	+0.26	+0.14 to +0.37	16.15
Overall student self-concept	12	+0.09	−0.00 to +0.19	11.11
General self-concept	6	+0.16	+0.02 to +0.31	3.33
Academic self-concept	6	+0.04	−0.09 to +0.16	6.15

* $p < .05$

TABLE 9
Overall effects of within-class grouping on other student outcomes: Grouping versus no grouping findings

medium-ability students, and high-ability students all benefitted from being placed in small groups ($d+ = +0.37$, +0.19, and +0.28, respectively), the effects were not uniform. In particular, low-ability students achieved significantly more than medium-ability students.

Within-class grouping positively affected student learning in all subject areas. However, the effect of within-class grouping was significantly larger in math and science ($d+ = +0.20$) than in reading, language arts, and other courses ($d+ = +0.13$). We were able to identify studies on within-class grouping at grade levels ranging from first grade to college, but the number of studies at any one level was small, and the findings appeared variable. The largest effect sizes were obtained in the late elementary grades (Grades 4–6; $d+ = +0.29$). Within-class grouping had a significantly positive effect for small (less than 25), medium (26–35), and large (more than 35) classes. The grouping effect was stronger in larger classes ($d+ = +0.35$) than in small ($d+ = +0.22$) or medium ($d+ = +0.06$) classes.

Whether the experimental treatment was brief (less than 4 weeks), medium (4 to 16 weeks), or long (more than 17 weeks) was not significantly related to the size of the effect. However, treatment intensity seemed to be a significant moderator of the grouping effect. The effect was larger in studies of high treatment intensity (more than 1 period per week, $d+ = +0.22$) than in studies of low treatment intensity (less than or up to 1 period per week, $d+ = +0.08$).

Overall Effects of Within-Class Grouping on Other Student Outcomes. The literature included a sufficient number of studies to allow a rudimentary exploration of the relationship between the use of within-class grouping and outcomes other than achievement. The mean effect sizes for student attitudes and self-concept are reported below.

Student attitudes. Thirty independent findings extracted from 21 studies compared student attitudes from within-class groups with student attitudes in no-grouping conditions. Measures of student attitudes included attitudes toward the subject matter, the instructional approach, and others (peers, school, etc.). Results of the homogeneity analyses on student attitudes are presented in Table 9. Overall, within-class grouping was positively related to student attitudes ($d+ = +0.18$, 95% confidence interval is +0.13 to +0.23). In particular, students in the grouped classes had significantly more positive attitudes toward the subject matter concerned ($d+ = +0.18$). However, attitudes toward the instructional approach were not significantly different between students in the grouped and ungrouped classes.

Student self-concept. Ten studies investigated the effects of within-class grouping on student self-concept. From those studies, 12 independent findings were extracted and analyzed (see Table 9). Measures of self-concept included general self-concept and domain-specific academic self-concept. Overall, the mean weighted effect size for student self-concept was +0.09, which is not significantly different from zero (95% confidence interval is −0.00 to +0.19). However, students in grouped classes had significantly higher general self-concept than students in the ungrouped classes ($d+ = +0.16$). Domain-specific academic self-concept was not significantly different between the grouped and ungrouped classes.

Analysis 2: Homogeneous Grouping Versus Heterogeneous Grouping

Twenty findings from 12 studies directly compared the effects of homogeneous ability grouping with heterogeneous ability grouping. All the studies employed interactive small-group learning. Methods of instruction were held constant

Variables	Q_B	n	$d+$	95%CI	Q_W
Type of small-group instruction	1.48	20			
Relative ability of students	11.42*	13			
Low		4	−0.60	−1.11 to −0.09	7.27
Medium		4	+0.51	+0.11 to +0.90	1.72
High		5	+0.09	−0.25 to +0.42	0.56
Subject area	8.61*	20			
Math/science		16	−0.00	−0.15 to +0.14	25.74
Reading		4	+0.36	+0.16 to +0.55	9.55*

* $p < .05$

TABLE 10
Study features analyses: Homogeneous ability grouping versus heterogeneous ability grouping findings

across the two conditions. Most studies employed experimental designs and implemented equivalent instructional treatments in terms of teacher training, reward strategies, and curriculum materials across the two conditions.

Overall Effect of Group Ability Composition on Student Achievement. The weighted mean effect size for group ability composition was +0.12, which is significantly different from zero (95% confidence interval is +0.01 to +0.24). Thus, the result of aggregating the 20 independent effect sizes indicated a slight superiority of homogeneous ability groups over heterogeneous ability groups in promoting student achievement. However, the slight superiority of homogeneous ability grouping was not uniform across findings, $Q_T(19) = 43.90$, $p < .05$. The effect sizes ranged from −1.75 to +1.12, with 13 effect sizes above zero favoring homogeneous ability groups, 1 effect size equal to zero, and 6 effect sizes below zero favoring heterogeneous ability groups. The heterogeneity of the effect sizes, therefore, warranted further analyses, which are presented in Table 10.

Moderators of the effects of group ability composition. There were sufficient differences in the design of the group composition studies to explore three study features. One of these, type of small-group instruction, did not explain variability in the effect sizes. The small advantage of homogeneous grouping compared to heterogeneous grouping was not modified by whether students learned cooperatively with outcome interdependence or students learned in small groups without outcome interdependence.

However, the effects of group ability composition were different for students of different relative ability. While low-ability students learned significantly more in heterogeneous ability groups than homogeneous ability groups ($d+ = −0.60$), medium-ability students benefitted significantly more in homogeneous ability groups than in het-

erogeneous ability groups ($d+ = +0.51$). For high-ability students, group ability composition made no significant difference ($d+ = +0.09$). Furthermore, the Q_Ws for the three mean effect sizes reported were all homogeneous, which indicated consistent and meaningful findings within each subset of results.

Subject area of instruction was also a significant moderator of the effect of group ability composition. In math and science, the effect of group ability composition was not significantly different from zero; overall, homogeneous groups performed as well as heterogeneous groups. However, four effect sizes compared homogeneous ability groups with heterogeneous ability groups in reading, and the mean effect size (d+ = +.36) revealed that, on average, homogeneous ability groups learned significantly more than heterogeneous ability groups in reading.

Discussion

This study quantitatively synthesized the literature on the effects of within-class grouping on student achievement, attitudes, and self-concept. The results complement and greatly extend the findings reported in other research integrations (Kulik & Kulik 1987, 1991; Slavin, 1987). Each of the reviews, including this one, reported positive effects of within-class grouping. Our review included far more studies, evaluated student learning and other outcomes, explored variability in study findings, and examined studies that directly compared types of small-group composition.

The results of this meta-analysis suggest that there are small but positive effects of placing students in groups within the classroom for learning. On average, students placed in small groups achieved more, held more positive attitudes, and reported higher general self-concept than students in nongrouped classes. However, the magnitude of the effect sizes varied across findings. Several study features significantly moderated the effect of within-class grouping on student achievement. These study features included outcome measure source and type, instructional treatment equivalence of the control and experimental groups, type of small-group instruction and amount of teacher training in the experimental condition, type of instructional method in the control condition, grouping basis and specificity, group size, group ability composition, relative ability of students, subject area, grade level, class size, and intensity of treatment.

Outcome Measure Source and Type

Measuring achievement by locally developed tests or by standardized tests can produce significantly different treatment effects. This phenomenon has been noticed by several meta-analysts. For example, Rosenshine and Meister (1994) in their review of reciprocal teaching found a significantly higher effect size for experimenter-made tests than standardized tests. One explanation Rosenshine and Meister offered was that experimenter-made tests were generally easier to answer, or more instructionally sensitive, than standardized tests. The topics in the experimenter-made tests were discussed during instruction, whereas those in the standardized tests were unfamiliar to the students.

In this meta-analysis, we found that the effect of small-group learning was much higher when achievement was measured with teacher-made tests than when researcher-made tests were used. Achievement measured with researcher-made tests was, in turn, higher than that measured with standardized tests. Similarly, we also showed that the effect sizes were higher when the outcome measures were geared to instruction than when they were not geared to instruction. Therefore, one explanation for the difference between locally developed tests and standardized tests is that teacher-made tests may have a closer match with local instructional objectives than researcher-made tests or standardized tests. Similarly, researcher-made tests may have a closer match to the local instructional objectives than standardized tests. Thus, locally made tests may reflect the large influence of within-class grouping on proximal instructional objectives, while standardized tests may reflect the small influence of within-class grouping on distal instructional objectives.

Another possible explanation is that teacher-made and researcher-made tests may be biased in favor of the experimental group. If the goal of the research is to measure acquisition of local instructional objectives, care should be taken to ensure that the tests measure what has been taught in both experimental and control conditions.

Instructional Treatment and Teacher Training

Differential instructional treatments can significantly moderate the effect of within-class grouping. Ungrouped classes usually employed a single set of materials for all the students in the class, but that did not always occur in grouped classes. In some studies, teachers employed the same set of materials for all the groups as well as the control classes; in others, teachers employed different materials across groups. The effect sizes were higher when instructional materials were varied for different groups than when the same set of materials was used for all the students. One argument for using small groups is to provide instruction which better meets the learning needs of individual students. Varying the instructional material is one means of providing more adaptive instruction (Kulik & Kulik, 1991).

The type of small-group instruction used in the experimental classes can moderate the achievement effects of within-class grouping. Often in cooperative small-group instruction, group members are positively interdependent for their learning outcomes. Each member contributes to the overall group goal and receives some form of group reward. The results of this meta-analysis suggest that small groups appeared to learn more when there was outcome interdependence among the group members.

Amount of training given to experimental and control teachers can significantly moderate the effect of within-class grouping. The largest effect sizes occurred in studies where the experimental teachers received much more or very different training than the control teachers. Even so, when teacher training was held constant across the control and experimental teachers, there was still a small positive effect for within-class grouping.

One anomaly to the linear effect of training occurred for teachers with moderate amounts of training. One tentative explanation is that teachers with little training adapt the new method to their existing practices and teaching philosophy, while teachers with extensive training adapt their practices and teaching philosophy to the new method. Teachers with moderate training may make neither adaptation successfully, which would minimize the benefits of small groups.

There were also variations in the instructional methods used in the ungrouped control classes. Within-class grouping had a significantly positive effect on student learning when compared with traditional whole-class instruction and individual seatwork or individualized mastery learning. However, when within-class grouping was compared with other methods of instruction (e.g., experiential whole-class learning), it was not always superior.

Overall, it appears that the positive effects of within-class grouping are maximized when the physical placement of students into groups for learning is accompanied by modifications to teaching methods and instructional materials. Merely placing students together is not sufficient for promoting substantive gains in achievement. Consequently, Slavin's (1987) practice of discarding studies where grouping method is confounded with other factors should be viewed with caution, since it may well remove not only instructionally relevant studies but those with the largest effects.

Grouping Strategies: Grouping Basis, Group Size, and Group Stability

Teachers employed a variety of strategies in grouping students for learning. Some groups were formed using standardized test results; others were formed using teacher-made test results or teachers' knowledge of students' abilities. Some group formations were based on general ability or specific ability in a subject matter, and others on a mixture of considerations. The basis and specificity on which small groups were formed significantly moderated the effect of within-class grouping on student achievement. Larger effects occurred when group formation was based on mixed sources and involved more considerations than ability alone. Just as the classroom or school is a social community, the small group where students learn together is also a small social community. Group interaction may be more positive when groups are cohesive, and teacher judgments of compatibility may help groups function well (Cohen, 1994).

Optimally sized groups for learning seem to be small, 3- to 4-member teams. While pairs achieved significantly more than students in ungrouped classes, the large, 6- to 10-member groups did not learn significantly more than students from ungrouped classes. Finally whether groups stayed together or changed members over time was not significantly related to the effect of within-class grouping on student achievement.

Subject Area and Class Size

The magnitude of the within-class grouping effect varied according to subject area and class size. There were larger effects of within-class grouping in math and science than in reading, language arts, and other courses. This may be due to the different nature of the learning tasks involved in these subject areas. Tasks in math are usually more hierarchical (i.e., where the level and complexity of the material to be learned must be adjusted to suit differences in the prior knowledge of students). Specific assistance from peers may help students progress through such hierarchical learning faster.

Large classes seemed to benefit more from within-class grouping. Grouping may provide a means for more adjusted instruction to the students in these classes and possibly greater opportunities for peer interaction and more active engagement of each pupil.

Group Ability Composition and the Relative Ability of Students

Group ability composition had a differential effect on student learning. In general, homogeneous ability groups achieved more than heterogeneous ability groups in studies that directly compared them. However, the superiority of homogeneous ability composition is not uniform for students of different relative ability. While low-ability students learned significantly more in heterogeneous ability groups than in homogeneous ability groups, medium-ability students benefited significantly more in homogeneous ability groups than in heterogeneous ability groups. For high-ability students, group ability composition made no significant difference.

Several mediational mechanisms are plausible explanations for these findings. First, according to Webb (1982a, 1982b, 1984), learning in small groups depends on giving and receiving explanations. Giving explanations helps tutors clarify and organize their own learning better. Receiving elaborated explanations helps tutees correct misconceptions and learn appropriate learning strategies. Not receiving an explanation—that is, receiving no response at all or receiving simply the answer—reduces achievement. Low-ability students may gain most in heterogeneous groups from having other students provide them with timely and elaborated homogeneous assistance and guidance. In contrast, when low-ability students are placed in homogeneous groups there may be no student capable of providing those explanations. High-ability students may benefit from being placed in heterogeneous groups to the extent that they are often called upon to provide elaborated explanations by their less able peers. Medium-ability students, however, may act neither as tutor nor tutee and, therefore, neither give nor receive explanations. Consequently, heterogeneous grouping is not as beneficial for these students. Homogeneous grouping may be better for medium-ability students because they may share in giving and receiving explanations among themselves.

Second, group cohesiveness can lead to increased performance by enhancing members' commitment to the group task (Mullen & Copper, 1994). In contrast to heterogeneous grouping, homogeneous grouping may be particularly conducive to group cohesiveness since students may share similar expectations about group goals. Medium-ability and high-ability students may especially benefit without compromising their aspirations or pace of learning to accommodate the lower ability students.

Third, adaptation of instruction may be important in realizing the benefits of homogeneous grouping. Appropriate tailoring of instruction for low-ability students may place extraordinary demands on the teacher. Furthermore, it may well be the case that low-ability students placed in homogeneous groups may suffer if the demands for learning are set too low; if these students feel isolated, inadequate, or incompetent; or if the teacher has negative performance expectations. Medium-ability groups may require the least adaptation of regular teaching materials and therefore exhibit the previously mentioned benefits of homogeneous grouping. Finally, high-ability students in homogeneous groups may work through the regular material at a faster pace and may challenge one another to elaborate their learning further.

Overall, then, we found no evidence that one form of grouping was *uniformly* superior for promoting the achievement of all students. Low-ability students gained most from being placed in heterogeneous groups with students who might provide them with individual guidance and assistance. The assistance provided may, in turn, be beneficial for the tutors in helping them develop a deeper, more structured understanding of the material. In contrast, medium-ability students gained most from being placed in homogeneous groups. For these students, sharing in giving and receiving explanations, high group cohesiveness, and appropriate instructional materials may be important factors and should be explored further.

Speculations, Limitations, and Future Directions

The myriad of factors which may distinguish among classroom grouping practices eventually come to influence one of two interrelated processes: students motivation to learn and students' processing, acquisition, and retention of information. Exploring these factors helps to understand the superiority of an instructional practice and the conditions for optimal implementation. But grouping practices themselves do not directly affect motivation and learning; it depends on how they are used.

For example, it is generally accepted that teacher, peer, and personal expectations influence student goal setting and motivation to learn. Teachers using whole-class instruction may negatively influence student expectations if they selectively encourage students to excel, give students unequal opportunities for responding, and praise (or criticize) students differentially when they are correct (or incorrect) according to ability (Cooper & Good, 1983). But if teachers provide equitable opportunities and proportionally uniform praise or otherwise exhibit facilitative behaviors

and attitudes, then the expectations of most students may be raised. Similarly, teachers using small-group instruction may positively influence student expectations if they assign group tasks that depend on the contributions of all students (Abrami et al., 1995). But if teachers assign group tasks that depend on the contribution of only the brightest students, the individual expectations for learning of most students may suffer.

Similarly, peer influences may either facilitate or discourage student performance. Students may establish a culture that promotes academic goals and achievement. In contrast, students may challenge teachers, obstruct academic activity, and misuse educational resources. These deleterious effects may be more likely in whole-class instruction when relatively weak students defend themselves against public academic humiliation and failure, but they are not unheard of in small groups (e.g., Salomon & Globerson, 1989). Abrami, Chambers, d'Apollonia, Farrell, and De Simone (1992) found negative effects of heterogeneous small-group learning for low-ability and learned helpless students whose groups had not succeeded at the learning task. They suggested that both self-deprecation and blame from teammates combine to provide a double disincentive for these students. In contrast, homogeneously grouped low achievers may suffer from a lack of appropriately behaving role models, which may increase the likelihood that they will mimic one another's off-task behaviors (Felmlee & Eder, 1983).

In undertaking this review, we attempted to explore the instructional and learning processes which distinguish whole-class instruction from small-group instruction and among heterogeneous and homogeneous small groups. However, the complexity of these processes and the paucity of evidence limited the extent to which we were successful. Now that we have moved closer to determining whether within-class grouping is effective, when it is effective, and with whom it is effective, it is time to devote greater energy to understanding why it is effective. We hope this review sets the stage for such inquiry.

We caution the reader that this meta-analysis, like others, does not allow one to make strong causal inferences, particularly with regard to explanatory features. Not only were we unable to extract information from every study about the existence of particular factors, which reduces the sensitivity of the analyses, but the study features were often intercorrelated while the heterogeneity within categories of study features were not resolved in many cases, which makes unambiguous interpretation impossible and untempered conclusions unwise.

It is possible that factors not identified by us or the primary researchers may explain some of the variability in study findings. It is also possible that some of the variability may be explained by substantive and methodological features which correlate or interact with those we identified. For example, in those studies comparing grouping with no grouping, the superiority of cooperative learning over other methods of instruction may be explained or exaggerated by the extra recent teacher training often involved in undertaking the former method. Contrariwise, it may be that differences in classroom experience with cooperative versus other methods attenuate the size of the relationship with study findings. Such explanations could not be adequately tested by us; they await verification through additional primary research.

Conclusions and Recommendations

The practice of within-class grouping is supported by the results of this review. Within-class grouping appears to be a useful means to facilitate student learning, particularly in large classes and especially in math and science courses. Small teams of three to four members seem more effective than larger groups. Low-ability students benefit most when placed in mixed-ability groups, but medium-ability students benefit most in relatively homogeneous ability groups. Cooperative learning with outcome interdependence helps facilitate small-group learning. Furthermore, teacher training in, and experience with, small-group instructional strategies helps maximize student learning. Finally, the best within-class grouping practices combine the physical placement of students into groups with the adaptation of instruction methods and materials for small-group learning.

Note

[1] Slavin (1990) also quantitatively reviewed the research on the effects of ability grouping on the achievement of secondary students. While the review focused on the effects of between-class grouping, Slavin also summarized the findings of several studies of within-class grouping, but without reporting effect sizes, and concluded that the effects of within-class grouping were largely nonsignificant.

References

References marked with an asterisk indicate studies included in the meta-analysis.

Abrami, P.C., Chambers, B., d'Apollonia, S., Farrell, M., & De Simone, C. (1992). Group outcome: The relationship between group learning outcome, attributional style, academic achievement, and self-concept. *Contemporary Educational Psychology, 17*, 201–210.

Abrami, P.C., Chambers, B., Poulsen, C., De Simone, C., d'Apollonia, S., & Howden, J. (1995). *Classroom connections: Understanding and using cooperative learning.* Toronto, Ontario, Canada: Harcourt-Brace.

Abrami, P.C., Cohen, P.A., & d'Apollonia, S. (1988). Implementation problems in meta-analysis. *Review of Educational Research, 58,* 151–179.

Abrami, P.C., d'Apollonia, S., & Cohen, P.A. (1990). Validity of student ratings of instruction: What we know and what we do not. *Journal of Educational Psychology, 82,* 219–231.

*Abu, R. B. (1993). The effects of cooperative learning methods on achievement, retention, and attitudes of selected vocational home economics students (Doctoral dissertation, North Carolina State University, 1993). *Dissertation Abstracts International, 54,* 3350A.

Allan, S. D. (1991). Ability-grouping research reviews: What do they say about grouping and the gifted? *Educational Leadership, 48,* 60–74.

*Allen, W.H., & VanSickle, R.L. (1984) Learning teams and low achievers. *Social Education, 48,* 60–64.

*Amaria, R.P., Biran, L.A., & Leith, G.O.M. (1968). Individual versus cooperative learning: Part 1–Influence of intelligence and sex, *Educational Research, 2,* 95–103.

*Armstrong, N. (1993). The effects of cooperative learning on gifted students in heterogeneous and homogeneous groups (Doctoral dissertation, Ball State University, 1993). *Dissertation Abstracts International, 54,* 2457A.

*Ballman, T.L. (1988). Is group work better than individual work for learning Spanish?: The findings of one study. *Hispania, 71,* 180–185.

*Bejarano, Y. (1987). A cooperative small group methodology in the language classroom. *TESOL Quarterly, 21,* 483–504.

*Berge, Z.L. (1990). Effects of group size, gender, and ability grouping on learning science process skills using microcomputers. *Journal of Research in Science Teaching, 27,* 747–759.

Bierden, J.E. (1970). Behavioral objectives and flexible grouping in seventh grade mathematics, *Journal for Research in Mathematics Education, 1,* 207–217.

*Blaney, N.T., Stephan, C., Rosenfield, D., Aronson, E., & Sikes, J. (1977). Interdependence in the classroom: A field study. *Journal of Educational Psychology, 69,* 121–128.

*Bright, G.W., Harvey, J.G., & Wheeler, M.M. (1980). Achievement grouping with mathematics concept and skill games. *Journal of Educational Research, 73,* 265–269.

*Campbell, A.L. (1965). A comparison of the effectiveness of two methods of class organization for the teaching of arithmetic in junior high school (Doctoral dissertation, Pennsylvania State University, 1964). *Dissertation Abstracts International, 813.*

*Carter, G., & Jones, M. G. (1993, April). *The relationship between ability paired interactions and the development of fifth graders' concept of balance.* Paper presented at the annual conference of the National Association for Research in Science Teaching, Atlanta, GA (ERIC Document Reproduction Service No. ED 361 175)

*Chang, S. (1993). The effect of group reward on student motivation, interaction, emotion, and achievement in cooperative learning small groups (Doctoral dissertation, University of California, Los Angeles, 1993). *Dissertation Abstracts International, 55,* 906A.

*Cignetti, M.J. (1974). A study of intraclass grouping and traditional groupings on students' terminal achievements during the last nine weeks in first semester typewriting (Doctoral dissertation, University of Pittsburgh, 1974). *Dissertation Abstracts International, 35,* 5765A.

Cohen, E. (1994). Restructuring the classroom: Conditions for productive small groups. *Review of Educational Research, 64,* 1–35.

Coldiron, J.R., Braddock, J.H., & McPartland, J.M. (1987, April). *A description of school structures and practices in elementary, middle, and secondary schools.* Paper presented at the Annual Meeting of the American Educational Research Association, Washington, DC.

Cooper, H.M., & Good, T.L. (1983). *Pygmalion grows up: Studies in the expectation communication process.* New York: Longman.

*DeVries, D.L., & Edwards, K.J. (1973). Learning games and student teams: Their effects on classroom process. *American Educational Research Journal, 10,* 307–318.

*Dewar, J.A. (1963). Grouping for arithmetic instruction. *Elementary School Journal, 63,* 266–269.

Eddleman, V.K. (1971). A comparison of the effectiveness of two methods of class organization for arithmetic instruction in grade five (Doctoral dissertation, Northeast Louisiana University, 1971). *Dissertation Abstracts International, 32,* 1744A.

*Evans, M.M. (1942). *The effect of variance grouping on reading achievement.* Unpublished doctoral dissertation, University of Pittsburgh.

*Fantuzzo, J.W., Polite, K., & Grayson, N. (1990). An evaluation of reciprocal peer tutoring across elementary school settings. *Journal of School Psychology, 28,* 309–323.

Felmlee, D., & Eder, D. (1983). Contextual effects in the classroom: The impact of ability groups on student attention. *Sociology of Education, 56,* 77–87.

Gage, N.L. (1959). Stanford achievement test. In O. K. Buros (Ed.), *The fifth mental measurements yearbook* (pp. 76–80). Highland Park: The Gryphan Press.

Gamoran, A. (1987). Organization, instruction, and the effects of ability grouping: Comment on Slavin's "best-evidence synthesis." *Review of Educational Research, 57,* 341–345.

Gleser, L.J., & Olkin, I. (1994). Stochastically dependent effect sizes. In H. Cooper & L. V. Hedges (Eds.), *The handbook of research synthesis* (pp. 339–355). New York: Russell Sage Foundation.

Glass, G.V., McGaw, B., & Smith, M.L. (1981). *Meta- analysis in social research.* Beverly Hills, CA: Sage.

Good, T.L., & Marshall, S. (1984). Do students learn more in heterogeneous or homogeneous groups? In P. Peterson, L.C. Wilkinson, & M. Hallinan (Eds.), *The Social context of instruction: Group organization and group processes* (pp. 15–38). Orlando, FL: Academic Press.

Hallinan, M. (1984). Summary and conclusions. In P. Peterson, L.C. Wilkinson, & M. Hallinan (Eds.), *The social context of instruction: Group organization and group processes* (pp. 229–240). Orlando, FL: Academic Press.

*Hallinan, M.T., & Sorensen, A.B. (1985). Ability grouping and student friendships. *American Educational Research Journal, 22,* 485–499.

*Harrah, D.D. (1956). A study of the effectiveness of five kinds of grouping in the classroom (Doctoral dissertation, University of Virginia, 1955). *Dissertation Abstracts International, 16,* 715.

*Hay, J.A. (1981). Effects of cooperative goal structuring on sixth grade science students' abilities to initiate task and maintenance group behaviours (Doctoral dissertation Michigan State University, 1980). *Dissertation Abstracts International, 41,* 3857A.

Hedges, L.V., & Olkin, I. (1985). *Statistical methods for meta-analysis.* Orlando, FL: Academic Press.

Hedges, L.V., Shymansky, J.A., & Woodworth, G. (1989). *A practical guide to modern methods of meta-analysis* (Report No. ISBN-0-87355-081-1). (ERIC Document Reproduction Service No. ED 309 952).

*Heller, L.R., & Fantuzzo, J.W. (1993). Reciprocal peer tutoring and parent partnership: Does parent involvement make a difference? *School Psychology Review, 22,* 517–534.

Hildreth, G.H. (1984). *Manual for interpreting Metropolitan Achievement Tests.* Yonkers, NY: World Book Company.

*Hudgins, B.B. (1960). Effects of group experience on individual problem solving. *Journal of Educational Psychology, 51,* 37–42.

*Hulten, B.H., & DeVries, D.L. (1976). *Team competition and group practice: Effects on student achievement and attitudes* (Rep. No. 212). (ERIC Document Reproduction Service No. ED 154 021)

Hunter, E.J., & Schmidt, F.L. (1990). *Methods of meta-analysis: Correcting error and bias in research findings.* Newbury Park, CA: Sage.

*Janicki, T.C., & Peterson, P.L. (1981). Aptitude treatment interaction effects of variations in direct instruction. *American Educational Research Journal, 18,* 63–82.

Johnson, B.T. (1989). DSTAT, software for the meta-analytic review of research literatures [Computer software]. Hillsdale, NJ: Erlbaum.

Johnson, D.W., & Johnson, R.T. (1989). *Cooperation and competition: Theory and research.* Edina, MN: Interaction Book.

Johnson, D.W., Johnson, R.T., & Skon, L. (1979). Student achievement on different types of tasks under cooperative, competitive, and individualistic conditions. *Contemporary Educational Psychology, 4,* 99–106.

*Jones, D.M. (1948). An experiment in adaptation to individual differences. *Journal of Educational Psychology, 39,* 257–273.

*Kamil, M.L., & Rauscher, W.C. (1990). Effects of grouping and difficulty of materials on reading achievement. *National Reading Conference Yearbook, 39,* 121–127.

*Kassem, C.L. (1990). *Cooperative versus individualistic learning strategies for undergraduate teaching: A comparative study.* Unpublished doctoral dissertation, Georgia State University, College of Education.

*Kenny, P.F. (1975). *Effects of group interaction stimulated by competition between groups as a motivating technique in a ninth grade mathematics classroom: Final report.* Washington, DC: National Institute of Education, Department of Health, Education, and Welfare, Office of Research, Basic Studies Division. (ERIC Document Reproduction Service No. ED 103 266)

*Knupfer, N.N. (1993). Logo and transfer of geometry knowledge: Evaluating the effects of student ability grouping. *School Science and Mathematics, 93,* 360–368.

*Kreider, P.S. (1992). Achievement in physical science using cooperative mastery learning (Doctoral dissertation, Florida Institute of Technology, 1992). *Dissertation Abstracts International, 53,* 3861A.

Kulik, J.A., & Kulik, C.-L. C. (1987). Effects of ability grouping on student achievement. *Equity and Excellence, 23,* 22–30.

Kulik, J.A., & Kulik, C.-L.C. (1991). *Research on ability grouping: Historical and contemporary perspectives.* Storrs: University of Connecticut, National Research Center on the Gifted and Talented. (ERIC Document Reproduction Service No. ED 350 777)

*Lawrenz, F. (1985). Aptitude treatment effects of laboratory grouping method for students of differing reasoning ability. *Journal of Research in Science Teaching, 22,* 279–287.

*Lawrenz, F.P., & Munch, T.W. (1984). The effect of grouping of laboratory students on selected educational outcomes. *Journal of Research in Science Teaching, 21,* 699–708.

*Macdonald, J.B., Harris, T.L., & Mann, J.S. (1966). Individual versus group instruction in first grade reading. *The Reading Teacher, 19,* 646–652.

*Marita, S.M. (1965). *A comparative study of beginning reading achievement under three classroom organizational patterns: Modified individualized, three to five groups, and whole class language experience.* Milwaukee, WI: Marquette University. (ERIC Document Reproduction Service No. ED 003 477)

*McHugh, W.J. (1959). Team learning in skills subjects in intermediate grades. *Journal of Education, 142,* 22–51.

*Mehta, J.I. (1993). Cooperative learning in computer programming at the college level (Doctoral dissertation, University of Illinois at Chicago, 1993). *Dissertation Abstracts International, 54,* 1309A.

*Merritt, P.W. (1972). *The effects of variations in instruction and final unit evaluation procedures on community college beginning algebra classes.* Unpublished doctoral dissertation, University of Michigan, Ann Arbor.

*Mevarech, Z.R. (1985). The effects of cooperative mastery learning strategies on mathematical achievement. *Journal of Educational Research, 78,* 372–377.

*—— (1991). Learning mathematics in different mastery environments. *Journal of Educational Research, 84,* 225–231.

*Mevarech, Z.R., & Susak, Z. (1993). Effects of learning with cooperative mastery method on elementary students. *Journal of Educational Research, 86,* 197–205.

Microsoft Corporation. (1993). Microsoft Excel (Version 5.0a) [Computer software]. Redmond, WA: Author.

Monroe, W.S. (1922). *Relation of sectioning a class to the effectiveness of instruction* (Bulletin No. 11). Urbana: University of Illinois, College of Education, Bureau of Educational Research.

*Moody, J.D., & Gifford, V.D. (1990, November). *The effect of grouping by formal reasoning ability, formal reasoning ability levels, group size, and gender on achievement in laboratory chemistry.* Paper presented at the annual meeting of the Mid-South Educational Research Association, New Orleans, LA. (ERIC Document Reproduction Service No. ED 326 443)

*Mortlock, R.S. (1969). Provision for individual differences in eleventh grade mathematics using flexible grouping based on achievement of behavioral objectives: An exploratory study (Doctoral dissertation, University of Michigan, 1969). *Dissertation Abstracts International, 30,* 3643A.

Mullen, B., & Copper, C. (1994). The relationship between group cohesiveness and performance: An integration. *Psychological Bulletin, 115,* 210–227.

Noddings, N. (1989). Theoretical and practical concerns about small groups in mathematics. *Elementary School Journal, 89,* 607–623.

Oakes, J. (1985). *Keeping track: How schools structure inequality.* New Haven, CT: Yale University Press.

*Park, I.H. (1993). Cooperative learning and individual learning with computer-assisted instruction in an introductory university level chemistry course (Doctoral dissertation, University of Texas at Austin, 1993). *Dissertation Abstracts International, 54,* 2972A.

*Peterson, P.L., & Janicki, T.C. (1979). Individual characteristics and children's learning in large-group and small-group approaches. *Journal of Educational Psychology, 71,* 677–687.

*Peterson, P.L., Janicki, T.C., & Swing, S.R. (1981). Ability × treatment interaction effects on children s learning in large-group and small-group approaches. *American Educational Research Journal, 18,* 453–473.

*Petty, M.C. (1953a). *Intraclass grouping in the elementary school.* Unpublished doctoral dissertation, University of Texas, Bureau of Laboratory Schools.

*Petty, M.C. (1953b) *Intraclass grouping in the elementary school.* Austin: University of Texas Press.

Piaget, J. (1954). *The construction of reality in the child.* New York: Ballatine Books.

*Putbrese, L.M. (1972). An investigation into the effects of selected patterns of grouping upon arithmetic achievement (Doctoral dissertation, University of South Dakota, 1971). *Dissertation Abstracts International, 32,* 5113A.

Rosenbaum, J.E. (1976). *Making inequality: The hidden curriculum of high school tracking.* New York: Wiley.

Rosenshine, B., & Meister, C. (1994). Reciprocal teaching: A review of the research. *Review of Educational Research, 64,* 479–530.

Rosenthal, R. (1991). *Meta-analytic procedures for social research* (Rev. ed.). Newbury Park, CA: Sage.

Salomon, G., & Globerson, T. (1989). When teams do not function the way they ought to. *International Journal of Educational Research, 13,* 89–99.

*Sandby-Thomas, M. (1983). The organization of reading and pupil attainment. *Journal of Research in Reading, 6,* 29–40.

Sedlmeier, P., & Gigerenzer, G. (1989). Do studies of statistical power have an effect on the power of studies? *Psychological Bulletin, 105,* 309–316.

Shields, J.M. (1927). Teaching reading through ability- grouping. *Journal of Educational Methods, 7,* 7–9.

*Slavin, R.E. (1978). Student teams and comparison among equals: Effects on academic performance and student attitudes. *Journal of Educational Psychology, 70,* 532–538.

—— (1987). Ability grouping and student achievement in elementary schools: A best-evidence synthesis. *Review of Educational Research, 57,* 293–336.

—— (1990). Achievement effects of ability grouping in secondary schools: A best-evidence synthesis. *Review of Educational Research, 60,* 471–499.

*Slavin, R.E., & Karweit, N.L. (1984a). Mastery learning and student teams: A factorial experiment in urban general mathematics classes. *American Educational Research Journal, 21,* 725–736.

—— (1984b, April). *Within-class ability grouping and student achievement.* Paper presented at the Annual Meeting of the American Educational Research Association, New Orleans, LA.

—— (1985). Effect of whole class, ability grouped, and individualized instruction on mathematics achievement. *American Educational Research Journal, 22,* 351–367.

*Smith, W.M. (1961). The effect of intra-class ability grouping on arithmetic achievement in grades two through five (Doctoral dissertation, Louisiana State University, 1960). *Dissertation Abstracts International, 21,* 563.

Spence, E.S. (1958). Intra-class grouping of pupils for instruction in arithmetic in the intermediate grades of the elementary school (Doctoral dissertation, University of Pittsburgh, 1958). *Dissertation Abstracts International, 58,* 5635.

SPSS, Inc. (1994). SPSS 6.1 for Windows update [Computer software]. Chicago: Author.

*Stern, A.M. (1972). Intraclass grouping of low achievers in mathematics in the third and fourth grades (Doctoral dissertation, University of California, 1971). *Dissertation Abstracts International, 32,* 5539A.

*Terwel, J., Herfs, P.G.P., Mertens, E.H.M., & Perrenet, J.C. (1994). Cooperative learning and adaptive instruction in a mathematics curriculum. *Journal of Curriculum Studies, 26,* 217–233.

*Tingle, J.B., & Good, R.G. (1990). Effects of cooperative grouping on stoichiometric problem solving in high school chemistry. *Journal of Research in Science Teaching, 27,* 671–683.

Vygotsky, L.S. (1978). Mind in society: *The development of higher mental processes.* Cambridge, MA: Harvard University Press.

*Wallen, N.E., & Vowles, R.O. (1960). The effect of intraclass ability grouping on arithmetic achievement in the sixth grade. *Journal of Educational Psychology, 51,* 159–163.

*Watson, S.B. (1988). *Cooperative learning and group educational modules: Effects on cognitive achievement of high school biology students.* Unpublished doctoral dissertation, University of South Florida, Tampa, FL.

*Webb, N.M. (1982a). Group composition, group interaction, and achievement in cooperative small groups. *Journal of Educational Psychology, 74,* 475–484.

*Webb, N.M. (1982b). Peer interaction and learning in cooperative small groups. *Journal of Educational Psychology, 74,* 642–655.

*Webb, N.M. (1984). Stability of small group interaction and achievement over time. *Journal of Educational Psychology, 76,* 211–224.

Webb, N.M. (1989). Peer interaction and learning in small groups. *International Journal of Educational Psychology, 13,* 21–39.

*Webb, N.M., Qi, S., Yan, K.X., Bushey, B., & Farivar, S. (1990, April). *Cooperative small-group problem solving in middle school mathematics.* Paper presented at the Annual Meeting of the American Educational Research Association, Boston, MA.

Wilkinson, L.C. (1986, June). *Grouping low-achieving students for instruction.* Paper presented at the Designs for Compensatory Education Conference, Washington, DC. (ERIC Document Reproduction Service No. ED 293 915)

*Wright, S., & Cowen, E.L. (1985). The effects of peer teaching on student perceptions of class environment, adjustment, and academic performance. *American Journal of Community Psychology, 13,* 417–431.

*Yager, S., Johnson, D.W., & Johnson, R. (1985). Oral discussion, group-to-individual transfer, and achievement in cooperative learning groups. *Journal of Educational Psychology, 77,* 60–66.

*Yueh, J.S., & Alessi, S.M. (1988). The effect of reward structure and group ability composition on cooperative computer assisted instruction. *Journal of Computer Based Instruction, 15,* 18–22.

*Ziegler, S. (1981). The effectiveness of cooperative learning teams for increasing cross-ethnic friendship: Additional evidence. *Human Organization, 40,* 264–268.

*Zisk, J.F. (1993). The effects of a cooperative learning program on the academic self-concept of high school chemistry students (Doctoral dissertation, Temple University, 1993). *Dissertation Abstracts International, 54,* 3711A.

Comments on the article by Cohen

A major theme of the following paper is that cooperative learning, like any pedagogical strategy, indeed learning and teaching itself, is an extremely complex matter. The relationships between approaches and outcomes can rarely be captured by single-valued functions of single variables. There are many factors that can intervene. For example, assigning very specific roles to individual members of a group can increase the observed amount of interaction, but might decrease the freedom of students to try to think about new ideas and unexpected phenomena. Or, studies may find that the effectiveness of a particular strategy can vary with the ability level of different members of a group. The relative value of a specific cooperative learning strategy can depend on whether the particular goal is learning an algorithm and how it can be applied, or understanding the relationship between components of the algorithm.

Cohen tries to bring some coherence to this chaotic situation by focusing on what specific studies of cooperative learning have to say about the quantity and quality of interaction within a group, the effect of the nature of specific tasks on productivity, and the different meanings of productivity in various learning situations. In this way she hopes to shed light on certain issues that have become controversial within the field of cooperative learning, such as rewards, interdependence and accountability. Her analysis attempts to move away from global questions about the effectiveness of cooperative learning towards more specific investigations of the conditions under which the use of small groups can be productive.

The paper is divided into two major parts. The first examines research on the relation between interaction and various kinds of productivity under varying task conditions. The second considers research on the factors that affect the quantity and quality of interaction.

A recurring theme is the importance of students learning interpersonal skills. Cohen argues that cooperative behavior may not occur and productivity may not increase unless something is done to help students develop these skills. At the end of the paper she returns to this question and describes research on training students for cooperation.

The literature discussed by Cohen suggests that there is not a simple causality between quantity of interaction among students in a group and performance. Not only does the effect on performance depend on the *kind* of interaction, but also on the nature of the task and the ability levels of students. An important factor affecting these relationships is the heterogeneity or homogeneity of the groups with respect to ability, gender, status and other characteristics. Another major factor is the extent to which the group operates as a group as opposed to a collection of individuals. Some studies have considered the effects on performance of using various structures that can effect how the group functions: positive goal interdependence, resource interdependence, and reward interdependence.

Cohen describes what the literature reports about attempts to increase interaction by structuring the group operations in certain ways. These methods include restraining the interaction, limiting exchange processes, and assigning different roles to members of a group. Again, the effectiveness of a structure depends on a number of factors.

The nature and amount of interaction, as well as how much each student participates is strongly affected by status issues. This is discussed at some length in another paper in this collection, by Cohen, Lotan, and Catanzarite.

A final factor affecting interaction is the role played by the teacher. Cohen describes some changes in teachers' roles, both planned and resulting from the environment created by cooperative learning. There are both positive and negative considerations here.

Discussion Questions

1. Write a one page or less outline of the contents of this paper.
2. After reading this paper, do you feel you have a greater global view of the literature on cooperative learning? How would you describe it?
3. Explain the various meanings for productivity that Cohen considers.
4. Cohen considers a very specific collection of articles. What is your opinion of her criteria for selection?
5. Briefly describe what the literature says about the relation between interaction and productivity.
6. What are Cohen's arguments for the need to help students develop interpersonal skills?
7. What methods can be used to help students develop interpersonal skills?
8. What are some different kinds of interactions among students in a group and how do they affect productivity on different kinds of problems and students of different abilities?
9. Summarize what, according to this paper, the literature reports on the issue of homogeneity versus heterogeneity. How has the paper affected your views on this issue?
10. What can be done to help a group operate more cooperatively rather than individually?
11. Explain the three kinds of interdependence discussed by Cohen. What is your view on their effects?
12. Describe the methods considered by Cohen for structuring the group operation. What is your opinion of the effectiveness of each of them?
13. Compare and contrast what Cohen says here about status issues with what appears in the paper by Cohen, Lotan, Catanzarite.
14. How do you see the role of the teacher in a cooperative learning environment?

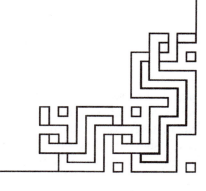

Restructuring the Classroom: Conditions for Productive Small Groups†

Elizabeth G. Cohen

Cooperative learning has gained increasing acceptance in classrooms here and abroad as a strategy for producing learning gains, the development of higher order thinking, prosocial behavior, interracial acceptance, and as a way to manage academic heterogeneity in classrooms with a wide range of achievement in basic skills. Theoretically, small groups offer special opportunities for active learning and substantive conversation (Nystrand, 1986) that are essential for authentic achievement, a goal recommended in the current drive to restructure schools (Newmann, 1991). Small groups have also been widely recommended as a means to achieve equity (Oakes & Lipton, 1990).

The purpose of this review of research is to move beyond the general question of effectiveness of small group learning to conceptualize conditions under which the use of small groups in classrooms can be productive. Reviews of research on cooperative learning have been mainly concerned with its effectiveness in comparison to traditional forms of instruction that are more competitive and/or individualistic. Early reviews (Sharan, 1980; Slavin, 1980) concluded that, in general, there were some significant positive effects on achievement and interracial relations that occur as a result of cooperative learning. Bossert (1988), in his review of research on cooperation, characterizes more recent meta-analyses on the now substantial body of research as suggesting that the benefits of cooperative learning activities hold for students at all age levels, for all subject areas, and for a wide range of tasks, such as those involving rote-decoding, retention, and memory skills as well as problem-solving abilities (Johnson, Johnson, & Maruyama, 1983; Johnson, Maruyama, Johnson, Nelson, & Skon, 1981). Bossert was, however, critical of the lack of knowledge about the ways in which various cooperative activities produce their positive effects. He was particularly critical of studies that employ a "black box approach" (p. 233) in which they compare a cooperative instructional method to a noncooperative method on outcome measures alone.

Despite the significant positive effects of cooperative learning in many studies, there was important variation in effectiveness between studies. In some of the early studies, cooperative learning was associated with results that were merely as good as those with more traditional forms of instruction and not necessarily superior. As research continued to accumulate, Davidson (1985), in a review of cooperative learning in mathematics education, found significant differences favoring cooperative versus traditional meth-

† *Review of Educational Research.* 64, pp. 1–35. Copyright © 1994 by the American Educational Research Association. Reprinted by permission of the publisher.

ods of instruction in a third of the studies; the remaining studies showed no significant differences according to type of instruction. A synthesis of "best evidence" taken from studies of secondary schools only (Newmann & Thompson, 1987) concluded that, of the 37 comparisons, 68% favored cooperative learning over traditional forms of instruction. Moreover, the results of cooperative learning sometimes differed according to the ethnic or racial group of the student (Widaman & Kagan, 1987). Slavin (1983b) argued in a best evidence synthesis that cooperative learning is only effective when group rewards and individual accountability are present.

This variability in findings suggests that the advantages that can theoretically be obtained from cooperative learning can actually be obtained only under certain conditions. A thorough search of the recent research literature reveals that numerous studies have progressed beyond the black box approach to one in which various features of cooperative learning are manipulated so as to highlight the importance of particular conditions for success on different kinds of instructional outcomes. In addition, observational studies that examine processes of interaction in relationship to outcome variables are useful in highlighting which features of interaction are more important in assuring particular outcomes. Analysis of the conditions under which optimal features of interaction are likely to occur permits an inference concerning conditions for productivity.

This is an inductive and conceptual review of research rather than a meta-analysis. Although much of this research does not contain powerfully developed theoretical frameworks, these findings will be built on to develop several testable propositions concerning the conditions for productive small groups. These propositions are consistent with all the research articles reviewed unless otherwise specified.

Some Definitions

For the purposes of this review, *cooperative learning* will be defined as students working together in a group small enough that everyone can participate on a collective task that has been clearly assigned. Moreover, students are expected to carry out their task without direct and immediate supervision of the teacher. The study of cooperative learning should not be confused with small groups that teachers often compose for the purpose of intense, direct instruction—for example, reading groups.

This definition is both broad and sociological in character. It is broad in that it encompasses what is called collaborative learning, cooperative learning, and group work. It is sociological in its stress on task and delegation of authority rather than the more psychological concepts of

common goals, rewards, and needs for other individuals in the group.

Techniques that are effective for one outcome variable may well be ineffective for another. Thus it is essential to distinguish among different meanings of productivity or effectiveness. The commonest definition of *productivity* for cooperative learning has been conventional academic achievement, of the kind that standardized achievement tests have measured in the past. This type of achievement stresses basic skills, memorization of factual materials, and the application of algorithms in areas such as mathematics.

Productivity can also be defined in terms of conceptual learning and higher order thinking. Some researchers advocate small groups because they believe that small-group processes contribute to the development of higher order thinking skills (Noddings, 1989). Noddings sees this school of thought as originating in the work of Dewey and the social constructivism of Vygotsky (1978). Because these researchers assume that such outcomes cannot be achieved without the creation of suitable discourse or conversation within the small groups or without a process of discovery, they define productive small groups as those that are engaged in high-level discourse. This alternative definition of productivity stresses conceptual learning and higher order thinking.

For those researchers concerned with equity, productivity is defined as the occurrence of equal-status interaction within the small groups. This is typically measured by comparisons of individual rates of participation for students of different statuses within the group. It is also possible to define productivity in this domain at the classroom level—that is, those classrooms in which there is very little difference between the participation rates for students of differing statuses within cooperative groups are more productive.

Finally, productivity may be defined in terms of desirable prosocial behaviors such as being cooperative or being friendly towards students of a different ethnic or racial group. Related to this type of outcome is a concern for the use of cooperative learning in a multiethnic setting. In this case, productivity is defined as positive intergroup relations.

Theoretical Focus of the Review

A central proposition of this review is that the relationship of the total amount of interaction within a group to achievement differs according to the nature of the task. Not all tasks assigned to cooperative groups are true group tasks. Some could be done as individuals and have the character of collaborative seatwork. In addition, some tasks have fairly clear procedures and may have "right answers," whereas others are what the sociologists call "ill- structured problems." Theoretically, the total amount of interaction should be far more critical for achievement gains when there is an ill-structured problem that is a true group task than when the task is more clear-cut and could be carried out by individuals.

Beyond sheer volume, the type of interaction that is the most effective, and thus the most desirable, will also vary with the nature of the task and the instructional objective. There is, for example, a major difference between the type of interaction useful for tasks with clear procedures and right answers when the objective is routine academic learning and the type of interaction desired when the objective is learning for understanding or conceptual learning and the task is ill-structured. For more routine learning, it is necessary for students to help each other to understand what the teacher or the textbook is saying, and it is helpful for them to offer each other substantive and procedural information. For conceptual learning, effective interaction should be more of a mutual exchange process in which ideas, hypotheses, strategies, and speculations are shared.

Given the most effective interaction for particular tasks and objectives, there are a number of factors that will affect how well that desired interaction is achieved. For example, if the main type of interaction desired is for students to offer each other assistance, then the motivation of students to do so as well as the preparation for constructive assistance of one another become important factors in predicting the relative success of the groups. If, on the other hand, an extensive mutual exchange of ideas and strategies is desired, then too sharp a division of labor or limited participation of low-status students may impede the very interaction necessary for the achievement of conceptual learning.

The discussion of specific studies is divided into two parts. The first part examines research on interaction and its relationship to productive small groups under varying task conditions. Having established the importance of interaction for attaining educational objectives under specified conditions, the second part focuses on factors that affect interaction.

With a focus on interaction, nature of the task, and productivity, this review is a reexamination of problems that have been debated for some time among researchers on cooperative learning. The hope is that by choosing to focus primarily on tasks and interaction rather than on interdependence, rewards, and individual accountability new light will be shed on some old problems. Rather than continue the current debate over which of the popular methods of cooperative learning are more effective, a less holistic

mode of analysis is used to examine the evidence for each of the selected variables.

In describing and analyzing relevant research, more general propositions are inferred about conditions under which small groups will be more productive. It is these general propositions that comprise recommendations for future research. The propositions are based on a post hoc analysis of the research literature and its contradictions. Future researchers would do well to put these propositions to a new and general test.

Collection of articles. The search of the literature was restricted to empirical research or to reviews of research and did not tap into the large literature written for practitioners on this subject. Eliminated were studies that contrasted a cooperative treatment to some kind of conventional academic instruction; selected were those studies or parts of studies that contrasted alternative forms of cooperative learning groups. Also omitted were discourse analyses and studies of peer response groups in the teaching of writing, peer tutoring, and studies of college-age students. Most of the studies selected for review took place in classrooms. A number of laboratory studies were dropped from consideration on the grounds that the experimental task bore no resemblance to a school task. A few laboratory studies were included because they used more applicable tasks and highlighted the effects of one of the factors under consideration. If the methodology were so grossly flawed that very little could be learned from a study, it was not included. Included were a number of modest qualitative studies of relatively few groups, detailing the nature of group interaction. The choice of which studies to include was dictated by the purpose of developing general propositions. All studies that met the above criteria were accepted for the review. Great care was taken to include studies that did not support the general propositions under development. Most of the relevant literature meeting these criteria was written in the 1980s.

Studies of Interaction

Several researchers have examined the nature of interaction taking place within cooperative groups. In these studies, students were given no special preparation for cooperative behavior. Students were typically instructed to work together, but there were no further attempts to structure interaction because the goal was to study "natural" cooperation.

Barnes and Todd (1977) carried out a pioneering study, recording detailed conversations of students engaged in a variety of creative problem-solving tasks. Many of their conclusions, based on a qualitative analysis of the interaction, foreshadowed issues that were to become central to the research of the 1980s. These included the nature of understanding that emerges from the group, the kinds of social and cognitive skills required of students for effective interaction, and the effects on interaction of variations in the type of tasks given to the group.

The transcripts from this study include some of the best examples in the literature of the social construction of knowledge. For Barnes and Todd, the meaning of a given contribution was often gradually negotiated through the interaction process. They cautioned researchers that meaning may not be explicit even to the speaker in an ongoing discussion, because criteria for relevance are negotiated moment by moment. Only when the conversation is over, by looking backwards, can a determinate meaning be assigned. These investigators made a distinction between operational meaning of the moment and subsequent reflective meaning.

Some of the groups studied by Barnes and Todd were far more effective than others. Useful behaviors included soliciting opinions, encouraging explicitness, pinpointing differences, and interrelating viewpoints. Some groups engaged in destructive interaction in which members were verbally attacked. These revealing transcripts produced the conclusion that students needed both social and cognitive skills for effective interaction. The social skills required included the ability to control progress through the tasks, the skills to manage competition and conflict, and the ability to modify and use different viewpoints as well as the willingness to give mutual support. Cognitive skills included constructing meaning for a given question, inventing a problem, setting up hypotheses, using evidence, and recreating experience.

Differences in the transcripts between groups carrying out different tasks led to the observation that the degree of unfamiliarity of the task to the students should be considered so as to keep the amount of uncertainty manageable. Other task dimensions that the investigators saw as important were how loosely or tightly structured was the task and whether there was one or multiple solutions to the problem. They also mentioned that having some concrete object for students to manipulate could make a difference in the effectiveness of the group.

Schwartz, Black, and Strange (1991) also take a constructivist view in trying to answer the question of why dyads are far more effective than individuals in inducing a general rule concerning a physical problem of the effects of multiple gears. Based on a study of interaction of dyads, they concluded that working pairs required subjects to create an agreed-on representation of the problem in order to communicate with each other. This representation allowed the group to abstract more successfully than single individuals. They recommend that cooperative learning should capitalize on the unique strengths of group learning by selecting tasks that involve abstractions and require and enable representational negotiation.

In contrast to these social constructivist views is the conclusion of Chang and Wells (1987) that, in order to be effective, groups must manage the process of solving problems with explicit talk. They define learning as problem-solving where the planning and execution of tasks are brought under conscious control. Groups support this process by making thinking explicit and available for inspection and revision. To work together, students have to specify goals more precisely, plan procedures, generate and select alternatives, and review or modify their plans. This problem-solving model deemphasizes the ongoing social nature of understanding.

Vedder (1985) also sees effective cooperative learning as a result of an explicit process. According to the theory of cooperative learning he developed from a more general view of teaching and learning, the children's role vis-à-vis each other should be that of teacher and pupil. For cooperative learning to be effective, Vedder reasoned that pupils must control and evaluate their partner's work. Also, help that is given should correspond to a model of a correct problem-solving process. After finding that cooperative groups did no better than the control condition on a set of geometry lessons, he performed an in-depth analysis of videotapes to see if students were actually regulating each other's problem-solving process. The pupils in the cooperative condition were taught how to regulate one another's solving of geometry problems. The analysis revealed that the students were fixated on finding the right answers which interfered with their attempting to regulate each other's process of problem-solving. They spent little time in thinking and talking about problem-solving strategies. They hardly used the resource card that contained useful information on problem-solving strategies.

Vedder was not the only researcher to be disappointed with the level of discourse that takes place in cooperative groups. In a study of small groups of students (ages 11 through 14) working with a computer and learning BASIC programming, Webb, Ender, and Lewis (1986) found that students performed all of their debugging statement by statement at the lowest abstract level. There was little long-range planning. Only with help from the instructor were they able to carry out plans at a more abstract level.

These studies suggest a useful generalization: If students are not taught differently, they tend to operate at the most concrete level. If teachers want high-level operation, particularly verbal, the students will require specific development of skills for discourse, either in advance of cooperative learning or through direct assistance when groups are in operation. The transcripts of Barnes and Todd suggest a similar proposition concerning interpersonal skills. These are not an automatic consequence of cooperative learning. Either through some kind of motivational device or through deliberate instruction in these social skills, something must be done to provoke the desired behaviors within cooperative groups.

Interaction and Achievement

There is an extensive literature on cooperative groups that correlates observed interaction with achievement, holding constant prior academic achievement. This literature presents a most interesting inconsistency, permitting the derivation of a general proposition concerning the conditions under which interaction will be related to achievement gains. On the one hand, there is a large body of meticulously conducted studies showing that the simple frequency of interaction on the part of individual students does not predict their achievement. Noreen Webb who is the investigator in many of these studies has also written several excellent reviews of this literature (1983, 1991). Most of these studies were conducted in mathematics classes where students were given problems to solve and were told to work together as a group, helping each other, and asking the teacher for help only when no one in the group could assist.

In contrast to this body of work stand a number of studies conducted on complex instruction in multilingual elementary classrooms. Complex instruction is a method of small group learning featuring open-ended discovery or conceptual tasks that emphasize higher order thinking skills. Each group in the classroom carries out a different task, all related to a central intellectual theme. Students have the opportunity to experience more than one of these tasks. *Finding Out/Descubrimiento,* a bilingual curriculum using concepts of science and math and designed to develop thinking skills, is used in conjunction with this method at the elementary level. Cohen and her colleagues consistently find that simple measures of frequency of task-related interaction are related to gains on computation and mathematical concepts and applications as well as on content-referenced tests. These results hold regardless of whether the unit of analysis is the individual learner or the percentage of students who are observed talking and working together in the classroom (Cohen & Intili, 1981; Cohen, Lotan, & Leechor, 1989). At the individual level, the frequency of students talking and working together in a task-related manner was positively correlated with the posttest scores on a content-referenced test in science, while holding constant the pretest scores (Cohen, 1984). This same variable of talking and working together had an independent effect on individual worksheet performance, as measured by quality of writing about results, conceptualization in mathematics, and inference (Stevenson, 1982). In an analysis of achievement on standardized tests of mathematics, Leechor (1988) concluded that task-related talk was a significant predictor of gains in mathematics for students who had reading scores at grade level or above as well as for students whose reading scores were below grade level. However, the linear correlation of participation with learning was more consistent in the low-achieving group than in the high-achieving group.

Task and interaction. What differences between these two bodies of studies could account for the differential effectiveness of simple interaction? The first difference lies in the working relationships between the group members. In the case of the group assignments in mathematics and the tasks given to the computer groups, the tasks could have been carried out by individuals. They were not inherently group tasks. A *group task* is a task that requires resources (information, knowledge, heuristic problem-solving strategies, materials, and skills) that no single individual possesses so that no single individual is likely to solve the problem or accomplish the task objectives without at least some input from others (Cohen & Arechevala-Vargas, 1987). The tasks used in complex instruction fit this definition of a group task. When working on a group task, members are interdependent in a reciprocal fashion. In other words, each actor must exchange resources with others before the task can be completed. This contrasts with many routine tasks used in cooperative learning where achievement depends on the stronger students helping the weaker students. This arrangement is also interdependent, but the interdependence is sequential as opposed to reciprocal—that is, one student's performance is dependent on another's, but the reverse is not true.

In the case of complex instruction, reciprocal interdependence is also produced by the system of classroom management in which each student is responsible for helping to ensure the success of all members. Each student has a role that has to do with the functioning of the group. Moreover, the students experience a week of skill-building activities in which they internalize norms of mutual assistance. Lastly, specific steps are taken to prevent the better students from doing all the helping and weaker students from accepting all of the help (Cohen & Cohen, 1991). In the studies reviewed by Webb, there was no such system of classroom management, nor was there any special training for cooperative relationships.

The second important difference lies in the nature of the work assigned to the groups. Computational or algorithmic mathematics assignments typically have a right answer that can be reached in well-structured ways while open-ended and discovery tasks, such as those used in complex instruction, do not have one right answer and are ill-structured problems; they are nonroutine problems for which there are no standard recipes or procedures. Under the conditions of a group task and an ill-structured problem, interaction is vital to productivity. In the case of a classroom setting, productivity is often defined in terms of achievement gains (see the first two definitions of productive small groups above). Unless the group members exchange ideas and information, they are unlikely to come up with creative solutions to their assignment or to discover underlying principles. This may be stated as a more general proposition:

Given an ill-structured problem and a group task, productivity will depend on interaction.

More specifically: given a problem with no one right answer and a learning task that will require all students to exchange resources, achievement gains will depend on the frequency of task-related interaction.

If general measures of interaction do not predict achievement when students are working on conventional school tasks with well-defined procedures that could be carried out as individuals, what does? The most consistent, positive predictor of achievement in these studies is the giving of detailed, elaborate explanations (Webb, 1983, 1991). In other words, the student who does the explaining is the student who benefits, controlling for how well he or she would have done based on past achievement/ability. Swing and Peterson (1982) also found that high achievers benefited from participation in heterogeneous groups, especially by giving explanations to others. Moreover, students with higher initial achievement/ability scores tend to give more explanations.

Giving of more detailed explanations is, in turn, related to the student's conception that better explanations are those that include specific content or information (Peterson & Swing, 1985). These concepts of a good explanation are significantly related to group achievement on seatwork with arithmetic tasks (Peterson & Swing, 1985).

The importance of giving explanations as a predictor of achievement gains did not hold up in studies of microcomputer learning. Webb summarizes the results of her first microcomputer study:

The importance of specific verbal interaction variables for learning was less in this study than in previous studies of small-group work in the classroom. In the present study in contrast to nearly all previous studies, giving explanations did not help students to learn computer programming. Receiving explanations, found in some previous studies to be beneficial for learning, in-

fluenced only learning of the basic commands. (Webb, 1984a, p. 1086)

Similarly, in a subsequent study of students learning BASIC, Webb and her colleagues (Webb, Ender, & Lewis, 1986) found that giving explanations was not a predictor and that receiving explanations related to knowledge of commands, but not to interpreting programs or to ability to generate programs.

Some of the favorable effects of giving explanations may stem from what Fletcher (1985) calls *cognitive facilitation*. In a computer task calling for solving equations in an earth spaceship game, individuals who were told to verbalize their decisions did as well in problem-solving performance on the game as groups told to come to consensus (Fletcher, 1985). Both these conditions had superior results to those found for individuals working silently. There is parallel evidence of the favorable effects of cognitive facilitation at the group level. King (1989) formed groups of fourth graders who were provided with videotape modeling of "think-aloud problem solving." The group task was to reproduce a stimulus design using *LOGO* computer graphics. Groups were instructed to think aloud as they performed their task. More successful groups asked more task-related questions, spent more time on strategy, and reached higher levels of strategy elaboration than did groups who were less successful on the task.

The helpfulness of helping.   How helpful are these elaborate explanations to the students who receive them? Receiving content-related explanations produced positive effects on achievement in only 3 of the 14 partial correlations in the studies surveyed (Webb, 1991). However, if students receive no answer when they request help, they clearly learn less than if they do get a response. Receiving no response to a request for help or a terminal response in which one is only given the right answer is consistently negatively related to achievement (Webb, 1991).

Webb (1991) points out that more important than the kind of help that a student receives is the match between the student's request for help and the kind of response received. For example, receiving less elaboration than is needed, such as asking for an explanation and being told only the correct answer, is negatively related to achievement. Another condition for effective helping, according to Webb (1992), is that the help received be applied to solve the problem. In a majority of cases, Webb found that students who expressed a need for help and met both these conditions performed well on an immediate and a later test. In contrast, students who did not meet these conditions were rarely successful on the delayed test. Navarrete (1985) also studied sequences of behavior surrounding help. The frequency of a sequence consisting of a student requesting help, receiving help, and returning to his or her task predicted gains in reading comprehension, while incomplete sequences such as receiving help without having asked for it or receiving no help when requesting it were unrelated to achievement.

Whether or not a student receives needed help has something to do with the nature of the request for assistance. Webb (1991) cites numerous studies that have found that specific requests are more successful than others in eliciting appropriate and adequate responses. The most extensive work on this subject has been done by Wilkinson and her colleagues (see, e.g., Wilkinson & Calculator, 1982).

Low-achievers undoubtedly are helped in the course of the interaction within cooperative groups in many ways outside of specific requests for help and adequate responses to those requests. Future research would do well to develop an understanding of the several different ways in which interaction in heterogeneous groups proves effective in assisting the learning of the low achiever. Available research often focuses on the fact that groups are heterogeneous or homogeneous with respect to achievement rather than on the nature of the interaction that occurs in the context of these two different kinds of groups.

Most models of cooperative learning advocate the use of heterogeneous groups because of the hypothesized benefits to low-achieving students of receiving instruction from high-achieving students or because of the desire to increase trust and friendliness between members of different social groups. There is considerable support in the research for the beneficial effects of heterogeneous groups on low-achieving students. Some researchers have focused specifically on this question of the effectiveness of heterogeneous versus homogeneous group composition. In studies of collaborative seatwork, Swing and Peterson (1982) found that students of low achievement benefited from participation in groups heterogeneously composed on achievement in comparison to participation in homogeneously low-achieving groups. Students of average achievement were the only ones not to benefit from their interaction with others of higher or lower achievement. They did better in homogeneous groups of average achievers.

In a study of homogeneous versus heterogeneous groups working on a computer-driven tutorial that did not relate to their work in the regular math classes, Hooper and Hannafin (1988) also report that low-achieving eighth-grade math students benefited from working with high-achieving students on a delayed posttest with questions covering factual recall, application, and problem solving. There were no differences in test performance by group composition, and group composition had little effect on the performance of high-achieving math students. The favorable effects for the low-achievers were restricted to the factual recall questions and not to the parts of the test that required higher level problem solving. Although Hooper and Hannafin wonder whether the higher level problem solving was inappropriate for the ability level of these students, it should be noted that the high-achieving students also did much worse on the application and problem-solving parts of the test than they did on factual recall. An alternative explanation for the failure of the cooperative learning to lead to gains in higher order thinking lies in the task instructions which had the students alternating roles of decision maker, advisor, and typist/advisor for every five questions. This sharp division of labor may have inhibited the type of interaction necessary for these more ill-structured problems.

There is evidence that lower achieving students are benefited by interaction with higher achieving students even when tasks demand higher order thinking. Children paired with a partner who had used a higher level cognitive rule on the pretest were significantly benefited and were able to function at a higher cognitive level on the posttest than on the pretest (Tudge 1990). Tudge (1990) concluded that it was exposure to high-level reasoning that made a difference as to whether a student would learn from another of greater competence. When the children's partner supported their predictions with reasoning at a higher level than that used by the target children, the latter were highly likely to improve. These effects of treatment conditions did not vary by age group; the study included pairs of kindergartners to fourth graders. By the same token, exposure to less-advanced reasoning in the course of interaction can have a negative effect on more developmentally advanced children. On a very challenging mathematical balance beam task, Tudge (1991) selected pairs homogeneous or heterogeneous as to the level of cognitive development they exhibited on a pretest on this task. Partners who were using more advanced rules to solve this problem, on the average, regressed in their thinking from pretest to posttest after interacting with a partner who had used a lower level rule on the pretest.

What can be concluded from this research? If the task is collaborative seatwork and if high-achieving students have the chance to give explanations, then heterogeneous groups will be especially beneficial for them. If the group is composed of only medium-achieving combined with low-achieving students, one would expect that the medium-achieving students would have the benefit of giving explanations. This proposition is predicated on the idea that the process of providing explanations is helpful for any student but that the better students in the group are more likely to engage in such behavior. If the task is very challenging and ambiguous and has an ill-structured solution, and if a heterogeneous pair is left alone to agree on an answer, then the confidence of the more developmentally advanced child can be shaken, and he or she may regress to a view of the matter that he or she held at a younger age. The only result that seems to hold unconditionally is the benefit to the low achiever of being in a heterogeneous group as compared to a homogeneously low-achieving group.

Interdependence and Interaction

Designers of cooperative learning tasks must contend with one consequence of using small groups. One may give a group a task, but, unless there is some reason for the group to interact, students may well tackle the task as individual work. This is especially the case if each individual must turn out some kind of worksheet or report. This is also the case if the instructor divides the labor so that each person in the group does a different part of the task; the group has only to draw these pieces together in sequential fashion as a final product. The consequence of either of these patterns is that there is comparatively little interaction; people do not gain the benefits of using one another as resources, nor is there any basis for expecting the prosocial outcomes of cooperation.

In the literature on cooperative learning, this problem is most typically addressed as one of the necessity for interdependence of the members of the group (Johnson & Johnson, 1990). In order to ensure interdependence through limiting resources or through setting a group goal, it is typically recommended that there be only one worksheet or report for the group. The object is to ensure that a group will be created because members are dependent on one another to achieve the group goal (positive goal interdependence) and will need to use one another's resources to attain that goal (resource interdependence).

Positive goal interdependence is a concept taken from Deutsch (1962) meaning that individuals perceive that they can achieve their goal if and only if the other individuals with whom they are cooperatively linked also achieve their goals (Johnson, Johnson, & Stanne, 1990). Positive resource interdependence exists when individuals can only achieve their goals when other group members provide needed resources. The Johnson model of cooperative learning advocates the use of both goal interdependence and resource interdependence. In a cognitively demanding computer simulation in which high school students had to apply both navigational and map reading skills to sail ships to the New World, conditions with both positive goal interdependence and resource interdependence led to better performance on the simulation than conditions with only one of these two types of interdependence (Johnson, Johnson, & Stanne, 1990).

However, interdependence of either type does not necessarily solve the problem of guaranteeing interaction. When there is a strong division of labor, but the group is committed to turn out a single end product, one may say the group is interdependent, but there is still no strong motivation for the group to interact and solve problems as a group. The limitation of goal interdependence is illustrated by the computer simulation study just cited; goal interdependence alone did not promote more effective performance. One may speculate that, although the three group members were given the same goal of getting all three ships to the New World, if they divided the labor and each attempted to sail one ship, then there might have been minimal interaction possibly reducing understanding and problem-solving success. Simple resource interdependence has similar problems with respect to interaction. When group members are simply dependent on one another for resources (sharing information in the case of the navigation task) but do not share a goal, achievement is also impaired because interaction consists of one person trying to get information from another but perhaps wanting to avoid wasting time by giving information. Simple resource interdependence, in this study, was associated with the poorest results (Johnson, Johnson, & Stanne, 1990).

Simple resource interdependence is also present in the *jigsaw* procedure (Aaronson, Blaney, Sikes, & Snapp, 1978) where members are oriented to their individual performance but obtain information from peers who become "expert" on their topic after work in specialized groups. There were no achievement differences in this study between jigsaw and traditional instruction even though the tasks were of the routine, social studies variety. Huber and Eppler (1990) note that slow-learning members of jigsaw teams do not necessarily return from their expert group sessions knowing more than their team members. There is, in this case, no particular motivation to interact with and to help these slow-learning team members to learn.

We propose a reformulation of this problem, not so much in terms of interdependence, but in terms of the type of interaction fostered by these differing task instructions. A proposition for future research is as follows:

- Effects of resource and goal interdependence on productivity will be mediated by the amount and type of interaction stimulated by these task arrangements.
- Resource interdependence alone will be associated with lower participation rates on the part of those students who stand to gain most by receiving assistance than will resource and goal interdependence combined.

- Resource and goal interdependence, taken one at a time, are not sufficient conditions for activating group participation.

The organizational concepts of sequential and reciprocal interdependence introduced earlier in this review pertain more directly to the type of interaction that takes place in the group and thus will have considerable heuristic value for research on productive small groups.

Reward interdependence. One task condition that has the power to stimulate students to participate and to help one another is the presence of rewards to the group based on the performance of each individual member. This is sometimes referred to as *reward interdependence.*

No aspect of cooperative learning has been as controversial as the issue of giving rewards to groups on a competitive basis. This issue has become enmeshed in the ideological controversy over cooperation versus competition as has the issue of extrinsic versus intrinsic rewards for students and their relationship to learning. The best known research and reviews of research on this topic have been those of Robert Slavin (1983a, 1983b, 1987). After reviewing 41 studies of cooperative learning that contrasted cooperative treatments of various types with traditional, individualistic learning, he came to the following conclusion: Achievement is enhanced by cooperative learning when cooperating pupils are rewarded as a group, while each pupil is individually accountable for his or her learning (1983a). In the most widely disseminated of the various models of cooperative learning developed by Slavin and his colleagues, a technique referred to as the STAD procedures, individuals take a test on their own learning and receive individual grades. For the purpose of public recognition, a group score or team score is awarded that is a composite of how well each individual has done relative to his or her own past performance. Certificates are awarded to the team with the highest score, or the winning score is published in the class newspaper or posted on a bulletin board. Slavin's conceptualization of how cooperation leads to achievement emphasizes individual accountability as strongly as group rewards. He states, "Learning is enhanced by provision of group rewards if and only if group members are individually accountable to the group for their own learning. Individual accountability can be created either by providing specific group rewards based on members learning or by having students perform unique tasks and providing incentives for students to learn from each other" (Slavin, 1983b, p. 59).

Because all the comparisons that Slavin uses are experiments contrasting one of the cooperative learning techniques with whole class or individual instruction, his generalization is based on how consistently cooperative learning conditions of various types bring superior results to a noncooperative situation. His strong generalization, however, implies a contrast between differing approaches to cooperative learning that systematically vary individual accountability and the presence or absence of group rewards. Bossert also makes this point in his review of the literature: "Slavin has not clearly tested the value of group contingencies within the Student Team Learning methods" (Bossert, 1988, p. 233). Vedder (1985) was highly critical of Slavin's review for the same reason as well as for counting as positive studies those where only the minority students made significant gains in achievement. He sharply disagrees with Slavin's characterization of some of the studies as having positive outcomes.

Slavin is, however, making an important theoretical point concerning the motivation of individuals to put out effort and to interact in the group setting. He is particularly critical of giving a group a single task that could conceivably be done by one person. In this case, he argues that positive goal interdependence is insufficient to motivate everyone's effort. In a study designed to make direct comparison of differing reward conditions for learning in cooperative settings, Yueh and Alessi (1988) contrasted three junior high school mathematics classes using computer-assisted instruction in groups. In a version of cooperative learning known as Teams Games Tournaments, the members of each group completed a drill with the computer accompanied by discussion; they then competed in new tournament groups composed homogeneously on a standardized mathematics achievement test. The competition went on for several days with the top-scoring student at each table moving on to a table of higher achieving students and the bottom-scoring student moving down a table. At the end of the tournament competition, actual prizes were awarded according to the reward conditions of the classroom. An achievement test with items based on application of principles was administered. One class received scores based on their individual performance in the tournament. A second class received scores based on the average of their group, while a third class was awarded scores on the combination of individual and group performance. In each case, prizes were awarded to the top-scoring individual, group, or those with the highest combined group and individual score. Data were analyzed at the level of the group. The class with the combined individual and group rewards did significantly better on the items measuring direct learning than the other two classes. There were no differences on the items requiring application.

Okebukola (1985) directly contrasted Teams Games Tournaments, STAD procedures, jigsaw, and the Learning Together model (based on the Johnsons' approach to cooperative learning). From a theoretical point of view, both Teams Games Tournaments and STAD procedures employ competitive, extrinsic reward interdependence as well as individual accountability. The jigsaw technique, as explained above, does not have an explicit group goal or reward, but students are dependent on one another for information. The Learning Together model (circa early 1980s) featured both goal and resource interdependence, but it did not employ competitive, extrinsic reward interdependence, nor did it allocate scores to individuals. Theoretically, it did not have a strong feature of individual accountability. On a test of science achievement employing both lower and higher level cognitive items, although all the cooperative methods were superior to independent study or to traditional whole class instruction, the Learning Together model produced the least favorable achievement results of the cooperative methods, and the STAD procedures produced the most favorable results. The Johnsons (1990) also describe several studies in which they have been involved in which the use of reward contingencies in connection with goal interdependence provided more favorable achievement results than goal interdependence alone.

The effectiveness of reward interdependence, however, should not be taken to mean that it is not possible to hold individuals accountable or to motivate them to participate without such reward contingencies. Such rewards are not used in Group Investigation, which compared favorably to STAD in producing achievement on items measuring higher order thinking (Sharan, et al., 1984), nor are they used in complex instruction where the activities are intrinsically interesting. Complex instruction has also been found to produce significant achievement gains (Cohen, 1991). Slavin's original proposition about the necessity of reward interdependence and individual accountability would appear to apply better to the kinds of collective or collaborative seatwork tasks that are so common in cooperative learning, where it is of vital importance to motivate those who could do the task by themselves to interact and to assist those who are having difficulty. These are not group tasks, as defined earlier in this article, because they could be carried out by one individual. Reward interdependence does not appear to be necessary for achievement when students are motivated to complete a challenging and interesting group task that requires everyone's contribution for a good outcome. This proposition appears to hold at least when individual accountability is maintained by other strategies such as requiring individual reports or making individuals responsible for some portion of the end product.

Offering rewards on a competitive basis, although effective in increasing motivation of team members to work together, may have negative effects on intergroup relations, more specifically on the perceptions that team members have toward other teams. Miller, Brewer, and Edwards (1985) report an experimental study in which the reward structure varied: In the cooperative condition, subjects were told that the problem solutions of the two teams would be evaluated jointly to determine their joint eligibility for a small monetary reward; in the competitive condition, they were told that the team with the better product would be eligible for a reward. After an initial phase of work as separate teams, the teams convened to discuss and to arrive at a final consensus. In the cooperative condition on a post-experimental measure, team members were more willing to allocate rewards to individuals on the other team and held more favorable perception of members of the other team than in the competitive condition. Similarly, a meta-analysis of studies of heterogeneous classrooms contrasting cooperation with and without intergroup competition showed that perceived personal attractiveness of nonteam members was lower with intergroup competition (Johnson, Johnson, & Maruyama, 1984).

In addition to this issue of the effect of competition on perceptions of outgroup members, there is some evidence that methods using competition such as Teams Games Tournaments and STAD procedures are ineffective for particular categories of students (Widaman & Kagan, 1987). While Anglo-American students showed significantly greater gains in spelling in the personally competitive technique of Teams Games Tournaments (TGT) than in STAD or in traditional classrooms, Mexican Americans showed significantly greater gains in traditional classrooms than in STAD or TGT. A study of TGT in the learning of mathematics has also shown that the failure of one's team can have a negative effect on one's individual achievement in a way that is independent of prior achievement and individual outcome (Chambers & Abrami, 1991). Moreover, the effect of participating on an unsuccessful team using STAD procedures was negative in mathematics achievement for those students characterized as "learned helpless" (p. 7) and had no effect on those students characterized as "mastery-oriented" (Abrami, Chambers, D'Apollonia, & De Simone, 1992, p. 7).

Despite these negative effects on achievement of some features of competitive reward systems, it should be noted that the evidence linking STAD to gains in cross-racial friendships is strong (Slavin, 1983a). The many studies documenting the connection between cooperative learning and improved intergroup relations, regardless of whether or not elements of competition are also employed, are not reviewed here because they compare the cooperative condition to traditional classroom structure.

Recommendations for the Study of Interaction

This section reviews studies of interaction in small groups and its relationship to effectiveness. I have recommended the use of a key distinction of whether or not the task of the group is a true group task and whether or not the nature of the assignment is routine with clear procedures and answers or is a problem with an ill-structured solution. This distinction helps to explain why the sheer volume of interaction fails to predict interaction in studies of collaborative seatwork using routine mathematical assignments, while it is a powerful predictor of learning when tasks are open-ended, conceptual in nature, and require reciprocal interdependence of the participants.

As have many other students of cooperative learning, I argue that the problem of motivating members to work as a group is of critical importance in ensuring effectiveness. However, the previous ways of looking at this problem in terms of resource, goal, and reward interdependence can be improved by introducing the variable of the type of task and interaction into propositions concerning the effects of interdependence. I examine propositions concerning the effects of resource and goal interdependence on interaction as well as effectiveness. I propose that the necessity for both resource and goal interdependence for effective groups arises because either of these conditions by themselves will not activate adequate group participation. Furthermore, task arrangements can have a direct effect on interaction that will mediate the effects of resource and goal interdependence. I also amend Slavin's propositions concerning the importance of reward interdependence and individual accountability as necessary and sufficient conditions for learning gains to apply more specifically to collaborative seatwork and routine learning. Clearly, there is evidence that cooperative learning groups with true group tasks and conceptual learning can be effective without reward interdependence.

Factors Affecting Interaction

Structuring the Interaction: Task Instructions

There are a number of ways in which the designers of group-work tasks attempt to ensure interaction from the participants. These range from simple task instructions, in which students are told to help one another or to discuss and come to consensus, to detailed procedures concerning how and what is to be discussed. In some cases, the interaction may even be scripted with specific conversational strategies that students practice before attempting the group task (e.g., Spurlin, Dansereau, Larson, & Brooks, 1984). In an attempt to raise the level of discourse and to ensure its effectiveness, some investigators and developers have in-

structed groups in specific ways that they should talk with one another. Assigning students particular roles is another way to get group members to take responsibility for active participation in the group. However, roles do not have a consistent effect on group interaction. If the labor is divided and each person is given a different role, such as artist, script writer, presenter, and so forth, the result may be each person quietly working on his or her task; there may be very little interaction at the group level. In contrast, a role such as group facilitator may have the effect of fostering interaction.

The problem as posed by some researchers (Brown & Palinscar, 1986; Yager, 1985) is whether it is effective to structure the interaction within small groups. Certainly, those investigators moving from a position of social constructivism would be opposed to such interference with the process of negotiation of meaning. From the perspective of this reviewer, the most useful research question to ask is not whether structuring interaction is productive but under what conditions it is productive. What conditions constrain the interaction or hinder full exchange from all participants in the group? Whether or not procedures that constrain and direct interaction are effective has to do with the kind of interaction that is necessary for optimal outcomes, given the nature of the learning outcomes that are desired.

Constraining the interaction. Let us start with two studies of the effects of structured oral discussion on tests of achievement and retention of map skills in social studies. Yager (1985) studied the effects of structured oral discussion on seventh- and eighth-grade students working on a map unit involving assignment sheets and desk-size world maps. Heterogeneous groups met 45 minutes per day for 25 days. Following 15 minutes of teacher instruction, students in the structured condition were randomly assigned the role of learning leader or learning listener. The responsibility of the leader was to restate and summarize the main points of the day's lesson while the learning listener was to ask probing questions, encourage the leader to explain better, recall areas of content left out, and discuss ideas or facts summarized incorrectly. This condition was contrasted with unstructured groups that were simply told to discuss the material after the teacher's initial instruction. The structured conditions did significantly better on the unit test and on a later test of retention. Similar results for this type of structured oral discussion were achieved with second graders working on a map unit where the instructional objectives were measured by factual recall (Yager, Johnson, & Johnson, 1985).

Structured oral discussion has some similarity to reciprocal teaching developed by Brown and Palinscar (1986). This technique also structures the interaction, not with roles but with specific strategies of questioning, clarifying, summarizing, and predicting. These strategies are designed to improve comprehension of reading and to serve as a self-testing mechanism. Reciprocal teaching has been shown to be effective on retention and comprehension of reading. However, with one exception, the research on reciprocal teaching does not fit the definition of cooperative learning used in this review because the teacher directly supervises the students who play the role of teacher. In one exploratory study (Palinscar, Brown, & Martin, 1987), students were allowed to play the role of teacher after 10 days of reciprocal teaching instruction, working with groups that operated independently of the classroom teacher. The gains indicated by the tutees in these groups on the comprehension assessments were comparable to those made by students working with their adult teachers in former studies.

The general inference that can be drawn from this research is that, when the learning task is factual recall, understanding of the assigned reading, or application of procedures and concepts in a relatively routine fashion, structuring the interaction through roles and scripts can be very effective. Such strategies probably owe their effectiveness to their capacity to raise the level of discourse and to ensure that disengaged students are drawn into participation.

Limited exchange processes.   Interaction can also be constrained by telling the groups that their principal task is to complete individual worksheets and that they should consult with one another and help one another. These are the task instructions used in the studies reviewed by Webb; Slavin's STAD procedures also use these instructions. In STAD procedures, there is an additional reward feature, discussed above. Important for this discussion are two features: (a) These instructions are typically given in connection with tasks that have well-structured solutions; (b) there are only a certain number of types of interaction that need take place in this context. Students can exchange information, explanations, or they can request assistance. They have no need to discuss how to proceed as a group, nor do they have to discover anything as a group or to negotiate any meanings. There is very little room for extensive controversy except for arguments over what is the right answer or procedure. It should be noted that this kind of limited cooperative interaction is typically used for conventional school tasks such as computational mathematics assignments, or understanding and being able to recall reading assignments.

In an extensive field experiment, Slavin's STAD techniques were compared to Sharan's Group Investigation method with respect to effects on learning outcomes as well as on the development of prosocial, cooperative behaviors (Sharan et al., 1984). Group Investigation fosters

more extensive kinds of interaction than the STAD method. Groups are given the task of developing elaborate presentations for the class. They must work together in planning this presentation and must develop procedures for dividing the labor on the component research tasks. After collecting the information, they must coordinate individual contributions into a unified group product. The experiment took place in a desegregated junior high school in Israel; classes were English as a Second Language and Literature, and they were untracked. Sharan et al. (1984) characterize important differences between the two techniques: With STAD, the teacher transmits the information, or a text transmits the information. The teacher emphasizes information and /or skill acquisition. In Group Investigation, the information is gathered by the pupils using a great variety of learning sources. The tasks stress problem-solving interpretation, synthesis, and application of information. In STAD, peer communication is primarily for rehearsal of teacher-taught materials. Pupils interact sporadically or in dyads as contrasted with group interaction necessary for the Group Investigation techniques where interactions are based on mutual exchange.

The results on the literature tests were instructive. On high-level questions, the Group Investigation classes did significantly better than the STAD classes. On the low-level questions, STAD classes performed significantly better than the Group Investigation classes. On the tests of English, both these cooperative methods were more effective than traditional instruction, but they were not different from each other with the exception of the listening comprehension scale, where the Group Investigation classes were superior. This study illustrates how differences in the type of interaction fostered by the task and task instructions are associated with different learning outcomes. For relatively low-level outcomes, the limited interaction model with its focus on acquiring information and correct answers is adequate and often superior. For higher order thinking skills, the interaction must be more elaborate and less constrained.

What about the STAD procedure is less effective for higher order thinking objectives? When Ross used STAD procedures for developing higher order thinking skills in two experiments (1988), he found that the cooperative groups using STAD procedures did no better than students working independently on practice worksheets following 20 minutes of teacher-directed dialogue. In the cooperative condition, students worked on the same worksheets as were used in the whole-class treatment. Each student was to complete his or her worksheet after conferring extensively with peers. Ross's worksheets take abstract problem-solving, such as learning how to represent problems effectively, and translate these skills into step-by-step problem solving through algorithms. The use of these worksheets was clearly more effective than a third treatment where problem solving was embedded in the content knowledge, but there were no worksheets and no explicit direction or encouragement for developing problem-solving skills. However, these experiments do not tell us how well students would have done with these materials if an exchange that was less constrained by worksheets were fostered between the students.

Inadvertently, we learn something about this alternative from a teacher who failed to follow detailed procedures for having students discuss the worksheets (Ross & Raphael, 1990). In this study, the interaction was supposed to be even more controlled than in Ross's previous studies of cooperative learning. Students were to read worksheets and work on the task individually, share answers, compare their answers to those on the feedback sheets, and then discuss discrepancies between student answers and the exemplary answer on the feedback sheet. The objective here was to develop the ability to make comparisons. One of the two teachers followed the procedure precisely, while the other allowed students to work out their own procedure. The latter teacher obtained much better results. More important than this result was the finding that there was much more interaction in her groups. Students made more factual and conceptual contributions in those unstructured groups with higher rates of interaction. Achievement outcomes were more favorable for groups where students more frequently contributed facts and concepts. These unintended results suggest that too much structure of a task that involves higher order thinking skills is dysfunctional because it impedes conceptually oriented interaction. As with scripting and roles that limit the nature of the interaction, the limited exchange processes (in conjunction with the reward features of the STAD procedures) are effective for acquiring information and other conventional school tasks. It should be noted that this effectiveness occurs in conjunction with teacher and textual presentation of information.

Hertz-Lazarowitz (1989) makes the distinction between low-cooperation group tasks, where students simply share materials or information or divide the labor so that each person's contribution can be joined together as a final product, and high-cooperation tasks where students must interact as they work together, discuss planning, decision making, and division of labor as well as substantive content. In a study of interaction among 782 students, grades 3–8, in Israel, she found that, of cooperative tasks, only 31% could be classified as high cooperative. Most relevant to this discussion is the finding that, whereas 56% of the interaction in low cooperative tasks was about information, in high cooperative tasks, 70% of the interaction had to do

with application. These findings suggest that more conceptual interaction takes place in high-cooperation tasks.

Nystrand, Gamoran, and Heck (1991) make a similar distinction between group-work tasks that are only collaborative seatwork and tasks that permit the students to define their problem and to engage in autonomous production of knowledge. On a test of understanding of literature that included conceptual questions, they found that ninth-grade classes spending more time in cooperative groups that demanded production of knowledge scored significantly higher on the test than classes spending less time in such groups. If the researchers did not divide the small group work in this way, the overall use of small groups had a negative relationship with scores on the test.

If, as was argued above, interaction is critical for achievement gains for group tasks with ill-structured solutions, then factors that affect the amount and richness of interaction will affect productivity for such tasks. Tasks with higher order thinking skills as their objectives are typically, but not necessarily (see Ross, 1988), seen by developers as open-ended tasks with ill-structured solutions. The general proposition to examine is the following:

> When the teaching objective is learning for understanding and involves higher order thinking, task arrangements and instructions that constrain and routinize interaction will be less productive than arrangements and instructions that foster maximum interaction, mutual exchange, and elaborated discussions.

Salomon and Globerson (1989) make a similar point:

> But such highly structured procedures as found in scripted cooperation, reciprocal teaching, or group attempts to gain rewards may not be the most desirable arrangements for when teams have to engage in more complex, free exploratory activities on a prolonged basis. (p. 96)

Hertz-Lazarowitz (1989) as well as Nystrand, Gamoran, and Heck (1991) imply that, unless groups determine their own procedures, their interaction will be less elaborated. However, there are studies of cooperative learning with rather elaborate procedures spelled out for the students that do not result in a limited or concrete type of interaction. On the contrary, the literature suggests that the way the instructions set up the problem, suggest procedures, and specify roles can do much to create interaction that is markedly superior to that produced by simply asking a group to reach consensus.

The research on the benefits of controversy within cooperative learning (Johnson & Johnson, 1985; Smith, Johnson, & Johnson, 1981) is the best example of how elaborate procedures and use of student roles can foster high level discussion leading to conceptual understanding. In these two studies, students in the controversy condition worked in four-person groups over several classroom sessions. First, two-person pairs, having been provided with relevant information, prepared opposing sides of a debate concerning conservation versus economic interests on the interesting topic of the proposed reintroduction of wolves into Minnesota. Within the pairs, each student played a relevant role such as farmer or rancher. Following this preparation, the pairs presented their opposing sides. The opposite pair was motivated to listen very carefully because the next phase required the pairs to switch sides and argue, using the information that had been presented. Finally, the entire group had to arrive at a consensual view of the issue and to write a group report.

In one study (Smith, Johnson, & Johnson, 1981), the controversy condition was compared to a concurrence condition where each small group could study the material in any way they wished, with the stipulation that they were to avoid arguing. The controversy condition not only promoted higher achievement on a test and better retention on a second test than the concurrence-seeking condition but, more pertinent to this discussion, there was a greater search for information and more cognitive rehearsal. On the achievement test, students were asked to take multiple perspectives in a way that tested their grasp of the concepts. Students who had experienced the controversy condition, not surprisingly, were better able to take multiple perspectives. In another study (Johnson & Johnson, 1985), the controversy condition was compared to a jigsaw debate in which students representing each role and position prepared their case in a first phase. In the next phase, the four-person groups were reassembled and carried out a formal debate. The students were told that they were responsible for learning about all these positions. The controversy condition promoted the most verbal rehearsal and exchange of assigned materials, the most active search for more information, and the most reevaluation of the students own position.

Note the elaborate way in which discussion was controlled in the controversy condition by the discipline of having to take sides and by having to play roles. Despite the elaborate structuring of interaction, the quality of the discussion in the controversy condition was superior to that in the concurrence or the debate conditions. The comparison with the debate condition illustrates that the power of this technique to foster higher level discussion does not lie solely in having to take sides. The instructions to the controversy groups fostered a reciprocal exchange in which the outputs of each actor became inputs of each other actor. Having examined the issue carefully from all sides, the group was well prepared for an in-depth discussion when they tried to come to consensus.

Roles.   When the group is working on problems with ill-structured solutions, roles can also be used to foster interaction that leads to conceptual gains. Working with classrooms using complex instruction, Zack (1988) showed that the use of a facilitator role was associated with an increase in talking and working together on discovery problems using math and science concepts. Talking and working together, in this setting, predicted gains in tests of mathematics concepts and applications (Cohen, Lotan, & Leechor, 1989). Using the same approach of complex instruction, Ehrlich (1991) studied a special adaptation of the commonly used role of the reporter. The reporter was given a special worksheet and time to discuss with the group the answers to a set of questions in preparation for his or her report to the class as a whole. The enhanced reporter's job was to encourage the group to think and talk together and, as a group, to create answers to the questions on the special form. These questions were timed at the beginning of the task, in the middle, and at the end. They were designed to encourage science-thinking behaviors. For example, the group was asked to specify their predictions for the science experiment, their observations, the inferences from their observations, and the extent to which their predictions were supported by their observations. Fourth-grade classes receiving this treatment were compared with classes using the same curriculum and techniques for cooperative learning, but the reporters were allowed to prepare their report for the class pretty much as they saw fit. Classroom observations revealed that there was a greater incidence of student interaction with one another when they used the reporter form than when groups were not using the form. On a criterion problem-solving task at the end of the year, groups from classes that had experienced the enhanced reporter form demonstrated more science-thinking behaviors. These behaviors included asking thinking questions, requesting justification, predicting, hypothesizing, inferring, and concluding (Ehrlich, 1991).

Here was the use of a role and a specific set of topics for the groups to discuss that fostered an abstract level of interaction, encouraging the children to use the language of science in a way that was distinctly new for all of them. Yet this interaction was not scripted or micromanaged. The children were free to search for the answers to these questions in ways they found productive. The distinction is a subtle one; task instructions can profitably set problems for discussion, specify roles, ask questions, determine procedures, all without constraining the full discussion of a problem with an ill-structured solution. However, this review would suggest that moving beyond these strategies for structuring the interaction to introduce worksheets that specify steps to solutions, to introduce strategies for talking about the content, or to constrain the discussion by having one student play the role of teacher and the other the learner would be counterproductive for solving problems with ill-structured solutions designed to foster the development of higher order thinking. Herein lies the dilemma: If teachers do nothing to structure the level of interaction, they may well find that students stick to a most concrete mode of interaction. If they do too much to structure the interaction, they may prevent the students from thinking for themselves and thus gaining the benefits of the interaction.

Ensuring Equity in Interaction

There are systematic inequalities in participation among members of cooperative groups. Moreover, these inequalities are related to academic status differences between students; low status students interact less frequently and have less influence than high status students (Hoffman, 1973; Rosenholtz, 1985; Tammivaara, 1982). *Status* is here defined as an agreed-on rank order where it is generally felt to be better to be high than low rank. In the studies cited, despite the fact that the tasks demanded no academic skills, those students who were perceived to be better readers or better at schoolwork were more active and influential than those students perceived to have less academic ability.

Several studies have further helped to rule out the possibility that some kind of actual ability difference is the source of this difference in rates of participation. In an analysis of interaction in cooperative learning groups of junior high school students of mathematics, Webb and Kenderski (1984) found that test scores did not predict the frequency of giving explanations. Rather, test scores relative to other members of the group predicted how frequently members gave explanations. The effect of measures of relative ability rather than absolute ability suggests that the determinant of interaction was the difference in perceived ability in mathematics within the small groups. Dembo and McAuliffe (1987) created an artificial distinction of average and above-average ability with a bogus test of problem-solving ability, described as relevant to an upcoming experimental task. Higher status students (defined as those publicly assigned above-average scores on the bogus test) dominated group interaction on the experimental task, were more influential, and were more likely to be perceived as leaders than low status students.

Academic status is the most powerful of the status characteristics in the classroom because of its obvious relevance to classroom activities. In responding to hypothetical learning groups on a questionnaire, students were much more likely to approve of leadership behavior on the part

of a good student than on the part of Whites or males (McAuliffe, 1991). Leadership behavior from those described as poor students was likely to be disapproved.

Differences in perceived academic ability are not the only sources of inequality within cooperative groups. Differences in perceived attractiveness or popularity—that is, peer status—can also act as the basis for status differentiation (Webster & Driskell, 1983). Popularity is often highly correlated with academic status, as in the classrooms studied by Rosenholtz and Wilson (1980).

Differences in social status such as gender, race, and ethnicity can also affect interaction of schoolchildren (Cohen, 1982). However, these effects have primarily been demonstrated in laboratory studies where students do not know each other. In classrooms, race and ethnicity often correlate with academic status; as a result, it has been difficult to document these effects separately in groups composed of students in a single classroom (Cohen, 1982). Only when academic status is uncontrolled can one see the effects of ethnicity in classroom studies. In a study of Middle Eastern and Western Jews in classrooms in Israel, Sharan and Shachar (1988) gave mixed-ethnic groups a discussion task and observed that Western Jews took significantly more turns at speaking than the Middle Eastern Jews and used significantly more words per turn.

Webb (1984b) found some strong evidence of the effects of gender in classroom groups of seventh and eighth graders studying mathematics. In majority-female groups, females directed most of their interaction to males and showed lower achievement than males. In majority-male groups, males tended to ignore females and showed somewhat higher achievement than did females. These differences were not observable in groups with equal numbers of males and females. Although girls are less active and influential than boys in cooperative groups of adolescents, gender does not appear to operate as a status characteristic in the early elementary years (Leal, 1985; Lockheed, Harris, & Nemceff, 1983).

Status problems make small group discourse nonproductive according to at least two of the definitions of productivity: inequitable interaction as well as unequal learning outcomes. Inequalities in participation based on gender, race, and ethnicity within cooperative groups should be a source of serious concern for those who recommend cooperative learning for heterogeneous settings. If the participants in cooperative learning have preexisting stereotypes about lesser competence of minorities and women confirmed in their group experience, then the effects of cooperation are far less desirable than many proponents of the technique would have us believe.

These inequalities in participation are worrisome for another reason: They are linked to learning gains. Cohen

(1984) demonstrated that the status of a student was correlated with interaction within the small group. Interaction, in turn, was a predictor of learning gains. This review has already cited research showing those conditions under which interaction is related to achievement gains. Clearly, the operation of these status effects is particularly detrimental to small-group productivity where interaction is critical for learning.

Status characteristic theory (Berger, Cohen, & Zelditch, 1966; Berger, Cohen, & Zelditch, 1972) provides an explanation for these effects of status as well as a basis for several interventions designed to equalize status within the groups. Status characteristics, a central concept of this theory, are defined as socially evaluated attributes of individuals for which it is generally believed that it is better to be in the high state than the low state.

Status generalization is the process by which status characteristics come to affect interaction and influence so that the prestige and power order of the group reflects the initial differences in status. When the educator gives a group a collective cooperative task, status differences based on academic ability become activated and relevant to the new situation, even if the task does not require the academic ability in question. The high status student will then expect to be more competent and will be expected to be more competent by others. The net effect is a self-fulfilling prophecy whereby those students who are seen as having more ability become more active and influential than those students who are seen as having less ability. When status generalization takes place, not only are low status students cut off from access to the resources of the group, but the group lacks the contributions and ideas of all its members. The process by which specific status characteristics generalize to new collective tasks is the same as that by which diffuse status characteristics such as race, ethnicity, and gender affect interaction.

The multiple ability treatment is an intervention in which teachers convince students that many different abilities are relevant to the group task (e.g., reasoning, creativity, and spatial problem solving). Moreover, if the teachers are successful in using the multiple ability treatment, students believe that each member of the group will be good at some of these abilities and that no member of the group will be good at all these abilities. In Tammivaara's laboratory study (1982) and in S.J. Rosenholtz's classroom experiment (1985), a multiple ability treatment substantially weakened status effects. In nonexperimental classroom conditions, Cohen, Lotan, and Catanzarite (1988) showed that the effects of status on interaction were reduced by a multiple ability treatment, though not eliminated. In a classroom setting, a successful multiple ability treatment requires the use of a multiple ability curriculum. If the assignments to

groups are restricted to conventional academic skills, then it is unlikely that students or teachers would believe that every student would have at least one of the requisite intellectual abilities or that no student would have all the abilities required.

Assigning competence to low-status students is a second intervention designed to ensure equity within cooperative groups. This treatment requires the teacher to observe students within groups as they work on multiple ability tasks. When a low-status student demonstrates competence on an important intellectual ability (such as spatial reasoning or scientific thinking), the teacher publicly provides an evaluation of that student describing specifically what he or she has done well, what ability he or she is displaying, and why this is an important resource for the group. Teachers who use these low status treatments more frequently have more equal-status interaction within their cooperative learning groups than teachers who use status treatments less frequently (Cohen, 1988).

Several propositions emerge from this review on equity within cooperative groups. In order to maximize productivity of cooperative learning, it is necessary to modify the effects of status. When the task is of a more routine variety, good effects can be achieved with scripted interaction and turn-taking, both of which will cut down on the possibilities for status to affect interaction. When the task is an ill-structured problem, however, it is necessary to treat differential expectations for competence in order to achieve maximum interaction and productivity.

When cooperative learning is used to improve intergroup relations, the concerns are not only that there be equal-status interaction but also that students of different groups learn to treat one another as persons rather than as members of social categories. On the basis of experimental work, Miller, Brewer, and Edwards (1985) caution teachers to avoid making the explicit use of racial or ethnic identity a basis for team formation. For the same reason, they advise against a mechanical composition of groups in which the percentage of each social category is always the same. For example, if a class were 30% African American, the teacher might make a third of each group African-American. In a laboratory analogue of this situation, these experimentalists created new social categories based on the results of a pretest in which subjects were randomly assigned to two groups called *dot overestimators* and *dot underestimators*. When assignment to groups was explicitly based on these categories, with one out-group member and two in-group members, those in the minority status showed more bias toward the other group than when assignment to groups was noncategorical. These findings on salience of social categories should also apply to gender; teachers should avoid composing groups so that they always have half males and females.

Classroom Factors Affecting Interaction

In addition to the design of the group-work task itself, several classroom strategies will affect the interaction and productivity of the small groups. Considerable attention is paid to these factors in many thorough staff development programs in cooperative learning.

Training students for cooperation. Many developers of cooperative learning models have observed that groups quite frequently fail to show behaviors that one might call cooperative; in fact, close examination of some groups reveals negative and insensitive behavior as well as refusal to assist one another in any meaningful way. The behavior called for in cooperative small groups is radically different from the behavior required in conventional classroom settings. Therefore, some developers of cooperative learning strongly recommend team-building or skill-building activities prior to cooperative learning that are designed to develop the prosocial behaviors necessary for cooperation as well as some specific skills for working successfully with others. Or, adapting techniques from group dynamics, they suggest that groups should become aware of their interpersonal and work processes as they work and take time to discuss how they are doing as a group.

Available research on the effectiveness of such strategies suggests that investing in such preparation and time spent on group process can definitely make for more productive groups. Swing and Peterson (1982) experimented with training fifth graders in task-related interaction and, more specifically, in improving explaining skills. The preparation included a practicum in explaining in which each student had the chance to explain a problem and to receive feedback from training personnel. The trained groups were compared on a test of mathematics achievement to control groups who participated in identical collaborative seatwork tasks but received no training in interaction. The trained groups had significantly higher rates of task-related interaction and provided and received more higher order explanations than the control groups. Although there were no statistically significant differences in achievement and retention between the two conditions, trained students with low scores on the pretest outperformed control students with similar scores on the pretests. Low-achieving students who more often provided and/or received conceptual explanations during seatwork obtained higher achievement scores.

Similarly, in collaborative seatwork on vocabulary words, Lew, Mesch, Johnson, and Johnson (1986) trained

students in collaborative skills of sharing ideas and information, keeping the group on task, praising and encouraging the contributions of others, and checking to make sure everyone in the group understood what was being taught. Moreover, the teacher awarded bonus points toward the quiz grade if all group members were observed to demonstrate three out of four cooperative skills. The addition of training in cooperative skills, plus the reward contingency for cooperative behavior, was necessary before cooperative groups produced superior achievement results to individual study. Positive goal interdependence and academic reward contingencies were not enough by themselves to produce superior achievement results.

Giving students specific feedback on their cooperative behaviors and asking them to reflect on how the group is behaving with respect to specific skills can have good results as well. A combination of these two strategies of teacher feedback and group processing proved more effective on a complex computer simulation problem than either the large-group processing alone or the condition where no processing took place (Johnson, Johnson, & Stanne, 1990; Johnson, Johnson, Stanne, & Garibaldi, 1990). The Group Investigation method also provides extensive feedback on cooperative behavior, a feature that is not present in the STAD procedures to which it has been compared (Sharan et al., 1984). In an evaluation of the effects of Group Investigation and STAD, students from both conditions were asked to copy a Leggo figure from a model. The students from the Group Investigation classrooms showed more cooperative behavior and less competitive behavior than the students from STAD classrooms (although either of these two cooperative methods produced more cooperative behavior and less competitive behavior than the classes that had received traditional whole-class instruction).

All these studies utilized very specific behaviors, whether in pretraining or in feedback and group processing. The importance of specificity is illustrated by the failure of a procedure utilized by Huber and Eppler (1990). Half the groups of fifth graders who participated in jigsaw learning with group reward contingencies rated their own cooperative process by means of a 6-point scale. They rated polarities such as friendly-hostile, hardworking-careless. Students were provided with the three most positive and three most negative ratings of their own group members on graph paper. They were then asked to discuss for 5 minutes what went wrong during the last session and how they could improve cooperation next time. The process feedback had no effect on achievement.

The behaviors must not only be specific but also directly relevant to the desired behaviors in the particular tasks that the teacher has assigned to the groups. In working with cultural diversity in the classroom, Miller and Harrington (1990) recommend a direct linking of group process skills to the team's task goals as opposed to human relations training programs that emphasize the general development of sensitivity, receptivity, openness, and reciprocity. Their rationale is that the former approach promotes more personalized interaction that helps people treat one another as persons rather than as members of categories. For example, Johnson, Johnson, Stanne, and Garibaldi (1990) selected for processing the behaviors of summarizing ideas and information of all group members, encouraging active oral participation of all members, and checking for agreement among members each time a decision was made that was relevant to a group working on a computer simulation. During the student-led processing, each member was assigned responsibility for ensuring that all members engaged in one of the three social skills.

When there is no preparation for cooperative interaction, mixed gender groups have been shown to work quite differently from single gender groups and can present problems of unwanted male dominance. Mixed-gender pairs working on a LOGO programming exercise exhibited social dominance by the boys; girls were less motivated and successful (Siann & Macleod, 1986). Underwood and Mc-Caffrey (1990) studied pairs of students (10 and 11 years of age) on a computer task filling in missing letters from words. They were not told how to work together. Single-sex pairs were more productive than mixed-sex pairs. Unlike the single-sex pairs, there was no improvement for mixed-sex pairs in their group performance over their individual performance. Single-sex pairs worked by discussion and agreement with each member of the pair contributing. Keyboard control was shared. In contrast, the mixed-gender pairs tended not to work by negotiation but simply divided the labor with one taking over the keyboard and the other instructing the typist with little discussion of alternative solutions.

In computer tasks, the students left to their own devices may well choose the division of labor of "thinkist" and "typist" in which there is relatively little interaction and argument. This is evidently especially likely to happen with young boys and girls who have often been observed to have strained and uneasy relationships with one another in the early elementary years. Students require preparation and instruction for the level of interaction that is considered desirable for the task. If this preparation had been undertaken, it is unlikely that mixed-gender groups would represent a special problem, although this is an empirical question for future research.

In sum, either pretraining or processing of the group while they are at work on the task can be effective in improving the productivity of small groups. There are several ways in which these procedures probably operate to improve the functioning of the group. They reduce interpersonal conflict; they increase the probability of specific behaviors that have been linked to learning outcomes, and they help the members of the group to take responsibility for one another and for what is happening in the group. Thus, they help to solve the key problem of motivation to participate. However, it is unlikely that these procedures will be effective unless they are both specific and relevant to behaviors that lead to the group goal. One note of caution: If the group is given an ill-structured problem, the procedures should not be so specific to what the group is supposed to say and think that they succeed in micromanaging the process of thinking and talking.

Teacher role. Obviously, when students are working independently in small groups, the teacher's role changes. She or he cannot be everywhere at once telling people what to do; whenever the teacher tries to tell the class something directly, the interaction in the small groups comes to an abrupt halt. Within small groups, the self-directed nature of student talk tends to disappear when the teacher arrives (Harwood, 1989).

The management of cooperative learning requires the teacher to deal with instruction that has become quite complex; instead of the whole class working on the same task, there may be as many as six or seven groups working at their own pace, or, in some cases, each group may be working on a different task. The sociologist refers to the latter pattern of work as a highly differentiated technology. What do teachers do when faced with such a complex mode of instruction? In a study of complex instruction, involving discovery learning with multiple learning centers and students permitted to move on to new centers when they finished their worksheets at the previous center, there was considerable variability in the number of learning centers in operation (Cohen & Intili, 1981). Some teachers simplified the technology by operating only three learning centers, each with an adult (a teacher, an aide, and a parent volunteer) directly supervising the center. Clearly, some teachers were unable or unwilling to delegate authority–that is to let go and to allow the children to solve problems for themselves. If the teachers were unable to delegate authority (as measured by the number of students under direct adult supervision), there were fewer learning centers in operation, the percentage of students talking and working together was lower, and, as a consequence, the average learning gains were precisely those where teachers were successful in delegating authority so that more children could talk and work together at multiple learning centers.

The larger the number of groups that a teacher is trying to manage, the lower the probability that she will use direct instruction and direct supervision in which she exerts detailed control over how tasks are executed (Cohen, Lotan, & Leechor, 1989). Moreover, when there are a larger number of groups, direct supervision is unrelated to student disengagement (Rosenholtz, 1981). When multiple groups are in operation, lateral relations or talk between the students, rather than direct supervision, predict engagement.

Cooperative learning can become complex along other dimensions besides the differentiation into multiple groups and materials. As discussed above, tasks given to the groups can be relatively routine procedures, or they can be problems with ill-structured solutions. If interaction is critical because the small-group task is a problem with an ill-structured solution, the extent to which the teacher applies direct supervision will diminish the possibilities and opportunities of students communicating with one another. If the teacher, as an authority figure, takes responsibility for their task engagement, students will not assume responsibility for solving problems related to the task. In two data sets, based on classrooms using complex instruction, Cohen, Lotan, and Leechor (1989) found that the rate at which the teacher used forms of direct instruction when students were working in small groups was negatively related to talking and working together among the students. Direct supervision is the obverse of delegation of authority. This research provides support for a general sociological principle formulated by Perrow (1967). Once technology has become more uncertain, two necessary changes should be made in order to maintain or increase organizational productivity: delegation of authority to the workers and more lateral communication among the workers. In educational terms, this means that, when cooperative learning tasks are nonroutine problem-solving or discovery tasks, it is necessary for the teachers to avoid direct supervision and to foster talking and working together within the small groups.

Learning to delegate authority to groups is not an easy task for teachers. Cohen and Intili (1981) found, as reported above, that teachers were afraid of losing control of the classroom and thus reduced the number of groups so that they could use direct supervision. These researchers responded by developing a new system designed to assure the teachers that they could still be in control of the classroom even though the authority was delegated to groups of students. They required that students move on to a new learning center only when the whole group had completed its task and worksheet. Furthermore, behavior was controlled through a system of systematic training in cooperative norms and the allocation of a different role to each group member. The introduction of this new system resulted in a significant increase in the percentage of students in small groups and a reduction in the use of direct supervision, along with a sharp increase in the proportion

of students observed talking and working together on the task (Cohen & De Avila, 1983).

Summary of Contextual Forces

In this section, I have reformulated the question of whether or not to structure interaction as a question of the conditions under which interaction should be structured to obtain maximal effectiveness. For example, it may be hypothesized that too much structuring may impede conceptually oriented interaction, particularly if it micromanages what group members are to say and think about. The same type of structure may be highly productive when groups are trying to learn a lesson the teacher has imparted or to absorb information on a given topic.

Status factors can affect interaction within small groups and, indirectly, their productivity. Particularly when the task is conceptual and nonroutine, one must treat expectations for competence so as to modify status effects if productivity is to be maximized.

Finally, there are two classroom factors that have been shown to affect interaction. Not only is training for cooperation necessary for effective groups, but the recommended behaviors should be specific and directly relevant to desired behaviors if cooperative interaction is desired. One cannot neglect the role of the teacher in fostering interaction within productive small groups. Our final proposition concerns the importance of delegation of authority in fostering interaction for groups engaged in group tasks with ill-structured solutions.

Conclusion

The research on cooperative learning has been moving past the necessity to defend this strategy as a legitimate method of instruction that can help students to learn. As the research has developed, there has been a tendency to become mired in ideological conflicts concerning the desirability of competitive elements embedded within cooperation and the use of extrinsic versus intrinsic rewards. Additionally, as questions are raised about what types of cooperative learning are the most productive, they tend to be answered by unconditional generalizations and by research designs that compare one of the popular models of cooperative learning with another.

By focusing on factors that make for a productive discourse within small groups, this analysis has raised questions concerning the kinds of discourse that are productive of different types of learning. Furthermore, the focus has been on the factors that affect discourse rather than factors that directly impact achievement gains. In other words, with interaction the central issue, the question becomes: What kinds of interaction are necessary for different kinds of outcomes? And what are the task instructions, student preparation, and teacher role that foster the desired type of interaction?

This analysis moves away from the fruitless debates about intrinsic and extrinsic rewards and goal and resource interdependence that have tied the field into theoretical and ideological knots for some time. Instead, I have recommended that propositions be conditionalized on whether or not it is a problem with an ill-structured solution. Research on the effects of interaction and on structuring interaction should be conditionalized according to these dimensions. Even the relationship of reward contingencies to achievement may vary as a function of whether or not the task is a true group task with high intrinsic interest. A focus on task and interaction can assist researchers, staff developers, and practitioners in moving on to a second generation cooperative learning that is more firmly based on detailed knowledge of what makes these groups productive.

References

Aaronson, E., Blaney, N., Sikes, J., & Snapp, M. (1978). *The jigsaw classroom.* Beverly Hills: Sage.

Abrami, P.C., Chambers, B., D Apollonia, M.F., & De Simone, C. (1992). Group outcome: The relationship between group learning outcome, attributional style, academic achievement, and self-concept. *Contemporary Educational Psychology,* 17, 1–9,

Barnes, D., & Todd, F. (1977). *Communication and learning in small groups.* London: Routledge & Kegan Paul.

Berger, J. B., Cohen, B.P., & Zelditch, M., Jr. (1966). Status characteristics and expectation states. In J. Berger & M. Zelditch, Jr. (Eds.), *Sociological theories in progress* (Vol. 1, pp. 29–46). Boston: Houghton-Mifflin.

Berger, J.B., Cohen, B.P., & Zelditch, M., Jr. (1972). Status characteristics and social interaction. *American Sociological Review,* 37, 241–255.

Bossert, S.T. (1988). Cooperative activities in the classroom. *Review of Research in Education,* 15, 225–250.

Brown, A., & Palincsar, A. (1986). *Guided cooperative learning and individual knowledge acquisition* (Tech. Rep. No. 372). Urbana-Champagne: University of Illinois, Center for the Study of Reading.

Chambers, B., & Abrami, P.C. (1991). The relationship between student team learning outcomes and achievement, causal attributions, and affect. *Journal of Educational Psychology,* 83, 140–146.

Chang, G.L., & Wells, G. (1987). *The literate potential of collaborative talk.* Paper presented at the meeting of the International Oracy Convention, Norwich, England.

Cohen, B.P., & Arechevala-Vargas. (1987). *Interdependence, interaction and productivity* (Working Paper No. 87-3). Stanford: Center for Sociological Research.

Cohen, B.P., & Cohen, E.G. (1991), From groupwork among children to R&D teams: Interdependence, interaction and produc-

tivity. In E.J. Lawler, B. Markovsky, C. Ridgeway, & H.A. Walker (Eds.), *Advances in group processes* (Vol. 8, pp. 205–226). Greenwich, CN: JAI.

Cohen, E.G. (1982), Expectation states and interracial interaction in school settings. *Annual Review of Sociology,* 8, 109–235.

—— (1984). Talking and working together: Status interaction and learning. In P. Peterson, L.C. Wilkinson, & M. Hallinan (Eds.), *Instructional groups in the classroom: Organization and processes* (pp. 171–188). Orlando: Academic.

—— (1988, July). *Producing equal status behavior in cooperative learning.* Paper presented at the convention of the International Association for the Study of Cooperation in Education, Shefayim, Israel.

—— (1991). Teaching in multiculturally heterogeneous classrooms: Findings from a model program. *McGill Journal of Education,* 26, 7–23.

Cohen, E.G., & De Avila, E. (1983). *Learning to think in math and science: Improving local education for minority children* (Final Report to the Johnson Foundation). Stanford University, School of Education.

Cohen, E.G. & Intili, J.K. (1981). *Interdependence and management in bilingual classrooms* (Final Report No. NIE-G-80-0217). Stanford University, School of Education.

Cohen, E.G., Lotan, R., & Catanzarite, L. (1988). Can expectations for competence be treated in the classroom? In M. Webster, Jr., & M. Foschi (Eds.,) *Status generalization: New theory and research* (pp. 27–54). Stanford: Stanford University Press.

Cohen, E.G., Lotan, R., & Leechor, C. (1989). Can classrooms learn? *Sociology of Education,* 62, 75–94.

Davidson, N. (1985). Small group learning and teaching in mathematics: A selective review of the research. In R. Slavin, S. Sharan, S. Kagan, R. Hertz-Lazarowitz, G. Webb, & R. Schmuck (Eds.), *Learning to cooperate, cooperating to learn.* New York: Plenum.

Dembo, M., & McAuliffe, T. (1987). Effects of perceived ability and grade status on social interaction and influence in cooperative groups. *Journal of Educational Psychology,* 79, 415–423.

Deutsch, M. (1962). Cooperation and trust: Some theoretical notes. In M.R. Jones (Ed.), *Nebraska symposium on motivation* (pp. 275–319). Lincoln, NE: University of Nebraska Press.

Ehrlich, D.E. (1991). *Moving beyond cooperation: Developing science thinking in interdependent groups.* Unpublished doctoral dissertation, Stanford University.

Fletcher, B. (1985). Group and individual learning of junior high school children on a micro-computer-based task. *Educational Review,* 37, 252–261.

Harwood, D. (1989). The nature of teacher-pupil interaction in the active tutorial work approach: Using interaction analysis to evaluate student-centered approaches. *British Educational Research Journal,* 15, 177–194.

Hertz-Lazarowitz, R. (1989). Cooperation and helping in the classroom: A contextual approach. *International Journal of Educational Research,* 13, 113–119.

Hoffman, D.E. (1973). *Students' expectations and performance in a simulation game.* Unpublished doctoral dissertation, Stanford University.

Hooper, S., & Hannafin, M.J. (1988). Cooperative CBI: The effects of heterogeneous vs. homogeneous grouping on the learning of progressively complex concepts. *Journal of Educational Computing Research, 4*, 413–424.

Huber, G., & Eppler, R. (1990). Team learning in German classrooms: Processes and Outcomes. In S. Sharan (Ed.), *Cooperative learning: Theory and research* (pp. 151–171). New York: Praeger.

Johnson, D., & Johnson, R. (1985). Classroom conflict: Controversy versus debate in learning groups. *American Educational Research Journal, 22*, 237–256.

——. (1990). Cooperative learning and achievement. In S. Sharan (Ed.), *Cooperative learning: Theory and research* (pp. 23–37). New York: Praeger.

Johnson, D., Johnson, R., & Maruyama, G. (1983). Interdependence and interpersonal attraction among heterogeneous and homogeneous individuals: A theoretical formulation and a meta-analysis of the research. *Review of Educational Research, 53*, 5–54.

—— (1984). Goal interdependence and interpersonal attraction in heterogeneous classrooms: A meta-analysis. In N. Miller & M. Brewer (Eds.), *Groups in contact: The psychology of desegregation* (pp. 187–212). Orlando: Academic.

Johnson, D., Johnson, R., & Stanne, M. (1990). Impact of goal and resource interdependence on problem-solving success. *Journal of Social Psychology, 129*, 507–516.

Johnson, D., Johnson, R., Stanne, M., & Garibaldi, A. (1990). Impact of group processing on achievement in cooperative groups. *Journal of Social Psychology, 13*, 507–516.

Johnson, D.W., Maruyama, G., Johnson, R., Nelson, D., & Skon, L. (1981). Effects of cooperative, competitive, and individualistic goal structure on achievement: A meta-analysis. *Psychological Bulletin, 89*, 47–62.

King, A. (1989). Verbal interaction and problem-solving within computer-assisted cooperative learning groups. *Journal of Educational Computing Research, 5*, 1–15.

Leal, A. (1985). *Sex inequities in classroom interaction: An evaluation of an intervention.* Unpublished doctoral dissertation, Stanford University.

Leechor, C. (1988). *How high achieving and low achieving students differentially benefit from working together in cooperative small groups.* Unpublished doctoral dissertation, Stanford University.

Lew, M., Mesch, D., Johnson, D., & Johnson, R. (1986). Positive interdependence, academic and collaborative skills, group contingencies, and isolated students. *American Educational Research Journal, 23*, 476–488.

Lockheed, M.E., Harris, A., & Nemcef, W.P. (1983). Sex and social influence: Does sex function as a status characteristic in mixed-sex groups of children? *Journal of Educational Psychology, 75*, 877–886.

McAuliffe, T. (1991, April). *Status rules of behavior in scenarios of cooperative learning groups.* Paper presented at the Annual Meeting of the American Educational Research Association, Chicago.

Miller, N., Brewer, M., & Edwards, K. (1985). Cooperative interaction in desegregated settings: A laboratory analogue. *Journal of Social Issues, 41*, 63–79.

Miller, N., & Harrington, H.J. (1990). A situational identity perspective on cultural diversity and teamwork in the classroom. In S. Sharan (Ed.), *Cooperative learning: Theory and research* (pp. 39–75). New York: Praeger.

Navarrete, C. (1985). *Problem resolution in small group interaction: A bilingual classroom study.* Unpublished doctoral dissertation, Stanford University.

Newmann, F. (1991). Linking restructuring to authentic student achievement. *Phi Delta Kappan, 72*, 458–463.

Newmann, F., & Thompson, J.A. (1987) *Effects of cooperative learning on achievement in secondary schools: A summary of research.* Madison, WI: University of Wisconsin-Madison, National Center on Effective Secondary Schools.

Noddings, N. (1989). Theoretical and practical concerns about small groups in mathematics. *Elementary School Journal, 89*, 607–623.

Nystrand, M. (1986). *The structure of written discourse: Studies of reciprocity between readers and writers.* New York: Academic.

Nystrand, M., Gamoran, A., & Heck, M.J. (1991). *Small groups in English: When do they help students and how are they best used?* Madison, WI: University of Wisconsin-Madison, Center on the Organization and Restructuring of Schools.

Oakes, J., & Lipton, M. (1990). *Making the best of schools: A handbook for parents, teachers, and policymakers.* New Haven: Yale University Press.

Okebukola, P.A. (1985). The relative effectiveness of cooperative vs. competitive interaction techniques in strengthening student performance in science classes. *Science Education, 69*, 501–509.

Palincsar, A.S., Brown, A.L., & Martin, S.M. (1987). Peer interaction in reading comprehension instruction. *Educational Psychologist, 22*, 231–253.

Perrow, C. (1967). A framework for the comparative analysis of organizations. *American Sociological Review, 32*, 194–208.

Peterson, P., & Swing, S. (1985). Students' cognitions as mediators of the effectiveness of small-group learning. *Journal of Educational Psychology, 77*, 299–312.

Rosenholtz, S.H. (1981). *Effect of task arrangements and management systems on engagement of low-achieving students.* Unpublished doctoral dissertation, Stanford University.

Rosenholtz, S.J. (1985). Treating problems of academic status. In J. Berger & M. Zelditch, Jr. (Eds.), *Status, rewards, and influence* (pp. 445–470). San Francisco: Jossey-Bass.

Rosenholtz, S.J., & Wilson, B. (1980). The effects of classroom structure of shared perceptions of ability. *American Educational Research Journal, 17*, 175–182.

Ross, J. (1988). Improving social-environmental studies problem solving through cooperative learning. *American Educational Research Journal, 25*, 573–591.

Ross, J., & Raphael, D. (1990). Communication and problem solving achievement in cooperative learning groups. *Journal of Curriculum Studies, 22*, 149–164.

Salomon, G., & Globerson, T. (1989). When teams do not function the way they ought to. *International Journal of Educational Research, 13*, 89–99.

Schwartz, D.L., Black, J.B., & Strange, J. (1991, April). *Dyads have a fourfold advantage over individuals inducing abstract rules.* Paper presented at the Annual Meeting of the American Educational Research Association, Chicago.

Sharan, S. (1980). Cooperative learning in small groups: Recent methods and effects on achievement, attitudes, and ethnic relations. *Review of Educational Research,* 50, 241–271.

Sharan, S., Kussell, P., Hertz-Lazarowitz, R., Begarano, Y., Raviv, S., Sharan, Y. (1984). *Cooperative learning in the classroom: Research in desegregated schools.* Hillsdale, NJ: Erlbaum.

Sharan, S., & Shachar, H. (1988). *Language and learning in the cooperative classroom.* New York: Springer-Verlag.

Siann, G., & Macleod, G. (1986). Computers and children of primary school age: Issues and questions. *British Journal of Educational Technology,* 17, 133–144.

Slavin, R. (1980). Cooperative learning. *Review of Educational Research,* 50, 315–342.

—— (1983a). *Cooperative learning.* New York: Longman.

—— (1983b). When does cooperative learning increase student achievement? *Psychological Bulletin,* 94, 429–445.

—— (1987). Developmental and motivational perspectives on cooperative learning: A reconciliation. *Child Development,* 58, 1161–1167.

Smith, K., Johnson, D.W., & Johnson, R.T. (1981). Can conflict be constructive?: Controversy versus concurrence seeking in learning groups. *Journal of Educational Psychology,* 73, 651–63.

Spurlin, J.E., Dansereau, D.F., Larson, C.O., & Brooks, L. (1984). Cooperative learning strategies in processing descriptive text: Effects of role and activity level of the learner. *Cognitive and Instruction,* 1, 451–463.

Stevenson, B.J. (1982). *An analysis of the relationship of student-student consultation to academic performance in differentiated classroom settings.* Unpublished doctoral dissertation, Stanford University.

Swing, S., & Peterson, P. (1982). The relationship of student ability and small-group interaction to student achievement. *American Educational Research Journal,* 19, 259–274.

Tammivaara, J.S. (1982). The effects of task structure on beliefs about competence and participation in small groups. *Sociology of Education,* 55, 212–222.

Tudge, J. (1990). Vygotsky: The zone of proximal development and peer collaboration: Implications for classroom practice. In L. Moll (Ed.), *Vygotsky and education: Instructional implications and applications of sociohistorical psychology.* New York: Columbia University Press.

—— (1991, April). *Age and gender as moderators of the effects of peer collaboration.* Paper presented at the Annual Meeting of the American Educational Research Association, Chicago.

Underwood, G., & McCaffrey, M. (1990). Gender differences in a cooperative computer-based language task. *Educational Research,* 32, 44–49.

Vedder, P. (1985). *Cooperative learning: A study on processes and effects of cooperation between primary school children.* Groningen, The Netherlands: University of Groningen.

Vygotsky, L. (1978). *Mind in society.* Cambridge, MA: Harvard University Press.

Webb, N. (1983). Predicting learning from student interaction: Defining the interaction variable. *Educational Psychologist,* 18, 33–41.

——(1984a). Microcomputer learning in small groups: Cognitive requirements and group processes. *Journal of Educational Psychology,* 76, 1076–1088.

—— (1984b). Sex differences in interaction and achievement in cooperative small groups. *Journal of Educational Psychology,* 76, 33–44.

—— (1991). Task-related verbal interaction and mathematics learning in small groups. *Journal of Research in Mathematics Education,* 22, 366–389.

—— (1992). Testing a theoretical model of student interaction and learning in small groups. In R. Hertz-Lazarowitz & N. Miller (Eds.), *Interaction in cooperative groups: the theoretical anatomy of group learning* (pp. 102–119). New York: Cambridge University Press.

Webb, N., Ender, P., & Lewis, S. (1986). Problem-solving strategies and group processes in small groups learning computer programming. *American Educational Research Journal,* 23, 243–251.

Webb, N., & Kenderski, C.M. (1984). Student interaction and learning in small group and whole-class settings. In P.L. Peterson, L.C. Wilkinson, & M. Hallinan (Eds.), *The social context of instruction: Group organization and group processes* (pp. 153–170). Orlando: Academic.

Webster, M., Jr., & Driskell, J. (1983). Beauty as status. *American Journal of Sociology,* 89, 140–165.

Widaman, K.F., & Kagan, S. (1987). Cooperativeness and achievement: Interaction of student cooperativeness with cooperative versus competitive classroom organization. *Journal of School Psychology,* 25, 355–365.

Wilkinson, L., & Calculator, S. (1982). Request and responses in peer-directed reading groups. *American Educational Research Journal,* 19, 107–120.

Yager, S. (1985). *The effects of structured oral discussion during a set of cooperative learning lessons on student achievement and attitude.* Unpublished doctoral dissertation, University of Iowa.

Yager, S., Johnson, D., & Johnson R. (1985). Oral discussion, group-to-individual transfer and achievement in cooperative learning groups. *Journal of Educational Psychology,* 77, 60–66.

Yueh, J., & Alessi, S. (1988). The effect of reward structure and group ability composition on cooperative computer-assisted instruction. *Journal of Computer-Based Instruction,* 15, 18–22.

Zack, M. (1988, July). *Delegation of authority and the use of the student facilitator role.* Paper presented at the meeting of the International Association for the Study of Cooperation in Education, Kibbutz Shefayim, Israel.

Comments on the article by Heller, Keith, and Anderson

The following paper, by Heller, Keith, and Anderson, is about teaching and learning physics. It considers some important questions and contains interesting information about them, so we must ask what relevance the results in this paper have for mathematics.

The context of the study which this paper describes is Introductory Physics at the University of Minnesota where this course is taught in classes with enrollments of about 120 students. The authors have designed and regularly implement a pedagogy which combines teaching a problem-solving strategy and having students work in cooperative groups to implement and practice that strategy. The specific questions which the study investigates are:

1. Are problem solutions or particular aspects of solutions worked out in cooperative groups better than the work of the best students in the groups?
2. Does individual problem-solving ability change during this course, and if so, is the change different for the better students than for the average and weaker students?
3. How does the problem-solving ability of students who take this course compare with students who take a traditional version of the course?

Several features of this study are of particular importance: the use of cooperative learning in large classes is discussed; the question of whole group performance versus the performance of the best student in a group is considered directly; comparisons are made with classes using traditional pedagogy; and attention is paid not only to performance with specific material in a single course, but also to the overall effects on students' problem-solving ability.

Two other issues are treated in this paper: the effectiveness of using what the authors call "context-rich" problems; and the use of grading practices that reflect both cooperative-group problem solving and the use of a prescribed strategy. The paper describes in some detail all of the components of the instructional strategy and the measurement procedures used in the study. Data is presented on all of the questions which the study addresses.

Finally, the authors summarize their results, which are fairly positive regarding the use of their pedagogical strategies and conclude that cooperative-group problem solving is a viable alternative to large lectures and recitation sections. The paper concludes with some comments on the "costs" of their approach in terms of reduced coverage and increased staff required and raises the question of what effect a focus on problem solving might have on students' development of conceptual understanding.

Discussion Questions

1. Summarize the results of the study reported in this paper.
2. What exactly do these results convince you of regarding the pedagogical strategies described? For example, do you take the authors' conclusions at face-value or do you see any confounding factors that might detract from their results?
3. How would you balance the gains which students may have made with the costs associated with this approach?
4. What do the authors mean by "context-rich" and what is your opinion about it?
5. How important is the fact that the problems were "context-rich"?
6. How important is the use of a prescribed problem solving strategy?
7. How does the grading described in this paper relate to what is reported in other papers in this collection?
8. What can be said about the transferability of these results to mathematics?

Teaching Problem Solving Through Cooperative Grouping Part 1: Group versus Individual Problem Solving[†]

Patricia Heller, Ronald Keith, and Scott Anderson

I. Introduction

Problem solving is one of the primary tools of college physics instruction. Unfortunately, many students in introductory courses consider problem solving to be independent of physics concepts and principles being taught (e.g., "I understand the material, but I just can't solve the problems."), or they believe that specific patterns of mathematical solutions are the physics to be learned (e.g., "I can follow the example in the textbook, but your test problems are too different."). For the past 3 years the University of Minnesota has been developing and testing an instructional approach to help students in a large introductory physics course integrate the conceptual and mathematical aspects of problem solving. This approach combines the explicit teaching of a problem-solving strategy with a supportive environment to help students implement that strategy. The supportive environment is provided by having students practice solving problems in cooperative groups.[1] The results of experiments on the structure and management of well-functioning cooperative groups are described in a companion article.[2]

Cooperative-group problem solving was adopted for two reasons. First, it has been shown to be an effective technique for helping students learn a complex skill.[3-5] We hypothesized that in well-functioning groups, students share their conceptual and procedural knowledge as they solve a problem together. During this joint construction of a solution, individual group members can request explanations and justifications from one another. This mutual critique would clarify all the members' thinking about the physics concepts and principles to be used, and how those concepts and principles should be applied to the particular problem. Moreover, each member can observe others perform the varied thinking strategies that he or she must perform independently and silently on individual problem assignments. The second reason for adopting cooperative grouping is more mundane and practical. Of the recommended teaching techniques for helping students become better problem solvers, cooperative grouping places the least demand on the instructors. With minimal training, graduate student teaching assistants can implement cooperative groups in recitation and laboratory sections.[6]

The purpose of this study was to investigate the effectiveness of our problem-solving instructional approach, particularly the cooperative grouping aspect. Although research in precollege education suggests that all students benefit from group work,[5,7] we are not aware of any studies that have been done on group problem solving in col-

[†] Reprinted with permission from *American Journal of Physics,* 60 (7), July 1992, pp. 627–636. Copyright © 1992 American Association of Physics Teachers.

lege physics. We assumed that if well-functioning cooperative groups were established, then group problem solutions would surpass those of any single group member on equivalent problems, even those of the highest ability member. In addition, if all students acquired individual problem solving skills, then there would be an increase in the quality of students' individual problem solutions over time, independent of their increasing knowledge of physics. If, on the other hand, the desired collaborative behaviors did not occur in the groups, then the group solutions would simply reflect the performance of the best (highest ability) student in the groups, and little benefit would accrue to anyone from the exercise. In that case, extensive group work might actually hinder the learning of the best students, who would spend their time dealing with other students rather than extending their own knowledge and skills.

This paper reports the results of our investigations to answer the following questions:

1. Are problem solutions worked out in cooperative groups better than the work of the best students in the groups?

2. If group problem solutions are better than individual problem solutions, which aspects of problem solving are accomplished better in the groups?

3. Do students' individual problem-solving performances improve during the course of instruction. If so, does the performance of the best students show the same improvement as that of the other students?

4. Are students taught with our instructional approach better individual problem solvers than students in a traditional course?

Of course no educational research is independent of the context in which it is done. The first section below outlines the introductory physics course and the problem-solving instructional approach employed. The following sections describe measurement procedures and the investigation methods and results. The last section summarizes our conclusions and discusses some implications of the results and unresolved issues for further research.

II. DESCRIPTION OF THE COURSE

A. Organization and goals

The University of Minnesota offers a two-quarter, algebra based physics course that is required by 24 different departments (e.g., architecture, agricultural engineering, geology, food science and nutrition, pharmacy, veterinary medicine, fishery and wildlife, soil science). The course consists of four 50-min lectures, a 50-min recitation section, and a 2-h laboratory per week. The course traditionally covers about two-thirds of the chapters in an introductory text for this level.[8] The enrollment is about 120 students in the lecture section, with 15–20 students in the recitation sections and laboratories, which are taught by graduate student teaching assistants.

We recently surveyed the faculty in the departments that require this physics course to determine what they want their students to learn. The survey revealed that their important goals are for students to: (1) learn the fundamental principles of physics (e.g., force laws, conservation of energy, conservation of momentum); (2) learn general qualitative and quantitative problems solving skills that they can apply to new situations; and (3) overcome their misconceptions[9] about the behavior of the physical world. To meet these goals, several changes were implemented in one experimental section of the course. These changes were based on recommendations in the physics instructional literature.[10-13] For the sake of brevity, only the problem-solving instructional approach is described here.

B. Problem solving instructional approach

The problem-solving instructional approach had several integrated components. First, students were taught a general problem-solving strategy that is based on a variety of research and instructional literature describing the nature of effective (or "expert") problem solving in physics. Second, a set of context-rich practice and test problems were constructed that reinforce the usefulness of the strategy. Third, during recitation and laboratory sessions students worked in carefully managed cooperative groups to practice using the prescribed strategy to solve context-rich problems. Finally, grading practices were changed to reflect the importance of both cooperative-group problem solving and the use of the prescribed strategy. The following sections describe these four components of the problem-solving instructional approach.

1. The prescribed problem-solving strategy. There is an expanding body of research comparing expert and novice problem-solving strategies in physics.[14-16] Novices typically begin to solve a problem by plunging into the algebraic and numerical solution—they search for and manipulate equations, plugging numbers into the equations until they find a combination that yields an answer.[17] All too often they neither use their conceptual knowledge of physics to qualitatively analyze the problem situation, nor do they systematically plan a solution before they begin numerical and algebraic manipulations of equations.[15,16,18] When they arrive at a numerical answer, they are usually satisfied—they rarely check to see if the answer makes sense.

The instructional literature recommends several strategies to help students integrate the conceptual and proceptual aspects of problem solving.[19,20] These strategies are very similar. The basic form of the five-step strategy designed for our students was strongly influenced by the work of Frederick Reif and Joan Heller,[21] but it has many elements in common with Alan Schoenfeld's framework for mathematics problem solving.[22] It requires students to make a systematic series of translations of the problem into different representations, each in more abstract and mathematical detail.

The five steps of the strategy are defined below in the context of the solution to a dynamics problem involving an airplane, which is shown in Table I. This problem gives the take-off angle and speed of a plane, its cruising speed and altitude, its weight, and the thrust of the plane. Students are asked to find the life and the drag on the plane during takeoff. Prior to this test question, the students had not been taught the specific concepts of lift, drag, and thrust. Figure 1 illustrates how a typical group used the following five steps to solve this problem:

1. Visualize the problem: This step is a translation of the problem statement into a visual and verbal understanding of the problem situation. In the airplane problem, students sketched the plane moving down the runway, taking off, and leveling off at cruising altitude. They determined the relevant information they were given to answer the question, and the general approach to take to the problem.

2. Physics description: This step requires students to use their qualitative understanding of physics concepts and principles to analyze and represent the problem in physics terms (e.g, vector diagrams). In the airplane problem, students drew a free-body and vector force diagram of the plane, and a kinematics diagram showing its position, velocity, and acceleration when it takes off and when it levels off. They then identified symbolically the relevant variables in the problem.

3. Plan a solution: This step involves translating the physics description into an appropriate mathematical representation of the problem (equations of the principles and constraints), determining if there is enough information represented to solve the problem, then specifying the algebraic procedure to extract the unknown variable(s). In the airplane problem, the students used their vector diagrams to generate the correct force and kinematics equations. From the ordering and position of statements in their written solution, we inferred that when they reached Eq. (5), they realized that they did not have enough information to solve the problem.[23] At that point, they went back to their physics description and determined that they could use a trigonometric relation to find the distance the plane traveled while accelerating to cruising altitude.

4. Execute the plan: Students use mathematical rules to obtain an expression with the desired unknown variable on one side of the equation and all the known variables on the other side. Specific values are then substituted into the

---

Airplane problem (group). One morning while waiting for class to begin, you are reading a newspaper article about airplane safety. This article emphasizes the role of metal fatigue in recent accidents. Metal fatigue results from the flexing of airframe parts in response to the forces on the plane, especially during take-off and landing. The reporter uses as an example a plane with a weight of 200,000 lbs and a takeoff speed of 200 mph which climbs at an angle of $30°$ with a constant acceleration to reach its cruising altitude of 30,000 ft with a speed of 500 mph. The jet engines provide a forward thrust of 240,000 lbs by pushing the air backwards. The article then goes on to explain that a plane can fly because the air exerts an upward force on the wings perpendicular to their surface called "lift." You know the air resistance is also a very important force on the plane and is in the direction opposite to the velocity of the plane. The article tells you this force is called the "drag." Although the reporter writes that some metal fatigue is primarily caused by the lift, and some by the drag, she never tells you their size for her example plane. Luckily, the article contains enough information to calculate them, so you do.

Elevator Problem (matched individual). You have been hired to design the interior of a special express elevator for a new office building. This elevator has all the latest safety features and will stop with an acceleration of $g/3$ in case of any emergency. The management would like a decorative lamp hanging from the unusually high ceiling of the elevator. You design a lamp with three sections that hang one directly below the other. Each section is attached to the previous one by a single thin wire that also carries the electric current. The lamp is also attached to the ceiling by a single wire. Each section of the lamp weighs 7.0 N. Because the idea is to make each section appear as if it is floating on the air without support, you want to use the thinnest wire possible. Unfortunately, the thinner the wire, the weaker it is. To determine the thinnest wire that can be used for each stage of the lamp, calculate the force on each wire in case of an emergency stop.

Moving problem (easier individual). You are helping a friend move into a new apartment. A box weighing 150 lbs needs to be moved to make room for a couch. You are taller than the box, so you reach down and push it at an angle of 50 deg from the horizontal. The coefficient of static friction between the box and the floor is 0.50 and the coefficient of kinetic friction between the box and the floor is 0.30. If you want to exert the minimum force necessary, how hard would you push to keep the box moving across the floor?

TABLE I

Examples of context-rich group and individual problems

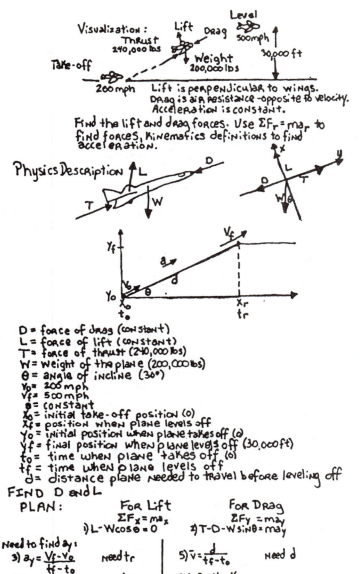

FIGURE 1
A cooperative solution of the airplane problem (Table 1),
illustrating the five steps of the problem-solving strategy.

expression to obtain a numerical solution. In the airplane problem, the students made an algebraic error.

5. Check and evaluate: Finally, the students evaluate the reasonableness of their answer–are the sign and units correct and does the answer match their experience of the world and/or their expectations of how large the numerical answer should be. In the airplane problem, the students first checked for correct force units. They evaluated the reasonableness of their answers by comparing the lift to the given weight, and the drag to the given thrust. They concluded that they had made a mistake somewhere (it was in the algebra) because their drag was larger than the thrust.

An outline of the five-step strategy is shown in Table II. The strategy was presented early in the first quarter and modeled subsequently in all lectures. To encourage the use of the strategy, students were given (1) flow charts that outlined a procedure and major decision points for each step of the strategy, and (2) problem-solving format sheets for solving homework problems. The format sheets reserved a section of the paper for each step of the problem-solving strategy, and each section included brief prompts for the type of information to include in the space provided. For example, the three prompts for planning a solution were: "State relevant general equations. Introduce specific variables into general equations; which specific equations are needed to determine the target quantity? Check—are there as many equations as unknowns?"

2. Context-rich problems. The rationale for constructing context-rich problems is described in detail in a companion article.[2] Briefly, context-rich problems, illustrated in Table I, are designed to focus students' attention on the need to use their conceptual knowledge of physics to qualitatively analyze a problem before beginning to manipulate equations. They are essentially short stories that include a reason for calculating some quality about a real object or event. In addition, they may have one or more of the following characteristics in common with real-word problems: (1) The problem statement does not always explicitly identify the unknown variable; (2) More information may be available than is needed to solve the problem; or (3) Information may be missing, but can easily be estimated or is "common knowledge", (4) Reasonable assumptions need to be made to solve the problem.

3. Cooperative group environment. In both the recitation and laboratory sections, students worked in carefully managed cooperative groups to practice the five-step problem solving strategy. In the recitation sections, they practiced using the strategy to solve context-rich problems like the ones shown in Table I. In the laboratories, which were coordinated with the lectures and recitation sections, they practiced using the strategy to solve concrete, experimental problems. Students had the same instructor (graduate teaching assistant) and worked in the same groups for both

---

1. Visualize the problem.   Translate the words of the problem statement into a visual representation:

- draw a sketch (or series of sketches) of the situation;
- identify the known and unknown quantities and constraints;
- restate the question;
- identify a general approach to the problem–what physics concepts and principles are appropriate to the situation.

2. Describe the problem in physics terms (physics description).   Translate the sketch(s) into a physical representation of the problem:

- use identified principles to construct idealized diagram(s) with a coordinate system (e.g., vector component diagrams) for each object at each time of interest;
- symbolically specify the relevant known and unknown variables;
- symbolically specify the target variable (e.g., find v_0 such that $h_{\max} \geq 10$ m).

3. Plan a solution.   Translate the physics description into a mathematical representation of the problem:

- start with the identified physics concepts and principles in equation form (e.g., $\bar{a}_x = \Delta v_x / \Delta t$, $\sum F_x = ma_x$);
- apply the principles systematically to each object and type of interaction in the physics description (e.g., $N_1 - W_1 \cos\theta = m_1 a_{1x}$ and $W_1 = m_1 g$);
- add equations of constraint that specify the special conditions that restrict some aspect of the problem (e.g. two objects have the same acceleration, $a_1 = a_2$);
- Work backward (from target variable) until you have determined that there is enough information to solve the problem (the same number of independent equations as unknowns);
- Specify the mathematical steps to solve the problem (e.g., solve equation #2 for N_1, then substitute into equation #1, etc.).

4. Execute the plan.   Translate the plan into a series of appropriate mathematical actions:

- use the rules of algebra to obtain an expression with the desired unknown variable on one side of the equation and all the known variables on the other side;
- substitute specific values into the expression to obtain an arithmetic solution.

5. Check and evaluate.   Determine if the answer makes sense:

- check—is the solution complete?
- check—is the sign of the answer correct and does it have the correct units:
- evaluate—is the magnitude of the answer reasonable?

TABLE II
Outline of the five-step problem solving strategy.

their recitation and laboratory section. This allowed students more opportunity to work with the same group members.

The experiments which resulted in the structure and management procedures for cooperative groups are described in a companion article.[2] Briefly, students worked in cooperative groups of three (or occasionally four) members. The composition of the groups changed about three times each quarter. The first groups were formed randomly. After the first test, however, students were assigned to groups by ability: a group consisted of a student from the top third, a student from the middle third, and a student from the lower third of the class based on past test performance. The students were assigned "roles" of Manager, Skeptic, and Checker/Recorder, which were rotated each week. These roles reflect the mental planning and monitoring strategies that individuals must perform when solving problems alone.

4. Testing and grading.   The testing and grading practices were designed to reinforce the use of the five-step problem solving strategy and the importance of cooperation.[2] In addition to individual final exams, the students took four tests the first quarter, and three tests the second quarter. Each test was given in two parts, (1) a context-rich problem to be solved in cooperative groups during the 50-min recitation section, and (2) a short qualitative question and two context-rich problems to be solved individually during the 50-min lecture period the following day. On most tests, one of the context-rich problems was more difficult, and one was easier, as defined below in Sec. IIIB. An example of the context-rich problems from one test are shown in Table I.

For the first three tests, students were required to solve the problems on the problem format sheets; thereafter, problems were solved on blank paper in the standard "blue books." For the group problem students turned in only one solution for their group, and each member of a group received the same grade. All problems, group and individual, were graded on a 20-point scale, and students received points for following the steps of the problem-solving strategy as well as for a correct solution. To reduce competition and encourage cooperation, letter grades were based on set criteria (above 70% was a grade of A, 50%–70% was a grade of B, etc.) rather than based on a curve.

III. MEASUREMENT PROCEDURES

The comparisons made in this study required the creation of two measurement scales: a valid and reliable measure of students' problem solving performance independent of the grading, and a rating scale of problem difficulty. In 1989, several performance and problem difficulty scales were developed, tested and refined. These scales were used to analyze the 1990 data reported in this study. The first section below describes the problem-solving performance rating scales. The second section describes the problem difficulty rating scale.

A. Problem-solving performance

The determination of whether one set of problem solutions are better than another requires a definition of "better..." Simply scoring the correctness of an algebraic or numerical solution and comparing average scores is not a good determination of better problem-solving performance. Students can make any number of mistakes solving problems, some more serious than others. Consequently, we defined "better" solutions as those which exhibit characteristics similar to the solution an expert produces when faced with a real problem. The scoring scheme adopted for measuring problem solving performance is similar to but more rigorous than, the standard grading practice of giving students partial credit for different characteristics of their problem solution. The following six characteristics of expert-like problem solutions were scored.

1. Evidence of conceptual understanding: Does the physics description reveal a clear understanding of physics concepts and relations? For example, does the description indicate curvilinear trajectories for projectiles or incorrect straight-line trajectories: Does the solution employ unbalanced forces for an accelerating object, or incorrect balanced forces?

2. Usefulness of description: Is the essential information needed for a solution present? For example, do the force diagrams include all the relevant forces? For collision problems, and the momentum vectors both before and after an interaction clearly indicated?

3. Match of equations with description: Are the specific equations used consistent with the physics described? For example, are vector equations used to relate vector quantities? Are the described forces appropriately included in specific force equations?

4. Reasonable plan: Does the solution indicate that sufficient equations were assembled before the algebraic manipulations of equations was undertaken? Does the solution include an indication of how to combine equations to obtain an answer?

5. Logical progression: Does the mathematical solution progress logically from general expressions of physics principles to a problem-specific formulation using defined variables? Are numbers substituted for variables only after

an algebraic solution for the unknown variable was obtained?

6. Appropriate mathematics: Aside from minor mistakes, is the mathematics used reasonable? Or does the solution employ invalid mathematical claims in order to obtain an answer (e.g., the mass is small, so set $m = 1$)?

The ratings for these six characteristics were equally weighted and normalized to yield an ordinal problem-solving scale with a maximum score of 100.

Several tests of the 1989 data were made to check the validity and reliability of the scoring scheme. First, we checked that the same mistake was not counted more than once. For example, it is impossible to solve a dynamics problem correctly if all relevant forces are not included in the vector diagram. The scoring scheme counted this type of mistake only once (e.g., to judge whether the equations matched the physics description, the equations were compared with the student's description, not the correct description). Second, we verified that the scoring scheme allowed for the increased sparseness of solution as students' expertise increased. That is, we checked that students independently judged to have gained problem-solving expertise, but who wrote less, received progressively higher problem-solving scores. Procedural neatness was not scored, although we noted that as students gained expertise, their solutions also became procedurally neater. Finally, we made sure that our rating criteria were sufficiently detailed for reliable scoring of solutions by different people.

B. Problem difficulty

A detailed comparison of students' performance on pairs of 1989 individual problems indicated that the following six characteristics contribute to the difficulty of context-rich problems:

1. Problem context: Contexts familiar to the majority of introductory students through direct experience, newspapers, television, or solving standard textbook problems are easier than problems with contexts unfamiliar to the students (e.g., ion beam, protons from the Sun, x-ray signals from pulsars).

2. Problem cues: Problems that cue a standard application of a set of related principles to solve the problem are easier than problems that do not explicitly cue a standard approach. For example, force problems that specify a force as the unknown variable (e.g., What is the lift on the airplane?) are easier than force problems that specify a mass as the unknown variable (e.g., What is the mass of the planet?).

3. Given information: Problems with no extraneous information or missing information in the problem state-

ment are easier than problems with irrelevant information or missing information that must be recalled or estimated.

4. Explicitness of question: Problems that specify a particular unknown variable (e.g., What is the muzzle velocity of the bullet?) are easier than problems for which the desired unknown variable must be determined (e.g., Will this design for the lunar lander work?).

5. Number of approaches: Problems that can be solved with one set of related principles (e.g., kinematics or energy conservation) are easier than problems that require the application of more than one set of related principles for a solution (e.g., both kinematics and energy conservation).

6. Memory load: Problems that require the solution of five or less equations are easier than problems that require the solution of more than five equations.

For each problem, each of these six characteristics was scored as 0 (easier) or 1(more difficult). We found that the sum of the six characteristics accurately predicted the relative difficulty of the course problems. That is, students had lower performance scores on problems with a total difficulty rating of 4 than they did on problems with a difficulty rating of 3, and so on. This scale was used to rate the difficulty of all 1990 group and individual problems.

IV. INVESTIGATIONS

A. Are problem solutions worked out in cooperative groups better than the work of the best students in the groups? It is difficult to design an experiment to determine if group problem solutions are better than the individual solutions of the best problem solvers from each group. Since students have memories and learn from the experiences, we could not give students the same test problem to solve individually that they had solved in groups the day before. Two alternative research designs are possible; either students are matched, or problems are matched. Creating subsets of matched students within an ongoing class is difficult at best, as is matching classes which may have different student populations. For example, one year the experimental section of the course consisted of 50% freshmen students, while the next year only about 25% of the students in the experimental section were freshmen. Consequently, we decided to match problems. Two criteria were used to select an individual problem from each test that matched the group problem: (1) the individual problem must be equal to or less difficult than the group problem, but (2) the individual problem could not be more than two ratings less difficult than the group problem. An individual problem was found that met these criteria for six of the seven class tests.

The best problem solver in each group was defined as the student receiving the highest total grade on the individual test and final exam problems each quarter. If group problem solutions reflect the work of the best problem solvers in the groups, then the problem-solving scores of the group problem solutions should be the same (statistically) as the scores of the "best-in-group" students on the matched individual problem. The null hypothesis, then, is that there is no statistical difference between the group (G) and best-in-group (B) problem-solving scores on matched problems, $H_o : G - B = 0$. The alternative hypothesis is that group problem-solving performance is significantly better than the performance of the best-in-group students on matched problems; $H_a : G - B > 0$.

The median scores of the group problem solutions and the matched best-in-group individual problem solutions for each test are shown in Table III. For all six tests, the median problem-solving score on the group problem is higher than the median score on the matched individual problem. The Wilcoxon Rank-Sum Test[24] for two matched samples were used to test for significant differences. Since the Z statistics shown in Table III are all larger than 1.65, the null hypothesis was rejected at the $p \leq 0.05$ level. Group problem solutions are significantly better than the best-in-group individual solutions on matched problems. We concluded that group problem solutions are not simply the work of the best problem solvers in the groups.

There are two potential sources of systematic error in this analysis. The first source of error occurs in the inherent inability to exactly match the problems. There are three design features of this study that counterbalance this error. First, criteria for judging the difficulty of context-rich problems were developed and tested. Using these criteria, all group problems were judged to be more difficult than

	N	Group problem median	Best-in-group individual problem median	Wilcoxon Z statistic
Winter text 1	33	78	53	4.43[a]
Winter test 3	32	66	60	1.95[b]
Winter test 4	30	85	61	3.36[a]
Spring test 1	30	89	58	4.19[a]
Spring test 2	24	93	53	4.95[a]
Spring test 3	30	78	55	3.50[a]

[a]$p < 0.01$.
[b]$p < 0.05$.

TABLE III
Group medians, best-in-group medians, and the Wilcoxon Z statistic for each class test.

the matched individual problems. This error works in favor of the individual problem solutions, not the group solutions. Second, all group problems were completed (and solutions posted) before the individual problems, so any learning effect favors the individual problem solutions. Finally, six different sets of problems in different content areas were matched over the two-quarters of the course. For any given content area, it is possible that the problems were not well-matched due to a conceptual difficulty evoked by the individual problem, but not the group problem. It is unlikely, however, that this would occur in every physics context.

The second potential source of error is the time factor. Students had 50 min to complete a group problem, and the same time to complete one qualitative question and two problems on an individual test. It could be argued that the group problem solutions were better than the matched best-in-group individual problem solutions simply because the students had more time to complete the group problem. On the other hand, the three students in each group had to discuss all steps, explain, argue, and finally agree to everything written down. Thus it could be argued that the "effective" time each student had to contribute to the group solution (50 min/3 students = 17 min per student) was probably about the same as the time the student had to solve the matched individual test problem (50 min/3 problems = 17 min per problem). Moreover, the group problems were more difficult than the matched individual problems, so they require more time to solve, reducing any error caused by the time factor.

Since students were given unlimited time to complete the final exams, the significance of the time factor could be tested. The pattern of complete and incomplete problems on the individual tests and finals was compared to check if time were a significant factor in lowering students' problem-solving performance on the individual problems. If students had insufficient time to complete the individual test problems, then there would be a pattern of complete final problem and incomplete test problems. (Of course, other factors could product this pattern, such as student learning or higher motivation to finish the final problems in order to improve their grade.) If a student completed 50% (or above) more final problems than test problems each quarter, then time was considered a potential factor in lowering a student's individual problem-solving performance. About 20% of the best-in-group students from each test met this criteria and were removed from the sample.

The remaining students completed approximately the same percentage of time test problems as unlimited-time final problems each quarter. For these students, time presumably was not a significant factor influencing problem completion. The Wilcoxon Rank-Sum tests were recalculated for these students. The results are shown in Table

	N	Group problem median	Best-in-group individual problem median	Wilcoxon Z statistic
Winter test 1	25	78	56	3.55[a]
Winter test 3	25	66	62	2.05[b]
Winter test 4	23	85	62	3.30[a]
Spring test 1	25	89	60	3.73[a]
Spring test 2	20	93	53	3.62[a]
Spring test 3	26	76	58	3.00[a]

[a] $p < 0.01$.
[b] $p < 0.05$.

TABLE IV
Group medians, best-in-group medians, and the Wilcoxon Z statistic of a sample of students for whom time is not a factor in problem completion.

IV. The Z statistics were all larger than 1.65, so the null hypothesis was again rejected. For a sample of students for whom time is not a factor influencing problem completion, group problem solutions are significantly better than best-in-group solutions on matched individual problems.

B. Which components of problem solving are performed better in groups?   To determine which components of problem solving were performed better in groups, we calculated the difference between the percent of group problem solutions and the percent of best-in-group individual problem solutions that received the *highest* rating on each of the six measured characteristics of problem solutions: evidence of conceptual understanding, usefulness of the physics description, match of the equations with the physics description, reasonable solution plan; logical mathematical progression of the solution, and appropriate mathematical procedures. The resulting differences are shown in Table V. As expected, there are variations in the differences that depend on the particular physics concepts and principles covered by each test. Averaged across the content of the two-quarter course, the biggest differences occurred for the three characteristics that measure the qualitative analysis of the problem: conceptual understanding (46%), usefulness of the physics description (35%), and the matching of the physics description with appropriate mathematical expressions of physics concepts and principles (45%). In groups, students generated more useful physics descriptions with fewer conceptual difficulties and a better match to the mathematical expressions of the physics principles than did the best problem solvers from each group on matched individual problems.

Correct conceptual understanding of physics	Useful physics description	Equations match physics description	Reasonable solution plan	Logical mathematical progression in solution	Appropriate mathematical procedures
Winter test 1	38	44	53	9	15	18
Winter test 3	28	41	44	−7	0	0
Winter test 4	−7	50	37	10	10	10
Spring test 1	73	−1	18	11	51	44
Spring test 2	74	49	63	36	47	44
Spring test 3	73	28	55	21	18	49
Average	46	35	45	13	24	22

TABLE V. Difference between percent of groups and percent of best-in-group students receiving the highest problem-solving ratings on matched problems from each test.

The problem solutions in Figs. 1 and 2 illustrate the differences described above in the qualitative analysis of groups and individuals. Figure 1 shows the solution generated by three students to a dynamics problem involving an airplane (see Table I). Their solution was discussed in detail in Sec. IIB. Although the solution is not perfect, the group generated a correct and useful description of the problem that they translated into appropriate force and kinematics equations with no major conceptual errors. In contrast, Fig. 2 shows how the best individual from this group solved the matched individual problem involving an elevator (Table I). This problem requires students to calculate the tension in the wires of a three-section lamp hanging in an elevator in the case of an emergency stop. The student started with a correct and rather clever approach to the problem. Instead of considering each section of the lamp separately, he considered the sections hanging from each lamp wire as one combined object. However, he was unable to translate his physics description into the correct mathematical expressions of the forces acting on each combined object. In addition to an error in the direction of the forces, he confused the mass of the combined object (m) with the mass of each lamp section (m_1, m_2, and m_3). That is, he did not recognize that the total mass to be accelerated is the sum of the individual lamp sections. He also made an algebraic mistake that resulted in incorrect force units.

This solution is typical of many good students who try to skip steps or carry out steps in their heads. If the student had done a more careful qualitative analysis of the problem (e.g., drawn the free-body diagrams as well as the vector diagrams), he might have caught his error. Our studies of group interactions indicated that although the best problem solver in each group usually provided the leadership in generating approaches to the problem, the medium and lower ability students often provided the monitoring and checking to make sure that conceptual and procedural mistakes were not made.[2] In this way, the group process can give valuable assistance to the best students to help them integrate self-monitoring into their problem solving.

C. Did students' individual problem-solving performance improve over time? If our problem-solving instructional approach was effective, then the individual performance of all students should improve over the two quar-

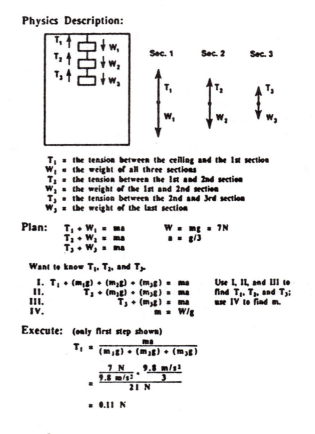

FIGURE 2
The incorrect solution of the highest-ability student from the cooperative group on the matched elevator problem (Table I).

ters of instruction. One possible outcome of working in cooperative groups, however, is that the problem-solving performance of the best students would either not improve, or not improve as much as the other students in the class, since the best students would spend their time dealing with the other students instead of improving their own skills. To test these possibilities, the class was divided into thirds on the basis of total individual grades on the tests and final exams. We then compared the performance pattern over time of the top third, middle third, and bottom third of the students on the least difficult of the context-rich individual problems. These problems, such as the moving problem shown in Table I, were defined as those with a difficulty rating (Sec. III B) between 0 and 2. Although they were the least difficult problems given in the experimental section, they were more difficult than any problems given in the traditional sections of the course.

The results indicated that the problem-solving performance of the top third, middle third, and lower third of the class improved over the two quarters of instruction. For example, Fig. 3 shows the percentage of students whose problem solutions followed a logical mathematical progression. Although there are fluctuations for problems of different difficulties and content areas, the pattern of improvement is roughly the same for all students, including the best students. This improvement pattern was similar for the other five measured characteristics of problem solutions (Sec. IIIA), with the exception of conceptual understanding. There was no appreciable change over time in the percentage of students in any ability group whose problem solutions indicated a correct conceptual understanding of the physics principles involved in the problems.

We concluded that an instructional approach that combines the explicit teaching of a problem solving strategy with practice implementing the strategy in cooperative

groups is effective in improving the problem-solving skills of all students on the less difficult context-rich problems. The highest-ability students improved at approximately the same rate as the other students in the class, indicating that working in cooperative groups is not detrimental to these students. None of the ability groups showed any significant change over time in their performance on the most difficult individual problems, which were matched to the group problems.(See, for example, the problem-solving medians of the best students in Table III.) Although these context-rich problems were solved reasonably well by cooperative groups of students, they appear to be too complex for beginning students to solve individually in a test situation.

D. Are students in the experimental section better individual problem solvers than students in a traditional section? If our problem-solving instructional approach was effective, then students in our experimental section of the introductory course should become better individual problem solvers than students in a traditional section of the course. Instructors teaching the traditional sections of the course were asked to include some context-rich problems on their final exams. However, the context-rich problems, even the least difficult ones, were judged by those instructors to be too difficult for their students. Consequently, two standard exercises from the first-quarter final of a traditional section were included on the first-quarter final of the experimental section of the course. These exercises, which are shown on Table VI, consist of a series of questions that lead students through the problem. For example, in the first inclined plane exercise, the normal force on the block (Question a) is needed to find the force of friction (Question b), which is needed to find the acceleration

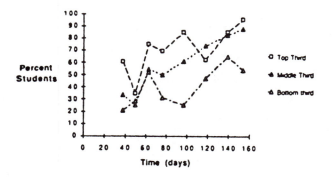

FIGURE 3

Percentage of the top third, middle third, and lower third of the class whose solutions followed a logical mathematical progression. The dashed lines are included for ease of reading the graphs.

---

1. A 60-kg block slides down a plane inclined at an angle of 35° to the horizontal. The coefficient of kinetic friction between the block and the plane is 0.25.

   (a) What is the normal force of the plane on the block?

   (b) What is the force of friction of the plane on the block?

   (c) What is the acceleration of the block?

   (d) If the block starts from rest, how far along the inclined plane does it travel in 1 min?

2. A 450-g ball on a 65-cm string is swung in a VERTICAL circle at a constant rate of 0.85 revolutions per second.

   (a) What is the centripetal acceleration of the ball?

   (b) What is the tension in the string when the ball is at the highest point in the circle?

   (c) What is the tension in the string when the ball is at the lowest point in the circle?

TABLE VI

Standard exercises used in comparison of experimental and traditional students.

of the block (Question c), which is needed to find how far the block lacks in 1 min (Question d). Therefore, unlike context-rich problems, these exercises require minimal planning to solve the problem.

Questionnaire results indicated that the students in the traditional and experimental sections had similar backgrounds and characteristics. The students' solutions to the exercises were scored using the rating scales for the six characteristics of problem solutions described in Sec. IIIA. The Wilcoxon Rank-Sum Test was used to compare the medians of the total problem-solving scores of the students in the two sections. The results are shown in Table VII. The students in the experimental section scored significantly higher than the students in the traditional section on both exercises. An examination of the scores on the six characteristics of problem solutions indicated that the biggest difference between the two groups was in the qualitative analysis of the problem. For example, all students in the experimental section who solved the problem drew useful force diagrams, compared to only 57% in the traditional section. In addition, the solutions of students in the experimental section exhibited more logical mathematical progressions than those of the students in the traditional section. We tentatively concluded that students who are taught an explicit problem-solving strategy and practice implementing the strategy in cooperative groups solve standard physics exercises better than students who receive traditional instruction. "Better" in this context means that their solutions exhibit more expert like characteristics.

V. SUMMARY AND IMPLICATIONS

The primary purpose of this study was to test one aspect of our problem-solving instructional approach. In well-functioning cooperative groups, students can share conceptual and procedural knowledge and argument roles, and request clarification, justification, and elaboration from one another, so a better solution emerges than could be achieved by individuals working alone. The results of this study suggest that this type of collaboration did occur. Group problem solutions were significantly better than those produced by the best problem solvers from each group on matched individual problems, particularly with respect to the qualitative analysis of the problems. In addition, the individual problem-solving performance of students improved over time at approximately the same rate for students of high, medium, and low ability. Comparisons with students taking a traditional section of the same course indicated that students in the experimental section exhibited more expert like problem solving. We concluded that teaching an explicit problem-solving strategy and having students practice using the strategy in cooperative groups is an effective instructional approach.

	Experimental section median ($N = 91$)	Traditional section median ($N = 118$)	Wilcoxon Z statistic
Problem #1	82	62	8.17[a]
Problem #2	71	50	4.20[a]

[a]$p < 0.0001$.

TABLE VII
Experimental and traditional medians and Wilcoxon Z statistic for two standard physics exercises.

These results suggest that cooperative-group problem solving is a viable alternative to traditional recitation sections. Instead of the instructors answering students' questions or modeling problem solving, the instructor monitors the group work and gives feedback and help only as needed. Many student difficulties can be addressed quickly and efficiently by peers. Moreover, instructor teaching skills need be less well developed to assist groups, since the group process provides a mechanism by which students can clarify the instructor's vague statements or correct simple instructor errors. This is of practical importance when the recitation instructors are inexperienced graduate teaching assistants.

Although the use of cooperative groups in standard recitation sections has no implications for course coverage, the implementation of our entire instructional model required a reduction in the number of topics taught in the course. In 20 weeks the course covered about one-half of the chapters from an introductory text, instead of the traditional two thirds of the chapters. This reduction in topics allowed the lecturer to teach and model the five-step problem-solving strategy, as well as address the other goals of the course (emphasizing the fundamental principles, teaching qualitative reasoning skills, and challenging students' misconceptions). Implementing the entire model with graduate assistants also required more time on the part of the lecturer to organize and coordinate the different components of the course, and to educate the TA's about the goals and structure of the course, common student misconceptions, the five-step problem-solving strategy, how to grade problems, and how to form and maintain well-functioning groups.[6]

Finally, one unresolved issue is whether the instructional emphasis on a problem-solving strategy detracts from students' development of conceptual understanding. We have reason to believe that teaching the five-step strategy and having groups practice using the strategy to solve context-rich problems actually enhances students conceptual understanding of the course material. When we observed and videotaped groups, we noticed that peers were often effective "teachers" when they discussed a problem with one another. In the process of justifying statements, clarifying ideas, and elaborating on explanations, students appear to be deepening their understanding of physics concepts and principles. At this time, however, we have only preliminary data indicating that our problem-solving instructional strategy enhances students' conceptual understanding of physics.

Notes

1. R. Johnson, D. Johnson, and E. Holubec, *Circles of Learning: Cooperation in the Classroom* (Interaction, Edina, MN, 1986).

2. P. Heller and M. Hollabaugh, "Teaching problem solving through cooperative grouping. Part 2: Designing problems and structuring groups," *Am. J. Phys.* 60, 637–644 (1992).

3. A. Collins, J.S. Brown, and S.E. Newman, "Cognitive apprenticeship: Teaching the crafts of reading, writing, and mathematics," in *Knowing, Learning, and Instruction,* edited by L. B. Resnick (Lawrence Erlbaum Associates, Hillsdale, NJ, 1989) pp. 453–494.

4. A.L. Brown and A.S. Palincsar, "Guided, cooperative learning and individual knowledge acquisition," in *Knowing, Learning, and Instruction,* edited by L.B. Resnick (Lawrence Erlbaum Associates, Hillsdale, NJ, 1989), pp. 393–451.

5. V. N. Lunetta, "Cooperative learning in science, mathematics, and computer problem solving," in *Toward a Scientific Practice of Science Education,* edited by M. Gardner, J. Greeno, F. Reif, A. Schoenfield, A. diSessa, and E. Stage (Lawrence Erlbaum Associates, Hillsdale, NJ, 1990), pp. 235–249.

6. F. Lawrenz, R. Keith, P. Heller, and K. Heller, "Training the TA," *J. Coll. Sci. Teach.,* in press.

7. D. W. Johnson and R.T. Johnson, *Cooperation and Competition: Theory and Research,* (Interaction, Edina, MN, 1989), pp. 35–55.

8. A. Van Heuvelin, *Physics: A General Introduction* (Harper Collins, New York, 1986). 2nd ed.

9. For examples of student misconceptions, see D.E. Trowbridge and L. C. McDermott, "Investigation of student understanding of the concept of acceleration in one dimension," *Am. J. Phys.* 49, 242–253 (1981); L. C. McDermott, "Research on conceptual understanding in mechanics," *Phys. Today* 37, 24–32 (1984); J. Clement, "Students' preconceptions in introductory mechanics," *Am. J. Phys.* 50, 66–71 (1982); M. McClosky, A. Caramazza, and B. Green, "Curvilinear motion in the absence of external forces: Naive beliefs about the motion of objects," *Science* 210, 1129–1141(1980); F.M. Goldberg and L. C. McDermott, "An investigation of student understanding of the real image formed by a converging lens or concave mirror," *Am. J. Phys.* 55, 108–119 (1987); R. Cohen, B. Eylon, and U. Ganiel, "Potential difference and current in simple electric circuits," *Am. J. Phys.* 51, 407–412 (1983).

10. A.B. Arons, "Phenomenology and logical reasoning in introductory physics courses," *Am. J. Phys.* 50, 13–20(1982); "Student patterns of thinking and reasoning," *Phys. Teacher* 21(9), 576–581 (1983); 22(1), 21–26(1984); and 22(2), 88–93(1984).

11. F. Reif, "Scientific approaches to science education," *Phys. Today* 39, 48–54 (1986); "Transcending prevailing approaches to science education," in *Toward a Scientific Practice of Science Education,* edited by M. Gardner, J. Greeno, F. Reif, A Schoeneld, A. diSessa, and E. Stage (Lawrence Erlbaum Associates, Hillsdale, NJ, 1990), pp. 91–109.

12. F. Reif, "Acquiring an effective understanding of scientific concepts," in *Cognitive Structure and Conceptual Change,* edited by L.H. West and A.L. Pines (Academic, New York 1985), pp. 133–151.

13. L.C. McDermort, "A view from physics," in *Toward a Scientific Practice of Science Education,* edited by M. Gardner, J. Greeno, F. Reif, A. Schoenfeld, A. diSessa, and E. Stage (Lawrence Erlbaum Associates, Hillsdale, NJ, 1990), pp. 3–30.

14. M.T. H. Chi, R. Glaser, and E. Rees, "Expertise in problem solving," in *Advances in the Psychology of Human Intelligence:* Volume II (Lawrence Erlbaum Associates, Hillsdale, NJ, 1983), pp. 7–75.

15. J.H. Larkin, J. McDermott, D. P. Simon, and H.A. Simon, "Expert and novice performance in solving physics problems," *Science* 208, 1335–1342 (1980).

16. For a review of the expert-novice research, see J. Larkin, "Cognition of learning physics," *Am. J. Phys.* 49, 534–541(1981); see also the "I'S Corner" by D.R. Woods in the *J. Coll. Sci. Teach:* "Novice vs. expert research suggests ideas for implementation," 18(1), 77–79 and 18(2), 138–141(1988), and "Novice versus expert research," 18(3), 193– 195 (1988-1989).

17. For an example of how novices typically solve textbook exercises, see Ref. 2.

18. See also M.T.H. Chi, P.J. Feltovich, and R. Glaser, "Categorization and representation of physics problems by experts and novices," *Cog. Sci.* 5, 121–152(1981).

19. See, for example, F. Reif, J.H. Larkin, and G.C. Brackett, "Teaching general learning and problem solving skills," *Am. J. Phys.* 44 (3), 212–217(1976); J. I. Heller and F. Reif, "Prescribing effective human problem-solving processes: Problem description in physics," *Cog. Instr.* 1(2), 177–216 (1984).

20. For comparisons of different problem-solving strategies, see L.B. Greenfield, "Engineering student problem solving," in *Cognitive Process Instruction: Research on Teaching Thinking Skills,* edited by J.Lockhead and J. Clement (Franklin Institute, Philadelphia, PA, 1979). pp. 229–238; and D.R. Woods, "Problem solving in practice," in *What Research Says to the Science Teacher: Volume Five, Problem Solving.* edited by D. Gabel (National Science Teachers Association, Washington, D.C. (1989). pp. 97–121.

21. F.Reif and J.I. Heller, "Knowledge structures and problem solving in physics," *Ed. Psych.* 17(2), 102–127(1982).

22. A.H. Schoenfeld. *Mathematical Problem Solving* (Academic, San Diego, CA, 1985).

23. In our evaluation of the group functioning (Ref.2), we observed many similar instances of groups planning a solution, determining that they did not have enough information to solve the problem, and going back to their physics description.

24. J.L. Devore, *Probability and Statistics for Engineering and the Sciences* (Brooks/Cole, Monterey, CA, 1987), 2nd ed., pp. 608–614.

Comments on the article by Vidaković

Do individuals really learn better in a group? Do they learn differently? What is it about interactions within a group which helps (or hinders) individual learning?

In the next paper, Vidaković reports on a study of students who are learning concepts related to the idea of *function*—composition of functions, inverse of a function. The author interviews a group of five students working together on some learning activities, and she interviews five individuals working alone on the same tasks. She concludes that the learning processes are essentially the same whether one is working individually or in a group, but there are certain characteristics which occur with students working in groups—and tend to happen only to a lesser degree (if at all) when students are working alone.

Discussion Questions

1. What do students need to know in order to understand the concept of *inverse function?* What are the principle components identified by this author? Would you add anything to this list? Subtract anything from it?

2. What is it about the group interaction which seems to enhance cognitive development?

3. Do the author's observations ring true in your own experience as a learner?

4. What are some characteristics of study groups which differentiate them from an individual mode of solving problems? How do these support or hinder the learning process of each of the individuals in the group?

5. In this author's view, what characteristics of group work seem important to facilitate cognitive development among the group members? What implications does this have for your own classroom?

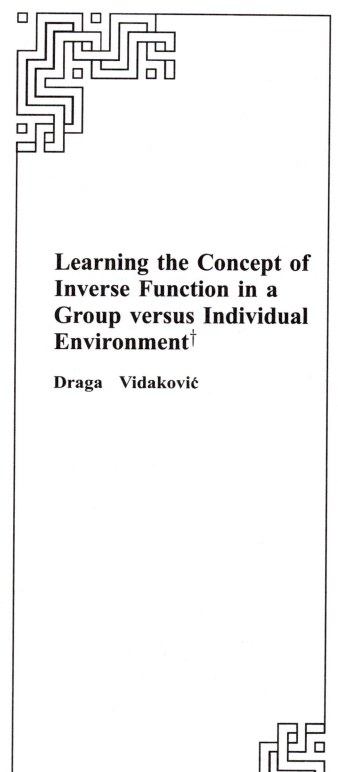

Learning the Concept of Inverse Function in a Group versus Individual Environment[†]

Draga   Vidaković

Introduction

Background of the problem

Cooperative or small-group learning has been used in education, with varying intensities for a long time. Interest in the use of small-group instruction in mathematics classes is increasing, especially at the elementary and secondary level. Many studies have found that cooperative learning has a positive effect on achievement outcomes. Lately, several researchers (Dees, 1991; Davidson, 1985, 1990; Davidson & Kroll, 1991; and others) have reported about different aspects of cooperative learning in college mathematics classes.

Reviews of the literature on cooperative learning in mathematics (Davidson, 1985; Slavin, 1985) indicate that a majority of the studies have focused on documenting the effect of cooperative learning on students' mathematical achievement. For example, studies done by Swing and Peterson (1982), Moskowitz et al. (1983), and Sharan (1980) have focused on the relationship between the students' interaction during small-group learning and academic achievement. All of them found a relationship between group interaction and achievement which suggests that the group setting can have a significant effect on an individual student's learning behavior.

Some other aspects of cooperative learning in mathematics were studied. For example, Webb (1991) reviewed studies done from 1979 to 1985 and concluded that certain characteristics of the grouping procedures, such as ability, gender, and the kinds of questions they asked each other and explanations they gave, had a major influence on the interaction in the group. These results were independent of the mathematical concepts studied and the grade level.

It seems that the benefits of using cooperative learning in the mathematics classroom are undeniable. But can we explain why cooperative learning has a positive effect on students achievement? What components of cooperative learning are important in individual learning?

Statement of the problem

The purpose of the study is to try to answer the question: "How is learning a concept—in particular, the concept of inverse function—as an individual different from learning it in a group?"

In this paper we will concentrate on the question "What are the processes of social interaction which are involved in the group problem-solving situation, and how

[†] This study was supported by NSF Award No. 9053432-USE at Purdue University.

175

might these affect the learning process of the individuals?" The description of how the concept of inverse function can be learned, and hence should be taught have been presented elsewhere (Vidaković, 1993; Vidaković, 1994).

The study is based on the Piagetian theory of cognitive learning. In particular, our focus in Piagetian theory is on the role of social factors in cognitive development. Piaget's view was that everyone's development originates within themselves, arising from their actions upon the environment, acknowledging the necessity of social interactions for individual development. In contrary to Piaget, Vygotsky (1978) argued that social interaction creates zones of proximal development that operate initially only in collaborative interactions. Gradually these newly awakened processes are internalized and become part of the subject's developmental achievement.

The importance of social interaction on cognitive development according to Piagetian theory

Although Piaget did not write very much about social factors, there are many places in his work showing that he was aware of the importance of social factors. In discussing the interdependence of social and intellectual development, Piaget (1950) differentiates several separate but interrelated processes that are closely synchronized with one another. These are: de-centration, de-egocentration, development of logic, and 'grouping'.

Let us now explain how the above processes were considered in Piaget's work. The preoperational child's thinking is characterized by centration. Perceptions of events tend to center on single or limited perceptual aspects of a stimulus and do not take into account all the salient features of the stimulus. Thus, as could be seen in the number conservation problems, preoperational children tend to center on the initial and final states of a given situation neglecting the intervening events which are responsible for the changes. For example, consider the situation in which the child is given two rows of the same number of marbles. After the marbles are spread out in one row the child says that there are more marbles in the longer row. The child has centered on the lengths and ignored a number of other factors. He or she has failed to consider the density of the rows, as well as their length, and has ignored the intermediary transformation (the spreading of the marbles). Thus, the child focuses mainly on the initial and final states and fails to integrate these impressions with all else that has occurred (Piaget, 1952).

Social interaction provides the opportunity to elaborate actions with another child, and thus to coordinate centrations, even though these may initially be different. This difference, as long as it is perceived without being assimilated into a joint system, may give rise to conflict among children. Contradictions coming from others, whatever their levels of development, serve to bring the cognitive differences between the two views into sharp focus, and thus lead to a coordination which will reduce the conflict.

Piaget suggested that opportunities for becoming less egocentric (able to see another's viewpoint) are much more common when students discuss things with one another (Piaget, 1968, 1970; Piaget & Inhelder, 1969a, 1969b). The child who wishes to communicate and to be understood must adapt to the informational needs of his listener.

He or she cannot continue to assimilate reality to private schemas, but must also accommodate to the point of view of the other. The individual cannot make contradictory statements and continue to remain unaware of their contradictory nature. The child is forced to face the reality of different human perspectives when he or she is involved in active group discussion. Cooperation with other students in the discussion helps the child learn how to take different points of view into account. When students share a goal, the result of trying to reach it can, because of different perspectives, lead to cognitive conflict. Resolving that conflict leads directly to cognitive development.

In the *The Psychology of Intelligence,* Piaget stated that the child's logic could not develop without social interactions because it is in interpersonal situations that the child feels an obligation to be coherent. As long as he or she is by her- or himself, the child can say whatever he or she pleases for the pleasure of the moment. It is when he or she is with others that the child feels a need to be consistent from moment to moment and to think about what to say to be understood and believed. While logical thinking cannot be taught directly, social interactions have the powerful effect of making the child feel obliged to make sense and be logical.

During the study of the operations underlying the system of different concepts (number, measurement, physical quantities, logical classes and relations), the need arose for structural models which would explain the processes involved in the formation of concepts. Piaget's view was that the appropriate model is that of algebraic grouping, defined by analogy to mathematical groups (grouping is defined as a coordination of operations, i.e. of actions accessible to the individual).

In terms of social interaction Piaget posed the question of whether such operational grouping is the cause or the effect of cooperation. In response to the question, he said that an individual would never come to group her or his operations into a coherent whole without interchange of thought and cooperation with others. So, in that sense, operational grouping presupposes social life. On the other hand, the "exchange of thought obeys a law of equilibrium which again could only be an operational grouping, since to cooperate is to coordinate operations. The grouping is therefore a form of equilibrium of inter-individual actions as well as of individual action, and it thus regains its autonomy at the very core of social life." (Piaget, 1950, p. 164).

There could be no change from intuitive representations into transitive, reversible, identical, and associative operations (grouping of operations) without interchange of thought. "The grouping consists essentially in a freeing of the individual's perceptions and spontaneous intuitions from the egocentric viewpoint, in order to construct a system of relations such that one can pass from one term or relation to another belonging to any viewpoint. The grouping is therefore by its very nature a coordination of viewpoints and, in effect, that means a coordination between observers, and therefore a form of cooperation between several individuals." (Piaget, 1950, p. 164).

What we said above does not mean in any sense that the "laws" of operational grouping are superior to cooperation and individual thought. It means only that the laws of grouping apply to the process of equilibration, where equilibrium is reached by solving the 'conflict situation' emergent from social interaction.

Methods

Research design

In order to explain and substantiate the methods designed and applied, we reiterate the goals of the study. The first goal was to examine the dynamic processes of learning through the observation of cognitive constructions in a problem solving situation, both in a group environment and individually. The second purpose was to investigate the possible differences between the processes of learning the concept as an individual versus learning it in a group.

The above goals and the research question listed at the beginning suggest a qualitative research design. Qualitative research is ideally suited to explore the meaning of social science phenomena (Patton, 1980).

The setting

Data for this research were collected during the Fall semester of 1992. The participants were students enrolled in Ma 161A, *Calculus, Concepts, and Computers with Co-operative Learning* classes at Purdue University. Students in Ma 161A sections were selected for participation on a volunteer basis. They were introduced to the program and the teaching philosophy before they registered for the classes. During the Fall semester there were three sections,

two sections with 33 students each and one section with 14 students. On the second day of the semester, each section was separated into small heterogeneous groups of 3 to 5 students, based on the information from the questionnaire administered on the first day of school, to work together for the rest of the semester. Groups were formed so as to be heterogeneous with respect to gender, mathematics background, computer and programming background, and typing skills.

Group work in all sections was organized in the following way:

(a) **In class.** The method of instruction was not traditional lecturing. The lessons were designed for guided discovery leading to mathematical generalization, and were suited to the cooperative learning mode. During the class period the teacher would assign tasks for group work. Usually there were 4–8 tasks during one class period. After assigning a problem, the teacher would ask students to work on it in groups for approximately 2-5 minutes. The next step was a discussion of the task in the whole class. That was the opportunity for groups to interact with other groups.

(b) **On laboratory activities and homework assignments.** The laboratory activities were mostly done in groups during the laboratory time that was scheduled two times per week for two hours each time. In cases when the work could not be completed during the regular laboratory time, the groups had to meet outside the laboratory time. The students' work on laboratory activities consisted in investigating the new mathematical concepts. The computers played an important role in this type of assignment. Another type of assignment was the homework assignment. The homework assignment was done after the new concept had been investigated and discussed in class. The goal with this type of assignment was for students to apply their knowledge about some concept to the problem solving situation and sometimes to practice some computational skills. The students had one set of laboratory activities and one homework assignment each week. Each group had to submit one set of solutions for the problems, with the signature on the front page of those students who fully participated in completing the assignment. There were no individual homework assignments.

(c) **On one test.** The first test (out of three) was a group test. Each group submitted one copy of the test to be graded and the group members received the group grade as an individual grade.

Data gathering—Instruments

The data were collected in the previously described setting.

Participants. Participants for this study were five groups of students in the Ma 161A course who had been assigned to work together for the whole semester and five individual students from the Ma 161A classes. Since the author was teaching one of the sections, the participants for this study were selected from the two remaining sections. Criteria for selecting the groups were the quality of their functioning. One well-functioning, one poorly-functioning, and three average-functioning groups were selected. As the well-functioning group, the group was chosen which accomplished all the group tasks together and on time. All its members shared the responsibilities, showed respect toward each other and willingness to help each other. The poorly functioning group had many interpersonal conflicts, and the group work consisted in splitting the task among the group members and finishing it without much communication. The average functioning groups had, from time to time, some problems due to personality differences and with time schedules and, consequently, with accomplishing the group task on time. But, with students' effort and sometimes with the instructor's help, those problems were resolved. To select such groups, recommendations of their teachers were considered as well as the students' and researcher's opinions. The individual students were selected from the remaining set of students in Ma 161A, i.e., those students who were not in the five selected groups. The criteria for selecting the individual students were academic performance. One high-, one poor-, and three average-skilled students were chosen.

Interviews.   Because of the nature and the goal of this study, we thought that the clinical interview was best suited as a method for gathering information. In order to gather sufficient information, an interview guide was made. The interview guide contained the core questions, leaving the researcher to pose other questions depending on the situation and the participant's response. The interview guide consisted of a set of questions on the mathematical concept of inverse functions (see Appendix). The questions were suggested by the researcher and evaluated by experts in the field. The interviews were conducted in the computer laboratory where the subjects had the freedom of using the computers in their work. The use of computers by groups and individuals was observed.

Complete group interviews were videotaped and audiotaped, while the individual interviews were only audiotaped. Both video and audio recording were used in group interviews because of the complexity of the observation of social interaction within a group. The videotapes were to be used during the process of data analysis as the source for observation of the interaction processes involved in the problem solving.

Data analysis

Based on the researcher's understanding of the mathematical concept of inverse function (see Vidaković, 1993, 1994) and the theoretical framework described in Asiala, et al. (1996), we made a 'preliminary' version of a genetic decomposition representing the sequence of steps (construction processes) through which students might go in learning the mathematical concept of inverse function. All that the genetic decomposition represents at this moment (before the study) is a possible schema or collection of schemas that appear in the researcher's mind consistent with her or his understanding, and that will possibly be related to the observation of students in the process of learning of that particular concept (Dubinsky, 1991a).

Given below is the 'preliminary' version of a genetic decomposition for the inverse function:

(1) Student has developed a process or object concept of a function (see operational definition in Table 1).

(2) Student coordinates two or more function processes to define the composition of two functions, in notation $h = f \circ g$.

(3) Student uses previously constructed schema of a function and the composition of functions to define an inverse function.

(4) Student understands and applies the inverse process to specific situations.

We start with the assumption that the student has developed the process or object concept of the function. Starting with two objects (functions), the student should de-encapsulate them to form two processes (functions) which then could be coordinated to form a new process (function). The new process should be encapsulated into the final object (function). The above-mentioned coordination is called the composition of two functions. The student may start with one object (function), de-encapsulate it into a process and then by reversing that process form another process. The reversed process is called the inverse function. The process of inverse function could also be found starting with the function process and obtaining a process which coordinated with it gives the identity. By coordinating the processes of a function, the composition of function and the inverse function, the student may apply the concept in many different situations.

For a further description of this method of analysis see Asiala, et al. (1996).

Based on the preliminary version of the genetic decomposition of the inverse function, we derived five main categories of all subjects' responses (see Table 1).

Results and interpretations

This section contains the analysis and interpretation of our data. In the first subsection we will give some basic operational definitions of the categories of students' responses derived from the data. Also, this subsection will contain a placement of each individual and each group at appropriate categories in the categorization. In the second subsection we will present some excerpts from the individual interview protocols which support each category. The third subsection will contain an in-depth analysis of a selected group involved in the process of problem-solving and a description of the social interaction that took place while that particular group was involved in the problem-solving situation. A depiction of the development of individual participants' contributions during the ongoing problem-solving process, as well as a depiction of the flow of the problem-solving process of a subject working individually, will be presented in the fourth subsection.

Categories

We believe that the construction of the concept of inverse function progresses through various steps, some of which include misconceptions. We want to emphasize that we do not expect that this progress is linear and fixed. It is not unreasonable to have a subject at one level of process and at a higher level of action for the same concept. Our goal is to find out what are the steps which subjects must pass through in learning the concept of inverse function, and to design instruction which will help them.

Within the framework of a 'preliminary' genetic decomposition, described on page 7, we classify subjects' responses into five main categories. A description of each category is given in Table 1.

Based on the above description of the categories, each individual and each group were placed at appropriate levels in the categorization (see Table 2). The individual or the group was placed in Category 0 if they showed an action level of understanding of the concept of function or composition of functions and no understanding of the concept of inverse function and its application. The subject was assigned to Category I if there was evidence of a process or object understanding of the concept of the function. The subject was assigned to Category II, if besides having a process (object) understanding of the function, he or she also demonstrates the ability to do at least one of the following: (i) to define the composition of two functions; or (ii) to solve the equation $h = f \circ g$ for given functions f and g; or (iii) to define or find the domain of the composition of two functions. The individual or the group was placed in Category III if they showed understanding and ability to

do at least one of the following: (i) to define the inverse function (as (a) something that inverts each operation and performs them in reverse order; or (b) something that flips the original function around the line $y = x$; or (c) neither of the above—it's just a procedure of switching x and y); (ii) find the inverse function (algebraically, graphically, or by describing it in words). The individual or the group was assigned to Category IV if they showed understanding and ability for at least one of the following: (i) to apply the concept of inverse function to solve the equation $h = f \circ g$ for given functions h and f (or h and g); or (ii) to apply the concept of inverse function to find the inverse of the composition of two functions.

Analysis of the individual responses

In this subsection we will describe and analyze the individual answers that best illustrate each category in the above categorization. We will not make the distinction between the subcategories in Categories II, III, and IV and will consider that the subject belongs to one and the same category if there is evidence that he or she belongs to, at least, one of the subcategories of that category.

Category 0. The subjects in this category clearly had no more than an action concept of function, although they were sometimes actually able to perform some of the tasks that define a higher category, but only at an action level (as we will see in the following case of Tom).

In the first excerpt, subject Tom describes the composition of two functions in the following way:

Draga: How would you define the composition of two functions f and g?

Tom: It just would be f composed with g of variable. I don't understand, I know like the definition, I know that the process of the composition is, is say you take the number and plug in g of x which would give you the answer to your function basically and then you plug in that number to f of x and then that is the process of it and then the domain would be, would have to be the domain of g, well, it has to be a domain that satisfies both of them g and f. For example if it was, if f was from here [he graphed two arbitrary functions] and g was from here then this couldn't be included in f. That's how I understand it.

From the above excerpt Tom could be placed in category II(i) but the next excerpt shows what keeps him out of that category. In a similar situation, a subject that has constructed an object concept of function might consider a function g as an object to which a process of f could be applied (see excerpt of Marsha in Category I). This is a new idea which emerged from our data. It is obvious that for Tom both functions, f and g, were actions performed

	Category	Subcategory	Operational definition
0	Action concept of function		The subject expresses the action concept of function or the composition of functions.
I	Process or object concept of function		The subject is capable of imagining a function as a dynamic transformation which, for the same input, always produces the same output; or, he or she also understands the concept of function as something to which actions and processes may be applied.
II	Composition of functions	(i)	The subject defines the composition of two functions.
		(ii)	The subject solves the equation $h = f \circ g$ for given functions f and g.
		(iii)	The subject defines and finds the domain of the composition.
III	Inverse function	(i)	The subject uses a previously constructed function schema to define inverse function in at least one of the following ways: (a) 'Something' that inverts each operation and performs them in reverse order. (b) 'Something' that flips the original function around the line $y = x$. (c) Neither of the above—it's just a procedure of switching x and y.
		(ii)	The subject finds the inverse function (algebraically, graphically, or describes it in words).
IV	Application of the inverse function	(i)	The subject applies the inverse function to solve the equation $h = f \circ g$ for given functions h and g (or h and f).
		(ii)	The subject applies the inverse function to find the inverse of the composition.

TABLE 1
Categories of responses

on some numbers and he defined the composition in that manner.

When finding a composition $h = f \circ g$ given by

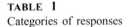

$$f(x) = \begin{cases} |x - 1| & \text{if } x > 1 \\ 2 & \text{if } x \leq 1 \end{cases} \quad \text{and} \quad g(x) = x - 2.$$

Tom still shows an action level in finding the seam point of the composition.

Tom: OK. So, I need each function. [he was trying to write a code for h but had problems in getting graphs. Then he started to plot f and g by hand, point by point.] . . . so I'm trying to keep myself confused. If x is three it should be two. [he was plugging different values for x into the expression for h in order to find the seam point] Do you have a lot of these to do? Ha-ha-ha. I know what I want, but I don't know how to get it. . . . [mumbling] . . . [pause] . . . [mumbling] . . .

Draga: So, what is the seam point?

Tom: That's what I'm trying to figure out. I just keep starting over and over.

Draga: Would it be the point one as you said before?

Tom: No. That's what I'm trying to figure out now. I had the idea I didn't check. I only checked one. . . . negative two is two . . . [mumbling, checking different values to find the seam point in h]. So for x less than four is two and if x is five it should be true. So, when x equals two than you put in four it gives . . . So it's when x is greater or equal than four. It took me for ever but I did my best.

Tom was not able to answer the questions regarding the definition of inverse function or its applications. In spite of that, he made a comment that through the course of the interview he had learned something about the composition of functions that he had never understood before. It is interesting to mention that Tom was the only individual subject who tried to use the computer during the interview. He wanted to graph a composition of two functions using the computer language ISETL, but he gave up after realizing that he did not know how to write a code for the composition.

Category I. Subjects in this category should have constructed a process or object concept of function, meaning that they are able to think of a function as a dynamic process or as also a static object on which some actions could be performed. Those actions presumably would transform the function into a new object. It is important to mention that a subject who has an object concept of function should be able to go back and forth between an object and a process concept of the function.

We found that most of the subjects had constructed an object concept of function in one situation while not having it in another, or at least not showing evidence of it. The most common situations in which some subjects showed that they had constructed an object concept of function were the following:

a. when defining and finding a composition of two functions.
b. when finding an inverse function which is given by its geometrical representation.
c. when solving an equation $h = f \circ g$ for f given g and h.

Below are some excerpts from our interviews which show different situations in which we consider that the subject has an object concept of function. In the first excerpt, Marsha has encapsulated a function and is able to think about it as an object to which another function could be applied.

When asked what is a composition of two functions, Marsha said

Marsha: ... OK. f of g would be taking a function f and applying it to a function g.

It seems that Marsha constructed a process T_f in which $T_f(g) = f \circ g$. This is different from the genetic decomposition of the composition of functions described in Ayres et al. (1988). Below is a situation which also indicates that the subject may have an object concept of function. Asked what is the process of the function f in Question 3 (Appendix), Mary said:

Mary: Aaa... process of f is to manipulate g of x to be equal h of x.

Although the issue of 'manipulating' could be discussed here we expect that Mary has encapsulated the function g and is thinking of it as an object which can be 'manipulated' by f. We conjecture that Mary, as Marsha, is also thinking of the process T_f.

In the next situation it is even clearer that Mary has an object concept of the function. When asked to sketch the inverse function of a function given by its graph, Mary says:

Mary: First thing I would do is I draw a straight line, straight as I can.
Draga: OK.
Mary: And then I just kind of, I know since it goes to one on the x it's gonna go to one on the y.
Draga: Aha.
Mary: And then I just try to mirror the whole thing as much as I can across the line of x equals y because since they are inverse functions x is going be equal what y used to be equal and whatever you have for x it is going to be on the y axes. So, they are just a mirror image of each other with respect to the y equals x.

As could be seen in the above situation, Mary was considering a graph of the function as a 'whole thing' which she 'mirrored' around the line $y = x$. She used only one point as a reference point.

Category II. A subject in this category should be able to define or find a composition of functions correctly, should be able to solve the equation $h = f \circ g$ for h given functions f and g, or should be able to discuss the domain of a composition. Dubinsky (1991b) emphasized that the notion of domain and range have no place in the schema of function for those students who have a 'function-as-formula-schema'. We found that the notion of domain of the composition of two functions was a big obstacle regardless of the subject's 'function schema'. Among the students working individually, there were some who were able to define a composition correctly, to solve the equation $h = f \circ g$ for any two given functions, but were not able to deal with the domain of the composition. Also, we found some evidence that a composition of function does not require object conception of function, but only process conception of function. That was originally hypothesized by Harel and Kaput (Harel & Kaput, 1991). Some answers in this category among the individual students are described below. The first is a situation in which the subject was not able to state the domain of the composition of two functions clearly and, when given a particular problem situation, was able to find it only after the interviewer's prompting. We consider this subject to be in transition from Category I to Category II.

Linda: ... Aaaa ... domain of that composition would be all values of ... those values in the domain of g that are also in the domain of f. ...
Draga: Find an expression for a function h so that h is a composition of f with g where f and g are functions given by these two expressions. [f and g were given by:

$$f(x) = \begin{cases} |x - 1| & \text{if } x > 1 \\ 2 & \text{if } x \le 1 \end{cases}$$
$$g(x) = x - 2.]$$

Linda: OK. Hmmm .... here is h.
Draga: OK. How ... If I ask you to find what is h of two how would you do that?
Linda: If x is two?
Draga: Ah-hah.
Linda: OK. So g of x gives a value zero.
Draga: Ah-hah.
Linda: So I'd put zero for x in function f.
Draga: Ah-hah. And what would you get?
Linda: I'll have the negative three and the absolute value of negative three would be three.
Draga: If x is two then g is zero and then f of zero ... Is that what you said? What would be f of zero?
Linda: Oooo ... Zero is less or equal than one. So I'll put it in this expression, and the value would be two.
Draga: OK. What is the value of the composition if x is one?
Linda: If x is one this would be the negative one, negative one is less than or equal to one and the value would be two.
Draga: Should you get the same if you plug in h?
Linda: If I plug in the value of one for x?

Draga: Yah.

Linda: Yes, the same thing.

Draga: OK. What if x is two now?

Linda: If x is two then x is greater than ...

Draga: Ah-hah.

Linda: ... one. Ammm ... I have a value of zero minus three is negative three absolute value of negative three is three ...

Draga: OK. So, this is when you plug into the expression for h. What if you go through this composition? What would you get?

Linda: Hmmm ... yeah. I see what you mean there because if I go to expression I'll have a zero, if x is equal zero ... ammm and zero is less or equal than one so the value is two.

Draga: OK. So?

Linda: So I have to change my h and see ... mmm why I don't understand this now? Aaa ......

Draga: How did you find your h?

Linda: How did I find this right here? By taking the expression g of x and placing it in the x in f of x because if I had a composition taking the function of the function g of x. So therefore you ...

Linda: So, x minus two minus three where x has to be greater than one, so x has to be ...

Draga: What should be greater than one? You said that now in f you have x minus two for x.

Linda: Oooo ... x minus two is greater than one, I didn't think of that.

It seems that Linda felt comfortable in finding the expression for the composition of two functions (except for the seam point) and in evaluating it at the given point. However, she needed a lot of prompting to realize that the seam point in the composition would also change from that in the function f.

In the following excerpt, we can see how Mary discusses the domain of the composition of two functions.

Mary: You gotta check where your function, your first function is defined ... you are checking ... that's where you reach, reach your domain of your x and you gotta see where is that is equal to what's your other domain was and then that changes your domain that far and then you just do what you would do with normal composition.

As can be seen, Mary considers the relationship between the range of one function and the domain of the other, as well as the domain of the first function.

In the following situation, Mary explains how to solve the equation $h = f \circ g$ if h and g are given (see Question 4, Appendix). She says that she would find f by reversing the process of g.

Mary: Hmmm ... OK. What I did is I kind of looked for values, equations that when I plugged two minus x in for x for first part it would eliminate two, so when I plug, when I ... it was two minus x, when I plug in two minus x for the x and that was a minus two plus x which these two cancel and what is left is just positive x and so I also had to amm shift my amm domain for that portion so that when I would plug in two in the original

graph in g ... ammm ... that I would be plugging the same value in if ... I get the same ... If you are plugging in the same value for x that would be ... if I plug two in g and I plug that value in for the x in f I get the same value. [She wrote the following $(2 - x) = x$, $-x = x - 2$, $x = -(x - 2)$, $f(x) = -x + 2$]. So in that way my seam point would match up with both of these graphs and that way after I would compose g with f and end up just with an x, my seam points would still match up. Then for the second portion I looked for aaa ... equation that would make my x positive and eliminate the two's then I, when I plug in x minus two in the x plus two, two's are kind of turning the equation, x plus two and x minus two cancel out and then because I'm only using two portions of, two ... only got two areas where is defined our g and if I shift my seam point in there so that they are both the same and they match up then I only need to portion the seam in f, and then f be composing just it have to find all the same values for every x. If they both equal zero or x and f and g compose these two portions and then it fits x for all, all values so that on that way we can just say h of x equals x. So then the process is like the last one, it's just looking for or try to find ways that we can get plug in our, or originally using our x into equation to get what we are trying to find which is the h of x.

Although Mary had difficulties explaining how she found the function f in the composition $h = f \circ g$, where h and g were given, it seems from what she wrote that she was finding it by reversing the operations in g. Keeping in mind that the result of the composition of f with g should be x, she first subtracted 2 from x and then multiplied $(x - 2)$ by negative one.

Category III. A subject in this category gives a correct description of the definition of the inverse function or is able to find the inverse function (algebraically, geometrically, or describe it verbally). What is significant about this category is that the subjects expressed different levels of action-process-object development regarding the situation. In another words, the subjects appropriately used different concepts regarding the given situation. For example, when asked to find an inverse function in Question 5 (see Appendix), most of the subjects expressed an action (pure procedure) level of understanding of the inverse function (see example with Linda below). In discussing Question 4 (Appendix), some subjects were at a transitional level from action to process, while in the situation of applying the inverse function concept to the composition of functions, there were some subjects who were at the object level.

Below is a situation in which Cantor defines an inverse function in terms of the composition of functions. Since this subject had a strongly developed function schema, we suppose that his definition assumes 'uniqueness to the right'.

Draga: OK. How would you define the inverse of a function?

Cantor: Aaa ... any function such that, any function g of x such that f of g is equal to x.

Draga: What do you think what would be g of f in that case?

Cantor: g of f?

Draga: From your definition.

Cantor: Yeah, it's x.

Draga: Do you think that works for any two functions?

Cantor: Yes, it should because the inverses multiplied together in any order should be equal to one and like normal numeric, algebraic, so yeah, any function g of x such that f of x is equal to x and g of f is equal to x.

Linda's answer to Question 5 summarizes pretty well the way in which most of the subjects responded to that question.

Linda: I know that ... let me think, I inverted, I switched the y and the x and then what I want to do from that is to solve from that, is solve for y. That's what I did here. So ... aaa ... that's about it.

The following is an excerpt in which we can see that Mary is at a higher level than that of an action. The procedure of finding an inverse function, as described above, obviously has some meaning for her.

Draga: Question number five: Find the inverse of f and state its domain. The function is given by this expression: two x minus one.

Mary: Ammm ... OK. f of x equals one half x plus one half and so, and the domain would be for all x.

Draga: Can you tell me how did you find the inverse function?

Mary: Ammm ... basically what should you, this is what you do when you find the inverse. You just switch your f of x and x in the equation and then solve for f of x because what it, what the inverse does is when you compose the two functions you get a straight line which is x equals, or f of x equals x.

Draga: Which two functions do you compose?

Mary: Aaa ... the f of x that we had and then the inverse of it. Those two functions when you compose them give you a straight line of y equals x.

This is a nice example in which good notation alone does not help. Mary probably learned this concept using the notation of x and y. Now she has "grown up" to x and $f(x)$, but the ideas did not grow. The notation $f(x)$ is encapsulated and treated as y.

Category IV. A subject in this category should be able to apply the concept of inverse function, to find the inverse of a composition of two functions, or to solve the equation $h = f \circ g$ for f given h and g.

In the first excerpt, the subject Mary says that the inverse of two functions is the composition of their inverses in opposite order. Though she needed a little prompting, we think that she has a process concept of inverse function.

Draga: So, if f and g have their inverses what would be the inverse of the composition of f and g?

Mary: I think it would just be aaa ... well ... I think it just gonna be the composition of the two inverses.

Draga: In which order? Would it be f inverse composed with g inverse? Is that what you wrote?

Mary: Ammm ... No, probably it will be reversed. It reverse the ...

Draga: Why would you reverse?

Mary: Because you wanna undo what the other one did, so it would be g, inverse of g composed with the inverse of f because if I come and graph what you have for your x values now become your y values, and what you have for y values now become your x values so in order to undo them you gonna do them in reversed order. Since the f was what you are using, since f is what you are plugging into with the inverse you gonna plug in that value first and then plug into ... OK. With compositions you wanna, with array of your compositions you gonna start on the ... with the smallest you gonna work out so you don't wanna start on the out what you let in, so if you have f of g in order to undo it you don't wanna start with f and so that's the one you would compose into the other one and then undo the g, f of g is that one.

In discussing Question 4 (Appendix), Marsha says that the problem of finding the function f in the equation $h = f \circ g$ is actually the problem of finding the inverse function of g.

Draga: If you think of those functions again what would be the process of f?

Marsha: Probably dividing ... aaa ... not dividing but finding a, finding an f of x that when multiplied by g of x is equal to one, so it would be the inverse of that I guess and finding inverse of it so that ammm something multiplied by something else is equal to just x.

Analysis of group responses and social interaction through different levels of categorization

For the purpose of detailed analysis, one group (GR1) was chosen and analyzed in depth. The results of the analyses of all groups are shown in Table 2.

The group which has reached the highest level in the categorization of understanding of inverse functions given earlier was chosen for in-depth analysis. It was a group of four male freshmen (Ervin, Ken, Mark, and Harry), who were functioning satisfactorily during the semester.

We consider that the group is at a certain level of understanding of the concept according to the final group answer. The group answer sometimes would be the answer of the most advanced group member, sometimes it would be the result of the mutual effort, or, as in the group which we choose to analyse here, it would be the answer of the most talkative group member. In general, saying that the group is at a certain level of understanding of the concept

		Function	Composition			Inverse		Application	
	Category 0	Category I	Category II			Category III		Category IV	
			i	ii	iii	i	ii	i	ii
Mary		*	*	*	*	*		*	... *
Linda		*	*	*	*	*	*		
Marsha		*	*	*		*	*	*	
Tom	*								
Cantor		*				*	*		
GR1		*	*	*	*	*	*	*	... *
GR2		*	*	*	*	*	*	*	... *
GR3		*				*	*		
GR4		*		*		*	*		
GR5		*	*	*	*	*	*	*	

TABLE 2
Individual and group placement

does not necessarily mean that all its members are at that level. Having in mind that groups are heterogeneous with respect to achievement, we expect the group members to be at different levels of understanding some concepts.

Category I & Category II. By analyzing a part of the interview which contains the group answer to Question 1 (Appendix), we concluded that the members of the group are at different levels in understanding the definition of the composition of two functions. The following excerpt illustrates that clearly.

Ervin: Composition of f of g to me would mean, you know, you take whatever a function you have for g you substitute your function f in that function.
Ken: OK. So substitute that for the, you have like an f of x function substitute your g of x function substitute into x value.
Ervin: Yeah.
Ken: OK. I understand. So if we had an f of x equals to x squared and a g of x equals three minus x then f of g would yield a three minus x the quantity squared.
Ervin: Ah-hah

We notice that Ervin defines the composition of f with g considering g to be an object to which process f could be applied. His response made sense to Ken, who had to reinterpret it in his way by thinking of an example (action level). Obviously, Ken was able to understand what Ervin was talking about but, because of his need to use one concrete example, we consider that he may be in tran-

sition from the action to the process level of the concept of composition of two functions.

In the following excerpt (in which Draga is the interviewer) we will see how this group dealt with the question about the domain of the composition, theoretically as well as in one concrete situation. The task was to find the composition of two given functions of which one was with the split domain (Question 2, Appendix).

Ken: OK. And then the domain of that composition ...
Ervin: Domain would depend on either the function was limited ... values where it is not defined.
Ken: OK. In this particular case there would be no limit. It will be all real numbers.
Harry: Yeah, all real numbers are domain of the function.
Draga: What do you mean by this if it is limited or not?
Ervin: Well, it could be ... aaa ... something like x squared over maybe x minus one, couldn't find x equals to one, so it will leave the function to be undefined at that point.
Ken: OK. In this case
Mark: separate intervals for f of x where like f is like broken up into .... expressions, define each expression at different location
Harry: and then you say how, then you have to say how the domain for g of x relates to the composition. You have to see like what happens to all the values when it's composed into the f of x and then you have to change
Ken: and also if it is, if the g of x composed with ... parts of it f of x is only one part then you have to substitute in your f of g into .... two parts because you have to deal with all limits

of the function. And so, the domain of the function we decided just gonna deal with all once . . .

Mark: well it can't.

Ken: just with all of the limits in this particular case three minus x the quantity squared.

Draga: What do you mean by "all the limits"?

Harry: Yeah, I wanna know that too.

Ken: The same thing as Ervin just said it's just any case . . .

Ervin: It's like all the restrictions would be a better word.

Harry: Restrictions would be a better word.
Yeah. So, that's all.

Mark: All the restrictions for g and for . . .

Ken: and also for f. Yes.

We may notice in the situation above that, although the group members had some difficulty in expressing themselves, they did not have any problem in understanding each other. It seems that the word "limits" had the same meaning for Ken, Mark and Ervin. When Ervin said ". . . the restrictions would be a better word", all of them agreed immediately and they used this word later in the interview.

This is a good example of the particular characteristics of group work: discussion in the group opens more varied possibilities for outcomes in problem solution because of more varied input and greater number of approaches to defining the elements of the problem.

Ken: OK. The next question: Find an expression for a function h so that h is f of g, where f and g are functions given by (and reads the functions f and g).

Draga: So, first find the expression for h.

Ken: OK. First expressions. Ervin [he turned his head toward Ervin calling him to respond but kept talking]? We need, we need f, f of g of x it's gonna equal to h.

Ervin: We have f of x.

Ken: Yeah, we have . . .

Mark: We have both.

Ken: We have f of x and we have g of x, so it's what we talked about in the last problem, we are to worry about the restrictions

Mark: just break it up into these two.

Ken: Right. So if x is greater than one then f of g of x . . . plugging a value of g of x . . .

Mark & Ken (together): x minus the square root x . . . it'll be absolute value of x minus five.

Ken: So it will be the square root . . . aaa . . . it's gonna be the absolute value of x minus two minus three which would be the absolute value of x minus five if x is greater than one. Agree?

Mark: Aha-hah. If x is less or equal than one it still be two, right?

Harry: Oh, yeah.

Ken: Yeah, f of g of x when x is greater than, less than equal to one . . . if your f of x is two there is no, there is no independent variable to plug in g of x into it, therefore it's gonna always be two so you don't have to worry about the g of x. Well, the process of h is gonna, just gonna be plugging the value for g of x into the independent variable for f of x. Any decent comments, anything you wanna add?

Ervin: You summed it up pretty much.

Mark: OK. All right. Cool.

Harry: Wait. Because this kind of f of x and when x is equal to g of x then you have to change these restrictions for g of x and make sure it fits in the . . .

Ken: OK. That makes sense. All right. Cause you are plugging in your g of x for your x, you are replacing independent variable with another variable. OK. I understand that.

Draga: And then what would you get?

Harry: Ha-ha.

Ken: What did you ask, I'm sorry?

Harry: We have to . . .

Mark: Why don't you put just x minus two in there and into so it would be x is greater than three . . .

Ken: OK. Yeah, it make sense. If x minus two is greater than one so it will yield if x is greater than three

Harry: I'm not sure if that's right.

Ken: if x minus is less then equal to one if x is less then equal to three. So, that is gonna work because g of x is equal to that in when every . . . if something is equal you can just replace like that. So . . .

Mark: Cool

Ken: that's the absolute value of x minus five if x is greater than three or two if x is less than equal to three.

Harry: Does that sound good? Ha-ha-ha.

Draga: I don't know. I'm asking you. Whatever you say.

Ken: I can agree with my own ideas so . . .

Mark: Great, great.

The last two excerpts show that, with joint effort, Mark and Harry gave a reasonable description of the domain of the composition ("Mark: Separate intervals for f of x where like f is like broken up into . . . expressions, define each expression at different location; Harry: and then you say how, then you have to say how the domain for g of x relates to the composition. You have to see like what happens to all the values when it's composed into the f of x and then you have to change"). How much that made sense to other members of the group could be seen later in the interview, from Ken's comment when finding a composition of two particular functions: "We have f of x and we have g of x, so it's what we talked about in the last problem, we are to worry about the restrictions." But further on, Mark's comment "Just break it up into these two," could have influenced Ken to consider a seam point in f as a fixed point in the composition. If there was no Harry in the group, who said: "Wait, because this kind of f of x and when x is equal to g of x when you have to change these restrictions for g of x and make sure it fits in the . . .", the rest of the group would probably remain satisfied with their previous answer concerning the seam point. Harry's comment made some sense to (at least) some of the group members. Ken expressed it in the following way: "OK. That makes sense. All right. Cause you are plugging in your g of x for your x, you are replacing independent variable with another variable. OK. I understand that." Again, Ken shows indication of the action level of the concept of composition of two functions. Anyhow, this group came up with the correct answer to Question 2 (Appendix) without any interviewer's prompting. It remains questionable whether the group would have come up with a correct answer if all members of the group had not fully participated in the discussion.

Category III. This group has shown a reasonable understanding of the concept of inverse function. Through the course of the interview, the group expressed a variety of interpretations of the meaning of inverse function. We go on to present excerpts which indicate the level of the concept which the group as a whole might be considered as having attained. In the first excerpt, the group defines the inverse function, at first as a procedure and then using the composition of two functions. This is an obvious example that shows that, when working in a group, subjects are exposed to a variety of definitions/solutions and each member has an opportunity to reflect on all of them.

Harry: OK. Well it's pretty much when y equals something x, or something like and then you got to reverse the roles. Well, the independent becomes the ... The independent variable becomes your dependent variable ...

Ken: You are switching your independent and dependent variables and then you wanna still solve for your original dependent variable.

Ervin: In terms of composition, f of g of x has to equal g of f of x [he wrote $f(g(x)) = g(f(x)) = x$.] ... that's the inverses

Mark: That's true, that's it. OK.

Ervin: So, ...

Ken: Because when you do inverses you can switch the two variables around like that and they need to equal to each other, so all you are doing is gonna end up with like when you have one f and then you take the reverse ... What's that?

Mark: This is ... [Mark was using a function and it's inverse from the previous question and composed them to show that Ervin's explanation is OK. They used the computer.]

Ken: They are actually inverses ...

Mark: Yeah, just trying to ...

Ken: You take ...

Ervin: Take this is ... You wanna plug two values for x and then try to ... Aaa, yeah.

Mark: That's f of x, not g of x.

Ken: Right. Equals x plus one ... just to make sure it works. Oooo, OK. I understand.

This time, Harry defined an inverse function at a pure action level but Ervin brought in a more sophisticated definition, in terms of composition. As we have seen earlier in a similar situation, some members had to use an example in order to give some meaning to the comment. That, in general, indicates their level of understanding of the inverse function. Recall that, earlier, Ken had to reinterpret Ervin's definition of the composition of two functions through an example. This time Mark reflected on Ervin's definition of

the inverse function by applying it to one example. Ken felt good about that, too, and he expressed this by saying "... just to make sure it works. Oooo, OK. I understand."

Another observation we can make here is that the group used the computer (successfully) to check if the composition of a function and its inverse is equal to the identity. In the same situation three other groups used the computer too. One group used the computer even when working on the first two problems.

The fact that the group considered 'uniqueness to the right' when talking about the inverse function could be seen from the following conversation. This is a discussion about the side question: Does every function have an inverse?

Mark: If there is no variable, like if there is y equals two.

Ken: Yeah. That's good case of ... if y equals two it's linear function there is no gonna be inverse for that. OK.

Draga: Why not?

Ervin: Do you want specific one?

Mark: Wait ... You would have for that ...

Ken: Because there is no independent variable ...

Ervin: If you have y equals two ...

Draga: What would be ...

Ervin: y equals two is a horizontal line.

Mark: Inverses are perpendicular ...

Ervin: No, you switch x and y. If independent and dependent variable, you switch your x you are actually rotating your graph.

Mark: I just think f of g of x, g of f of x is equal x.

Harry: Actually you could argue that y equal two is ... could actually be y equals zero times x plus two. You could say that.

Mark: What that actually does?

Harry: Just, and if you are to switch x and y that would make the vertical line at x equals two which does not pass the vertical line test.

The above situation shows not only that the group came to the correct conclusion, but also shows the way in which they came to it. Joint effort and full participation (as in this example) were two very important components in the process of answering the question. Mark, Ervin, and Harry, with their complementary comments, succeeded in arriving at the 'correct' explanation that not every function has an inverse. Ken's role here was mostly to listen and possibly clarify for himself others' comments. This situation also shows that the different group members had different levels of understanding. It seems that only Mark indicated a higher level of understanding from an action level. It is also important to mention that although Mark showed the highest level conception he did not dominate the group.

In another situation, the group interpreted the inverse function in the following way:

Ken: ... Also, it sort of make sense that I think you might be right Ervin that f of g of x equals g of f of x equals x

because when you are taking an inverse you are switching your independent and dependent variables and then solving still for the y value for the dependent variable and when you start out with the three x minus two equals f of x then you gonna end up with an x plus two divided by three it's gonna be exactly the opposite of the ... ammm ... Of the mathematical plus, minus, divided, times ... the mathematical tools. Is that good enough word?

Ervin: Operations. Operations.

Ken: And so, when you solve, when you plug into each other they gonna cancel each other out. Do you see what I mean?

Harry: Yeah, they are inverses.

Ken: Yeah. And so they cancel each other out and all it's gonna do is to solve for your x because you are trying, what you are trying to do is you go back to your x as your independent variable with everything else outside of that.

As could be seen from the above excerpts, the group discussed the inverse function from several very different perspectives. For them, the inverse function is a function which composed with another function gives the identity; then it is a process of inverting all the operations of the original function in order to get identity (action level of understanding); and it is also a pure action of inverting the x and the y and solving it for y. Even though they have in some cases demonstrated that knowledge only at an action level, the value of the multiplicity of perspectives participating in the shared interaction and therefore feeding into the individual construction of mental schemas is not diminished. If a statement by another student triggers a developmental change in a subject, the level of understanding of that student did not really matter.

Category IV.   When discussing the inverse of the composition of two functions, the group members went back and forth between the answer that it is a composition of the inverses of the functions in direct order and the answer that it is a composition of the inverses in opposite order. Ken approached the problem from his standpoint—by taking an example. The rest of the group agreed, and they proceeded to 'experiment' with possibilities of what the inverse of the composition would be. They started with the assumption that the inverse of the composition is the composition of the inverses in direct order. Below is an excerpt showing their 'experiment'.

Harry: Let me think of an example and see what happens in that example. Like an experiment. [He wrote: $f = x^2$]

Ken: No, because there is no inverse of x squared because you have plus or minus the square root of x. You can't have two, any power really.

Mark: Like two x plus four over three.

Ken: x plus four. x plus nine, OK.

Ken: The inverse cosine of x minus eleven ...

W: It's secant ...

Ken: Equals what?

Harry: And so then how would we deal with this and how is this relate to two functions that we have put to there? Is that necessarily the ...

Ken: Ammm, no, no, we need to do though, we need ... this is the inverse of f of g we need to prove that the composition of the inverse of f of x and the inverse of the g of x equals that. So we have is if f of x equals x plus nine is gonna be equal y equals x plus nine so is gonna be x equals y plus nine and is gonna be y equals x minus nine and then g of x equals $\cos(x)$ plus two you gonna have y equals cosine x plus two, x equals cosine y plus two, x minus two the arc cosine of that, then you have to prove that f of x the inverse of g of x inverse is gonna equal to h of the x inverse so you gonna have to plug this into that as you have an arc cosine of x minus two minus nine which is ... Which is really very close ...

Mark: Wait, wait a second, wait a second. This is x, this is minus two should be in the parentheses, shouldn't it?

Ken: Cosine, arc cosine x plus two, x equals cosine y plus two, x minus two equals to cosine y, arc cosine of x minus two. Although, if you think about it here ... I see a problem. This is arc cosine of x minus eleven equals y, so the whole thing...

Ken: Is not gonna be the inverse, if you had an inverse of f of x and inverse of g of x you gonna have to take g of f of x in order, in order for that to equal the inverse of f of g because you are plugging in your values for your f of x—the inverse which in this case we have x minus nine into a values for the g of x inverse which is arc cosine of x minus two and you get arc cosine of x minus eleven which is the same thing as your h of x. So if you have your inverse of f of x and your inverse of g of x in order for a composition of that to equal the inverse of f of g you have to take the g of x which is just ...

Harry: Is the order like the inverse of g and the inverse of f?

Ken: So, this is wrong. It should be g inverse of f inverse equals f of g of x inverse. So you gonna switch the order of f and g in order to work. That is just an example that prove it ... it make sense because since you are taking the inverse of the functions you gonna need to switch them around in order to compensate for a ... for the ... word, what is the word I want. I don't know. You gonna ...

Harry: It seems to work for this one particular example.

Draga: But if you think of the processes involved does it make some sense?

Ken: It does make sense because since you are switching the g and the f you gonna need, no since you are taking the inverse of the g and the f that means that all your pluses is gonna be minuses, all your divides is gonna be times ... I don't know the best way to say that, all your mathematical tools but you gonna have switch g and f in order for your final products, your final sums, and your final signs to come up in correct way because everything is gonna be switched around in opposite. Does that make sense?

Ervin: Yeah.

Ken: I mean that's just like ... no the way I explain it but ... I don't really know better way to explain that. So we were wrong about that because we just showed an example that proved that's wrong.

Draga: Are you sure now that this is true for any two functions?

Harry: For any two functions that have their inverses.

Ken: I think it will work for any two functions that have an inverse.

Mark: That's right.

Harry: I guess I would agree but I can't be a hundred percent sure.

Ervin: It makes common sense.

Ken: Since it is not something . . .

Ervin: But something . . .

Ken: I don't know the better way to explain. So, in our best guess, an educated guess that's what.

Ervin: I agree.

Mark: If we are wrong we are wrong.

Harry: We intend to think that this is true.

Ken: We would say that we are 98.97% sure.

Although the group did not apply the concept of inverse function at the process level in this example, they came up with the correct answer with relatively little prompting. A process conception of function that several group members displayed here could be some explanation for that. It is interesting to see the way of reasoning through which they came upon this solution. Recall that the group assumed that the inverse of the composition is the composition of the inverses in direct order. After completing their example, in which they did not get support for their assumption, Ken made the following conclusion: 'So, we were wrong about that because we just showed an example that proved that's wrong.' It seems that they assumed there were only two possible answers to the original question. Using the 'method of counterexample' and being aware that one example is not sufficient for a proof, they decided that the answer must be the remaining situation, which is that the inverse of the composition is the composition of the inverses in reversed order. This is an indication that for students, a statement is always true or always false.

The above example indicates that the coordination of the processes of the inverse function and the composition of functions should be the next step in learning the concept of the inverse function, before applying it in different situations.

A depiction of the development of individual participants' contributions during the ongoing problem-solving process

It is impossible to compare, one by one, all levels in the above categorization between the individuals and the groups. In this subsection we will present two things. First, we will try to depict the development of the individual participants' contributions during the ongoing group problem-solving process on Question 2. Second, we will present a corresponding excerpt (about the same question) from one individual interview. This will allow us to compare indi-

viduals' functioning in situations of individual and group problem solving. This might give us some idea about the kinds of mechanisms that are differentially involved in individual and group work. We will present one excerpt from the group interview and analyze it in two ways. First, we will analyze the discussion of all members of the group as it went in the interview. Then, we will extract all responses for each member of the group in the discussion, and analyze how they were developed and how they may have possibly contributed to the students' understanding of the concept. A question that students were discussing in this situation was to find a composition of two functions f and g given by

$$f(x) = \begin{cases} |x - 1| & \text{if } x > 1 \\ 2 & \text{if } x \leq 1 \end{cases}$$

and $g(x) = x - 2.$

Group excerpt:

Ken: OK. First expressions Ervin [he turned toward Ervin]. We need, we need f, f of g of x it's gonna equal to h.

Ervin: We have f of x.

Ken: Yeah, we have . . .

Mark: We have both.

Ken: We have f of x and we have g of x, so it's what we talked about in the last problem, we are to worry about the restrictions.

Mark: Just break it up into these two.

Ken: Right. So if x is greater than one then f of g of x . . . plugging a value of g of x . . .

Mark & Ken (together): x minus the square root x . . . it'll be absolute value of x minus five.

Ken: So it will be the square root, aaa it's gonna be the absolute value of x minus two minus three which would be the absolute value of x minus five if x is greater than one. Agree?

Mark: Ah-hah. If x is less or equal than one it still be two, right?

Harry: O, yeah.

Ken: Yeah, f of g of x when x is greater than, less than equal to one . . . if your f of x is two there is no, there is no independent variable to plug in g of x into it, therefore it's gonna always be two so you don't have to worry about the g of x. Well, the process of h is gonna, just gonna be plugging the value for g of x into the independent variable for f of x . . . h. Any decent comments, any thing you wanna add?

Ervin: You summed it up pretty much.

Mark: OK. All right. Cool.

Harry: Wait. Because this kind of f of x and when x is equal to g of x then you have to change these restrictions for g of x and make sure it fits in the . . .

Ken: OK. That makes sense. All right. Cause you are plugging in your g of x for your x, you are replacing independent variable with another variable. OK. I understand that.

Draga: And then what would you get?

Harry: Ha-ha.

Ken: What did you ask, I'm sorry?

Harry: We have to . . .

Mark: Why don't you put just x minus two in there and into so it would be x is greater then three . . .

Ken: OK. Yeah, it make sense. If x minus two is greater than one so it will yield if x is greater than three

Harry: I'm not sure if that's right.

Ken: if x minus is less then equal to one if x is less than equal to three. So, that is gonna work because g of x is equal to that in when every . . . if something is equal you can just replace like that. So, . . .

Mark: Cool

Ken: that's the absolute value of x minus five if x is greater than three or two if x is less then equal to three.

Harry: Does that sound good? Ha-ha-ha.

Draga: I don't know. I'm asking you. Whatever you say.

Ken: I can agree with my own ideas so . . .

Mark: Great, great.

Let's trace individual responses as they went in the above discussion. It could be of some importance to know that Ken was the person who wrote most of the group responses during the interview and read the questions loudly for the group. It was a group decision that Ken would read the questions since he is the 'loudest' person in their group.

It could be noticed throughout the interview that Ken was not very confident in his understanding of some concepts but also that he was not afraid to share his thoughts with the rest of the group. Ken's very first comment in this excerpt could be interpreted as Ken's uncertainty how to start the problem. Ervin was a member to whom they addressed the question in several 'crucial' situations. After Mark's indication that the first step should be to find the composition of f with g for each of the two branches in f, Ken made the comment: "So, it will be the square root, aaa it's gonna be the absolute value of x minus two minus three which would be the absolute value of x minus five if x greater than one. Agree?" It could be interpreted as Ken's ability to follow what Mark was saying. But, we can notice that Mark did not mention the seam point and Ken keeps the same seam point as in the function f. Further on, Mark agrees with Ken about the seam point and at the same time adds the comment about the second branch ("Aha-hah. If x is less or equal than one it still be two, right?"). At the first moment Harry agrees with them. Ken's comment about Mark's observation that the second branch is equal to the constant two may indicate that he himself needed an explanation (". . . if your f of x is two there is no, there is no independent variable to plug in g of x into it, therefore it's gonna always be two. So you don't have to worry about the g of x."). While Ken was summarizing their answer to the question, Harry had time to reflect on what they had said earlier about restrictions for the domain of the composition of two functions, and by making the comment "Wait, because this kind of f of x and when x is equal to g of x then you have to change these restrictions for g of x and make sure it fits in the . . ." he changed the group answer

from 'incorrect' to 'correct'. Again, Ken's comment ". . . Cause you are plugging in your g of x for your x, you are replacing independent variable with another variable," could be interpreted as his own need for an explanation of Harry's comment. His additional comment "OK. I understand that." confirms that interpretation. An even clearer example of Ken's need to reinterpret somebody's comment in his way (action level of understanding) could be seen in the following situation. After Mark notes what should be done algebraically ("Why don't you put just x minus two in there and into so it would be x is greater then three . . .") Ken says: "OK. Yeah, it make sense. If x minus two is greater than one so it will yield if x is greater than three . . . if x minus is less than equal to one if x is less than equal to three. So, that is gonna work because g of x is equal to that in then every . . . if something is equal you can just replace like that. So, . . . that's the absolute value of x minus five if x is greater than three or two if x is less than equal to three."

This dynamic of question-answer-confirmation illustrates the potential of the group to pull the individual (Ken in our examples) to the limits of her or his current development, pulling her or him up to a higher developmental level. This process is comparable to what Vygotsky describes as interaction in the "zone of proximal development" (Vygotsky, 1962).

We can also notice the externalization of the problem-solving strategy as an aspect of the role division in group work. Whereas in individual work the subject creates and follows a strategy of her or his own, involving a part of her or his mental energy in the meta-cognitive function, the strategy of problem-solving in the group situation is created and followed within the interaction of individuals, as a form of implicit agreement.

Let us now extract all responses for each individual and summarize what was their contribution in the above discussion. Below are Ken's responses:

Ken: OK. First expressions Ervin.

Ken: Yeah, we have . . .

Ken: Right. So if x is greater than one then f of g of x . . . plugging a value of g of x . . .

Mark & Ken (together): x minus the square root x . . . it'll be absolute value of x minus five.

Ken: Yeah, f of g of x when x is greater than, less than equal to one . . . if your f of x is two there is no, there is no independent variable to plug in g of x into it, therefore it's gonna always be two so you don't have to worry about the g of x. Well, the process of h is gonna, just gonna be plugging the value for g of x into the independent variable for f of x . . . h. Any decent comments, any thing you wanna add?

Ken: OK. That makes sense. All right. Cause you are plugging in your g of x for your x, you are replacing independent variable with another variable. OK. understand that.

Ken: What did you ask, I'm sorry?

Ken: OK. Yeah, it makes sense. If x minus two is greater than one so it will yield if x is greater than three

Ken: if x minus is less than equal to one if x is less than equal to three. So, that is gonna work because g of x is equal to that in when every ... if something is equal you can just replace like that. So, ...

Ken: that's the absolute value of x minus five if x is greater than three or two if x is less then equal to three.

Ken: I can agree with my own ideas so ...

It is obvious that Ken participated in the discussion much more than any other member of the group. Following his contribution in this discussion we may notice that he openly expressed his reflections on others' comments. His constant need to reinterpret others' comments indicates that he might be at an action level of understanding of the concept of the composition of two functions. Although we can not evaluate how much (if any) this group discussion contributed to Ken's cognitive growth, his comments of the type "OK. That make sense. All right. ... I understand that," indicate that, at least, it made some sense to him. We can only say that he was able to follow the discussion and had an opportunity to hear different (from his own) ways and views of approaching the question. Regarding the role that Ken took in this group discussion, we may notice that he was the one to start the discussion, even if it consisted in calling upon somebody else to start with the first attempt to answer the question. He was also the one who tended to summarize the group answer and reinterpret it in some other way.

Below are Mark's responses.

Mark: We have both.

Mark: Just break it up into these two.

Mark & Ken (together): x minus the square root x ... it'll be absolute value of x minus five.

Mark: Aha-hah. If x is less or equal than one it still be two, right?

Mark: OK. All right. Cool.

Mark: Why don't you put just x minus two in there and into so it would be x is greater then three ...

Mark: Cool

Mark: Great, great.

We interpret that Mark was following the discussion and was satisfied with their answers ("OK. All right. Cool. ... Great, great). For him, too, a comment about the seam point made sense. That could be seen from his comment "Why don't you put just x minus two in there and into so it would be x is greater than three ..."). On the other hand, in terms of the individual roles within the group, it seems that Mark took the role of suggesting what to do ("Just break it up into these two."), reminding the group of what should be the next step in their work ("Why don't you put just x minus two ..."), and also he had the role of rewarding verbally the whole group ("Cool. ... Great.").

In the following excerpt we present Harry's comments in the group discussion.

Harry: O, yeah.

Harry: Wait. Because this kind of f of x and when x is equal to g of x then you have to change these restrictions for g of x and make sure it fits in the ...

Harry: Ha-ha.

Harry: We have to ...

Harry: I'm not sure if that's right.

Harry: Does that sound good? Ha-ha-ha.

From the above we may notice the following about the flow of Harry's responses. First, he participated in the discussion by confirming somebody's statement ("O, yeah.") with a dose of surprise. As if he didn't expect, or forgot, about that statement. His next statement ("Wait. Because this kind of f of x and when x is equal to g of x then you have to change these restrictions for g of x and make sure it fits in the ...") indicates that he reflected on what has been said earlier about the domain of the composition. His point about that fact was a very significant step in this problem-solving situation. His comment influenced the thoughts of other members of the group who found a way to justify it. Later in the discussion Harry expressed some doubt in the correctness of his statement ("I'm not sure if that's right.") but since the rest of the group ignored it he finished the conversation with the question to the interviewer "Does that sound good?" and the sound of relief "Ha-ha-ha".

The last excerpt is a set of Ervin's responses in the discussion.

Ervin: We have f of x.

Ervin: You summed it up pretty much.

In this particular situation we are unable to conclude much about Ervin's participation in the group discussion. If we recall from the first excerpt in this section, Ervin was called to respond first to the question. After being interrupted by some other members of the group he stayed quiet most of the time. His greatest contribution in this discussion was nodding his head as a sign of his agreement with the group response.

In the case of the excerpt from the individual interview, we will analyze the flow of the individual answer. The criteria for selecting the excerpts is the 'correctness' of the answer to Question 2 from the interview.

Below we present an excerpt in which Mary is answering the Question 2.

Mary: OK. (pause) That would be ...

Draga: OK. What you wrote is that the first branch is the absolute value of two minus three if x is greater than 1 and two if x is less or equal than one.

Mary: Right, because if it's less than one for every new, having g is no matter it still will do whatever we plug in there and then the top one we would just have whatever the value of

g plug it in where the x is and subtract the 3 and then take the absolute value of it and then for all x greater than one.

Draga: So what would be the domain of h?

Mary: It'd be all x.

Draga: Aha, and you said ...?

Mary: Because you define h you have to define for all x you really will have to split up.

Draga: OK. So what you are saying you'll keep the same seam point...

Mary: You keep the same domain ...

Draga: So you would keep the same point where the function splits ...

Mary: Right, because your g was defined for all x and so the only thing to split would be your f.

Draga: OK. So, what is the process of h in this case?

Mary: Ammm ... You are going to have a seam point wherever there is a break in either of these two functions. Since there is a break in only one function that's going to define where your graph is gonna break at. If it's in both of them you just gonna break in more than, it's gonna break in more than two parts.

Draga: OK. And the process of h in this case would be what?

Mary: Aaa ... aaa. Let see. You have to look at what x you ... let me change that in a minute. This would shift because in your original function there you have less or equal than one. So if you put in something like, like one here you'd have less than one, you plug it back in the original you get two. So this would be to change to ... (pause) ... let see ... I need to change to three ...

Draga: Ah-hah, so you need to change your seam point.

Mary: ... because you get to look where the g equals ... according to x, or according to your f, function f, where the seam point was.

Draga: Ah-hah.

Mary: So it would change.

Draga: OK.

Mary: I just remember that. You gotta check where your function, your first function is defined ... you are checking ... that's where you reach, reach your domain of your x and you gotta see where is that is equal to what's your other domain was and then that changes your domain that far and then you just do what you would do with normal composition.

From the above situation, we may observe that Mary started her response from one action standpoint ("... we would just have whatever the value of g plug it in where the x is and subtract the 3 and then take the absolute value of it and then for all x greater than one."). Initially, Mary said that the seam point would be the same in f and h because "your g was defined for all x and so the only thing to split would be your f." But soon she realized her mistake and corrected it, explaining "You gotta check where your function, your first function is defined ... you are checking ... that's where you reach, reach your domain of your x and you gotta see where is that is equal to what's your other domain was and then that changes your domain that far ...". Mary's comment "I just remember that" makes us wonder whether she would be able to conclude that if she

did not know it before. Another thing which could be noticed in the above excerpt is that Mary needed a significant amount of prompting by the interviewer.

Summary

Differences between group and individual construction processes of the concept of inverse function

We may recall that we started this research with the assumption that students learn the concept of inverse function in the following order: learning the function concept first, and then the composition of function, then the definition of inverse function, and finally the application of the concept of inverse function. After data analysis we may see (see Table 2) the following: There were some subjects who were able to define (in terms of switching x and y) and find (by switching x and y, or by trial and error) the inverse function without understanding the concept of the composition of two functions (Cantor, GR3). Also, there were some subjects (GR4) who understood the concept of the composition of two functions, and the concept of inverse function but could not apply it in the particular situation. We consider it as an indication that the coordination of the processes of inverse function and the composition of functions is an important step which subjects should attain before being able to apply those two concepts. On the other hand, there were some subjects (Mary, GR1, GR2) who were able (at least on the action level) to apply both, the concepts of composition and inverse function, in the given problem-solving situation.

As regards the differences between learning the concept of inverse function in a group versus learning it individually, we may conclude that there are no differences in the steps of genetic decomposition, but there are differences in the process of learning it. The transcripts show clearly that group members take on different roles in the social interactive process of problem-solving. It is our hypothesis that it is exactly this social structuring of the group that differentiates group problem-solving from individual problem-solving. Namely, the role division in a group creates a more complete and more flexible support system for problem-solving. It is obvious that a greater number of people, taking on different roles, both social and cognitive, in the problem-solving process, will bring a greater variety of approaches and modes of understanding, that may be used in increasing the efficiency of the problem-solving. On the other hand, a certain flexibility is brought to the process through the simultaneous availability of various possible directions of thought.

Below we will summarize the most frequent characteristics of the process of learning the concept of inverse function that appeared in our protocols of the selected group of four subjects, and then we will discuss those characteristics (as they appear) in the process of individual learning. These characteristics differentiate between the process of learning the concept in a group and in the individual situation.

Characteristics of the group process in problem-solving

Disequilibrium. The members of the group were exposed, most of the time, to confrontations between various ideas and views. Let us recall that Piaget emphasized that equilibration (the process of seeking mental equilibrium) is the mechanism for growth and transition in cognitive development. This confrontation in some cases led to the assimilation of the new conceptual matter into existing schemas, while in some other cases and for at least some of the group members it led to the creation of new schemas or the modification of old schemas (accommodation). For example, the excerpt on page 162 describes the following situation: the group was discussing how to find the composition of two given functions.

In any individual problem solving situation Mark suggested to "... put just x minus two in there and into so it would be x greater then three", Ken's reaction was "OK. Yeah, it make sense. If x minus two is greater than one so it will yield to x is greater than three." By assimilating the new information into existing schemas, Ken was able to see why x should be greater than three, and the equilibrium was restored ("OK. Yeah, it make sense."). We see another example in the situation where the group defines the inverse function. When Ervin defined the inverse function in terms of composition, Ken was confused (disequilibrium) and tried to make sense out of that ("Because when you do inverses you can switch the two variables around like that and they need to equal to each other, so all you are doing is gonna end up with like when you have one f and then you take the reverse ... What's that?"). At the first moment, his attempt to make sense out of Ervin's definition was unsuccessful, but later, after discussing it with others, Ken obviously created a new schema of the inverse function (accommodation), which he expressed by "Oooo, OK. I understand.".

It is our hypothesis that even if a contradiction is engendered at the social level between two or more individuals, a key factor in this event concerns an individual's realization that her or his idea is incompatible with another. In line with Piaget's ideas of the role of disequilibrium in driving cognitive development the greater incidence of situations of confrontation in the group situation in comparison to the individual situation of problem-solving creates more ample opportunity for the construction of new schemas.

Diversity of approaches.   Group work encouraged each student to become aware of her or his own ideas through their explication, and also provided a supportive social environment with a multiplicity of questions that furthered the clarification of these ideas and viewpoints that put them in perspective. Each member of the group had the opportunity to reflect upon different views (approaches) at the same time and, by coordinating them, to gain some better understanding of the concept. From our protocols we have seen that the group discussed the inverse function from several very different perspectives. For them, the inverse function is a function which, when composed with another function, gives the identity, "Ervin: In terms of composition, f of g of x has to equal g of f of x ... [he wrote $f(g(x)) = g(f(x)) = x$].", or "Mark: I just think f of g of x, g of f of x is equal x.); then it is a process of inverting all the operations of the original function to get identity ("Ken: ... it's gonna be exactly the opposite of the ... ammm ... of the mathematical plus, minus, divides, times ..."); and it is also a pure action of inverting the x and y and solving it for y, "Harry: ... The independent variable becomes your dependent variable ..." and then Ken takes over and says "You are switching your independent and dependent variables and then you wanna still solve for your original dependent variable."). It is significant that in the above cases, different ideas came from different members of the group. Notice that Ervin defined the inverse function in terms of composition, Ken defined it as a reversed process, and Harry gave the idea of the inverse function as the action of switching variables. It remains in question whether any member of the group who worked alone would have come up with all these different definitions.

Building mathematical language.   It is very often mentioned in the literature (Sharan & Sharan, 1992) that students working in a group have less problems to understand their partners than to understand the instructor. Also, the group discussion helps them to accept some new, common terminology regarding the concept. In our protocols, we have seen how the group accepted the new term 'restrictions' for the term 'limitations' and used it later in the course of the interview. We saw that Ken had a problem with finding the appropriate word for addition, subtraction, division and multiplication. He called it 'mathematical tools', but Ervin helped him by saying that they are called operations.

In the process of interaction, the group of students constructs the assigned problem, in order to go on to the construction of its solution. Whereas an individual student interprets and solves a problem on the basis of her or his previous knowledge, without any additional input, the students in a group develop a shared construction of the problem, which has a defined structure at the level of the group, but individual interpretations which may vary in their scope of understanding and the associations related to it. When one member of the group uses some term or way of expressing her or his understanding of some aspect of the problem, this is readily understood by others on the basis of the shared problem structure. In this way, individuals may fill in their idiosyncratic gaps in knowledge, building at the same time a shared pool of terminology and perspectives for the group.

Taking different roles.   Our transcripts showed clearly that group members take on different roles in the social interactive process of problem-solving. We have seen the situation in which all members who participated in the discussion took on different roles (starting the discussion, calling upon some member to respond, suggesting what to do, clarifying comments, reflecting on what has been said in the past, summarizing, writing the solution . . .). We believe that it is precisely thanks to role distribution in the group that Harry in this example had time (while others were discussing the expression for the composition of two given functions) to reflect upon what the group had discussed earlier about the domain of the composition and to remind the rest of the group about that fact. It turned out that that fact changed the group solution from 'incorrect' to 'correct'.

We hypothesize that it is exactly this social structure of the group that differentiates group problem-solving from individual problem-solving in important ways. As indicated in our data it is obvious that a greater number of people, taking on different roles, both social and cognitive, in the problem-solving process, will bring a greater variety of approaches and modes of understanding, that may be used in increasing the efficiency of the problem-solving. On the other hand, a certain flexibility is brought to the process through the simultaneous availability of various possible directions of thought.

In addition to the characteristics of group work described above, we have noted two important conditions created in our group that seemed to facilitate the positive outcome of problem-solving. These conditions, unlike the ones previously described, are not necessary characteristics of group work. They are rather variables which might differentiate successful groups from less successful ones.

These consist in the full participation of all members in group work and in their mutual encouragement and verbal support.

Full participation of all group members and mutual encouragement.   In order to stimulate a greater diversity of ideas and a smooth flow of the discussion, it is important to motivate all group members to participate in the discussion. From our protocol we have seen that the members of this group were all active in the group discussion most of the time though the ability and understanding levels of the individuals were very different. Sometimes, the group answer to the given problem-solving situation would depend on the full participation of all its members. For example, we have seen that the group found the correct expression for the composition of two given functions including the correct domain of the function. It remains questionable whether the group would have come up with a correct answer if all members of the group had not fully participated in the discussion.

Working in a group also gives students an opportunity to develop their self-esteem. It is very important for all students who are working together to learn how to encourage each others' participation. Giving some verbal reward could be one way to do so. Throughout our protocols we have seen several such situations in which some members expressed their satisfaction and rewarded the whole group. For example, we see that Mark used words *cool, all right,* or *great* to encourage his teammates for good work.

Characteristics of the individual process in problem-solving.   Any problem-solving situation provides opportunities for the creation of cognitive conflict (disequilibrium). In the individual problem-solving situation, therefore, as in the group situation, there are plenty of opportunities for disequilibrium. The difference between the disequilibrium in the group and the disequilibrium in individual problem-solving is in their cause. In the individual problem-solving situation, disequilibrium is usually induced only by the problem itself, while in the group problem-solving situation there is an additional source—the other members of the group. In addition, it is much easier for an individual than a group to ignore a contradiction. Also, the process of restoring equilibrium in some cases could be quicker in the group, because of the help which one individual may get from her or his teammates.

Of course, an individual may have more than one approach (view) to the given problem situation. What is the difference between an individual who has more than one approach and the group having and sharing more than one approach? In a group whose members share different approaches, most likely, there will be at least one member who does not know all the approaches and has an opportunity to learn them. In the individual case, all different approaches have an internal character, stay inside just one individual.

In individual work, a student has less opportunity to be corrected or to get help. Also, he or she lacks the opportunity to be encouraged as much as an individual when working in the group.

While working alone, an individual focuses on one thing at a time. As we have seen in our example for taking different roles in the group, one group member had time to think about something else while somebody else was working on the problem. We believe that this creates a more complete and more flexible support system for problem-solving.

In any individual problem-solving situation an individual must participate fully in order to come up with some solution. But that participation is linear in the sense that its focus is usually just the problem situation. In the group environment full participation involves not only focusing on the problem-solving situation but also on others' comments. The only encouragement that one may get while working individually is her or his success. In case of failure an individual may get discouraged very quickly and gives up. In a group in such a situation, there is a greater probability that there will be somebody who will have an idea and will persist to the solution.

Conclusions

In conclusion, in this work we make two recommendations with regard to circumstances of learning the concept of inverse function at the undergraduate level. The first recommendation relates to the choice between group work and individual problem-solving. On the basis of inductive empirical investigation of the process of the construction of problem solutions in a group of students we have found a number of characteristics of study groups that differentiate them from the individual mode of problem-solving. These are:

1. Fostering disequilibrium
2. Diversity of approaches
3. Building mathematical language
4. Taking different roles

We believe on the basis of the comparative analysis of these characteristics of groups and comparable conditions in individual problem-solving, that the inherent characteristics of the group problem-solving process positively con-

tribute to the development of the students' schemas related to the inverse function.

We have also noted two characteristics of group work which we believe differentiate between more effective and less effective groups. These are:

1. Full participation of all group members
2. Encouragement

We would like to stress that these findings reflect the structure of particular individuals and groups observed during the problem-solving process, and further studies of a more experimental character would have to be planned in order to make generalizations.

Acknowledgments.   The author would like to express her gratitude to Ed Dubinsky and Neil Davidson for their thoughtful comments and criticisms of earlier drafts of this manuscript.

Bibliography

Asiala, M., Brown, A., DeVries, D. J., Dubinsky, E., Mathews, D., & Thomas, K. (1996). A framework for research and development in undergraduate mathematics education. *Research in Collegiate Mathematics Education,* II, 1–32.

Ayres, T., G. Davis, E. Dubinsky, & P. Lewin. (1988). Computer experiences in learning composition of functions. *Journal for Research in Mathematics Education,* 19(3). 246–259.

Davidson, N. (1985). Small-group learning and teaching in mathematics: A selective review of the research. In R. E. Slavin, S. Kagan, R. Hertz-Lazarowitz, C. Webb, & R. Schmuck (Eds.), *Learning to Cooperate, Cooperating to Learn* (pp. 221–230). New York: Plenum.

—— (1990). *Cooperative learning in mathematics: A handbook for teachers.* Menlo Park, CA.: Addison-Wesley Publishing Co.

Davidson, N., & Kroll, D. L. (1991). An overview of research on cooperative learning related to mathematics. *Journal for Research in Mathematics Education,* 22, (5), 362–365.

Dees, R. L. (1991). The role of cooperative learning in increasing problem-solving ability in a college remedial course. *Journal for Research in Mathematical Education,* 22, 409–421.

Dubinsky, E. (1991a). Reflective abstraction in advanced mathematical thinking. In Tall, D. (Ed.), *Advanced Mathematical Thinking,* London: Riedel.

—— (1991b). Constructive aspects of reflective abstraction in advanced mathematics. In L. P. Steffe (Ed.), *Epistemological foundations of mathematical experience,* New York: Springer-Verlag.

Harel, G., & Kaput, J. (1991). The role of conceptual entities and their symbols in building advanced mathematical concepts. In Tall, D. (Ed.), *Advanced Mathematical Thinking,* London: Riedel.

Moskowitz, J. M., Malvin, J. H., Schaeffer, G. A., & Schaps, E. (1983). Evaluation of a cooperative learning strategy. *American Educational Research Journal, 20,* 687–696.

Patton, M. Q. (1980). *Qualitative evaluation methods.* Beverly Hills, CA: Sage Publications.

Piaget, J. (1950). *The psychology of intelligence.* Routledge & Kegan Paul LTD, Broadway House, Carter Lane. London, E. C. 4.

—— (1952). *The child's conception of number.* New York: The Humanities Press Inc.

—— (1968). Six psychological studies. (A. Tenzer, Trans.). New York: Vintage Books. (Original work published 1964).

—— (1970). *Science of education and the psychology of the child.* (E. Denoel, Trans.). Grossman Publishers, Inc.

Piaget, J., & Inhelder, B. (1969a). *The Psychology of the Child.* (H. Weaver, Trans.). New York: Basic Books. (Original work published 1966).

—— (1969b). *The early growth of logic in the child.* (E. Lunzer & D. Papert, Trans.). W. W. Norton & Company, Inc., NY.

Sharan, S. (1980). Cooperative learning in small groups: Recent methods and effects on achievement, attitudes and ethnic relations. *Review of Educational Research, 50,* 241–271.

Sharan, Y., & Sharan, S. (1992). *Expanding cooperative learning through group investigation.* Teachers College Press, NY.

Slavin, R. E. (1985). Team-assisted individualization: Combining cooperative learning and individualized instruction in mathematics. In R. Slavin, S. Sharan, S. Kagan, R. Hertz-Lazarowitz, C. Webb, & R. Schmuck (Eds.), *Learning to cooperate, cooperating to learn,* (pp. 177–209). New York: Plenum Press.

Swing, S. R. & Peterson, P. L. (1982). The relationship of student ability and small-group interaction to student achievement. *American Educational Research Journal, 19,* 259–274.

Vidaković D. (1993). Differences between group and individual processes of construction of the concept of inverse function. Doctoral dissertation.

—— (1994). Learning the concept of inverse function. To be submitted to the *Journal of Computers in Mathematics and Science Teaching.*

Vygotsky, L. S. (1962). *Thought and language.* Cambridge, MA: MIT Press.

—— (1978). *Mind in society: The development of higher psychological processes.* (M. Cole, V. John-Steiner, S. Scribner, & E. Souberman, Eds.), Cambridge, MA: Harvard University Press.

Webb, N. M. (1991). Task-related verbal interaction and mathematics learning in small groups. *Journal for Research in Mathematics Education, 22* (5), 366–389.

Appendix

1. Let f and g be two functions. How would you define a composition of f with g? What is the process of that composition? What is the domain of the composition?

2. Find an expression for a function h so that $h = f \circ g$, where f and g are functions given by:

$$f(x) = \begin{cases} |x - 1| & \text{if } x > 1 \\ 2 & \text{if } x \le 1 \end{cases}$$

and

$$g(x) = x - 2.$$

What is the process of h?

3. Find an expression for a function f so that $h = f \circ g$, where g and h are functions given by:

$$g(x) = \cos(x)$$
$$h(x) = 2\big(\cos(x)\big)^2 - 7.$$

What is the process of f?

4. Find an expression for a function f so that $h = f \circ g$, where g and h are functions given by:

$$g(x) = \begin{cases} 2 - x & \text{if } x \le 2 \\ x - 2 & \text{if } x > 2 \end{cases}$$
$$h(x) = x.$$

What is the process of f?

5. Find the inverse of f and state its domain.

$$f(x) = 2x - 1.$$

6. What is the inverse of a function?

7. If f and g are inverse functions of each other, what would be $g \circ f$? Explain.

8. For the function f given by the sketch below, make a sketch of its inverse.

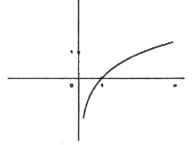

9. If $f \circ g$ represents a composition of f and g, what would be the inverse of that composition? Explain.

PART III
Implementation Issues

One conclusion that can be drawn from the papers we have considered up to this point is that cooperative learning can make a substantial contribution to students' learning mathematics, and that this can significantly improve the results obtained by traditional teaching methods—all provided that, in a given implementation, the system actually works the way in which one intends for it to work. This raises a number of issues regarding how cooperative learning can be implemented, and in this section we present papers that consider some of these issues.

First there are two papers that consider very specific issues. Johnson and Johnson argue that interpersonal and small-group skills should be taught and they describe a method for doing that. They also recommend a procedure for providing rewards. Heller and Hollabaugh present a system of structural and management procedures for problem solving in a physics course.

Cohen, Lotan, and Catanzarite introduce a very different issue—status problems and how they might be treated. Many of the fundamental goals of cooperative learning, such as students of different abilities and backgrounds working together productively can be difficult to achieve if communication is affected by variations in status that students have in the eyes of their peers. Cohen et al. discuss this issue and ways of dealing with it.

Finally, we present two papers, by Davidson and by Dubinsky and Schwingendorf, which describe the operation of cooperative learning within a total pedagogical system. In both cases the course is calculus and, like most of the papers in this collection, the pedagogical innovations under consideration involve cooperative learning in a major way, but also go beyond that single pedagogical strategy.

Comments on the article by Johnson and Johnson

This paper takes the position, in agreement with several other works, that only under certain conditions will co-operative learning methods increase students' efforts to achieve. According to the authors, these conditions are: positive interdependence, face-to-face interaction, individual accountability, social skills, and group processing.

The authors feel that students should be taught interpersonal and small-group skills. They describe a series of steps for teaching such skills and describe both short-term and long-term outcomes.

Another method advocated in this paper for getting students to work cooperatively is the use of rewards. The authors recommend a system of group points and describe a procedure for implementing a structured program for awarding such points.

The paper concludes by arguing that teaching interpersonal and small-group skills is as important as the academic content in a course.

Discussion Questions

1. Explain each of the items on the authors' list of conditions for the success of cooperative learning.

2. Do you agree with the authors' list of conditions for the success of cooperative learning? Would you add things to the list? Would you drop anything?

3. In a college course that uses cooperative learning, how much time should be spent in teaching students to work in cooperative groups? What are the ways in which you would do this?

4. What do you think are the relative importance in a college mathematics course of learning to work in cooperative groups and learning the mathematical content?

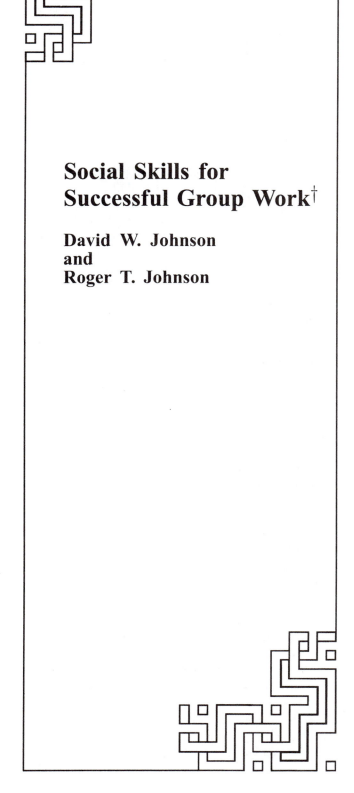

Social Skills for Successful Group Work†

David W. Johnson
and
Roger T. Johnson

In a 4th grade classroom the teacher is trying out learning groups. "This is a mess," she thinks. In one group, students are bickering over who is going to do the writing. In another group, one child sits quietly, too shy to participate. Two members of a third group are talking about football while the third member works on the assignment. "My students do not know how to work cooperatively," she sighs.

What is a teacher to do in such a situation? Simply placing students in groups and telling them to work together does not, in and of itself, produce cooperation—and certainly not the higher achievement and positive social outcomes that can result from cooperative learning groups. The reason? Traditional group efforts may go wrong in many ways. Group members sometimes seek a free ride on others' work by "leaving it to George" to complete the group's tasks. Students who are stuck doing all the work sometimes decrease their efforts to avoid being suckers. High-ability group members may take over in ways that benefit themselves at the expense of lower achieving group members (the "rich get richer" effect). Pressures to conform may suppress individual efforts. Or group work may break down because of divisive conflicts and power struggles.

Only under certain conditions can we expect cooperative efforts to achieve and improve the quality of their relationships with classmates and their psychological health. These conditions are positive interdependence, face-to-face (promotive) interaction, individual accountability, social skills, and group processing (Johnson and Johnson 1987, Johnson et al. 1988). Each of these elements mediates the relationship between cooperation and its outcomes (Johnson and Johnson 1989). And they are all interrelated. Using social skills, for example, makes sense only when there is positive interdependence. In competitive and individualistic situations, trust and empathy are inappropriate.

Teaching Cooperative Skills

People do not know instinctively how to interact effectively with others. Nor do interpersonal and group skills magically appear when they are needed. Students must be taught these skills and be motivated to use them. If group members lack the interpersonal and small-group skills to cooperate effectively, cooperative groups will not be productive.

In order to coordinate efforts to achieve mutual goals, students must (1) get to know and trust one another, (2) communicate accurately and unambiguously, (3) accept and support one another, and (4) resolve conflicts construc-

† *Educational Leadership,* 48 (7) pp. 29–33. Reprinted with permission of the Association for Supervision and Curriculum Development. Copyright © 1990 by ASCD. All rights reserved.

tively (Johnson 1986, Johnson and Johnson 1987). Interpersonal and small-group skills make possible the basic nexus among students; and if students are to work together productively and cope with the stresses of doing so, they must have at least a modicum of these skills.

Teachers can follow a series of steps in teaching students interpersonal and small-group skills. First, students must see the need to use the skill. To want to learn the skill, students must believe that they will be better off if they know it. Teachers can highlight the need for the skill by explaining why it is important, displaying what it looks like on posters and bulletin boards, and informing students they will be rewarded for using it.

Encouraging Participation	
Looks Like	Sounds Like
Smiles	What is your idea?
Eye contact	Awesome!
Thumbs up	Good idea!
Pat on back	That's interesting.

TABLE 1
T-Chart

Second, students must understand what the skill is and when it should be used. This information is most commonly conveyed through a "T-Chart" (Johnson et al. 1988) and through modeling the skill. (See Figure 1 for an example of a T-Chart.) The teacher lists the skill (e.g., encouraging participation) and then asks the class, "What would this skill look like?" After several nonverbal behaviors are generated, the teacher asks, "What would this skill sound like?" Several phrases are listed. The teacher then models the skill until the students have a clear idea of what the skill sounds and looks like.

Third, to master a social skill, students must practice it again and again. Immediately after defining the skill, the teacher should ask students to role-play the skill several times with the persons sitting next to them. The social skill may also be assigned to students as a role to be engaged in during group meetings. For example, the teacher could assign the roles of reader, encourager, summarizer, and elaboration-seeker to the members of a cooperative group. The roles could be rotated daily until every student has been responsible for each role several times. At the end of each cooperative lesson, teachers can announce how many times the skill was observed. New skills need to be cued consistently and reinforced for some time. Teach-

ers should be relentless in encouraging prolonged use of cooperative skills.

Fourth, students must process how frequently and how well they are using the skill. Students need to discuss, describe, and reflect on their use of the skill in order to improve their performance. To ensure that they do so, teachers should provide a regular time for group processing and give students group processing procedures to follow. A standard processing task is, "Name three things your group did well, and name one thing your group could do better next time." Such group processing will not only increase students' interpersonal and small-group skills, it will also increase achievement (Johnson et al. in press, Yager et al. 1985) and the quality of the relationships developed among students (Putnan et al. 1989).

Fifth, students must persevere in practicing the skill. Students have to practice cooperative skills long enough to go through the stages of awkward enactment, phony (role-playing) enactment, and mechanical use of the skill to automatic, routine use where the skill is fully internalized. Ways to ensure that the students persevere include continuing to assign the skill as a group role, continuing to give students feedback as to how frequently and how well they are performing the skill, and rewarding the groups when members use the skill.

Using Bonus Points

Many teachers want to use a structured program to teach students the interpersonal and small-group skills they need. Such a program will give students the opportunity to earn bonus points for their groups by using targeted cooperative skills. We have found that students, even socially isolated and withdrawn ones, learn more social skills and engage in them more frequently when the group is given bonus points for their doing so (Lew et al. 1986a, 1986b). Bonus points can be accumulated for academic credit or for special rewards, such as free time or minutes listening to one's own choice of music. We recommend the following procedure:

1. Identify, define, and teach a social skill you want students to use in working cooperatively with one another. This skill becomes a target for mastery. Skills include staying with the group, using quiet voices, giving direction to the group's work, encouraging participation, explaining answers, relating present learning to past learning, criticizing ideas without criticizing people, asking probing questions, and requesting further rationale (Johnson et al. 1988).

2. Use group points and group rewards to increase the use of the cooperative skill:
   a. Each time a student engages in the targeted skill, the student's group receives a point.
   b. Points may be awarded only for positive behavior.

c. Points are added and never taken away. All points are permanently earned.

3. Summarize total points daily. Emphasize daily progress toward the goal. Use a visual display such as a graph or chart.

4. Develop an observational system that samples each group for the same amount of time. In addition, use student observers to record the frequency of students' use of the targeted skills.

5. Set a reasonable number of points for earning the reward. Rewards can be both social and tangible. A social reward is having the teacher say, "That shows thought," "I like the way you explained it," "That's a good way of putting it," "Remarkably well done." The points earned can be traded in for a tangible reward: free time, computer time, library time, time to play a game, extra recess time, and any other activity that students value.

6. In addition to group points, class points may be awarded. For example, the teacher might say, "Eighteen people are ready to begin and helped the class earn a reward," or "I noticed 12 people worked the last 25 minutes." Class points may be recorded with a number line, beans in a jar, or checks on the chalkboard.

7. In addition to social skills, potential target behaviors include following directions, completing assigned tasks, handing in homework, behaving appropriately in out-of-class settings such as lunch or assemblies, or helping substitute teachers.

Long-Term Outcomes

Teaching students interpersonal and small-group skills produces both short-term and long-term outcomes (Johnson and Johnson 1989). Short-term outcomes include greater learning, retention, and critical thinking. Long-term outcomes include greater employability and career success.

Most people realize that a college education or vocational training improves their career opportunities, but many are less aware that interpersonal skills may be the set of skills most important to their employability, productivity, and career success. Employers typically value verbal communication, responsibility, initiative, and interpersonal and decision-making skills. A question all employers have in mind when they interview a job applicant is, "Can this person get along with other people?" Having a high degree of technical competence is not enough to ensure a successful career. A person also has to have a high degree of interpersonal competence.

For example, in 1982 the Center for Public Resources published "Basic Skills in the U.S. Workforce," a nationwide survey of businesses, labor unions, and educational institutions. The Center found that 90 percent of the respondents who had been fired from their jobs were fired for poor job attitudes, poor interpersonal relationships, and inappropriate behavior. Being fired for lack of basic and technical skills was infrequent. Even in high-tech jobs, the ability to work effectively with other personnel is essential, as is the ability to communicate and work with people from other professions to solve interdisciplinary problems.

In the real world of work, the heart of most jobs—especially higher-paying, more interesting jobs—is getting others to cooperate, leading others, coping with complex problems of power and influence, and helping solve people's problems in working together. Millions of technical, professional, and managerial jobs today require much more than technical competence and professional expertise. Such jobs also require leadership. More and more, employees are asked to get things done by influencing a large and diverse group of people (bosses, subordinates, peers, customers, and others), despite lacking much or any formal control over them and despite their general disinterest in cooperating. Employees are expected to motivate others, negotiate and mediate, get decisions implemented, exercise authority, and develop credibility—all tasks that require interpersonal and small-group skills. Thus, the skills developed within cooperative efforts in school are important contributors to personal employability and career success. In addition, social skills are directly related to building and maintaining positive relationships and to keeping psychological health. Maintaining a set of good friends, being a caring parent, maintaining a loving relationship with your spouse—all directly relate to how interpersonally skilled you are. One's quality of life as an adult depends largely on one's social skills. Furthermore, the more socially skilled people are, the healthier they tend to be psychologically. For these and many other reasons, we should teach students the skills necessary to build and maintain cooperative relationships with others.

As Important as Academic Content

If the potential of cooperative learning is to be realized, students must have the prerequisite interpersonal and small-group skills and be motivated to use them. These skills should be taught just as systematically as mathematics, social studies, or any subject. Doing so requires that teachers communicate to students the need for social skills, define and model these skills, have students practice them over and over again, process how effectively students perform the skills, and ensure that students persevere until the skills are fully integrated into their behavioral repertoires. If teachers do so, they will not only increase student achievement, they will also increase students' future employability, career success, quality of relationships, and psychological health.

References

Johnson, D.W. (1986), *Reaching Out: Interpersonal Effectiveness and Self-Actualization.* Englewood Cliffs, NJ: Prentice Hall.

Johnson, D.W., and F. Johnson. (1987). *Joining Together: Group Theory and Group Skills.* Englewood Cliffs, NJ: Prentice Hall.

Johnson, D.W., and R. Johnson. (1989). *Cooperation and Competition: Theory and Research.* Edina, MN: Interaction Book Company.

Johnson, D.W., R. Johnson, and E. Holubec (1988). *Cooperation in the Classroom.* Edina, Minn.: Interaction Book Company.

Johnson, D.W., R. Johnson, M. Stanne, and A. Garibaldi. (in press). "The Impact of Leader and Member Group Processing on Achievement in Cooperative Groups." *Journal of Social Psychology.*

Lew, M., D. Mesch, D.W. Johnson, and R. Johnson. (1968a). "Positive Interdependence. Academic and Collaborative-Skills Group Contingencies and Isolated Students." *American Educational Research Journal* 23: 476–488.

—— (1968b). "Components of Cooperative Learning: Effects of Collaborative Skills and Academic Group Contingencies on Achievement and Mainstreaming." *Contemporary Educational Psychology* 11: 229–239.

Putnan, J., R. Johnson, J. Rynders, and D.W. Johnson. (1989). "Effects of Cooperative Skill Instruction on Promoting Positive Interpersonal Interactions Between Moderately-Severely Mentally Handicapped and Nonhandicapped Children." Submitted for publication.

Yager, S., D.W. Johnson, R. Johnson, and B. Snider. (1985). "The Effect of Cooperative and Individualistic Learning Experiences on Positive and Negative Cross-Handicap Relationships." *Contemporary Educational Psychology* 10: 127–138.

Comments on the article by Heller and Hollabaugh

This paper is a continuation of the paper by Heller, Keith and Anderson, which was discussed in our earlier section on Research and Effectiveness. In the previous paper, the authors presented a study of the effectiveness of a pedagogy which combines teaching a problem-solving strategy with having students work in cooperative groups to implement and practice that strategy. The present work focuses on the nature of the physics problems which the students were asked to solve and takes a first step towards generalization by considering a different kind of physics course at a different kind of university.

The previous paper emphasized what was called "context-rich" problems and considered the introductory physics course taught to a large class at a major midwestern university. In this paper, the authors return to the data of the first study and compare it with data from a similar study, this time in a sophomore-level physics course for physics and pre-engineering majors at a community college. They consider the following specific questions.

1. What type of physics problems promotes students' use of an effective problem-solving strategy?
2. What structural and management procedures result in well-functioning cooperative groups for problem-solving in physics?
3. Are some types of problems more suitable for cooperative learning than others? Are some types of problems only suitable for cooperative learning? Are some not suitable at all?

The main interest for us in this paper lies in the second of these three questions. In trying to understand how to form and maintain well-functioning cooperative groups, the authors provide data and discuss in some detail issues of group size, ability and gender composition, dominance of a group by a single student, conflicts within a group, and getting students to be concerned about the performance of all group members as well as their own performance. Data is presented about each of these questions and the authors explain how their research supports various choices they made, or led to changes in their procedures for working with groups.

The authors feel that their methods are effective in making cooperative learning work well at two different kinds of universities with two different kinds of courses, and that their data supports this position.

Discussion Questions

1. To what extent do you feel that the fact that similar results were obtained at two different kinds of schools with two different kinds of physics courses affects the likelihood that the methods used can be applied to mathematics courses at your kind of school?
2. For each of the five cooperative learning issues, to what extent do you think the authors have made their case? After reading this paper, what is your position?
3. Do you see any interaction between the issue of kinds of problems and cooperative learning?

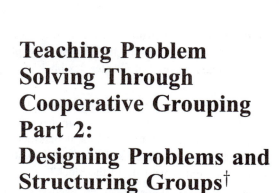

Teaching Problem Solving Through Cooperative Grouping Part 2: Designing Problems and Structuring Groups[†]

Patricia Heller
and
Mark Hollabaugh

I. Introduction

This is the second of two articles which reports investigations of an instructional approach for the effective teaching of physics problem solving. The approach combines explicit teaching of a problem-solving strategy with a supportive environment for helping students implement the strategy. The prescribed problem-solving strategy is based on the nature of effective (or "expert") problem solving in physics.[1,2] This strategy, which is described in detail in the first article,[3] emphasizes the qualitative description and analysis of the problem situation, planning a solution before the mathematical manipulation of equations, and checking and evaluating the answer to see if it makes sense. Cooperative groups were used to provide a supportive environment in which students practiced using the problem-solving strategy.

The results reported in the first article indicate that the instructional approach is effective in improving the individual problem-solving performance of all students in a large introductory physics course. The success of the approach is dependent, however, on two factors. The first factor is the type of problems students are given to solve. The problems must discourage the use of novice problem-solving strategies and promote the use of the more effective, prescribed strategy. The second factor is the formation and maintenance of well-functioning cooperative groups. Unlike traditional groups, cooperative groups are carefully structured and managed to maximize the active and appropriate participation of all students in the group.[4] In well-functioning groups, students share their conceptual and procedural knowledge in the joint construction of a problem solution, so that all students are actively engaged in the problem-solving process and differences of opinion are resolved in a reasonable manner.

Most of the previous research in cooperative grouping has been done with precollege students.[5-7] This article reports the results of investigations at the college level to answer the following questions:

1. What type of physics problems promotes students' use of an effective problem-solving strategy?

2. What structural and management procedures result in well-functioning cooperative groups for physics problem solving?

3. Is the instructional approach adaptable to different settings?

[†] Reprinted with permission from *American Journal Physics* 60 (7), July 1992, 637–644. Copyright 1992 American Association of Physics Teachers.

II. Procedure

For the past 3 years, we have been experimenting with ways to adapt and modify some general recommendations for cooperative grouping[8] to the specific context of teaching physics problem solving at the college level. A standard formative evaluation procedure[9] was used to monitor, modify, and adjust the structure and management of the problem-solving groups. Observations of student interactions were made of groups solving different types of problems, groups with different structures, and groups with different management procedures. The groups were observed by the instructors and other science educators, and a sub-sample of groups were videotaped for later analysis. Group problem solutions were photocopied so the problem-solving performance of groups with different problem types, structures, or management procedures could be examined and compared. A random sample of groups was interviewed, and questionnaires which asked for students' perceptions of their cooperative group experiences were collected from all students. Approximately 400 students participated in this study. The evaluation procedure yields a large and rich collection of varied data. For the sake of brevity, we have not described all the types of data collected in each investigation.

The experiments were conducted in two different settings, a large state university and a community college. The algebra-based, introductory physics course for nonmajors at the University of Minnesota enrolls about 120 students per quarter and uses cooperative problem-solving groups in recitation sections of about 18 students. The recitation sections are taught by graduate teaching assistants (TAs) who receive training in cooperative-grouping in the quarter prior to the course.[10] The TAs also conducted laboratories with the same groups of students. At Normandale Community College, cooperative groups are used in a sophomore-level modern physics course for physics and pre-engineering majors. In this course, which enrolls 10–12 students, the cooperative problem-solving groups are led by the instructor (MH). In both educational settings, the lecturer (not the TAs) outlined the development of the physics concepts and modeled the prescribed problem-solving strategy.

The first two sections below report the results of investigations in the large introductory physics course. The following section reports the results of investigations in the smaller modern physics classes at a community college. The final section summarizes our current approach for structuring and managing cooperative problem-solving groups.

III. Designing Physics Problems to Promote Effective Problem Solving

The determination of the types of physics problems that are most effective in promoting students' use of the prescribed

problem-solving strategy was accomplished in three phases. First, we examined student problem solutions and group interactions for standard textbook problems and characterized the typical novice strategy for solving these problems. Second, we compared textbook problems with real-world problems to determine (a) the characteristics of textbook problems that encourages the continued use of the novice strategy, and (b) the characteristics of real problems that require the use of an expert strategy. Finally, we designed "context-rich" problems based on the structure of real problems and tested the effectiveness of these problems in promoting the application of the prescribed strategy. The results of each of these phases are described below.

A. Standard textbook problems. The first problems given to cooperative groups in the introductory physics course were standard, end-of-chapter textbook problems such as the following:

> A 5.0-kg block slides 0.5 m up an inclined plane to a stop. The plane is inclined at an angle of 20° to the horizontal, and the coefficient of kinetic friction between the block and the plane is 0.60. What is the initial velocity of the block?

While solving these problems, the group discussions tended to revolve around "what formulas should we use" rather than "what physics concepts and principles should be applied to this problem." Figure 1 is an illustration of a typical group solution for this problem. The students in this group did not begin with a discussion and analysis of the

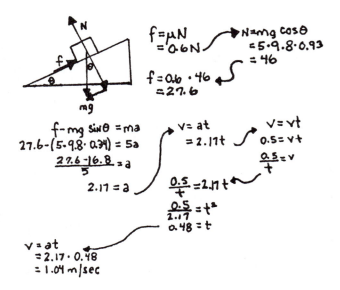

FIGURE 1

A typical incorrect solution of a group for a standard textbook problem. The arrows show the progression of the mathematical solution.

forces acting on the block in this situation. Instead, they attempted to recall the force diagram and formulas from their text, which were for a block sliding *down* an inclined plane. Consequently, their solution has the frictional force in the wrong direction and the force equation has a sign error. The students did not plan a solution before the mathematical manipulation of equations, but haphazardly plugged numbers into formulas until they had calculated a numerical answer. Their conversations concerned finding additional formulas that contained the same symbols as the unknown variables. ("Can't we use this distance formula $[x = vt]$? It has v and t in it.") They did not discuss the meaning of the symbols or formulas, and they incorrectly combined a formula containing an instantaneous velocity ($v = at$) with a formula continuing an average velocity ($x = \bar{v}t$) to calculate the initial velocity of the block.

From observations, interview data, and the examination of group problem solutions, we estimated that about two-thirds of the groups used this "formulaic" problem-solving approach instead of the prescribed strategy that was taught by the lecturer. We concluded that standard textbook problems were not effective in promoting the type of group discussions that would help the students become better problem solvers.

B. A comparison of textbook and real problems.

An analysis of standard textbook problems suggested several characteristics that encourage students' continued use of the formulaic strategy, despite the instructors's effort to teach a more effective strategy. Typically, textbook problems refer to idealized objects and events (e.g., a block sliding on an inclined plane) that have no connection with the student's reality. This would seem to reinforce the student's predilection to memorize sets of formulas and techniques (algorithms), each of which applies to a very specific idealized object or situation (e.g., inclined plane problems are different from circular motion problems).[11,12] In addition, the unknown variable is specified in the last sentence and all the variables needed to solve the problem are concisely reported in consistent units. This feature appears to reinforce a strategy of selecting the memorized formulas that contain all the given variables and then plugging in numbers until a combination is found that gives an answer. For textbook problems such as the inclined-plane problem shown above, there is no need for the student to consider the units of the quantities involved or solve the problem with reference to physical variables (algebraically) before doing arithmetic.

On the other hand, in real-world problems there is a motivation or reason for wanting to know about actual objects or events with which the students are familiar. Before mathematical manipulation of formulas can begin, the prob-

lem solver must decide (1) which specific variable(s) would be useful to answer the question, (2) what physics concepts and principles could be applied to determine that variable, (3) what information would be needed, and (4) where or how that information could be obtained or estimated. That is, the appropriate physics concepts and principles must, of necessity, be decided upon early in the problem-solving process in order to organize the gathering of pertinent information. We hypothesized that solving real problems emphasizes the application of physics concepts and principles, because they force these decisions to be made. Most textbook problems have removed the necessity of making decisions, so solving physics problems appears to the students to be an exercise in algorithmic applications.

C. Design and testing of "context-rich" problems.

To encourage students to practice using the prescribed problem-solving strategy, "context-rich" problems were designed that have many characteristics in common with real problems. Examples of these problems are given in Table I. Context-rich problems are short stories that include a reason (if sometimes far-fetched or humorous) for calculating specific quantities about real objects or events. In addition, they may have one or more of the following characteristics:

1. The problem statement does not always specify the unknown variable (e.g., Will this design for the lunar leader work?); the students must decide upon an appropriate target variable that will answer the question.

2. More information may be available than is needed to solve the problem; the appropriate information must be selected based on the particular physics principles that are applied to solve the problem.

3. Some of the information needed to solve the problem may be missing; students must first determine the physics principles that will solve the problem, then use their common knowledge of the world to recall specific values (e.g., the boiling temperature of water) or estimate values of relevant quantities (e.g., the length of a table).

4. Reasonable assumptions may need to be made (e.g., assume constant acceleration) to simplify the problem and allow for a meaningful solution.

Because context-rich problems are complex and involve making decisions about physics concepts and principles new to beginning students, they are difficult and frustrating even for the best students. In cooperative groups, however, students share the thinking load and can solve these problems. Because decisions must be made, context-rich problems forced the groups to discuss physics issues while practicing effective problem-solving techniques. The group practice enhanced the students' ability to handle this

Traffic ticket: Introductory physics problem.   While visiting a friend in San Francisco, you decide to drive around the city. You turn a corner and find yourself going up a steep hill. Suddenly a small boy runs out on the street chasing a ball. You slam on the brakes and skid to a stop, leaving a skid mark 50 ft long on the street. The boy calmly walks away, but a policeman watching from the sidewalk comes over and gives you a ticket for speeding. You are still shaking from the experience when he points out that the speed limit on this street is 25 mph.

After you recover your wits, you examine the situation more closely. You determine that the street makes an angle of 20° with the horizontal and that the coefficient of static friction between your tires and the street is 0.80. You also find that the coefficient of kinetic friction between your tires and the street is 0.60. Your car's information book tells you that the mass of your car is 1570 kg. You weigh 130 lbs, and a witness tells you that the boy had a weight of about 60 lbs and took 3.0s to cross the 15-ft wide street. Will you fight the ticket in court?

Lifetime of the Sun: Modern physics problem.   One day at the office, you and another engineer are discussing the design of a new computer circuit. In the background a radio is on and you both hear a popular song proclaiming, "Baby, I'll be yours until the Sun no longer shines." Your colleague exclaims, "Wow, I wonder how long that would be?" You had astronomy in college and recall the lifetime of the Sun is billions of years. Being the curious sort, you decide to calculate the lifetime of the Sun. You recall the Sun generates energy with the proton-proton cycle and that four protons (hydrogen) are fused into one helium nucleus (4H → He). You also remember that thermonuclear reactions occur only in the hot, dense, core of the Sun, and so only 10% of the available protons are actually used up in the proton-proton cycle. Fortunately a reference book gives you the mass of the Sun, 1.99×10^{30} kg, and the solar luminosity, 3.86×10^{26} J/s. Recalling the age of the Earth to be about 4.5 billion years, you rush into your associate's office to announce the duration of the relationship with "baby."

TABLE I
Examples of context-rich group problems.

type of problem individually, as reported in the preceding article.[3]

From observations, questionnaire data, and an examination of written problem solutions, we estimated that about three-fourths of the groups practiced implementing the prescribed strategy to solve context-rich problems. The students had to pool their knowledge of the actual behavior of the objects and the physics concepts and principles that describe this behavior to solve these problems. For example, Fig. 2 shows how a well-functioning group solved the traffic ticket problem shown in Table I. This problem is the inclined-plane textbook problem discussed above, rewritten in context-rich form. The students first sketched the situ-

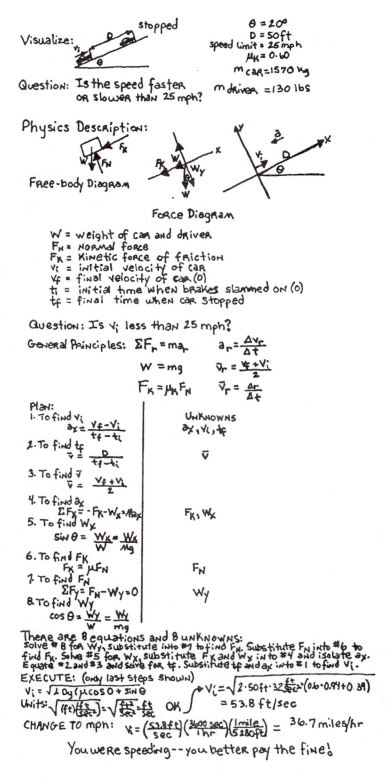

FIGURE 2
The solution of a well-functioning group for the traffic ticket problem shown in Table I.

ation and discussed what variable was needed to answer the question: "Will you fight the ticket in court?" They decided they should calculate the initial velocity of the car just before the brakes were applied to see if this velocity was above the speed limit of 25 mph. After drawing the kinematics diagram, they then discussed what information they needed to find the initial velocity. They decided they could ignore the information about the child, since "the car stopped before it hit the child." They then spent several minutes drawing free body diagrams of the car and discussing whether they needed to use static friction, kinetic friction, or both. During this discussion, they referred several times to the friction experiments they were doing in the laboratory. Once this issue was resolved and the force diagram agreed upon, they systematically planned a solution, following the planning procedure modeled during lectures.

Context-rich group problems refocused students' discussions on "what physics concepts and principles should be applied to this problem" rather than "what formulas should we use." The students' attitudes toward using the prescribed problem-solving strategy also improved. When groups were interviewed by science educators who were not instructors of this course, students said that they found the strategy "annoying" or "frustrating" to use on simple textbook problems because the strategy required them to write down more than they thought was necessary. (It should be noted, however, that these students were not usually successful at solving these problems using the formulaic strategy they preferred.) These same students agreed that the prescribed strategy was very useful for solving the more difficult textbook problems and context-rich group and individual problems given on the tests and final exams.

IV. Forming and Maintaining Well-Functioning Cooperative Groups

We investigated several issues related to the structure and maintenance of well-functioning cooperative groups. What is the optimal group size for successful physics problem solving? What ability and gender composition of groups results in the best problem-solving performance? How can problems of dominance by one student and conflict avoidance within a group be addressed? How can groups be structured so students are concerned about the performance of all group members as well as their own? The results of the investigations of each of these issues are described in the following sections.

A. What is the "optimal" group size for physics problem solving?   Group sizes between two and six are rec-

ommended in other contexts, depending on the nature of the task and the experience of the group members.[13] We experimented with groups of two, three, and four members. An examination of written group problem solutions indicated that three- and four-member groups generated better plans for solving problems and a solution with fewer conceptual mistakes than pairs. For example, to solve the traffic ticket problem shown in Table I, most pairs (80%) included an incorrect "force of the car" or "force of the engine" on their force diagram of the car. Very few groups of three or four members (10%) made this mistake. These results were typical of group performances on other problem solutions examined.

Observations of group interactions suggested several possible causes of the poorer performance of pairs. Groups of two did not seem to have the "critical mass" of conceptual and procedural knowledge for the successful completion of context-rich problems. They tended to go off track or get stuck on a single approach to a problem, which was often incorrect. With larger groups, the contributions of the additional student(s) allowed a group to jump to another track when it seemed to be following an unfruitful path. In some groups of two, one student dominated the problem-solving process, so the pair did not function as a cooperative group. A pair usually had no mechanism for deciding between two strongly held viewpoints except the constant domination by one member, who was not always the most knowledgeable student. This behavior was especially prevalent in male-female pairs. In larger groups, one student often functioned as a mediator between students with opposing viewpoints. When an impasse was reached, these larger groups often relied on voting. While not an ideal strategy for resolving differences of opinion, voting at least focuses on the issue rather than the personality trait of a particular student.

In groups with four members, one student was invariably left out of the problem-solving process. Sometimes this was the more timid student who was reticent to ask for clarification. At other times, the person left out was the most knowledgeable student who appeared to tire of continually struggling to convince the three other group members to try an approach, and resorted to solving the problem alone. To quantify these observations, the number of contributions each group member made to the solution of a constant acceleration kinematics problems was counted from the videotapes of a three-member and a four-member group. Each member of the group of three made 38%, 36%, and 26% of the contributions to the solution. For the group of four, each member made 37%, 32%, 23%, and 8% of the contributions to the solution. The only contribution of the least involved student (8%) was to check the numerical calculations.

For our students, who have no real experience working in cooperative groups, we concluded that the "optimal" group size for problem solving is three members. That is, a three-member group is large enough for the generation of diverse ideas and approaches, but small enough to be manageable so all students can contribute to the problem solution. The physical arrangement of the students did, however, influence the functioning of the cooperative groups.[14] When three students sat side-by-side, two of the students were often observed engaged in on-task conversations, while the third member was either completely off task (e.g., reading the newspaper) or working in isolation. This did not occur when the students were seated facing each other.

B. What ability and gender composition of groups results in the best problem-solving performance?

In this experiment, students were assigned to groups by ability based on their individual test scores. Students were never allowed to form their own groups. An examination of written problem solutions indicated that instructor-assigned groups of mixed ability (e.g., a high, medium, and low ability student) performed as well as groups consisting of only high-ability students, and better than groups with students of only low or medium ability. For example, on a problem that asked for the energy of light emitted when an electron moves from a larger to a smaller Bohr orbit, 75% of the mixed-ability groups solved this problem correctly, while only 45% of the homogeneous-ability groups solved this problem. This result was typical of other problem solutions examined, and is consistent with other research on the ability composition of cooperative groups.[15]

Observations of group interactions indicated several possible explanations for the better performance of heterogeneous groups. For example, on the Bohr orbit problem homogeneous groups of low or medium ability students had difficulty identifying energy terms consistent with the defined system. They did not appear to have a sufficient reservoir of correct conceptual or procedural knowledge to get very far on context-rich problems. Most of the homogeneous high-ability groups included the gravitational potential energy as well as the electric potential energy in the conservation of energy equation, even though an order-of-magnitude calculation of the ratio of the electric to gravitational potential energy had been done in the lectures. These groups tended to make problems more complicated than necessary or overlooked the obvious. They were usually able to correct their mistake, but only after carrying the inefficient or incorrect solution further than necessary. For example, in the heterogenous (mixed ability) groups, it was usually the low or medium ability student who pointed out that the gravitational potential energy term was not needed.

("But remember from lecture, the electrical potential energy was many times bigger than the gravitational potential energy. Can't we leave out the gravitational term?") Although the higher-ability student typically supplied the leadership by generating the new ideas and approaches to the problem, the low or medium ability student often kept the group on track by pointing out obvious, simple ideas.

In heterogeneous groups, the low or medium ability student also frequently asked for clarification of the physics concept or procedure under discussion. While explaining or elaborating, the higher ability student often recognized a mistake, such as overlooking a contributing variable or making the problem more complicated than necessary. For example, in one group it was the higher-ability student who first thought that both the static and kinetic frictional forces were needed to solve the traffic ticket problem (Table I). This is the same group whose solution is shown in Fig. 2. When the lower-ability student in the group asked for an explanation, the higher-ability student started to push her pencil up an inclined notebook to explain what she meant. In the process of justifying her position, she realized that only the kinetic frictional force was necessary.

With a group of three members there is always a gender imbalance, unless a group is all of the same gender. An examination of the written problem solutions indicated that homogeneous gender groups and mixed gender groups of two females and one male performed better than groups with two males and one female. Observations of group interactions indicated that groups composed of two males and one female tended to be dominated by the male students. This was true even when the female member was articulate and the highest-ability student in the group. For example, during their work on a projectile motion problem, a group with a lower-ability male, a medium-ability male, and a higher-ability female had a vigorous discussion concerning the path a projectile would follow. The men insisted on a path following the hypotenuse of a right triangle, while the woman argued for the correct parabolic trajectory. At one point, she threw a pencil horizontally, firmly commenting as it fell to the floor. "There, see how it goes—it does *not* travel in a straight line!" Even so, she could not convince the two men, who politely ignored her arguments.

C. How can problems of dominance by one student and conflict avoidance within a group be address?

Even with mixed-ability, three-member groups, two major difficulties prevented some groups from functioning effectively:

1. Dominant personalities: Some groups had a dominant student who railroaded the group into an approach or problem solution. At the other end of the personality spectrum, a timid student would be reticent of participating and often became the silent record-keeper for the group.

2. Conflict avoidance: Even groups that functioned well in other respects had a tendency to resolve issues too quickly by either accepting the first idea proposed or by voting (e.g., "Yes it is! No it isn't! Well, let's vote."). Particularly in the introductory physics class, students initially did not critically examine ideas and suggestions or appropriately argue for or against a particular position. This tendency often resulted in conceptual mistakes in the problem solutions (e.g., frictional forces in the wrong direction).

Two strategies recommended in the cooperative group literature were introduced to address these problems.[7] The first strategy is to define and assign specific roles to each student. The second strategy is for the each group to discuss how well they worked together and what they could do next time to improve their group functioning. Both of these strategies were helpful and are described below.

1. Assigning, defining, and rotating roles.   When faced with a difficult task, members of a well-functioning group spontaneously adopt a variety of roles, such as (a) the executive or manager, who designs plans for action and suggests solutions; (b) the skeptic, who questions premises and plans; (c) the educator, who takes on the burden of explanation and summarization; (d) the record keeper, who organizes and keeps track of the results of the discussion; and (e) the conciliator, who resolves conflicts and strives to minimize interpersonal stress. In well-functioning groups, members share these roles and role assumption usually fluctuates over time.[1] The majority of our students, however, were not skilled at performing and sharing these roles. Consequently, instructors assigned specific roles that students were to perform during group problem solving each week.

For groups of three, the roles of Manager, Skeptic, and Checker/Recorder were assigned. The instructor defined each role and gave key phrases a person in that role might say.[16] For example, the Manager keeps the group on task, organizes the task into subtasks, and manages the sequence of steps. Possible phrases for this role are: "We also need to consider. . ." "We need to move on to the next step." "Let's come back to that if we have time later." The Skeptic plays the role of devil's advocate. This person helps the group avoid quick agreement, asks questions that will lead to understanding, and pushes members to explore all possibilities. This person would say things like: "What else could we say about this?" "Are there other possibilities?" "Before we agree, maybe we should consider..." Finally, the Checker/Recorder checks for consensus among group members, obtains members' consent upon completion of each step, writes the group solution, and turns in the completed problem. Phrases for this include: "Can you explain how we got this." "Let's summarize what we've decided." "Does everyone agree?"

Observations of group interactions indicated that after roles were assigned by the instructor, the number of dominance and conflict avoidance problems decreased. Assigning roles empowered students to take actions they would not spontaneously perform. By rotating roles, students practiced critically examining and discussing a physics problem from different perspectives. Interviews confirmed that students in groups with assigned and rotated roles were more comfortable with their group interactions, particularly at the beginning of the course.

2. Discussing group functioning.   The second strategy adopted for addressing problems of dominance and conflict avoidance was to give the groups about 5 minutes at the end of each activity to discuss how well they worked together.[17] To initiate this discussion, the following instructor-posed questions were used: (1) "What are three ways you worked well together in this problem-solving activity?" or "What did your group like best about this way of solving problems?" (2) "What problems did you have interacting as a group?" (3) "What could you do better next time to interact as a group more effectively?" At the beginning of the course, students wrote individual responses to these questions, then discussed their responses with their group. This was followed by a class discussion of the answers to the third question, so students could consider a wider range of ways groups could function better. Common answers included: Come better prepared; Listen better to what people say; Make better use of our role (e.g., "Be sure the Manager watches the time so we can finish the problem." or "Be sure the Skeptic doesn't let us decide too quickly."). After students became more comfortable working in groups, a discussion of group functioning was needed only occasionally.

Interview data indicated that when students were given a chance to discuss their group's functioning, their attitude about group problem solving improved. There was also a sharp decrease in the number of students who visited instructors during office hours to complain about their group assignment. In addition, groups that were not functioning well improved their subsequent effectiveness following these discussions. For example, in groups with a dominant student, the other group members were more willing to say things like: "Hey, remember what we said last week. Listen to Kerry. She's trying to explain why we don't need all of this information about the lunar lander's descent." In groups that suffered from conflict avoidance, there were comments like: "Oops! I forgot to be the Skeptic. Let's see. Are we sure friction is in this direction? I mean, how do we know it's not in the opposite direction?" This result is consistent with the research on precollege students.[18]

D. How can groups be structured so students are concerned about the performance of all group members as well as their own?   One of the educational advantages of cooperative-group problem solving is that the roles of Manager, Skeptic, Explainer, and Record Keeper are executed overtly. This verbalization of procedures, doubts, justifications, and explanations helps clarify the thinking of all group members. In addition, students can rehearse and observe others perform these roles, which correspond to the planning and monitoring strategies that they must perform independently and silently on individual problem-solving assignments. These advantages are not experienced when students simply sit in a group but work independently on a problem solution. Research in cooperative group learning indicates that two conditions must be met for students to collaborate on the joint construction of a problem solution, positive interdependence and individual accountability.

Positive interdependence exists when students believe that they are linked with others in a way that one cannot succeed unless the other members succeed. There are many recommended ways of structuring positive interdependence.[19] We experimented first with goal interdependence: students were requested to produce one problem solution and agree on the answer and the solution strategy. An examination of written solutions and observations of group interactions revealed two major difficulties. In many groups, the students did not take the assignment seriously. They talked primarily about their social life, and rarely finished solving the problem. In other groups, students worked independently to solve the problem, usually using a formulaic strategy instead of the prescribed strategy, then compared their solutions. To address these problems, we adopted a second tool for structuring positive interdependence, namely reward interdependence. Each class test was changed to include a group problem which counted as one-fourth of a student's grade for that test. The group test problem was given in the recitation section the day before the individual test problems. Each group turned in one solution, and all members received the same grade for that problem. For all problems, group and individual, students were given points for following the steps of the prescribed strategy as well as for a correct solution.

An examination of written group solutions after these grading practices were adopted indicated a marked improvement in the problem-solving performance of the groups, especially on the group tests. These results were confirmed by our observations of group interactions. The amount of social talk during problem solving decreased, more groups completed the problem, and fewer groups were observed with students working independently. Comments like: "We really have to figure out how to draw vector diagrams before the group test next week!" were common in problem-solving sessions. During these sessions, the general atmosphere was one of "getting the job done." On the group test days, however, the emphasis was on getting the problem *right* rather than just getting it done. Consequently, the most constructive discussions and significant learning appeared to occur during the group tests. These results are consistent with research on precollege students.[20]

Individual accountability exists when students take personal responsibility for mastering the assigned material. In physics classes, individual accountability is most commonly accomplished by giving individual tests. After the test, each group member knows how well he or she has mastered the problem-solving assignment. Individual accountability is also important so that group members know (1) which student needs to be helped and encouraged, and (2) that they cannot "hitch-hike" on the work of others.[21] In our experience, these two aspects of individual accountability in cooperative-group problem solving were the most difficult to structure. For example, some students consistently missed the problem-solving sessions, but showed up for the group test (expecting to hitch-hike on the previous work of their partners). We established the rule that if a student were absent from the problem-solving session previous to the test, then that student could not take the group test problem and would receive a grade of zero. The students agreed that this procedure was "fair," and very few students subsequently missed the problem-solving sessions. Two additional strategies were adopted to encourage groups to make sure each member understood the group solution to a problem and how that solution was obtained. While monitoring group work, the instructor questioned the student who seemed to be the least involved in the problem-solving task. During subsequent class discussions, individual students were randomly called on to present their group's answer.[22]

V. Applying Cooperative-Group Problem Solving to a Community College Setting

Given the success of the initial use of the instructional approach in the university setting, we tested the applicability of the method in a community college setting. At Normandale Community College, cooperative groups were used in a sophomore-level modern physics course for physics and pre-engineering majors. This course, which enrolls 10–12 students, has a prerequisite of one year of general physics. Most of the students subsequently transferred to the University of Minnesota electrical engineering program. A major difference from the university introductory physics course was that the cooperative problem-solving groups were led by the course instructor (M.H.). This gave the instructor complete control over the management and structure of the groups as well as the selection and grading of the problems. Some reduction in content (about one chapter of the text) was necessary to allow time for the instructor to model the prescribed problem-solving strategy, as well as time for students to work problems in cooperative groups.

In implementing cooperative-group problem solving in this more advanced context, we investigated similar issues of problem type and group structuring and management procedures. Initially, students solved standard textbook problems, which often dealt with abstract concepts or derivations of physical laws. They were also allowed the use of their textbook and notes. Observations revealed two related difficulties. First, like the introductory students, the modern physics students persisted in their formulaic approach to problem solving. Second, the students spent a great deal of time searching the textbook for appropriate formulas or solutions of example problems similar to the given problem. ("Look on page 89. The problem solved there also uses the photoelectric work potential. Can't we use the same formulas in this problem?")

The first difficulty was solved by designing context-rich problems based on principles having direct technological applications, such as tunneling or binding energy. An example of a context-rich modern physics problem is shown in Table I. The solution to the open-book difficulty was to give each group a sheet with any necessary equations or constants. Observation of group interactions indicated an improvement in group functioning. Fewer groups had students who worked in isolation. More group time was spent discussing which physics principles should be applied to the problems, and how to apply those principles.

The structure and management procedures that produced well-functioning groups in the introductory physics course were also effective in the modern physics course. Groups of three, based on mixed ability levels, were assigned the roles of Manager, Skeptic, and Checker/Recorder. However, there was a different resolution to the problem of the gender composition of the groups. Engineering and physics are still primarily male fields, so the women need to develop their skills in justifying and defending their position. The modern physics class consisted of two women and ten men. The women were good friends and frequently studied together outside of class. However, they were never in a problem-solving group together. At the end of the course, they both expressed their appreciation for the experience of "standing their ground" in male dominated groups.

The Lifetime of the Sun problem shown in Table I provides an example of the effectiveness of this cooperative group problem solving in the modern physics class. Before the course employed cooperative groups, this problem was given to individual students on a test. Although the students knew they needed to calculate the energy released in the proton-proton cycle, they did not know what to do with the result of that calculation. None of the students solved the problem. A year later when the same problem was given as a group test, all groups arrived at a reasonable solution. This is consistent with the results of the investigation reported in the companion article,[3] in which we found that group problem solutions were significantly better than the solutions of the best problem solvers from each group on matched individual problems.

VI. Summary

We have found cooperative grouping to be an effective means of teaching physics problem solving in two very different kinds of courses: a university introductory physics course and a community college sophomore-level modern physics course. Our current approach to structuring and managing cooperative groups evolved as we gained experience from the experiments recounted in this paper. Students are now assigned to three-member groups on the basis of ability (a higher-ability, medium-ability, and lower-ability student in each group). In the introductory physics course, two women are assigned with one man, or same-gender groups are assigned. In the modern physics course, each woman in the class is assigned to a group with two men. In classrooms with movable chairs, groups are requested to move their three chairs into a circle facing each other. In classrooms with long tables, two students on one side of the table face the third member on the other side of the table. In classrooms with theater-style seating, a student in one row turns around to face her or his other two partners in the second row.

Once each week students work together on a problem that is more context-rich than standard textbook exercises. They are not allowed to consult textbooks or class notes. The students are assigned the roles of Manager, Checker/Recorder, and Skeptic. These roles are rotated each group session. At the end of a problem-solving session, the instructor occasionally directs the groups in a discussion of the groups' functioning. Approximately three or four times during the 10-week quarter, a problem is treated as a group test and all students in a group receive the same grade on the problem solution. Students are reassigned to a new group after each test. They always have at least two sessions with their new group before the next test.

While it was our intention to implement an effective method for teaching physics problem solving, not necessarily a popular one, student questionnaire data indicate a high satisfaction with cooperative-group problem solving. In the introductory physics course, 72% of the students agree with the statement: "The discussion with my group helped me understand the course material," 21% were neutral, and only 11% disagreed with this statement. Similarly, 68% agreed that "Taking tests as a group helped me to do better on the individual tests," 12% were neutral, and 19% disagreed with the statement. One modern physics student noted, "The group work and problem solving is very helpful in understanding the material. The cooperation of students in each group, by discussing the problem and generating ideas, shows how things are related."

Acknowledgements.   We wish to thank many colleagues who assisted us with out efforts in cooperative learning: Professors Kenneth Heller, Roger Johnson, Konrad Mauersberger, and Frances Lawrenz at the University of Minnesota. We also wish to thank Professor Lillian McDermont for her constructive comments on the manuscript, and Ron Keith and Scott Anderson, who devoted many hours observing and videotaping groups and photocopying tests. We are grateful to the graduate teaching assistants at the University of Minnesota and to our students at Normandale Community College and the University of Minnesota who participated in the cooperative groups. We also gratefully acknowledge financial support from the University of Minnesota for this project in the form of an Educational Development Grant (P.H.) and a Graduate Student Research Award (M.H.).

References

1. D.R. Woods, "Problem solving in practice," in *What Research Says to the Science Teacher: Volume Five, Problem Solving*, edited by D. Gabel (National Science Teachers Association, Washington, DC, 1989), pp. 97–121.

2. F. Reif and J. I. Heller, "Knowledge structures and problem solving in physics," *Ed. Psych.* 17(2), 102–127(1982).

3. P. Heller, R. Keith, and S. Anderson, "Teaching problem solving through cooperative grouping. Part 1: Group versus individual problem solving," *Am. J. Phys.* 60, 627–636(1992).

4. D.W. Johnson, R. T. Johnson, and E. J. Holubec, *Circles of Learning: Cooperation in the Classroom* (Interaction, Edina, MN, 1986), pp. 6–10.

5. A. L. Brown and A. S. Palincsar, "Guided, cooperative learning and individual knowledge acquisition," in *Knowing, Learning, and Instruction*, edited by L.B. Resnick (Lawrence Erlbaum Associates, Hillsdale, NJ, 1989), pp. 393–451.

6. V. N. Lunetta, "Cooperative learning in science, mathematics, and computer problem solving," in *Toward a Scientific Practice of Science Education*, edited by M. Gardner, J. Greeno, F. Reif, A. Schoenfeld, A. diSessa, and E. Stage (Lawrence Erlbaum Associates, Hillsdale, NJ, 1990), pp. 235–249.

7. D. W. Johnson and R. T. Johnson, *Cooperation and Competition: Theory and Research* (Interaction, Edina, MN, 1989).

8. The structure and management recommendations adapted for this study were from Ref. 4. For recent college teaching recommendations, see D. W. Johnson, R. T. Johnson, and K. A. Smith, *Active Learning: Cooperation in the College Classroom* (Interaction, Edina, MN, 1991).

9. P. H. Rossi and H. E. Freeman. *Evaluation: A Systematic Approach* (Sage, Beverly, CA, 1985). 3rd ed., pp. 38–40 and 78–80.

10. F. Lawrenc, R. Keith, P. Heller, and K. Heller, "Training the TA," *J. Coll. Sci. Teach.*, in press.

11. M.T.H. Chi, R. Glaser, and E. Rees, "Expertise in problem solving," in *Advances in the Psychology of Human Intelligence: Volume II* (Lawrence Erlbaum Associates, Hillsdale, NJ, 1983), pp. 7–75.

12. J. H. Larkin, J. McDermott, D. P. Simon, and H. A. Simon, "Expert and novice performance in solving physics problems," *Science* 208, 1335–1342 (1980).

13. Reference 4, pp. 35–38.

14. Reference 4, p. 41.

15. Reference 7, pp. 46–47 and references therein.

16. Reference 4, pp. 82-83.

17. Reference 4, pp. 52–53 and 83–84.

18. Reference 7, pp. 74–75 and references therein.

19. Reference 4, pp. 58–60.

20. Reference 7, pp. 58–60 and references therein.

21. Reference 7, p. 63 and references therein.

22. Reference 4, p. 45.

Comments on the article by Cohen, Lotan, and Catanzarite

Some research provides data suggesting that cooperative learning groups should be organized so that students with different characteristics, such as ability level, are together in the same group (Good and Marshall). The paper by Cohen, Lotan and Catanzarite however, points to research that raises a problem in connection with "mixed-status" groups, that is, groups whose members have different statuses in each other's eyes. It seems that in such cases there is a tendency for the high-status members to dominate and the low-status members to withdraw. Thus, if intra-group interaction between students with different characteristics is important to learning, then the effect of status is of concern.

This paper begins by explaining what is meant by status problems and describes various forms these can take. There is a brief review of research documenting status problems of children in classrooms. Treatments designed to moderate the effects of status on interaction are proposed and two sets of data are presented. In the first set, a bilingual approach to cooperative learning developed by Edward De Avila is used. In the second set, several changes are made including the proposed treatments to moderate status effects, a new classroom management strategy, and longer teacher training.

The authors present some detail on how the studies they are describing measure status, student interaction and achievement. They also provide specifics about the students, their environment and the instructional treatments that were used in the classrooms from which their data was obtained. All of the students involved were in grades 2–4. The paper presents a path model analysis of the relations that were found between status, interactions and learning.

In considering the two sets of data, the authors are interested in three major issues and how they compared in the two sets: the relationship between status and interaction, changes in perceived status, especially for the low-status children, and achievement. They found that in the second set of data, although they did not disappear, the effects of status on both rates of interaction and on learning were weakened. The authors also infer from their data that there was a considerable change in status differences in the eyes of the children. The classroom became a friendlier place.

In spite of the progress that is reported in this study, the authors still believe that status problems are highly resistant to change and, according to them, learning problems are easier to treat than status problems.

The paper ends with a discussion of implications of this study for cooperative learning. The issues considered are: use of norms and roles, curricular materials, multiple ability treatment, consistency of implementation, and the potential of changed expectations for competence.

Discussion Questions

1. What do Cohen et al. mean by status?
2. Describe the method(s) proposed in this paper to treat status problems. What do you think of them?
3. What other methods of treating status problems should be considered? What are their advantages and disadvantages?
4. How do the studies in this paper measure status, student interaction, and achievement?
5. To what extent can the results of this paper be transferred from elementary school pupils to college students?
6. Explain the path model analysis and what conclusions can be drawn from it.
7. What do you think was accomplished by the instructional treatments that were used? Can these results be generalized?
8. Why do the authors feel that learning problems are easier to treat than status problems? Do you agree?
9. What, if any, implications do you think this paper has for cooperative learning? Will it have any effect on your teaching practice?

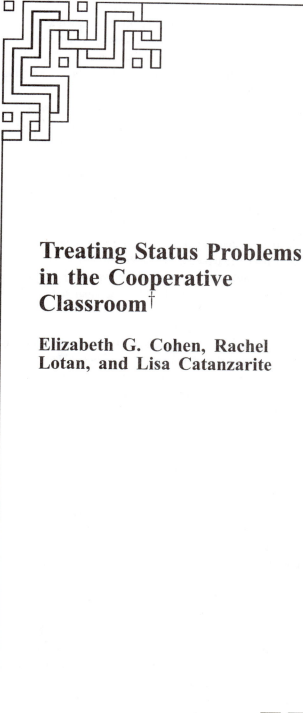

Treating Status Problems in the Cooperative Classroom[†]

Elizabeth G. Cohen, Rachel Lotan, and Lisa Catanzarite

Cooperative groupwork has a strong potential for engaging students, improving friendliness and trust between students and, under some conditions, producing superior achievement gains in comparison to traditional individualistic modes of education (Johnson et al. 1981; Sharan 1980; Slavin 1983). There are, however, some important problems that remain to be solved in connection with designing classroom settings for cooperative learning. One of these problems arises from status differences between students in the classroom. It has been repeatedly shown that mixed-status groups engaged in collective tasks are dominated by high-status members and do not receive the benefit of the contribution of some low-status members (Berger, Rosenholtz, and Zelditch 1980). Research on mixed-status groups of classmates shows the same pattern of high-status dominance and low-status withdrawal (Rosenholtz 1985). If cooperative learning techniques depend on interaction for their desirable effects on learning, then access to interaction that differs according to the status of the student is of practical concern.

What is a status problem?

Status characteristics are social rankings in which it is generally believed that it is better to be in the high state than the low state. The process by which status characteristics come to affect interaction and influence is described by expectation states theory (Berger et al. 1966, 1972).

Race and ethnicity are examples of diffuse status characteristics that can have an impact on the behavior of schoolchildren as they interact on collective tasks. When, for example, a racial status characteristic becomes salient in the situation, the prestige and power order of the small group working on a collective task comes to reflect the broader social status ranking of the races in a kind of self-fulfilling prophecy. Whites turn out to be more active and influential than blacks. (For a full description of this process, see Berger, Rosenholtz, and Zelditch 1980.) Using a standardized game task, it has been shown repeatedly in the United States, Canada and Israel that race and ethnicity can act as characteristics so that high-status students are more active and influential than low-status students (Cohen 1982).

When a status characteristic is diffuse, there are general expectations for competence and incompetence that are attached to the characteristic. The status organizing process is related to these expectations for competence held by the self and the other in collective task groups. It bears no rela-

† In S. Sharan (ed.), *Cooperative learning: Theory and Research,* 203–229. New York: Praeger. Copyright 1990 by Praeger. Reproduced with permission of Greenwood Publishing Group, Inc., Westport, CT.

tionship to feelings of friendliness. Theoretically, the use of cooperative interracial groups in desegregated classrooms can, at one and the same time, confirm stereotypes concerning the lesser competence of some races and, simultaneously, generate increased feelings of friendliness between the races.

There are other status characteristics at work in the classroom that have an impact on interaction in collective tasks. The most powerful are academic status characteristics (Hoffman and Cohen 1972; Rosenholtz 1985; Tammivaara 1982). When the educator gives a group a collective, cooperative task, status differences based on academic ability become activated and relevant to the new situation. The high-status students will then expect and will be expected to be more competent. The net effect is a self-fulfilling prophecy whereby the high-status student is more active and influential than the low-status student. When students see themselves and are seen by classmates as having more or less academic ability or reading ability, those who are seen as having more ability will be more active and influential than those who are seen as having less ability.

The classroom is a multi-characteristic situation. Students vary on three different types of status characteristics: social, academic, and peer. Social status characteristics are those ascribed characteristics brought into the classroom from the outside society (race, ethnicity, sex). Academic status characteristics are created and maintained in the classroom setting. Peer status characteristics are created in the informal relationships between students. There are very few studies that have specifically tested the operation of peer status on behavior. One of the studies that has done so is that of Webster and Driskell (1983) on attractiveness as a status characteristic. Maruyama and Miller (1981), in reviewing the literature on physical attractiveness, conclude that physically attractive individuals are seen as more capable in short-term interactions. This generalization would also suggest the operation of attractiveness as a status characteristic.

From a practical point of view, these status effects constitute a significant problem to those who work with cooperative learning situations. Theoretically, the introduction of interdependence in a group task is sufficient to activate differential expectations for competence based on status characteristics. Once these expectations have become activated and relevant to the new cooperative task, low-status students will interact less than high-status students. If one argues that interaction is of great benefit to the student, then the net effect of the process of status generalization is that low-status students receive less of the benefit of interaction than high-status students.

This line of reasoning is not inconsistent with the research findings that in cooperative learning in desegregated

situations, blacks make even greater achievement gains than whites (Slavin 1983). Cooperative groupwork will engage students who are ordinarily disengaged and will assist those who cannot read the curricular materials. Thus low-achieving students are often better off in the cooperative group than they would be in the traditional class. However, it can still be the case that these students are less active and influential than their high-status classmates. Furthermore, it is still possible that low-status students could show even greater gains if their expectations for competence were raised and if they were more active in the group.

Expectation states theory has been used to create various interventions that modify the operation of status characteristics. These interventions have been successful in the laboratory and in controlled classroom settings (Cohen 1982; Cohen, Lockheed, and Lohman 1976; Rosenholtz 1985). Despite these successes, the classroom is one of the most difficult places to produce lasting equal-status behavior because of the strong relevance of academic ranking as a status characteristic. Many features of conventional classrooms help to create an agreed-upon status order, running from the smartest students to the "dumbest." The evaluation system of most classrooms lets everyone know who are the winners and who are the losers in this academic ranking process. (For a full review of this literature see Cohen 1986.)

The Treatment of Status Problems: Plan for Analysis

Analyses of two comparable data sets are reported in this chapter. Initially, we will review research documenting status problems of children in classrooms as they interact cooperatively on learning tasks. This research demonstrated that the learning gains of low-status children can be inhibited by their failure to have as much access to interaction as high-status children (Cohen 1984b).

The data collected in 1979–80 on 307 children in nine classrooms is referred to as data set I. The instructional approach implemented in these classrooms was *Finding Out/Descubrimiento,* a bilingual approach to the development of thinking skills developed by Edward De Avila. Classrooms contained multiple learning centers, each with different materials and activities. The centers operated simultaneously; four or five children worked at each. They were assigned challenging tasks requiring repeated use of the same mathematics and science concepts in different ways and with different media. Over a period of 15 weeks, four days a week, for 45 minutes per day, children had to complete the task at each learning center and fill out the worksheet that accompanied the task.

In 1982–83 several important changes were introduced to the implementation of *Finding Out/Descubrimiento*. These changes included a new classroom management strategy, longer teacher training, and a special emphasis on the use of treatments designed to moderate the effects of status on interaction in cooperative classroom groups. Despite these strategic changes, the curriculum materials and the pattern of multiple materials and learning centers described above were identical in the two years. In the second part of the paper, the comparison of this second set of data (referred to as data set II) with the 1979–80 data (referred to as data set I) allows us to investigate the answers to several research questions concerning the possibility of moderating status effects in cooperative learning.

Research Questions.   Of particular interest is an examination of the effects of the new classroom management system. Did it increase interaction? Did it reduce the effect of status on interaction as well as the effect of status on learning gains in comparison to the effects observed in data set I? These questions are investigated by correlating measures of status gathered from sociometric data with observed rates of behavior among a set of selected "target children" and with standardized test scores on the children's achievement in the fall and spring of each school year studied. The strength and nature of the observed relationships are compared for the two data sets.

The focus of a second set of research questions is an examination of shifts in status at the classroom level as measured by sociometric questions between fall and spring in data set II. In absolute terms, is there evidence of some improvement in the standing of low-status children during the school year? In relative terms, did the standing of low-status children in comparison with that of high-status children improve over the school year? Is there any evidence that classrooms showing reduced effects of status on the distribution of sociometric choices are classrooms that experienced superior implementation of the program? And finally, what is the relationship of status differences as measured by sociometric data to status difference as measured by talk between peers?

Measurement.

Measures of status.   The instrument used for both data sets consisted of sociometric questions, each of which was followed by a list of names of the students in that particular classroom. The sociometric questionnaires were administered in the fall and spring of each year. The students were asked, for example, to circle the names of those in their class who were "best at math and science," their "best friends," or "best at games and sports." Students then identified their choices by circling the appropriate names on the

list following each question. There was an English and a Spanish version of the instrument. A group of trained test administrators tried to make sure that each child could understand the directions and could recognize the names of classmates on the questionnaire.

Since students could circle any number of names, the number of choices indicated for each criterion question varied between students and between classrooms. The distribution of choices for each question was divided into quintiles for each classroom. Each child was then assigned a score ranging from one to five, depending on the fifth of the distribution in which lay the number of times that child's name was chosen.

The two questions from the fall questionnaire requiring choices on who was "best at math and science" and who was "a best friend" made up the measure of status. In both data sets, there was a high level of correlation between being chosen on one of these criteria and being chosen on the other. In data set I, the correlation for the fall measures was .50 ($p < .001$); in data set II, the correlation coefficient was .64 ($p < .001$). In other settings, measures of peer status may or may not be positively associated with academic status (Cohen 1984a).

The specific status characteristic of ability in mathematics and science was the one most directly relevant to the learning materials. The question on "best friends" was used as an indicator of the status characteristic of unattractiveness/popularity; it represents peer status. In order to derive a single measure of status in a multi-characteristic setting, the two quintile scores were added together. This measure is referred to as the co-status score. The rationale for the construction of this index was the combining principle that theoretically operates in a multi-characteristic setting (Humphreys and Berger 1981). According to this principle the actor combines all units of status information to form aggregated expectation states for the self and the other. If the information is inconsistent, such that there are both positive and negative expectations for the competence of an actor, then these can cancel each other out.

Analysis of the sociometric data in data set I showed a high level of correlation among all the sociometric indexes (see Cohen 1984b). Even being chosen as best in games and sports was highly correlated with being chosen as best in reading. One should not assume that there is a generalization from academic status characteristics to nonacademic status characteristics. In some cases the generalization appears to operate from attractiveness/popularity to perceived academic ability; some children with limited English proficiency who were perceived as attractive were given high ratings on the academic criteria despite low objective scores on achievement tests. In general, however, there is a relationship between classmate selection as best in an academic subject and objective test scores; for example, the quintile score on "best at math and science" showed a significant correlation with scores on the achievement tests in mathematics ($r = .41$, $p < .001$ in fall; $r = .60$, $p < .001$ in spring).

Observed behavior. Observers visited classrooms once a week to obtain timed observations of the task-related behavior of target children working at learning centers. They used a device for scoring interaction that measured performance outputs of the child relevant to the task. Measures of interaction were closely related to the small-group scoring system developed on the basis of status characteristics and expectation states theory and used on small-group interaction in more controlled settings (Cohen 1982). During each 30-second interval of a three-minute period, the observer recorded the frequency of task-related talk and of selected nonverbal behaviors: working alone or together on the curriculum, behavior not related to the task, and behavior not directly relevant to this analysis.

In order to assess the reliability of the target-child instrument, each classroom observer was paired with a supervisor who acted as a criterion scorer. The supervisor scored alongside the observer. No observer was allowed to score independently until a satisfactory level of agreement with the supervisor's scoring was reached. A percentage agreement was calculated by comparing the total number of checks made by the observer and by the supervisor for each category on the scoring instrument during the scoring period. If 90 percent of the judgments were in agreement, the level of reliability was deemed satisfactory. During the data collection, each observer received visits from one of the supervisors. Reliability checks were made at that time. The average percentage agreement for this instrument was 90 percent over the 24 times reliability was assessed for data set I. For data set II, the average percentage agreement was also 90 percent over the 26 times reliability was assessed.

The two variables of interest here are the rates of task-related talk with peers and the observed frequency of working together on the curriculum with peers. A task-related speech was scored by a single check as long as it was not interrupted by another student talking or by a change to a subject that was not related within the 30-second interval. If the speech extended to the next time interval, the observer recorded another check. To calculate an average rate of talking across observations, the total frequency of these speeches was divided by the number of observations for that child.

In order to be sure that there was sufficient stability in the measures taken of a given child to justify this aggregation procedure, an analysis of variance was carried out on frequency of talk for different observations taken on the same child. This analysis showed that in both data sets, there was a substantial difference between observations taken on different children as compared with the set of observations taken on the same child; the value of F was statistically significant for this analysis on each data set.

The other critical variable was the rate of working together with peers. As with rate of talking, the child was a significant source of variance in the frequency of this behavior per observation ($F = 1.28$; $p < .033$). Rate of talking and working together is an indicator of task-related interaction in an interdependent work relationship. (For details of the information of this index, see Cohen 1984b). This index of talking and working together has the effect of weighting talk by the frequency with which it occurs in an interdependent context. Because young children quite frequently talk to themselves about the task, not all talk takes place in an interdependent context.

Achievement data. The achievement test data consisted of fall and spring scores on the CTBS (Comprehensive Test of Basic Skills) math concepts and application and reading subscales. The spring testing took place after students had all experienced a substantial number of curriculum units. Only those students who took the English CTBS in the fall *and* in the spring were included in the sample for achievement analysis. Thus, those students who moved away during the school year, those who transferred into the school after the fall testing date, those whose English was judged insufficient to take the examination in the fall, and those who were absent on either test day were omitted. The achievement data are in national percentile scores in both data sets.

Data set I also included two additional tests. One, called the Mini-Test, was given orally in English and in Spanish; it was specifically constructed to reflect the content of the curriculum. This test was used to measure the relationship between status, interaction, and learning in the initial documentation on the effects of status in *Finding Out* (Cohen 1984b). The other set, the Language Assessment Scale, was a measure of English proficiency developed by De Avila and Duncan.

PART I
Documentation of Status Problems in Data Set I

Data set I contains nine bilingual classrooms (grades 2–4) from five districts in the San Jose, California, area; there were nine teachers who were volunteers and 307 children. Classes were largely composed of children of Hispanic background with a small proportion of Anglos, blacks, and Asians. Parental background was working class and lower white collar, with a few children from families on welfare. There was great diversity of academic skills as measured by the Comprehensive Test of Basic Skills, with many students functioning far below grade level.

The data used for this analysis were the behavioral observations, sociometric questionnaires, and test scores collected on two sets of target classroom within each of the nine classrooms (grades 2–4). One set was selected for varying levels of proficiency in English and Spanish; the other set was selected by the teacher as likely to have the most difficulty in activities requiring mathematics and science. All students filled out a sociometric questionnaire (the source of the measures of status) in the fall of the experimental year. Achievement data for this first analysis included scores on a content-referenced test (the Mini-Test) especially constructed to measure learning outcomes of this curriculum. Test scores on this instrument were used as the dependent variable. In addition, the score on the reading subscales from the Comprehensive Test of Basic Skills was used as a control variable along with a measure of English proficiency from the Language Assessment Scale developed by DeAvila and Duncan. Both of these tests were administered in the fall. The behavioral measures of target children consisted of the talking and working together index described above and a simple notation for each three-minute observation period as to whether or not the child was seen reading or writing (a 0, 1 variable).

Analysis of Collective Task Conditions in Data Set I

Unlike previous work on expectation states with schoolchildren, the method of instruction in 1979–80 rarely required children to work together to produce a joint product or to make joint decisions. Instead, children worked in shifting groups at learning centers. They were individually responsible for completion of the task and worksheet at each learning center.

However, there were some special features that produced brief interdependencies between the students. Teachers gave the following two rules: You have the right to ask anyone at your learning center for help; you have the duty to assist anyone at your learning center who asks for help. Since the tasks from *Finding Out* are highly challenging, uncertain, and always novel, and the students are compelled to complete their tasks and worksheets, there was strong motivation for students to look to one another as resources.

Grouping was temporary and heterogeneous. After finishing one center, a student would select a new center that did not already have the posted limit of students working at it. Over time, each student had the chance to work with practically every other student in the class.

Path Model Analysis of Status, Interaction, and Learning

The path model depicting the relations between status, interacting, and learning is presented in Figure 9.1 (see also Cohen 1984b). All of the paths in this model have statistically significant path coefficients. The data show a clear relationship between status characteristics and peer interaction, even when the amount of knowledge about the curriculum prior to its start is controlled. The statistically significant path coefficient between interaction and learning is particularly important in light of the multiple controls; other significant predictors of the post-test score on the criterion-referenced test are the pre-test score on this same instrument, the CTBS Reading pre-test score, and the observed frequency of reading and writing.

Cohen interpreted these results as follows:

At the same time that the path model depicts the favorable effects of peer interaction on learning, it shows the negative effects of status. In this interactional system, those children with high social status have more access to peer interaction that, in turn, assists their learning. In other words, the rich get richer. This is the dilemma of using peer interaction; at the same time that it

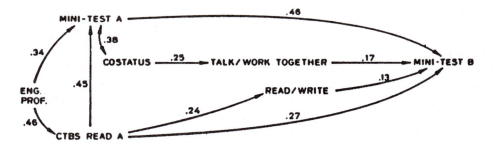

FIGURE 9.1
Path Model of Relations between Status, Interaction, and Learning

increases engagement and provides a strong potential for learning, it makes the status structure of the classroom salient and allows it to become the basis of the prestige and power order within the interacting classroom group. (Cohen 1984b; 184)

This analysis documents status problems among children who have been allowed and encouraged to work interdependently. The fact that some of the low-status children fail to have equal access to the interaction constitutes a barrier to their learning. Some low-status children who have inadequate reading skills are particularly dependent on peers for help in understanding the nature of the task; it is therefore critical to prevent situations in which there are children who never really understand what is expected of them because they cannot ask peers for assistance.

PART II
Moderating Status Effects

Despite gains in achievement test scores in the 1979–80 study (data set I), there was much room for improvement, particularly in training teachers to work with children at multiple learning centers. Teachers needed more help in delegating authority than they received in the three-day workshop that we held prior to the start of school in the summer of 1979. The failure of some teachers to delegate authority and to allow multiple learning centers to function without constant supervision limited opportunities for children to talk and work together and thus limited their opportunities for learning. An analysis of these problems led to the introduction of a more elaborate teacher training program and a new system of classroom management.

Revision of Rules and Roles: 1982–83 Study

In 1982–83, although we used the same curriculum materials, we made substantial changes in the way children worked at the learning centers. Teachers assigned children to heterogeneous groups (mixed as to academic achievement, language proficiency, and sex) and to particular learning centers. A child could not move on to a new learning center until the whole group had finished the task, thus increasing interdependence of group members.

We introduced a new system of group management in a two-week workshop for teachers. Teachers learned how to inculcate a set of cooperative norms in the children by means of a series of training games played prior to initiation of the curriculum. These norms of cooperation included asking questions, listening to others, helping another person without actually performing the task, explaining to others, showing other people how things work, and giving other people what they need.

In addition to new behavioral norms, children were assigned specific roles to play in the group. An important role was that of facilitator, a person who sees to it that all members of the group get the help that they need. Other roles were that of checker, who makes sure that everyone finishes the worksheet; reporter, who discusses what the group learned during the wrap-up session held at the end of every learning center session; clean-up supervisor; and safety officer. Each child had a role to play, and the roles were rotated.

To increase the achievement of low-status children, we sought to increase their opportunities for talking and working together and to treat the status problems documented in the 1979–80 data set. The purposes of the norms and roles were to help teachers delegate authority and to ensure that children were using each other as resources so that everyone might participate fully in the learning activities. Obviously, this approach would increase the probability of children talking and working together. The teaching of norms that encourage cooperation has been shown to prevent dominance by high-status members of the group (Morris 1977). When a group believes that everyone ought to participate, it will force members to share materials and will not permit one member to do all the talking. The use of such norms to equalize participation, however, does not alter expectations for competence.

The 1982–83 teacher training program gave emphasis to the use of multiple ability treatments, in which teachers attempt to modify competence expectations by convincing students that many different abilities are relevant to the tasks at hand (Tammivaara 1982; Rosenholtz 1985). In *Finding Out,* teachers discuss with students the many different abilities that are needed for the learning centers of each unit of the curriculum. They explain that reading and computational ability are only two of the relevant abilities and state specifically: "No one is going to be good at all these abilities; everyone is going to be good on at least one." The goal is for each student to have a mixed set of expectations for competence, some high, some low, for the multiple abilities relevant to the task. The multiple ability treatment is an adaptation of the laboratory study of Tammivaara (1982) and of the classroom experiment of Rosenholtz (1985). In these studies, the assignment of a set of competence expectations, some of which were high and some of which were low, substantially weakened status effects. In 1979 a brief but unsuccessful attempt was made to train teachers to use this approach. Persuading teachers to perceive tasks in terms of multiple abilities and to believe that every student will be good on some of these abilities is a difficult strategy to implement; it appears to run counter to some persistent beliefs. There is a tendency among teachers to believe that students are either competent or incompetent to perform a wide range of tasks.

Evaluation of the operation of learning centers in 1982–83 showed that teachers consistently maintained multiple and different learning centers in simultaneous operation (Cohen and DeAvila 1983). In data set II, the average percentage of children observed in small groups was 93.65 percent, whereas the average percentage in data set I was only 38.21 percent. The average percentage of students talking and manipulating the materials was increased to 32 percent in data set II from 24 percent in data set I.

Results: Comparison of Data Sets I and II

Did the introduction of the new system of classroom management weaken the relationship between status and interaction? Did low-status children interact more with their peers under the new system? These are particularly important questions because many low-status children were poor readers or nonreaders who needed the assistance of peers to understand the instructions on the activity card and on the worksheets. If they did not ask for help or if peers did not voluntarily help them, their access to the excellent learning materials was limited.

If the new system was successful, then low-status children should have higher rates of interaction in 1982–83 than in 1979–80. If we were successful in improving expectations for competence during the school year in 1982–83, then we could expect a direct effect of improved expectations for competence reflected in test scores as well as the indirect effects mediated through peer interaction and participation in activities designed to teach concepts. Still another question is whether teachers were successful in convincing the children that everyone had a contribution to make. If they were not, then high-status children would believe they were more expert and therefore more capable of offering assistance.

Description of Data Set II. During the school year 1982–83, 391 children in ten schools in three school districts, as well as 18 volunteer teachers and eight assistants, participated in the program. (Some of these assistants were teachers' aides and some were credentialed teachers.) Sociometric measures as well as standardized achievement tests were administered to all students in each classroom in the fall and spring. We were able to gather sociometric and achievement data for the pre- and post-test for 176 children in 13 classrooms of grades 2–5. Observational data were collected on a subsample of target children chosen to produce variability in academic achievement and in English language proficiency. There were 131 target children on whom we had a sufficient number of observations as well as sociometric data.

	1979/80		1982/83	
	Mean	S.D.	Mean	S.D.
	(N=111)		(N=131)	
Peer Task-Related Talk	2.170	1.303	3.998	1.707
Offering Assistance	0.425	0.426	0.629	0.581

* Rate = Frequency per 3 minutes observation period.

TABLE 9.1

Comparison of Mean Rates* of Task-Related Talk and of Offering Assistance, 1979–80 versus 1982–83

Changes in the relationship of status to interaction and learning. Table 9.1 presents observational data from the subsample of target children. It gives the mean rates of task-related talk that the target children directed to their peers in 1979–80 and 1982–83 and the mean rates of offering assistance to peers in those two years. With the introduction of norms and roles, the mean rate of talk increased sharply from 2.17 times per three minutes to four times per three minutes ($t = 4.83$; $p < .001$). There was also a statistically significant increase in the rate of offering assistance ($t = 7.05$; $p < .001$).

Table 9.2 gives the mean rates of task-related talk for three categories of the co-status scores in the two data sets. The distribution of co-status scores is divided into three groups, with approximately a third of the distribution falling into each group. In 1979–80, the low- and medium-status students talked less than the high-status students, but the former two groups were not significantly different from each other. The comparison of mean rates of low- and high-status students' talk in 1979–80 yielded a t value of 1.14 ($p < .05$); the comparison of mean rates of medium- and high-status students' talk yielded a t value of 2.65 ($p < .005$).

CoStatus*	Task-Related Talk			
	1979/80		1982/83	
	Mean	S.D.	Mean	S.D.
Low (2–4)	2.075	1.257	3.662	1.605
	(N = 32)		(N = 44)	
Medium (4–7)	1.879	1.061	4.046	1.492
	(N = 48)		(N = 40)	
High (8–10)	2.720	1.541	4.272	1.936
	(N = 31)		(N = 47)	

* CoStatus = Quintile of Choice Distribution for "Best in Math and Science" + "Best Friend".

TABLE 9.2

Mean Rates of Task-Related Talk for High-, Medium-, and Low-Status Students, 1979–80 and 1982–83

A comparison of the two data sets by status group allows an estimate of how much the new system changed rates of interaction. One important finding is that each group in data set II talked significantly more than its counterpart in data set I. The increases in rates of talk between 1979–80 and 1982–83 were much greater for the medium- and high-status groups than for the low-status group. Moreover, there were no significant difference between the status groups in data set II, while in data set I, significant differences were found (as reported above). This is one measure of our success in equalizing rates of interacting for students participating in the 1982–3 implementation.

We examined the effects of status on three behavioral measures and test scores in the two data sets using correlational techniques. The original index scores for the behavioral measure of talking and working together were transformed to z-scores. Table 9.3 presents the correlations of the co-status score with task-related talk, with the z-score of talking and working together, with the rate of offering assistance, and with the individual's gain in achievement test score on a subscale of the Comprehensive Test of Basic Skills called Math Concepts and Application. This particular subscale is closely related to the problem-solving focus of the curriculum and has proven to be very sensitive to opportunities for interaction in the classroom. For example, the average gain per classroom in test scores on this subscale significantly correlates with the average percentage of students talking and manipulating materials, a measure of opportunities to interact in the classroom ($r = .72$ in data set II).

The correlation between co-status and task-related talk fell from .195 in 1979–80 to .165 in 1982–83. Whereas the first correlation coefficient was statistically significant, the second only reached the .06 level of significance. However, the *difference* between these two correlation coefficients is not statistically significant. The correlation of co-status with the z-score of talking and working together did not show the same pattern. The correlation was, if anything, slightly stronger in 1982–83. Most noticeable is the relatively strong correlation between co-status and rate of offering assistance in 1982–83 ($r = .257$; $p = .003$). The same correlation was much lower and not statistically significant in 1979–80. Examination of the difference between these two correlation coefficients shows that one is barely within the confidence interval of the other; thus the correlations are not significantly different.

The correlation between the co-status and gain scores in Math Concepts and Application fell from .278 in 1979–80 to .151 in 1982–83 (a nonsignificant difference). The correlation in data set II was still statistically significant ($p < .05$). We also examined the relationship of the co-status score to the achievement test score by performing regression analyses of the post-test scores from Math Concepts and Application on the pre-test scores and on the co-status scores. This analysis, for which we used data from the entire sample, not just the subsample of target children, revealed that co-status was a statistically significant predictor of the post-test scores in data set I but not in data set II (see Table 9.4). The beta weight for the co-status score as a predictor of post-test scores in 1979–80 was 1.54; in 1982–83 it was .069.

Interpretation. Introduction of the new classroom management system in 1982–83 resulted in significant increases in rates of interaction and of offering assistance. These changes reflect the fact that groups were responsible for seeing to it that everyone received the help needed and did not move on to the next learning center until the whole group had finished. New norms for interaction had

| | Correlations with CoStatus | | | | | |
| | 1979/80 | | | 1982/83 | | |
	N	r	P	N	r	P
Task-Related Talk*	111	.195	(.041)	131	.165	(.060)
Z Scores of Talk + Works Together	111	.175	(.067)	131	.181	(.039)
Offers Assistance	111	.152	(.110)	131	.257	(.003)
Gain Score in Math Concepts and Application	153	.278	(.001)	176	.151	(.0449)

* Because of skewness, this correlation was computed with square roots of the original rates of talk.

TABLE 9.3

Correlation of Co-status with Rates of Talk, Offering Assistance, and Gain Scores in Achievement Test, 1979–80 and 1982–83

1979/80

| | $N = 151$ | | |
| Dependent Variable: | Math Concepts and Applications, Post-Test | | |
Predictors	Beta	T	P
Pre-Test	.584	3.26	<.001
CoStatus	1.540	5.51	<.001

$R^2 = .512$

1982/83

| | $N = 176$ | | |
| Dependent Variable: | Math Concepts and Applications, Post-Test | | |
Predictors	Beta	T	P
Pre-Test	.693	10.21	<.000
CoStatus	.069	1.02	<.310

$R^2 = .496$

TABLE 9.4

Regression of Post-test Scores of Achievement Test on Co-status: 1979–80 and 1982–83

the desired effect: everyone's interaction rate increased, regardless of status. Because low-status students were significantly more active in 1982–83 than in 1979–80, they probably were more likely to gain access to the learning materials by discussing the instructions on activity cards. In one second-grade classroom where the teacher stressed reading the activity cards, the conversation turned largely on what these cards instructed them to do (Navarrete 1985).

In 1982–83 the increased rates of interaction weakened the effect of status on interaction, but by no means did it disappear. Whether this was in fact the result partly depends on the index used. The relatively strong correlation in Table 9.3 between offering assistance and co-status ($r = .257$) in 1982–83 reveals the continuing operation of status characteristics; high-status children were more likely to offer assistance than low-status children. High-status children probably perceived themselves as more competent and, in terms of skills measured by the standardized achievement tests in mathematics and reading, many of them were. Even if low-status children were expected by classmates to possess some of the skills required at the learning centers, continued effects of the co-status variable might be anticipated because expectations based on the original status distinctions and those stemming from the new status characteristics relevant to the curriculum would combine. On the average, expectations for competence of high-status children would still be higher.

The effect of status on learning was much weaker in 1982–83. This is a highly desirable result because, from an educational point of view, the major disadvantage of allowing status to affect interaction is that it indirectly affects learning. In an absolute sense, the sizable learning gains in 1982–83 show that the teaching methods and materials were highly effective. Furthermore, we did much to remove the inequalities in interaction that prevented the low-status students from learning as much as the high-status students.

It is ironic that learning problems should be easier to treat than status problems. One explanation is that these learning materials are extraordinarily well engineered to facilitate the understanding of math concepts and the solution of word problems. They consist of many different media so that, for example, children who understand things spatially or who can visually grasp abstract concepts are not deprived of learning because they may not understand as well by listening or by reading. Assuming that the management system helped to solve the problem of giving non-readers access to the materials, the materials themselves are capable of teaching in a powerful fashion.

Results: Change in Status over Time within Data Set II

In addition to comparing the relationship between status and interaction for two years, another way to tell whether status treatments attempted in 1982–83 were at all successful is to examine changes in perceived status at the classroom level from fall to spring of that school year. Sociometric data were collected in the fall and in the spring of 1982–83. One can compare the choices received by the group of children who were classified as "low status" by the sociometric questionnaire given in the fall to choices received by the low-status group in the spring. Did the low-status group receive more choices in the spring on the two sociometric items of "best friend" and "being good in math and science" than in the fall?

The sociometric data presented a considerable challenge for analysis. There were marked classroom differences in the number of choices in response to the sociometric questions. We had to find a measure that standardized for the variable number of choices made in different classrooms and at two points in time. Moreover, the measure had to provide us with a way to look at choices received by high-status students versus choices received by low-status students within the same classroom.

Changes in classroom climate. Analysis of data at the classroom level revealed some important changes in the pattern of choosers and the recipients of choices on the two sociometric questions used for the co-status scores. We examined the percentage of choosers who directed their choices to the lowest third of the distribution of co-status scores in the fall and in the spring. The average percentage of all possible choosers in the classroom who chose children in the lowest third of the co-status score distribution with regard to either criterion question rose from 22.65 in fall to 35.24 in spring. In contrast, a smaller percentage of classmates chose high-status students in the spring (74.25) than in the fall (79.62). Both of these changes were statistically significant. Stated differently, in every classroom but one there was an average gain in the percentage of classmates choosing low-status children; in 10 out of 13 classrooms there was an average loss in the percentage of classmates choosing high-status students.

We should emphasize that this analysis focuses on classroom rather than on individual effects. We are not examining the change in number of choices received by individuals who were in the extremes of the distribution in the fall measures. Rather, we are examining all those who received relatively fewer choices at either of these points in time. They may or may not be the same individuals. This analysis avoids the danger of over-interpreting changes that may simply be regression toward the mean of initially extreme scores.

Another critical finding is that the distributions of choices had less of a variance in the spring than in the fall, a consequence of having more choices directed at the low-status end of the distribution and fewer choices directed at the high end of the status distribution. This change is measured by a statistic called the coefficient of variation, which is the standard deviation of a distribution divided by its mean. The average value for this statistic, calculated across all classrooms, was 57.3 for the pre-test and 50.5 for the post-test. This decline in the coefficient of variation between fall and spring was found in every classroom but two.

This analysis is similar to that of Hallinan (1976) who examined the average mean and variance of the number of choices received on a friendship question in open and traditional classrooms. She argued that a larger variance in the distribution of choices might imply the presence of more sociometric stars and isolates. In support of her argument she found that the variance of the distribution was markedly lower in open classrooms than in traditional classrooms.

Similar to Hallinan's findings, there was evidence in data set II for the association between a reduction in the variance of the choice distribution between fall and spring and opportunities for interaction in the classroom. We correlated the difference between the coefficient of variation in the fall and the spring for each classroom with a measure of the quality of implementation of the program. This measure consists of the percentage of students found talking or talking while manipulating the materials. The relationship between these variables yielded a Pearson r of .48 ($p < .05$). In other words, those classrooms where teachers fostered more talking and working together tended to be the same classrooms that developed fewer underchosen and overchosen students over time.

A friendlier place. What is the meaning of these changes? And how do they relate to the status treatments? We interpret these findings to mean that these classrooms were friendlier places, where the supply of esteem was less likely to be the exclusive property of a few students in the spring than it was in the fall. This is a well-documented effect in classrooms in which there is a high level of peer interaction, especially cooperative interaction (Hallinan 1976; Epstein and Karweit 1983; Slavin 1983).

Such a favorable change in climate does not mean that all status-generated problems have been eliminated, however. Status characteristics can continue to operate in cooperative groups whose members enjoy friendly relationships. Two factors can affect the number of times a given student's name is chosen in response to a sociometric question about "best friend": the general friendliness of the classroom and the relative popularity of the student. The increase in the number of those choosing a low-status student is more likely to be explained by a change in the friendliness of the classroom than by a change in the student's relative popularity. The analysis above does not take into account the relative position of high- and low-status students in a given classroom. The results are, nonetheless, worth reporting because low-status students in these classrooms certainly had more friends in the spring than did low-status students in the fall. The changes in classroom social structure described here did succeed in improving the social situation of the low-status child in comparison to what it would have been in a more traditional classroom.

Change in status advantage. Because we sought a way to measure status changes that (1) would be less affected by the increasing friendliness of these classrooms and (2) would indicate the *relative* status differences within classrooms, we decided to use an index of status advantage. In laboratory work on status characteristics and expectation states theory, a similar index, called the expectancy advantage, is typically calculated by subtracting the aggregated expectations held for the low-status actor from those held for the high-status actor. In applied research on free interaction in mixed-status, four-person groups, Cohen has interpreted expectancy advantage as an indicator of the status effect *at the group level* and has calculated it by subtracting the mean influence or interaction rate of all low-status actors from that of all high-status actors (Cohen 1982). The index of status advantage is an extension of the expectancy advantage to the classroom level; this is justified on the assumption that at some time during the school year each student performed a collective task with every other student at least once. (Teachers were instructed to compose groups to this end.) Thus it is possible to compare high-status and low-status students at the classroom level and to talk about the status advantage of high-status students over that of low-status students in the performance of collective tasks *at the classroom level.*

The data in this case were responses to the sociometric question asking which classmates were the best in math and science. This was one of the two items making up the co-status score; it was much less reflective of general friendliness than the other item, the choice of best friend. The status advantage was based on the *average percentage of all choices* made, in a given classroom, naming children who were classified as low or high status according to the fall sociometric data. The percentage of *choices* rather than *choosers* avoids the problem of classroom differences and differences over time on the number of choices made. Since children had an unlimited number of choices in answering the sociometric questions, in many classrooms the total number of choices made by all children was very large. It ranged from 80 to 265 in the fall and from 98 to 335 in the spring in response to the question about who was best in math and science. (There were more respondents in the spring than there were in the fall.)

To make the initial determination of status in the fall, we divided the distribution of percentages of choices made in response to the math and science question into thirds, with low status defined as being in the lowest third and high status defined as being in the highest third. Next we calculated the status advantage for each classroom using the average percentage of all choices made—that is, an average percentage of all choices made by all classrooms. Since the denominator of this figure can be as large as 335, the average percentage tends to be a small number. The status advantage is calculated as follows. The average percentage of choices of children who were initially classified as low status was subtracted from the average percentage of choices of children who were initially classified as high status. Table 9.5 presents the status advantages for fall and spring for each of 13 classrooms. Because we selected high- and low-status groups on the fall distribution of choices, all status advantages in the fall were, by definition, positive. As it turned out, the fall status advantages were large in many classrooms. By spring, the status

advantage for each classroom was smaller than it had been in the fall.

Table 9.5 also includes descriptive statistics derived by creating a grand mean across classrooms of the average percentage of choices naming high- and low-status target children. The average percentage of choices naming high-status children in the fall was 5.98; low-status children were named in only 0.99 percent of the choices, on the average. By spring, the comparable figures were 5.18 percent for high-status children and 1.93 percent for low-status children. The overall difference, obtained by subtracting the average percentage of all choices naming low-status students from the average percentage naming high-status students, was 4.99 percent in the fall and 3.25 percent in the spring. This difference was statistically significant ($p = .001$) according to the Mann-Whitney U test.

The decrease in status advantage over time was produced by an increase in the percentage of choices naming low-status children and a decrease in the percentage of choices naming high-status children. In all probability, this means that some low-status children were perceived as more competent as the school year progressed.

Status advantage: sociometric data versus observed behavior. A final question concerns the relationship of questionnaire evaluations of competence on a relevant status characteristic and observed behavior of mixed-status collective task groups. To answer this question, we examined the relationship of status advantages calculated from sociometric data to status advantages calculated from data on task-related talk at the classroom level.

The only children for whom we had both sets of data were the target children. To derive a status advantage from the data on task-related talk, we defined low- and high-status groups as previously described, according to the lowest and highest third of the percentage distribution of choices in response to the question on math and science in the fall sociometric questionnaire. We then subtracted the average rate of talk for the low-status group from that for the high-status group. (In four classrooms there were too few target children defined as low or high status to be included in the analysis.) The Pearson correlation coefficient between the spring sociometric status advantage and the status advantage based on peer talk was .58 ($p < .01$).

Interpretation of change in status advantage. In all classrooms, status advantages were smaller in the spring than in the fall. From this it can be inferred that some children who were not perceived as best in math and science prior to the experience of *Finding Out* were likely to be perceived as very competent by at least some of their classmates at the end of the instruction. Since the regular math program in these classrooms was taught in ability groups, in which there are few mechanisms that enable the

Class	Fall Status[+] Advantage	Spring Status Advantage
1	4.47	4.14
2	6.64	4.79
3	4.06	2.81
4	5.31	4.53
5	4.45	4.06
6	4.91	2.99
8	3.42	1.62
9	6.92	2.66
10	5.17	4.30
11	4.21	2.67
12	3.99	2.12
13	6.25	3.88
14	5.94	1.55
All Classrooms Means Status Advantage	4.99	3.25**

[+] Status Advantage = Mean % of all Choices on Math/Science Given to High Status Students − Mean % of all Choices on Math/Science Given to Low Status Students.

** $p < .001$ for difference between Spring and Fall status advantage: Mann-Whitney U Test.

TABLE 9.5
Status Advantage of High- over Low-Status Students in Percentage of Choices as Best in Math and Science, Fall versus Spring Measures for Treated Classrooms

low-achieving student to display competence, and since science was not taught outside the *Finding Out* curriculum, we can presume that something about the *Finding Out* experience brought about this change in perception. But this change should not be taken to mean that the differential competence initially perceived had disappeared. Although the status advantages were smaller in the spring, they remained positive.

The correlation between status advantage based on peer talk and that based on sociometric choices in the spring suggests that this change in perception is related to the prestige and power order of small groups engaged in collective tasks. Thus we have some confidence that the sociometric analysis partly reflects the extent to which status differences were successfully treated in the classroom.

An alternative explanation for the decreased percentage of choices received by high-status students and the increased percentages of choices received by low-status students is that the changes are caused by a statistical artifact, a regression toward the mean of initially extreme values of the variable. Without a control group of sociometric measures taken on comparable classrooms that did not experience this intervention, we cannot rule out such an interpretation.

Nevertheless we have strong grounds for arguing that this observed change is unlikely to be a product of measurement error. The reduced status advantages in the spring are correlated with observed status advantages based on peer talk, an entirely independent behavioral measure. Second, the shape of the distributions changed between fall and spring showing a reduced variance, an occurrence that cannot be attributed to measurement error. Moreover, these changes in the distribution, as measured by the coefficient of variation, are correlated significantly with a measure of program implementation: the proportion of students talking or talking while manipulating the materials. We argue that insofar as the changes in status advantages are related to changes in the shape of the distribution and insofar as they have a demonstrated association with independent measures, they are unlikely to be a product of measurement error.

Discussion

The discussion of results centers on two questions: (1) Why does it appear to be easier to treat learning problems than status problems? and (2) Why are expectations for competence relatively resistant to change in classroom situations and what, if anything, can be done to alter them?

Treatment of Learning Problems.   Although the consistency of classroom implementation resulted in stronger

gains in achievement in data set II, low and high achievers made highly significant gains in both years. Analyses of the correlation of status with learning gains should not obscure this fact. The children in data set II consistently improved their standing in comparison to that of the nationally normed population across all the subscales of the Comprehensive Test of Basic Skills. This improvement brought the average of many of the classrooms up to the fiftieth percentile even though most of them had started out far below grade level (Cohen and DeAvila 1983).

This analysis thus focuses, in part, on the results of using a powerful set of instructional materials. The study shows that if a teacher allows children to work together on these materials and encourages them to use each other as resources, scores on standardized achievement tests can be considerably improved. The high-status students in data set I gained more than the low-status students, as indicated by scores on the Math Concepts and Applications test. In 1979–80, lateral relations between students were permitted but not required. A student who was too inhibited to ask for assistance might well be excluded from the instructional activity. Teachers did not then hold regular orientation sessions to explain the learning centers and activity cards. Furthermore, teachers in some of the classrooms were using only a few learning centers attended by larger groups at each of them. This situation would make it particularly difficult for some children to "get their hands on" the learning materials.

In 1982–83 the introduction of cooperative norms and roles solved both the problem of helping teachers to encourage children to work together on their own at the learning centers and the problem of making sure that all children had access to the learning materials and activities. The norms of cooperation increased the level of interaction and taught children how to ask for and give assistance. The role of facilitator was designed to prevent children from being left out either intellectually or physically. The role of checker enforced the rule that each child had to complete the worksheet. In addition, teachers regularly held orientations and wrap-up sessions at which they explained the activities to the students. When ensured access to the learning materials low-status students made dramatic learning gains. In contrast, it is not uncommon for the standardized achievement scores of low achievers in conventional classrooms to decline between fall and spring.

Learning problems will not always be easier to treat than status problems. The results obtained in this study can be ascribed to instructional activities that enable students to learn through doing. We also utilized an elaborate system of classroom management that requires extensive teacher training and provides teachers with organizational support (Cohen and DeAvila 1983). Given the highly motivating nature of the materials, once we had solved the problem of ensuring access to the learning materials and activities, we could begin to remove the effects of status on learning outcomes.

There were several features of the new management system that increased the rates of interaction of all students. Whatever else the students did, they were supposed to play their roles. Each role led to interaction with other members of the group. The norms of cooperation included standardized ways of asking for and giving help; each child took turns practicing these new behaviors during the training period. In the scoring of interaction, no distinction was made between procedural talk that was specifically related to norms and roles, and talk that was more directly relevant to the task. When one considers the interaction arising from prescribed talk and from the responsibility that the children took for each other's performance, it is not surprising that the correlation between status and task-related talk was weaker under the new system. This does not necessarily mean that competence expectations were changed. What probably happened was that differential competence expectations no longer prevented children from interacting. In this way we solved the problem of the differential access of low-status students to the learning materials and activities.

The Challenge of Changing Competence Expectations.
Can we change expectations for competence in a classroom situation where children differ on at least one status characteristic that is directly relevant to the activity we are trying to treat? The children in this study differed on the status characteristic of ability in math and science, which was seen as directly relevant to the math and science activities of the *Finding Out* curriculum. A direct path of relevance between a status characteristic and a new set of tasks should, from a theoretical point of view, have maximum power to affect behavior (Humphreys and Berger 1981).

Despite the salience of the status characteristic, there were several features of the activities and the teaching technique that encouraged the students to see themselves as competent on intellectual abilities that were distinct from traditionally defined ability in math and science. The activities presented excellent opportunities for children to display previously hidden intellectual abilities. The multiple abilities treatment, utilized by teachers in 1982–83, also helped children to see themselves as competent on some of the intellectual abilities required by the learning activities. After discussing the different abilities required by each new set of learning centers, teachers specifically explained to the students that reading and computational skills were only two of the relevant skills required. Teachers stated that every-

one could expect to be good on at least one of the required abilities.

To some extent we were successful in changing the perceptions of children's competence in math and science; status advantages of high-status students were reduced although by no means eliminated. Nonetheless high-status children were more likely to offer assistance than low-status children in data set II. This suggests that children who initially had better test scores and were perceived as more competent in the fall were more likely to adopt a tutorial role. Even if expectations for competence for low-status children were raised by the multiple abilities treatment, we might still expect that the initially high-status children would have an advantage because of a combining effect.

We were dealing with a specific status characteristic on which the children received many evaluations in connection with daily instruction in mathematics. In many of these classrooms, ability grouping was used for the teaching of math outside of *Finding Out*. Thus, to some extent, the status order we were trying to modify was probably being reconstructed as fast as we weakened it.

In addition, we were trying to change the teachers' and students' ideas about academic ability: we were introducing a multidimensional view of ability in mathematics and science. The majority of teachers have difficulty accepting the idea that children from lower social classes who show limited proficiency in English and Spanish and whose reading and writing skills in either language are minimal might have multiple intellectual abilities, such as reasoning, hypothesizing, and visual and spatial thinking. Perhaps this was the underlying source of the resistance to change of competence expectations for low-status students.

Implications for Cooperative Learning

The major implication of this work is the realization that the implementation of cooperative learning should consider the status problems that have been described. Fostering interdependence may activate these very status problems, so that failure to deal with them may shut off access to interaction for low-status children.

The Use of Norms and Roles.   The use of training for cooperative behaviors such as listening to each other and giving everyone a chance to talk in combination with the assigning of rotating roles to each member of the group will do much to solve the problem of access of low-status students to interaction. If the learning materials are sufficiently stimulating and well-related to the criterion test, then this in itself will do much to equalize the learning gains for low-and high-status students.

Curricula for Cooperative Learning. Another implication is the importance of the curricular materials that are used in conjunction with cooperative learning. They should be rich and not entirely dependent on reading so that different children are able to make different kinds of contributions. In the case of *Finding Out*, the activities themselves presented excellent opportunities for children to display previously unrecognized intellectual abilities; the activities were certainly far richer in required intellectual abilities than any set of school activities labeled as science or math. Even for adults, these activities create uncertainty and required aptitudes far beyond what is tested in ordinary achievement tests.

Multiple Ability Treatment Required. However, rich curriculum materials will not, by themselves, prevent status problems from arising. Unless they are used in conjunction with a multiple ability treatment, students will view the new tasks as requiring the same academic abilities as other school tasks. In 1982–83 teachers were trained to introduce each set of activities as requiring multiple abilities. After discussing the different abilities involved, they specifically explained to the students that reading and computational skills were only two of the relevant skills required. The point here is that if the children are persuaded by the teacher that the tasks involve multiple abilities, rich and stimulating materials can do much to equalize learning gains as a consequence of the cooperative curriculum for low- and high-status students.

Consistency of Implementation. The implementation of cooperative learning techniques is a great challenge for the in-service developer. The inclusion of techniques to deal with status problems requires special attention to teacher training and organizational support for the teacher. Teachers need to have a fundamental understanding of what status problems are and how their actions in the classroom affect those problems. Furthermore, the changes in behavior for most teachers are sufficiently great that there must be careful follow-up and feedback on exactly how consistently they are utilizing the recommended strategies. The initial workshops must be followed up by a systematic concern with how well treatments for status problems are being implemented in each classroom.

Potential of Changed Expectations for Competence. If the effects of status on learning can be weakened by equalizing participation and access, then why is it important to continue attempts to alter competence expectations? The low-status children we selected were socially isolated and were not perceived as especially competent in any academic endeavor. The public educational system is typi-

cally least successful with these children. Being defined as unattractive and incompetent in a highly evaluative setting and forced to participate five days a week is not an enviable fate for any human being. Theoretically, such children would be better if they were free of general expectations for their incompetence. Although status has indirect effects on learning as a result of students' interactions with peers, there are other ways in which expectations based on status affect learning. High-status students are more likely to initiate interaction with the teacher; this probably is a source of their superior test performance. As a result of low expectations for competence, low-status students are more likely to show low levels of effort in performing school tasks; and this behavior is a barrier to their academic success. If general expectations for competence could be raised, we should see an even greater improvement in oral proficiency and in academic achievement, to say nothing of improved social acceptance and self-esteem.

A new status treatment in which teachers assign competence to low-status children has been developed that can be integrated with the multiple-ability treatment described here. The teacher is a high-status source of evaluations for students. If teachers make evaluations of students, students are likely to believe those evaluations. Theoretically, this treatment ensures that competence expectations for low-status children are raised because they will accept the teacher's evaluation of themselves as competent on relevant skills. These evaluations must be both specific and public. For example, the teacher will specifically describe how competent a low-status student is in reasoning, in skills requiring spatial ability, or in activities requiring precision. This is a difficult set of skills to learn. Video techniques can help teachers learn to identify and to analyze student reasoning, visual and spatial thinking, and precision, and to rehearse the giving of evaluations. The advantage of continuing to try to change expectations for competence lies in the tremendous potential that cooperative learning in combination with successfully treated expectations for competence has in academically heterogeneous classrooms. We have the potential to help the most unsuccessful students to achieve.

References

Berger, J. B., Cohen, B.P., and Zelditch, M., Jr. (1966). Status characteristics and expectation states. In J. Berger and M. Zelditch, Jr. (Eds.), *Sociological theories in progress* (Vol. 1, pp. 29–46). Boston: Houghton-Mifflin.

——— (1972). Status characteristics and social interaction. *American Sociological Review*, 37: 241–255.

Berger, J., Rosenholtz, S. J., and Zelditch, M., Jr. (1980). Status organizing processes. *Annual Review of Sociology* 6: 479–508.

Cohen, E.G. (1982), Expectation states and interracial interaction in school settings. *Annual Review of Sociology*, 8: 209–35.

—— (1984a). The desegregated school: Problems in status power and interethnic climate. In *Desegregation: Groups in Contact: Psychology of Desegregation,* edited by N. Miller and M. B. Brewer. San Diego, CA: Academic Press.

—— (1984b). Talking and working together: Status interaction and learning. In *The Social Context of Instruction: Group Organization and Group Processes,* edited by P. L. Peterson, L. C. Wilkinson, and M. Hallinan. San Diego, CA: Academic Press.

—— (1986). On the sociology of the classroom. In *The Contributions of the Social Sciences to Educational Policy and Practice: 1965–1985,* edited by J. Hannaway and M. E. Lockheed. Berkeley, CA: McCutchan.

Cohen, E.G., and De Avila, E. (1983). *Learning to Think in Math and Science: Improving Local Education for Minority Children.* Final Report to the Johnson Foundation. Stanford University, School of Education.

Cohen, E.G. and Intili, J.K. (1981). *Interdependence and Management in Bilingual Classrooms.* Final Report, NIE Grant. Stanford, CA: Center for Educational Research, Stanford University, School of Education.

Cohen, E.G., Lockheed, M.L., and Lohman, M. (1976). The center for interracial cooperation: a field experiment. *Sociology of Education* 49: 47–58.

DeAvila, E.A., and Duncan, S.E. (1980). *Finding Out/Descubrimiento.* Corte Madera, CA: Linguametrics Group.

Epstein, J.L., and Karweit, N. (1983). *Friends in School: Patterns of Selection and Influence in Secondary Schools.* New York: Academic Press.

Hallinan, M. (1976). Friendship patterns in open and traditional classrooms. *Sociology of Education* 49: 254–65.

Hoffman, D., and Cohen, E. G. (1972). An exploratory study to determine the effects of generalized performance expectations upon activity and influence of students engaged in a group simulation game. Paper read to the American Educational Research Association, Chicago.

Humphreys, P., and Berger, J. (1981). Theoretical consequences of the status characteristics formulation. *American Journal of Sociology* 86: 953–83.

Johnson, D.W., Maruyama, G., Johnson, R.T., Nelson, D., and Skon, L. (1981). Effects of cooperative, competitive, and individualistic goal structures on achievement. *Psychological Bulletin,* 89: 47–62.

Maruyama, G., and N. Miller (1981). Physical attractiveness and personality. *Progress in Experimental Personality Research* 10: 203–80.

Morris, R. (1977). A normative intervention to equalize participation in task-oriented groups. Ph.D. dissertation. Stanford, CA: Stanford University.

Navarrete, C. (1985). Problem resolution in small group interaction: A bilingual classroom study. Ph.D. dissertation, Stanford, CA: Stanford University.

Rosenholtz, S.J. (1985). Treating problems of academic status. In *Status, Rewards, and Influence,* edited by J. Berger and M. Zelditch, Jr. San Francisco, CA: Jossey-Bass.

Sharan, S. (1980). Cooperative learning in small groups: Recent methods and effects on achievement, attitudes, and ethnic relations. *Review of Educational Research,* 50: 241–271.

Slavin, R. E. (1983). *Cooperative learning.* New York: Longman.

Tammivaara, J.S. (1982). The effects of task structure on beliefs about competence and participation in small groups. *Sociology of Education,* 55: 212–222.

Webster, M., Jr., and Driskell, J. (1983). Beauty as status. *American Journal of Sociology,* 89: 140–65.

Comments on the article by Davidson

As we saw in the research survey by Davidson, there are a myriad of different classroom practices which are lumped together under the heading of cooperative learning. The present article by Davidson provides a detailed look at one particular cooperative learning methodology called the small group discovery method. The current paper is intended to at least partially answer questions about how one might implement cooperative learning in a collegiate mathematics course, as well as why one might choose to do this.

Davidson begins the article by describing the forces which led him to develop the small group discovery method in mathematics. He then provides an overview of this method through addressing such issues as motivating students, sequencing of course material, providing instruction on interaction, forming groups, pacing and evaluating student achievement. For this reason, this paper may be considered as a compendium of the issues and options associated with this particular cooperative learning strategy.

After outlining the classroom practices associated with small group discovery learning, Davidson provides a brief overview of a number of fundamental studies in social psychology and group interaction which, taken as a whole, may be used to inform the countless choices which confront the instructor who is attempting to implement pedagogy based on small group cooperative learning. It should be noted that the studies cited and inferences made by the author appear to be equally applicable to virtually all forms of cooperative learning, not only the small group discovery method.

Having established the framework upon which a small group discovery-based course may be constructed, and having sketched an overview of empirical studies informing such a course organization, Davidson provides a fairly extensive example of a particular calculus course organized according to this structure. Included in this discussion are sample problems, discussion of successes achieved and a discussion of difficulties encountered.

Discussion Questions

1. How important is the discovery aspect of the cooperative learning activities described by Davidson?
2. What mathematics in the undergraduate curriculum is it reasonable for students to discover?
3. Are cooperative learning activities which don't involve a discovery component more or less valuable than those that do?
4. Is there value in students working on problems geared toward discovery if they ultimately do not make the discovery? Why or why not?
5. Compare and contrast the teacher's role in small group discovery with that of Professor C in the Finkel and Monk article.

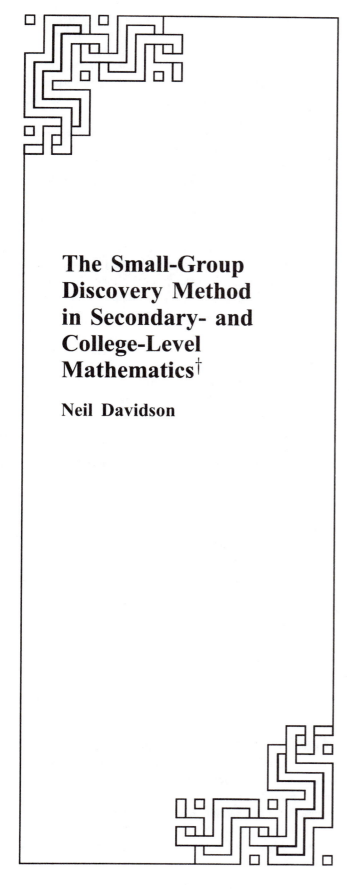

The Small-Group Discovery Method in Secondary- and College-Level Mathematics[†]

Neil Davidson

Introduction

Let me begin with a personal story with three strands, which, when woven together, led me to develop the small-group discovery method. In 1966, I thought that I needed a course in experimental psychology but was denied admission because of lack of prerequisites. On my way out of the psychology building, I noticed something that riveted my attention: a class with small groups of students sitting and talking with each other. After watching in amazement for a few moments, I approached the professor, explained my status as a doctoral student, and asked permission to join the class, whatever it was. The teacher, David Bradford, generously agreed, and I enrolled as a student in theories of social and organizational change and later in his course in group dynamics. Thus began my exposure to group processes in learning.

During this same period of time, I was tantalized by Dewey's (1916, 1938) philosophy of education, which emphasized learning through active personal experience; learning by doing nonroutine, thought-provoking activities; learning as a social process; and much more. This philosophy actually provided the impetus for much of the work in classroom group dynamics. The philosophy seemed highly appealing and yet not quite practical in mathematics, or so I thought at the time.

For several years prior, I had taken a series of graduate courses in point set topology, taught by the Moore method (Moise, 1965). This is a highly competitive, individualistic method in which students independently develop conjectures, prove theorems, and construct counterexamples to propositions in topology. The students work alone outside of class, without recourse to books or to other people, and then are called upon to present to the entire class the problems that they claim to have solved. This method has produced some spectacular successes, including a number of world-renowned topologists (Moise, 1965). It also produced among many of my classmates a sense of isolation and discouragement, even though they did well in other branches of mathematics. I wondered whether there might be a way to retain the challenging problems and intellectual excitement of the Moore method but to change the social patterns to foster more human contact and greater success for the majority of students.

One day, in a moment of insight, I saw an answer: Using Dewey's philosophy as the theoretical foundation, I would try to combine the intellectual challenge of the Moore method with the social support inherent in the group dynamics approaches. That insight, which was perfectly obvious after the fact, was the beginning of the small-group discovery method. Little did I know that others, whose work is represented in this volume, were beginning to develop different forms of small-group teaching in mathematics at about the same time. In retrospect, it seems this was an idea whose time had come, perhaps a seed in the collective consciousness of humanity.

After a semester of informal experimenting with teaching calculus by small-group problem solving, I was ready for my first systematic attempt at small-group teaching. This was a year-long course in calculus of one variable, taught by the small-group discovery method. That first trial took place under favorable conditions: a small class with better-than-average students. After the first anxious month, I could see that the method really was working and had some promise. Since that time, other instructors and I have used the method in a number of secondary- and college-level courses, including precalculus, calculus, math for elementary teachers, linear algebra, abstract algebra, number theory, foundations of geometry, advanced calculus, topology, and complex variables.

The remainder of this chapter is organized as follows: a description of principles from Dewey's philosophy, an overview of classroom practices, an elaboration based on practices in group dynamics, a description of the interaction between the students and the mathematics content in calculus, and an evaluation of the strengths and limitations of the method.

Practices Derived from Educational Philosophy

Let us turn our attention to the philosophical basis of the small-group discovery method. Polya (1965) placed emphasis upon student thinking, active learning, and interest in mathematics. These factors are particular aspects of a general philosophy of education and of life, whose foremost advocate in education was John Dewey (1916, 1938). While a description of Dewey's philosophy is beyond the scope of this paper, there follows a summary of classroom practices derived from Dewey's philosophy and applied in the design of the small-group discovery method.

In this method, students learn through personal experience; they learn mathematics by doing mathematics. The students, with limited subtle guidance from the teacher, formulate some definitions, make conjectures, state theorems, prove theorems, construct examples and counterexamples, solve specific problems, and develop techniques for solving various classes of problems. (For any given class, these challenges are realistically adjusted to fit the background and capabilities of the students.)

The approach to the subject matter is one of guided discovery in which thought-provoking topics are introduced

as questions for investigation by the students. Some questions in calculus are: *How can we find the tangent line to a curve? How can we find the area under a curve? How can we find the volume of the surface obtained by revolving a curve around an axis?* Questions such as these can be raised in brief discussions with the entire class to set the stage for group explorations and activities.

The classroom activities take place in small groups of students. Within each group there is to be a cooperative atmosphere in which students can freely discuss mathematical ideas and work together to solve the problems at hand. The work is done "...as a social enterprise in which all individuals have an opportunity to contribute and to which all feel a responsibility" (Dewey, 1938, p. 56).

The teacher adopts a democratic leadership style by facilitating the activities of the students in a manner that is not highly directive. The teacher spends most of the class period with the small work groups, providing guidance and support in a variety of ways to be described later.

Motivation

Interest in mathematical topics and activities is intended to provide the major source of motivation. Problems are often given that arise in real life or in concrete physical situations, such as projectile motion, velocity and acceleration, distance required to stop a car, spring displacement, radioactive decay, and profit or loss functions. An occasional paradox is introduced, such as the arrow that never seems to hit the target because it always travels half of the remaining distance. Whenever possible, visual images are linked with and used to enliven symbolic expressions. Many situations involve a search for hidden patterns and relationships in data.

The teacher attempts to determine which topics are of intrinsic value, which appear to be useful (instrumental), and which have little interest or value from the student viewpoint. The ideal goal is to provide a learning environment in which all topics are perceived as interesting, valuable, or useful to the students. (This is not easy to achieve in practice, as is described later.)

Approaching the Mathematics

The sequencing of subject matter proceeds from the more concrete to the more abstract, as seen from the viewpoint of the learner. Abstract, theoretical considerations are postponed, pending the occurrence of a good deal of concrete experience. For example, students gain facility in finding limits of many functions and combinations thereof before encountering the definition of the limit and theorems about limits.

Emphasis is placed upon the discovery of new ideas, more than upon the expression of the ideas in the most impeccable form. Professional standards of rigor are not imposed upon the beginner, and the initial development is informal in character. The need for increased precision and theoretical security becomes apparent to the students with the handling of increasingly difficult and abstract problems over the course of time. For example, the need for proofs or counterexamples becomes clear when there is genuine doubt about the truth of a conjecture. This is one of the greatest departures from more formal traditional teaching.

Skills are formed under conditions where thought is necessary. Whenever possible, the students themselves develop the techniques for solving each class of problems. The remaining practice occurs with problems that differ from one another and that require some judgment for the solutions. The skills are attained, whenever possible, by solving problems of intrinsic value for the students.

The teacher proposes problems and questions in order to guarantee that all major and essential topics are covered during the course. Within this basic framework provided by the teacher, many questions occur to the students. The investigation of student-generated questions is a frequent activity of the class members.

Emphasis is placed on learning rather than upon evaluation. The teacher can often rely on students' internal sources of motivation—such as curiosity, interest in the mathematical topics or activities, and desire to develop a sense of competence or mastery. Some teachers may choose to reduce concern about external motivators such as grades by giving the students some voice in determining grading policies—for example, the frequency, timing, and type of exams or projects.

Classroom Procedures

In this method the class is divided into small groups, usually with four members each. Each group has its own working space, preferably including a section of the chalkboard. Each group discusses mathematical ideas and solves problems cooperatively during class. In some courses, group members also prove theorems, make conjectures, and construct examples and counterexamples. The teacher moves from group to group, checking the students' work and providing assistance as needed.

To facilitate cooperative group problem solving, the teacher states a set of guidelines, such as the following:

1. Work together in groups of four.
2. *Cooperate* with other group members.
3. Achieve a group solution for each problem.
4. Make sure that everyone understands the solution before the group goes on.
5. Listen carefully to others and try, whenever possible, to build upon their ideas.
6. Share the leadership of the group.
7. Make sure that everyone participates and no one dominates.
8. Take turns writing problem solutions on the board.
9. Proceed at a pace that is comfortable for your own group.

A teacher with small groups introduces new material and poses problems and questions for discussion or investigation. This can be done orally with a class discussion at the beginning of a period or with individual groups at appropriate moments. New material can also be introduced in written form via teacher-made worksheets or special texts designed for small-group learning. There are texts in elementary algebra (Stein and Crabill, 1986), plane geometry (Chakerian, Crabill, and Stein, 1986), algebra II/trigonometry (Stein, Crabill, Chakerian, 1986), abstract algebra (Davidson and Gulick, 1976), and mathematics for elementary-education or liberal-arts majors (University of Maryland Mathematics Project, 1978; Weissglass, 1979).

In discussions with the whole class, the teacher may need to answer certain questions, serve as discussion moderator, and clarify and summarize what the students have found. An overall synthesis by the teacher is needed from time to time, since students in the groups sometimes "see the trees but lose sight of the forest."

The teacher provides guidance and support during small-group activities. The teacher observes the group interaction and solutions on the board and, in visits to particular groups, checks their solutions, gives hints, clarifies notations, makes corrections, answers some questions, provides encouragement, and helps the groups function more smoothly. It is to be hoped that the teacher behaves in a friendly and constructive manner and strikes a balance between giving too much and too little assistance.

Forming Small Groups. There are several options for forming small groups.

1. The teacher can form groups that are as heterogeneous as possible in terms of mathematical achievement, sex, and race (Slavin, 1980).
2. The teacher can form homogeneous groups based on some criteria such as mathematical achievement or aptitude. This tends to be disastrous for the very slow learners.
3. The teacher can use random assignment or some arbitrary numerical scheme to form the groups.
4. Groups can be formed on the basis of natural seating patterns in the class.
5. The teacher can administer a psychological test and use the results to form groups. For example Schutz's

(1966) FIRO-B instrument can be used to form groups of persons with mutually compatible needs for inclusion, control, and affection.

6. Students can participate in choosing their own group members. If students do not know each other at first, the groups membership can be switched daily for several class periods. In one variation of this procedure, students are helped to get acquainted by talking together in pairs for a few minutes each day. After this initial period, students then choose groups in one of two ways. In one procedure, the students stand up and form themselves into groups during class. In a second procedure, the sociometric choice method, the students write confidentially on paper the names of those people with whom they prefer to work and perhaps those they would rather avoid. The teacher then forms groups that respect these written preferences and avoidances.

Space does not permit a detailed discussion of the pros and cons of the various group-formation procedures. Generally, if greater care and attention are given to group formation, there will be better group functioning and less need to switch groups later on. There is some experimental evidence showing positive effects of mixed-ability heterogeneous grouping (Slavin, 1980; Webb, 1985), sociometric choice procedures (Stam, 1973; Grant, 1975), and random assignment (Cohen, 1986). My personal preference is the use of sociometric choice after several days of group switching and interaction exercises.

In college-level courses that meet only once or twice per week, it may be best to choose groups that remain together for the whole semester. However, in courses such as calculus, which meet every day, the groups may rotate members every few weeks.

An experienced teacher can usually work comfortably with as many as six or seven groups. In very large classes, the teacher may need an aide for help in group supervision; a more advanced student can often be an effective aide.

Pacing and Evaluation.   Some groups move more quickly than others. If all groups begin each new topic on the same day, the teacher should have some challenging extra problems ready for groups that finish early.

The small-group method can be used as a total instructional system or in combination with other methods. Groups can be used all the time, on specific days of the week, during portions of any class period, or for specific topics. I personally prefer to use small groups for most of the class time, except in a few multisection departmentalized courses taught on a rigid time schedule at breakneck pace with uniform hour exams.

A variety of grading schemes are compatible with small-group instruction. These include in-class tests and quizzes, take-home tests, group tests, group projects, homework, classwork (attendance, participation, cooperation), self-evaluation, and peer evaluation. If a teacher gives tests on a specific date, that date should realistically allow all groups to finish the material beforehand without rushing. If a teacher gives grades for classwork (attendance, participation, cooperation), he or she should *not* grade individual mathematical performance during class–doing so will foster competition and destroy group cooperation.

Classroom Practices Derived from Social Psychology

Supporting evidence and further elaboration for the previously described practices are provided by empirical studies in social psychology and group dynamics. This chapter includes a few major findings from these studies and inferences drawn from them in the design of the small-group discovery method.

White and Lippitt (1960) and Anderson (1963) found that the use of a democratic (learner-centered) style of leadership, in contrast to an autocratic or laissez-faire style, produces higher morale and satisfaction in groups. Accordingly, I recommend the use of a democratic leadership style by the teacher with the small-group discovery method. This is done as follows. The teacher provides a perspective on each day's mathematical activities in a brief discussion with the entire class. He or she spends most of the period working with the small groups, as described earlier. The teacher refrains from giving orders or disrupting commands. There is only a minimal amount of objective, constructive praise and criticism, usually directed to the work group as a whole rather than to particular individuals. The teacher offers guiding suggestions at times when they are needed and might be appreciated; these include mathematical hints and suggestions about work organization and group functioning. The teacher sometimes provides technical information upon request and stimulates self-direction by encouraging group members to think through and elaborate upon their ideas and to detect group errors. The teacher develops a friendly relationship with the students and behaves in an egalitarian manner, which might, for some teachers, include being on a reciprocal first-name basis. Finally, certain policies in the class, such as the timing of exams and the frequency of switching groups, can be arrived at through group discussion and decision making by a majority vote.

Decisions about cooperation or competition within the work groups are made on the basis of a classic study conducted by Deutsch (1960) at MIT. He found that in a cooperative situation, as compared with a competitive situation, the group members were more friendly, listened more attentively, better understood the ideas of others, and had fewer conflicts. Moreover, the productivity of the cooperative group discussion was higher in terms of the quantity and quality of ideas agreed upon for solving the problem. In accordance with these results, the mathematics teacher can promote cooperation within each work group by stating guidelines for cooperative group behavior, as given earlier. When interacting with a group, the teacher can check the group solution without asking who was responsible for it. He or she emphasizes the need for joint efforts to solve difficult problems, the importance of listening carefully and building upon the ideas of others, the fact that one person's good idea helps the entire group, and the goal of solving the problem in such a way that all members understand the group solution.

Studies have shown that conformity pressure to go along with a group can lead to the modification or distortion of individual judgment or perception (Asch, 1960). Fortunately, it is possible to reduce conformity in problem solving by developing group standards that encourage members to respect their own judgment. The teacher in a mathematics class develops such standards by emphasizing the importance of independent judgment, the legitimacy of disagreement, and the obligation of group members to give reasons to support their statements. The teacher intervenes as a mediator when students look puzzled or confused or when several group members put undue pressure on a dissenting member. The teacher emphasizes the distinction between thoughtless conformity and a change of opinion based upon a thoroughly understood argument. Moreover, he or she discourages conformity without promoting the other extreme of stubborn refusal to listen to the views of others.

A commonly held misconception is that every group must have a leader (Cartwright and Zander, 1960). In a discovery-oriented mathematics class, there is no clear case for establishing the need for a leader in each group. Therefore, the work groups operate without designated leaders. Although it is not possible to create a completely egalitarian work group in which all members have exactly the same influence, it is possible to place some limitations upon the discrepancy in power between the most active and the least active group members. No person is allowed to dominate the discussion in a manner that excludes or severely limits contributions from others. Whenever necessary, the teacher influences the dynamics of particular groups by drawing certain members into the discussion, by suggesting that different people assume primary responsibility for writing the solutions to different problems on the chalkboard, and by using other techniques to promote cooperation.

It is necessary to keep work groups small, since the opportunity for active participation decreases as the group size increases. There is some empirical evidence available concerning the effects of group size upon group interaction in nonmathematics discussions. In two-person groups there is no one to resolve differences, and either member can bring the group to a halt by disagreement or withdrawal (Bales and Borgatta, 1961). Three-person groups tend to break up into a pair and an isolated member. Four-person groups can split into two subgroups of equal size and thereby produce a protracted argument or deadlock (Bales and Borgatta, 1961; Mills, 1960). Groups with five, six, or seven members entail the possible dangers of competition, exclusion of members from the discussion, and the need for a definite leader (Slater, 1958).

The experimental evidence, combined with my classroom experience, points to the following tentative generalization: Groups of four are large enough to generate ideas for discussion and solution of challenging problems, and large enough not to be bothered by the absence of one member. Groups of four are small enough to permit active participation, to allow clustering around a chalkboard panel, and not to require a leader or elaborate organizational structure. Groups of four can also split into pairs for occasional computational practice or simple application problems.

Examples of the Leadership Style of the Teacher

In giving a perspective on each day's mathematical activities, the teacher might raise questions for investigation such as these: *What happens at a high or low point on a curve? What can you say about a function that vanishes at the endpoints of its interval of definition? Let's see if we can find a formula for the derivative of a product.* These questions set the stage for the main activity of student problem solving in groups. Just enough input is provided in class discussions so that the groups can function productively for the rest of the class period. This discussion period may be reduced if special texts or developmental worksheets are employed.

The teacher finds it easy to keep track of group progress if students write their problem solutions on the chalkboard. With experience, the teacher learns when to wait for a request for assistance and when to jump in and offer a suggestion. Often, a visit with a particular group takes a minute or less—for example, if it is necessary only to point out an arithmetic mistake, ask the reason for a step, or check a simple solution. However, on difficult proofs the groups need considerable assistance, and visits last longer. If the teacher stays too long with any one group, members of the other groups may begin calling for help.

The teacher checks the group solutions of all the *difficult* problems or theorems. In other problems, checking preferences vary. Some members always want their group's solution checked; other group members are quite confident and erase their solutions without teacher checking. When enough board space is available, some groups leave one solution up for checking while working on another problem.

Guiding suggestions of a mathematical nature are given in the form of hints, sometimes using the heuristic techniques of Polya (1965). Here are a number of examples in calculus:

1. The teacher frequently asks the students to concentrate on the given data, the desired result, and relationships between the two. This helps, for example, in the proof that differentiability implies continuity and in many proofs that involve the definition of the limit.

2. The teacher sometimes suggests use of an analogy with previous results. For example, if students have trouble deciding whether a function such as

$$f(x) = \begin{cases} 2 & \text{if } x \geq 0 \\ -2 & \text{if } x < 0 \end{cases}$$

has no limit or two limits at $x = 0$, the teacher might suggest a comparison with certain sequences such as $2, -2, 2, 2-, \ldots$, where a similar issue has previously been settled.

3. General results are sometimes formulated by considering special cases. The students can correctly conjecture the fundamental theorem of calculus after computing:

$$\int_a^b x^k dx, \qquad k = 1, 2, 3$$

This is described in more detail later in the chapter.

4. It is sometimes useful to suggest that the students discover or confirm results by drawing pictures. This is suggested, for example, in stating the mean value theorem or when students cannot remember if $\frac{d}{dx}(\sin x)$ is $\cos x$ or $-\cos x$.

5. A slight shift in notation occasionally makes a big difference in problem solving. In their first encounter with implicit differentiation, students may have great difficulty in finding $\frac{dy}{dx}$ for $x^2 + y^2 = 1$. The hint to replace y by $f(x)$ readily enables students to find $f'(x)$ if they are more used to functional notation.

6. The suggestion to guess the answer to a problem sometimes leads to some surprises. Students are usually convinced that the derivative of a product should turn out to be the product of the derivatives.

7. Sometimes, there are occasions when a hint is given only once and it does not need to be repeated for the remainder of the year. In the proof of the formula for the derivative of a product, the hint can be given to add and subtract the same term. For the rest of the year the students tend to use this technique correctly as needed.

8. It is sometimes helpful to suggest that students consider a simple instance of a general problem. This is done with $n = 2$ and $n = 3$ in guessing the formula for the derivative of a product of n functions.

The teacher sometimes offers guiding suggestions with respect to the work organization and functioning of a particular group. Students often write four or five attempted solutions all over the board, and no one can tell where one idea ends and the next begins. Many students omit key symbols—for example, writing $\sin x = \cos x$ instead of the equation

$$\frac{d}{dx} \sin x = \cos x \qquad \text{or} \qquad \int \cos x \, dx = \sin x + c.$$

This causes great confusion on complicated problems. Hence, suggestions about chalkboard technique and recording on paper are definitely needed.

The teacher provides technical information on request if the development or recall of that information is not a key part of the problem at hand. For example, a request for an approximation of the number e to five decimal places might be honored. A request to provide the formula for $\frac{d}{dx} f(x)^n$ is not honored. Other items of information, for example, an identity for $\cos 2\theta$, are provided for some problems but not others, depending on the context.

The teacher attempts to stimulate self-direction by encouraging students to look for errors in their group's solutions. Many errors are caught by the students themselves; others are detected by the teacher. There are computational errors, incorrect applications of basic formulas such as ($\frac{d}{dx} \sin 3x = \cos 3x$), errors in basic algebraic facts, logical errors of many types (circular reasoning, proving a conclusion without using the hypothesis, and so on), errors of overgeneralization ($\frac{d}{dx} e^x = x e^{x-1}$), and errors of notation (if $f(x) = x^3$, then $f'(x^3) = 3x^2$). The teacher might be surprised by the students' frequent shifts from erroneous to insightful thinking and back again.

The Interaction Between the Students and the Mathematics

This section includes a number of additional examples of student responses to the mathematics content. For simplicity, this discussion is limited to the subject matter of calculus; numerous examples could also be given from abstract algebra, foundations of geometry, topology, and the like. I have selected examples from the first-year course in calculus, which I have taught for a number of years using the small-group discovery method. On the whole, the students were successful with limited guidance in making conjectures, proving the main theorems of calculus, developing techniques for solving various classes of problems, and in coming up with problem solutions and proofs not previously known to the teacher. The students sometimes alternated between moments of brilliance and moments of ineptitude. This section begins with a number of success stories and concludes with accounts of difficulties and surprising responses to the subject matter of calculus.

Situation 1. Rolle's theorem was introduced as an openended problem for exploration by the students. The problem was stated as follows: "Let f be a function defined on $[a, b]$ such that $f(a) = f(b) = 0$. Assume that f is differentiable on the open interval, (a, b) and continuous at the endpoints. What conclusions can you draw about f?" The groups then generated a collection of conjectures involving the existence of a positive maximum or a negative minimum under certain conditions—numbers of zeros of the functions, existence of inflection points, and so on. They also correctly stated Rolle's theorem: There is a point c in (a, b) such that $f'(c) = 0$. However, they were disappointed to find this result labeled as a theorem. "You mean the least interesting theorem is the one with the name?"

Situation 2. The mean value theorem was introduced with the following question. "Let f be defined on (a, b) satisfying the hypotheses of Rolle's theorem, but remove the restriction that $f(a) = f(b) = 0$. What conclusions can you draw about f?" When the students had difficulty formulating a conclusion, the hint was given to draw a picture and to state the conclusion of Rolle's theorem in geometrical language. After stating that the tangent line at some point was parallel to the x-axis (in Rolle's theorem), a student in each group made the appropriate analogy and stated that the tangent line at some point was parallel to the chord line joining the endpoints of the curve.

After the groups expressed their conclusions as mathematical statements involving a derivative, the hint was given to begin the proof by constructing a new function that satisfied the conditions of Rolle's theorem. Within a few minutes, someone in each group set $h(x) = f(x) - g(x)$, where $y = g(x)$ was the equation of the line joining the endpoints $(a, f(a))$ and $(b, f(b))$. Until this time, matters had progressed roughly in accordance with the expectations of the teacher. However, each group then made the following argument: By construction, $h(a) = h(b) = 0$. By Rolle's theorem, there is a point c in (a, b) such that $h'(c) = 0$. Then $f'(c) = g'(c)$, and $g'(c)$ is just the slope of the chord line, namely, $[f(b) - f(a)]/(b - a)$.

Much to my surprise, the groups had completed the proof without any of the usual complications involving the equation of the line $y = g(x)$. Their proofs were more clear and comprehensible than the one found in many calculus books.

Situation 3. *Exploration:* Let f be a continuous positive function on $[a, b]$. How can you find the area under the curve (that is, the area between the graph of f and the x-axis from a to b)?

Students came up with a variety of approaches for finding the area. In one group, three members wanted to compute the area under a curve by making approximation with the areas of rectangles. The fourth member insisted that it was better to use little squares (as in the double integral). The argument went on rather intensely for a few minutes. I then intervened and attempted to lower the tension level by pointing out that both sides were right but in different ways. The majority was right, as shown by several previous problems, in claiming that it was computationally easier to use rectangles than to use little squares. The fourth member was right in claiming that the use of little squares theoretically gave the same answer as the use of rectangles. This illustrated that there may be more than one right way to solve a problem.

In other groups, there were heated arguments about the merits of approximating the area by rectangles underneath the curve, rectangles above the curve, and trapezoids. These were resolved by some computational problems showing that all techniques gave the same answer for the limit, but that it was computationally easier to use rectangles than trapezoids. Upper and lower sums were defined after students had computed the same answers for all the techniques with simple functions.

Situation 4. The following exploration was given as a preliminary step in computing integrals of simple polynomials: Find formulas for the sum of the first n even integers, the sum of the first n integers, and the sum of the first n integers cubed.

The following chart helped guide the students' work:

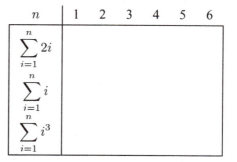

n	1	2	3	4	5	6
$\sum_{i=1}^{n} 2i$						
$\sum_{i=1}^{n} i$						
$\sum_{i=1}^{n} i^3$						

The hint was given to fill in the sums for the indicated values of n, to look for patterns, and to do the problems in the order stated. All groups successfully conjectured the results.

$$\sum_{i=1}^{n} 2i = n(n+1)$$

$$\sum_{i=1}^{n} i = \frac{n(n+1)}{2}$$

$$\sum_{i=1}^{n} i^3 = \left[\frac{n(n+1)}{2}\right]^2$$

By using summation formulas, the students correctly computed

$$\int_0^b x\,dx = \frac{b^2}{2}$$

$$\int_0^b x^2\,dx = \frac{b^3}{3}$$

$$\int_0^b x^3\,dx = \frac{b^4}{4}$$

They then easily extended these results to an interval $[a, b]$ with $0 \le a < b$, obtaining

$$\int_a^b x\,dx = \frac{b^2}{2} - \frac{a^2}{2},$$

and so on.

They noticed that each expression for the result of the first, second, or third integral, if it were rewritten with x instead of b, would be a function whose derivative is the integrand. In response, I then suggested for the first problem,

$$\int_0^b x\,dx = \frac{b^2}{2}$$

that they use the name $F(x) = \frac{x^2}{2}$. They picked up this suggestion for all the problems, and then conjectured that

$$\int_a^b f(x)dx = F(b) - F(a), \quad \text{where } F'(x) = f(x).$$

They were amazed when I labeled this result (with appropriate hypotheses) as the fundamental theorem of calculus.

Observations.   For certain problems students found a variety of possible paths to the solution. For example, in evaluating

$$\int x\sqrt{1 - x^2}\,dx$$

the four members of one group suggested the following correct approaches:

    a. Let $x = \sin\theta$.

    b. Let $x = \cos\theta$.

    c. Let $u = 1 - x^2$.

    d. Write the answer by inspection.

The group members argued about which approach to take, without reaching agreement. I then commented as follows: "Let's agree to just pick one approach to start the problem. Then, whether it works or not, you can still try out those other ideas afterward. It might be interesting to see how many different ways you can solve the problem." The students then went on to solve the problem correctly using each of the four approaches in turn.

In evaluating $\int \tan x \sec^2 x\,dx$, two students obtained different correct answers, namely, $\frac{1}{2}\sec^2 x + c$ and $\frac{1}{2}\tan^2 x + c$. Each student insisted that he was right and the other student was wrong. I then asked, "Is there any possibility that you're both right? Could the answers be equivalent?" The students then established the equivalence by using the identity $1 + \tan^2 x = \sec^2 x$.

Misconceptions, Difficulties, and Surprises

Through daily conversations with the students and daily observations of their work, I learned much about the student reactions to the subject matter. In addition to many strikingly successful experiences, there were also many misconceptions, difficulties, and surprising responses to the subject matter. If I hadn't seen the students working and heard their arguments, I would not have known these things; they don't normally surface in expository instruction.

The students frequently did not test incorrect identities or formulas by using specific instances of them. Examples of this included the incorrect formulas $1 + \sec^2\theta = \tan^2\theta$, $\cos(x + y) = \cos x \cos y - \sin x \sin y$, and $\frac{d}{dx}\sec x = \tan^2 x$. Each time the students wrote down such incorrect identities, I asked if there was any easy way to test the truth of their statements. It was usually necessary to suggest that the students try their statement with a particular value of x.

The students were not used to thinking in terms of definitions, and they tended to forget the definitions of the limit, the definite integral, and continuity. However, the definition of the derivative fared somewhat better than the others, perhaps because it was a simple formula that was frequently used. I often reminded students to write an appropriate definition and use it to approach a problem.

There was a noticeable tendency for the students to treat all problems as separate entities that were not related to one another. For instance, the groups first evaluated

$$\int \frac{dx}{a^2 + x^2}$$

by means of the substitution of $x = a\tan\theta$. Instead of using this result, the groups then evaluated

$$\int \frac{dx}{9 + x^2}$$

by the substitution $x = 3 \tan \theta$. Although some repetition can be a useful aid in learning up to a certain point, I often had to remind people to use the result of one problem in order to solve another one.

In working with derivatives of composite functions, most students did not perceive the need for applying the chain rule in new situations. Although the student groups correctly developed the formula for the derivative of each major new function, they then made erroneous statements such as

$$\frac{d}{dx} \sin 2x = \cos 2x, \quad \frac{d}{dx} e^{3x} = e^{3x}, \quad \frac{d}{dx} \ln 4x = \frac{1}{4x}.$$

In each instance it was necessary to remind students that they were dealing with a composite function.

In problems that could be solved in several different ways, the students often preferred to use the technique they learned first. For example, the technique of integration by trig substitution was first introduced by the problem of computing the area of a circle. In order to evaluate

$$\int_{-r}^{r} \sqrt{r^2 - x^2} \, dx$$

the groups used polar coordinates and set $x = r \cos \theta$. Then, in many other integrals involving the expression $r^2 - x^2$, the students always used the substitution $x = r \cos \theta$ rather than the more standard substitution $x = r \sin \theta$. Several students said that $x = r \sin \theta$ would work but that they liked their first approach better.

The students' intuitive notions about sequences were surprising to me. Almost all the students believed initially that the listing $1, 1, 1, 1, \ldots$ did not describe a sequence, since the nth term did not change and was not specified by a formula involving n. After resolving this issue, almost all students stated that the sequence $1, 1, 1, 1, \ldots$ did not have a limit, since "it's not getting close to any number; it's there already." A similar response occurred with constant functions.

Most students stated that the sequence $0, 2, 0, 2, 0, 2, \ldots$ converged to two different limits and were upset when I said that the sequence had no limit. Their discomfort was alleviated somewhat when I introduced the notion of a subsequence.

In trying to solve problems or write proofs using the formal ϵ-δ definition of the limit of a sequence or a function, the students encountered great conceptual and technical difficulties. Comments from several students indicated that they did not perceive the statement as a reasonable definition. "If that's a definition, it's the weirdest one I've seen in my entire life." Moreover, most students did not find the proofs of limit theorems to be useful. "There's no reason to prove a theorem unless there is some doubt about the result, and I never had any doubt about the sum of the

limits being the same as the limit of the sum." Many students were not convinced by proofs of the limit theorems. "That proof is nothing but a bunch of equivalent statements with complicated notation. It doesn't prove anything to me." These attitudes and difficulties were not caused by lack of prior concrete experience; the students had spent several weeks working with a variety of sequences before encountering the formal definition of the limit.

The student concept of a function seemed to include several basic but unstated assumptions. Students invariably drew the graph of a function as a smooth curve with a small number of relative maxima or minima. A student said, and others agreed, that "there are only three possibilities at an endpoint of an interval. Either the curve comes in level or it comes in from below or from above." It appeared that student's concepts of a function on a closed interval actually meant a continuous, differentiable function with finitely many maxima and minima. Students viewed as "very peculiar" certain functions with infinitely many oscillations in their graphs, such as

$$f(x) = \begin{cases} x \sin \frac{1}{x} & \text{if } x \neq 0 \\ 0 & \text{if } x = 0 \end{cases}$$

Most students felt that there was something unnatural or artificial about functions with discontinuities. As they put it, these functions were "made up" by moving points out of their proper locations, by adding points that did not belong in the domain, or by putting in artificial steps.

The students seemed to think at times that all functions were differentiable. For example, for the function $f(x) = |x|$, the students stated that they were going to find $f'(0)$. When the right-hand and left-hand limits of the difference quotients turned out to be different, most students thought that they had made an arithmetic mistake somewhere. They found it hard to reconcile their belief with their correct computational result.

Many students made a distinction between theory and problems. As one student put it, "Calculus should be 25 percent theory and 75 percent problems." The distinction between theory and problems seemed to depend largely on the presence or absence of arbitrary functions. Although most students preferred problems over theory, they sometimes distinguished between useless theory and useful theory. Useless theory consisted of propositions intended to "prove the obvious" or "straighten out things we already know." Most students deemed as useless the definition of the limit and the development of the natural logarithm as an integral. Useful theory consisted of general propositions that had applications to interesting problems with specific functions. Many students accepted as useful theory the proof of the fundamental theorem of calculus and the development of the formula for the volume of a surface of a revolution.

In summary, the close contact with the students in the groups helped me gain much insight into the student perceptions of the calculus content. The difficulties that occurred should not obscure the success of the student groups in proving the major theorems of calculus, in developing techniques for solving classes of problems, in stating some insightful conjectures, and in coming up with problem solutions and proofs not previously known to me.

Evaluation of the Method

In studies of student achievement by Davidson (1971), Loomer (1976), and Brechting and Hirsch (1977), the experimental treatment was the small-group discovery method or a variation upon it, and the control treatment was the lecture-discussion method in calculus. Davidson and Urion (n.d.) compared these same types of experimental and control treatments in half a dozen courses ranging from general mathematics in junior high school through differential equations at the college level. In most comparisons there was no statistically significant difference in student achievement; when significant differences did occasionally occur, they favored the small-group treatment. Hence, it is safe to say that students taught by the small-group discovery method have performed at least as well as those taught by more traditional lecture-discussion procedures.

Over a number of years I have given attitude surveys to students and teachers involved with the small-group discovery method. The main problem areas reported most frequently by teachers and students include concerns about covering enough material, initial difficulties in forming effective groups, barriers to fostering cooperation among students, occasional conflict or frustration with overly difficult mathematical problems, and providing high-quality instructional materials. Although student attitudes toward the method of instruction are generally favorable, the degree to which they are favorable depends upon the teacher's experience and skill in handling the problem areas just described.

There are many advantages to learning mathematics in cooperative groups. The following positive points are frequently mentioned by teachers and students responding to attitude surveys. Students learn mathematics by working actively at a comfortable pace. They learn to cooperate with others and to communicate in the language of mathematics. The classroom atmosphere tends to be relaxed and informal, help is readily available, questions are freely asked and answered, and even the shy student finds it easy to be involved. Students tend to become friends with their group members, and the teacher-student relationship tends to be more relaxed, more pleasant, and closer than in a traditional approach. The usual "discipline" problems of talking and moving around are eliminated by definition. In addition, many students maintain a high level of interest in the mathematical activities. Many students like math more—or at least hate it less—than in teacher-centered approaches. Finally, students have an opportunity to pursue the more challenging and creative aspects of mathematics while they achieve at least as much information and skill as in more traditional approaches.

Attitudes of several students can be conveyed vividly by quoting their responses from a questionnaire given in a successful calculus class: (1) "Other students, no matter who, force you to learn more." (2) "Most classes stress being able to use formulas while this stresses total understanding." (3) "It is my most interesting and liked class. I enjoy coming to it." (4) "I think I learned a lot more this year than in all three years of high school math." (5) "It showed me that I can do things that before looked impossible. All it takes is a little understanding. Math doesn't scare me as much now." (6) "I simply feel it was a great experiment (and experience) and more subjects should be adapted to this general method." (7) "This type of class was, in my estimation, the closest possible setup to an ideal learning situation."

References

Anderson, R.C. 1963. Learning in discussions: A Résumé, of the Authoritarian-Democratic Studies. In *Readings in the social psychology of education,* edited by W.W. Charters and N.L. Gage. Boston: Allyn & Bacon.

Asch, S.E. 1960. Effects of group pressure upon the modification and distortion of judgments. In *Group dynamics: Research and theory,* edited by D. Cartwright and A. Zander. 2d ed. New York: Harper & Row.

Bales, R.F., and E.F. Borgatta. 1961. Size of group as a factor in the interaction profile. In *Small groups, studies in social interaction,* edited by A.P. Hare, E.F. Borgatta, and R.F. Bales. New York: Alfred A. Knopf.

Brechting, Sister M.C., and C.R. Hirsch. 1977. The effects of small-group discovery learning on student achievement and attitudes in calculus. *MATYC Journal* (2): 77–82.

Cartwright, D., and A. Zander. 1960. *Group dynamics: Research and theory,* 2d ed. New York: Harper & Row.

Chakerian, G.D., C.D. Crabill, and S.K. Stein. 1986 *Geometry: A guided inquiry.* Pleasantville, NY: Sunburst.

Cohen, E.G. 1986. *Designing groupwork: Strategies for the heterogeneous classroom.* New York: Teachers College Press.

Davidson, N. 1971. *The small-group discovery method of mathematics instruction as applied in calculus.* Ph.D. diss., University of Wisconsin, 1970. Technical Report No. 168, Wisconsin Research and Development Center for Cognitive Learning, Madison, Wisconsin.

———. 1971. The small-group discovery method as applied in calculus instruction. *American Mathematical Monthly* (August-September): 789–91.

——. 1976. Motivation of students in small-group learning of mathematics. *Frostburg State College Journal of Mathematics Education* (11): 1–18.

——. 1979. The small-group discovery method: 1967–77. In *Problem solving studies in mathematics,* edited by J. Harvey and T. Romberg. The Wisconsin Research and Development Center for Individualized Schooling, University of Wisconsin, Madison.

——. 1985. Small-group learning and teaching in mathematics: A selective review of the research. In *Learning to cooperate, cooperating to learn,* edited by R. Slavin. New York: Plenum Press.

Davidson, N., L. Agreen, and C. Davis. 1978. Small-group learning in junior high school mathematics. *School Science and Mathematics* (January): 23–30.

Davidson, N., and F. Gulick. 1976. *Abstract algebra: An active learning approach.* Boston: Houghton Mifflin.

Davidson, N., R. McKeen, and T. Eisenberg. 1973. Curriculum construction with student input. *The Mathematics Teacher* (March): 271–75.

Davidson, N. and D. Urion, n.d. "Some results on student achievement in small-group instruction versus teacher-centered instruction in mathematics." (In press.)

Deutsch, M. 1960. The effects of cooperation and competition upon group process. In *Group dynamics: Research and theory,* 2d ed., edited by D. Cartwright and A. Zander.

Dewey, J. 1916. *Democracy and education.* New York: Macmillan. (Republished: Collier Books Paperback Edition, New York, 1966.)

——. 1938. *Experience and education.* New York: Kappa Delta Pi. (Republished: Collier Books Paperback Edition, New York, 1963.)

Gallicchio, A. 1976. The effects of brainstorming in small group mathematics classes. Ph.D. diss., University of Maryland, College Park.

Grant, S. 1975. The effects of three kinds of group formation using FIRO-B compatibility, sociometric choice with group dynamics exercises, and in-class choice on mathematics classes taught by the small-group discovery method. Ph.D. diss., University of Maryland, College Park.

Klingbeil, D. 1974. An examination of the effects of group testing in mathematics courses taught by the small-group discovery method. Ph.D. diss., University of Maryland, College Park.

Loomer, N.J. 1976. A multidimensional exploratory investigation of small-group heuristic and expository learning in calculus. Ph.D. diss., University of Wisconsin, Madison.

McKeen, R., and N. Davidson. 1975. An alternative to individual instruction in mathematics. *American Mathematical Monthly* (December): 1006–9.

Mills, T.M. 1960. Power relations in three-person groups. In *Group dynamics: Research and theory,* 2d ed., edited by D. Cartwright and A. Zander. New York: Harper & Row.

Moise, E.E. 1965. Activity and motivation in mathematics. *American Mathematical Monthly* 72 (4): 407–12.

Polya, G. 1965. *Mathematical Discovery,* Vol. 2. New York: John Wiley.

Schutz, W.C. 1966. *The interpersonal underworld.* Palo Alto, Calif.: Science and Behavioral Books.

Slater, P.E. 1958. Contrasting correlates of group size. *Sociometry* 21 (2): 129–39.

Slavin, R.E. 1980. Cooperative learning. *Review of Educational Research.* 50: 315–42.

Stam, P.J. 1973. The effect of sociometric grouping on task performance in the elementary classroom. Ph.D. diss., Stanford University.

Stein, S.K., and C.D. Crabill. 1986. *Elementary algebra: A guided inquiry.* Pleasantville, N.Y.: Sunburst.

Stein, S.K., C.D. Crabill, and G.D. Chakerian. 1986. *Algebra II/Trigonometry: A guided inquiry.* Pleasantville, N.Y.: Sunburst.

Thoyre, H. 1970. A pilot study on the use of small-group discussion in a mathematics course for preservice elementary teachers. Ph.D. diss., University of Wisconsin, Madison.

University of Maryland Mathematics Project (M. Cole, N. Davidson, J. Fey, J. Henkelman et al). 1978. *Unifying concepts and processes in elementary mathematics.* Boston: Allyn & Bacon.

Webb, N.M. 1985. Verbal interaction and learning in peer-directed groups. *Theory into Practice,* Vol. 24, 32–39.

Weissglass, J. 1976. Small groups: An alternative to the lecture method. *The Two-Year College Mathematics Journal* VII (February): 15–20.

——. 1977. Mathematics for elementary teaching: A small-group laboratory approach. *American Mathematical Monthly* (May): 377–82.

——. 1979. *Exploring elementary mathematics: A small-group approach for teaching.* San Francisco: W. H. Freeman.

White, R., and R. Lippitt. 1960. Leader behavior and member reaction in three "Social Climates." In *Group dynamics: Research and theory,* edited by D. Cartwright and A. Zander. New York: Harper & Row.

Comments on the article by Dubinsky and Schwingendorf

Our beliefs about how people learn influence the choices we make as teachers. Before beginning to read this article, *reflect on your own beliefs*: What does it mean for someone to *know* mathematics? What implications does this have for *learning* mathematics?

In this article, cooperative learning is presented as one of several components in the classroom/laboratory setting for a calculus course. Students working in a technologically-rich environment use computers to construct mathematical functions and, as a result (according to the authors) simultaneously construct mathematical ideas in their minds. In the computer laboratory, students work in small groups, discussing and explaining ideas to each other. The computers provide a context in which students *experiment* with various mathematical expressions and receive immediate feedback regarding how the expression is interpreted by the computer. Perhaps because the computer is more consistent and rigid than the (human) instructor, the students are directly challenged to adapt their mental images to fit the computer's feedback.

Working in small groups provides students a (humanly) supportive network of persons— peers engaged in learning the same concepts—with whom to reflect on and discuss the problems they are trying to solve. Not only is the small group process supportive of learning mathematics, the experience of working in groups is valuable preparation for life beyond the mathematics classroom as well.

This article provides a specific extended example of a particular pedagogical strategy applied within a college-level calculus course in the spirit of the framework described in the paper by Asiala et al. It discusses the performance of students in this course in relation to students in parallel sections of the same course at the same university.

Discussion Questions

1. What are your own beliefs about how people learn mathematics? How has this shaped the way you teach?
2. Think about your own experiences as a learner. What have been effective elements in your own learning environment? What structures, activities, strategies have helped you to learn new concepts?
3. How can (how does) technology affect the learning environment? How can you as a teacher set up the classroom/laboratory so that computers are used to enhance thinking and problem-solving activities among students?

Constructing Calculus Concepts: Cooperation in a Computer Laboratory[†]

Ed Dubinsky
and
Keith Schwingendorf

Although an important part of any mathematical endeavor is individual thinking, the construction of mathematical ideas does not really flourish in solitude. From the superstar research mathematicians who invariably take off from the results of others ("stand on the shoulders of giants" in the words of Isaac Newton) and feel a deep seated need to communicate (i.e., publish) their results, to the struggling students who take comfort in the realization that mathematics is just as challenging for everyone else as it is for them, there is every indication that mathematics is a social activity.

We believe that mathematical knowledge, in education as well as research, grows as a result of people constructing their own mathematical concepts and synthesizing their individual thoughts with the ideas of others. We will try to show in this paper how a computer laboratory can be a very good teaching environment in which to get students constructing mathematical ideas by working together as a team.

Our work is based on a developing theory of learning so we begin with a sketch of this theory. We consider its relation to other points of view and give an indication of the role of computer labs in fostering the construction and cooperation that this theory calls for. In Section 2 we go into some detail on the particular programming language we use in our laboratory and give some examples of how it can help get students to make mental constructions appropriate for learning mathematics. In Section 3 we describe our particular laboratory environment and all of the nuts and bolts that go into this particular implementation of our approach to helping students learn calculus. In Section 4 we consider one major mathematical topic—the Fundamental Theorem of Calculus—and give a full explanation of our treatment, including some indication of its effectiveness. Finally we offer some overall evaluations of our approach from various sources.

1. Theoretical basis for construction and cooperation in computer labs

Construction. We start with the observation that how you teach is determined by what you believe about how people learn and about the nature of the subject you would like to help your students learn. We are convinced that the ineffectiveness of mathematics education at all levels is largely due to the teaching methods chosen by mathematics fac-

[†] L. Carl Leinbach et al. (eds.), *The Laboratory Approach to Teaching Calculus,* Washington, DC: MAA, 1991, pp. 47–70.

ulty based on traditional beliefs about learning and about mathematics.

We reject these beliefs and the choices they imply, and we propose below alternatives based on a constructivist[1] theory of knowledge and its development in an individual. It turns out that it is possible to design instruction in mathematics that is consistent with our theories and the beliefs to which they lead us. Moreover, our experience has been that a computer lab can be used to implement such instructional treatments, and the results in terms of student learning can be refreshingly positive.

Our description, in the following pages, of our theoretical analysis and the corresponding instructional treatments is necessarily brief. A more complete discussion, together with references to the literature that reports on our results, is given in [6,7,8].

Beliefs and choices—what we reject

We reject the idea that people learn mathematics spontaneously by listening or watching while it is being presented. We do not feel that mathematics is learned effectively by working with many examples and trying to extract their essential features. Nor do we believe that having students solve problems in other fields is the only way to motivate them to study mathematics.

Regarding the nature of mathematics in general or Calculus in particular, we do not believe that it is a body of knowledge existing outside ourselves and waiting to be discovered. Moreover, we insist that mathematics is more than a collection of techniques for solving standard problems or for solving "real-world problems."

Because of these beliefs, we do not choose a teaching methodology that is restricted to giving lectures, showing applications, having students work on set problems, and testing their performance on examinations.

Admittedly, these rejections are sharply at variance with "conventional wisdom" but, after all, we are in a situation in which conventional methods (of teaching mathematics) do not appear to work. Perhaps it is time to reconsider our basic beliefs about the nature of mathematics and how it is learned.

Our beliefs and choices—what is mathematical knowledge

We believe that mathematics is a set of ideas created by individual and collective thought over many hundreds of

years. But its nature is dynamic, not static. Mathematical knowledge is not something you *have* but rather something you (might) *do*. Let us offer a definition as a basis for discussion.

A person's mathematical knowledge is her or his tendency to respond to certain kinds of perceived problem situations by constructing, reconstructing and organizing mental processes and objects to use in dealing with the situations.

This is a very general statement that might apply to many disciplines, but when we consider some of the details of the responses we are talking about, it will become clear how our definition applies to mathematics.

All of us who teach are familiar with the distinction between the problem which the teacher sets before the student and the student's perception of that problem. We have every opportunity to make the situation as clear as we can, but eventually the time comes when the student decides what he or she thinks the problem is and it is that perception that determines the student's response. We might think, for example, that the "problem" is to understand that the derivative of a particular function is a useful linear approximation to it near a point. But our students will often conclude that the "problem" is to find a formula for the derivative of that function. It is not very easy to get them to revise their interpretations so it is very important to be concerned with how our students initially perceive the problems we set before them.

Another familiar experience is the inconsistency of mathematical understanding within a single person. Like the athlete, the mathematics student is sometimes able to function at a very high level of sophistication, but on other days, with similar or even identical problems, he or she is much less successful. Thus mathematical understanding is not about what a person is surely able to accomplish, but what he or she has a tendency to do.

In connection with this, we can think of a person faced with a problem situation, not as bringing forth immutable pieces of mathematical knowledge, but rather as reconstructing what he or she has previously constructed in order to deal with the present situation. It is this reconstruction which is at the root of this inconsistency. Sometimes it produces tools that are less powerful than those which the person has previously used. On other occasions, stimulated by the special difficulty of the actual problem, it can produce something that is more powerful, more sophisticated and more effective. In the latter case, we can say that growth of the person's mathematical knowledge has taken place.

If what we are saying has any relation at all to what really goes on with students, then it has some very disturbing implications for testing, indeed for our overall system

---

[1] We refer here to the epistemological constructivism of J. Piaget and not the mathematical constructivism of L.E.J. Brouwer. See [13] for an introduction to the former and its distinction from the latter.

of evaluation. If inconsistency is a normal aspect of a person's intellectual performance, if it is actually an important part of intellectual growth, then it is not clear what is being measured by an examination which is a one-shot, do or die situation. If we decide that learning mathematics is both constructive and cooperative, then in addition to rethinking how we teach, we must also reconsider the means by which we evaluate the results of that teaching.

Our beliefs and choices—what is learning mathematics and how computer labs can help

The part of our definition that has to do specifically with learning mathematics is the construction and reconstruction of mental processes and objects. It is in this area that we can become specific to mathematics, and it is here that we encounter the mental activities that are so amenable to group work in a computer laboratory.

Roughly speaking, processes are built up out of actions on objects and ultimately converted into new objects which are used for new actions that are converted into new processes and so on, as a person's mathematical knowledge spirals up to higher and higher levels of sophistication. Let's look at some details.

Numbers are *objects*. *Actions* such as arithmetic calculations can be performed on them. When an action such as adding three to a number is repeated with different numbers, there is a tendency to become aware of and *interiorize* this action into a *process*, $x + 3$. This leads to algebra. Processes can also be constructed by composing two processes, say adding three and squaring, which gives $(x + 3)^2$, or by reversing a given process, say adding three, to obtain the process of subtracting three or $x - 3$. A single process such as adding 3 can be *encapsulated* to become an object, in this case, the expression $x + 3$. Now the standard algebraic manipulations with expressions can be seen as actions on these new objects. Figure 1 is a schematic display of these different kinds of constructions.

Here we can introduce a major connection between our use of the computer and this theoretical analysis. It turns out that each of these mental steps: actions on objects, interiorization of actions into processes, composing processes, inverting processes and encapsulating processes into objects can be represented in terms of computer tasks. Moreover, when students are set to performing these tasks, we believe that they tend to perform the corresponding mental activities and begin making constructions. This is our basic justification for using a lab in connection with calculus instruction.

Of course the computer tasks that are reasonable to perform depend on the particular computer system and how it is used. For example, the mathematical notation $(x + 3)^2$

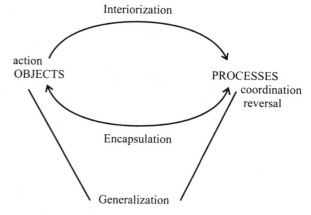

FIGURE 1
Construction of objects and processes

can represent two kinds or mental constructions. One is the process obtained by composing the "add 3" process with the "square" process. The other construction is the object obtained by squaring the object $x + 3$. Both representations are important, although the former carries greater mathematical content, whereas the latter is more formal and can lead to performing manipulations quickly and efficiently, but perhaps without much understanding of their content.

In any case, there are computer systems appropriate to either interpretation. Computer Algebra Systems emphasize the object view of expressions like $(x + 3)^2$. On the other hand, having students write procedures that implement the functions given by such expressions emphasizes the nature of a function as a process.

There are, of course, much more mathematically sophisticated situations. In Calculus, most of the examples in which mathematical concepts are interpreted in terms of objects and processes have to do with functions. The input/output point of view treats a function as a process, as does the interpretation that points on a graph come from evaluating the function at the x-coordinate and taking the answer for the y-coordinate. Lab work that has students implementing functions by writing computer procedures tends to get the students interiorizing the processes of those functions.

On the other hand, considering differentiation as an operation that transforms one function into another, thinking about iterating the composition of a function with itself, or seeing that the solution of a differential equation must be a whole function (rather than a number or even a structured collection of numbers) requires the interpretation of a function as an object.

In order to model such an interpretation, a computer language should treat functions as what computer scientists call *first-class objects*. This means that functions are data like numbers and can be operated on, collected together in sets or sequences, accepted as inputs to other functions and can be the resulting object output by the execution of a procedure. Research [14] suggests that one way of helping students construct mathematical objects in their minds is to let them perform operations on what is to become an object.

Sometimes it is necessary to conceptualize a function simultaneously as a process and as an object. To understand the notation $f'(3)$, for example, requires the idea of transforming a function to its derivative (object) and evaluating at 3 (process). We suggest that this can only happen if the object conception of the function was constructed by encapsulating the process conception corresponding to evaluation. In this case, the subject is able to go back and forth between the two interpretations. Thus the computer language should not only allow functions as processes (procedures) and functions as objects (first-class objects), but also its syntax should allow easy passage between the two interpretations.

Functions are not the only context in which this theory operates. Mathematical induction is an important tool in Calculus which is often (wrongly) assumed to be well understood by the students. Predicate Calculus is critical for understanding the ϵ-δ formulation of the limit, and it seems likely that the difficulty students have with limits and related concepts is at least partly due to their poor comprehension of quantification. For details about these and other relations between the theory described here and various mathematical topics, we refer to [4,5,6,7,8,9,11].

Other ways computer labs help mental construction

In addition to the specific construction of mental objects and processes, several other mental constructions can be specifically benefitted by a calculus laboratory. One is the issue of *generalization*. It is important to distinguish between generalization and reconstruction. Both involve using previous mental schemas to deal with new situations. In the case of generalization the schema that is used in the new situation is completely unchanged. This works sometimes, but it often leads to trouble.

Mathematics education abounds with examples of false generalization. Looking a little bit at computational understanding that precedes Calculus, consider the "classic" error of writing

$$\sqrt{x + y} = \sqrt{x} + \sqrt{y}$$

This is not a random mistake. A student who thinks this relation holds may have a strong schema for the distributive rule. So strong that it is applied whether or not it is

appropriate. A similar example is the error of thinking that the derivative of $\sin^2 x$ is $2\sin x$. This could come from a misguided application of the power rule.

Reconstruction on the other hand, involves taking a rule, or schema apart to see what makes it tick and putting it together in the new situation—not just to get an answer, but to make some kind of sense. When the schema is related to something which the student has constructed on a computer, such as a procedure, it is more concrete and there a greater possibility that the action, being explicit for the student, can change.

Returning to the general definition of mathematical knowledge, we note our assertion that a person constructs mathematics in order to deal with perceived problem situations. This means that the student must know what the problems are. One important use of a computer laboratory is to give students experience with a number of problem situations. Even when students have not yet developed the mathematics necessary to solve these problems, computer tools can help them to see clearly what the problem is. Often, for example in the case of approximating derivatives at a point or areas under a curve, the computer will allow students to work with a problem and even get a "solution" that might be a satisfactory approximation. Then the mathematics becomes a methodology for organizing and formalizing activities which are already in the students' mental repertoires. This can provide a motivating factor that we suggest is at least as important as the fascination we are all supposed to have with "real world" problems.

Finally, we can mention the issue of timing. The mental constructions that a person makes in learning mathematics amount to building new knowledge based on knowledge that already exists for her or him. There must be objects for processes to transform and processes to encapsulate into objects. Whatever takes place in the classroom, it will not be successful if it is based on incorrect assumptions about what mathematical entities are present in a student's mind. Another purpose of a computer laboratory is to give all students a chance to get in their minds the phenomena that subsequent mathematical discussion will help them explain and understand.

Cooperation

Cooperation as a basis for introducing a laboratory aspect into a Calculus course is, at least for us, a relatively new idea. Indeed our original design did not emphasize group work. It has grown with us as we have become experienced with having our students work in small groups, and as we have come to understand the benefits of this kind of approach. We consider three aspects of cooperation in a laboratory environment: reflection, support systems, and "preparation for life."

Reflection.   In the previous section we considered mental activities such as interiorization, encapsulation, coordination, and reversal, and indicated in a general way how the use of computer activities can get students performing these mental activities so as to make appropriate constructions. There is another ingredient that is essential in order to interiorize an action to a process or encapsulate a process to an object. That is reflection. According to constructivist theory, both interiorization and encapsulation arise, at least in part, as a result of conscious reflection on the problem situation and methods of dealing with the problem—both successful and unsuccessful.

One way to heighten your awareness of what you are doing, for example when making calculations, is to explain it or teach it. Some of the computer tasks we have students perform are by way of "teaching their actions to a computer," by writing programs.

Another way of getting students to be aware of mathematical relationships is to have them explain them to each other in a group. In addition to establishing formal teams and allowing group submission of assignments, we have tried to set up our labs so that students are encouraged to work together and talk to each other.

A lab can have an atmosphere in which as soon as one student figures something out it spreads throughout the group and then throughout the entire class. It is of course true that sometimes what spreads is more of a "how to" than an understanding. Nevertheless, whenever a student is forced to make an explanation to someone else the act of explanation carries with it a modicum of intellectual growth.

A computer lab allows us to give large assignments with many parts and encourages students to divide the work. Often, the parts are similar enough so that no one loses any value by not doing all of them. Moreover, the collection of several parts can lead to a group result that is not feasible for a single student to achieve. The only thing that is really lost is the repetition.

On another plane, we use the computer lab to enhance the learning of students after they have taken our course (or even other courses). Some of our students become lab assistants who play an essential role in helping new students with minor technical details. With our encouragement, however, the role of the undergraduate lab assistants is expanded to include the role of explaining mathematical ideas to students who may be no more than half a year younger than themselves. This form of cooperation leads to mathematical awareness and reflection, and hence the construction of mathematical concepts, on the part of the lab assistant.

Support systems.   Recent research [15] and development projects [3] suggest that students will do much better in mathematics if they have the right kind of human support system. This is not only important for developing self confidence and helping a student deal with the many kinds of frustration that are endemic to doing mathematics. It is also the case that working with a group can help one form and reinforce effective study habits. Many young people need little more in the way of support than acknowledgment from their peers that working hard, studying and doing well in school are reasonable ways to live one's life. Others need more specific assistance such as models for allotment of time and organization of work. In general, most students will do better in mathematics (and other intellectual activities) if they find themselves in an environment where a positive attitude towards studying mathematics is not only accepted but is an admired mode of behavior.

What does all that have to with a lab? Not much more than that a lab can become a place where an atmosphere such as we have been describing is developed and nurtured.

Preparation for life.   Finally we offer a simple observation about how mathematics is done and used in "real life": that is, in the workplace. Although we remain convinced that not even research in mathematics at the highest levels is a solitary activity, this point is arguable. But for the kind of relationship to mathematics that most of our students will have after they leave school and work in industry or education or government, there is little question that doing mathematics is a team sport in the workplace.

The first thing anyone should think of doing when stuck is to ask a co-worker. This is not always easy to do nor is it easy to respond to. The questioner needs to learn how to formulate questions. The respondent needs to know how to share information, to answer the question that was asked and not the question one thinks should be asked, or to point out that the wrong question has been asked. All of these are skills that can be learned through teamwork in a computer laboratory. And then, perhaps, our students will not feel so strongly that what they did in school has little to do with what they are supposed to do in work.

2. Fostering mental constructions via programming

We use three different software systems in our Macintosh computer labs—ISETL, a mathematical programming language, MAPLE, a symbolic computer system, and graphics software. Actually, there are only two distinct systems because the graphics system is already contained in one of the others (MAPLE at the moment, but we are switching to the new graphics capabilities of ISETL in Fall, 1990). We keep them separate because there are conceptual differences.

The three software systems correspond neatly to three different ways of thinking about functions. For MAPLE, as for all symbolic computer systems, a function is basically an algebraic/trigonometric expression and is an object as such. For ISETL a function is a process in that it is implemented by a computer procedure (called `func` in ISETL) that students write, and it is an object in that `funcs` are first class objects and are treated as data. A graph is also an object with the main feature of being visual as opposed to the analytic nature of the other two interpretations.

Incidentally, as a technical point, we should mention that, strictly speaking, the statements in the above paragraph are not completely true. It is possible to write procedures in MAPLE (and other symbolic computer systems). These procedures have some, but not all, of the properties of first class objects (in particular, the result of applying a function in MAPLE cannot be a function). In ISETL, procedures have full status as first-class objects and can be returned by other procedures. On the other hand, although it would be possible to implement symbolic manipulation in ISETL this would not be very convenient and there are no plans to do so. Finally, both MAPLE and ISETL have (or shortly will have) graphics capabilities sufficient for calculus.

It may well be that the development of software will be in the direction of constructing a single software system that will combine all features of all three of these systems. We are not sure that would be a good idea (for Calculus). In our course, we have used the differences to help our students develop an awareness of the different interpretations of functions and to reflect on the (very important) activity of using several representations and switching back and forth between these representations within a single problem situation. Now that graphics are coming to ISETL and it will be feasible to reduce work with MAPLE to a minimum, it is not clear whether this is the best thing to do. We have inaugurated a research project to help us answer that question.

In this section we give some details about how we use each of the three software systems to help students construct mathematical concepts in their minds. First, we consider MAPLE which is, in our opinion, most valuable in helping students develop the necessary manipulative skills for doing mathematics. Our use of MAPLE is not very different from what most projects are doing and so our discussion is very brief. Next, we explain how we coordinate two systems in our approach to graphics. Finally we have

a long discussion of ISETL, its general features and how we use it to help students interiorize actions to construct processes and encapsulate processes to construct objects.

Learning manipulative skills with MAPLE

The laboratory work that we do with the symbolic computer system MAPLE alone involves students using the system to simplify complex expressions, find derivatives and antiderivatives, evaluate limits and definite integrals, and solve the standard problems of calculus as well as some new problems that are accessible to them because they have such powerful tools.

This work has considerable merit and students learn the manipulative skills of calculus about as well (and sometimes better) than they do in traditional courses. Since this is about *all* that most students learn in the traditional courses today, we are satisfied that our laboratory course achieves at least as much as the traditional courses. We will also be arguing in this paper that since manipulation is only a small part of what happens in our laboratory course, our students learn much more than do those in traditional courses.

Having said this, we hasten to add that our use of a symbolic computer system and the results we are obtaining do not differ very much from what other people have achieved. For a more detailed description of the effect of symbolic computer systems on students learning manipulative skills in Calculus, see [12].

Doing graphics in a different way

As we indicated above, at the beginning of our project, the only powerful graphics system we had was the one embedded in MAPLE. This is a reasonable system, provided that one is content to produce graphs of functions that come from expressions. There are, however, other kinds of functions that are important in Calculus. These include functions defined in parts—that is, given by different expressions in different parts of the domain, functions created by a procedure (such as an approximation to the derivative of a given function), and functions which are sequences.

The mathematical programming language ISETL can implement all of these kinds of functions (and more), so we had to devise a means of using ISETL for defining a function and MAPLE for its graph. This is not very difficult. Suppose, for example, it is desired to sketch a graph of the following function (which results from fitting a curve to data giving the compressibility of a substance as a function of its volume—the different branches correspond to the state of the substance, solid, liquid, gas).

$$Z(V) = \begin{cases} 1 + \dfrac{(V-2)^3(V-6)}{54} & \text{if } 0 \le V < 6 \\[2ex] \dfrac{V^3}{3 \times 10^3} - 0.048V^2 + 1.73V - 7.7 & \text{if } 6 \le V < 90 \\[2ex] \dfrac{4V^{3/2}}{\sqrt[5]{V^3 - 8 \times 10^5}} - \dfrac{1}{V - 100} & \text{if } 90 \le V \end{cases}$$

The first thing that must be done is to implement this expression with an ISETL procedure and assign it to a variable name, say Z. This is easy to do and we will see how it looks when we discuss ISETL syntax in some detail below.

Next, the student decides on the region of the independent variable over which to sketch the graph, for instance the interval [0,300], and the number of points to sample, say 100 (here the student learns about the trade-off between using many points for greater accuracy and waiting a long time for the graph). The following command is then given in ISETL

```
graph(Z,0,300,100, "data");
```

The result is to create a file named "data" outside of ISETL containing a set of 100 ordered pairs of data points for this function. The student then leaves ISETL (this is unnecessary if Multifinder is available), enters MAPLE and gives the following two commands,

```
read data;
sketch(");
```

The result of the first command is to display the data on the screen and the second causes the graph to be drawn.

This complex use of (what is conceptually) three systems has its advantages and disadvantages. It is cumbersome and does not lend itself to quickly displaying different parts of the same graph. On the other hand, it forces the student to act and to wait, and there is hope that this will enhance awareness of and reflection on how the computer is making this graph. In particular, our approach could improve the student's understanding of the connection between a function and its graph. Hopefully the research project, in which we will compare our approach with approaches using a single software system, will help us decide whether to keep this method or move to something that will be much more convenient when the ISETL graphics are ready.

A final point about graphs. As far as we know, every graphics system samples points and uses splines to connect them. This can lead to difficulties when a function has singularities and we have seen examples in which the system will connect dots smoothly across a discontinuity. To avoid dealing with a problem that is, as far as a computer lab for calculus is concerned, purely technical, our `sketch` tool simply puts the dots on the screen. This is admittedly primitive because the same density of dots is used no matter what the function is doing. It will have to be improved. It

does give us some interesting tasks to set before the student, however. We have them put the graphs of several functions on the screen and make a hard copy. Then it is their task to connect the dots. They have to use their understanding of the processes of the functions to distinguish between the several collections of dots.

Fostering mental constructions with ISETL

The syntax of ISETL consists of very simple and standard control statements together with a number of expressions that correspond very closely in meaning and notation to fundamental mathematical concepts. Our experience is that students have very little difficulty learning to use the language. Their main efforts are devoted, as they should be, to understanding the ideas behind various mathematical constructs so as to be able to use them in writing ISETL programs.

Because of ISETL's clear mathematical structure, we are able to introduce the reader to its basic operations with a minimum of detailed explanation. We do this in the next paragraph. In the following paragraphs we give a number of examples of specific ISETL constructs that we use to get students to make several important mental constructions. For interiorization we consider using ISETL `funcs` to express functions with split domains, the ISETL `tuple` for sequences and series, and the `func` again for constructing a process corresponding to the composition of two functions. For encapsulation, we explain how implementing composition in ISETL as a binary operation on two functions that produces a function helps students construct an object conception of function. We also consider the operation of approximate differentiation (for which there is a simple ISETL implementation) as having a similar effect.

Generalities about ISETL

ISETL, which stands for *interactive set language* is an interactive, interpreted, high-level programming language that runs on the Macintosh or PC (under MS-DOS). It contains the usual collection of statements common to procedural languages but a richer set of expressions than is usually available. The objects of ISETL include integers, floating point numbers, the two boolean values (true and false), character strings, finite and heterogeneous sets and tuples (sequences), funcs (procedures) and maps (sets of ordered pairs).

One uses ISETL by entering an expression to which the system responds by evaluating and returning a result. An expression can involve arithmetic operations on numbers (integers or floating point), boolean operations, or operations on character strings. Assignments can be made to variables, and expressions can combine variables and constants. The domain of a variable is determined in context dynamically by the system and there is no need to declare data types, sizes, etc. Many important mathematical operations on these data types are implemented directly in ISETL and are used with a single command. In addition to the usual arithmetic, they include mod, max/min, even/odd, signum, absolute value, random, greatest integer less than, concatenation (of strings) and the standard trigonometric, exponential and logarithmic functions.

The power of ISETL begins to appear with the complex data types of set, tuple, func, and map. Syntax such as

```
{7..23};
{-4,-1..40};
{9,7..0};
```

can be used to construct sets of finite arithmetic progressions of integers. It is also possible to construct a set containing any data types whatsoever (including other sets) simply by listing them. For example, the following set has cardinality 5.

```
{8-1,  "t"  +  "he",  1.2,  {1,3,4,2},
{1..4},3<2, "the",7,false};
```

Students don't often see this right away because they count elements of this set which are sets (such as $\{1,3,4,2\}$) according to their cardinality and will count repeated elements twice. Working with ISETL helps them learn about elementary properties of mathematical sets.

Once such sets have been constructed, one can then construct complicated subsets by using a set former notation that can generally be understood by anyone who knows the mathematics. Consider the following ISETL code.

```
{k**3:k in {-N,-N+2..N} | k**2 mod 4 = 2};
```

This is the set of cubes of even integers (of absolute value less than or equal to N) whose squares are congruent to 2 mod 4.

Standard set operations are implemented with single command syntax. They include union, intersection, difference, adjunction, tests for membership or subset, power set, cardinality, and selection of an arbitrary element. It is possible to iterate over a set to make loops conveniently but the operations of existential and universal quantification over a set are implemented and they often render loops superfluous. For example, in the following code, the first and second lines construct respectively the sets of all positive even integers and all primes less than or equal to N and the third checks the Goldbach conjecture up to N. The last line returns the value true.

```
E:={2,4..N};
P:={p:p in {2..N} |
```

```
(forall q in {2..p-1} | p mod q/=0)};
forall n in E |(exists p,q in P | n = p+q);
```

All of this is very interesting and has been used in important ways to help students learn various topics in mathematics [1,4,5,9,10], but it has little to do with calculus directly. We will consider funcs and tuples in the next few paragraphs and see how they are used to get students to make mental constructions that are essential for understanding calculus. Our introduction to ISETL is far from complete (for example we made no mention of smaps). For more information see [1].

Interiorization—the func

Consider the compressibility function that was described (mathematically) on page 231. The mathematical expression defining Z as a function of V has great deal of meaning for the mathematician, but usually it is totally incomprehensible to the calculus student.

Before explaining how we deal with this difficulty, let's review what we would like to be going on in the student's mind relative to this function. We would like her or him to construct an action and interiorize it as mental process. What is this process? One can think of it in terms of a transformation of the volume V. One has a particular value for V. It is necessary first to check that this value is nonnegative and, if so to determine whether it is less than 6. If that is the case, then a particular calculation is made with V. If not, then one must see if it is less than 90. If that is so, then a different calculation is made. If not, then still a different calculation is required. Thus, in one way or another, a value for V is transformed into a value for Z.

This is the sort of dynamic activity that we would like to be going in the student's mind. We would like her or him to be able to work with it, to realize that the choices correspond to something meaningful in the situation (the state of the substance) and to be able to imagine various mathematical operations performed on it. The way we get students to perform such an interiorization is to ask them to write a procedure that implements this function and to perform various operations on the procedure in the computer laboratory. Here is how that procedure looks as an ISETL func (note that almost all of the complications are due to the mathematical formulas—and not the programming):

```
Z:= func(V);
 if V < 0 or V = 100 return
  "Out of domain"; end;
 if V <=6 then return
  1 + ((V-2)**3 * (V-6))/54;
 elseif V <= 90 then return
  V**3/3.0e3 - 0.048*V**2 + 1.73*V -7.7;
 else return
  4*V**(3/2)/(5*sqrt(V**3-8.0e5))-1/(V-100);
```

```
end;
 end;
```

Our claim is that writing this `func` requires the student to go through precisely the same mental manipulations as we described above. In this way, students construct the process in their minds as they construct the `func` on the computer.

Interiorization—the tuple

The concepts of sequence and sum can also be seen as processes which the student must construct. One can imagine the process for a sequence as running through the positive integers, and at each step, one grabs a number. That is an infinite sequence.

The process for sum can come from the sequence of partial sums. Here the student must encapsulate the sequence process to get an object. Then he or she again imagines running through the positive integers. This time at each step say n, the sequence is grabbed (it is, after all, an object) and de-encapsulated to its process, at least up to n and all the numbers are added up. This gives the nth partial sum. There are a number of ways of dealing with this in ISETL. Let us suppose for simplicity that "infinity" is not an issue. (There are ISETL approaches that take infinity into account, but we are only beginning to learn how to use them.) We "approximate" infinity with large positive numbers N. With this point of view, one can express the alternating harmonic sequence in ISETL as follows.

```
a:= [(-1)**(i+1)/i : i in [1..N]];
```

Then, the sequence of partial sums can be written (the symbol %+, is what ISETL uses for $\sum$)

```
Sa :=%+[a(1..i) : i in [1..N]];
```

We do not suggest that these expressions are any easier to understand than standard mathematical notation—they are almost identical. What we claim is: the fact that they are computer objects and students can calculate with them leads to the students constructing useful mental models for these mathematical entities. For example, students can investigate convergence of this series just by writing

```
Sa(I);
```

for large values of I (making sure to increase N when necessary) and see that it appears to converge.

An interesting alternative investigation comes from replacing the original sequence by the following,

```
b :={x : x in a};
```

b is the *set* of all elements of the *sequence* a. Then computing Sb analogously to Sa will give interesting results because each time b is evaluated, its elements will appear in a different order. Riemann's theorem is not far away at this point.

Interiorization—composing two processes

Understanding the composition of two specific functions requires that the student has constructed processes for the individual functions and then that he or she coordinate these two processes in series to form a new one. Once the individual processes are constructed, the coordination or composition is simple. This process is similar in mathematics, and, psychologically, students who have written `funcs` to construct the two functions can immediately form a new `func` corresponding to their composition.

Suppose for example, one is investigating the function Z for compressibility in terms of volume V. It is possible to imagine an apparatus that varies the volume with time, but keeps the temperature constant so that the expression for Z remains valid. Suppose for example, the volume is varied with time according to the following function:

$$V(t) = \begin{cases} 26.7t^2 & \text{if } 0 \leq t \leq 50 \\ \frac{4}{3}\pi t^3 & \text{if } t > 50 \end{cases}$$

At this point, students do not have much difficulty in implementing this with an ISETL `func`:

```
V:=func(t);
    if t < 0 return "Out of domain"; end;
    if t <=50 then return
        26.7*t**2;
    else return
        (4/3) * Pi * (t**3);
    end;
end;
```

The student can now easily write a `func` representing the function Z_t that gives compressibility in terms of time.

```
Zt:= func(t);
        return Z(V(t));
    end;
```

This helps students coordinate two processes. They have little difficulty figuring out the meaning of expressions like

$$Z_t(10) = Z\big(V(10)\big)$$

and they can overcome the difficulty presented by the branches. Working with this kind of composition of functions sets students up for a more meaningful experience with the chain rule.

Encapsulation—the operation of composition

Once students have a good grasp of the composition of two specific functions, they are ready to think about an operation that takes two functions and produces a new function. This requires several encapsulations. The functions to be composed (general, not specific) must be thought of as objects and then—a major psychological difficulty for students—it is necessary to imagine an operation whose result is not a number, *but whole function*. The code is simple, but students labor over it. It is the right struggle, for it consists of their developing the ability to convert processes to objects and then go back and forth between the two. Here is the ISETL code.

```
co := func(f,g);
    return func(x);
        return f(g(x));
    end;
end;
```

It is a great triumph for students to write such code and then come to understand the meaning of an ISETL expression like

```
(Z .co V)(10);
```

Once students have it well in hand, issues such as the compatibility of the range of V with the domain of Z or various properties (such as limit or continuity) of the composition of two functions become accessible to them.

Encapsulation—approximate differentiation

There is an even more important example that is very similar to what we have done with having students compose two functions and then construct an operator that will compose any two functions.

Return again to the compressibility function Z. We will discuss below some of the investigations we ask students to make with a func like the following,

```
Zs := func(V);
        return (Z(V+0.0001) - Z(V))/0.0001;
    end;
```

Once again we note that the value of 0.0001 is not the issue here (although we do have students make investigations in which it is). We can have students make tables of this function, draw its graph and compare it with the original function Z. Obviously there is great interest in what happens in the different branches and at the cut points.

Psychologically, the above func corresponds to using the process of the function Z to produce another process, the difference quotient function, or what we call the approximate derivative of Z. In analogy with composition, the next step is clear. We have students write the following func.

```
D :=func(f)
    return func(x);
        return (f(x + 0.0001) - f(x))/0.0001;
    end;
end;
```

After the experience with composition, this is not so hard. The student must imagine the incoming function as

an object to be acted on, take it apart to get its process, use the process to construct the new process for the difference quotient, and wrap that up as a function (object) which is sent back as the answer.

Mathematically, the student who has written this func has a tool that will allow her or him to use things like D(Z) as a function whose properties can be investigated. Issues like different expressions for the derivative in different branches and computation of the derivative at the seam by using the definition tend to become accessible to students who have made these constructions. Finally, as we will see below, it forms a critical step in the student's construction of the ideas surrounding the fundamental theorem of calculus.

3. Environment and Implementation

In this section we describe our computer laboratory and its operation. We begin with some principles that established our goals and helped us with the main design decisions. The question of hardware and configuration was dealt with in detail in the article in Part 1 of this volume. The major considerations for software selection were given in the previous section of this article. We believe that our principles were reflected in each of these aspects of a computer laboratory.

Principles

We were guided in our design of the laboratory by the following principles or goals.

The lab should be a place where students engage in guided discovery relative to the mathematical phenomena of calculus.

The lab activities should stimulate the students to make some of the specific mental constructions of objects and processes discussed in the previous section.

The atmosphere of the laboratory itself and the activities that are assigned should encourage the students to engage in group work.

Students should think of the computer lab as a comfortable place to go and to work in the company of their colleagues and with the support and encouragement of faculty, staff and assistants.

Every effort should be made to minimize distractions and frustrations that students might experience in trying to get the hardware and the software to function as it should.

The two variables that we have a chance to manipulate in trying to live up to these principles and achieve these goals are first, the lab itself and the way in which it operates and second, the design of instruction that is at least partly implemented in the lab. In this section we concentrate on the former.

Hardware

In this day and age the selection of computer hardware is not critical once one has decided to have a networked microcomputer laboratory. Networking is essential for the practical requirements of distributing material to the students, printing and submitting completed assignments. It also has the pedagogical value of fostering communication between students (if it has a mail facility) and encouraging group work.

The decision to use microcomputers (rather than terminals linked to a mainframe or workstation) is a temporary choice dictated by the fact that, today, the most developed, convenient to use and inexpensive computing systems appropriate for educational purposes exist on microcomputers. There is no educational reason why this has to be the case forever. If the situation should change, then alternative choices would be reasonable.

Given the choice of a networked microcomputer laboratory, one must decide between Macintosh and PC compatible computers and one must determine various parameters such as size, speed, numbers, etc. Of course, the equipment must be sufficient to run the software that will be used and accommodate the number of students one expects to serve. Beyond that, the selection can be determined by personal preference and the resources available. At the present time we are using 20 Macintosh SE computers and a laser printer linked with Appleshare networking.

Software

The most important things that we have to say about software are contained in the previous section. This is because the only thing that really matters about software is how it is used and the extent to which it is effective.

There is one major point that we should make about software that is more connected with the computer laboratory than with the content of the course. The software should be as easy as possible for the students to use. This means not only that it should be "user-friendly" but there should be documentation that is readable, accurate and helpful. We had to spend a fair amount of time trying to produce documentation for both ISETL and MAPLE that had these properties.

Configuration

Purdue University is experiencing a serious space problem. It was easier to get financial support for the equipment than it was to get a room to house it. The room we got was small and poorly ventilated. It had the advantage of being readily accessible for both students and faculty. The figure below shows the configuration of the laboratory.

The Macintosh next to the LaserWriter (LW) was used for a file server and was not otherwise available. There were 20 computers available to the students with a total of 40 chairs. The machines were very reliable so that we never had less than 18 functioning computers. In general, there were about 25 students in the laboratory during the course.

The configuration of the lab encouraged group work in two ways. The fact that there were more students than machines meant that they had to work in teams. Also, the arrangement of machines on tables encouraged groups of varying size. The five tables accommodate 6,6,8,8, and 12 students, respectively. The nature of the groups tended to vary throughout a lab session. A table with 8 students would sometimes have 4 groups of 2 members each, and other times it would be only 2 groups with 4 members each. On occasion the students at the table would form a single group of 6–8, all talking, sometimes heatedly, and often about the work at hand.

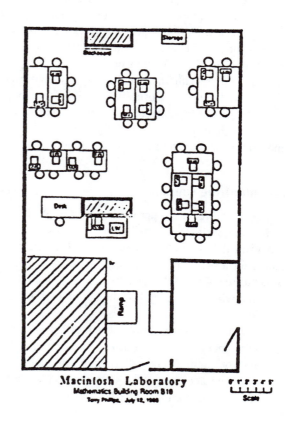

Macintosh Laboratory
Mathematics Building Room 818
Tony Phillips, July 12, 1988

Scale

This arrangement of tables and the flexibility supported individual differences as well as the fact that there were times when a student might want to work alone and other times when he or she benefited from being part of a team. We could observe the students as they flowed back and forth between groups and set their work situation according to the task at hand and/or their needs at the moment. This relaxed, friendly atmosphere contrasted with the intensity of the work that was set before them and the former made the latter considerably more palatable. We made every effort to contribute to both the friendliness and the intensity.

The laboratory is one place where we tried to contribute towards our goal of minimizing distraction and frustration that can be a part of working with computers. The software itself is relatively free of programming distractions. Although the students had a great deal of difficulty, most of it was mathematical, and this is as it should be. After all, if the students were *not* having difficulty because of the mathematics involved in working their computer tasks, then it is likely that they were not learning very much.

Relation to the other sections of this calculus course

This same course was taken by about 2150 students. The first two semesters each carry 5 semester hours of credit. It meets three times a week in large lecture sections (about 450 students) and twice a week in recitation sections of about 40 students. For the third semester, the course is reduced to four credit hours and it meets four times per week in classes of about 30 students.

By agreement with the department, our course was constrained to follow, as closely as possible, the content and syllabus of the regular course. Our students did not take the same hourly exams, but they did take the same common final exam in the first two semesters.

Operation of the course

Our course met three times per week (Monday, Wednesday and Friday) in a classroom and twice per week (Tuesday, Thursday) in the computer laboratory. Each meeting was scheduled for a period of 50 minutes. In addition, the students had a free period scheduled after each of the lab sessions during which time they had the option of continuing to work in the lab.

Each week the students were given a lab assignment with a list of (mainly) computer tasks to perform in the lab and a homework assignment with (mainly) problems from the text assigned according to a schedule similar to that used by the regular sections. The homework assignments

we gave were not as extensive as those given to the regular sections but, together with the lab assignments, the students had considerably more work to do than was required in the regular sections.

The students were expected to do a significant amount of work on the lab assignments during the scheduled lab hours but were not expected to complete them without returning to the lab during its open hours. The discussions in the class meetings were based on the work that students were expected to have done on the computer tasks.

The lab assignments were due each Monday and the homework assignments were due each Tuesday. They were corrected by a student grader based on an answer sheet prepared by us and were returned to the students. The examinations during the course were given in the evenings. They consisted of questions designed to elicit the understandings that students had constructed of various concepts in calculus. There was no time restriction for the exams.

4. A case study—The Fundamental Theorem of Calculus

The example we give here is not a single lab assignment, but a coherent sequence of assignments that were given over a period of time. In this sense, our example is not typical (almost all of the other tasks were given in a single assignment). It is, however, typical of our assignments in several aspects. First, this assignment involves a coordinated use of both ISETL and MAPLE. Second, it is typical in that it involves not only an opportunity for students to discover important mathematical ideas, but also it offers a stimulus for students to make various important mental constructions. Finally, this assignment, as did many others, makes use of certain mathematical and programming tools that we had to provide.

The Fundamental Theorem of Calculus is not mentioned in the course until the 13th week of the semester. There is a series of computer assignments, however, that are spread throughout the previous 12 weeks and are designed to help the students make a number of mental constructions that will prepare them for a discussion of this theorem.

About half of these assignments are designated as Lab Assignments. The others are called Homework Assignments. This distinction only refers to whether the students are expected to do most of the assignment during scheduled lab hours or entirely on their own time. All of the work is to be done on the computer in the laboratory either during scheduled lab times (Lab Assignments) or during open hours in the lab that are scheduled at various times (Homework Assignments).

Appendix 1 contains copies of the 11 assignments that were given on this topic. We discuss each of them briefly to indicate our expectations of what the student should gain from working on the task. These tasks represent only one problem in the entire Lab or Homework Assignment indicated. Generally there were 10-12 such tasks in each assignment.

Lab Assignment 2. A partition is a process consisting of marking points on a line. It is also an object in that it is a sequence of demarcation points. Because the process is so simple, we consider that doing it once is sufficient to get the students to interiorize it. Collecting the points in a `tuple` is expected to help the students encapsulate the process into an object.

Homework Assignment 2. The purpose of this assignment is to move the student from thinking about a single partition to being able to consider the formation of partitions in general. We hope that they will coordinate the `tuple`, the `func` and mathematical notation into a single scheme for partitions.

Homework Assignment 3. The purpose of this assignment is to get the students to interiorize a process of concatenating two partitions to form a new one. This is done by having them write ISETL code to implement such an action. Our goal is to get them ready to think about the fact that if $a < b < c$ then the integral over $[a, c]$ is the sum of the integral over $[a, b]$ and the integral over $[b, c]$. (See Homework Assignment 12.)

Homework Assignment 5. The process to be interiorized this time consists of forming the usual Riemann sum for a partition and a function, with the evaluation point chosen to be the left endpoint of each interval. This is applied to a reasonably complicated function. It is one, however, that the students have worked with so it is not completely unfamiliar.

Actually, we consider the Riemann sum to be two processes. One is the analytic calculation of the sum of values of the function multiplied by lengths of subintervals and the other is the graphical interpretation as an approximation to the area under a curve. The purpose of this assignment is to get the students to coordinate these two process into a single process. Our intention is that coordinating the ISETL and MAPLE implementations will help achieve this synthesis.

Homework Assignment 6. As with partitions, we now would like the students to deepen their process conception of Riemann sum from something that is done with a particular function to a process that can be applied to any

function. We try to achieve this by having them write an ISETL `func` that implements the process, and having them apply that process to several functions. Naming the process (`RiemLeft`) may also get them to encapsulate it into an object, although this is not an important goal for us at this point.

The fact that the three functions to which they apply their `func` are not very specific (a mystery function, a function obtained as the result of a previous operation) is intentional. The vagueness is expected to contribute to their sense of generality for this process.

Note also that we have them apply their `func` for Riemann sums to the result, `Df`, of applying the approximate derivative operator to a function. This is, of course, not an accident but is designed to start them on the road to the Fundamental Theorem.

Lab Assignment 8. If the process of adding up all of the small rectangles from left to right to get an area is interiorized, it should be possible to reverse it in the sense of going from right to left. The students make the simple discovery that this has the effect of negating the result obtained by going from left to right. Our intention is that they should also discover the reason for this in the details of the calculation.

Lab Assignment 9. Another variation of the `RiemLeft` process consists of taking the evaluation point at the right of each interval. The students are expected to discover this just from the name `RiemLeft`.

Lab Assignment 10. This is in the same spirit as the previous assignment, this time for midpoints. Another point of this task is to discover something about the relation between the mesh size and the accuracy of the approximation. The examples given are intended to point out that this relation can depend on the particular function.

Lab Assignment 11. The purpose of this assignment is to further deepen the students' process conception of Riemann sums by coordinating it with another activity, of comparable difficulty, on which they worked in previous assignments. This is the process of estimating the maximum value of a function on an interval by partitioning the interval and picking the demarcation point at which the function takes on its largest value.

The coordination of the two processes leads to a fourth version of Riemann sums, `RiemMax`. Again, the method by which we help the students construct these processes is to have them implement the actions in ISETL.

Lab Assignment 12. This is the *pièce de résistance*. We can discuss it more easily in terms of the solutions that we hope for. First of all, the func `Int` could look like this.

```
Int:=func(f,a,b);
    return func(x);
        if a <= x and x <= b then
            return RiemMid(f,a,x,25);
        end;
    end;
end;
```

We feel that the student really must encapsulate the Riemann sum process into an object in order to be able to use it here with a variable upper endpoint. Related work in class and on assignments has them apply this mental construction to defining functions by integration. Next there are the last two columns which `print3` is supposed to produce. The values, for a particular x are given by

```
Int(D(f),a,b)(x)
```

and

```
D(Int(f,a,b))(x)
```

Make no mistake about it, these two pieces of code are extremely difficult for the students to come up with. They struggle with it for long periods of time, but most of them do eventually produce this code and apply it to get results that are reasonable enough for them to try to interpret.

The two pieces of code are, of course, ISETL implementations of the two parts of the Fundamental Theorem of Calculus. We see in the code all of the mental constructions that the student must make. In the first, it is necessary for the function `f` to be an object which is transformed by the *process* `D` to another object `D(f)`. Only then can the process `Int` transform this into yet another object which is a function. This function, which is an object, must be de-encapsulated to obtain its process (which is known only through a deep knowledge of `Int` and `D`) and applied to the value x. This is how the student is expected to interpret the numbers that appear in the third column of `print3`.

For the second piece of code, the whole thing is reversed. The process `Int` transforms the object f into another object which is again transformed into a new object by `D`. This object is again de-encapsulated to its process and applied to the value x. This is how the student is expected to interpret the numbers that appear in the fourth column of `print3`.

The student cannot miss the fact that the second and fourth columns of this table agree. It is interesting, amusing, and above all gratifying to watch their reactions to the third column. They seem to feel intuitively that this column should also agree and many of them think that an error has been made. They puzzle over this for a while and discuss it among themselves. After not too much time

in the laboratory, a few students will notice, and the point spreads around the room like wildfire, that this column differs from the second and fourth by a constant. Someone pipes up with a phrase like, "Oh, so that is what the constant of integration is all about!" One can almost see the light bulbs illuminating over the heads of the students.

At this point, they are ready for a proof of the Fundamental Theorem of Calculus.

Homework Assignment 12. Here we coordinate the earlier work (Homework Assignment 3) on concatenating two intervals with what we expect is a serious understanding of the Riemann integral and give the student an opportunity to discover the fact that the integral is additive over unions of adjacent intervals.

Evaluation

It is extremely difficult to evaluate the effects of giving students a sequence of tasks such as these. We have already suggested that a person has only a tendency to display knowledge and this makes traditional "objective" tests somewhat suspect. We did not make observations (as in research such as [2,4,9]) to determine if the students appeared to making the mental constructions that were intended. We do have various results on the students' performance and these were quite high, but so much was going on that it is nearly impossible to identify this particular collection of tasks as one of the causes.

The only direct data that we have is the number of correct and partially correct submissions on the assignments. This information must be treated with care for a number of reasons. The assignments had deadlines, but we did not enforce them. (This is an overall weakness of our first implementation that will be discussed later). The students worked together in groups and although we believe that almost all of them made sincere efforts to complete these tasks and tried individually to understand the work, there is no way to tell how many, in the end, got their final results from their colleagues without understanding them. After all, their scores helped determine their grades and these students were no more free of the pressures to obtain good grades than are most students in higher education.

Finally, we point out that the idea behind the Lab Assignments is that the students were supposed to do serious work on each of them *before* the topics were considered in class. They were not necessarily expected to complete the task successfully, only to "wrap their minds around the issues." We can give a subjective evaluation in that our ob-

	A	B	C	D
Lab Assignment 2	18	6	1	0
Homework Assignment 2	19	3	2	1
Homework Assignment 3	24	0	0	1
Homework Assignment 5	20	1	1	3
Homework Assignment 6	16	4	1	4
Lab Assignment 6	9	12	3	1
Lab Assignment 9	20	2	2	1
Lab Assignment 10	14	9	0	2
Lab Assignment 11	18	3	2	2
Lab Assignment 12	12	6	4	3
Homework Assignment 12	15	1	1	8

Results of Computer Tasks on the Fundamental Theorem

servations of students working in labs indicated that they did indeed give serious thought to these problems.

Given all of this, the reader is free to interpret the Table of their scores on submissions of their results on these tasks. The code "A" indicated that the task was completed successfully or nearly so. The code "B" indicates that they made significant progress but did not fully succeed on the task. The code "C" indicates that they were, essentially, wrong and the code "D" indicates that they did not submit anything on this task.

We can perhaps summarize the results by pointing out that, in the end, most students turned in something reasonable on most of the tasks. The sharp drop in the number of those who turned in the last assignment probably has to do with end of semester difficulties that are fairly typical.

There is one final subjective discussion we would like to include relative to these tasks. At the end of the three semesters, we gave an assignment to write an essay (about three pages) entitled "What I learned in Calculus." Many students referred to Riemann sums, definite integrals and their applications. Here are some excerpts from those essays. First, from one of the brightest students in the class who is an engineering major.

"The integral is equal to the area under the curve of a function. In order to learn this, I dealt with Riemann sums. This is basically just dividing the independent variable into a number of parts within the limits of integration. These parts can then form rectangles by using the value of the function at one of the points as the height. Summing the areas of these rectangles then gives an approximation to the integral. Increasing the number of rectangles under the curve until there are an infinite number of them would actually give you the exact integral. This can be done simply by taking the limit as the number of subdivisions of the independent variable goes to in-

finity. While I also learned many different techniques for solving integrals and applying them, I feel this initial basic description of the integral was the most important thing I learned, allowing me to solve many different varied problems later."

And second, from a student who, throughout the three semesters, had more difficulty than anyone, almost dropped out on several occasions, and will probably not major in anything connected with mathematics.

"When taking the integral of equations in a double integral the first integral would divide the region w/respect to that variable and then the next would do it with respect to the other and the limit of the sums of all these was the area. You had to decide the order and limits of integration by looking at the picture of the region and the equations and then decide."

And finally, a student who also did quite poorly in the course tried to be humorous in his essay and ended it by saying that one of the "ultimate truths" he learned in Calculus was

"Every math problem can be solved by using small boxes."

Nothing decisive, of course, and there is nothing surprising about good responses from the best students. But if we can have even our weakest students walking away from Calculus with thoughts like those expressed in the last two quotes, then perhaps there is some hope for us.

5. Overall Evaluations

The difficulties that we mentioned in connection with evaluating the effects of our instructional treatment of the fundamental theorem of calculus are endemic to evaluation of any aspect of our project, or, in our opinion, to evaluation of any educational activity. Short of conclusions which amount to little more than "those who do well, do well," we do not really understand very much about deciding whether one instructional treatment is better than another, or even if a particular approach is worth the trouble it takes.

The reason for this is that we continue to use variations or polishings of evaluation instruments that are based on implicit assumptions about learning—assumptions we believe are not justified. For example, as we have indicated earlier, a person may know something, but not display that knowledge with any reliability.

There are other difficulties, and we are convinced that a major effort of research and development on evaluation techniques will be necessary before much progress can be made. Such an effort should start with the question, "What is learning?" and go on to ask what it means to have learned something, how does one display what one has learned, and a host of other questions before beginning to think about what reasonable instruments might look like.

In the meantime, we are reduced to presenting what data we have obtained, and letting the reader draw whatever conclusions he or she deems appropriate. Our information is in several categories: performance of students of finals taken in common with all sections of the corresponding calculus course at Purdue, performance of students on exams we designed, comments of students, and comments of various visitors.

Performance of Students on Common Finals

In the first two of three semesters, the students in our special class took a common final examination together with all Purdue students (over 2000) taking first year calculus. These exams are timed (three hours), multiple choice and are designed to test the lowest common denominator of student skills in manipulations and solving the same problems they have practiced throughout the semester.

In our course, we spent very little time with this kind of problem and almost no time in drilling students on these kinds of calculations. After 13 weeks of the 15 week first semester we changed this abruptly. We told the students that the course had ended and that the remaining two weeks would be spent in preparing for the final examination. We spent two weeks engaging the students in the same kind of practice and memorization that the students in the regular sections had been doing all semester.

In the second semester we did this for only a week and with somewhat less intensity.

In the first semester, our class average of the final was 75% as opposed to 69% for the regular sections. In the second semester, our class average was 59.25% as opposed to 59% for the regular sections.

Thus our students, after spending most of the semester in conceptual development relative to calculus and only a short time practicing with techniques, performed on these exams as well as, or better than, students who spent the entire semester practicing techniques. This result is a replication of the findings of Heid [12] and others. In the second run-through of our course taking place at the time of this writing and with different instructors, the results do not seem to be very different.

In the third semester we made a decision not to make this comparison and our students did not take the common final exam. There were two reasons for this. In the first place, there seems little information to be gained, because

every time the "experiment" is performed the results are the same.

The second reason is more serious. As the students moved, at the end of the semester, from trying to understand mathematics to trying to memorize it, we began to suspect that this may be doing more harm than good. All semester we worked hard to convince the students that they should think about what they are doing, that even if they do not see how to solve a problem immediately, continued thought over time could lead to success, problems don't necessarily have unique, short answers, and so on. These are new ideas and attitudes for them and they are inconsistent with other messages they are getting in their educational experiences. The students only begin to come around to this way of thinking gradually over a period of time. Then we suddenly shift gears and organize activities that seem to deny everything we have been telling them. We thought we detected a negative effect on their thinking about mathematics from this reversal and we decided that, when not required to do so by the department, our students would not take common final examinations.

Performance of Students on Our Exams

During each of the three semesters we gave two class exams to the students in our section. These tests were designed to elicit information about the students' understanding of the concepts that were studied in class. More than half of the questions were unfamiliar to the students and the questions that were similar to ones they had worked on before tended to be more difficult than, for example, their homework problems.

These exams were given in the evening with no time limit. Students were not permitted to use books or notes, but hand calculators were allowed.

Semester 1, Exam 1	76.9
Semester 1, Exam 2	80.8
Semester 2, Exam 1	63.6
Semester 2, Exam 2	72.9
Semester 3, Exam 1	73.2
Semester 3, Exam 2	78.4

Class Average Percentage Scores on Exams

The exams were graded by the instructor (Dubinsky) and partial credit was given. For this reason, even the numbers in the preceding Table have a subjective component.

The actual distribution is interesting. In general, about half of the students scored above 85%. Most of the rest were in the 55–75 range and two or three (usually the same individuals) had very low scores.

Comments of Students

The students had many opportunities to make written comments about their experiences, usually anonymously. They were uniformly positive. The full set of comments is available from the authors. Following are some excerpts that are typical of the students' attitudes toward the lab and computer component of the course at the end of the three semesters.

". . . our use of the computer was not for technology's sake, but to help us think."

". . . piecing together of information...had to be done on computers in the lab where everything had to be reduced to general format. Although the process of breaking down a problem, however complex, into coherent parts took place mostly on a subconscious level, there where times when this process brought an ordinary confusing problem into a much more logical light. Riemann sums are the first example that comes to mind. I've heard many people from Ma161 tell me how they didn't understand Riemann sums, but after plodding through the code on the Macintosh and having to understand everything about them, I felt somewhat unable to help the ordinary Ma161 student who didn't have such appropriate means to learn what was going on."

"...working with Riemann sums on the computer put a physical significance on the work we did in class. It made the physical aspects of the theory recognizable."

"Since our class went quite in depth into understanding theories and physical aspects of calculus, I felt that the computer work and class work went very well together."

"Programming definitely strengthened what we learned because in order to program the computer we first had to understand exactly what was going on and break it down into parts. So not only did I learn how to use ISETL and Maple to calculate things quicker than I would be able to by hand, but I also greatly strengthened my calculus knowledge by doing so."

"In my opinion, Labs are the most beneficial part of this class. Labs indicate to the student what he/she doesn't understand. It helps students to formulate questions."

"The Macintosh Lab was a great asset to the class because its usage required an understanding of the processes involved and made us "learn" calculus not just "plug and chug" like the "normal" calculus classes. The major lesson I learned was how to attack problems."

"Placing the problems on the computer also further embodied the spirit of the course by presenting us with the difficulty of implementing and understanding the method, versus subjecting us to the repetition of many similar problems and much busywork."

"The use of computers enabled me to work with the concepts behind the mathematics, while the homework made sure I could function by hand. The exploration of the concepts gave, and still promises, greater understanding than is possible through hand written solutions in the same length of time. Indeed, the increased versatility given by the computer increases experimentation and depth of understanding exponentially."

"The way a concept becomes clearer when a person writes a function in ISETL to do it is amazing, and actually being able to manipulate graphs also helps out a bunch when working with functions."

"In my opinion the labs helped me better understand the meaning behind the things that we covered."

The future

Naturally, we have our own evaluation and, of course, it is completely subjective. We feel that our approach is a vast improvement over traditional methods of teaching calculus. The results that have been obtained are, no doubt, due in part to the small class size, the enthusiasm of the teachers and the newness of it all (Hawthorne effect). But this is not the first time the authors have taught, nor is it their first experiment in innovative methods. Indeed we have, between us, more than half a century of undergraduate teaching experience. Both of us have always been interested in improving our teaching and have tried many things. Never before have either of us achieved the level of success (relative to the particular students) that we are having with this approach. We are convinced that our use of computer activities and small group problem solving to implement a theory of learning mathematics has shown itself to be an extremely promising direction for improving the learning of mathematics.

There are many things that still need to be done and many ways in which our course must be improved. The most important has to do with the content of the course. At the insistence of the mathematics department, we have made our content and the order in which it is taken up essentially identical to that of the regular sections. For the next stage, beginning Fall 1990, we will have two classes of about 60 students each and the only restriction on content is that at the end of each semester any of our students who desire to transfer to regular sections will have the appropriate background to do so.

There are also areas within the context of our present method that need to be improved. The most important has to do with the timing of Lab Assignments. An important component of our method is that the appropriate lab activity must be completed before the matter is considered in class. Our students did not always achieve this and in a few cases they fell seriously behind. We had deadlines but did not enforce them because we were concerned about the effect this might have on the class atmosphere. We were under considerable pressure from the students (who could leave at any time) to minimize the extent to which the demands of our course exceeded that which students experienced in other sections. The workload in our course was greater and initial difficulties with our overall laboratory system (unavoidable for new projects) made the burden on the students frightening.

In our next phase, we should solve most of the external problems and our software systems (especially ISETL) will be considerably more convenient to use. We intend to use this easing of pressure from external effects to increase the intensity of the work. In particular, deadlines will be enforced.

The same could be said with respect to participation in class. Not everyone answers questions. This can mean that some people just don't do their thinking in ways that allow them to formulate reasonable responses to questions. But there is the danger of degenerating into a situation where only a few students do all the talking. Measures will be taken in the next phase to avoid this issue.

Within the parameters of a first attempt we feel that our approach has been very successful. We hope that in the next phase of our course, we will take advantage of our first step and take a number of subsequent steps towards a calculus course that results in students learning a significant amount of mathematics.

References

1. Baxter, N., Dubinsky, E. & Levin, G., *Learning Discrete Mathematics with ISETL,* Springer, New York, 1989.
2. Breidenbach, D., Dubinsky, E., Hawks, J. & Nichols, D., Development of the process conception of function, preprint.
3. Conciatore, J., From flunking to mastering calculus, *Black Issues in Education,* pp 5–6, February (1980).
4. Dubinsky, E., Teaching mathematical induction I, *The Journal of Mathematical Behavior,* 5 (1986), pp 305–317.
5. Dubinsky, E., Teaching mathematical induction II, *The Journal of Mathematical Behavior,* 8 (1989), pp 285–304.
6. Dubinsky, E. (In press) Constructive aspects of reflective abstraction in advanced mathematical thinking, in L.P. Steffe (ed.), *Epistemological Foundations of Mathematical Experience,* New York: Springer-Verlag.
7. Dubinsky, E., Reflective abstraction in advanced mathematical thinking, in (D. Tall, ed.) *Advanced Mathematical Thinking* (in preparation).
8. Dubinsky, E., A learning theory approach to calculus, *Proceedings of the St. Olaf Conference,* St. Olaf (1989) (preprint).
9. Dubinsky, E., F. Elterman & C. Gong, The student's construction of quantification, *For The Learning of Mathematics* 8, 2 pp 44–51 (1988).
10. Dubinsky, E., On Learning Quantification (preprint).
11. Dubinsky, E. & P. Lewin, Reflective abstraction and mathematics education: the genetic decomposition of induction and compactness, *The Journal of Mathematical Behavior,* 5 (1986), pp. 55–92.
12. Heid, K., Resequencing skills and concepts in applied calculus using the computer as a tool, *Journal for Research in Mathematics,* 19 (1988), pp 3–25.
13. Selden, A. & J. Selden, Constructivism in mathematics education: a view of how people learn, *UME Trends,* E. Dubinsky (ed.), 2, 1 (1990) p 8.
14. Sfard, A. Operationals vs. structural methods of teaching mathematics—a case study, *Proceedings of the 11th Annual Conference of the International Group for the Psychology of Mathematics Education* (A. Borbas, ed.) Montreal (1988) 560–567.
15. Treisman, U., A study of the mathematical performance of Black students at the University of California, Berkeley, Thesis, University of California, Berkeley (1985).

Appendix I

Laboratory Assignments Relative to the Fundamental Theorem of Calculus

MA161 Lab Assignment 2. Tuples can have more than two components. One use for tuples with many components is to represent partitions of an interval. Here is a `tuple` that represents a partition of the interval from −1.5 to 0.7 with 5 equal subdivisions.

$$[-1.5. -1.06, -0.62, -0.18, 0.26, 0.7]$$

SUBMIT
1. A partition of the interval from 0.05 to 12 into 17 equal subdivisions. (Handwritten)
2. A diagram of a line with the endpoints of the interval and subdivisions clearly marked.

MA161 Homework Assignment 2. A `tuple` such as the one in Lab Assignment 2, #2 is often expressed in mathematical notation more compactly as

$$-1.5 + 0.44(i-1), \qquad i = 1, 2, \ldots, 6$$

In general to express the partition of the interval from a to b into n equal subdivisions, in mathematics, we write

$$a + (b-a)\frac{i-1}{n}, \qquad i = 1, 2, \ldots, (n+1)$$

A very similar notation is used in ISETL. For example the first `tuple` can be represented in ISETL as

```
>[-1.5 + 0.44*(i - 1) : i in [1,2..6]];
```

Enter this expression and see the resulting `tuple` written out explicitly. Such an expression is called a *tuple former*.

SUBMIT

1. A `tuple` former that produces the partition of the interval from 0.05 to 12 into 17 equal subdivisions.

2. A `func` that will accept numbers a, b with $a < b$ and a positive integer n and will return the `tuple` of the partition from a to b into n equal subdivisions. *Don't submit an untested* `func`—*try it on the examples first.*

MA161a Homework Assignment 3. For this problem, review the work that you did on partitions in Week 2 (Lab Assignment 2, #2 and Homework Assignment 2, #7). Also, notice that you will have to record your ISETL session.

If `t1` and `t2` are tuples in ISETL, then `t1+ t2` is a `tuple` formed by tacking `t2` onto the end of `t1`. Suppose then that we have a partition `P1` of the interval from a to b into n subintervals and a partition `P2` of the interval from b to c of k subintervals. Then `P1+P2` is *essentially* a partition of the interval from a to c into $n + k$ intervals. The only thing is that point b appears twice. Actually, in all of our applications of partitions this will not matter, but we can remove it for neatness. This is done by removing the first component of `P2` before tacking it onto `P1`. (This value is stored in x but we do not use it.) Here is ISETL code that will do it and display the new partition.

```
> take X fromb P2;
> P3:= P1 + P2;
> P3;
```

Use `tuple` formers (see Homework Assignment 2, #7) to construct a partition from -17.63 to 0.0005 with 14 equal subdivisions and a partition from 0.0005 to $\sqrt{3/2}$ with 9 subdivisions. Then use code such as the above to construct a partition from -17.63 to $\sqrt{3/2}$ with 23 (definitely nonequal) subdivisions.

SUBMIT

1. A record of your ISETL session, once it is correct.

2. The last partition, copied from the screen. One decimal place accuracy will be sufficient.

MA161a Homework Assignment 5. The ISETL operation `%+` can be used to add up all of the quantities of a `tuple`, or even quantities depending on the values in a `tuple`. For example, if P is a partition of the interval from a to b into n equal parts and f is some function whose domain includes this interval, then there are many situations in calculus where one would like to consider each subinterval and multiply the value of f at, say, the left endpoint times the length of the subinterval and then add up all of these products. The mathematical notation for this quantity

is

$$x_i = \left(a + \frac{(b-a)}{n}(i-1) \right), \qquad i = 1, \ldots, n+1$$

$$\sum_{i=1}^{n} f(x_i)(x_{i+1} - x_i)$$

and using `%+`, the ISETL code for obtaining it is very similar.

```
x:=[a+((b-a)/n)*(i-1) : i in [1..n+1]];
%+[f(x(i))*(x(i+1)-x(i)) : i in [1..n]];
```

1. Use the following function and a partition of the interval form -3 to 2 into 17 equal parts to compute the above quantity.

$$H(y) = \begin{cases} \frac{1.3y^2+6y-4}{y^2+2y+1} & \text{if } y \leq -2.6 \\ y + 1 & \text{if } -2.6 < y \leq 1 \\ \frac{1}{3y-2} & \text{if } 1 < y \end{cases}$$

2. Use ISETL and Maple to produce a graph of H on the interval from -3 to 2, make a hardcopy of it and indicate on the graph a representation of what is being computed here.

SUBMIT

1. An ISETL record of your calculations.

2. The numerical answer.

3. Your graph with the indicated representation.

MA161a Homework Assignment 6. In Homework Assignment 5, Problem #4, you worked with using ISETL to compute the quantity

$$\sum_{i=1}^{n} f(x_i)(x_{i+1} - x_i)$$

where f is a function and $[x_i : i = 1, \ldots, n+1]$ is a partition of the interval from a to b into n subintervals. In this problem you are to put it all together and write an ISETL `func` which accepts a `func`, say f which represents a function, the endpoints a, b of an interval contained in the domain of f, and a positive integer n. Your `func` is to construct the partition of the interval from a to b into n equal subintervals and then return the value of the above expression. Call your `func` by the name `RiemLeft`, apply your `RiemLeft` in the following situations. Choose your own value of n.

1. The function is `mys2`, $a = -1$, $b = 4$.

2. The function is the absolute value, $a = -1$, $b = 2$.

3. The function is `Df` where f is the absolute value function and D is the operator you developed in Lab 5, #5 $a = -1$, $b = 2$.

SUBMIT 1. A copy of your RiemLeft

2. Your three answers, copied from the screen.

MA 161a Lab Assignment 8. Return to Homework Assignment 6, Problem #4 and your `func RiemLeft`. Run this `func` on the same three examples you used then except reverse a and b. Compare your answers with the answers you got originally.

SUBMIT

1. What is the effect of this reversal?
2. Go through `RiemLeft` and explain exactly why you get this effect.

MA161 Lab Assignment 9. Return again to Homework Assignment 6, Problem #4 and consider the first function, `mys2` on the interval $[-1, 4]$. Sketch a graph of this function and, using a value of $n = 10$, shade in the quantity on the graph that is represented by the calculation that `RiemLeft` would make.

Repeat this precess except this time, use the calculation that `RiemRight` would make. Of course you have to guess what `RiemRight` would be!

SUBMIT
1. Your sketch using `RiemLeft`.
2. Your sketch using `RiemRight`.

MA161a Lab Assignment 10. In the spirit of Lab 9, Problem #2, write a `func` called `RiemMid`. Apply `RiemMid` to the functions given by the following expressions on the interval $[0, 1]$.

$$t^2$$
$$u^{100}$$

You must experiment to determine the choice of n as follows. The exact values that are being approximated as larger and larger values of n are taken (that is, smaller and smaller "meshes") are $1/3$ and $1/101$ respectively. You must choose your value of n so as to get 3 significant figures accuracy.

SUBMIT
1. A copy of your `func RiemMid`.
2. The values of n you used to get the required accuracy.
3. An explanation of why the accuracy improves an n increases.

MA161a Lab Assignment 11. You will write a function `RiemMax` which will be the same as the others except for the following.

1. `RiemMax` will accept an additional parameter `crit` which is a `tuple` consisting of a list of all points at which the function in question could have a relative maximum.

2. Instead of computing

$$\sum_{i=1}^{n} f(x_i)(x_{i+1} - x_i)$$

The quantity $f(x_i)$ will be replaced by the maximum value of f on the interval $[x_i, x_{i+1}]$. This is given by the ISETL code

`%+max[f(t) : t in T];`

where `T` is a `tuple` of all possible values in the interval $[x_i, x_{i+1}]$ at which f could attain a maximum.

HINT: if S is a tuple, p and q numbers, then the tuple of all numbers in S that are in the interval [p,q] together with these two endpoints is given in ISETL code,

`[p] + [s : s in S | p < s and s < q] + [q];`

As part of your `func`, you will have to have a construction of a `tuple` of `tuples`, corresponding to your partition that gives the possible points at which the maximum could occur.

Run your `func` on `mys2` with the three following choices of the interval $[a, b]$

1. $[-1, 4]$
2. $[-1, 0]$
3. $[0, 4]$

Use $n = 100$ in all cases.

Of course you must figure out the `tuple crit` by hand.

Think about the following questions. What property of the function on the interval will guarantee that the results of `RiemMax` and `RiemLeft` are the same? What will guarantee that `RiemMax` and `RiemRight` are the same? That the results of `RiemRight` and `RiemLeft` are the same?

SUBMIT
1. Your `func RiemMax`.
2. The results of applying it in the three given cases.
3. Your answers to the questions.

MA161a Lab Assignment 12. In this problem, which is perhaps the most important of all, you will put together several things that you have been using this semester. First, the approximate derivative `func D` from Week 5 (use a value of 0.000001 for e), then `RiemMid` and finally `func print1` from Week 6.

The first step in the problem is to write a `func Int` which accepts a `func` representing a function f and two numbers a and b representing the interval $[a, b]$ and returns a `func` whose value, for a number x in $[a, b]$ is the result of applying `RiemMid` to f with the interval from a to x (note this is x, not b) and 25 subdivisions.

Next adjust the `func print1` to obtain the `func print3` which will accept only one `func` representing a function f, an interval $[a, b]$, positive integer n and a filename. The result of `print3` is to place in the file four columns of values. The first gives the numbers x at $n + 1$ evenly spaced points in the interval $[a, b]$; the second gives f at x; the third gives the value obtained by applying D to f, applying Int to the resulting `func` and then evaluating the resulting `func` at x; and the last column gives the value obtained by applying Int to f, applying D to the resulting `func` and then evaluating the resulting `func` at x;

SUBMIT

1. A hard copy of your `func Int`.

2. A hard copy of your `func print3`.

3. A hard copy of the result of applying `print3` to the function $x \sin x^2$ on the interval from 0 to $\pi/2$. Use $n = 10$.

4. Your interpretation of the resulting data.

5. A hard copy of the result of applying `print3` to the function $\sqrt{1 - x^2}$ on the interval $[0, 1]$. Use $n = 10$.

6. Your interpretation of the resulting data. In particular, is there any way in which this example differs from the previous one? If not, explain why they are the same. If so, explain the cause of the difference.

MA161 Homework Assignment 12.   Let $a < b < c$ be three real numbers. Suppose that you applied `RiemLeft` three times to the same function with the same n but three different intervals, $[a, b]$, $[b, c]$, and $[a, c]$. Find a simple relationship between the three answers that you would get.

You can try this on several examples to guess the answer, but you should also attempt to understand, from the meaning of `RiemLeft`, why your relation must be true.

SUBMIT

1. The relation you came up with.

2. Your explanation of why it holds.

Appendix II

A Sample Exam Given in M161a

We have been asked what difference does teaching Calculus as a laboratory course make in terms of what our students learn? We feel that we can answer this question best by showing an exam that we have given to our students. The average score on the exam was 80.8. This exam was the second exam given in Math 161a. It was given on November 21, 1988. The first exam was given on October 6, 1988.

Math 161a Test 2.   Each Problem is worth 10 points (A = 100 points)

1. Find the equation of the normal line to the curve defined by the equation:

$$3x^4 + 4y - x^2 \sin y = 3$$

at the point $[1, 0]$.

2. For each of the following two curves, give a graphical description of how Newton's method, starting at the indicated x_0, would succeed or fail to approximate the indicated zero. Label each situation as success or failure, and indicate what happens by drawing right on the graph.

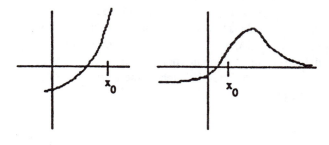

3. Following are the graphs of two equations:
graph1

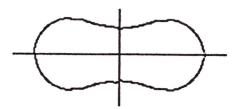

$$(x^2 + y^2 + 25)^2 - 100x^2 = 10^8$$

graph2

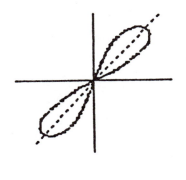

$$(x^2 + y^2)^2 = 4xy$$

(a) On graph 1, label the intersections of the graph with the coordinate axes and on graph 2, label points at which the graph is farthest from the origin. Your labels should be the approximate numbers at which these points occur.

(b) For each, draw intervals on the coordinate axes to restrict the graph so that it defines a function, u for graph1 and v for graph2, but do this in such a way that the composition $v \circ u$ is defined.

4. Find the third Taylor polynomial for the function given by

$$x\sqrt{4-x}$$

about the point 1.

5. Suppose that you applied the `func RiemLeft` and the `func RiemMax` to the same function f on the same interval $[a, b]$. Can you be certain of any relation between the two results? Explain your answer.

6. Make a careful sketch of the graph of the function given by the expression:

$$x^{2/3}(3x + 10)$$

Label with values the important points and show the shape of the curve clearly.

7. Boyles Law for gases states that $pv = c$ where p denotes the pressure, v the volume, and c is a constant. At a certain instant the volume is 75 in^3 and the pressure is decreasing at a rate of 2 (lbs/in^2)/sec. At what rate is the volume changing at this instant?

9. A package can be sent by parcel post only if the sum of its height and girth (the girth is the perimeter of the base) is not more than 96 in. What is the maximum volume that can be sent if the base of the box is a square?

10. The Campbell Soup Company has come to its senses and designed its can so as to minimize the amount of material used. If the radius of the can is increased by 1 percent and the basic design is maintained, what is the corresponding increase in the amount of material?

11. Use the Mean Value Theorem to show that if f is a function whose domain is the interval $[\alpha, \beta]$ and whose derivative is constant value k on $[\alpha, \beta]$, then f is a linear function.

12. Let f be the function given by

$$f(x) = \begin{cases} 2x & \text{if } x \leq 1 \\ 3 + x^2 & \text{if } x > 1 \end{cases}$$

find f' and explain the method you used for determining $f'(x)$ for each x.

Epilogue and Comments on the bibliography
by Cooper and Robinson

It is perhaps ironic that in science, mathematics, engineering, and technology—fields in which much important progress has been achieved through collaboration and building on the work of others—our teaching in these fields has tended to emphasize individual and competitive, rather than cooperative and collaborative, paradigms. We are only just beginning to understand how to use cooperative strategies effectively in the classroom to promote problem solving and deeper understanding of important concepts. Until recently, much of the literature has addressed issues of cooperative learning in elementary schools; very few papers have addressed issues of cooperative learning in higher education. But that is beginning to change.

In this volume of *Readings,* we have been able to include a very small, carefully chosen, selection of papers. If you have read, reflected on, and discussed these papers with your colleagues, you have begun to think about some important issues in cooperative learning. We have not attempted to include everything. In fact, we have made some difficult choices about what to include and what to leave out.

At this point you may be ready to continue your study of cooperative learning. Where might you look for additional resources? In the following annotated bibliography, Cooper and Robinson offer (in their words) "a snapshot of the field" at this point in time, providing the interested reader with suggestions for further study. Although this bibliography contains nearly 100 citations, it is a selection and not an exhaustive review of the literature. Section 1 contains references which deal with research and theory, while Section 2 focuses on references which make applications to the classroom. Each section is subdivided into two parts, the first addressing general cooperative learning issues, and the second focusing on resources more directly applicable to science, mathematics, engineering, and technology in higher education.

In compiling this bibliography, Cooper and Robinson have used as guiding principles three questions which are frequently asked by faculty and administrators as they begin to use cooperative learning in their own classrooms:

1. What is cooperative learning, and how does it differ from other forms of small group instruction?

2. Is there a research base which supports the use of cooperative learning, particularly at the college level? Is there research evidence that cooperative learning is an effective pedagogical strategy in the sciences, mathematics, engineering, and technology?

3. What resources are available which offer specific suggestions for implementing cooperative learning in college-level classes in these disciplines?

Each reference included in this bibliography has been annotated to guide the interested reader to those resources which may prove to be helpful. Cooper and Robinson often include their own recommendations for the works cited. An index is included which makes it easier to find resources which address issues in specific disciplines.

Annotated Bibliography of Science, Mathematics, Engineering and Technology (SMET) Resources in Higher Education[†]

James Cooper
and
Pamela Robinson

Introduction

In constructing this bibliography we had rather specific readers in mind: faculty members or administrators involved in science, mathematics, engineering and/or technology (SMET) who are interested in teaching and learning issues. Specifically, these persons would be interested in research, theory and/or practice in small-group instruction focusing on SMET disciplines in higher education.

This document is not an exhaustive description of research, practice and theory in small-group instruction relating to SMET or the individual disciplines which SMET encompasses. Rather, we intend to give readers a sense of the field of cooperative and collaborative learning in SMET disciplines, without constructing an overly technical document. We want to give readers a snapshot of historical and contemporary work in cooperative learning that furnishes a context from which to view the field. Readers may choose from a number of resources, depending on interests and needs.

Organizational Plan

We have organized this bibliography into two major sections, one dealing with Research and Theory and the other dealing with Applications. Each of the two major sections is subdivided into two portions, one related to General Cooperative-Learning Issues and one that is specifically focused on SMET-Related Cooperative-Learning Issues.

Our reasoning for including a number of general cooperative-learning resources in this bibliography is that SMET-related research on cooperative learning in higher education is a relatively new and undeveloped area of inquiry. Many of the authors in the SMET sections of this bibliography were influenced by others who have published work dealing with general applications of cooperative and collaborative learning. For readers to have a more complete understanding of cooperative learning in higher education and help set a context for the SMET-related contributions, a number of significant historical and contemporary general contributions to teaching and learning are included.

Section 1.A. This section in the bibliography addresses general cooperative-learning issues dealing with research, theory and practice. The definition of cooperative learning, and how it is similar to and different from other forms

† Preliminary work on this document was supported, in part, by the Los Angeles Collaborative for Teacher Excellence (LACTE). This document was written for the National Institute for Science Education, an NSF-supported institute housed at the University of Wisconsin, Madison. The copyright is held by James Cooper. Copies of the final draft of this document may be obtained by contacting NISE (1025 West Johnson St., Madison, WI 53706).

of active-learning strategies are among the issues treated. We identify sources documenting the empirical base for cooperative learning and place it in a general theoretical setting.

Section 1.B. This section identifies sources which document theoretical and empirical support for the power of cooperative learning as it is used in SMET disciplines. Resources are described which assess the impact of cooperative learning on several student outcome measures. The majority of these sources have been published in the 1990s.

Section 2.A. This section focuses on general applications of cooperative learning to the classroom. There are many types of cooperative learning. Spencer Kagan (Citation 66 in this document) reports that there may be over 100 different forms. The intent of this section is to identify resources which may help readers get a sense of the broad range of structures implemented by some of the leaders in the field, structures which have been used at all levels of education, with many disciplines and many student populations. Some SMET-practitioners may be unaware of the rich variety of techniques available, which are often field-tested by those working with more generic applications of cooperative learning.

Section 2.B. This section which addresses SMET-related applications of cooperative learning gives readers a sense of the variety of applications of cooperative learning in a number of SMET-related fields.

Guiding Questions

Faculty and administrators often ask the same fundamental questions about cooperative learning. We identify those questions which many readers of this report may also have and suggest specific resources in the bibliography that will address each question or concern.

What is cooperative learning and how does it differ from other forms of small-group instruction such as lab groups, study groups, collaborative learning and problem-based learning? Matthews, Cooper, Davidson and Hawkes (10) have written a short piece using non-technical terminology that describes differences between cooperative and collaborative learning. For more detailed treatments of a number of small-group procedures readers may be interested in an article by Jean MacGregor and Barbara Leigh Smith in the Goodsell et al. book (62) or the fairly detailed taxonomy provided by Joe Cuseo (5). A number of other authors included in this document also address the distinctions between cooperative learning and other forms of small-group and active-learning strategies.

Is there research and theory which supports the use of cooperative learning? Is there supporting research at the college level? In SMET disciplines generally? In my discipline? The short answer is that there is considerable evidence that cooperative learning is effective in fostering a number of cognitive, affective and other outcomes. Much of the work has been done at the pre-collegiate level, as documented by the 1981 meta-analysis performed by David and Roger Johnson (9) and by their 1989 research and theory text (8). They also include research performed at the college level, as do Cooper (13) and his associates in three annotated bibliographies published in 1989, 1991 and 1995. Some of the citations from these bibliographies are included in the current annotated bibliography.

The best documentation that cooperative learning is effective in SMET disciplines in higher education can be found in the meta-analysis recently completed for NISE by Leonard Springer, Marybeth Stanne and Samuel Donovan (49). The NISE group found that SMET classes taught using cooperative learning achieved robust effect sizes when measuring the impact of cooperative learning on student achievement, student persistence and student attitudes. They have identified an ambitious line of future research which will address questions relating to the impact of cooperative learning on a number of student outcomes, types of students, and disciplinary areas.

Regarding the impact of cooperative learning on specific SMET-disciplinary areas, the college-level research is still relatively new and has yet to be systematically organized. Treismann (52) in mathematics, Felder (76, 77) in engineering, Heller (34) in physics and Cooper (23, 24) in chemistry have led colleagues within disciplinary groups demonstrating that small-group work can have a powerful impact on achievement, attrition and attitudes among students, particularly women and minorities.

The research and theory section of this bibliography identifies a number of qualitative and quantitative studies which are beginning steps in what we hope will be a long-term commitment by NISE, NSF and others to further assess the impact of cooperative learning within and across disciplines, and to organize this information in order to stimulate additional research and applied work.

Where can I find specific information regarding how to implement cooperative learning? I am specifically interested in college-level applications, preferably ones that are specific to my field. There are a number of workbooks that are useful. Spencer Kagan (66) has written a very applied text that identifies nearly 100 cooperative-learning techniques. The book is designed for K-12 personnel though it can be useful to higher-education practitioners. Philip Abrami and his colleagues (56) have written a general sourcebook which is designed for both collegiate and precollegiate audiences and combines a good mix of research, theory and practice. David and Roger Johnson and Karl Smith (64) have written an excellent workbook that is very popular. Designed for college teachers, it focuses on general applications of cooperative learning. Susan Nurrenbern has recently published a very useful cooperative-learning workbook (92) specifically designed for chemistry teachers. McNeill and Bellamy (89) have written a very applied workbook describing how cooperative learning can be used in engineering classes. Hagelgans et al. (1995) wrote a good workbook designed for college-level math teachers. Readers will want to consult the general and the SMET-related applied sections of the bibliography for many additional applications of cooperative learning.

Craig Bowen is working with NISE to develop a web site (http://144.92.236.220/main.html) that specifically addresses cooperative/collaborative learning issues in postsecondary SMET disciplines. We encourage readers to monitor this web site for information and resources on a variety of SMET teaching and learning issues, including new initiatives undertaken by NISE.

I'm new at this—what is a good reference to begin with if I want to try cooperative learning in my class? I am particularly interested in seeing college-level examples from my own discipline. For those in chemistry, the Nurrenbern workbook (92) is probably the best single source; those in mathematics will want to start with the Hagelgans et al. math workbook; for those in engineering the McNeill and Bellamy workbook (89) is probably the best reference with which to begin. The best general sourcebook for the beginner wishing to start using small-group instruction is the Johnson, Johnson and Smith workbook (64). It contains an introduction to the history of cooperative learning and addresses the research and theory base for the technique. It identifies a variety of small-group techniques in clear terms and treats assessment and grading issues. It even contains a sample syllabus. For brief, readable overviews of cooperative learning, the resources written by Barbara Millis (68, 69) are recommended.

The index for this bibliography identifies sources within specific disciplinary areas. The citations in italics identify resources within each discipline that we believe may be particularly useful for the person new to small-group instruction who is interested in very applied materials.

In Summary

This collection of resources dealing with cooperative learning in college-level SMET disciplines has been a challenge to assemble. We examined hundreds of documents in selecting the resources contained in this report. As noted earlier,

this bibliography is a work in progress that will change and grow as the work in cooperative learning continues to grow. We would like to hear from readers who wish to suggest materials for inclusion in future bibliographies.

Our intent with this document is to give readers a snapshot of the field at a point in time. It is incomplete and not entirely consistent, just as the research, theory and application of cooperative learning in SMET are incomplete and, at times, inconsistent. The work of NISE, NSF and other groups will ultimately provide more focus for this developing body of knowledge. But we believe that an interim report on the state of cooperative learning in SMET disciplines in higher education may serve to stimulate interest in more work which may bring greater coherence to this very young field.

Section 1. RESEARCH and THEORY

Section 1.A. General Cooperative-Learning Issues.

1. Bouton, C., & Garth, R. (Vol. Eds.) & K. E. Eble, & J. F. Noonan (Series Eds.). (1983). Learning in groups. *New directions for teaching and learning, no. 14.* San Francisco: Jossey-Bass.

A text in which a number of different chapter authors describe research and practice in collaborative learning. A good overview concerning how collaborative learning can be applied in a variety of college disciplines. Recommended for the new practitioner, and those already implementing collaborative techniques. The text includes an influential chapter dealing with the Atlas complex by Finkel and Monk. The Atlas complex is thinking that the instructor must take total responsibility for students' success. Finkel and Monk argue that instructors should work collaboratively with students in sharing responsibility for success in the classroom.[1]

2. Carrier, C. A., & Sales, G. C. (1987). Pair versus individual work on the acquisition of concepts in a computer-based instructional lesson. *Journal of Computer-Based Instruction,* 14(1), 11–17.

A very short-term study in which concept formation taught via computer-assisted instruction was compared for college students learning the information in pairs or individually. Although the pairs scored higher on an immediate posttest and a retention test given one week later, the differences were not statistically significant. The paired students asked for more elaborate feedback from the computer.[2]

3. Chickering, A. W., Gamson, Z. F. (1987). Seven principles for good practice in undergraduate education. *AAHE Bulletin,* 3–7.

A report published by AAHE identifying principles of good practice in undergraduate education. Among the principles identified are active learning, cooperation among students and frequent contact between faculty and students.[2]

4. Cohen, E. G. (1994). Restructuring the classroom: Conditions for productive small groups. *Review of Educational Research, 64*(1), 1–35.

A powerful and persuasive conceptual piece which identifies "conditions under which small groups in classrooms can be productive." The author examines type of discourse between students in both routine learning and more conceptual learning and suggests how task instructions, student preparation and teacher role can be differentially effective in the two types of learning. The author also address status problems in group learning. Not an easy read for most, but well worth the effort.

5. Cuseo, J. (1992, Winter). Collaborative & cooperative learning in higher education: A proposed taxonomy. *Cooperative Learning and College Teaching, 2*, 2–5.

This excellent article attempts to identify the variety of cooperative and collaborative techniques used in higher education by developing a taxonomy based on the types of interaction: a) student-student, b) teacher-teacher, and c) student-teacher. Cuseo describes procedures which are often not clearly distinguished, including cooperative learning, collaborative learning, peer teaching and learning communities. He is a contributing editor to the *Cooperative Learning and College Teaching* newsletter and has written many articles dealing with empirical and theoretical issues relating to teaching and learning. Topics Cuseo has examined include cooperative learning and its effects on student diversity, emotional development, critical thinking, and writing across the curriculum.

6. Davidson, N., & Worsham, T. (Eds.). (1992). *Enhancing thinking through cooperative learning.* NY: Teachers College Press.

A powerful book which addresses research, theory and practice concerning how cooperative learning can foster critical thinking. Among chapter authors are many leaders in cooperative learning as well as leaders in critical thinking, such as Robert Marzano, Arthur Costa and Toni Worsham. Most chapters deal with applications of small-group instruction to develop critical thinking, including a chapter dealing with science instruction and one dealing with math instruction. Highest recommendation.

7. Hertz-Lazarowitz, R., & Miller, N. (Eds.). (1992). *Interaction in cooperative groups: The theoretical anatomy of group learning.* Cambridge: Cambridge University Press.

This is an excellent sourcebook for those interested in academically rigorous discussions of empirical and theoretical issues in cooperative learning, focusing on K–12 populations.

8. Johnson, D. W., & Johnson, R. T. (1989). *Cooperation and competition: Theory and research.* Edina, MA: Interaction Book.

A research summary which describes the impact of cooperative learning on a variety of outcome measures. Results are reported separately for students of varying ages/grades (grades 1 though college and adult). Over 600 studies are cited in this meta-analysis. Must reading for anyone interested in research on cooperative learning at any level.

9. Johnson, D. W., Maruyama, G., Johnson, R. T., Nelson, D., & Skon, L. (1981). Effect of cooperative, competitive and individualistic goal structures on achievement: A meta-analysis. *Psychological Bulletin, 89*, 47–62.

Influential meta-analysis of cooperative-learning research. A review of 122 studies (largely K–12) which compared the effect of cooperative, competitive and individualistic goal structures in promoting student achievement and productivity. Results of the meta-analysis indicated that cooperation was considerably more effective than competitive or individualistic goal structures. Potential mediating variables accounting for the results are described.[1]

10. Matthews, R. S., Cooper, J. L., Davidson, N., & Hawkes, P. (1995, Fall). Building bridges between cooperative and collaborative learning. *Cooperative Learning and College Teaching, 6*, 2–5.

An interesting description of the similarities and differences between cooperative and collaborative learning, co-written by authors identified with each of the two approaches. Includes a good annotated bibliography of resources in both fields.

11. Millis, B. J. (1991). Fulfilling the promise of the "seven principles" through cooperative learning: Action agenda for the university classroom. *Journal on Excellence in College Teaching, 2*, 139–144.

A good article which indicates how cooperative learning implements the Seven Principles of Good Practice in Undergraduate Education reported by Chickering and Gamson in *The Wingspread Journal* (AAHE). Highly recommended.[2]

12. O'Donnell, A. M., & Dansereau, D. F. (1992). Scripted cooperation in student dyads: A method for analyzing and enhancing academic learning and performance. In R. Hertz-Lazarowitz, & N. Miller (Eds.), *Interaction in cooperative groups: The theoretical anatomy of group learning* (pp. 120–141). Cambridge: Cambridge University Press.

A thought-provoking chapter by two leaders of cooperative-learning research in higher education. They detail their decade-long research assessing the impact of various manipulations of cooperative-learning features on a number of outcome measures. Among the emerging principles they report: a) active engagement rather than passive involvement resulted in better performance on a variety of outcome measures (many relating to scientific technical information), b) use of cooperative learning for one task resulted in successful transfer of skills to other individually-completed tasks, c) teacher-structured cooperative-learning activities rather than student-structured dyadic activities generally produced better cognitive and affective performance, and d) heterogeneous dyads performed better than homogeneous dyads (largely due to increased performance by the lower-achieving member of the dyad). Most of this chapter deals with a specific cooperative-learning technique using dyads, called Scripted Cooperation, used in short-term laboratory studies. However, this chapter is for serious students of cooperative learning in higher education. Dansereau and O'Donnell have conducted many studies of cooperative learning in higher education, most of which have been well-controlled, short-term studies using dyads. O'Donnell has summarized some of her recent work in Vol. 4, No. 2 of *Cooperative Learning and College Teaching*.

13. Robinson, P., & Cooper, J. (1995). *An annotated bibliography of cooperative learning in higher education: Part III—the 1990s*. Stillwater, OK: New Forums Press.

The third in a series of annotated bibliographies completed by Cooper and his associates, all dealing with cooperative and collaborative learning in higher education (the others were published in 1989 and 1991). The 1995 bibliography contains 55 citations and is indexed by academic discipline (e.g., Physical Science, Engineering and Math, Biological and Health Sciences, Management and Business). There are separate sections for Research and Theory and for Applied work.

14. Sharan, S. (Ed.). (1990). *Cooperative learning: Theory and research*. New York: Praeger.

Although written with K–12 applications in mind, this book is must reading for anyone interested in research, theory and practice in cooperative learning. Twelve chapters written by various authors deal with such issues as causal mechanisms and cooperative learning, cooperative learning and achievement, and a perspective on research and practice in cooperative learning. Chapter authors include many of the influential thinkers in the cooperative-learning community, including Slavin and the Johnsons. Highly recommended.[2]

15. Sharan, Y., & Sharan, S. (1992). *Expanding cooperative learning through group investigation*. NY: Teachers College Press.

A well-written explication of Group Investigation, one of the most powerful cooperative learning procedures for fostering higher-order thinking. Group Investigation is a complex cooperative procedure in which students take responsibility for planning, carrying out and reporting on research projects which can last many weeks. Sharan and Sharan, who popularized the technique, describe the approach and offer example of Group Investigation within several disciplines. They also discuss the history of the approach and its effects on students. The examples use K–12 populations but the book is of value to all audiences.

16. Totten, S., Sills, T., Digby, A., & Russ, P. (1991). *Cooperative learning: A guide to research*. New York: Garland.

A book of 390 pages in which the authors present annotated bibliographies of the research in cooperative learning. Separate chapters contain bibliographies for various types of cooperative learning (e.g., Jigsaw, Group Investigation), subject areas, student outcomes affected by cooperative learning (e.g., mathematics, science, social skills) and other topics. The authors also present information on films, games, newsletters and organizations associated with cooperative learning. An excellent 18-page overview and introduction is also provided. The focus is largely on precollegiate work, reflecting the historical emphasis of cooperative-learning researchers. Must reading for anyone interested in research on cooperative learning (and interesting reading for practitioners wanting to find out more about applications of cooperative learning).[2]

Section 1.B. SMET-Related Cooperative-Learning Issues.

17. Basili, P. A., & Sanford, J. P. (1991). Conceptual change strategies and cooperative group work in chemistry. *Journal of Research in Science Teaching*, 28, 293–304.

An outstanding article comparing cooperative learning to a more traditional method of teaching introductory chemistry at a suburban community college. The researchers found that cooperatively-taught students had significantly lower misperceptions concerning chemistry concepts than traditionally-taught students and scored higher on an achievement test. The authors discuss four conditions for bringing about conceptual change in students first identified by Posner, et al. (1982): a) dissatisfaction with their present concepts, b) the correct concept must be intelligible, c) the correct concept must be plausible, and d) the correct concept must be useful. The authors present a fascinating discussion of how these conditions relate to conceptual change in chemistry using quantitative and qualitative data collection.

18. Bonsangue, M. (1994). An efficacy study of the calculus workshop model. *CBMS Issues in Collegiate Mathematics Education*, 4, 117–137.

An examination of an adaptation of Treisman's calculus workshop model for students at California State University, Pomona. Bonsangue found: a) no significant differences on a variety of pre-enrollment measures of achievement between minority students participating in the program and those not participating, b) minority students participating in the workshop had mean .6 higher GPA in calculus than minority non-participants and a much higher completion rate for the calculus sequences and math-based majors, c) the effects on academic achievement and persistence were particularly powerful for women, d) black and Latino workshop participants achieved at or above the level of all other ethnic groups at CSU Pomona, as measured by GPA in calculus and number of attempts required to complete the calculus sequence.

19. Bonsangue, M. (1991, January). *Achievement effects of collaborative learning in introductory statistics: A time series residual analysis.* Paper presented at the Joint Annual Meeting of the Mathematical Association of America/The American Mathematical Society, San Francisco, CA.

A study showing the benefits of collaborative/cooperative learning in an introductory statistics class. Comparison of control and experimental groups showed no difference on the first examination but significant differences in favor of the experimental group at measurement points thereafter. The study found evidence to support collaborative/cooperative learning as a useful alternative teaching method in mathematics.[2]

20. Burron, B., James, M. L., & Ambrosio, A. L. (1993). The effects of cooperative learning in a physical science course for elementary/middle level preservice teachers. *Journal of Research in Science Teaching, 30,* 697–707.

A comparison of traditionally- versus cooperatively-structured laboratory sections of a physical science course for preservice teachers. Two sections of the lab were taught using the Johnson's Learning Together technique and two using a traditional format. No significant differences were found in student achievement between the two instructional formats. Classroom observations of the two groups revealed that the cooperatively-taught students demonstrated more gains in collaborative behavior than comparison students. A posttest of student satisfaction with the course given only to the cooperatively-taught students indicated high levels of satisfaction.

21. Chang, G., Cook, D., Maguire, T., Skakun, E., Yakimets, W. W., & Warnock, G. L. (1994). Problem-based learning: Its role in undergraduate surgical education. *Canadian Journal of Surgery, 38*(1), 13–21.

A report of the appropriate role of problem-based learning (PBL) in the undergraduate clinical surgery course.

The authors report that meta-analyses of the effects of PBL in medical education indicate that it is equal to more traditional forms of instruction in fostering knowledge (rote) skills such as those tested in the National Board of Medical Examiners' tests. However, according to the authors, PBL produces more enthusiasm and more positive attitudes toward learning than more traditional methods.

22. Committee on the Mathematical Sciences in the Year 2000. (1991). *Moving beyond myths: Revitalizing undergraduate mathematics.* Washington, DC: National Academy Press.

A 65-page report of a committee of 20 academics, leaders of industry and public-policy makers, sponsored by the National Research Council. The report calls for: a) engaging college math faculty in issues of teaching and learning, b) elevating mathematics teaching to the same level as mathematics research, c) achieving parity for women and minorities in mathematics, and d) teaching in ways that engage students. The report decries overreliance on passive modes of instruction, including the lecture method, in favor of small-group instruction focusing on higher-order math skills.

23. Cooper, M. M. (1995). Cooperative chemistry laboratories. *Journal of Chemical Education, 71,* 307.

A description of cooperatively-taught chemistry labs at Clemson University which enroll as many as 2000 students per semester. Student teams work on three open-ended, multi-step projects per semester, rather than more traditional one-lab-period-closed exercises. TAs are trained to work with students as coaches and facilitators rather than teacher-experts. The author reports the results of a study in which half of the students in introductory chemistry received cooperatively-taught labs and the other half were taught using traditional procedures (all received the same lecture). She indicates that students in the cooperatively-taught labs reported more positive lab experiences and believed they learned more. Lecture-students' grades were 2–10% higher for women in cooperative labs than women in traditional labs. Course drop-out rate for women in the cooperatively-taught labs was 13%, compared with 21% for women in traditional labs. No achievement or drop-out rate differences were observed for men in the two lab formats.

24. Cooper, M. M. (1995). Cooperative learning: An approach for large-enrollment courses. *Journal of Chemical Education, 72,* 162–164.

The author describes the advantages and disadvantages of cooperative learning in general, and in large-lecture classes. She offers advice to instructors regarding preparation for cooperative-learning classes, with an emphasis on preparing for large classes. She reports on student attitudinal responses ("overwhelmingly positive") in a class of

190. Eight sample group-quiz problems that could be used in mid-lecture to stimulate discussion are also included. See Eric Mazur's article describing his work in physics for a similar lecture/quiz technique.

25. Courtney, D. P, Courtney, M., & Nicholson, D. (1992, November). *The effect of cooperative learning as an instructional practice at the college level.* Paper presented at the Annual Meeting of the Mid-South Educational Research Association, Knoxville, TN. (ERIC Document Reproduction Services No. ED 354 808)

A comparison of cooperative learning and a traditional lecture approach to the teaching of graduate-education statistics. The authors found no differences in achievement between the two sections on two multiple-choice achievement tests. They report highly favorable qualitative responses made by the cooperative learning students about self motivation, self efficacy, level of anxiety and social cohesiveness. This study has significant methodological flaws.[3]

26. Davis, R. B., Maher, C. A., & Noddings, N. (Eds.). (1990). *Constructivist views on the teaching and learning of mathematics* (Journal for Research in Mathematics Education Monograph No. 4). Reston, VA: National Council of Teachers of Mathematics.

A powerful exposition of the constructivist position as it relates to theory and practice in mathematics. A variety of authors in this theme issue of the journal describe the history and philosophy of constructivism and the implications of this position for learning and teacher training. Highly recommended.

27. DeClute, J., & Ladyshewsky, R. (1993). Enhancing clinical competence using a collaborative clinical education model. *Physical Therapy, 73,* 683–697.

A study which compared a 2:1 student to instructor ratio in the teaching of clinical skills in physical therapy with a more traditional 1:1 ratio. The authors found that the 2:1 ratio (which they characterized as a collaborative- or cooperative-learning model) produced higher performance on the clinical competence assessment form generated by the university. Three commentaries are appended to the article critiquing the collaborative model and the study itself. The authors' responses to the commentaries are also included.

28. Dees, R. L. (1991). The role of cooperative learning in increasing problem-solving ability in a college remedial course. *Journal for Research in Mathematics Education, 22,* 409–421.

A comparison of cooperatively- and traditionally-structured discussion sections of a remedial mathematics college course enrolling approximately 100 students per semester. The researcher found that cooperatively-taught students developed better higher-order math skills than the traditionally-taught students. The cooperatively-taught students had more skill in solving word problems in algebra and proof writing in geometry. The procedures used in the sections identified as using cooperative learning implemented somewhat informal small-group techniques, rather than formal cooperative-learning structures.

29. Duckwall, J. M., Arnold, L., Willoughby, T. L., Calkins, E. V., and Hamburger, S. C. (1990). An assessment of the student partnership program at the University of Missouri-Kansas City School of Medicine. *Academic Medicine, 65,* 697–701.

A report of a partnership program at the University of Missouri-Kansas City School of Medicine. The program combines a bachelor's degree with a medical degree in a six-year course of study. Third-year students are paired with fifth-year students in a two-month internal-medicine rotation required of all students during the last four years of the program. Teams of 12 students are supervised by medical faculty. Survey and interview results presented in this article report generally positive results of the student pairings. The authors recommend that those wishing to maximize success in similar programs should: a) have training sessions for students and teachers to clarify expectations, teach interpersonal skills and engender commitment to the program, b) use teacher-directed assignment of pairs (rather than random assignment), and c) create an environment of cooperation rather than competition for grades.

30. Frierson, H. T. (1986). Two intervention methods: Effects on groups of predominantly black nursing students' board scores. *Journal of Research and Development in Education, 19,*(3) 18–23.

A study of 139 nursing students who attended a predominantly black state college. Students studying cooperatively for the state nursing board exam and who also received instruction in test-taking strategies received higher board exam scores than nursing students who received no intervention or who received just test-taking strategies instruction.[1]

31. Frierson, H. T., Jr. (1987, Spring). Academic performance in predominantly black nursing classes: Effects associated with intervention designed for standardized test preparation. *Journal of Research and Development in Education, 20*(3) 37–40.

A follow-up to the Frierson (1986) article dealing with the effects of cooperative learning on the performance of nursing students at a minority institution taking the state nursing certification exam. In the study described in this article one group of students was exposed to a traditional-instruction method, another group received regular instruction plus eight hours of test-taking instruction.

A third group of students received regular instruction plus twelve hours of instruction combining test-taking strategies with cooperative learning. Both experimental groups received higher GPAs than the traditionally-taught comparison group. However, the students receiving the cooperative-learning intervention had a substantially higher GPA than the students in the other two groups. In addition, the students in the cooperative-learning group increased their GPA from a Fall semester mean of 2.21 to a Spring semester mean of 3.09.

32. Garland, M. (1993). The mathematics workshop model: An interview with Uri Treisman. *Journal of Developmental Education, 16, 14–16, 18, 20, 22.*

An interview with Uri Treisman whose work with minority students in calculus brought national attention to small-group instruction in the 1980s. Treisman indicates that to increase the academic performance of at-risk students a fundamental re-examination of the curriculum and related services must be instituted (including but not limited to cooperative learning). An interesting insight into the mind of a successful educational change agent examining twenty years of tilting at the status quo.

33. Hagelgans, N. L., Reynolds, B. E., Schwingendorf, K., Vidakovic, D., Dubinsky, E., Shahin, M., & Wimbish, J. G., Jr. (1995). *A practical guide to cooperative learning in collegiate mathematics* (MAA Notes No. 37). Washington, DC: Mathematical Association of America.

A relatively short book designed to introduce the college math instructor to cooperative-learning research, theory and practice. A number of sample activities are described from several math courses. The authors also describe the results of a survey returned by 42 college math teachers who use cooperative procedures. Very applied and easy to read.

34. Heller, P., Keith, R., & Anderson, S. (1992). Teaching problem solving through cooperative grouping. Part 1: Group versus individual problem solving. *American Journal of Physics Teachers, 60, 627–636.*

Heller, P., & Hollabaugh, M. (1992). Teaching problem solving through cooperative grouping. Part 2: Designing problems and structuring groups. *American Journal of Physics Teachers, 60, 637–244.*

A fascinating description of how cooperative learning can be combined with explicit ("expert") problem-solving strategies to foster improved problem solving in college physics classes (although this article would be of interest to those in math, engineering and a variety of other science-related fields as well). Part 1 of the article details how the authors taught a five-step problem-solving strategy to their students and combined the techniques with the use of context-rich, real-world problem sets (as opposed to rote, textbook problems). The problem sets were solved in cooperative-learning groups. The authors found that such a curricular and instructional approach had a significant impact on conceptual understanding, usefulness of the physics description and the matching of the description with the mathematics needed to solve the problems. They also found that the positive effect of the intervention was significant for students at all ability levels (including the best students). When students in the classes described above were compared with students taught with more traditional instruction on two exercise problems, the cooperative learning students performed at a much higher level. Part 2 of the article describes practical advice for implementing the techniques described in Part 1. The authors offer their advice on such issues as optimal group size (three or four on a team is better than two, and teams of three are the best) and gender composition of the three-person teams favored by the authors (same sex teams, and teams with two females and one male are better than teams with two males and one female). The authors favor heterogeneously-formed teams based on achievement. They also give advice on forming and testing "context-rich" problems. Highest recommendation for college teachers in all disciplines.[3]

35. Hooper, S., Sales, G., & Rysavy, S. D. M. (1994). Generating summaries and analogies alone and in pairs. *Contemporary Educational Psychology, 19, 53–62.*

A short-term study in which students worked alone or in pairs to master a 6200-word text passage dealing with marine life. Some students were given instructions to use analogies in learning the content of the passages, others were given instructions to generate summaries of paragraphs within the passages and others were given neither analogy nor summarizing (cognitive elaboration) strategies. Students working alone scored higher than students working in pairs on a test of rote knowledge of the passage content. Students using cognitive-elaboration strategies scored higher than those using analogies. Learning rates or efficiency was higher for students working alone. The authors hypothesize that the relatively poor performance for pairs may be that the dyads did not perceive positive interdependence between each other and did not participate in self evaluation, factors considered essential in small-group learning, according to Johnson, Johnson, and Smith (1991) and other cooperative-learning theorists.[2]

36. Jones, J. D., & Brickner, D. (1996, June). *Implementation of cooperative learning in a large-enrollment basic-mechanics course.* Paper presented at the American Society for Engineering Education Annual Conference, Washington DC.

A well-designed comparison of two sophomore-level basic-mechanics classes lasting one year and having enrollments of around 100. The cooperatively-taught class used a highly-structured procedure consisting of mini-lecture, sample problem analysis and collaborative problem sets which were completed during each class meeting. The traditionally-taught class used a lecture method of instruction. The cooperatively-taught classes generally achieved at a higher level on in-class exams, GPA and reported more positive attitudes on a survey of work habits and attitudes, particularly attitudes toward the teacher. There were positive anecdotal responses concerning the course from 90–95% of the students in the cooperatively-taught section. The authors suggest that random formation of groups is as effective as teacher formation of heterogeneous groups. They base their perceptions about group formation on their in-class experiences rather than more formal research procedures.

37. Kacer, R., Rocklin, T., & Weinholtz, D. (1992). Individual versus small group instruction of computer applications: A quantitative and qualitative comparison. *Journal of Computing in Teacher Education,* 9(1), 6–12.

   A study in which groups of students in a computer-applications class were randomly assigned to work either alone or in cooperative-learning groups. Quantitative measures revealed no difference between the groups on achievement or attitude. Qualitative measures suggested that the cooperative-learning students engaged in more planning activities and had better conceptual understanding of the content.

38. Lawrenz, F., & Munch, T. W. (1984). The effect of grouping of laboratory students on selected educational outcomes. *Journal of Research in Science Teaching,* 21, 699–708.

   A study comparing three ways of forming teams in a laboratory science class taught to undergraduate education students. Students in groups formed heterogeneously and homogeneously (based on reasoning ability) received higher scores on a posttest of science knowledge relative to students in self-selected teams. Students in classes using heterogeneously-formed teams did not differ in achievement from students in classes using homogeneous grouping. No differences between the three grouping conditions were observed in measures of students' perceptions of classroom environment.

39. Lord, T. R. (1994). Using constructivism to enhance student learning in college biology. *Journal of College Science Teaching,* 23, 346–348.

   A short article in which the author presents a detailed description of a cell-division lesson in a biology class for non-majors. The author uses as his constructivist conceptual base a 5E model attributed to Rodger Bybee. The five

elements of the teaching model are Engage, Explore, Explain, Elaborate and Evaluate. Must reading for biology teachers and others interested in keeping students actively involved in science classes.

40. Lundeberg, M. A., & Moch, S. D. (1995). Influence of social interaction on cognition: Connected learning in science. *Journal of Higher Education,* 66, 312–335.

   A qualitative study that uses Supplemental Instruction in health-science classes taken by female nursing students. Based on a variety of data-collection procedures, the authors suggest that female students in science classes may learn best when: a) a sense of cooperation and community is fostered in the classroom, b) risk taking is encouraged, c) power is shifted from the instructor to the students, d) students assess their own and their colleagues' knowledge in an ongoing fashion, and e) abstract concepts are related to the students' lives.

41. Marks, M. (1991). *Cooperative learning in chemistry.* College Park, MD: Center for Teaching Excellence.

   Marks describes the process of designing and implementing cooperative learning in an honors chemistry class at a university. He reports favorable results from questionnaires administered to the students regarding attitudes about cooperative learning, and includes some of the dialogue from student interviews about the cooperative-learning techniques used in the class. This honors chemistry class had a higher average on a final exam that was also administered to a regular section of chemistry and another honors section not using cooperative-learning techniques. The instructors were also interviewed and said that cooperative learning "keeps the students involved," and that they do not teach but "provide a way for students to learn."[2]

42. Mohr, P. H. (1995). Cognitive development in college men and women as measured on the Perry scheme when learning and teaching styles are addressed in a chemical engineering curriculum. (Doctoral dissertation, North Carolina State University, 1995). *Dissertation Abstracts International,* 56(08), 3020A.

   A study comparing differences in Perry's cognitive-development positions for undergraduate chemical-engineering students exposed to cooperatively-taught classes versus those exposed to more traditional forms of instruction. Students (both male and female) exposed to the cooperatively-taught classes demonstrated greater gains in Perry positions than students exposed to traditional-instructional formats.

43. Posner, H. B., & Markstein, J. A. (1994). Cooperative learning in introductory cell and molecular biology. *Journal of College Science Teaching,* 23, 231–233.

   A study comparing the use of cooperative learning to more traditional methods of teaching discussion sections of large enrollment introductory cell and molecular biology courses. The researchers found that: a) retention rates for minority students in cooperatively-taught sections substantially exceeded rates for similar students in traditional sections, b) grades for regularly-admitted minority students were higher in the cooperatively-taught sections, c) student attitudes in cooperatively-taught sections were generally positive, and d) minority-student enrollment in advanced biology courses increased after implementation of cooperative learning in the introductory course. However, cooperatively-taught sections did not produce significantly differential effects on minority students' grades among special-admissions students. Also, the study was confounded in that cooperatively-taught sections had more than one discussion leader per section.

44. Posner, G. J., Strike, K. A., Hewson, P. W., & Gertzog, W. A. (1982). Accommodation of a scientific conception: Toward a theory of conceptual change. *Science Education, 66*, 211–227.

A fascinating article that argues that for conceptual change (accommodation) to occur in students four conditions must be present. First, there must be dissatisfaction with existing conceptions. Second, the new conception must be intelligible to the learner. This intelligibility is often fostered by the use of analogies and metaphors. Third, the new conception must appear initially plausible. Often this involves consistency of the new concept with existing knowledge. Fourth, the new concept should suggest the possibility of a fruitful extension to new areas of inquiry. The authors discuss the implications of their formulation for curriculum and teaching. Although the authors do not specifically discuss cooperative learning, their recommendations for teaching are consistent with cooperative-learning techniques (e.g., creating cognitive conflict, organizing instruction so the teacher is a facilitator not a lecturer, using multiple presentation modes and multiple modes of assessment for student errors in thinking). Highest recommendation.

45. Roth, W., & Roychoudhury, A. (1993). Using vee and concept maps in collaborative settings: Elementary education majors construct meaning in physical science courses. *School Science and Mathematics, 93*, 237–244.

A qualitative study of the impact of using collaborative learning, concept maps and Vee mapping in a course in physics methods for elementary education ($n = 27$). Authors report that over the term the use of collaborative learning and mapping caused students to produce maps containing larger numbers of meaningful, relevant concepts and increased positive affect (attitude) of students toward the pedagogy.[2]

46. Ryan, M. A., Robinson, D., & Carmichael, J. W., Jr. (1980). A Piagetian-based general chemistry laboratory program for science majors. *Journal of Chemical Education, 57*, 642–645.

Describes a chemistry program at a historically-black college based on the principles of collaborative learning and Piaget. Data-analysis focus is on a chemistry lab taught using a Piagetian/collaborative approach versus a more traditional approach. Authors conclude that students performed equally well on a "skills-based" final exam but that experimental-group students performed better on a Piagetian-like test, rated the course higher on a post-course evaluation and had better attendance.[2]

47. Shaw, M. E., Ackerman, B., McCown, N. E., Worsham, A. P., Haugh, L. D., Gebhardt, B. M., & Small, P. A., Jr. (1979). Interaction patterns and facilitation of peer learning. *Small Group Behavior, 10*, 214–223.

A study conducted on first-year medical and dental students enrolled in an immunology course. The authors found that group members who gave information to peers in their small groups were perceived as facilitating group performances. However, group members asking for information were more important in actual facilitation of group learning, based on Bales' method for interaction process analysis.

48. Shearn, E., & Davidson, N. (1989, March). *Use of small-group teaching and cognitive developmental instruction in a mathematical course for prospective elementary school teachers.* Paper presented at the Meeting of the American Education Research Association, San Francisco.

Two groups of teacher trainees taking an introductory math course were exposed to cooperative learning. Cognitive development (based on Perry's model) and students' self concept increased from pretest to posttest.[2]

49. Springer, L., Stanne, M. E., & Donovan, S. (1997, January). *Effects of cooperative learning on academic achievement among undergraduates in science, mathematics, engineering, and technology: A meta-analysis* (Unpublished Report). Madison, WI: University of Wisconsin-Madison and National Center for Improving Science Education, The National Institute for Science Education.

A significant addition to the literature on cooperative learning in SMET disciplines in higher education. The authors provide a brief introduction to cooperative-learning research and theory, then detail their meta-analysis methodology, results and conclusions. They focused on classroom-based research using academic achievement as their outcome measure. Their conclusion that "cooperative learning is more effective than traditional forms of instruction" in science and mathematics courses is based on an effect size in excess of .50.

50. Steen, L. A. (1992). 20 questions that deans should ask their mathematics department (Or, that a sharp department will ask itself.). *AAHE Bulletin,* 44,(9), 3–6.

A highly readable brief article that calls for a re-examination of the ways in which mathematics is taught at the college level. The author, a contributor to the National Research Council publication *Moving Beyond Myths: Revitalizing Undergraduate Mathematics,* summarizes the findings of that 1991 report. He also describes the 1989 report of the National Council of Teachers of Mathematics. Both publications call for more active learning/teaching and a greater emphasis on higher-order thinking in the math classroom. The central role of mathematics in influencing retention rates, particularly for women and minorities, is also addressed. The author calls for greater attention to professional development for college mathematics teachers dealing with such topics as effective teaching and assessment.

51. Tobias, S. (1990). They're not dumb. They're different. A new "tier of talent" for science. *Change,* 22, 110–30.

An excerpt from Tobias' well-known book *They're Not Dumb. They're Different.* Tobias conducted a qualitative study in which seven auditors attended physics and chemistry classes as if they were students and kept logs of their responses to the classes. Tobias found that women perceive science classes as unfriendly and are "uncomfortable" working in the intensely competitive environment of many introductory science classes. Tobias' findings coincide with a University of Michigan study that found that women (and other students who were academically qualified to major in science but chose not to) would perform better in "cooperative and interactive modes of learning" and if "scientific knowledge were more closely linked to important societal issues."

52. Treisman, U. (1985). A study of the mathematics performance of black students at the University of California, Berkeley (Doctoral dissertation, University of California, Berkeley, 1986). *Dissertation Abstracts International,* 47, 1641-A.

A description of Treisman's important research concerning collaborative learning with minority math and science students at Berkeley. Black students enrolled in this enrichment program received significantly higher grade-point averages in freshman calculus, graduated in math-based majors four times more often and had significantly lower attrition rates than comparable black students not enrolled in the program. Treisman's model is now used at a number of colleges in math, science and engineering programs, with minority and other students.[1]

53. Valentino, V. R. (1988). A study of achievement, anxiety, and attitude toward mathematics in college algebra students using small group interaction methods. (Doctoral dissertation, West Virginia University, 1988). *Dissertation Abstracts International,* 50(02), 379A.

A comparison of a highly-structured form of cooperative learning known as STAD (Slavin, 1995) with a lecture method of teaching college algebra. Students in the cooperatively-taught section had higher course completion rates, lowered math anxiety and more positive attitudes toward mathematics. Math achievement scores were generally higher in the cooperatively-taught class (though not statistically significant).

54. Watson, B. B., & Marshall, J. E. (1995). Effects of cooperative incentives and heterogeneous arrangement on achievement and interaction of cooperative-learning groups in a college life science course. *Journal of Research in Science Teaching,* 32, 291–299.

A relatively well-controlled study of cooperative incentives and heterogeneous grouping in a college life-science course for education majors. The treatment lasted four weeks and involved using a Jigsaw instructional technique with a multiple-choice science-achievement test used as the dependent measure. Jigsaw is a technique in which each team member is responsible for learning different elements of an assignment, then teaching that element to teammates. The researchers reported no achievement differences for students put in 3–4 person cooperative teams formed heterogeneously versus homogeneously (based on science achievement pretest scores). No achievement differences were found for students given grade incentives for group performance relative to students given individual performance grades. The authors report that these findings are inconsistent with research and practice reported at the precollegiate level (although they report that the research on homogeneous versus heterogeneous team formation at precollegiate levels is inconsistent).

55. Weissglass, J. (1993). Small-group learning. *The American Mathematical Monthly,* 100, 662–668.

A personal account of how one mathematics professor came to use small-group learning in his college classes. The author offers advice on a number of issues relating to small-group instruction, including how to get started, how to address student needs and concerns and how to develop institutional support.

Section 2. APPLICATIONS

Section 2.A. General Cooperative-Learning Issues.

56. Abrami, P. C., Chambers, B., Poulsen, C., De Simone, C., d'Apollonia, S., Howden, J. (1995). *Classroom connections: Understanding and using cooperative learning.* Toronto, Ontario, Canada: Harcourt Brace.

A very good handbook that covers empirical, theoretical and practical issues regarding cooperative learning. The authors treat such topics as theoretical explanations for the efficacy of cooperative learning (e.g., cognitive, behavioral, humanistic) and the research base for its effectiveness. They also treat a variety of specific approaches to cooperative learning (e.g., STAD, Jigsaw, Group Investigation). A good contribution to the field. Written for both precollegiate and college teachers.

57. Abercrombie, M. L. J. (1974). *Aims and techniques of group teaching.* London: Society for Research into Higher Education, Ltd.

A short book describing a variety of small-group techniques, including syndicate learning, peer tutoring and associative group discussion. Emphasis is on work conducted in Britain. Abercrombie's work on collaborative learning with medical students at the University of London is considered by Kenneth Bruffee and others as seminal.[1]

58. Cooper, J. L., Prescott, S., Cook, L., Smith, L., Mueck, R., & Cuseo, J. (1990). *Cooperative learning and college instruction: Effective use of student learning teams.* Long Beach, CA: The California State University Foundation on behalf of California State University Institute for Teaching and Learning.

A 50-page workbook designed for college instructors interested in incorporating cooperative learning into their courses with minimal disruption to existing teaching formats such as lecture and lecture-discussion. Among the topics treated are the benefits of using cooperative learning, critical features, organizing the classroom, trouble-shooting problems in implementation, and tips on getting started. Very practical.[2]

59. Feichtner, S. B., & Davis, E. A. (1984–1985). Why some groups fail: A survey of students' experiences with learning groups. *The Organizational Behavior Teaching Review,* 9(4), 58–71.

A description of good and bad collaborative learning procedures in college settings. Very practical.[1]

60. Forest, L. (Ed.). *Cooperative Learning.*

Special-theme issues of the magazine have dealt with the teaching of math and science. In 1993 they published a theme issue dealing with higher education, though most issues tend to focus on precollegiate applications. A good blend of applied research, theory and practice, with a de-cided emphasis on practice. Persons interested in subscribing may contact the magazine at (514) 848-2020.

61. Gabelnick, F., MacGregor, J., Matthews, R. S., & Smith, B. L. (1990). Learning communities: Creating connections among students, faculty, and disciplines. In R. E. Young (Series Ed.), *New directions for teaching and learning,* no. 41. San Francisco: Jossey-Bass.

An excellent source which describes a number of learning communities. Among the issues treated are the history of learning communities, faculty and student perspectives and curriculum issues relating to the subject. The last chapter describes a variety of resources for those wishing to find out more about learning communities. Recommended.

62. Goodsell, A., Maher, M., & Tinto, V. (1992). *Collaborative learning: A sourcebook for higher education.* University Park, PA: National Center on Postsecondary Teaching, Learning, & Assessment.

A good sourcebook which contains a number of reprints and original articles by leaders in the cooperative- and collaborative-learning movement, including Kenneth Bruffee, Barbara Leigh Smith, Jean MacGregor, Karl Smith and Roger and David Johnson. Leigh Smith and MacGregor contributed an excellent article which identifies a variety of collaborative techniques, including discussions of problem-based learning, guided design, cooperative learning, writing groups and learning communities. The sourcebook includes an annotated bibliography and a listing of sites and networks where collaborative learning is used. National Resource Center materials can be ordered by calling (814) 865-5917.[2]

63. Johnson, D. W., Johnson, R. T., & Smith, K. A. (1986). Academic conflict among students: Controversy and learning. In R. S. Feldman (Ed.), *The social psychology of education: Current research and theory* (pp. 199–231). Cambridge: Cambridge University Press.

A textbook chapter which describes a specific form of cooperative learning known as structured controversy. In structured controversy, members of the same learning team assume different positions concerning an issue in an attempt to ultimately maximize learning for all team members through discussion and research relating to the positions. Authors conclude that this technique sparks conceptual conflict within students, creates epistemological curiosity and promotes higher-level thinking skills.[1]

64. Johnson, D. W., Johnson, R. T., & Smith, K. A. (1991). *Active learning: Cooperation in the college classroom.* Edina, MN: Interaction Book.

An excellent workbook which provides a wealth of practical information concerning cooperative learning and college teaching. This is the book to buy if you only purchase one general source of information on the subject. Highest recommendation. To purchase this book and other materials call (612) 831-9500.[2]

65. Kadel, S., & Keehner, J. A. (1994). *Collaborative learning: A sourcebook for higher education,* vol. II. (K. Parsley, Ed.). University Park, PA: National Center on Postsecondary Teaching, Learning, & Assessment.

The second sourcebook published by the National Center (which was funded by the U.S. Department of Educational Research and Improvement). The book begins with the text of a keynote presented by Zelda Gamson, which presents her view of collaborative learning from both a historical and a contemporary perspective. This is followed by a series of short articles by a number of figures in cooperative and collaborative learning. There is also a series of somewhat sketchy one- and two-page descriptions of both generic applications of collaborative learning and applications in specific disciplines, including a few in SMET.

66. Kagan, S. (1994). *Cooperative learning.* San Juan Capistrano, CA: Resources for Teachers.

Kagan's workbook is a rich source of ideas concerning applications of cooperative learning to a host of outcomes and issues. Over 100 activities or cooperative-learning structures are reported in the index, most of which appear to be field-tested. An invaluable source of ideas, checklists, lesson plans and materials are provided. The workbook is clearly focused on elementary teachers but the structures described can easily be adapted to the college classroom. To purchase this text and additional cooperative-learning materials call 1-800-933-2667.

67. Michaelsen, L., Watson, W. E., & Sharder, C. B. (1984–1985). Informative testing—a practical approach for tutoring with groups. *The Organizational Behavior Teaching Review,* 9 (4), 18–33.

A description of a collegiate collaborative-learning technique using organizational behavior as a framework. Focus is on the use of highly-structured criterion-referenced testing combined with highly-structured group activities designed to diagnosis and remediate students' learning.[1]

68. Millis, B. J. (1990). Cooperative-learning strategies for continuing-education faculty. In M. C. Natelli, & T. F. Kowalik (Eds.), *Continuing Education: A Critical Reflection.* Proceedings of the 1990 Annual Conference of Region II, National University Continuing Education Association (pp. 41–49). Binghamton, NY: National University Continuing Education Association. (ERIC Document Reproduction Service No. ED 324 455)

Millis outlines the critical features of cooperative learning and relates cooperative learning to characteristics of the adult learner. She also outlines a number of specific cooperative-learning procedures. Highly recommended.[2]

69. Millis, B. J. (1991). Helping faculty build learning communities through cooperative groups. In L. Hilsen (Ed.), *To improve the academy: Resources for student, faculty, and institutional development* (pp. 43–58). Stillwater, OK: New Forums Press.

An excellent source describing a variety of cooperative-learning techniques at the college level. Although research support is cited, the focus is on very practical applications of cooperative learning across all disciplines. Highly recommended for new practitioners as well as more experienced users.[2]

70. O'Donnell, A., & Adenwalla, D. (1989, July). Scripted cooperation and knowledge maps: Information processing tools applied to deaf education. In D. Martin (Ed.), *International symposium on cognition, education, and deafness,* 2 (pp. 836–854). Washington, DC. (ERIC Document Reproduction Service No. ED 313 849)

O'Donnell and Adenwalla describe the uses of scripted cooperative learning and the use of knowledge mapping. Scripted cooperation is a method for structuring cooperative learning which uses student pairs. Students alternate roles as recaller of information and checker of the correctness of the recall. Both members of the dyad attempt to elaborate and use other metacognitive strategies to assist retention. In knowledge mapping, information is presented in two-dimensional representations. Idea units are connected to other ideas using a series of links in order to render relationships more explicit to the teacher and students. Both scripted cooperation and knowledge mapping are potentially powerful metacognitive additions to cooperation which should be considered by cooperative-learning practitioners interested in enhancing long-term retention and critical thinking. Highly recommended.[2]

71. Prescott, S. (1996, Fall). Trouble-shooting. *Cooperative Learning and College Teaching,* 7, 5–6.

This article is one in a series of very helpful articles written by the author for the *Cooperative Learning and College Teaching* newsletter. In this article she focuses on the importance of clarity of content in designing cooperative-learning tasks. She notes that many instructors are much too global in their thinking about course content and what knowledge students should be able to demonstrate regarding that content. She also indicates that many instructors are unclear when telling cooperative groups how to complete exercises. Prescott writes a regular Trouble-shooting column for the newsletter which addresses implementation issues in cooperative learning. She has addressed such topics as cooperative learning and: a) students' reflective thinking, b) teacher planning, c) when to use small-group work, d) graphic organizers, and e) student empowerment.

72. Whitman, N. A. (1988). *Peer teaching: To teach is to learn twice* (ASHE-ERIC Higher Education Report No. 4) Washington, DC: Association for the Study of Higher Education.

An excellent short book which describes five major approaches to peer teaching and summarizes the empirical support for each. The techniques described include the use of teaching assistants, tutors, and counselors within and outside of the classroom. Student partnerships and student work groups which closely approximate the critical features of cooperative learning are described. Text includes a good reference section.[2]

Section 2.B. SMET-Related Cooperative-Learning Issues.

73. Davidson, N. (Ed.). (1990). *Cooperative learning in mathematics.* Menlo Park, CA: Addison-Wesley.

A handbook focusing largely on cooperative learning at the K–12 level. However, many of the exercises and descriptions can be adapted for use in college-level mathematics. Chapter authors include many of the leaders in application of cooperative learning to mathematics, including Elizabeth Cohen, Julian Weissglass, Marilyn Burns and Neil Davidson. Davidson's introduction and review chapter are especially good.

74. Dedic, H., Rosenfield, S., d'Apollonia, S., & De Simone, C. (1994, Spring). Using cooperative concept mapping in college science classes. *Cooperative Learning and College Teaching, 4,* 12–15.

The authors describe a combination of cooperative learning and concept mapping in college science courses. They indicate that Cooperative Concept Mapping enhances students' knowledge acquisition, organization and metacognition. The authors offer advice to teachers interested in introducing this strategy. They provide an example of how a team of students interact using Cooperative Concept Mapping in solving a physics problem. The authors report success in implementing the procedures in college physics, biology, statistics and astronomy classes.

75. Della-Piana, C. K., Villa, E. Q., & Pinon, S. D. (1996, June). *Using cooperative learning in a freshman summer engineering orientation program.* Paper presented at the American Society for Engineering Education Annual Conference, Washington, DC.

Describes a required summer bridge program for 200–300 computer science and engineering students at the University of Texas at El Paso, the largest university in the US with a majority Hispanic student population. The program

lasts for one week and is based on cooperative-learning principles. Program-evaluation information indicated that the program was rated successful on several criteria. Ratings information was obtained by a questionnaire regarding the quality of the math workshops, group projects and work related to academic success. Ninety-seven percent of respondents reported that they would recommend the summer session to friends.

76. Felder, R. M., & Brent, R. (1994). *Cooperative learning in technical courses: Procedures, pitfalls, and payoffs.* Raleigh: North Carolina State University. (ERIC Document Reproduction Service No. ED 377 038)

A very practical discussion of how Felder implements cooperative learning in his five-course chemical-engineering sequence. The authors introduce the features of cooperative learning and describe a number of cooperative exercises that have worked well in Felder's courses (both in-class and out-of-class). They also present a brief case study of the five-semester sequence. Finally, the authors address common concerns expressed by faculty members considering adoption of cooperative learning and the authors' responses to these concerns. Highest recommendation.

77. Felder, R. M. (1991). It goes without saying. *Chemical Engineering Education, 25,* 132–133.

This interesting short article takes the reader step-by-step through a one-hour small-group problem-solving exercise for a sophomore course in chemical engineering. Felder set up a problem for his students and then guided them through a series of interim solutions which ultimately led to the final resolution of the problem. In his article, Felder points out how the exercise required his students to use information related to a number of important concepts within the course and related courses, yielding a level of understanding much more profound than that achieved with his former teaching style, the lecture. Although the lesson dealt with a very technical area of engineering, the step-by-step Guided Design approach taken can be used in a variety of courses.[3]

78. Hart, F. L., & Groccia, J. E. (1994, February). *An integrated, cooperative learning oriented freshman civil engineering course: Computer analysis in civil engineering.* Paper presented at the Freshman Year Experience Conference, Columbia, SC.

Summary of a presentation which describes innovative approaches being used at Worcester Polytechnic Institute in the undergraduate curriculum. This description focuses on the use of formal- and informal-learning teams and computers in the teaching of a civil-engineering class. Both graduate and undergraduate aides are used to facilitate group functioning. At Worcester a premium is put on oral presentation of laboratory findings and integration of knowledge.

79. Hassard, J. (1990). *Science experiences: Cooperative learning and the teaching of science.* Menlo Park, CA: Addison-Wesley.

A useful workbook of science activities using a number of cooperative-learning structures. Although designed for elementary classrooms, the ideas presented may be of value to science teachers at all levels. The first three chapters include introductory material related to experiential learning, brain research, holistic instruction and shifts in instructional paradigms from product/outcome orientations to process/student-oriented approaches.

80. Johnson, D. W., & Johnson, R. T. (Eds.). (1991). *Learning mathematics and cooperative learning: Lesson plans for teachers.* Edina, MN: Interaction Books.

A set of lesson plans developed by teachers, administrators, adult educators and college professors. The focus is on K–12 math instruction but the procedures can easily be adapted for collegiate applications.

81. Klemm, W. R. (1995, Spring). Computer conferencing as a cooperative learning environment. *Cooperative Learning and College Teaching, 5,* 11–13.

A description of the use of cooperative computer conferencing in a neuroanatomy class. The author criticizes the use of E-mail and listservs in college courses and argues for his method of conferencing using hypermedia links to address weekly issues relating to brain organization and functioning. The weekly computer-based activities include student ratings of one anothers' performance and required "insights" relating to lecture content. A very elaborate organizational plan for combining cooperative learning and technology in the classroom.

82. Laws, P. W., Rosborough, P. J., & Poodry, F. J. (1995). Women's responses to an activity-based introductory physics program. In J. Gainen, & F. W. Willemsen (Eds.), *Fostering student success in quantitative gateway courses. New Directions for Teaching and Learning* 61, (pp.77–87). San Francisco: Jossey-Bass.

An interesting short chapter that describes the physics workshop curriculum at Dickinson College. The authors use a variety of collaborative-learning procedures and often use a four-part learning technique based on the work of cognitive psychologist David Kolb. The authors report that students taught using their small-group procedure mastered higher-order physics concepts in much larger numbers than students taught more traditionally, and generally have more positive attitudes toward a variety of learning experiences. Women students at Dickinson were as likely to major in physics as their male colleagues. The authors also note that a number of students, including about 20% of the female students, did not express positive attitudes about the small-group workshop approach. The authors attribute much of this to prior negative experiences working in small groups and to feelings that the instructors should present the information in a clear and straight-forward lecture format.

83. Leron, U., & Dubinsky, E. (1995). An abstract algebra story. *American Mathematical Monthly,* 102, 227–242.

An outstanding article in which the authors describe teaching three concepts in algebra using small-group instruction with computers. The authors include typical student discussions that take place as they work collaboratively on the problems. This is a very detailed discussion with step-by-step explications of how students construct meaning using small-group procedures. The authors also present and respond to objections to their procedures. Highly recommended.

84. Long, G. A. (1989). Cooperative learning: A new approach. *Journal of Agricultural Education,* 30(2), 2–9.

An article which describes a variety of cooperative-learning techniques such as STAD, Jigsaw I and II, as well as team building and other elements of cooperative learning. The focus is on university-level agricultural classes but the techniques can be applied in a variety of college-level disciplines. Recommended as a brief overview of a number of cooperative-learning practices.[2]

85. Mattila, L. (1990). *Using cooperative learning groups in teaching computer science.* Unpublished manuscript.

A very brief report describing the application of cooperative learning to a community-college computer-science class. Very applied.[2]

86. Mazur, E. (1997). *Peer instruction: A user's manual.* Upper Saddle River, NJ: Prentice Hall.

A useful manual which details Eric Mazur's Peer Instruction procedure and provides many examples of curricular and assessment materials for use in introductory physics. Mazur uses a variety of testing strategies at the start of his classes to ensure that students have read the assigned work, then uses additional brief assessment procedures during his classes to stimulate higher-order thinking and interactive peer instruction. Mazur's manual details his use of multiple "ConcepTests" embedded within sixty-minute "Peer Instruction lectures." Highest recommendation.

87. McEnerney, K. (1989). Cooperative learning as a strategy in clinical laboratory science education. *Clinical Laboratory Science,* 2, 88–89.

Describes the features of cooperative learning and how it can be applied in a college classroom. Although clinical science is the course content used in this paper the information presented can be generalized to a variety of academic disciplines. Very practical. Recommended.[1]

88. McEnerney, K. (1992, Spring). Cooperative learning: Experience in a professional curriculum. *Cooperative Learning and College Teaching, 2*, 2–4.

McEnerney describes the use of cooperative learning in both undergraduate and graduate clinical-science courses at a diverse campus of the California State University system. The author discusses using cooperative learning to address such issues as the special concerns of students who major in clinical science, cultural diversity, peer editing and adult learners.

89. McNeill, B. W., & Bellamy, L. (1995). *Engineering core workbook for active learning, assessment & team training.* Section edition. (ERIC Document Reproduction Service No. ED 384 315).

A very useful and complete workbook designed for Arizona State University's core engineering program students. Among the content presented in this text are rationales for using small-group instruction, active-learning exercises, student-assessment materials and team-training information. Over 200 pages of practical material that could be adapted by SMET faculty in many disciplines. Highly recommended.

90. Miller, J. E. (1996, Spring). Learning to think like a scientist: Cooperative learning in an introductory college biology course. *Cooperative Learning and College Teaching, 6*, 4–7.

A description of a project-based cooperative-learning approach to teaching General Biology I and II for 100–150 students per class at Worcester Polytechnic Institute (WPI). Teams of students are assigned four projects per term and are assisted by undergraduate teaching assistants. Interactive lectures are combined with team conferencing with the assistants in an attempt to focus on having students act and think like scientists rather than simply listen to lectures. A sample project is described, dealing with the evolution of the AIDS virus.

91. Neff, G., Beyerlein, S., Apple, D., & Krumsieg, K. (1995, October). *Transforming engineering education from a product to a process.* Paper presented at the World Conference on Engineering Education. St. Paul, MN.

A description of Process Education in engineering courses, which is a set of principles and techniques that the authors indicate represents a paradigm shift from content mastery to problem solving and critical thinking. Among the features of the Process Education approach are the use of cooperative learning, discovery learning, journal writing and assessment. The authors provide a 13-step planning template for designing activity sheets that would be useful to instructors in any field.

92. Nurrenbern, S. C. (Ed.). *Experiences in cooperative learning: A collection for chemistry teachers.* Madison, WI: University of Wisconsin-Madison, Institute for Chemical Education.

A very useful workbook designed for chemistry professors. Nurrenbern offers a rationale for the use of cooperative learning, and advice on such issues as managing groups and the role of the teacher in cooperative learning. SMET faculty may be most interested in the 80 pages devoted to descriptions of a variety of cooperative tasks and exercises in chemistry. Enough detail is included to enable instructors to easily use these activities in teaching a number of SMET concepts. Highest recommendation.

93. Pence, H. E. (1993). Combing cooperative learning and multimedia in general chemistry. *Education, 113*, 375–380.

A description of how technology and cooperative-learning partner pairs can be combined in teaching general chemistry. The author briefly describes a sequence of instruction and reports that students' attitudes were favorably affected by the use of cooperative learning and technology (including laser disk and computer simulations). Student drop-out rates were reported as lower in classes taught using cooperative learning.

94. Roth, W. (1990, April). *Collaboration and construction in the science classroom.* Paper presented at the Annual Convention of the American Educational Research Association, Boston, MA. (ERIC Document Reproduction Service No. ED 318 631)

Roth argues that knowledge is a social construction and is "shared through social transactions in a community of knowers, rather than being descriptive of an absolute, knower-independent reality." He then describes his basic beliefs and central metaphors which he uses in the teaching of science. The last section of this conference paper describes specific collaborative procedures Roth uses in the teaching of physics, including collaborative learning and cognitive mapping. This paper is of particular interest to those teaching in the physical sciences.[2]

95. Schamel, D., & Ayres, M. P. (1992). The minds-on approach: Student creativity and personal involvement in the undergraduate science laboratory. *Journal of College Science Teaching, 21*(4), 226–229.

A clearly-written short article that describes how two biologists use a small-group cooperative technique as an alternative to more traditionally-taught lab formats. In addition to briefly describing their "Minds On" active-learning approach, the authors describe six problems in traditionally-taught laboratory instruction and how their approach represents an improvement to that format. They report that 81–92% of their students prefer the cooperative-group lab format.

96. Smith, K. A. (1984). Structured controversies. *Engineering Education, 74,* 306–309.

An application of cooperative-learning techniques to collegiate engineering courses. Of interest to those teaching at the collegiate level in any discipline. Recommended.[1]

97. Smith, K. A. (1986). Cooperative learning groups. In S. F. Schomberg (Ed.), *Strategies for active teaching and learning in university classrooms* (pp. 18–26). Minneapolis, MN: University of Minnesota.

An excellent chapter on how to get started using cooperative learning at the college level. Includes applications of cooperative learning in two college engineering classes. Recommended for teachers within all disciplines.[2]

---

[1] This citation was included in: Cooper, J. L., & Mueck, R. (1989). Cooperative/collaborative learning: Research and practice (primarily) at the collegiate level. *The Journal of Staff, Program, & Organization Development, 7,* 143–148.

[2] This citation was included in: Cooper, J., McKinney, M., & Robinson, P. (1991). Cooperative/collaborative learning: Part II. *The Journal of Staff, Program, & Organization Development, 9,* 239–247.

[3] This citation was included in: Robinson, P., & Cooper, J. (1995). An annotated bibliography of cooperative learning in higher education: Part III—the 1990s. *Cooperative Learning and College Teaching.*

INDEX TO THE BIBLIOGRAPHY

Research and Theory
> Section 1.A. Citations 1–15 General Cooperative Learning Resources
> Section 1.B. Citations 17–55 SMET Cooperative Learning Resources

Applications
> Section 2.A. Citations 56–72 General Cooperative Learning Resources
> Section 2.B. Citations 73–97 SMET Cooperative Learning Resources

Discipline	**Citation Numbers**

Italicized numbers are recommended for new practitioners interested in applications of small-group instruction to a specific discipline.

Discipline	Citation Numbers
Agriculture	84
Biology	*39* 43 *90 95*
Chemistry	*17* 23 *24* 41 46 *92* 93
Clinical Science	*87 88*
Computer Science	37 *85*
Dental (see Medical/Dental)	
Engineering	36 75 *90 91 96 97*
Chemical	42 *76 77*
Civil	*78*
Mathematics	22 26 28 33 50 *55* 73 *80*
Algebra	53 *83*
Calculus	18 32 52
Statistics	19
Graduate Education	25
Teacher Education	48
Medical/Dental	21 29 47
Physical Therapy	27
Nursing	30 31 *40*
Physics	*34* 74 82 *86 94*
Science	35 44 51 54 *79*
Laboratory	38
Physical Science for Ed.	20 45
Veterinary Medicine	81

Not Discipline Specific	**Citation Numbers**
Annotated Bibliographies	13 16
General Works Including: Overviews, Issues, Procedures, Sourcebooks/ Workbooks	1 2 3 4 5 6 7 10 11 12 14 15 56 57 58 59 60 61 62 63 64 65 66 67 68 69 70 71 72 84
Meta-analyses	
General	8 9
SMET	49